TRANSFORMING
TRAUMA

NEW DIRECTIONS IN THE HUMAN-ANIMAL BOND
Series editors: Alan M. Beck and Marguerite E. O'Haire, Purdue University

A dynamic relationship has always existed between people and animals. Each influences the psychological and physiological state of the other. This series of scholarly publications, in collaboration with Purdue University's College of Veterinary Medicine, expands our knowledge of the interrelationships between people, animals, and their environment. Manuscripts are welcomed on all aspects of human-animal interaction and welfare, including therapy applications, public policy, and the application of humane ethics in managing our living resources.

Other titles in this series:

TRANSFORMING
TRAUMA

RESILIENCE AND HEALING THROUGH OUR CONNECTIONS WITH ANIMALS

Edited by Philip Tedeschi and Molly Anne Jenkins
Foreword by Dr. Bruce D. Perry

Purdue University Press, West Lafayette, Indiana

Library of Congress Cataloging-in-Publication Data

Names: Tedeschi, Philip, 1961– editor. | Jenkins, Molly Anne, 1979– editor.

Title: Transforming trauma : resilience and healing through our connections with animals / [edited by] Philip Tedeschi, Molly Anne Jenkins.

Other titles: New directions in the human-animal bond.

Description: West Lafayette, Indiana : Purdue University Press, [2019] | Series: New directions in the human-animal bond | Includes bibliographical references and index.

Identifiers: LCCN 2019008633 | ISBN 9781557537959 (pbk. : alk. paper) | ISBN 9781612495200 (epub) | ISBN 9781557538505 (epub open access knowledge unlatched) | ISBN 9781612495194 (epdf)

Subjects: | MESH: Animal Assisted Therapy—methods | Trauma and Stressor Related Disorders—therapy | Bonding, Human-Pet | Resilience, Psychological

Classification: LCC RM931.A65 | NLM WM 450.5.A6 | DDC 615.8/5158—dc23 LC record available at https://lccn.loc.gov/2019008633

Cover image: "Safe" by Elicia Edijanto, 2014, watercolor on paper. From the artist: "My art is my cathartic release, just like a journal or diary where I can share my feelings. For me, nature is always the best remedy. River flowing, herd of horses running, sun setting, moving grasses of the savanna, and so forth can always bring tranquility and reassure my mind. The relationship between human and animals and nature is very beautiful. I use children and animal as my subjects because they're honest and sincere. They both have inimitable compassion toward each other. It's so easy to catch the subtleties in their gestures and expressions because they're unpretentious. Back in the old days, we used to live in nature, side by side with all its elements—human, animals, plants, in harmony. We used to live in balance and complement each other. This thought has such a calming effect on me, and when I put it in a painting, I feel a wonderful peace inside. I want people to feel it too. I want to share this beautiful feeling."

Dedications

Philip Tedeschi

Some of my most trusted and reliable friends are nonhuman animals. Fortunately, in my own life, the human-animals who raised and loved me were trustworthy as well. I want to express my deepest gratitude to my parents—John and Anne Tedeschi, both inspired intellectuals and scholars—whose commitment to issues of social justice, respect for others, and learning is only surpassed by the love they have for their children. In the safe harbor of our home, my sisters and I were encouraged to learn, to think for our ourselves, and to seek adventure and exploration. Throughout my life, these gifts have helped me connect with animals and the natural world, as well as raise a family of my own. This book and its penetrating message of wonder and hope is dedicated to the loves of my life: my wife, Rebecca Albright, and my children, Gemma, Ruby, and Micah Tedeschi. You power my world, and it has been my genuine honor to share this life with you.

My heartfelt gratitude goes out to my fantastic colleagues and the indomitable team at the Institute for Human-Animal Connection at the Graduate School of Social Work, University of Denver. You are many and you know who you are. Namaste.

Molly Anne Jenkins

I owe a great debt of gratitude to my dear ones—both human and animal, too many to count or mention here—who offered insight and surrounded me with encouragement throughout the creation of this most exciting book. Thank you, Phil, for always inspiring me to come into my own and to take the conversation in new, unexplored directions. To mom, my first editor: thank you for your unwavering dedication to the causes that matter, for your support of me and my writing, for giving me Riley when I needed him most. With all my love, I dedicate the pages that follow to my sweet little family—Queenie, whose friendship swells my heart; Murray, who keeps me ever on my toes; and my wondrous Nick, who believes in me and says so, day in and day out.

Contents

Foreword

Trauma, resilience, healing, and connection—these words have permeated the young field of traumatology for the last thirty years. Indeed, hundreds of articles, book chapters, and books have these words in the titles; thousands of researchers and clinicians study and write about trauma, resilience, connection, and healing. Yet the current book is so important because of a unique and powerful lens applied to these issues—the human-animal relationship. The capacity of human-animal interactions to play a central role in the therapeutic approach to trauma is, at once, ancient and unappreciated. These authors are pioneers. They share their thoughts and experiences in these chapters. This is a refreshing perspective in the current climate where the "evidence-based" loop tends to inhibit creative exploration of promising clinical practices. Evidence of effectiveness is essential for us to move our field forward; yet, without systematic exploration of plausible practice and program elements, no progress will take place. And what could be a more plausible and effective source of healing than that provided by centuries of convergent evidence, independently collected from multiple cultures on different continents?

This capacity for strong, nurturing (and helping) relationships is an essential element of therapeutics. In studies of the effectiveness of therapy, one common (and most powerful) factor emerges: the capacity to form a helping relationship is the best predictor of outcomes independent of clinical technique or therapeutic perspective. Reflect a moment on the intense emotional connections between humans and animals—you may have one yourself. Our literature and arts celebrate these relationships— *Black Beauty*, *National Velvet*, *The Black Stallion*, *Old Yeller*, *One Hundred and One Dalmatians*—and remember Toto, Lassie, and so many more.

It stands to reason then, that the human-animal connection could be used for therapeutic purposes. The rationale and practice are outlined throughout this book.

Another emerging, important factor in therapeutic work in trauma is the importance of regulation as a key factor in effective engagement. A dysregulated child (or adult) is difficult to connect with and impossible to reason with. And, of course, a sensitized, overly reactive stress response is a major characteristic of most trauma-related syndromes. This sensitization frequently interferes with the capacity to utilize any cognitive dominant interventions (e.g., Trauma-Focused Cognitive Behavioral Therapy or TF-CBT). The organization of the central nervous system (CNS) is such that all sensory input (read as "all experience"—including therapeutic engagement) first is processed and, if appropriate, acted on by lower, more reactive networks in the brainstem and diencephalon before limbic and cortical networks have a chance to process or act. This means a clinician attempting to engage a dysregulated individual with these lower neural networks on hyperdrive will be fundamentally frustrated. The sequence of engagement dictated by our neuroanatomy is to regulate first, then relate, and then reason. Our capacity to get to the most important and most "human" part of our brain depends upon a minimal level of regulation. Enter man's coevolutionary partners, the dog and horse.

In the codependent evolution of humankind and animals, dogs, specifically, were major regulators for humans. For possibly 32,000 years, humans and dogs have depended upon each other. When a known dog is present and projecting nonverbal, nurturing signals, part of the human brain knows "the camp is safe." Dogs, with their superior capabilities in hearing and smell, expanded the sensory alarm radius for their human clan dramatically. Deep in our brain we know that if the dog is relaxed and playfully engaged, we are safe. The mere presence of a calm dog will calm us down. In contrast, a shift in vigilance or an alarm bark tells us something is afoot. Similar shifts in a horse's behavior can have comparable impact on our regulatory state. The horse has been our coevolutionary partner for less time than dogs, probably 8,000 years or so, but this capacity to read and respond to the subtle emotional cues of a human in ways that are regulating and reassuring is equally strong. Certainly, this coregulatory capacity is a major component of therapeutic work with animals.

A second and equally important regulating element of interacting with our animal partners is the impact that repetitive, rhythmic somatosensory activity has on our stress-response systems. Petting, grooming, riding, and walking with our animals will provide a powerful regulating rhythmic input that is known to calm a dysregulated individual.

The combination, then, of human-animal connectedness to regulate and relationally engage (relate) provides a perfect matrix for the therapeutic process with an individual experiencing trauma. This is most helpful if the trauma has been in the context of early life relationships resulting in attachment problems; in these cases, the individual has developed human-specific relational evocative cues that can disrupt attempts to use traditional therapies that are relationally mediated. The client will be escalated and dysregulated by attempts to "connect." In these situations, the animal-specific sensory cues that are present during the regulating and relationship-building processes are not "evocative" and disruptive. The client can engage, learn, grow, and heal in context of the human-animal relationship, preparing them for healthier human connectedness in the future.

The authors of this book provide an exciting and promising exploration of the power of our connections to animals. These ancient and important connections may prove to be some of our most effective and flexible ways to engage and heal. Certainly, these insights will improve our current limited capacity to meet the needs of the vast numbers of maltreated and traumatized children, youth, and adults.

Bruce D. Perry, M.D., Ph.D.
Senior Fellow, The ChildTrauma Academy, Houston, TX
Professor (Adjunct), Department of Psychiatry and Behavioral Sciences,
    Feinberg School of Medicine, Northwestern University, Chicago, IL
Professor (Adjunct), School of Allied Health, College of Science, Health
    and Engineering, La Trobe University, Melbourne, Victoria, Australia

Human Trauma and Animals: Research Developments, Models, and Practice Methods for Trauma-Informed Animal-Assisted Interventions

Philip Tedeschi, MSSW, LCSW; and Molly A. Jenkins, MSW, AASW

Throughout the writing and editing of this book, Samara has been by our side, providing levity and support through countless brainstorming sessions, discussions, and rewrites. Her head and body are generally pointed in our direction, even through the snores that characterize her deepest sleep. With just a small squint of her resting eyes, we take comfort in knowing she is observing our various actions, behaviors, and moods—rarely missing a thing or skipping a beat. Samara is a black Labrador retriever who lives and works with Philip Tedeschi, and plays an integral role at the University of Denver's Graduate School of Social Work. Through our collective time together on this project, she has taught the two of us a great deal. Originally adopted from Colorado's Prison Trained K9 Companion Program (PTKCP), Samara now works with students in our graduate-level animal-assisted social work program, with several other clinical assignments ranging from visiting with children who have experienced developmental trauma to assisting adults with persistent mental illness and homelessness. As such, we have spent a lot of our time with her, and although we know dogs as a species well, we are routinely amazed by her intuition and emotional attunement, as well as her personality, which seems to be fully

Samara in her element: wide open spaces.

committed to our work of caring for people and educating students. It is difficult not to be amazed by the patience and level of consistency she offers to establish her side of a relationship. On most days, you can be sure you'll find her right in the thick of it.

ORIGINS

Every book concept has a birthplace. This particular book has two influential origins that captured our attention, and increased our already ardent interest in exploring how animals consistently play a profound and facilitative role in human trauma recovery. However, the pages that follow are not so much a story of our own journey to explore this topic as a significant window that we hope both frames and clarifies a paradigm in need of greater understanding. In the process of editing this volume, we have encountered many important concepts, new findings, and influences, all of them shaped by intimate testimonials, accounts of actual implementation of programs and practices, and emerging and well-established research. We are pleased to be able to present the meaningful and varied work of each of the contributing authors in the forthcoming chapters.

One of the first catalysts for this book was a conference entitled, "Transforming Trauma: Research Developments and Methods for Trauma-Informed Animal-Assisted Interventions," held in 2015 at the University of Denver and organized by the Institute for Human-Animal Connection as part of the "Animals on the Mind" Conference Series. The Institute for Human-Animal Connection has existed at the University of Denver (housed in the Graduate School of Social Work) since 2007. This conference offered two days of focused presentations on contemporary research to practice models to illuminate the discourse and new research directions occurring in the field of human-animal interaction (HAI). Overall, this learning event was an impactful step toward highlighting the emerging evidence basis for animal-assisted intervention (AAI) in a variety of trauma recovery domains, including developmental trauma, adult post-traumatic stress, and crisis response.

Equally important were the compelling accounts among conference participants, many of them students, who frequently shared a resolute certainty regarding the power and transformative capacity of human-animal connection. More often than not, these participant convictions stemmed from personal experiences where animals and animal relationships served as critical elements in their own recovery, in some cases literally saving their lives. Over the last decade, many students enrolled in the animal-assisted social work program at the University of Denver (in which Tedeschi directs and Jenkins graduated and serves as affiliated faculty) have shared that their interest in incorporating animals into social work and therapeutic settings emanated from personal experiences where an animal helped them cope and find the resilience to move forward from the impacts of child abuse, parental divorce, and grief related to other losses (among others). It is difficult to argue with someone who has personal experience as his or her proof of concept, much less many "someones." These powerful personal testimonials of human-animal connection, as well as an intention to enrich the AAI field's understanding and therapeutic application of them, have offered important emphasis in shaping the focus and narratives of this book.

THE ETHICS OF HUMAN-ANIMAL CONNECTION

Above all, we hope the most powerful takeaway from this volume will be a commitment toward an emerging new ethical mandate in AAI. It is inevitable in the offering of a book such as this, where we have examined with some detail the complex situations in which we place animals, to wonder if we should, in fact, be promoting these activities. For example, we might wonder what it is like to be a dog who is assigned to live with an angry, depressed, or potentially suicidal individual diagnosed with post-traumatic stress disorder (PTSD), or who is asked to respond to the inconsolable grief of a community responding to the losses inflicted after a school shooting. In compiling this text, we have been humbled by the remarkable capacity of animals to be at our sides, often through no choice of their own, during these moments of adversity. Nevertheless, we are just as certain that sustained practice and research improvements are essential to ensuring that our expectations of animals who take part in this work are fair, reasonable, and informed.

In the chapters to come, you will likely find agreement among the contributors that we must offer optimum support for animal well-being in AAI, and that our current welfare standards—developed to support visiting therapy dogs through the application of basic animal welfare standards, such as the Five Freedoms—will no longer suffice to fully meet our obligation. The worst possible outcome of this amazing field of HAI would be to succeed in our pursuit for evidence that animals do in fact improve human health, but then systematically launch yet another problematic and exploitative mode of interacting with them on a large scale. The risk that this could be an unintended outcome of progress developments within the field is likely. We say this because human-centric agendas often fail to build in adequate, critical review from the perspective of how our actions impact nonhuman animals. In the context of trauma response, it may be even more likely that the consideration offered to the animals involved might be overshadowed by the gravity of responding to the crisis or to the intensity of need among human clients. As we move forward with the processes of defining the potential of HAI, developing and continuously refining AAI protocols to support effective intervention, and documenting outcomes through improved scientific study, we must also seek—as a stipulation—a rethinking of our relationships with other animals and our ethical obligations as stewards of their comfort and well-being.

THERAPEUTIC EFFECTS OF HUMAN-ANIMAL INTERACTIONS AND EMERGING PRACTICES

Throughout this book, every effort was made to articulate and examine the unique, therapeutic, and diverse ways that animals seem to help humans overcome trauma. The AAI field is growing in remarkable ways. Importantly, the significance of the origins for this book's development is largely based on the current prevalence of AAI practice, with thousands of programs, nationally and internationally, beginning to incorporate animals for specific human health objectives and outcomes. This increase in interest may be due, at least in part, to the challenges encountered in finding effective treatment for persons who have experienced trauma, including that which is associated with the complexity of decades of war; various forms of child maltreatment; large-scale disaster, violence, and inhumanity; and mass victim events. This difficulty might be especially true in cases of treatment-resistant forms of trauma, as well as large numbers of people needing services with urgency due to high rates and risk of suicide. For example, the Veteran's Administration Health Care System (VAHCS) reports that 50% of clients with PTSD admitted to its evidence-based programs quit within the first three sessions, with 66% of those who actually completed treatment still meeting the criteria for a PTSD diagnosis (National Intrepid Center of Excellence, 2014).

Increasingly, research suggests that HAIs have a positive impact on human emotional health. A prominent conclusion is that HAI provides overall emotional support, and correlates with reductions in depression, anxiety, and stress (McCardle, McCune, Griffin, & Maholmes, 2011). Some researchers suggest that the reason for AAI's success is rooted in an animal's ability to create relationship, offer affection, and provide a less-threatening opportunity to connect with the helper or intervention (Kruger & Serpell, 2006). There is general consensus in the field that AAI's quality of enhancing rapport-building between client and therapist is one of the greatest strengths that animals offer in trauma-informed settings (Beetz, 2017). For instance, AAI can be employed to develop safety in the therapeutic alliance and increase the retention of clients, both of which serve as significant challenges in trauma treatment. Enhanced motivation increases retention, which is the best predictor of positive results, increased likelihood of bonding with treatment providers, actively participating in treatment, and endorsing treatment goals (Lefkowitz, Paharia, Prout, Debiak, & Bleiberg, 2005).

Moreover, animals are often perceived as being more genuine than humans, given that they do not hold human biases (Chandler, 2005; Pichot & Coulter, 2007). In this way, clients often trust a therapy animal more readily than they do humans, and this can serve as a precursor to developing trust with a human therapist. The presence of an animal may also reduce the client's overall anxiety about being in treatment, and offer additional and regular opportunities to have a client reevaluate the trustworthiness of his or her therapist. In addition, the therapeutic animal may provide the client with a surrogate for therapeutic touch, allowing for the use of physical touch in an ethical and appropriate manner (Chandler, 2005).

ANIMALS' ROLE IN GROWTH AND RESILIENCE IN TRAUMA RECOVERY

What happens when we are not able to trust people? Or when a life event so completely shakes the foundation of our willingness to have human relationship that a traditional therapeutic "trusting relationship" is no longer a viable approach to therapeutic intervention? These types of deep trauma experiences have the potential to establish long-term patterns of functioning that can interfere with an individual's normal development and healthy living. For example, childhood trauma can disrupt normative emotional development, as well as negatively influence a child's ability to experience emotional security (Perry, 2008). Childhood trauma is associated with biological stress reactions that influence brain development and can disrupt motor, emotional, behavioral, language, social, psychosexual, moral, and cognitive skill development. In turn, challenges to behavioral and emotional regulation contribute to disruption in attachment and likely impact all relationships throughout the life span. These developmental disruptions can leave a child at risk for developing internalizing disorders, such as separation anxiety disorder, dysthymia, major depressive disorder, and externalizing disorders (e.g., attention deficit hyperactivity disorder or ADHD and oppositional defiant disorder) (van der Kolk, 2002). Notably, they may also result in a diagnosis of PTSD.

Increased research and scholarship in this area appears regularly, and a significant level of interest seems directed at the potential that animals offer for recovery and resilience in response to trauma. Research methods have expanded to explore the underlying mechanisms at work, including the changes that animals can have on our physiological and neurobiological functioning (Beetz, 2017). Time and again, people also reflect that the presence of a trusted nonhuman animal allows them to experience the comfort that comes only from feeling physically and emotionally safe; indeed, the importance of feeling safe with animals in trauma recovery is highlighted throughout the chapters of this book, and even influenced our choice of cover art ("Safe," by Elicia Edijanto) and design. Further, animal-assisted treatment of complex trauma, and particularly as it manifests in PTSD, is at the forefront of clinical research and public discourse, particularly given the increasingly visible social challenges amongst post-9/11 veteran and active service member communities.

Within this text, we have utilized in places the concepts of *resilience* and *post-traumatic growth*. These concepts remain somewhat controversial, in part because they lack the full authority of significant evidentiary support. Briefly defined, post-traumatic growth (or PTG) suggests that trauma for some persons, and under some circumstances, is beneficial (including psychologically and physically), with recognition that trauma is not experienced uniformly and that not all individuals react to trauma experiences in the same way. Resilience has been described as "the ability of an individual, family, group, community, or organization to recover from adversity and resume functioning even when suffering serious trouble, confusion, or hardship" (Kirst-Ashman & Hull Jr., 2012, p. 22). Presumably, developing or emphasizing a person's resiliency following the adverse event(s) may improve his or her well-being, and ease the challenges and symptoms of the trauma so that the person may achieve a higher level of functioning and, thus, quality of life. That is to say, greater resiliency may lead to PTG.

Through experience, research, review, and discussion of material, we have encountered the inclusion of animals (companion, therapy, service, and those living in nature) in the lives of individuals as offering opportunity for significantly improved functioning. As such, we postulate that one reason why animals may be so helpful in trauma recovery is because of their capacity to foster resiliency in those affected. Throughout this book, we hope that readers will consider the following questions time and again: 1) What factors might impact the reframing of PTSD to PTG? and 2) Is the presence of, or connection with, an animal a significant or particular contributor to this transformative process?

RESEARCH AND IMPLEMENTATION SCIENCE

The primary purpose of research is to test theories through the discipline of sustained and sound inquiry, thereby building authoritative scientific knowledge. Clear terminology, testable protocols, and robust objective measures that underpin strong methodological evaluation are all advantageous research components. Like other AAI investigators before us, we will fall short here in establishing absolute certainty and specificity in regard to particular models, and in providing unassailable endorsement of their scientific, clinical, and practical applications. We will, however, begin to see appearing from the underbrush of these chapters, concepts that hold consistency and structure, have basis in existing practice and research, and offer promise as emerging trauma-informed interventions that deserve our attention.

In virtually every article published in the existing HAI literature, the author bemoans the scarcity of supportive research and calls for more. But more of what, exactly? From our perspective, the needs that continue to hamper AAI and HAI research efforts, primarily, are related to a lack of monetary (and other resource), innovation, and implementation support. Recent trends in funding new research with rigorous standards, while well-intentioned, may inadvertently have their own drawbacks, particularly in terms of feasibility and practicality. Therefore, in addition to meeting expectations for refined research with scientific gold standard, we may also want to refocus on—and fund—more testable theories and methodologies in order to boost the certainty in these ideas and the impact of these interventions.

As alluded to above, there exists a significant research-to-practice gap in the field of AAI, in that practical applications often fail to be manifested in reproducible fidelity to the research models or protocols. The inclusion of animals in trauma-informed programs is diverse in both practice setting and client population. As the field moves forward to investigate the health-related potential of AAI, it is clear that the evidence base needed to ensure that treatment models are effective and implemented with quality has not kept pace with expansions in practice. Furthermore, individual organizations involved in delivering AAI often have limited capacity for program and staff development, quality implementation, and practice evaluation, all of which can affect the quality and efficacy (or lack thereof) of the wider field. Researchers are likewise hindered as a result of this research-to-practice gap because they are often attempting to examine interventions that are loosely defined and/or inconsistently administered. Thus, we contend that greater emphasis on "real-world" research, as well as increased resources to bring these findings into implementation, are critical to consider as the field continues its growth in the areas of trauma treatment and recovery.

On the whole, two new goals of investigative research in trauma-informed AAI settings should be to establish a general, consensus-based literacy related to the underlying conceptual frameworks that can inform practitioner training programs, and to examine specific methods under which this knowledge might be utilized to achieve greater methodological fidelity and approaches to evidence-based practice outcomes in AAI. As editors, we attempted to ensure that each chapter offers clear, coherent, and factual content. However, given that this emerging field of trauma-informed AAI is still in an "information-gathering phase" of sorts, we did not attempt to substantively change the terminology or central concepts presented by each author or set of authors.

As such, we realize and have accepted that the discussion of certain concepts—specifically related to the definitions, use, and application of select terminology (e.g., the biophilia hypothesis)—will differ somewhat due to the divergent approaches and professional backgrounds of our contributing authors. As editors, we might have approached this challenge by forcing a shared definition and set of formal agreements on the use of these key terms. Instead, we were compelled to offer the flexibility for each contributor to discuss these terms in his or her distinct and intentional manner (as long as accuracy was maintained). Although this may require an expansive intellectual effort on the part of the reader, we have concluded it may, in time, serve to offer a more robust and comprehensive understanding of these core concepts at this early stage in the field's growth. Eventually, we believe that requiring a shared set of definitions and terminology will likely be important and worth seeking agreement for the purpose of accurate translation, as well as the enhancement of practice and research protocols. At the same time, we support the need to create sufficient space to explore the diversity of ideas and models, and to allow for innovation and integration of new knowledge. We hope that the use of terminology and concepts in this volume offers adequate attention to both of these objectives, and that the diversity of thought strengthens, rather than hinders, the ultimate potency of the text.

CONCLUSION

In the following chapters, we are honored to introduce you to our contributing authors whose insight and generosity of spirit in sharing their ideas we wish to acknowledge and celebrate. They represent a diverse and highly qualified array of experts on the topics offered. In this volume, we and our contributors will primarily focus on three categories of human trauma experience: 1) child and family violence; 2) crisis response and intervention; and 3) post-traumatic stress, particularly among military service members and veterans. As discussed earlier, this compendium of chapters and associated ideas were not written with the intention that they would necessarily coalesce with one another or be vetted for agreement between authors. It is, however, our hope that the organization of chapters builds toward consilience of a more integrated knowledge on these subjects.

Edward Wilson has stated that "the greatest enterprise of the mind has always been and always will be the linkage of the sciences and the humanities" (Wilson, 1998, p. 9). He reflects openly on the limitations and fragmentation that often define our approach to education, scholarship, and research, and in turn, presents a stunted way in which we tend to gain knowledge and understanding. In an effort to address these challenges, Wilson imagines a process that reaches far beyond transdisciplinary integration. He indicates that the concept of consilience occurs when inductive knowledge obtained from one core branch coincides with another, allowing for the true testing of theory. According to Wilson (1998), "the strongest appeal of consilience is in the prospect of intellectual adventure and, given even modest success, the value of understanding the human condition with a higher degree of certainty" (p. 9).

Here, we feature contributions from a diverse set of professions and disciplines. To name a few, we have academics involved in the social and biological sciences; practitioners in education, psychotherapy, and human and nonhuman medicine and public health; and clinicians serving the continuum of the human condition across the life span. This book's contents include those proffered by scientists oriented toward analysis and measurement who might dispute the suggested best methods and tools, or even the most important questions to ask, posed by therapists or teachers (and vice versa). This, again, is reflective of divergent methodologies and differing standards of illuminating fact-based knowledge and, thus, of reporting different colors and dimensions of the truth. Indeed, the present contributors routinely use a lexicon and language indicative of their unique lens and disciplines, placing differing weight on what is significant and what constitutes relevant knowledge. In linking together the chapters, we sought to gain greater consilience among the core branches of knowledge that engineer our progress and certainty. As you read this book, moving from one chapter to the next, consider taking on the enterprise of linking knowledge, rather than ranking information hierarchically. Valuable knowledge will come at you from differing perspectives, even from non-human perspectives if you listen carefully.

People have a way of placing themselves first. One of the more important lessons learned from the creation of this work is that humans can often be lazy and careless about our relationships with one another, even when attempting to help. Spoken and increasingly written language appear to be the only information and methods of communication we tend to offer our human counterparts in order to understand and to be understood. Animals, on the other hand, use everything except verbal language in which to communicate and understand others and the world around them. Even when trying to understand the contributions offered by our nonhuman relationships, we often fail to appreciate the emotional, cognitive, and communicative diversity of other animals. Greater attention must be paid to how animals communicate their needs, preferences, and support, particularly in the context of AAI for trauma.

As we finish writing this introductory piece, Samara has not abandoned her post. She lays quietly close to the desk and, per usual, offers us her ever-reliable patience and good nature. We have attempted in this book to both encourage and retain the authentic voice of each contributor. In the process, we hope we have captured hers as well.

REFERENCES

Beetz, A. M. (2017). Theories and possible processes of action in animal assisted interventions *Applied Developmental Science, 21*(2), 139–149.

Chandler, C. K. (2005). *Animal assisted therapy in counseling.* New York, NY: Routledge.

Kirst-Ashman, K. K., & Hull Jr., G. H. (2012). *Understanding generalist practice* (6th ed.). Boston, MA: Brooks/Cole Publishing.

Kruger, K. A., & Serpell, J. A. (2006). Animal-assisted interventions in mental health: Definitions and theoretical foundations. In A. H. Fine (Ed.), *Handbook on animal-assisted therapy: Theoretical foundations and guidelines for practice* (2nd ed., pp. 21–38). San Francisco, CA: Elsevier.

Lefkowitz, C., Paharia, I., Prout, M., Debiak, D., & Bleiberg, J. (2005). Animal-assisted prolonged exposure: A treatment for survivors of sexual assault suffering posttraumatic stress disorder. *Society & Animals: Journal of Human-Animal Studies, 13*(4), 275–295.

McCardle, P., McCune, S., Griffin, J. A., & Maholmes, V. (Eds.). (2011). *How animals affect us: Examining the influence of human-animal interaction on child development and human health.* Washington, DC: American Psychological Association.

National Intrepid Center of Excellence (NICoE). (2014). Fact sheet. Retrieved from http://www.nicoe.capmed.mil/Shared%20Documents/NICoE_Updated _One_Pager_3_4_2014.pdf

Perry, B. (2008). Child maltreatment: A neurodevelopmental perspective on the role of trauma and neglect in psychopathology. In T. Beauchaine & S. P. Hinshaw (Eds.), *Child and adolescent psychopathology* (pp. 93–129). Hoboken, NJ: John Wiley & Sons.

Pichot, T., & Coulter, M. (2007). *Animal-assisted brief therapy: A solution-focused approach.* New York, NY: The Haworth Press.

van der Kolk, B. A. (2002). The assessment and treatment of complex PTSD. In R. Yehuda (Ed.), *Treating trauma survivors with PTSD* (pp. 127–156). Arlington, VA: American Psychiatric Association Publishing.

Wilson, E. O. (Ed.). (1998). *Consilience.* New York, NY: Vintage Books, Random House.

ABOUT THE AUTHORS

Philip Tedeschi is the executive director of the Institute for Human-Animal Connection, and faculty at the University of Denver's Graduate School of Social Work. Recognized for his expertise in clinical methods for animal-assisted interventions, he is the founder and supervisor of the University's Animal-Assisted Social Work and Animals and Human Health Professional Development certificate programs. His teaching, research, and scholarship focus on the bioaffiliative connection between people and animals, human-animal interactions, animal welfare, interpersonal violence and animal cruelty, social ecological justice, One Health, and bioethics.

Molly Anne Jenkins is an affiliated faculty member and adjunct professor at the Graduate School of Social Work's Institute for Human-Animal Connection at the University of Denver. She previously served as research analyst and human-animal interaction specialist for American Humane Association, where her research focused on the effects of animal-assisted intervention for children with cancer and their parents, as well as therapy dogs. Her background and primary interests center on human-animal relationships; animal welfare, sentience, and behavior; veterinary medicine; social and ecological justice; and One Health. She currently serves on the Boards of Youth and Pet Survivors at Children's Hospital Colorado and the American Psychological Association's HAI Section.

CHAPTER 1

The Impact of Human-Animal Interaction in Trauma Recovery

Marguerite E. O'Haire, PhD; Philip Tedeschi, MSSW, LCSW; Molly A. Jenkins, MSW, AASW; Sally R. Braden, MSW, AASW; and Kerri E. Rodriguez, MS

BACKGROUND

There is a documented call for adjunctive and integrative treatments to address the needs of individuals who have experienced trauma (Imel, Laska, Jakupcak, & Simpson, 2013; Najavits, 2015). Concurrently, there are new advances toward an evidence base for human-animal interaction (HAI), as well as efforts to develop and refine professional standards and competencies in the HAI field (O'Haire, Guérin, & Kirkham, 2015a). Given powerful anecdotal and scientific accounts of the benefits of HAI, a growing number of practitioners have begun to incorporate animals into their mental and physical health services.

The inclusion of animals in therapeutic applications is known as animal-assisted intervention or AAI (Kruger & Serpell, 2010). AAI ranges from informal activities with animals to provide enrichment (animal-assisted activities or AAA); to individualized and structured sessions with animals, targeted at meeting the client's therapeutic goals (animal-assisted therapy or AAT); to the incorporation of animals in educational settings to achieve academic objectives (animal-assisted education or AAE). The premise of AAI is that the animal's presence is expected to provide a unique and therapeutic benefit, above and beyond other complementary approaches

(Chandler, 2012). For people who have experienced trauma, these benefits may include a source of nonjudgmental support, stress-reducing companionship, positive outlets for joy and laughter, a safe haven for physical touch and emotional vulnerability, and "bio-affiliative safety" (Chandler, 2012; O'Haire, et al., 2015a; Taylor, Edwards, & Pooley, 2013; Yount, Ritchie, Laurent, Chumley, & Olmert, 2013).

The concept of bio-affiliative safety offers promising explanations and known processes for how we become vigilant of, and responsive to, various threat-related stimuli. Concurrently, these same systems allow us to recognize safe environments and relationships. Bio-affiliative safety is best explained through the important contributions of Dr. Stephen Porges, whose work has focused uniquely on how our neural system processes threats. Specifically, when a threat exists, our preconscious neural capacities are engaged to offer adaptive threat and defensive responses. According to Porges (2004),

> Neural circuits provide physiological mechanisms that reflexively organize mobilization or immobilization behaviors before we are consciously aware of what is happening. When, on the other hand, neuroception tells us that an environment is safe and that the people [or animals] in this environment are trustworthy, our mechanisms of defense are disenabled. We can then behave in ways that encourage social engagement and positive attachment. (p. 24)

In Porges' explorations of the polyvagal system and the concept of neuroception, we can begin to understand how the presence of a nonhuman animal interaction may offer critical information for accurate responses to our immediate actual or perceived safety (or lack thereof). For those persons working to overcome trauma, the significance of an animal companion in providing a sound sense of safety and well-being (in times of uncertainty and otherwise), an increased capacity for self-regulation, and the impetus for functional reengagement with the social environment cannot be underestimated.

History

Though humans have experienced animal companionship for millennia, our understanding of the benefits of these relationships has evolved considerably, especially over the last 50 years (Serpell, 2006). As we have begun to comprehend the ways in which animals help humans thrive, their inclusion in our therapeutic interventions has inherently followed. At times, these beginnings have stemmed from fortuitous chance. This was certainly the case for Smoky, a small Yorkshire terrier who is often heralded as the first therapy dog (Wynne, 1996). She was found by an American soldier during World War II, and accompanied him and his comrades through numerous missions. Through interacting with Smoky, the soldiers found respite and an impetus for positive emotion; the trauma and terror of their combat seemed to somehow lessen through connecting with the mere four-pound dog. Since the war, the story of Smoky has spread and is often credited with leading to a boom in the use of therapy and service dogs for individuals in recovery from traumatic physical and psychological injuries.

By the 1970s, there were dedicated organizations and groups focused on AAI. Today, thousands of therapy animal and handler teams interact with trauma survivors during their healing processes. Recently, service animals have also begun to be specially trained to assist those who have experienced trauma (Taylor et al., 2013; Yount et al., 2013). While historically service animals have solely been enlisted for physical assistance, their application has broadened into the psychological realm to build upon the growing acknowledgment of the effects of animals on human well-being (Tedeschi, Fine, & Helgeson, 2010).

Overview of Trauma

A majority of people will experience trauma at some point in their lifetime (Breslau et al., 1998). Not all of these individuals will face ongoing struggles after a traumatic event, but many will. Trauma can take on numerous forms and stems from a variety of different causes—many more than we are able to comprehensively cover in this single chapter alone. As such, our focus here is on the following three core categories of trauma: child and family violence, post-traumatic stress, and crisis response.

Child and Family Violence

Child maltreatment and family violence are devastating and pervasive. Though public awareness of these issues has grown over time, many cases still go unreported (Gracia, 1995). Children are at particular risk of poor outcomes due to the negative and traumatic impacts of witnessing and/or experiencing family violence, abuse, and/or neglect on early developmental trajectories (Anda et al., 2006; McCloskey & Walker, 2000). Importantly, child maltreatment can establish developmental trauma impacts, such as an impaired capacity for trust and attachment. Seeking assistance can also be frightening and even dangerous if a perpetrator suspects that a survivor may leave. In these situations, the presence of an animal may serve several purposes.

In the home environment, pets often function as sources of perceived unconditional positive regard and consistent support for members of the family (Walsh, 2009). In the fearful cycle of violence or neglect, a companion animal may provide a refuge, friendship, source of positive emotional exchange, and safe outlet for warmth and affection. In some cases, when domestic violence and child maltreatment are present, family pets are also at risk of significant harm (known commonly as "the Link") (Ascione & Arkow, 1999). For example, animals may be hurt by the abuser as a way to threaten, control, or punish family members who love them. In such situations, people may place themselves in harm's way by trying to protect their animals from abuse and, although not always correlated, children who are abused may even learn to hurt animals themselves (Arluke, Levin, Luke, & Ascione, 1999; Currie, 2006).

In the clinical environment, the presence of an animal may enhance the tone of the room and the therapeutic relationship by providing a positive impetus for connection and rapport between the client and the professional (Prothmann, Bienert, & Ettrich, 2006). Physical contact involved in stroking the animal may release tension and assist those with trauma to achieve physiological self-regulation (Nagengast, Baun, Megel, & Leibowitz, 1997). Watching or playing with the animal may also lessen the gravity of the situation (Hansen, Messinger, Baun, & Megel, 1999). For children in particular, the animal may play a critical role in reducing fear and distress during otherwise unpleasant and challenging interactions with adults, such as reliving traumatic events for the purposes of reporting or testifying (Parish-Plass, 2008).

CASE STUDY

In 2015, two black Labradors, Dozer and Lupe, were officially sworn in as the newest "staff members" to California District Attorney Michael Ramos. Serving on a special victims' canine unit, Dozer and Lupe work inside courtrooms to support children and families as they provide testimony of physical and sexual trauma. One of Ramos' clients, a young boy sexually abused by a relative, was understandably stressed over having to publicly relive his trauma. When Lupe nudged the child's leg, prompting for a pet, the boy began rubbing Lupe's ears, which allowed him to relax and disclose his story with greater ease (McCleery, 2016). The presence of such "courtroom facility dogs" is becoming increasingly common in cities across the United States.

Post-Traumatic Stress

A proportion of individuals who experience trauma, including children who have experienced maltreatment, will go on to develop post-traumatic stress disorder (PTSD) (Breslau, 2009; Kilpatrick et al., 2013). The source of trauma can vary, from traumatic experiences during war, family violence, sexual assault, serious illness, and natural or manmade disasters. PTSD is characterized by clinical symptoms of reexperiencing, such as flashbacks or nightmares; avoidance, such as staying away from certain places; memory loss; and hyperarousal, such as being on high alert or startling easily (American Psychiatric Association, 2013). It can develop at any point throughout the life span, and is related to marked impairments in everyday functioning at work and at home. Notably, experts in the field of treating trauma among our military populations have increasingly begun to use the term *post-traumatic stress* (PTS). PTS is now often differentiated from PTSD in recognition that normal and adaptive responses to experiencing stressful or life-threatening events may trigger at least some of the symptoms of a PTSD diagnosis in almost anyone who experiences them (Regel & Joseph, 2010). In an attempt to destigmatize the very natural fight-or-flight response to a traumatic event, we feel it is most accurate to use the term PTS interchangeably with PTSD *where appropriate* (e.g., when not discussing diagnostic criteria). The inclusion of this nomenclature will hopefully lend support to the notion that symptoms such as reexperiencing, avoidance, and hyperarousal in response to trauma can be normal, rather than pathological. Additionally, acknowledgment of these normative responses may even help foster resilience in those who have been traumatized.

While there are many available treatments for PTS, it is a challenging condition to effectively treat. There is a strong evidence base for the effectiveness of some treatments, such as eye movement desensitization and reprocessing (EMDR) and exposure therapy, among others (Foa et al., 1999; Rothbaum, Meadows, Resick, & Foy, 2000). Exposure therapy, for example, involves both imagined and real-life exposure to reminders or components of the traumatic event in a gradual progression that enables the person to build up to facing, rather than avoiding, his or her fears (Foa, Chrestman, & Gilboa-Schechtman, 2008). In the hierarchical series of exposure events, the individual habituates to specific, anxiety-producing stimuli or environments associated with the traumatic event (e.g., being in a dark room or crowd). The progression is slow and follows the pace of the individual. Although effective, this treatment is often perceived as unpleasant and aversive to many clients (Becker, Zayfert, & Anderson, 2004). Nevertheless, it is important that people with PTS persist and engage in these sorts of evidence-based treatments, because they can help to achieve improved outcomes.

As a complement to existing practices, animals often provide unique, additional benefits to the alleviation of PTS symptoms. For example, the presence of an animal often offers a source of safety and support (Marr et al., 2000; Yount et al., 2013). Animals can also reduce loneliness (Banks & Banks, 2002) and create connections among friends and family members through positive interactions (McNicholas & Collis, 2006; Wood et al., 2015), which may be especially important for individuals with PTS who are often socially isolated. In a more formal capacity, animals can be involved in AAIs or trained as service animals to assist with individualized needs, and to address specific, daily challenges caused by PTS.

For example, a core role of many psychiatric service dogs is to promote a biofeedback function to reduce anxiety or arousal. Service dogs are trained or naturally learn to sense when an individual is experiencing a heightened state of stress, which may lead to an anxiety or panic attack. In many such cases, the animal alerts the individual by nudging and/or licking them, and thus encourages the person to concentrate on the dog, take deep breaths, and use mindfulness techniques to refocus on the present. The service dog will continue to nudge the person until they take these actions. The biofeedback notification, along with an anxiolytic interaction, can help to decrease anxiety and instill calm among people in situations of stress.

Other trained tasks or AAIs can also be undertaken, based on the individual's specific needs. However, it is important to note that the inclusion of animals in PTS services should not be perceived as a stand-alone or replacement treatment. The current body of evidence suggests that social support may be the single most important variable needed for trauma recovery and, for some individuals, the support that animals provide can enhance and expedite their treatment and healing processes (Flannery Jr, 1990; Guay, Billette, & Marchand, 2006).

CASE STUDY

Staff Sargent Brad Fasnacht was clearing mines on an Afghanistan road in 2009 when he was injured by an IED blast, causing a broken spine, two broken ankles, and a traumatic brain injury—consequently exacerbating his PTS. After learning how to walk again, Brad decided to get a service dog, named Sapper, to help alleviate his PTS symptoms. Brad was in a constant hypervigilant state, scanning streets and trees for snipers. With Sapper, Brad's anxiety improved and prevented what would have often previously resulted in a panic attack. Because Brad lost some of his hearing in the blast, Sapper would notify Brad of necessary sounds, alarms, or even if someone was approaching him from behind. Like many other individuals with PTS, Brad also had nightmares, but he was able to wake from them when Sapper licked his face (Thompson, 2012).

Crisis Response

The aforementioned forms of trauma represent ongoing and often lifelong issues. We are devoting a separate chapter of this book to crisis response, because of the unique and acute elements that define it. In the wake of crisis (e.g., natural disasters, acts of community violence and terror), communities are shaken. Normalcy seems a distant memory and panic, loss, and numbness pervade. In these times, many people take great comfort in the presence of a friendly animal, such as a therapy or companion animal (Chandler, 2005; Crawford, 2003). Given the myriad studies showing that animals, particularly dogs, can reduce and buffer physiological and endocrine stress responses (Beetz, Uvnäs-Moberg, Julius, & Kotrschal, 2012b), it is no surprise that incorporating animals into crisis response has become increasingly prevalent (Chandler, 2005).

Animal-assisted crisis response (AACR) or disaster stress relief (DSR) is a specific type of AAI that incorporates a working team of a therapy dog and a certified first responder. The first contact with an individual who has undergone trauma can be fragile; incorporating a therapy dog into a crisis response team can: 1) help build rapport by developing a bridge between the individual and a responder or mental health professional; 2) act as a safe and calming presence; 3) provide certain relief through interaction that does not require effortful or verbal communication; and 4) encourage physical movement (Greenbaum, 2005). The animal can also act as a transitional "object" to encourage present-minded thoughts and provide those in crisis with a reality-orienting focus (Greenbaum, 2005).

The first example of a major disaster response that incorporated animals was during the 1995 bombing of the Murrah Building in Oklahoma City. Twenty therapy dog-handler teams were sent to provide comfort during the initial trauma recovery of victims and their families. As first responders are known to experience secondary trauma, compassion fatigue, and burnout (Alexander & Klein, 2009; Figley, 1995; Palm, Polusny, & Follette, 2004), the addition of therapy dogs into the crisis response protocol was found to be as important to the responders and handlers as to those actually being served in the community. During the terrorist attacks of September 11, 2001, approximately 500 therapy animal-handler teams from three surrounding states were deployed to provide relief for traumatized individuals, displaced persons, police officers, firefighters, US Army Reserve troops, and other professional and volunteer relief workers. In recent years, national standards and protocols have been developed to facilitate safe crisis response for both the dogs and people involved as practice continues to grow and gain national acceptance (National Standards Committee for Animal-Assisted Crisis Response, 2010).

CASE STUDY

Just days after one of America's deadliest massacre shootings and hate crimes at Pulse, an LGBT nightclub in Orlando, Florida, K-9 Comfort Dogs and handlers were brought forth to help console victims of the attack and their loved ones, as well as others in need of support. Comfort dogs were present in hospitals, churches, and even attended memorial services in order to help those in distress feel, even if just temporarily, a sense of calm and security during such tragedy. Many hospitalized victims could not get out of bed, but were seen smiling, and in a few cases, started talking again through their interaction with the dogs (Bromwich, 2016).

THEORY AND POTENTIAL MECHANISMS

Various theories and mechanisms have been proposed to explain the unique benefits of animals and animal relationships for people, including those who have experienced trauma. The increasing popularity of AAI in clinical environments is, perhaps, rooted in the evolutionary benefits of our bonds with animals, as well as the theory that humans have an innate need to be in connection with other living beings, including animals and the natural environment (Wilson, 1984; Fine, O'Callaghan, Chandler, Schaffer, Pichot, & Gimeno, 2010; Melson & Fine, 2010). This instinctive pull toward nature ("biophilia") and/or beneficial connection with it ("bio-affiliation") are just two explanations for why so many people consider their relationships with animals to be amongst their most significant. In the specific case of trauma-informed applications, some mechanisms are rooted in empirical evidence, while others remain anecdotal and challenging to define with a singular theory. The most commonly cited theories and mechanisms in this area are explored below, categorized broadly by psychological and physiological bases.

Psychology

The benefits of animals for trauma recovery are often framed by biopsychosocial theories that explore the relationships between social beings, including social support, attachment, and cognitive perception. These theories generally relate to interactions between humans, but are reframed here to highlight their relevance to HAI.

Social Support Theory

The social support theory proposes that animals provide both direct and indirect support to humans. In a direct way, animals act as sources of nonjudgmental support, perceived unconditional positive regard, and companionship (Friedmann, Katcher, Lynch, & Thomas, 1980; Kruger, Trachtenberg, & Serpell, 2004; Wood et al., 2015). Indirectly, animals often serve as social lubricants or facilitators of interaction between humans (Gunter, 1999; McNicholas & Collis, 2006; O'Haire, McKenzie, Beck, & Slaughter, 2013).

Not only is a lack of social support one of the strongest predictors of developing PTS (Ozer, Best, Lipsey, & Weiss, 2003), but the presence of socially supportive connections often plays a critical role in the recovery from experiencing a traumatic event (Guay et al., 2006). In this context, a positive relationship with an animal provides a unique form of supportive companionship that may be unavailable or unsolicited from human social interaction (Serpell, McCune, Gee, & Griffin, 2017). Moreover, the emotional support received from an animal may also act as a "buffer" to attenuate perceived or anticipated stress (Polheber & Matchock, 2013). In the face of trauma, people can feel ostracized, stigmatized, and alone, with intrusive thoughts, flashbacks, and nightmares further isolating them from their communities and social networks. As a social facilitator, the trusted presence of an animal may help foster social engagement for these individuals, as well as their meaningful reconnection with society (Taylor et al., 2013; Wood et al., 2015).

Attachment Theory

There are many different ways to define attachment. Here we refer to attachment as the social bond created between two individuals, whether human or animal (Budge, Spicer, Jones, & George, 1998). It is most often characterized as a relationship that provides feelings of safety as a secure base (Bowlby, 2005). For individuals who have experienced trauma, there is a need for feelings of safety and security (Pearlman & Courtois, 2005), and in many cases, animals can offer this form of attachment in unique ways (Beck & Madresh, 2008; Kurdek, 2008). This is consistent with findings that humans gain social and emotional support from animals during stressful contexts (e.g., Beetz, Julius, Turner, & Kotrschal, 2012a; McNicholas & Collis, 2006). Additionally, the attachment relationship is often mutually beneficial, in which the animal may obtain emotional and physical security from a trusted human's care and presence (Prato-Previde, Custance, Spiezio, & Sabatini, 2003; Topál, Miklósi, Csányi, & Dóka, 1998).

There is some debate as to whether this form of attachment between humans and animals is adaptive in the long term, or whether it is most effective as a transitional relationship, similar to the use of transitional objects with children (Winnicott, 1953). In this scenario, the animal provides a source of comfort during the time of greatest need, which is slowly transitioned into security independent of the animal (Triebenbacher, 1998). The timing and duration of the attachment or transitional relationship likely depend on the severity and source of the trauma, the availability of the animal (e.g., whether a service animal or visiting therapy animal), and the needs of the individual.

Cognitive Perception

One of the least appreciated ways in which animals can benefit trauma survivors is through their ability to change people's perception. People with animals are perceived as friendlier, happier, less threatening, and more approachable (Eddy, Hart, & Boltz, 1988; Friedmann & Lockwood, 1991; Lockwood, 1983; McNicholas & Collis, 2000; Wells, 2004); such perceptions may serve to further facilitate interactions and support between people. Likewise, these perceptual differences also extend to environmental settings; the simple presence of an animal changes the way we discern our surroundings. Imagine the terrifying emotions that overwhelm individuals following a hurricane disaster. If the arrival of a friendly therapy dog can change the tone of the scene, this in and of itself is an important functional role of the animal. This perceptual change can also be useful in initial therapeutic encounters or in a wide range of clinical environments, including treatment approaches and settings for PTS. The clinician's office may be perceived as more welcoming and less threatening if an animal is present (Fine, 2010; Kruger, Serpell, & Fine, 2006; Wells & Perrine, 2001). It has also been suggested that the clinician will appear more approachable, which could in turn accelerate a therapeutic alliance necessary to achieve positive change (Wesley, Minatrea, & Watson, 2009).

Psychophysiology

Beyond the psychological theories that endeavor to explain our relationships with animals, there are several complementary psychophysiological mechanisms suggested to underlie HAIs. Such mechanisms highlighted here include arousal modulation and neuroendocrine changes.

Arousal Modulation

One of the core symptoms of PTS is hyperarousal, which includes a heightened state of alert (American Psychiatric Association, 2013). Often, individuals with PTS feel that danger is around every corner, and they cannot relax or feel at ease. It has been posited that the presence of an animal can reduce anxious arousal and encourage feelings of safety. For example, research in nontraumatized populations has demonstrated that being with or stroking an animal can lead to reductions in physiological indicators of arousal, such as lowered heart rate, blood pressure, and skin conductance (Friedmann, Katcher, Thomas, Lynch, & Messent, 1983; Nagengast et al., 1997; Odendaal & Meintjes, 2003; O'Haire, McKenzie, Beck, & Slaughter, 2015b; Vormbrock & Grossberg, 1988). Interacting with animals also significantly reduces self-reported fear and anxiety (Barker, Knisely, Schubert, Green, & Ameringer, 2015; Barker, Pandurangi, & Best, 2003; Lass-Hennemann, Peyk, Streb, Holz, & Michael, 2014). For individuals who experience intrusive flashbacks from trauma, anecdotal reports suggest that animals can alleviate hyperarousal and distress by promoting feelings of calmness and security (Taylor et al., 2013; Yount, Olmert, & Lee, 2012). Thus, the presence of an animal may act as an effective complementary strategy to modulate arousal in trauma populations to more productive levels for everyday functioning.

Neuroendocrine Changes

Neuroendocrine regulation plays a large role in current psychophysiological theories relevant to our connections with animals (Borgi & Cirulli, 2016), with various hormones having been proposed to underlie changes following HAI and AAI. One frequently researched biomarker relevant to arousal and stress is the hormone cortisol. Reductions in cortisol levels, as well as neurotransmitters like epinephrine and norepinephrine, during and following HAI demonstrate the stress-reducing capacity of animals (Beetz et al., 2012a; Cole, Gawlinski, Steers, & Kotlerman, 2007; Handlin et al., 2011; Odendaal, 2000; Odendaal & Meintjes, 2003). Moreover, the dysregulation of cortisol levels has been shown to impact brain functioning, specifically in the amygdala and hippocampus (which has implications for emotional response, memory, learning, and decision making) (Shin, Rauch, & Pitman, 2006; Yehuda, 2002). Perhaps not surprisingly, dysregulated cortisol levels are common among those with a PTSD diagnosis (Shin et al., 2006). Therefore, interventions that either help reduce or regulate cortisol—such as HAI—could likely be of multifaceted benefit for those with trauma histories.

Another primary target in current psychophysiological theory is the hormone oxytocin, which is often informally called "the love hormone" due to its relevancy in mother-infant bonding, as well as other attachment relationships (Beetz et al., 2012b; Galbally, Lewis, Ijzendoorn, & Permezel, 2011; Hurlemann & Scheele, 2016). Oxytocin also has far-reaching effects on social interaction (i.e., increasing trust, empathy, generosity) and stress (i.e., inhibiting stress-related activity), while also acting as an anxiolytic (MacDonald & MacDonald, 2010). Thus, oxytocin may modulate such PTS symptoms as hyperarousal, anxiety, and difficulty with interpersonal relationships. In fact, recent studies have begun to examine the potential therapeutic effects of intranasal oxytocin for individuals with PTS (e.g., Flanagan, Sippel, Wahlquist, Moran-Santa Maria, & Back, 2018). In HAI research, oxytocin has been shown to increase in both humans and pet dogs following short interactions, particularly those that involve gazing into one another's eyes (Handlin, Nilsson, Ejdebäck, Hydbring-Sandberg, & Uvnäs-Moberg, 2012; Miller et al., 2009; Nagasawa et al., 2015). These human and canine changes in hormone regulation are thought to provide physiological evidence for a long-held and (hopefully) mutually beneficial bond between humans and other animals (Beetz et al., 2012b).

EMERGING PRACTICES

As appreciation of our bonds with animals has gained momentum, so too has the field of HAI as a serious focus of academic and professional pursuit. Graduate-level programs in social work, psychology, counseling, public health, education, and veterinary medicine have increasingly begun to understand how important these relationships can be for both human and animal health (Jenkins, Ruehrdanz, McCullough, Casillas, & Fluke, 2012). For example, the Center for the Human-Animal Bond at Purdue University's College of Veterinary Medicine is a recognized pioneer in AAI education, as is the University of Denver's Graduate School of Social Work's (GSSW's) Institute for Human-Animal Connection. In fact, animal-assisted social work (or AASW), which is an empowerment-based AAI approach applicable across multiple settings, disciplines, and populations, has expanded GSSW's clinical- and practice-based education, and has brought many social workers in-training to the university.

Organizations such as Pet Partners, Therapy Dogs International (TDI), Alliance of Therapy Dogs, and the Professional Association of Therapeutic Horsemanship International (PATH Intl.) (to name a few) have spearheaded the promotion of AAI practice, as well as the registration and/or certification of therapy animals and their handlers to provide these services in a variety of settings. Likewise, many Assistance Dogs

International (ADI)-accredited organizations now specialize in the training and placement of service dogs with people who have disabilities, including PTSD. Worldwide, practitioners—ranging from mental health professionals to teachers to service dog trainers to community members and volunteers—are implementing diverse AAI applications in their efforts to help people recover from trauma.

Approaches to animal-assisted trauma recovery vary and are often tailored according to the following factors: 1) the client's source of trauma and/or diagnoses; 2) the client's individual needs and treatment goals; 3) the client's age, gender, race, socioeconomic status, and other key demographics; 4) the practitioner's discipline, training, theoretical framework(s), therapeutic methods, and resources; 5) the geographical location in which treatment is taking place; 6) the species, individual characteristics, and cultural perceptions of the animal(s); and 7) whether or not the animal is owned by the practitioner (i.e., a "therapy animal" who visits with a client) or the client (i.e., a "service animal," "emotional support animal," or "companion animal"/pet who lives with a client).

Given these various factors, it is somewhat difficult to provide a complete and accurate summary of what comprises typical or even prevailing AAI practice. Indeed, there is nothing typical about working with living animals (who also have unique needs and idiosyncrasies) to improve the lives of people. Further, even in comparable clinical situations where these factors are more or less controlled, AAI protocol fidelity is anything but commonplace. While a lack of pure practice fidelity is understandable, and in select cases necessary or even preferable, it can make determining "what works best" in AAI practice a significant challenge. This reality has, in part, contributed to the complexity of conducting sound and meaningful AAI studies across diverse populations (Trujillo, Tedeschi, & Williams, 2011).

Additionally, while it is true that rigorous experimental designs (e.g., randomized controlled trials or RCTs) are desirable for strong evidence of AAI effectiveness, it also is important to note that many relational aspects of HAIs are subtle or inherently qualitative and, thus, difficult to capture in quantitative methodologies alone. Some may dismiss the anecdotal and qualitative research that pervades the literature on HAI and AAI, but these data should not be rejected out of hand; just as quantitative data can inform issues of causation, generalizability, and mechanism, qualitative data often provides rich, detailed accounts of actual day-to-day applications and personal experiences. Of significance, embedded in these accounts we might seek or uncover specific approaches to support previously undefined needs of trauma survivors and/or the well-being of animals.

Because research and study methodology in the area of trauma-informed AAIs are just beginning to take shape and gain attention, we are hesitant to characterize and/or endorse any one practice model as being more effective than another. In truth, the AAI practice approaches and protocols outlined throughout this book, as well as others presently being implemented across the globe, should really be considered "emerging practices" that have a strong foundation in what we now know to be effective in both trauma and general AAI work. Concurrently, these existing and innovative practices should not be dismissed simply because research has not yet fully supported their use. Rather, this work should be encouraged and thoughtfully implemented to address the current needs of those with trauma and to inform research, thereby strengthening future practice (i.e., a "practice-to-research-to-practice" model).

As such, we proffer that the following are necessary steps in AAI practice and research development: 1) improve the ethical standards for all animals involved in AAI; 2) apply implementation science approaches toward AAI practice fidelity, including understanding what factors increase the effectiveness of these interventions and challenging the research to service delivery knowledge gap; 3) expand the confines of what is considered fundable research in this field, through more progressive and inclusive approaches, to spur scientific inquiry; and 4) foster intervention research and the inclusion of AAI practice in established degree programs. We hope to provide a resource for practitioners and the public-at-large on what is working feasibly and effectively as we speak, as well as identify knowledge gaps to optimize future study endeavors in the AAI field.

Practice With Therapy Animals

AAT and AAA are included under the umbrella term of AAI, and were developed primarily to complement more traditional treatment and therapeutic services. While many types of animals can be therapy animals, dogs—followed by horses—are by far the most common (Friedmann, Son, and Tsai, 2010; Granger & Kogan, 2006; Nimer & Lundahl, 2007; O'Haire et al., 2015a). As stated earlier, AAT is defined as a targeted intervention that incorporates a trained therapy animal to help clients or patients meet specific treatment goals. AAT sessions typically include a therapist or doctor, and the client is often matched with the same animal-handler team over the course of treatment. In contrast, AAAs are less formal, and are often characterized by brief therapy animal visits in hospitals, schools, libraries, and other settings. AAA visits, which tend to be more spontaneous than AAT sessions, seek mainly to provide people with comfort and enrichment. Of note, those in the HAI field often use these terms interchangeably or inconsistently when referring to their work, which, in turn, can cause confusion regarding practice intentions and specifics (Barker & Wolen, 2008; Palley, O'Rourke, & Niemi, 2010).

There is some debate among those in the field over how AAT sessions should be defined and structured. For example, some believe that in order for an intervention to be considered AAT, it must include: 1) the recipient; 2) the interventionist; 3) the animal-handler (often a volunteer); and 4) the therapy animal (Delta Society, 2008; Kruger & Serpell, 2010). Other schools of thought assert that the interventionist can also serve as the handler, and that this may even be the best option as the professional is likely knowledgeable about the particular recipient population and their needs. Conversely, others argue that having an interventionist serve as both professional and handler may place the client and the animal at risk, since the individual is unable to fully attend to either participant simultaneously (Jenkins et al., 2012).

At present, those who are interested in integrating therapy animals into their practice or volunteer work need not obtain any formal credentials to do so. That said, it is strongly recommended, and often required (depending upon the setting), that the individual not only seek AAI education, but also train, register, and insure the individual's therapy animal through such organizations as Pet Partners, TDI, or PATH Intl. Each registering body has their own specific standards of practice, and many require that the handler and animal be reregistered on a regular basis. Examples of such practice standards with dogs specifically include: the dog must be at least one year of age and be in good physical health; the dog's behavior must be predictable in a variety of unfamiliar settings; the dog and handler must complete repeated training courses and pass evaluations; the animal-handler team should visit for no more than two hours at a time, to allow for the dog to rest and express normal behaviors; and the dog should actively seek interaction with people during visits (Pet Partners, 2017).

Further, central to the registration process is for the handler to develop a keen understanding of the animal they are partnering with, including the animal's suitability for therapy work, their individual and species-specific needs, and their typical and stress-related behaviors (VanFleet, Fine, O'Callaghan, Mackintosh, & Gimeno, 2015). Equally important is to be knowledgeable about the population served, and how best to meet their needs while ensuring that the animal is safe and enjoying the therapeutic interaction. Taken together, these proficiencies are necessary to support a mutually beneficial experience for the people and therapy animals involved.

Practice With Service Animals

Service or assistance animals (most commonly dogs) differ from therapy animals in that they live with the person they are serving, and are trained to perform specific, quantifiable tasks to ease the challenges associated with that person's physical and/or psychiatric disability (Sutton, 2015). The 1990 Americans with Disabilities Act (ADA) stipulates legally covered disabilities among service dog owners, including visual and hearing impairments, physical mobility issues, multiple sclerosis, diabetes, epilepsy, autism, and a PTSD diagnosis (American Humane, 2016; U.S. Department of Justice, 2011). At the turn of the last century, it was estimated that approximately 10,000 dogs were service dogs. With time and increased interest in how animals impact our well-being, the number of service dogs (and the individuals and organizations that provide them) have also experienced steady growth (Sandler, 1996).

That said, there currently is a lack of universally recognized service dog training, certification, and identification standards, and professional trainers, organizations, and laypersons may all train service dogs. This lack of evidence-based standardization often presents confusion regarding practice and even the rights of those with service dogs, such as in their access to housing, public places, and travel (American Humane, 2016). At a minimum, service dogs should be individually trained in the essential functions or tasks that a person could not otherwise perform due to his or her disability. In addition, service dogs should be well behaved in the community and with strangers (as specified by the Public Access Test), and have a strong sense of loyalty to their handler (Psychiatric Service Dog Partners, 2017). Yet, given the needs of those they serve, much more is often required of these dogs. Several organizations and stakeholders are currently responding to the growing need for qualified PTS service dogs by developing and optimizing additional training and evaluation standards.

Recent research advancements indicate that service dogs may be able to help veterans with PTS or traumatic brain injury (TBI) confront their symptoms by providing a sense of security and serving as a motivator to engage positively with people and the world around them (U.S. Department of Veterans Affairs or VA, 2014). While some organizations specialize in providing dogs to veterans (e.g., K9s For Warriors, Paws Assisting Veterans, paws4people), others focus on having veterans train service dogs for fellow veterans with disabilities (e.g., Warrior Canine Connection). Both K9s For Warriors and Warrior Canine Connection are the subjects of ongoing research, via the VA, the Center for the Human-Animal Bond at Purdue University, and others, with initial efficacy data indicating positive outcomes for veterans (i.e., reduced PTSD symptomology, increased quality of life, and positive social relationships) (Kloep, Hunter, & Kertz, 2017; O'Haire et al., 2015a; Yarborough et al., 2017).

EVIDENCE-BASED RESEARCH

To validate the growing accounts of positive outcomes from HAI and AAI practices, scientists have begun to conduct an increasing number of studies to better understand if, how, and when animals can benefit humans. As discussed previously, practice is vastly outpacing research with respect to trauma populations. However, there are a small group of studies that have paved the way for this emerging and critical field of research.

A recent systematic review identified ten studies on AAI for trauma, of which four were unpublished theses (O'Haire et al., 2015a). Since that time, we have identified a handful more, including a few unpublished theses, which have now been published in peer-reviewed scientific journals. Though sparse, the studies have been notably positive. The majority of the research to date has focused on child victims of abuse, with little to no research on military veterans and/or those in need of crisis response (see figure). Most study populations were children and adolescents, with some focused on adults. The dearth of research on adults with military trauma is quickly changing, however, with many ongoing studies on the topic. The most common animals in this review were dogs and horses, with some studies including a broad range of farm animals that often also included dogs and horses.

The characteristics of the intervention in research were wide-ranging, yet there were some patterns. Outside of service dogs, AAI interventions

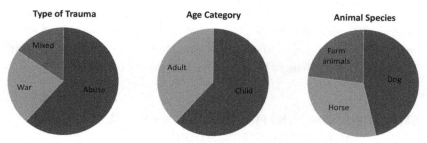

Breakdown of key elements of current research on AAI for trauma.

with a therapy animal included a set number of sessions of time-limited duration. Sessions typically occurred 1–2 times per week over the course of 7–8 weeks. Roughly half of the sessions were conducted with groups of clients, while the other half were one-on-one with an individual and interventionist. Session duration was highly variable, ranging from 20 minutes to four hours. The interventionists had varying backgrounds, from clinical psychologists to animal trainers to untrained volunteers. There was no standardized procedure described for intervening, and/or training the animal, handler, or team. Likewise, whether or not the animal and handler were registered to provide AAI was not well-documented. Thus, across all studies, the main unifying component was simply an animal's presence. This illustrates that the field of research, as well as practice, is emerging and has not yet identified the most effective, or best, protocols to follow.

Though most studies were small and preliminary, several findings emerged as areas that may be promising for further investigation. That said, they should be interpreted with caution, as the research in this area is in its infancy, requiring much larger and more rigorous designs to validate initial outcomes. One of the most commonly reported outcomes concerned depression, with seven studies reporting reduced depressive symptoms in participants from before to after AAI sessions. PTSD symptomology and anxiety were also key outcome measures. One notable study compared the mental health and functioning of 153 children, ages 7–17 years, undergoing group treatment for childhood sexual abuse either with (treatment) or without (control) AAT with a therapy dog. Results indicated that children in the AAT group exhibited lower anxiety, depression, anger, and PTSD symptoms than those receiving usual group treatment (Dietz, Davis, & Pennings, 2012). Additional outcomes across fewer studies included increased positive emotion, life satisfaction, and social engagement in conjunction with AAI. Further positive outcomes were reported, yet the aforementioned areas emerged across multiple studies, and thus, may be the most reasonable areas to anticipate changes from AAI for trauma as a broad category.

ETHICAL FOUNDATIONS FOR THE HUMAN-ANIMAL BOND AND ANIMAL-ASSISTED INTERVENTION

Equally important to supporting human well-being and trauma recovery via AAI is the need to ensure that the animals who provide this important work—often when incorporated or deployed in traumatic working environments—are offered optimum support, care, protection from harm, and respect in terms of their own individual needs and preferences. Throughout this book, we intend to celebrate, clarify, and advocate for the roles of animals in our lives, while also honoring the principles of mutuality in human-animal relationships and ensuring that the emerging AAI field does not ignore the responsibility to animal well-being. We also feel it is critical to draw specific attention to the procedure, practices, and issues related to animal well-being, as well as to the ethical responsibilities we have to animals who are activated to the agenda of human health.

As Dr. Leo Bustad reflected on over 20 years ago in his timeless book, *Compassion: Our Last Great Hope*, with sensitivity and responsibility guiding the development of new AAI practices, we must also seek specificity related to ensuring that we are not establishing yet another homocentric or exploitive approach to our relationships with nonhuman animals (Bustad, 1990). Accordingly, those who involve animals in their work to help improve the lives of others have a strict, moral, and enduring responsibility to the animal participants. The American Veterinary Medical Association (AVMA, 2017) has offered the following widely circulated definition of the human-animal bond (HAB)—one that not only describes the features of our relationships with animals and the environment, but also highlights the importance of mutuality:

A mutually beneficial and dynamic relationship between people and animals that is influenced by behaviors that are essential to the health and well-being *of both* [emphasis added by this chapter's authors]. This includes, but is not limited to, emotional, psychological, and physical interactions of people, [other] animals, and the environment. (para. 1)

Of note, the conceptualization and place that nonhuman animals hold in status and value may render oversimplified notions about the nature of these relationships. It is important to acknowledge that the HAB has existed in numerous forms, and that accounts of human-animal relationships and AAI vary across cultures and countries. These connections include many types of nonhuman animals who have historically served as rich sources of social support, protection, and "objects" of bidirectional affection and attachment.

As noted previously, the most common species of animals selected for use in AAIs are dogs and horses, although some organizations permit the registration of other species. Likewise, many therapeutic farms maintain a variety of animals, such as pigs, miniature horses, goats, sheep, chickens, turkeys, birds, cows, reptiles, small animals (e.g., guinea pigs), and even wildlife. In-the-wild interactions, such as swimming with dolphins or riding elephants, have increasingly gained in popularity despite a lack of consensus regarding their efficacy, impact on animals, and ethical implications (Serpell, Coppinger, Fine, & Peralta, 2010; Zamir, 2006). Zamir (2006) makes a strong argument against the use of any wildlife in AAIs; indeed, Zamir attests that due to the domestication process and the likelihood of severe species reduction or elimination among wildlife populations, only dogs and horses are suitable for inclusion in AAIs. Despite potential for animal harm in animal-assisted work due to rough handling, injuries, illness or stress, Zamir (2006) ultimately concludes that both dogs and horses live healthier, longer, and more comfortable lives symbiotically with humans, and that "a world in which practices like AAT exist is an overall better world for these beings than one that does not include them" (p. 195). It should be noted, however, that many agencies and organizations do not adopt this position and continue to utilize a wide variety of both wild and domestic species for the anticipated benefit to humans via these animal interactions. Although we are not endorsing that only specific species participate in AAI, this lack of cohesion across the HAI field, along with other factors, emphasizes the necessity to establish and constantly refine ethical standards that address these discrepancies and prioritize well-being as a condition for any animal's inclusion in AAI applications.

Current Approaches to Advocacy and the
Support of Animal Well-Being

The development of an ethical framework for the conscientious inclusion of animals for therapeutic purpose has historically been contentious. Experts in animal welfare, behavior, and ethics continue to debate issues surrounding consciousness, sentience, and the rights of animals (Bekoff, 2007). For example, some contend that if society demands strictly scientific or quantifiable data prior to the enactment of policy or standards, we may continue to struggle for some time with the requisite assessment and measurement of animals' more subjective internal states, such as emotion, quality of life, and pain. Conversely, others argue that by accepting the "face value" of human perception of animal well-being, the risk is unacceptably high that competing motivators or factors (i.e., economics, personal gain, ignorance, and/or consciously or unconsciously placing a higher priority on human [both client and handler] needs, rather than animal needs) may unduly influence and compromise the integrity of one's perspective (Tedeschi, Bexell, & NeSmith, 2013). Therefore, as discussions regarding subjective internal states remain important in furthering our understanding of non-human animals and their experiences, we may be unable to wait for such debates to be settled in the abstract while animals are being asked to work now under a host of increasingly complex AAI conditions (many of them "high-stress" in nature). With that said, below are some current, important contributions that attempt to provide a grounded, ethical framework when working and living with animals in the context of AAI.

IAHAIO Definitions and Guidelines

In 2014, the International Association of Human-Animal Interaction Organizations (IAHAIO), one of the key professional organizations advancing the HAI field, released a white paper entitled *The IAHAIO Definitions for Animal Assisted Intervention and Animal Assisted Activity and Guidelines for Wellness of Animals Involved* (Jegatheesan et al., 2014). This succinct report provides a clear discussion regarding ways to improve attention to both the physical and emotional health of the participating animal. For example, many animals are particularly sensitive to anger and emotion. Interventions that place an animal at the center of a family working through conflict, and/or encourage an individual to share their traumatic experiences with the animal present, may pose a stressful experience for participating animals.

Often, the enthusiasm surrounding the field's potential can create a rush to incorporate animals in therapeutic situations without careful concern for efficacy and safety, as well as ethical regard for the nonhuman participant(s). Yet, the integrity and welfare of our animal participants need to be imminently addressed to ensure conscientious, responsible, and effective AAI practice. The matter is all the more urgent as the incorporation of AAIs in therapeutic settings continues to expand and diversify. As such, an immediate priority for AAI practice should be the development and finesse of a dynamic code of ethics that parallels and evolves to match actual AAI practices. At present, this IAHAIO report seeks to identify the welfare needs of therapy animals, and serves as a valuable resource for professionals who include animals in their practices and services.

The Five Freedoms

The Five Freedoms, originally published in the *Brambell Report* in 1965, are arguably the most frequently referenced framework for assuring animal welfare. Initially developed to address the welfare needs of farm animals, they are also relevant in other HAI and AAI applications. The Five Freedoms state that animals are entitled to: 1) freedom from thirst, hunger, and malnutrition; 2) freedom from discomfort; 3) freedom from pain, injury, and disease; 4) freedom from fear and distress; and 5) freedom to express normative behavior (Brambell, 1965).

In the most recent and currently available edition of *The Handbook on Animal-Assisted Therapy* (Fine, 2015), veterinarian Dr. Zenithson Ng and his colleagues reflect on a useful expansion of the Five Freedoms into three key areas (*physical, affective,* and *nature*), and provide several examples of the well-being issues facing animals in therapeutic settings (such as sensitivity to anger and high emotion, as discussed above). In addition, they make a point of identifying the animal-handler as critical to ensuring attention to these details (Ng, Albright, Fine, & Peralta, 2015). Of note, Dr. Ng also discusses the Five Freedoms in the context of AAI in chapter 2 of this volume.

The Therapy Animal's Bill of Rights

In her recent book, *Teaming with Your Therapy Dog* (2015), longtime animal-assisted social worker Ann Howie offers a unique juxtaposition by suggesting a Therapy Animal Bill of Rights. Howie has written this Bill of Rights—with selected, key elements included below—from the perspective of therapy dogs to exemplify the importance of their needs, preferences, and experiences (Howie, Fine, and Rojas expand upon these in chapter 9). Howie (2015) writes,

> As a therapy dog, I have the right to a handler who:
>
> - Provides gentle training to help me understand what I am supposed to do
> - Is considerate of my perception of the world
> - Helps me adapt to the work environment
> - Guides clients, staff, and visitors to interact with me appropriately
> - Takes action to reduce my stress
> - Provides a well-rounded life with nutritious food, medical care, physical and intellectual exercise, social time, and activities beyond work
> - Respects my desire to retire from my work when I think it is time (p. 125)

The Capabilities Approach

Nussbaum's Capabilities Approach (2006), with its focus on dignity, respect, and justice, offers an ethical practice framework that is both extensive and flexible enough to account for each AAI participant, as well as a wide variety of treatment modalities. The ten capabilities that apply to both human and animal participants in AAI include: 1) life; 2) bodily health; 3) bodily integrity; 4) senses, imagination, and thought; 5) emotions; 6) practical reason; 7) affiliation; 8) other species; 9) play; and 10) control over one's environment.

In the context of human healing professions, the dignity of all participants involved must be considered. From this view, adopting a code of ethics where the integrity and welfare of the animal participants is valued at least as much, or even more highly, than the perceived benefit to human recipients should again be an imminent goal for organizations, educational institutions, and individual practitioners. Arguably, only when an animal is properly cared for will there actually be a therapeutic transfer. The Capabilities Approach provides a sound, practical, and ethical foundation of justice and respect for all beings involved in AAI (to be established at the outset and continued throughout the therapeutic process), and offers a common ground to move forward in a unified effort to improve the lives of both humans and animals. According to Nussbaum (2006),

> Animals are entitled to a wide range of capabilities to function, those that are most essential to a flourishing life, a life worthy of the dignity of each creature. Animals have entitlements based upon justice. (p. 392)

Physiological measures have been both the traditional "gold standard" and elusive "holy grail" in the inquiries regarding the welfare of therapy and service animals, despite frequent calls for the addition of more holistic approaches that assess the whole animal (Taylor & Mills, 2007; Yeates & Main, 2009). Vital to the discussion of ethics, welfare, and the quality of life of animal participants in AAIs are centered concerns regarding working conditions (i.e., length and frequency of working time and breaks, setting familiarity, temperature, water accessibility, amount of space, and tasks/weight loads); positive versus negative training methods; (chronic) stress; calming signals, displacement, and/or stereotypic behaviors; communication; and social/activity needs (Ng et al., 2015). However, current limitations should neither halt inquiry nor should an ethical AAI framework that is too rigid to allow for scientific growth or the development of more progressive models be adopted. Rather, enhancing awareness and understanding of these various issues, and their relationship to animal welfare, are important components of continued research progress and AAI practice advancement.

GAPS AND NEXT STEPS

It is an exciting and important time to be involved in research on AAI for trauma because the evidence base has received so little attention to date. Preliminary studies have begun to establish proof-of-concept by demonstrating positive outcomes from interacting with animals (O'Haire et al., 2015a). The next step in this direction is to convincingly demonstrate that the benefits of including an animal in trauma treatment are above and beyond what would be expected from the presence of another novel, appealing entity (i.e., a toy, game, or activity), which would presumably be less costly or logistically complex to incorporate/implement if effective.

It is also vital to evidence that the outcomes are not simply reported because people want to see them happen. This is often called an "expectancy bias," and occurs when people are invested in seeing change and thus report that there is change (and often believe there is change) even when there is not (Rosenthal & Rosnow, 1991). Common ways to address this threat to the validity of the research are to include reports from people who are not invested in the outcomes (or do not even know the treatment occurred) or to incorporate physiological measurements, which should be inherently less biased. Thoughtful measurement and research design are the keys to advancing the reputation and credibility of AAI for trauma.

Other critical areas to pursue are intervention development and quality enhancement. All of the AAI programs for trauma that have been published in research studies have used different formats, programs, and timing (O'Haire et al., 2015a). Few have published a protocol or manual that can be replicated. Thus, even if research shows that one program works, how can another program in another state or country expect the same outcomes? Without a manual, replicable protocol, or an evidence base for the core components of the program, it is nearly impossible to expect the same outcomes to occur and/or to systematically enhance the program's practices. Some practitioners are understandably hesitant to move toward manualization due to the individualized nature of their practice (Addis, Wade, & Hatgis, 1999). However, manualized modules could arguably allow for flexibility if they were selected for independent use (i.e., where an interventionist selects the specific modules that best suit the individual). Likewise, recommendations could be customized for specific populations, and a set of standardized options could be provided to suit a variety of species, settings, and practitioner preferences. The need for evidence-based protocols should not be hindered by individual differences; rather, these needs should drive the creation and evaluation of tailored and adaptable components and modules that can be scientifically evaluated and improved over time (Connor-Smith & Weisz, 2003).

An additional important gap in the current research is evidence of the components that are most important and effective to drive positive outcomes from AAI for trauma specifically. For example, we do not know if it is more effective to have 1 session versus 10 versus 100. We do not know the "dose" required to see a treatment response or the most effective frequency (e.g., once weekly versus once monthly). These are important research questions to address following preliminary efficacy studies. Conducting a components analysis of the intervention can assist practitioners in knowing which activities may be most effective with animals, which animals to include, how important bonding with the same animal is versus the importance of novelty, and the multitude of other choices interventionists make when designing and implementing AAI "best practices" for trauma. Instead of viewing one's own AAI program as superior and complete, we recommend a continued process of testing and collecting data, no matter how small or technical the scale, to enhance and provide the best possible services to individuals who are seeking assistance through HAI.

A final and immensely important gap in the current research is further study of the well-being of the animals involved. This goes beyond a simple determination of whether or not the animals are safe and well overall. It involves a component analysis to ensure that we understand which activities are best for *both* the human and the animal. We suspect that the most optimal outcomes occur when both parties are engaged and benefiting from the interaction. Without the animal, AAI does not exist. Both quantitative and qualitative research should place more emphasis on this essential partnership to maximize mutually beneficial outcomes and ethical standards.

CONCLUSIONS

The emerging landscape of HAI for trauma deserves attention. It has anecdotally saved lives and created hope for others. From incorporating animals into first response crisis teams to therapeutic interventions for those who have faced the anguish of war and violence, AAI continues to permeate into trauma treatment and recovery. However, the scientific foundation of these various practices is currently limited and, as such, federal (and other) support for programming has been sparse. Research is being far outpaced by current AAI practice, and it is clear that additional scientific inquiry is needed to quantify outcomes and create a solid evidence base.

While animals may not be appropriate for all individuals who have experienced trauma, it is essential to identify and validate those whom they can help. Understanding bidirectional effects is also of paramount importance, with welfare implications for both participating human and nonhuman animals. Existing and innovative AAI applications and inquiries should continue to address the urgent needs of those with trauma, ensure the well-being of animal participants, inform future research, and optimize practice. We hope this chapter, as well as others in this volume, will contribute to these efforts by shining a light on how trauma-informed AAIs are currently understood and realized, as well as how they may be strengthened as the field continues to advance.

REFERENCES

Addis, M. E., Wade, W. A., & Hatgis, C. (1999). Barriers to dissemination of evidence-based practices: Addressing practitioners' concerns about manual-based psychotherapies. *Clinical Psychology: Science and Practice, 6*(4), 430–441.

Alexander, D. A., & Klein, S. (2009). First responders after disasters: A review of stress reactions, at-risk, vulnerability, and resilience factors. *Prehospital and disaster medicine, 24*(02), 87–94.

American Humane. (2016). *Wags4Patriots guide to getting a PTS service dog.* Unpublished report. Retrieved from https://www.americanhumane.org/app /uploads/2016/08/Wags4Patriots-guide-to-getting-a-PTS-service-dog.pdf

American Psychiatric Association. (2013). *Diagnostic and statistical manual of mental disorders: DSM-5* (5th ed.). Washington, DC: Author.

American Veterinary Medical Association. (2017). *Human-animal bond.* Retrieved from https://www.avma.org/KB/Resources/Reference/human-animal-bond /Pages/Human-Animal-Bond-AVMA.aspx

Anda, R. F., Felitti, V. J., Bremner, J. D., Walker, J. D., Whitfield, C., Perry, B. D., Dube, S. R., & Giles, W. H. (2006). The enduring effects of abuse and related adverse experiences in childhood. *European Archives of Psychiatry and Clinical Neuroscience, 256*(3), 174–186.

Arluke, A., Levin, J., Luke, C., & Ascione, F. (1999). The relationship of animal abuse to violence and other forms of antisocial behavior. *Journal of Interpersonal Violence, 14*(9), 963–975.

Ascione, F. R., & Arkow, P. (1999). *Child abuse, domestic violence, and animal abuse: Linking the circles of compassion for prevention and intervention*: West Lafayette, IN: Purdue University Press.

Banks, M. R., & Banks, W. A. (2002). The effects of animal-assisted therapy on loneliness in an elderly population in long-term care facilities. *The Journals of Gerontology, Series A: Biological Sciences and Medical Sciences, 57*(7), M428–M432.

Barker, S. B., Knisely, J. S., Schubert, C. M., Green, J. D., & Ameringer, S. (2015).

The effect of an animal-assisted intervention on anxiety and pain in hospitalized children. *Anthrozoös, 28*(1), 101–112.

Barker, S. B., Pandurangi, A. K., & Best, A. M. (2003). Effects of animal-assisted therapy on patients' anxiety, fear, and depression before ECT. *The Journal of ECT, 19*(1), 38–44.

Barker, S. B., & Wolen, A. R. (2008). The benefits of human-companion animal interaction: A review. *Journal of Veterinary Medical Education, 35*(4), 487–495.

Beck, L., & Madresh, E. A. (2008). Romantic partners and four-legged friends: An extension of attachment theory to relationships with pets. *Anthrozoös, 21*(1), 43–56.

Becker, C. B., Zayfert, C., & Anderson, E. (2004). A survey of psychologists' attitudes towards and utilization of exposure therapy for PTSD. *Behaviour research and therapy, 42*(3), 277–292.

Beetz, A., Julius, H., Turner, D., & Kotrschal, K. (2012a). Effects of social support by a dog on stress modulation in male children with insecure attachment. *Frontiers in Psychology, 3*, 352.

Beetz, A., Uvnäs-Moberg, K., Julius, H., & Kotrschal, K. (2012b). Psychosocial and psychophysiological effects of human-animal interactions: The possible role of oxytocin. *Frontiers in Psychology, 3*, 234.

Bekoff, M. (2007). *The emotional lives of animals.* Novato, CA: New World Library.

Borgi, M., & Cirulli, F. (2016). Pet face: Mechanisms underlying human-animal relationships. *Frontiers in Psychology, 7*, 298.

Bowlby, J. (2005). *A secure base: Clinical applications of attachment theory* (Vol. 393): Taylor & Francis.

Brambell, F. W. R. (1965). *Report of the technical committee to enquire into the welfare of animals kept under intensive livestock husbandry systems: Command Paper 2836.* London, UK: Her Majesty's Stationary Office.

Breslau, N. (2009). The epidemiology of trauma, PTSD, and other posttrauma disorders. *Trauma, Violence, & Abuse, 10*(3), 198–210.

Breslau, N., Kessler, R. C., Chilcoat, H. D., Schultz, L. R., Davis, G. C., & Andreski, P. (1998). Trauma and posttraumatic stress disorder in the community: The 1996 Detroit Area Survey of Trauma. *Archives of general psychiatry, 55*(7), 626–632.

Bromwich, J. E. (2016, June 16). *In a Shaken Orlando, Comfort Dogs Arrive With "Unconditional Love."* Retrieved from http://nytimes.com/2016/us/in-a-shaken-orlando-comfort-dogs-arrive-with-unconditional-love.html?_r=0

Budge, R. C., Spicer, J., Jones, B., & George, R. S. (1998). Health correlates of compatibility and attachment in human-companion animal relationships. *Society & Animals, 6*(3), 219–234.

Bustad, L. K. (1990). *Compassion: Our last great hope.* Renton, WA: Delta Society.

Chandler, C. K. (2005). Crisis and disaster response counseling with therapy animals. In C. K. Chandler (Ed.), *Animal assisted therapy in counseling* (1st ed., pp. 271–287). Boca Raton, FL: CRC Press.

Chandler, C. K. (Ed.). (2012). *Animal assisted therapy in counseling* (2nd ed.). New York, NY: Routledge.

Cole, K. M., Gawlinski, A., Steers, N., & Kotlerman, J. (2007). Animal-assisted therapy in patients hospitalized with heart failure. *American Journal of Critical Care, 16*(6), 575–585.

Connor-Smith, J. K., & Weisz, J. R. (2003). Applying treatment outcome research in clinical practice: Techniques for adapting interventions to the real world. *Child and Adolescent Mental Health, 8*(1), 3–10.

Crawford, J. J. (2003). *Therapy pets: The animal-human healing partnership.* Amherst, NY: Prometheus Books.

Currie, C. L. (2006). Animal cruelty by children exposed to domestic violence. *Child Abuse & Neglect, 30*(4), 425–435.

Delta Society. (2008). *Pet Partners team training course: Student manual* (7th ed.). Bellevue, WA: Delta Society.

Dietz, T. J., Davis, D., & Pennings, J. (2012). Evaluating animal-assisted therapy in group treatment for child sexual abuse. *Journal of Child Sexual Abuse, 21*(6), 665–683.

Eddy, J., Hart, L. A., & Boltz, R. P. (1988). The effects of service dogs on social acknowledgements of people in wheelchairs. *Journal of Psychology, 122*(1), 39.

Figley, C. R. (1995). Compassion fatigue: Toward a new understanding of the costs of caring. In B. H. Stamm (Ed.), *Secondary traumatic stress: Self-care issues for clinicians, researchers, and educators* (2nd ed., pp. 3–28). Lutherville, MD: Sidran.

Fine, A. H. (2010). Incorporating animal-assisted therapy into psychotherapy: Guidelines and suggestions for therapists. In A. H. Fine (Ed.), *Animal-assisted therapy: Theoretical foundations and guidance for practice* (3rd ed., pp. 169–191). San Diego, CA: Elsevier.

Fine, A. H. (Ed.). (2015). *Handbook on animal-assisted therapy: Foundations and guidelines for animal-assisted interventions* (4th ed.). San Diego, CA: Academic Press.

Fine, A. H., O'Callaghan, D., Chandler, C., Schaffer, K., Pichot, T., & Gimeno, J. (2010). Application of animal-assisted interventions in counseling settings: An overview of alternatives. In A. H. Fine (Ed.), *Animal-assisted therapy: Theoretical foundations and guidelines for practice* (3rd ed., pp. 193–222). San Diego, CA: Elsevier.

Flanagan, J. C., Sippel, L. M., Wahlquist, A., Moran-Santa Maria, M. M., & Back, S. E. (2018). Augmenting prolonged exposure therapy for PTSD with intranasal oxytocin: A randomized, placebo-controlled pilot trial. *Journal of Psychiatric Research, 98*, 64–69.

Flannery Jr, R. B. (1990). Social support and psychological trauma: A methodological review. *Journal of Traumatic Stress, 3*(4), 593–611.

Foa, E. B., Chrestman, K. R., & Gilboa-Schechtman, E. (2008). *Prolonged exposure therapy for adolescents with PTSD emotional processing of traumatic experiences: Therapist guide.* Oxford, UK: Oxford University Press.

Foa, E. B., Dancu, C. V., Hembree, E. A., Jaycox, L. H., Meadows, E. A., & Street, G. P. (1999). A comparison of exposure therapy, stress inoculation training, and their combination for reducing posttraumatic stress disorder in female assault victims. *Journal of Consulting and Clinical Psychology, 67*(2), 194.

Friedmann, E., Katcher, A. H., Lynch, J. J., & Thomas, S. A. (1980). Animal companions and one-year survival of patients after discharge from a coronary care unit. *Public Health Reports, 95*(4), 307–312.

Friedmann, E., Katcher, A. H., Thomas, S. A., Lynch, J. J., & Messent, P. R. (1983). Social interaction and blood pressure: Influence of animal companions. *Journal of Nervous and Mental Disease, 171*(8), 461–465.

Friedmann, E., & Lockwood, R. (1991). Validation and use of the animal thematic apperception test (ATAT). *Anthrozoös, 4*(3), 174–183.

Friedmann, E., Son, H., & Tsai, C. (2010). The animal/human bond: Health and wellness. In A.H. Fine (Ed.), *Handbook on animal-assisted therapy: Theoretical foundations and guidelines for practice* (3rd ed., pp. 85–107). San Diego, CA: Elsevier Inc.

Galbally, M., Lewis, A. J., Ijzendoorn, M. v., & Permezel, M. (2011). The role of oxytocin in mother-infant relations: A systematic review of human studies. *Harvard Review of Psychiatry, 19*(1), 1–14.

Gracia, E. (1995). Visible but unreported: A case for the "not serious enough" cases of child maltreatment. *Child Abuse & Neglect, 19*(9), 1083–1093.

Granger, B. P., & Kogan, L. (2006). Characteristics of animal-assisted therapy: Animal-assisted therapy in specialized settings. In A. H. Fine (Ed.), *Handbook on animal-assisted therapy: Theoretical foundations and guidelines for practice* (2nd ed., pp. 213–236). San Diego, CA: Academic Press.

Greenbaum, S. (2005). Introduction to working with animal assisted crisis response animal handler teams. *International Journal of Emergency Mental Health, 8*(1), 49–63.

Guay, S., Billette, V., & Marchand, A. (2006). Exploring the links between posttraumatic stress disorder and social support: processes and potential research avenues. *Journal of Traumatic Stress, 19*(3), 327–338.

Gunter, B. (1999). *Pets and people: The psychology of pet ownership.* London: Whurr Publishers Ltd.

Handlin, L., Hydbring-Sandberg, E., Nilsson, A., Ejdebäck, M., Jansson, A., & Uvnäs-Moberg, K. (2011). Short-term interaction between dogs and their owners: Effects on oxytocin, cortisol, insulin and heart rate—An exploratory study. *Anthrozoös, 24*(3), 301–315.

Handlin, L., Nilsson, A., Ejdebäck, M., Hydbring-Sandberg, E., & Uvnäs-Moberg, K. (2012). Associations between the psychological characteristics of the human-dog relationship and oxytocin and cortisol levels. *Anthrozoös, 25*(2), 215–228.

Hansen, K. M., Messinger, C. J., Baun, M. M., & Megel, M. (1999). Companion animals alleviating distress in children. *Anthrozoös, 12*(3), 142–148.

Howie, A. R. (2015). *Teaming with your therapy dog.* West Lafayette, IN: Purdue University Press.

Hurlemann, R., & Scheele, D. (2016). Dissecting the role of oxytocin in the formation and loss of social relationships. *Biological Psychiatry, 79*(3), 185–193.

Imel, Z. E., Laska, K., Jakupcak, M., & Simpson, T. L. (2013). Meta-analysis of dropout in treatments for posttraumatic stress disorder. *Journal of Consulting and Clinical Psychology, 81*(3), 394–404.

Jegatheesan, B., Beetz, A., Choi, G., Dudzik, C., Fine, A., Garcia, R. M., Johnson, R., Ormerod, E., Winkle, M., & Yamazaki, K. (2014). *White paper: The IAHAIO definitions for animal assisted intervention and guidelines for wellness of animals involved.* Unpublished report. Retrieved from http://www.iahaio.org /new/fileuploads/4163IAHAIO%20WHITE%20PAPER-%20FINAL%20 -%20NOV%2024-2014.pdf

Jenkins, M. A., Ruehrdanz, A., McCullough, A., Casillas, K., & Fluke, J. D. (2012). *Canines and Childhood Cancer: Examining the effects of therapy dogs with childhood cancer patients and their families—Literature review.* Unpublished report. Pfizer Animal Health (currently Zoetis) and American Humane. Retrieved from https://www.americanhumane.org/app/uploads/2016/08 /january2012clcompressed.pdf

Kilpatrick, D. G., Resnick, H. S., Milanak, M. E., Miller, M. W., Keyes, K. M., & Friedman, M. J. (2013). National estimates of exposure to traumatic events and PTSD prevalence using DSM-IV and DSM-5 criteria. *Journal of Traumatic Stress, 26*(5), 537–547.

Kloep, M. L., Hunter, R. H., & Kertz, S. J. (2017). Examining the effects of a novel training program and use of psychiatric service dogs for military-related PTSD and associated symptoms. *American Journal of Orthopsychiatry, 87*(4), 425–433.

Kruger, K. A., & Serpell, J. A. (2010). Animal-assisted interventions in mental health: Definitions and theoretical foundations. In A. H. Fine (Ed.), *Handbook on animal-assisted therapy: Theoretical foundations and guidelines for practice* (3rd ed., pp. 33–48). San Diego: Academic Press.

Kruger, K. A., Serpell, J. A., & Fine, A. (2006). Animal-assisted interventions in mental health: Definitions and theoretical foundations. *Handbook on animal-assisted therapy: Theoretical foundations and guidelines for practice* (2nd ed., pp. 21–38). San Diego: Academic Press.

Kruger, K. A., Trachtenberg, S. W., & Serpell, J. A. (2004). *Can animals help humans heal? Animal-assisted interventions in adolescent mental health.* Philadelphia, PA: Center for the Interaction of Animals and Society, University of Pennsylvania School of Veterinary Medicine.

Kurdek, L. A. (2008). Pet dogs as attachment figures. *Journal of Social and Personal Relationships, 25*(2), 247–266.

Lass-Hennemann, J., Peyk, P., Streb, M., Holz, E., & Michael, T. (2014). Presence of a dog reduces subjective but not physiological stress responses to an analog trauma. *Frontiers in Psychology, 5*, 1010.

Lockwood, R. (1983). The influence of animals on social perception. In A. H. Katcher & A. M. Beck (Eds.), *New perspectives on our lives with companion animals* (pp. 64–72). Philadelphia, PA: University of Pennsylvania Press.

MacDonald, K., & MacDonald, T. M. (2010). The peptide that binds: A systematic review of oxytocin and its prosocial effects in humans. *Harvard Review of Psychiatry, 18*(1), 1–21.

Marr, C. A., French, L., Thompson, D., Drum, L., Greening, G., Mormon, J., Henderson, I., & Hughes, C. W. (2000). Animal-assisted therapy in psychiatric rehabilitation. *Anthrozoös, 13*(1), 43–47.

McCleery, K. (2016, May 27). Meet the 'courtroom dogs' who help child crime victims tell their stories. Retrieved from http://www.pbs.org/newshour/bb /meet-the-courtroom-dogs-who-help-child-crime-victims-tell-their-stories/

McCloskey, L. A., & Walker, M. (2000). Posttraumatic stress in children exposed to family violence and single-event trauma. *Journal of the American Academy of Child & Adolescent Psychiatry, 39*(1), 108–115.

McNicholas, J., & Collis, G. M. (2006). Animals as social supports: Insights for understanding animal-assisted therapy. In A. H. Fine (Ed.), *Handbook on animal-assisted therapy: Theoretical foundations and guidelines for practice* (2nd ed., pp. 49–71). San Diego, CA: Academic Press.

McNicholas, J., & Collis, G. M. (2000). Dogs as catalysts for social interaction: Robustness of the effect. *British Journal of Psychology, 91*(1), 61–70.

Melson, G. F., & Fine, A. H. (2010). Animals in the lives of children. In A. H. Fine (Ed.), *Animal-assisted therapy: Theoretical foundations and guidelines for practice* (3rd ed., pp. 223–245). San Diego, CA: Elsevier.

Miller, S. C., Kennedy, C., DeVoe, D., Hickey, M., Nelson, T., & Kogan, L. (2009). An examination of changes in oxytocin levels in men and women before and after interaction with a bonded dog. *Anthrozoös, 22*(1), 31–42.

Nagasawa, M., Mitsui, S., En, S., Ohtani, N., Ohta, M., Sakuma, Y., Onaka, T., Mogi, K., & Kikusui, T. (2015). Oxytocin-gaze positive loop and the coevolution of human-dog bonds. *Science, 348*(6232), 333–336.

Nagengast, S. L., Baun, M. M., Megel, M., & Leibowitz, J. M. (1997). The effects of the presence of a companion animal on physiological arousal and behavioral distress in children during a physical examination. *Journal of Pediatric Nursing, 12*(6), 323–330.

Najavits, L. M. (2015). The problem of dropout from "gold standard" PTSD therapies. *F1000Prime Reports, 7.*

National Standards Committee for Animal-Assisted Crisis Response. (2010). Animal-assisted crisis response national standards. Retrieved from http://www.hopeaacr.org/AACR%20National%20Standards%207%20Mar%202010.pdf

Ng, Z., Albright, J. A., Fine, A. H., & Peralta, J. (2015). Our ethical and moral responsibility: Ensuring the welfare of therapy animals. In A. H. Fine (Ed.), *Handbook on animal-assisted therapy: Foundations and guidelines for animal-assisted interventions* (4th ed., pp. 357–376). San Diego, CA: Associated Press.

Nimer, J., & Lundahl, B. (2007). Animal-assisted therapy: A meta-analysis. *Anthrozoös, 20,* 225–238.

Nussbaum, M. C. (2006). *Frontiers of justice: Disability, nationality, species membership.* Cambridge, MA: Belknap Press of Harvard University Press.

Odendaal, J. (2000). Animal-assisted therapy—Magic or medicine? *Journal of Psychosomatic Research, 49*(4), 275–280.

Odendaal, J., & Meintjes, R. (2003). Neurophysiological correlates of affiliative behaviour between humans and dogs. *The Veterinary Journal, 165*(3), 296–301.

O'Haire, M. E., Guérin, N. A., & Kirkham, A. C. (2015a). Animal-assisted intervention for trauma: A systematic literature review. *Frontiers in Psychology, 6.*

O'Haire, M. E., McKenzie, S. J., Beck, A. M., & Slaughter, V. (2015b). Animals may act as social buffers: Skin conductance arousal in children with autism spectrum disorder in a social context. *Developmental Psychobiology, 57*(5), 584–595.

O'Haire, M. E., McKenzie, S. J., Beck, A. M., & Slaughter, V. (2013). Social behaviors increase in children with autism in the presence of animals compared to toys. *PLOS One, 8*(2), e57010.

Ozer, E. J., Best, S. R., Lipsey, T. L., & Weiss, D. S. (2003). Predictors of posttraumatic stress disorder and symptoms in adults: A meta-analysis. *Psychological Bulletin, 129*(1), 52.

Palley, L. S., O'Rourke, P. P., & Niemi, S. M. (2010). Mainstreaming animal-assisted therapy. *Institute for Laboratory Animal Research Journal, 51*(3), 199–207.

Palm, K. M., Polusny, M. A., & Follette, V. M. (2004). Vicarious traumatization: Potential hazards and interventions for disaster and trauma workers. *Prehospital and disaster medicine, 19*(01), 73–78.

Parish-Plass, N. (2008). Animal-assisted therapy with children suffering from insecure attachment due to abuse and neglect: A method to lower the risk of intergenerational transmission of abuse? *Clinical Child Psychology and Psychiatry, 13*(7), 7–31.

Pearlman, L. A., & Courtois, C. A. (2005). Clinical applications of the attachment framework: Relational treatment of complex trauma. *Journal of Traumatic Stress, 18*(5), 449–459.

Pet Partners. (2017). *Become a Handler.* Retrieved from https://petpartners.org/volunteer/become-a-handler/.

Polheber, J., & Matchock, R. (2013). The presence of a dog attenuates cortisol and heart rate in the Trier Social Stress Test compared to human friends. *Journal of Behavioral Medicine,* 1–8.

Porges, S. W. (2004). Neuroception: A subconscious system for detecting threats and safety. *Zero to Three, 24*(5), 19–24.

Prato-Previde, E., Custance, D. M., Spiezio, C., & Sabatini, F. (2003). Is the dog-human relationship an attachment bond? An observational study using Ainsworth's strange situation. *Behaviour, 140*(2), 225–254.

Prothmann, A., Bienert, M., & Ettrich, C. (2006). Dogs in child psychotherapy: Effects on state of mind. *Anthrozoös, 19*(3), 265–277.

Psychiatric Service Dog Partners. (2017). *Public Access Test.* Retrieved from http://www.psychdogpartners.org/resources/public-access/public-access-test

Regel, S., & Joseph, S. (2010). *Post-traumatic stress.* Oxford, UK: Oxford University Press.

Rosenthal, R., & Rosnow, R. L. (1991). *Essentials of behavioral research: Methods and data analysis*. New York, NY: McGraw-Hill Humanities Social.

Rothbaum B. O., Meadows E. A., Resick P., & Foy, D. W. (2000). Cognitive-behavioral therapy. In E. B. Foa, T. M. Keane, & M. Friedman (Eds.), *Effective treatments for PTSD: Practice guidelines from the International Society for Traumatic Stress Studies*. New York, NY: Guilford Press.

Sandler, J. L. (1996). Care and treatment of service dogs and their owners. *Journal of the American Veterinary Medical Association, 208*, 1979–1981.

Serpell, J. A. (2006). Animal-assisted interventions in historical perspective. In A. H. Fine (Ed.), *Handbook on animal-assisted therapy: Theoretical foundations and guidelines for practice* (2nd ed., pp. 3–20). San Diego, CA: Academic Press.

Serpell, J. A., Coppinger, R., Fine, A. H., & Peralta, J. M. (2010). Welfare considerations in therapy and assistance animals. In A. H. Fine (Ed.), *Handbook on animal-assisted therapy: Theoretical foundations and guidelines for practice* (3rd ed., pp. 481–503). San Diego, CA: Associated Press.

Serpell, J., McCune, S., Gee, N., & Griffin, J. A. (2017). Current challenges to research on animal-assisted interventions. *Applied Developmental Science, 21*(3), 223–233.

Shin, L. M., Rauch, S. L., & Pitman, R. K. (2006). Amygdala, medial prefrontal cortex, and hippocampal function in PTSD. *Annals of the New York Academy of Sciences, 1071*(1), 67–79.

Sutton, H. (2015). Know the difference between service and support animals. *Disability Compliance for Higher Education, 21*(2), 9.

Taylor, K. D., & Mills, D. S. (2007). The effect of the kennel environment on canine welfare: A critical review of experimental studies. *Animal Welfare, 16*, 435–447.

Taylor, M. F., Edwards, M. E., & Pooley, J. A. (2013). "Nudging them back to reality:" Toward a growing public acceptance of the role dogs fulfill in ameliorating contemporary veterans' PTSD symptoms. *Anthrozoös, 26*(4), 593–611.

Tedeschi, P., Bexell, S., & NeSmith, J. (2013). Conservation social work: The interconnectedness of biodiversity health and human resilience. In M. Bekoff (Ed.), *Ignoring nature no more: The case for compassionate conservation* (pp. 223–235). Chicago, IL: University of Chicago Press.

Tedeschi, P., Fine, A. H., & Helgeson, J. I. (2010). Assistance animals: Their evolving role in psychiatric service applications. In A. H. Fine (Ed.), *Handbook on animal-assisted therapy: Theoretical foundations and guidelines for practice* (3rd ed., pp. 421–438). San Diego, CA: Academic Press.

Thompson, M. (2012, November 22). Bringing dogs to heal: Care for veterans with PTSD. *Time Magazine, 176*(21). Retrieved from http://content.time.com/time/magazine/article/0,9171,2030897,00.html.

Topál, J., Miklósi, Á., Csányi, V., & Dóka, A. (1998). Attachment behavior in dogs (Canis familiaris): A new application of Ainsworth's (1969) Strange Situation Test. *Journal of Comparative Psychology, 112*(3), 219.

Triebenbacher, S. L. (1998). Pets as transitional objects: Their role in children's emotional development. *Psychological Reports, 82*(1), 191–200.

Trujillo, K., Tedeschi, P., & Williams, J. H. (2011). Research meets practice: Issues for evidence-based training in human-animal interaction. In P. McCardle, S. McCune, J. A. Griffin, L. Esposito, & L. S. Freund (Eds.), *Animals in our lives: Human-animal interaction in family, community, & therapeutic settings* (pp. 199–215). Baltimore, MD: Paul H. Brookes Publishing Company.

U.S. Department of Justice. (2011, July 12). *ADA requirements: Service animals.* Retrieved from www.ada.gov/service_animals_2010.htm

U.S. Department of Veterans Affairs. (2014). *Dogs and PTSD.* Retrieved from http://www.ptsd.va.gov/public/treatment/cope/dogs_and_ptsd.asp

VanFleet, R., Fine, A. H., O'Callaghan, D., Mackintosh, T., & Gimeno, J. (2015). Application of animal-assisted interventions in professional settings: An overview of alternatives. In A. H. Fine (Ed.), *Handbook on animal-assisted therapy: Foundations and guidelines for animal-assisted interventions* (4th ed., pp. 157–177). San Diego, CA: Elsevier.

Vormbrock, J. K., & Grossberg, J. M. (1988). Cardiovascular effects of human-pet dog interactions. *Journal of Behavioral Medicine, 11*(5), 509–517.

Walsh, F. (2009). Human-animal bonds I: The relational significance of companion animals. *Family Process, 48*(4), 462–480.

Wells, D. L. (2004). The facilitation of social interactions by domestic dogs. *Anthrozoös, 17*(4), 340–352.

Wells, M., & Perrine, R. (2001). Pets go to college: The influence of pets on students' perceptions of faculty and their offices. *Anthrozoös, 14*(3), 161–168.

Wesley, M. C., Minatrea, N. B., & Watson, J. C. (2009). Animal-assisted therapy in the treatment of substance dependence. *Anthrozoös, 22*(2), 137–148.

Wilson, E. O. (1984). *Biophilia.* Cambridge, MA: Harvard University Press.

Winnicott, D. W. (1953). Transitional objects and transitional phenomena. *The International Journal of Psycho-Analysis, 34*, 89.

Wood, L., Martin, K., Christian, H., Nathan, A., Lauritsen, C., Houghton, S., Kawachi, I., & McCune, S. (2015). The pet factor: Companion animals as a conduit for getting to know people, friendship formation and social support. *PLOS One, 10*(4), e0122085.

Wynne, W. A. (1996). *Yorkie doodle dandy, a memoir*. Mansfield, OH: Wynne-some Press.

Yarborough, B. J. H., Owen-Smith, A. A., Stumbo, S. P., Yarborough, M. T., Perrin, N. A., & Green, C. A. (2017). An observational study of service dogs for veterans with posttraumatic stress disorder. *Psychiatric Services, 68*(7), 730–734.

Yeates, J., & Main, D. (2009). Assessment of companion animal quality of life in veterinary practice and research. *Journal of Small Animal Practice, 50*(6), 274–281.

Yehuda, R. (2002). Post-traumatic stress disorder. *New England Journal of Medicine, 346*(2), 108–114.

Yount, R. A., Olmert, M. D., & Lee, M. R. (2012). Service dog training program for treatment of posttraumatic stress in service members. *U.S. Army Medical Department Journal*, 63–69.

Yount, R. A., Ritchie, E. C., Laurent, M. S., Chumley, P., & Olmert, M. D. (2013). The role of service dog training in the treatment of combat-related PTSD. *Psychiatric Annals, 43*(6), 292–295.

Zamir, T. (2006). The moral basis of animal-assisted therapy. *Society & Animals, 14*(2), 179–199.

ABOUT THE AUTHORS

Marguerite (Maggie) O'Haire received her BA in psychology from Vassar College and her PhD in psychology from The University of Queensland. She is currently an associate professor of human-animal interaction in the Center for the Human-Animal Bond in the College of Veterinary Medicine at Purdue University. Dr. O'Haire's research focuses on the biopsychosocial impacts of interacting with animals for various populations, including children with autism spectrum disorder and military veterans with PTSD.

Sally R. Braden received her BS in psychology from Wofford College in Spartanburg, South Carolina. She was then employed as a foster care case manager for the Department of Social Services, and later moved to Raleigh, North Carolina, where she was employed as the program director for the Elizabeth Edwards Foundation. In 2015, Braden received her Master of Social Work and Animal-Assisted Social Work certificate from the University of Denver. Braden currently works at Denver Health Hospital in Psychiatric Emergency Services, and her research interests include animal-assisted interventions in acute psychiatric settings.

Kerri E. Rodriguez is currently a PhD student of human-animal interaction in the Center for the Human-Animal Bond at Purdue University's College of Veterinary Medicine, under Dr. Marguerite O'Haire. She received her BS from Duke University and her Master of Science from the University of St. Andrews. Her research focuses on the psychosocial and physiological effects of service dogs among individuals with physical disabilities and military veterans with PTSD.

Biographical sketches for **Philip Tedeschi** and **Molly A. Jenkins** can be found on p. 12 of this volume.

CHAPTER 2

Advocacy and Rethinking Our Relationships With Animals: Ethical Responsibilities and Competencies in Animal-Assisted Interventions

Zenithson Ng, DVM, MS, DABVP (Canine and Feline)

INTRODUCTION

We ask a lot of our animal companions. In reality, we don't even ask, but rather expect them to enter unfamiliar environments, to be approached and touched by strangers, to follow commands, and to act appealing or "cute," all for our own and other people's personal gain. While the human recipient benefits from interacting with the animal, and the handler benefits from seeing the animal bring joy to others, we have to ask if the animal is benefiting from their participation in animal-assisted interventions (AAIs), is unaffected by them, or is possibly even subjected to undue negative consequences as a result. If given free will, would an animal naturally remain in an interaction designed to comfort an individual or would it choose to flee from the situation at hand? With the limited amount of definitive evidence that animals truly have a significantly positive impact on humans, or that non-living animal substitutes, such as lifelike canine robots, may bring about similar positive impact and that there are potential risks of these activities to animal welfare, one may question the ethical use of animals for these interventions. As such, it is essential that the field of AAI keep animal welfare at the forefront of practice and research pursuits.

Animal welfare can be appropriately described as the "animal's attempt to cope with its environment at a physiological, behavioral, and medical level" (Broom, 1996, p. 24). Welfare is often graded on a scale from very good to very poor (Haverbeke, Diederich, Depiereux, & Giffroy, 2008). However, grading welfare in animals can be notoriously problematic and complex because it is usually based on an observer's subjective evaluation of the animal's well-being (Hetts, Clark, Arnold, & Mateo, 1992; Hiby, Rooney, & Bradshaw, 2006). When utilizing animals for purposes of providing a service for humans in the form of AAI, there is an ethical obligation for these animals to achieve "very good" welfare status. Good welfare and well-being can be characterized as a state in which an animal is free from distress most or all of the time, is in good physical health, exhibits a substantial range of species-typical behaviors, and is able to deal effectively with various environmental stimuli (Hetts et al., 1992; Novak & Drewsen, 1989).

Most animal welfare experts believe that animals are sentient beings, although it is difficult for research to definitively confirm this. A sentient being implies that the individual has the ability to experience emotional effects of pleasure and suffering. Research in cognitive ethology, psychology, and neuroscience is increasingly recognizing the complexity of animal emotions and consciousness (Bekoff, 2007; Panskepp, 2005; others). There is compelling evidence that some animals likely feel a full range of emotions, including fear, joy, happiness, shame, resentment, jealousy, rage, anger, love, pleasure, compassion, respect, relief, disgust, sadness, despair, and grief (Bekoff, 2000, 2007). For example, elephants have long been noted to express a high emotional intelligence similar to human beings (Bradshaw, 2004). Because of elephants' intricate bonds with one another, mother elephants have been observed mourning over a dead offspring for days after death, often touching and caressing the corpse, seemingly trying to bring the deceased back to life. Additionally, after the death of an elephant, the herd may grieve the corpse for years after death; when the skull of a deceased elephant was brought back to the herd in a zoo, the elephants gathered around and performed a ritual of touch and caressing (Moss, 1992). These deliberate behaviors demonstrate that animals form close attachments to other living beings and cope with the trauma of loss. In the case of domesticated animals, pet owners will often report behaviors that indicate depression or sadness in a pet after the death of a cohabitating animal companion.

Likewise, post-traumatic stress disorder (PTSD) has been recognized in animals that have experienced an event that is unpredictable and out of their control (Foa, Zinbarg, & Rothbaum, 1992). In military working dogs, for instance, canine PTSD is characterized by a collection of behavioral signs including hyperresponsivity and hypervigilance to environmental events; behaviors aimed at escaping or avoiding previously positive or neutral environments; changes in social interaction with their human handler; and failure to perform previously mastered critical tasks (Stampfl, 2012). This suggests that animals not only experience emotion, but can also suffer harmful consequences, including trauma, from such emotions and experiences.

One underlying reason for this is that adverse events are commonly ingrained in animals' memories, and recurrence of similar events evokes a variety of stress behaviors, physiologic changes, and likely emotional consequences. Based on a previous experience, animals quickly learn to fear specific conditions such as types of people, locations, and smells. The classic situation that is often associated with a traumatic experience for an animal is a visit to the veterinary hospital. As soon as an animal arrives at the vet, it recognizes what has occurred in the past, which often involves sensing the fear and anxiety of other animals, loud noises (i.e., dogs barking and cats yowling), forced restraint, and treatments involving injections, oral medication, and rectal exams. These feelings of discomfort may be exacerbated by the fact that the animal is often ill and requiring veterinary care in the first place. The fear, elevated blood pressure, retreat, and stress behaviors exhibited by these animals at the veterinary hospital are often characterized as "white coat" syndrome. These negative experiences shape the animal's behavioral and physiological stress response, and can be considered to be a form of trauma. A recognition of the negative experience for animals has resulted in the strong movement for veterinary clinics to practice low-stress or fear-free methods to elicit positive emotions in both animals and owners.

Similarly, the nature of working with people who have experienced various forms of trauma through AAI may be more intense and strenuous and, thus, may have certain stress implications for the therapy animal as compared to work with other populations. Individuals who have experienced trauma may be particularly emotional, unpredictable, and erratic in their behaviors and emotions. If a patient with an unstable temperament were to vocalize loudly or inflict physical harm on an animal in an outwardly violent manner, the animal will likely be fearful of the circumstances that led to the negative experience. These seemingly subtle circumstances may include the particular individual or identifying characteristics of that individual (i.e., gender, hair color, voice intonation, clothing color or pattern), the location of the event, or the inherent smells permeating throughout the experience. Any or all of these factors may result in trauma, where the animal would avoid/retreat from the stimulus or exhibit signs of stress and anxiety.

Treatment for animals with anxiety disorders often involves counter-conditioning, in which the fearful stimulus is paired with a positive reward, with the ultimate goal being to change the animal's emotional response to that stimulus. For example, in a therapy dog that has become fearful of men because a man had hit the dog during an AAI session, counter-conditioning would involve exposing the dog to a male giving treats and toys. For anxiety disorders not amenable to behavioral modification, or that impair the animal's ability to express normal behavior, the inciting stimulus should be avoided altogether or pharmaceutical intervention may be required. However, if AAI is traumatic enough to require that an animal take anti-anxiety medications to continue work, it is in the best interest of the animal to discontinue any future AAI involvement. Moreover, consultation with trainers or veterinary behaviorists would likely be necessary.

In addition to experiencing a variety of emotions themselves, animals are able to recognize different emotional states in other species as well. Most work investigating the human-dog relationship shows that dogs are uniquely suited to identify, and be sensitive to, the emotional cues from their owners (Duranton & Gaunet, 2015). Dogs are able to discriminate happy from sad human faces and respond differently to that specific emotion (Albuquerque et al., 2016; Muller, Schmitt, Barber, & Huber, 2015; Nagasawa, Murai, Mogi, & Kikusui, 2011). Moreover, specific areas of the dog brain are responsive to human voice and cues, demonstrating that they are able to recognize and process different human emotions (Andics, Gacsi, Farago, Kis, & Miklosi, 2014). Specifically, canine brain imaging reveals that dogs perceive specific words differently from the intonation of those words, similar to the way in which humans do (Andics et al., 2016). This remarkable finding demonstrates animals' innate ability to recognize and respond to other species.

While animals may be able to recognize different emotions in other species, we have to ask ourselves if they truly possess empathy. Empathy is a shared state phenomenon to feel what another living being is feeling

(Preston & de Waal, 2002). It is postulated that many creatures demonstrate and possess empathic abilities (Kuczaj, Tranel, Trone, & Hill, 2001). In humans, chemosensory anxiety signals can activate brain areas necessary to process emotional stimuli and recruit empathy-related resources (Prehn-Kristensen et al., 2009). If empathy is indeed present in nonhuman animals, it is likely that similar neuronal mechanisms exist in these species as well.

For example, the interspecies relationship between dog and human suggests that dogs have the ability to empathize with people (Silva & de Sousa, 2011). The most compelling evidence that animals are empathic creatures is the synchronization of hormones between human and dog. One study investigated the change in hormones in agility dogs and their handlers and found that testosterone levels in handlers were correlated with, and predicted change in, cortisol levels in their dogs (Jones & Josephs, 2006). Additionally, another study found that the change in cortisol levels in handlers simultaneously mirrored the change in cortisol levels in agility dogs in competition (Buttner, Thompson, Strasser, & Santo, 2015). These studies suggest a hormonal synchronization across species interacting with one another.

Aforementioned, in AAI, an animal may be exposed to, and affected by, a wide range of human personalities and mood states, especially in times of despair, loss, and trauma. Indeed, human therapists are known to suffer adverse effects on mental health and well-being in response to this type of work (Linley & Joseph, 2007; Pearlman & Mac Ian, 1995). The fundamental difference is that therapists go into this work out of their own volition; animals do not. If animals truly are empathic, it is possible that they too could suffer negative consequences from internalizing and harboring these emotions. Crying, an expression of emotion commonly observed in therapy sessions, may negatively impact therapy dogs. From a physiological perspective, researchers have found that cortisol levels in dogs increased after listening to a human crying (Yong, Ruffman, & Yong, 2014). Likewise, from a behavioral perspective, dogs have also demonstrated a submissive approach toward a human crying compared to when they were humming or talking (Custance & Mayer, 2012). Interestingly, one paper reported that shortly after completing a study where a trained therapy dog engaged in regular contact with college students reminiscing about negative or traumatic events, it developed unforeseen behavior problems and was permanently retired from work (Hunt & Chizkov, 2014).

This may suggest that AAI with people in distressed states can negatively impact the animal.

We have an ethical obligation to ensure that these adverse effects are prevented. We often select certain animals, especially dogs, for AAI because they are so sensitive and reactive to human cues (Udell & Wynne, 2008; Vitztum & Urbanik, 2016), and have a high drive to please people (Udell, Dorey, & Wynne, 2010). It has even been suggested that animals possess some degree of altruism (de Waal, 2008), making them ideal candidates for assisting in interventions seeking to improve human health and well-being. However, we must be careful that we do not take advantage of the gentle and compliant nature of these animals and put them into a state of learned helplessness (Peterson, 1993). This is the condition of powerlessness in which the animal has learned it is unable to escape or avoid aversive stimuli, giving it no option other than to forfeit itself to the situation. Since AAI animals are so obedient with a high desire to please, what can be perceived as a tolerant and quiet dog in the presence of an emotional human could actually be a dog suffering from learned helplessness. It is our duty to ensure that appropriate, evidence-based protocols are implemented to prevent these conditions.

The field of AAI currently is lacking in formal universal guidelines on the ethics of human-animal relationships (Antonites & Odendaal, 2004). It is presumed that most human-animal interaction (HAI) organizations emphasize that animal welfare be protected and enhanced wherever possible (Preziosi, 1997; Santori, 2011). However, specific guidelines are difficult to establish because research has not yet identified the precise criteria necessary to guarantee welfare. The International Association of Human-Animal Interaction Organizations (IAHAIO) (Jegatheesan et al., 2014) describes general guidelines to safeguard animal welfare in AAI, while select studies have measured and are continuing to measure the effects of AAI for therapy animals, but more work is necessary.

This chapter will address the ethical, practical, and research considerations and solutions for the welfare of the AAI animal. Animals should not merely be made tools for human advantage, but rather be recognized as partners and sentient beings that benefit us in so many ways. There are four key factors that deserve special consideration to ensure animal welfare in AAI: the handler, the animal, the recipient, and the environment. Additionally, it is necessary to provide practice guidelines for tasks to complete before, during, and after an intervention, especially one where human trauma is of focus. The importance of animal well-being in ensuring and guiding safe, humane, effective, and sound therapeutic interventions will be discussed.

ETHICAL CONSIDERATIONS IN AAI

When considering animal welfare in the context of AAI, a conceptual, ethical framework to apply are the Five Freedoms of animal welfare, first proposed by the Farm Animal Welfare Council (FAWC) (Brambell, 1965). These Five Freedoms include:

- Freedom from thirst, hunger, and malnutrition
- Freedom from discomfort
- Freedom from pain, injury, and disease
- Freedom from fear and distress
- Freedom to express most normal behavior

To ensure "good" welfare status, the animal must meet each of the conditions of the Five Freedoms. Violation of any of these freedoms can result in a poor welfare state via the incitement of stress.

While many would consider it unusual for a therapy animal to not meet each of the Five Freedoms, there are certain aspects of AAI that may challenge these freedoms. Concerning *freedom from thirst, hunger, and malnutrition*, an AAI animal (e.g., a therapy dog) is unlikely to suffer from these detriments due to the care provided by the owner/handler. However, these basic necessities may be affected when the animal is actively engaged in an AAI session. For example, it has been reported that handlers who are worried about dogs urinating in the facility during a session may withhold access to water, which can result in thirst and consequent dehydration (Hatch, 2007). Similarly, handlers may deny food to the animal for fear of accidental defecation in the facility, resulting in hunger. With *freedom from discomfort*, the actual animal-assisted activity (AAA)/animal-assisted therapy (AAT) facility may present certain risks that lead to discomfort. These facilities, particularly hospital environments, often subject animals to crowds of people, loud sounds, adverse smells, and unpredictable circumstances (King, Watters, & Mungre, 2011).

The *freedom from pain, injury, and disease* component is a relatively straightforward concept to guarantee for all animals. To ensure this freedom, steps should be taken to minimize the risk of disease or injury to participating animals. In addition, a plan should be in place to seek immediate medical assistance on the rare occasion that an animal becomes ill or is hurt while participating in AAI. Injury to the animal can occur due to being improperly handled by the human recipient of AAA or AAT, but these occurrences are infrequently reported (Hatch, 2007). Notably, however, handlers may refrain from reporting adverse events in these situations to avoid upsetting or embarrassing the visited client, especially if the individual has special needs and the animal does not appear to have suffered severe injury.

Freedom from fear and distress may be more of an abstract concept to ensure in therapy and service animals. This freedom is met if the animal is free of mental suffering. Mental suffering is a difficult parameter to objectively assess, but all attempts should be made to decrease fear and stress in AAI animals. Although there are limited studies to report how well dogs tolerate this type of work, stress may be quite prevalent in AAA and AAT (Glenk, Stetina, Kepplinger, & Baran, 2011; King et al., 2011). The presence of a human being has the potential to cause stress in animals (Jones & Josephs, 2006), and social interactions are reported to be among the most potent stressors an animal may endure (McEwen & Wingfield, 2003).

Finally, the *freedom to express most normal behavior* may be the greatest challenge to meet in AAI. This freedom requires that the animal be provided with sufficient space, proper facilities, and company of the animal's own kind. However, this freedom is difficult to apply in AAI because AAA/AAT environments are unlike any that the animal would naturally encounter. These animals did not choose to be trained for, or to engage in, AAI—the owners decided this fate for them. Even if an animal achieves AAA or AAT certification and registration, it does not necessarily mean that the animal has the desire to voluntarily participate in these activities. Because the handler is in control of the animal at all times, the animal is typically unable to vacate or escape these conditions if the need or desire arises (Serpell, Coppinger, Fine, & Peralta, 2010). AAI is unlike any other animal activity in that it requires an animal to endure intimate, unsolicited affections from a human stranger for extended durations of time (Butler, 2004). Animals in these contrived circumstances must remain steady and cope with the interaction of unfamiliar people and strange settings without being able to choose whether to stay or leave (Piva, Liverani, Accorsi, Sarli, & Gandini, 2008), which prevents expressing normal behavior.

HANDLER SELECTION: CALM, KNOWLEDGEABLE, AND PROACTIVE

The handler is the ultimate gatekeeper of animal welfare. An appropriate handler should be one who is motivated to help the human recipient, as well as safeguard the needs of the animal. The animal relies on the handler for guidance and leadership; without an appropriate leader, the interaction may not be safe or effective. Whether handlers are human health specialists or volunteers, they should be trained appropriately and be expected to comply with a certain standard of practice. It should be noted that an exuberant volunteer may disregard the animal's needs in order to meet his or her own agendas in ensuring patient satisfaction. At the most basic level, the handler should prioritize the animal's welfare above the recipient's emotional or health needs, even if that means leaving the visit prematurely or not holding it at all.

The ideal handler should be calm and controlled in his or her interactions. This would be a particularly desired quality for handlers working with patients and clients who have experienced trauma, as stability is essential to conveying a safe and trustworthy presence. Likewise, since handler and canine hormone synchronization exists, the handler may strongly influence the dog's performance and experience in any given interaction. Anxiety in an AAI handler can be sensed by, and reflected in, the dog (Hatch, 2007), so it is important that the handler maintain a natural level of calmness. It has also been shown that increasing stress levels in the owner decrease the accuracy of performance in working dogs (Sumegi, Olah, & Topal, 2014). Therefore, evaluation of personality characteristics and response to stressful situations, such as test-taking, may be helpful in selecting calm handlers.

The key to ensuring knowledgeable handlers is providing an appropriate level of training in animal behavior and health. It has been reported that most handlers are not properly educated in ethology (Fejsáková et al., 2009). Specifically, they should be knowledgeable about the species-specific behaviors that may indicate compromise to animal welfare, as humans are often poor at truly assessing animal welfare (Mariti et al., 2012). There exists the potential for the handler to harm the animal in AAI, as he or she may misread or fail to read stress signals and respond to them appropriately (Hatch, 2007). Being able to recognize the behavioral signs of stress is the first essential lesson for the handler; being proficient in responding to these signals is the second.

Dogs look to humans for guidance to react to certain circumstances (Call, Brauer, Kaminski, & Tomasello, 2003), demonstrating that these animals rely on the handler to provide the appropriate cues for them. In one study, researchers found that undue stress was placed on working dogs performing tasks because handlers frequently did not instruct the dogs properly, which put them at risk of injury and performance failure (Coppinger, Coppinger, & Skillings, 1998). Handlers should be trained on the importance of taking an active, rather than passive, role in guiding the animal through the interaction.

In addition, the handler should have excellent knowledge of, and relationship with, that particular animal, recognizing the animal's individual baseline behaviors when it is not in a stressful circumstance, such as the home setting. He or she should also recognize the behaviors exhibited when the animal is under circumstances that it finds stressful. Since stress-associated behaviors vary between individuals, recognizing that particular animal's behaviors in contrasting situations can be helpful in assessing the animal's comfort level in the AAI setting, and in anticipating the circumstances or triggers that may pose a risk to the animal.

Deciding whether a patient is safe to visit is also an important and often challenging task, and it is the handler's responsibility to assess the safety and stability of the potential recipient. Prior to engaging a visit, the handler may inquire with other staff members about cautions regarding specific individuals. Additionally, the handler is responsible for providing structure and guidelines for safe interaction with the animal prior to the intervention. This may include how to approach the animal, where it prefers to be touched, and the most appropriate volume and tone of voice. In one study, handlers were instructed to permit the visitation only if the breathing pattern between the dog and patient were matched (Braun, Stangler, Narveson, & Pettingell, 2009). Certain human recipients may be unpredictable, and if a patient has a temper or tendency for violence, visitation should be carefully considered and/or avoided. If aggression is encountered, the handler should remove the animal from the situation in a rapid and safe manner. The handler should possess the skills to respectfully inform the client that a visit or future interactions may not be appropriate under these circumstances. Furthermore, because the welfare of these animals is paramount, it is imperative that strong supervision for the safety of the animal and all individuals involved be provided for such situations.

On the opposite extreme, individuals who have experienced trauma may be withdrawn and disengaged due to a lack of trust in others, which may actually be an indication to integrate AAI in counseling. These recipients may show disinterest in engaging in HAI, and while this may appear to be unharmful to the animal, there is a possibility that motivated animals (e.g., dogs with high drive) may be frustrated by such circumstances because they exhibit engaging behaviors in exchange for positive human contact. As such, it may be important for handlers and mental health professionals to carefully consider the best animal-human matches for the AAI (e.g., pairing recipients who are slow to engage with animals who have more passive personalities).

Animal health education is another essential component to ensuring that handlers are animal-welfare conscious. First, handlers should recognize signs of illness or sickness in the animal. They should seek veterinary attention and not work with the animal if it is feeling unwell. In one study, it was reported that 76% of dogs with urinary tract infections and 86% of dogs with diarrhea were still taken on AAI visits (Lefebvre, Reid-Smith, Waltner-Toews, & Weese, 2009). These handlers may not have been aware (or lacked formal understanding) that continued work could worsen these conditions or that the animal could be carrying transmissible infectious diseases. In another study of 90 AAI handlers, 40% could not name at least one disease transmittable from animal to human (Lefebvre et al., 2006). Overall, these data demonstrate that handlers should receive basic training on the tenets of infection control and zoonotic diseases, especially when visiting hospital settings or immunocompromised patients. Likewise, the handler should have basic knowledge of first aid care for the animal in the event an accident occurs onsite. This should include management of simple wounds and toxins, as well as foreign body ingestion.

To assess the level of understanding from this training, the handler should be tested and retested periodically. A written examination in addition to performance in a role-playing simulation helps to ensure a minimum competency for handlers. The role-playing simulation is particularly important, not only to assess the animal's behavior, but also the handler's response to the animal and specific situations. One study validating an evaluation showed that dogs demonstrated a high rate of stress signals, and the authors postulated that handlers were unwilling or unable to advocate for the animal's welfare needs (Mongillo et al., 2015). A testing requirement exemplifies a high standard of practice and permits the organization to observe how a handler deals with stress, both of which influence animal health and welfare.

A handler who passes rigorous testing should be equipped with a foundation of knowledge and skills that supports the safety and welfare of the animal. This level of education should be appropriate to the capacity at which the handler is working, whether he or she be a volunteer, paraprofessional, or professional. For example, Pet Partners offers a tiered model of handler competencies that defines minimal core, intermediate, and professional knowledge, as well as skills and attitudes required of that specific animal-handler team (Stewart, n.d.). While every handler, regardless of role, should have core knowledge that relates directly to animal welfare (such as recognizing triggers to stress for his or her animal and preventing the spread of infectious disease), volunteers are not expected to have a deep understanding of a patient's diagnosis or to design theory-based interventions, which would be required of a professional. Catering a specific level of training based on the particular AAI work that the handler will do demonstrates an advanced initiative that ensures the safety, well-being, and welfare of both the animal and the recipient. It is reasonable to assume that a higher level of education and training for a handler results in better outcomes for AAI recipients. Future research should address how the handler's competency directly correlates with the welfare of the animal, as well as clinical outcomes for the patient. Regardless, entry-level AAI training and follow-up with continuing education for handlers are essential components to safeguard the interests of all parties involved.

ANIMAL SELECTION: HEALTHY, PREDICTABLE, RELIABLE, AND CONTROLLABLE

Selecting the appropriate AAI animal is essential in safeguarding animal welfare. We want an animal to not just tolerate the intervention, but to enjoy the experience and benefit from it. The animal that is physically healthy, predictable, reliable, and controllable will be the best suited for AAI.

It is imperative that veterinarians be involved in the approval process (Mongillo et al., 2015). Prior to advanced screening or evaluation, a veterinarian should deem the animal physically healthy and behaviorally sound to participate in AAI. With regard to physical health, animals with chronic disease may be considered for approval for AAI work. While well-managed diseases that would not be impacted by AAI may be permitted for approval, animals with conditions that could worsen or grow more painful from AAI activities should not be considered. For example, diseases affected by touching, walking, increased activity, travel, or unpredictable events such as cardiac, respiratory, neurological, or severe orthopedic disease pose an animal health risk. In addition, animals receiving medications that may be toxic to humans should be precluded.

Many organizations have also prohibited any animals receiving raw food diets from participating in AAI, as they are more likely to spread infectious disease (Lefebvre, Reid-Smith, Boerlin, & Weese, 2008). Because there has been a lack of scientific evidence proving the long-term effects of raw food diets, it has been a controversial topic that requires education and consideration for the health and welfare of human participants.

The veterinarian should ensure absence of zoonotic disease by confirming the animal is up-to-date on a preventive health protocol tailored to the animal's specific health risks. An appropriate preventive health plan includes routine vaccination, protection against endoparasites and ectoparasites, and verification of a negative fecal examination (as indicated by the absence of common parasites such as roundworms, hookworms, whipworms, and others) performed by centrifugation. It is important to note that a negative fecal examination indicates absence of potentially harmful parasites *at that current moment*, and does not guarantee the animal has not been infected thereafter.

Regarding vaccines, the rabies vaccination must always be given in accordance to local laws (National Association of State Public Health et al., 2016), and a legal rabies tag must be visualized on the animal at all times. It is at the veterinarian's discretion to dictate whether or not core and noncore vaccines are given in accordance with local disease states, as other vaccine-preventable diseases are less likely to pose a risk to humans. In addition, flea, tick, heartworm, and intestinal parasite prevention should be given regularly, typically on a monthly basis depending on the particular product. The method of administration may be a factor in choosing a preventive for the AAI animal. Oral preventives may be preferred over topical preventives, as topicals can leave a temporary residue and odor that may be off-putting to humans who are petting them. The veterinarian's pivotal role is to ensure that the animal is healthy enough to work and does not pose a health risk to others.

Once the animal has received medical clearance from the veterinarian, the animal can be behaviorally evaluated. While an appropriate therapy dog (for example) may be any age, sex, or breed, certain demographics may render an animal more successful in AAI than others. In regard to age, it is important that animals less than one year not participate. These animals are less likely to be calm and mature enough to handle the strict requirements of AAI. Since calmness is a desirable trait in AAI, age is an important consideration; it was recently found that the most calm dogs were older (greater than seven years of age) (Kubinyi, Turcsan, & Miklosi, 2009). With regard to dog breed, while breeds such as Golden and Labrador retrievers may be overrepresented as therapy and service animals because of their high affiliative index, any breed of dog may be appropriate for AAI. However, a high level of trainability is highly desired in potential candidates.

One factor that significantly impacts canine trainability is the number of professional training courses (e.g., obedience, agility) that the dog has experienced, with the most trainable dogs having completed three or more (Kubinyi et al., 2009). The quality of training may also impact the welfare of the animal, as there is potential for inhumane training protocols to be performed (Serpell et al., 2010). It has been shown that positive reinforcement training without punishment is more favorable than negative reinforcement training, as it results in decreased frequency of unwanted behaviors (Blackwell, Twells, Seawright, & Casey, 2008). Additionally, equipment for the AAI dog should consist of a nonretractable lead and collar or head halter. Choke chains or prong collars should be prohibited, as a dog that requires this aggressive method of control is not likely to be an appropriate candidate for AAI.

Prior to in-house full behavior evaluation, a behavioral screening tool may be utilized to screen for inappropriate AAI candidates. The Canine Behavioral Assessment and Research Questionnaire (C-BARQ) may be able to predict aggressive behavior tendencies (Hsu & Serpell, 2003), so further evaluation of an animal that scores with aggressive inclinations on the C-BARQ may not be necessary. In addition, approving an animal with a bite history may likely be controversial. It may be assumed that a dog that has bitten another human being or animal will not be appropriate for HAI work. However, the circumstances of a single, isolated bite incident may be explored if the animal otherwise passes a rigorous behavioral evaluation.

While basic obedience and following commands on cue are desirable characteristics in an AAI animal, the in-house behavior evaluation should focus primarily on the temperament of the animal and its reactivity to stressors. The animal should be placed in role-play scenarios representative of a typical AAI encounter. In general, the animal should "enjoy" and seek interaction with strangers without showing signs of stress, fear, aggression, shyness, or avoidance (Mongillo et al., 2015). The animal should be accepting of rough or awkward handling, loud noises, being approached and/or crowded by strangers, and exposure to medical equipment. For animals working in trauma-informed AAIs specifically, it may be important to role-play by exposing the animal to people performing unstable or erratic behaviors such as flailing arms and/or kicking, in addition to extreme verbal emotions such as yelling and/or excessive crying. Exposure to both individuals and crowds may also be useful in determining the suitability of the animal's participation in group therapy sessions or other interventions of similar intensity.

In addition, the frequency of behavioral indicators of stress should be closely evaluated. This is often overlooked in AAI evaluations. A recent study reported a high rate of stress signals (about 2.5 stress signals/minute) in a dog during the evaluation, suggesting that the evaluation process may itself be a stressful circumstance (Mongillo et al., 2015). Ultimately, this was not a factor in deciding whether the dog was suitable for AAI, but the frequency, duration, and type of animal stress signals should be strongly considered in AAI evaluations. A suitable animal may certainly demonstrate these behaviors in response to stressors, but the animal should be resilient and return to its normal state in a reasonable amount of time.

In dogs, behavioral signs of stress (often referred to as calming signals, appeasement behaviors, or displacement behaviors) include increased restlessness, snout licking, paw lifting, yawning, body shaking, nosing, circling, increased locomotor activity, and lowering of body posture (Beerda, Schilder, van Hooff, & de Vries, 1997; Beerda, Schilder, van Hooff, de Vries, & Mol, 1998; Beerda, Schilder, van Hooff, de Vries, & Mol, 2000; Schwizgebel, 1982). In horses, behavioral signs of stress include repetitive head movements, flightiness, restlessness, sweating, kicking, vocalizing, pinned back ears, tail swishing, and pawing (Fureix, Jego, Sankey, & Hausberger, 2009; Kaiser, Heleski, Siegford, & Smith, 2006; McBride, Hemmings, & Robinson, 2004). Cats are often subtler in demonstrating fear and anxiety by being more withdrawn and frozen. Outward indications of stress in cats include retreating, avoiding eye contact, low body posture while ambulating, vocalizing, hissing, pinning ears back, and tail swishing (Landsberg, Hunthausen, & Ackerman, 2012; Levine, 2008). It is important to note that demonstration of stress behaviors in all species varies greatly among individuals; rather than relying on a single behavioral indicator of stress, it is more important to note the frequency and duration of potential stress behaviors in the context of the situation, and compare these behavioral outcomes to the animal's normal baseline behavior in a relaxed setting.

Although the essential characteristics of being controllable, reliable, and predictable help to identify a good candidate, these qualities do not necessarily indicate that the animal "enjoys" human interaction. While enjoyment is difficult to objectively capture, the presence of attention-seeking behavior may suggest enjoyment. Unsolicited behaviors, such as approaching, sniffing, licking, nudging, and body contact with a stranger, indicate the animal actively solicits attention, which is a desirable characteristic to have in an AAI animal (Custance & Mayer, 2012). In addition, sustained eye contact may indicate the animal enjoys human interaction. Dogs with higher levels of oxytocin are able to maintain gaze with their owners and subsequently increase their levels of oxytocin (Nagasawa et al., 2015). Staring directly at a stranger with soft eyes in a relaxed manner is a highly desired behavioral skill/trait that indicates animal welfare is not threatened.

Once an animal has been deemed suitable for AAI, the animal's health and behavior should be constantly monitored, both inside and outside of work. After being tested in the role-play, the animal should be further evaluated in its actual working environment, as an animal deemed appropriate for one type of intervention may not necessarily be appropriate for a different application, human recipient, or setting. Generally, physical examination should be repeated annually, and behavioral surveillance should be repeated every 2–4 years. However, these specifications should be adhered to on a case-by-case basis. If health or behavior changes are noted sooner, it is the handler's responsibility to ensure the animal is reevaluated. For example, a dog that was stepped on by a human may exhibit panting and retreating behaviors that were not observed prior to the evaluation. The animal should be medically evaluated by a veterinarian and behaviorally evaluated by the overseeing organization to determine the cause. If the change in behavior is situational and not observed in the animal routinely, it may warrant an evaluator to observe the specific situation so he or she can accurately assess and address the condition. It is critical that the handler be educated and observant of these subtle signs of behavior change, as formal evaluations only provide a single snapshot of the animal's demeanor at that particular moment and may not be representative of overall welfare.

The assessment of temperament and reactivity to stress in identifying healthy animals that are predictable, reliable, and controllable apply to all species. However, it should be noted that specific characteristics and evaluation tools of species desirable for AAI other than dogs have yet to be validated. Cats, for example, are required to be nonaggressive, social, calm, and not stressed. They should tolerate being passed from person to person without struggle, and purring may be a desired behavior in AAI. Because cats are more flighty and thrive in predictable and consistent environments, they are typically less tolerant than dogs in being transported or adapting to new settings and people, but they can certainly be trained and conditioned if their temperaments allow.

Importantly, during any AAI, the safety of the client must be aligned with the safety of the animal, and methods to reduce risk of harm cannot be underemphasized. It is understood that an animal should not induce physical harm through bites or scratches toward a human, which is mostly preventable by selecting the appropriate animal that is nonaggressive and controllable. However, inadvertent scratches, play bites, or falls over animals can be injuries that the AAI participant may sustain even with the most well-mannered therapy animals. For example, scratches may occur if a dog unexpectedly jumps or paws at a person or if a cat moves on or off the lap of a person. Trimming and filing of nails on a regular basis is important to prevent such incidents. An open animal mouth that comes into contact with the recipient's skin, possibly from play or mouthing behavior, may result in pain and excessive bruising even if it does not break the skin. Any mouthing behavior should be stopped and corrected immediately by the handler. People should also be aware of where the animal is located at all times to avoid any trips or falls, as musculoskeletal injuries can be severe, especially in geriatric adults (Stevens, Teh, & Haileyesus, 2010; Willmott,

Greenheld, & Goddard, 2012). In addition, through appropriate medical and behavioral screening of animals, hand washing, and practicing safe interactions as discussed previously, the risk of zoonotic disease transmission from animal to human participant can be minimized.

Finally, it is critical that any adverse event be immediately reported to the appropriate administrative staff, whether it be the facility, the certifying AAI organization, or insurance provider. To date, there are no known scientific reports of the frequency of adverse events occurring in AAI, but these incidents are likely underreported. People are reluctant to describe any negative event associated with an AAI because they may perceive the event to be mild, believe that it was just an accident, or want to avoid negative repercussions for the animal, handler, or organization. However, it is very important that all details be recorded so the proper authorities can address the situation and apply any measures necessary to ensure the safety of all future participants. Nevertheless, the best method of avoiding adverse event reports is to prevent them from the beginning to ensure the safety of all parties involved.

RECIPIENT SELECTION: ACCEPTING AND APPROACHABLE

Just as we select for animals that are predictable, reliable, and controllable, we should select for AAI recipients with similar qualities. However, this is not always possible as many AAI interactions are spontaneous, and it is difficult to ensure that a stranger, especially one who is emotionally distraught from trauma, would possess any of these qualities. To best be prepared, the animal-handler team should anticipate that the client will be emotional and unpredictable. The ideal recipient of AAI is willing and accepting of the animal interaction and relates to the animal in a gentle, nonthreatening manner. A successful AAI is one in which mutuality is present, and where the human benefits from contact with a nonstressed animal.

There are people for whom AAI is inappropriate, as it may pose a risk to human well-being and/or animal welfare. The recipient should be informed of exactly what to expect during the visit, and be asked permission to visit before introducing the animal. People with active contagious infection should not be visited. A protocol should be in place to alert animal handlers of a potential infectious disease and to prohibit visitation. If a patient has open sores or wounds, visitation should be discontinued. Not only can animals acquire infection, but they can also pass infection on to others. In addition, caution should be used when working with immuno-compromised individuals to prevent transmission of zoonotic disease from animal to human. Appropriate medical screening of the animal, as well as deliberate hand washing before and after interacting with the animal, can mitigate the spread of infectious disease.

Overall, the animal should not be forced upon an individual who is unaccepting of a visit. Fear of, and allergies to, animals are common reasons for a patient to decline an animal visit; in some cases, a fear of animals may be directly linked with the history of trauma. In addition, the human individual may not be in an appropriate emotional state to receive a visitor, whether it be human or nonhuman. An individual suffering from trauma may exhibit high anxiety, cry uncontrollably, and/or speak loudly, all of which may result in a fear or stress response in the animal. However, notably, while crying may increase cortisol (Yong et al., 2014) and induce submissive behavior in dogs (Custance & Mayer, 2012), it was recently found that a stressed person had no significant effect on cortisol or behavior in AAI horses (Merkies et al., 2014).

In trauma-specific cases, the AAI animal may also not necessarily know how to respond to an individual with unpredictable behaviors and emotions. Consequently, the animal may engage in avoidant behaviors or exhibit signs of stress when exposed to this individual. In addition, people with anxiety disorders due to trauma are often hypervigilant and have difficulty concentrating. Such physiological and behavioral indicators can be unsettling to animals, which may result in higher anxiety or even mirroring the recipient's behavior. For example, a person who constantly needs to use his or her hands may stroke an animal too quickly with excessive pressure, which could then cause stress and restlessness in the animal. Fundamentally, animals may not understand the intention of a behavior; they only see and experience the outcome.

The age of the recipient may also play a role in affecting animal welfare, since children and their frequent erratic behaviors invoke higher levels of stress in animals as compared to adults (Marinelli, Normando, Siliprandi, Salvadoretti, & Mongillo, 2009). One case study reported that an AAI dog exhibited behavioral signs of stress and suffered from Cushing's disease, an endocrine disorder characterized by high levels of cortisol, after persistent engagement with children with disabilities (Heimlich, 2001). It has also been shown that service dogs for autistic children form stronger bonds with the parental figures than with the children (Burrows & Adams, 2008), indicating that dogs may be more comfortable with adults than with children. While many AAI handlers anecdotally state that their dogs "love" children, it is advised that handlers take a more proactive role in educating children how to safely interact with animals.

Just as an animal should not be forced upon a human, a human should not force himself or herself upon an animal. Some exuberant individuals may have the tendency to thrust themselves upon an animal or engage in forceful petting, hugging, grabbing, pulling, squeezing, or pinching. These individuals should be instructed how to safely interact with the animal, ideally allowing the animal to approach the human first. Techniques that may lessen the perception of threat to an animal include moving slowly, speaking softly, and avoiding direct eye contact. In addition, positioning oneself to be at the same level as the animal by crouching can be helpful. Guiding where the animal does and does not like to be touched, as well as demonstrating the amount of pressure to apply during petting, are helpful techniques in ensuring the animal's comfort and trust level. The handler can also be effective in teaching the recipient what behaviors indicate discomfort or stress, and to modify or discontinue the interaction if these signs occur. The recipient should recognize that an animal interaction should not be taken for granted, but rather earned when the animal learns it can trust him or her. This will lead to safer interactions for all participants.

ENVIRONMENT SELECTION: COMFORTABLE AND CONTROLLED

Even with the right handler, animal, and recipient, AAI may be unsuccessful if it does not take place in an appropriate environment. Once clearance for animal admission is granted by the facility, many factors should be considered when selecting the right environment conducive to the health and welfare of the animal in AAI. The setting should ideally be quiet and absent of sudden loud noises, as they may be distracting to animals, especially those with noise phobias. To ameliorate the stress with unpredictable commotion, background noise such as classical music may facilitate a more calming environment (Kogan, Schoenfeld-Tacher, & Simon, 2012). Similarly, the environment should be free of distractions. The presence of other people, dogs, and/or human food may be distracting and arousing to the AAI animal. If possible, the animal should be kept separated from other animals to ensure appropriate engagement with the humans involved. Although selection of the ideal AAI setting is preferred, this may not always be possible to guarantee when working with traumatized populations in shelters, hospitals, or disaster/crisis environments, settings that can be more unpredictable or stress-inducing to the animal. Therefore, it is imperative that proper handler and animal selection be performed in these cases.

The ambient temperature should be set at room temperature, typically where both handler and client are comfortable. However, pocket pets, birds, and reptiles often require warmer temperatures. If this is not possible, a heat source such as a warm pack or heating lamp should be available to the animal at all times. Likewise, it is important that the environment have secure footing for the animal. Most hospitals and institutional facilities have slick floors. While these are easier to sanitize, carpets or rubber flooring are preferred surfaces for animals to walk.

Throughout the interaction, the environment should remain as clean as possible. However, dogs have a keen sense of smell, and overwhelming scents of perfumes, cleansers, or deodorizers may be distracting and off-putting to animals. In addition, animals may have contact allergies or eye sensitivities to these aromatic compounds, so products should be used judiciously.

Importantly, the AAI location should have an area designated for the animal for rest and respite. This serves as a safe zone where the animal can take a "time-out" break and have access to water. If a space is not dedicated to freedom from human interaction, the handler should take regular breaks in a quiet area away from other activities. Therapy dogs should also have easy access to an outdoor area for urination and defecation.

The novelty of an environment appears to be an important factor to the welfare of the animal as well. Although cortisol levels were not different in AAI dogs between the home and AAI setting in a recent study, they were significantly higher in a novel setting (Ng et al., 2014). In addition,

researchers recently proposed that the novelty of the setting was a significant factor in the high frequency of stress behavioral signals observed in
AAI dogs (Mongillo et al., 2015). An unfamiliar location may be stressful
to an animal, and the more acclimated the animal is with the environment, the more comfortable it will be. Therefore, it may be reasonable to
introduce the animal to the AAI environment for the first time without
human interaction.

There is some evidence that species-specific pheromones infused into
the environment by manual spray or plug-in diffusers can reduce stress and
fear in dogs and cats in certain environments (e.g., Feliway spray or diffusers for cats) (Kronen et al., 2006; Tod, Brander, & Waran, 2005). This may
be a noninvasive method to make the AAI environment more comfortable
for the animal, especially when other factors cannot be controlled.

AAI may also take place outdoors, especially when working with
horses, engaging in farm settings and/or nature-based applications, or
visiting individuals in disaster locations (customarily with therapy dogs).
Extreme weather conditions, especially heat, should preclude visitation.
In outdoor environments, fresh water should be available at all times,
and shelter in a shaded area should be provided to avoid dehydration
and heat exhaustion. The most common ailments found in dogs working
in disaster areas are minor cuts and scrapes from debris, such as broken
glass, nails, or other sharp objects (Slensky, Drobatz, Downend, & Otto,
2004). Footwear on dogs may help in preventing some issues, but, again,
it is important that handlers are knowledgeable of basic first aid in these
situations.

Another concern in outdoor environments is exposure to air debris,
toxins, and allergens. For example, search and rescue dogs deployed for
9/11 showed higher liver values, suggesting that they were exposed to high
levels of toxins or antigens (Otto, Downend, Serpell, Ziemer, & Saunders,
2004). However, these abnormalities were clinically insignificant, as there
was no evidence of increased incidence of liver disease, cancer, respiratory
problems, or behavioral conditions in these dogs compared to nonworking
dogs five years later (Otto et al., 2010). While no long-term effects have
yet to be reported in dogs working in disaster settings, handlers should be
cognizant of the particular risks involved.

Additionally, outdoor environments where wildlife or unvaccinated
animals reside put AAI animals at risk of contracting a host of infectious

diseases. Animals can easily acquire parasites such as fleas, ticks, and intestinal worms, which can be prevented with regular administration of chemoprophylaxis. In addition, bacteria and viruses may be prevalent as well, so ensuring the animal is current on vaccines recommended by the veterinarian is essential in ensuring animal health.

BEFORE THE VISIT

Once the key factors of choosing the right handler, animal, recipient, and environment have been decided, securing animal welfare depends on how the AAI is conducted before, during, and after the session. To prepare the animal before the visit, it should be confirmed that the animal has had no medical or behavioral problems in the last 72 hours. As long as it is healthy and willing to go to work, it should be groomed to be clean and free of odors. While bathing regularly ensures a clean coat, bathing too frequently may strip the coat of its natural oils, predisposing it to dryness or other skin issues. Nails should be trimmed and filed down to reduce risk of injury from scratching. Teeth should also be brushed, if possible, to minimize halitosis and dental disease.

At a minimum, dogs and cats should wear a collar with identifying information. Pocket pets, birds, or reptiles should be confined to, and transported in, an appropriately sized container before, during, and after the session. If apparel, such as a scarf indicating it is an AAI animal, is worn for the visit, it should be nonobtrusive and placed on the animal immediately before entering the facility and removed immediately after. While many perceive that dressing animals in clothing or costumes makes them look cute, this practice should be avoided, especially in animals that do not typically wear them. Wearing clothes is not natural for the animal, prevents tactile interaction between the person and the animal, and may be uncomfortable or constricting.

Transportation to the AAI location may pose an issue to animals that are anxious during travel. Some animals may be anxious during travel if the only times they leave the home are for visits to the vet, which, as discussed earlier, may be an adverse experience. Counterconditioning by taking trips to positive locations and rewarding them may help mitigate this particular stress. In addition, some animals may demonstrate travel sickness, an issue that warrants management advice from the veterinarian. The animal should be given the opportunity to relieve itself upon arrival and prior to entering the AAI facility.

DURING THE VISIT

During the visit, it is the handler's obligation to advocate for the animal in regard to the duration, frequency, and intensity of the AAI. The handler should be mindful of the animal, environment, and people visited, and able to recognize when a situation may not be safe or comfortable. The handler should be vigilant in looking for an increase in stress-associated behaviors, and actively remedy distressing situations by modifying or concluding the visit.

The animal should be safely directed through the visit with attentive guidance, rather than tight restraint. For example, a dog should be held on a loose lead so it has some freedom to approach or remove itself from a stranger. If the interaction is in a confined environment, an appropriate AAI dog may not necessarily be required to be on-leash, as cortisol levels have been shown to be higher on-leash than off-leash (Glenk et al., 2013). A small pocket pet, bird, or reptile can be gently handled as long as its container is within reach.

The duration of the visit is an important factor in the welfare of the animal. Traditionally, most organizations recognize that visits should be limited to a maximum of one hour (Lefebvre et al., 2008). While recent research findings show that cortisol levels in dogs did not change significantly over the course of a one-hour AAI session to indicate increased levels of stress (Ng et al., 2014), the strict one-hour guideline is controversial and warrants further investigation. For example, some animals are readily accepting of a full hour of work, some may be unaffected by numerous hours, and others may fatigue after a 20-minute interaction.

One important variable in AAI that likely impacts animal fatigue is the intensity of the session. One study demonstrated that AAI dogs that worked shorter sessions (one hour) had higher cortisol levels than dogs that worked longer sessions (more than six hours) (Haubenhofer & Kirchengast, 2006). The likely explanation for this is that the shorter sessions were more intense while longer sessions were more relaxed and included frequent breaks. Therefore, the intensity and quality of the inter-action likely matter more than the finite amount of time spent working. For example, a dog may be able to tolerate a longer visit with one or two immobile geriatric patients than with five to ten active children. This is an important consideration regarding AAI with trauma, as sessions may be of a higher intensity, and discussion of sensitive topics may foment extreme emotions and actions in these clients. As a result, these sessions may be more stimulating or stress-inducing to the animal, which requires more frequent breaks and active monitoring for behavioral signs of stress.

No matter the session intensity, breaks for the animal are essential (King et al., 2011), and should serve as an opportunity for the animal to be free of human contact, to play or express normal behavior, to relieve itself, and to drink water. As previously mentioned, some handlers have expressed concern about providing water for the animal for fear of the animal hav-ing an accident in the facility (Hatch, 2007). Healthy, well-trained dogs should not have an accident if they are given the opportunity to go to the bathroom outside before and/or during the visit. In addition, restricting water during work can lead to dehydration and contribute negatively to the animal's welfare. While no specific guideline for timing of breaks has been validated, it should be given at least one during a session, especially when behavioral indicators of stress are observed.

Hand washing and/or sanitizing is essential to the health of the an-imal and to all individuals who come into contact with that animal. In fact, it is the most critical practice that can be implemented to combat the transmission of zoonotic disease. This is important in all visits, but particularly critical in hospital settings where contagious diseases such as methicillin-resistant *Staphylococcus aureus* (MRSA) and *Clostridium diffi-cile* (C. diff) are highly prevalent and can be easily transmitted. Although AAI dogs in hospitals were colonized with such diseases in one study, they were not found to be clinically infected or ill (Lefebvre et al., 2009). However, the potential for infection in the animal or transmission to other individuals still exists. Since practices such as shaking paws, getting up on beds, licking faces, and taking treats were risk factors for colonization of MRSA and C diff, these activities should be avoided or kept to a minimum whenever possible. Furthermore, excessive treats predispose the animal to obesity and can be distracting, so use of treats during AAI sessions should be limited, if not prohibited.

AFTER THE VISIT

After the session, the animal should be thoroughly rewarded to positively reinforce the event and ensure a positive experience. Whether it is enthusiastic praise, play/exercise, toys, or treats, it should be a high-value reward to that particular animal.

Monitoring forms should also be completed by the handler to record the details of the AAI session. Accurate record keeping permits the AAI organization or facility to monitor the progress of the visits and address any minor issues that may have occurred. This information may include how many people were visited, the duration of the session, session activities, and any adverse effects. A list of stress-associated behaviors may be provided as a reference for individuals to report what was observed during the visit.

To prevent infectious disease, hand washing at the completion of the session is essential. Since paw contact with contaminated surfaces is the typical source of colonization, it may be reasonable for the handler to wipe the paws with an antiseptic wipe as well. Bathing the animal after an AAI session is likely unnecessary, unless contact with an infectious individual is confirmed.

RECURRING VISITS AND RETIREMENT

The handler must be vigilant about monitoring for abnormal animal behaviors or symptoms in and out of work, paying close attention to the animal's response toward returning to the facility or to interactions with a particular recipient. If there is hesitation to visit demonstrated by freezing or an increase in stress signals or behavior before, during, or after the visit, further investigation is warranted. Any notable changes in behavior should be assessed by an animal behaviorist or animal health expert associated with the AAI organization. Of course, any abnormal health problems exhibited by the animal should allow for him or her to be temporarily relieved of duties and seen by a veterinarian. The return to work after illness should be at the discretion of the veterinarian.

Every being that has a job should be granted the reward of retirement. The decision to retire an animal from AAI work depends on a variety of factors. While the handler is the ultimate decision maker in this regard, he or she must be the voice and advocate for the animal. Two studies of AAI have reported that participating dogs passed away before the completion of the studies (Braun et al., 2009; King et al., 2011), although specific details about their fatalities were undisclosed. While their deaths are unlikely to be related to AAI work, it brings up the ethical question of why these animals were not relieved of their duties prior to death. Some may argue that animals still enjoy working until their final days, but this remains an important issue in the life span of an AAI animal.

With the physical changes associated with aging, the veterinarian should evaluate the animal on at least an annual basis. While senior animals can be affected by any chronic disease and/or cancer, one of the most common and important clinical signs to watch for is pain. Discomfort from osteoarthritis, exacerbated by obesity, is prevalent in older dogs, and recent research has revealed that musculoskeletal issues are the most common reason for guide dogs to retire early (Caron-Lormier, England, Green, & Asher, 2016). Maintaining a healthy weight through diet and exercise is crucial, and joint supplementation may be helpful in slowing the process. The handler must be cautious of activities that place physical stress on the animal's body during AAI, such as getting into and out of cars for transport.

CONCLUSIONS

Our current knowledge of the way in which AAI impacts the welfare of participating animals is limited, with few studies rigorously evaluating the short- and long-term effects. Since AAIs are so variable and dependent on the individuals and circumstance, controlled prospective trials are scarce. Likewise, research in this area has, to date, demonstrated mixed results regarding the stress-related welfare concerns of working therapy dogs (i.e., see Glenk et al., 2013; Haubenhofer & Kirchengast, 2006, 2007; King et al., 2011; Marinelli et al., 2009; McCullough et al., 2018; Ng et al., 2014). The study of animal emotion, stress, and welfare is generally challenging, as these concepts cannot be measured directly, but rather through behavior and physiology (Mendl, Burman, Parker, & Paul, 2009). Even with advances in measuring parameters such as cortisol, proper interpretation of this physiologic indicator is difficult, as an increase or decrease does not necessarily correlate with a positive or negative emotion (Edgar, Nicol, Clark, & Paul, 2012). Therefore, multiple physiological parameters should be interpreted in conjunction with behavioral signs. Future studies should incorporate advanced imaging and cardiovascular effects to obtain a comprehensive look at the animal. In addition, as evident throughout this chapter and others in this volume, the field of HAI is heavily canine focused, and research on all species used for this work will be valuable to the field in making future evidence-based and species-specific recommendations.

Although this discussion has focused on recognizing the potential negative consequences and risks of HAI (and especially AAT/AAA) on animals, we must acknowledge that there are likely beneficial effects for these animals as well. When we have done everything in our power to safeguard animal welfare, a positive AAI can be mutually beneficial for both the human and the animal. In selecting the right handler, animal, recipient, and environment, and following appropriate protocols, we will ensure the success of these interactions.

REFERENCES

Albuquerque, N., Guo, K., Wilkinson, A., Savalli, C., Otta, E., & Mills, D. (2016). Dogs recognize dog and human emotions. *Biology Letters, 12*(1), 20150883. https://doi.org/10.1098/rsbl.2015.0883

Andics, A., Gabor, A., Gacsi, M., Farago, T., Szabo, D., & Miklosi, A. (2016). Neural mechanisms for lexical processing in dogs. *Science, 353*(6303), 1030–1032. https://doi.org/10.1126/science.aaf3777

Andics, A., Gacsi, M., Farago, T., Kis, A., & Miklosi, A. (2014). Voice-sensitive regions in the dog and human brain are revealed by comparative FMRI. *Current Biology, 24*(5), 574–578. https://doi.org/10.1016/j.cub.2014.01.058

Antonites, A., & Odendaal, J. (2004). Ethics in human-animal relationships. *Acta Veterinaria Brno, 73*(4), 539–None.

Beerda, B., Schilder, M. B. H., van Hooff, J. A. R. A. M., & de Vries, H. W. (1997). Manifestations of chronic and acute stress in dogs. *Applied Animal Behaviour Science, 52*(3–4), 307–319.

Beerda, B., Schilder, M. B. H., van Hooff, J. A. R. A. M., de Vries, H. W., & Mol, J. A. (1998). Behavioural, saliva cortisol and heart rate responses to different types of stimuli in dogs. *Applied Animal Behaviour Science, 58*(3–4), 365–381.

Beerda, B., Schilder, M. B. H., van Hooff, J. A. R. A. M., de Vries, H. W., & Mol, J. A. (2000). Behavioural and hormonal indicators of enduring environmental stress in dogs. *Animal Welfare, 9*, 49–62.

Bekoff, M. (2000). Animal emotions: Exploring passionate natures: Current interdisciplinary research provides compelling evidence that many animals experience such emotions as joy, fear, love, despair, and grief—we are not alone. *BioScience, 50*(10), 861–870.

Bekoff, M. (2007). *The emotional lives of animals: A leading scientist explores animal joy, sorrow, and empathy—and why they matter.* Novato, CA: New World Library.

Blackwell, E. J., Twells, C., Seawright, A., & Casey, R. A. (2008). The relationship between training methods and the occurrence of behavior problems, as reported by owners, in a population of domestic dogs. *Journal of Veterinary Behavior: Clinical Applications and Research, 3*(5), 207–217. https://doi.org/10.1016/j.jveb.2007.10.008

Bradshaw, I. G. A. (2004). Not by bread alone: Symbolic loss, trauma, and recovery in elephant communities. *Society & Animals, 12*(2), 143–158.

Brambell, F. W. R. (1965). *Report of the technical committee to enquire into the welfare of animals kept under intensive livestock husbandry systems: Command Paper 2836.* London, UK: Her Majesty's Stationary Office.

Braun, C., Stangler, T., Narveson, J., & Pettingell, S. (2009). Animal-assisted therapy as a pain relief intervention for children. *Complementary Therapies in Clinical Practice, 15*(2), 105–109. https://doi.org/10.1016/j.ctcp.2009.02.008

Broom, D. M. (1996). Animal welfare defined in terms of attempts to cope with the environment. *Acta Agriculturae Scandinavica Section A Animal Science, 27*(Supplement 27), 22–28.

Burrows, K. E., & Adams, C. L. (2008). Challenges of service-dog ownership for families with autistic children: Lessons for veterinary practitioners. *Journal of Veterinary Medical Education, 35*(4), 559–566. https://doi.org/35/4/559 [pii]10.3138/jvme.35.4.559

Butler, K. (2004). *Therapy dogs today: Their gifts, our obligation.* Norman, OK: Funpuddle Publishing Associates.

Buttner, A. P., Thompson, B., Strasser, R., & Santo, J. (2015). Evidence for a synchronization of hormonal states between humans and dogs during competition. *Physiology & Behavior, 147*, 54–62. https://doi.org/10.1016/j.physbeh.2015.04.010

Call, J., Brauer, J., Kaminski, J., & Tomasello, M. (2003). Domestic dogs (*Canis familiaris*) are sensitive to the attentional state of humans. *Journal of Comparative Psychology, 117*(3), 257–263. https://doi.org/10.1037/0735-7036.117.3.257

Caron-Lormier, G., England, G. C. W., Green, M. J., & Asher, L. (2016). Using the incidence and impact of health conditions in guide dogs to investigate healthy ageing in working dogs. *Veterinary Journal, 207*, 124–130. https://doi.org/10.1016/j.tvjl.2015.10.046

Coppinger, R., Coppinger, L., & Skillings, E. (1998). Observations on assistance dog training and use. *Journal of Applied Animal Welfare Science, 1*(2), 133–144. https://doi.org/10.1207/s15327604jaws0102_4

Custance, D., & Mayer, J. (2012). Empathic-like responding by domestic dogs (Canis familiaris) to distress in humans: An exploratory study. *Animal Cognition, 15*(5), 851–859. https://doi.org/10.1007/s10071-012-0510-1

de Waal, F. B. M. (2008). Putting the altruism back into altruism: The evolution of empathy. *Annual Review of Psychology, 59*, 279–300. https://doi.org/10.1146/annurev.psych.59.103006.093625

Duranton, C., & Gaunet, F. (2015). Canis sensitivus: Affiliation and dogs' sensitivity to others' behavior as the basis for synchronization with humans? *Journal of Veterinary Behavior: Clinical Applications and Research, 10*(6), 513–524. https://doi.org/10.1016/j.jveb.2015.08.008

Edgar, J. L., Nicol, C. J., Clark, C. C. A., & Paul, E. S. (2012). Measuring empathic responses in animals. *Applied Animal Behaviour Science, 138*(3/4), 182–193. https://doi.org/10.1016/j.applanim.2012.02.006

Fejsáková, M., Kottferová, J., Mareková, J., Jakuba, T., Ondrašovičová, O., & Ondrašovič, M. (2009). *Ethical aspects related to involvement of animals in animal assisted therapy.* Paper presented at the 52nd Student Scientific Conference, Kosice, Slovakia, 28 April 2009.

Foa, E. B., Zinbarg, R., & Rothbaum, B. O. (1992). Uncontrollability and unpredictability in post-traumatic stress disorder: An animal model. *Psychological Bulletin, 112*(2), 218–238.

Fureix, C., Jego, P., Sankey, C., & Hausberger, M. (2009). How horses (Equus caballus) see the world: Humans as significant "objects." *Animal Cognition, 12*(4), 643–654.

Glenk, L. M., Kothgassner, O. D., Stetina, B. U., Palme, R., Kepplinger, B., & Baran, H. (2013). Therapy dogs' salivary cortisol levels vary during animal-assisted interventions. *Animal Welfare, 22*(3), 369–378. https://doi.org/10.7120/09627286.22.3.369

Glenk, L. M., Stetina, B. U., Kepplinger, B., & Baran, H. (2011). Salivary cortisol, heart rate variability and behavioral assessment in dogs during animal-assisted interventions (AAI) in neuropsychiatry. *Journal of Veterinary Behavior, 6*(1), 81–82.

Hatch, A. (2007). The view from all fours: A look at an animal-assisted activity program from the animals' perspective. *Anthrozoös, 20*(1), 37–50.

Haubenhofer, D. K., & Kirchengast, S. (2006). Physiological arousal for companion dogs working with their owners in animal-assisted activities and animal-assisted therapy. *Journal of Applied Animal Welfare Science, 9*(2), 165–172. https://doi.org/10.1207/s15327604jaws0902_5

Haubenhofer, D. K., & Kirchengast, S. (2007). Dog handlers' and dogs' emotional and cortisol secretion responses associated with animal-assisted therapy sessions. *Society & Animals, 15*, 127–150. https://doi.org/10.1163/156853007x187090

Haverbeke, A., Diederich, C., Depiereux, E., & Giffroy, J. M. (2008). Cortisol and behavioral responses of working dogs to environmental challenges. *Physiology & Behavior, 93*(1–2), 59–67. https://doi.org/S0031-9384(07)00299-5 [pii]10.1016/j.physbeh.2007.07.014

Heimlich, K. (2001). Animal-assisted therapy and the severely disabled child: A quantitative study. *Journal of Rehabilitation, 67*(4), 48–54.

Hetts, S., Clark, J. D., Arnold, C. E., & Mateo, J. M. (1992). Influence of housing conditions on beagle behaviour. *Applied Animal Behaviour Science, 34*, 137–155.

Hiby, E. F., Rooney, N. J., & Bradshaw, J. W. (2006). Behavioural and physiological responses of dogs entering re-homing kennels. *Physiology & Behavior, 89*(3), 385–391. https://doi.org/S0031-9384(06)00301-5 [pii] 10.1016/j.physbeh.2006.07.012

Hsu, Y., & Serpell, J. A. (2003). Development and validation of a questionnaire for measuring behavior and temperament traits in pet dogs. *Journal of the American Veterinary Medical Association, 223*(9), 1293–1300.

Hunt, M. G., & Chizkov, R. R. (2014). Are therapy dogs like xanax? Does animal-assisted therapy impact processes relevant to cognitive behavioral psychotherapy? *Anthrozoös, 27*(3), 457–469.

Jegatheesan, B., Beetz, A., Choi, G., Dudzik, C., Fine, A., Garcia, R. M., Johnson, R., Ormerod, E., Winkle, M., & Yamazaki, K. (2014). *White paper: The IAHAIO definitions for animal assisted intervention and guidelines for wellness of animals involved.* Unpublished report. Retrieved from http://www.iahaio.org/new/fileuploads/4163IAHAIO%20WHITE%20PAPER-%20FINAL%20-%20NOV%2024-2014.pdf

Jones, A. C., & Josephs, R. A. (2006). Interspecies hormonal interactions between man and the domestic dog (Canis familiaris). *Hormones and Behavior, 50*(3), 393–400. https://doi.org/S0018-506X(06)00122-X [pii]10.1016/j.yhbeh.2006.04.007

Kaiser, L., Heleski, C. R., Siegford, J. & Smith, K. A. (2006). Stress-related behaviors among horses used in a therapeutic riding program. *Journal of American Veterinary Medical Association, 228*(1), 39–45.

King, C., Watters, J., & Mungre, S. (2011). Effect of a time-out session with working animal-assisted therapy dogs. *Journal of Veterinary Behavior:*

Clinical Applications and Research, 6(4), 232–238. https://doi.org/10.1016/j
.jveb.2011.01.007

Kogan, L. R., Schoenfeld-Tacher, R., & Simon, A. A. (2012). Behavioral effects of auditory stimulation on kenneled dogs. *Journal of Veterinary Behavior: Clinical Applications and Research, 7*(5), 268–275. https://doi.org/10.1016/j
.jveb.2011.11.002

Kronen, P. W., Ludders, J. W., Erb, H. N., Moon, P. F., Gleed, R. D., & Koski, S. (2006). A synthetic fraction of feline facial pheromones calms but does not reduce struggling in cats before venous catheterization. *Veterinary Anaesthesia and Analgesia, 33*(4), 258–265. https://doi.org/10.1111/j.1467-2995.2005.00265.x

Kubinyi, E., Turcsan, B., & Miklosi, A. (2009). Dog and owner demographic characteristics and dog personality trait associations. *Behavioural Processes, 81*(3), 392–401. https://doi.org/10.1016/j.beproc.2009.04.004

Kuczaj, S., Tranel, K., Trone, M., & Hill, H. (2001). Are animals capable of deception or empathy? Implications for animal consciousness and animal welfare. *Animal Welfare, 10*(Supplement), S161–S173.

Landsberg, G., Hunthausen, W., & Ackerman, L. (2012). *Behavior problems of the dog and cat* (3rd ed.). Philadelphia, PA: Saunders.

Lefebvre, S. L., Golab, G. C., Christensen, E. L., Castrodale, L., Aureden, K., Bialachowski, A., Gumley, N., Robinson, J., Peregrine, A., Benoit, M., Card, M. L., Van Horne, L., & Weese, J. S. (2008). Guidelines for animal-assisted interventions in health care facilities. *American Journal of Infection Control, 36*(2), 78–85. https://doi.org/10.1016/j.ajic.2007.09.005

Lefebvre, S. L., Reid-Smith, R., Boerlin, P., & Weese, J. S. (2008). Evaluation of the risks of shedding Salmonellae and other potential pathogens by therapy dogs fed raw diets in Ontario and Alberta. *Zoonoses Public Health, 55*(8–10), 470–480. https://doi.org/10.1111/j.1863-2378.2008.01145.x

Lefebvre, S. L., Reid-Smith, R. J., Waltner-Toews, D., & Weese, J. S. (2009). Incidence of acquisition of methicillin-resistant Staphylococcus aureus, Clostridium difficile, and other health-care-associated pathogens by dogs that participate in animal-assisted interventions. *Journal of American Veterinary Medical Association, 234*(11), 1404–1417. https://doi.org/10.2460/javma.234.11.1404

Lefebvre, S. L., Waltner-Toews, D., Peregrine, A., Reid-Smith, R., Hodge, H., & Weese, J. S. (2006). Characteristics of programs involving canine visitation of hospitalized people in Ontario. *Infection Control and Hospital Epidemiology, 27*(7), 754–758. https://doi.org/10.1086/505099

Levine, E. D. (2008). Feline fear and anxiety. *Veterinary Clinics of North America: Small Animal Practice, 38*(5), 1065–1079.

Linley, P. A., & Joseph, S. (2007). Therapy work and therapists' positive and negative well-being. *Journal of Social and Clinical Psychology, 26*(3), 385–403.

Marinelli, L., Normando, S., Siliprandi, C., Salvadoretti, M., & Mongillo, P. (2009). Dog assisted interventions in a specialized centre and potential concerns for animal welfare. *Veterinary Research Communications, 33*(Supplement 1), S93–S95. https://doi.org/10.1007/s11259-009-9256-x

Mariti, C., Gazzano, A., Moore, J. L., Baragli, P., Chelli, L., & Sighieri, C. (2012). Perception of dogs' stress by their owners. *Journal of Veterinary Behavior: Clinical Applications and Research, 7*(4), 213–219.

McBride, S. D., Hemmings, A., & Robinson, K. (2004). A preliminary study on the effect of massage to reduce stress in the horse. *Journal of Equine Veterinary Science, 24*(2), 76–81.

McCullough, A., Jenkins, M. A., Ruehrdanz, A., Gilmer, M. J., Olson, J., Pawar, A., . . . O'Haire, M. E. (2018). Physiological and behavioral effects of animal-assisted interventions for therapy dogs in pediatric oncology settings. *Applied Animal Behaviour Science, 200*, 86–95.

McEwen, B. S., & Wingfield, J. C. (2003). The concept of allostasis in biology and biomedicine. *Hormones and Behavior, 43*(1), 2–15.

Mendl, M., Burman, O. H., Parker, R. M., & Paul, E. S. (2009). Cognitive bias as an indicator of animal emotion and welfare: emerging evidence and underlying mechanisms. *Applied Animal Behaviour Science, 118*(3), 161–181.

Merkies, K., Sievers, A., Zakrajsek, E., MacGregor, H., Bergeron, R., Borstel, U. K. v., & von Borstel, U. K. (2014). Preliminary results suggest an influence of psychological and physiological stress in humans on horse heart rate and behavior. *Journal of Veterinary Behavior: Clinical Applications and Research, 9*(5), 242–247. https://doi.org/10.1016/j.jveb.2014.06.003

Mongillo, P., Pitteri, E., Adamelli, S., Bonichini, S., Farina, L., & Marinelli, L. (2015). Validation of a selection protocol of dogs involved in animal-assisted intervention. *Journal of Veterinary Behavior: Clinical Applications and Research, 10*(2), 103–110. https://doi.org/10.1016/j.jveb.2014.11.005

Moss, C. (1992). *Echo of the elephants: The story of an elephant family.* London, UK: BBC.

Muller, C. A., Schmitt, K., Barber, A. L., & Huber, L. (2015). Dogs can discriminate emotional expressions of human faces. *Current Biology, 25*(5), 601–605. https://doi.org/10.1016/j.cub.2014.12.055

Nagasawa, M., Mitsui, S., En, S., Ohtani, N., Ohta, M., Sakuma, Y., Onaka, T., Mogi, K., Kikusui, T. (2015). Social evolution: Oxytocin-gaze positive loop and the coevolution of human-dog bonds. *Science, 348*(6232), 333–336. https://doi.org /10.1126/science.1261022

Nagasawa, M., Murai, K., Mogi, K., & Kikusui, T. (2011). Dogs can discriminate human smiling faces from blank expressions. *Animal Cognition, 14*(4), 525–533. https://doi.org/10.1007/s10071-011-0386-5

National Association of State Public Health Veterinarians Compendium of Animal Rabies Prevention and Control Commitee, Brown, C. M., Slavinski, S., Ettestad, P., Sidwa, T. J., & Sorhage, F. E. (2016). Compendium of animal rabies prevention and control. *Journal of American Veterinary Medical Association, 248*(5), 505–517. https://doi.org/10.2460/javma.248.5.505

Ng, Z. Y., Pierce, B. J., Otto, C. M., Buechner-Maxwell, V. A., Siracusa, C., & Werre, S. R. (2014). The effect of dog-human interaction on cortisol and behavior in registered animal-assisted activity dogs. *Applied Animal Behaviour Science, 159*, 69–81. https://doi.org/10.1016/j.applanim.2014.07.009

Novak, M. A., & Drewsen, K. H. (1989). Enriching the lives of captive primates: Issues and problems. In E. F. Segal (Ed.), *Housing, care, and psychological well-being of captive and laboratory primates* (pp. 161–185). Park Ridge, NJ: Noyes.

Otto, C. M., Downend, A. B., Moore, G. E., Daggy, J. K., Ranivand, D. L., Reetz, J. A., & Fitzgerald, S. D. (2010). Medical surveillance of search dogs deployed to the World Trade Center and Pentagon: 2001–2006. *Journal of Environmental Health, 73*(2), 12–21.

Otto, C. M., Downend, A. B., Serpell, J. A., Ziemer, L. S., & Saunders, H. M. (2004). Medical and behavioral surveillance of dogs deployed to the World Trade Center and the Pentagon from October 2001 to June 2002. *Journal of American Veterinary Medical Association, 225*(6), 861–867.

Panksepp, J. (2005). Affective consciousness: Core emotional feelings in animals and humans. *Consciousness and cognition, 14*(1), 30–80.

Pearlman, L. A., & Mac Ian, P. S. (1995). Vicarious traumatization: An empirical study of the effects of trauma work on trauma therapists. *Professional Psychology: Research and Practice, 26*(6), 558.

Peterson, C. (1993). *Learned helplessness*. Wiley Online Library.

Piva, E., Liverani, V., Accorsi, P. A., Sarli, G., & Gandini, G. (2008). Welfare in a shelter dog rehomed with Alzheimer patients. *Journal of Veterinary Behavior: Clinical Applications and Research, 3*(2), 87–94. https://doi.org/10.1016/j .jveb.2007.08.004

Prehn-Kristensen, A., Wiesner, C., Bergmann, T. O., Wolff, S., Jansen, O., Mehdorn, H. M., Ferstl, R., & Pause, B. M. (2009). Induction of empathy by

the smell of anxiety. *PLOS One, 4*(6), e5987. https://doi.org/10.1371/journal
.pone.0005987

Preston, S. D., & de Waal, F. B. (2002). The communication of emotions and
the possibility of empathy in animals. In S. G. Post (Ed.), *Altruistic love: Science, philosophy, and religion in dialogue* (pp. 284–308). Oxford, UK: Oxford
University Press.

Preziosi, R. (1997). For your consideration: A pet-assisted therapist facilitator
code of ethics. *The Latham Letter*, 5–6. Retrieved from https://www.latham
.org/Issues/LL_97_SP.pdf

Santori, P. (2011). Problems related to the use of animals for therapeutic and
care purposes: The Document of the National Committee for Bioethics. *Annali dell'Istituto Superiore Di Sanita, 47*(4), 349–352. https://doi.org/10.4415
/ann_11_04_05

Schwizgebel, D. (1982). Zusammenhänge zwischen dem Verhalten des deutschen
Schäferhundes im Hinblick auf tiergerechte Ausbildung. *Aktuelle Arbeiten zur
artgemäßen Tierhaltung 1982*, 138–148.

Serpell, J. A., Coppinger, R., Fine, A. H., & Peralta, J. M. (2010). Welfare considerations in therapy and assistance animals. In A. H. Fine (Ed.), *Handbook
on animal-assisted therapy: Theoretical foundations and guidelines for practice* (3rd
ed., pp. 481–503). San Diego, CA: Associated Press.

Silva, K., & de Sousa, L. (2011). "Canis empathicus"? A proposal on dogs' capacity to empathize with humans. *Biology Letters, 7*(4), 489–492. https://doi
.org/10.1098/rsbl.2011.0083

Slensky, K. A., Drobatz, K. J., Downend, A. B., & Otto, C. M. (2004). Deployment morbidity among search-and-rescue dogs used after the September
11, 2001 terrorist attacks. *Journal of American Veterinary Medical Association,
225*(6), 868–873.

Stampfl, B. (2012). Theorizing canine PTSD. In J. Pelkey (Ed.), *Semiotics* (pp.
159–168).

Stevens, J. A., Teh, S. L., & Haileyesus, T. (2010). Dogs and cats as environmental
fall hazards. *Journal of Safety Research, 41*(1), 69–73. https://doi.org/10.1016/j
.jsr.2010.01.001

Stewart, L. A. (n.d.). *Animal-assisted interventions competencies*. Pet Partners. Retrieved from https://petpartners.org/wp-content/uploads/2014/12/Tiered-AAI
-Competencies_2016.pdf

Sumegi, Z., Olah, K., & Topal, J. (2014). Emotional contagion in dogs as measured by change in cognitive task performance. *Applied Animal Behaviour*

Science, 160, 106–115. https://doi.org/10.1016/j.applanim.2014.09.001

Tod, E., Brander, D., & Waran, N. (2005). Efficacy of dog appeasing pheromone in reducing stress and fear related behaviour in shelter dogs. *Applied Animal Behaviour Science, 93*(3/4), 295–308.

Udell, M. A. R., Dorey, N. R., & Wynne, C. D. L. (2010). What did domestication do to dogs? A new account of dogs' sensitivity to human actions. *Biological Reviews, 85*(2), 327–345. https://doi.org/10.1111/j.1469-185X.2009.00104.x

Udell, M. A. R., & Wynne, C. D. L. (2008). A review of domestic dogs' (Canis familiaris) human-like behaviors: Or why behavior analysts should stop worrying and love their dogs. *Journal of the Experimental Analysis of Behavior, 89*(2), 247–261. https://doi.org/10.1901/jeab.2008.89-247

Vitztum, C., & Urbanik, J. (2016). Assessing the dog: A theoretical analysis of the companion animal's actions in human-animal interactions. *Society & Animals, 24*(2), 172–185. https://doi.org/10.1163/15685306-12341399

Willmott, H., Greenheld, N., & Goddard, R. (2012). Beware of the dog? An observational study of dog-related musculoskeletal injury in the UK. *Accident Analysis and Prevention, 46,* 52–54. https://doi.org/10.1016/j.aap.2011.10.004

Yong, M., Ruffman, T., & Yong, M. H. (2014). Emotional contagion: Dogs and humans show a similar physiological response to human infant crying. *Behavioural Processes, 108,* 155–165. https://doi.org/10.1016/j.beproc.2014.10.006

ABOUT THE AUTHOR

Zenithson Ng is a clinical assistant professor of veterinary medicine at the University of Tennessee. He earned his veterinary degree from Cornell University and completed an American Board of Veterinary Practitioners (ABVP) Canine/Feline residency, combined with a master's degree in human-animal bond studies, at Virginia Tech. His research and teaching interests span all aspects of the human-animal bond, including the effect of human-animal interaction on both humans and animals, the veterinary-client relationship, and stress reduction in veterinary and animal-assisted intervention settings.

CHAPTER 3

Clinical Objectives for Animal-Assisted Interventions: Physiological and Psychological Targets in Trauma-Informed Practice

Andrea M. Beetz, MA, PhD; and Ira Schöfmann-Crawford, MA

In their lifetimes, many humans will experience traumatic events. Some will cope successfully with such trauma and, within a certain amount of time, show resilience, and not suffer further negative effects. Others, in contrast, may develop post-traumatic reactions such as post-traumatic stress disorder (PTSD), which is frequently accompanied by other clinically relevant symptoms such as depression, anxiety, substance abuse, or sleeping disorders. Animal-assisted intervention (AAI), especially for PTSD, has become more popular as a form of treatment. In the United States, particularly organizations for war veterans have worked with dogs and horses to improve veterans' quality of life and reduce symptoms of PTSD. Research on this practice, as well as on AAI for other traumata—such as sexual abuse in childhood and natural disasters—remains scarce.

In the following chapter, an introduction to traumatization and PTSD and their neurobiological correlates will be given. Current forms of standard interventions will be described before the basis of AAI for trauma (i.e., the scientifically documented effects of human-animal interaction [HAI] and the theoretical frameworks employed to explain the positive effects of animals on humans) is introduced. Then, briefly, the different possible AAIs around trauma and their effects will be discussed, followed by the presentation of current empirical evidence.

TRAUMA, PTSD, AND RELATED DISORDERS

Experiencing a traumatic event can lead to several reactions, including acute stress reactions as well as the development of PTSD and comorbid disorders. One of the first difficulties when dealing with trauma-related reactions involves determining whether a reaction to a stressor is an abnormal, and therefore diagnosable, reaction or a common adaptive and normal stress reaction. Today, the following reactions to traumatic experiences are usually distinguished in accordance with the DSM-5 (the following information on trauma, PTSD, neurobiology, genetics/epigenetics, and therapy for PTSD is based on the edited book by Schnyder and Cloitre, 2015, which gives an up-to-date overview of the topic).

Acute Stress Disorder (ASD)/Acute Stress Reaction (ASR)

Acute stress disorder (ASD) can be considered a pre-stage of PTSD, and describes an acute stress reaction during the time directly after trauma exposure. As in the diagnosis of PTSD, a traumatic event must have been experienced and accompanied by feelings of fear, helplessness or horror, and symptoms of dissociation, reexperiencing, avoidance, and increased arousal. The nature of the trauma may vary widely, from physical or sexual abuse and torture to exposure to natural disasters, large-scale acts of violence, and accidents. However, for a diagnosis of ASD or PTSD, the event had to be an exposure to death, threatened death of others or oneself, or a violation of one's physical integrity.

Post-Traumatic Stress Disorder (PTSD)

According to the DSM-5, besides the exposure to death or threatened death, four other criteria need to be met for a PTSD diagnosis: reexperiencing of the event, avoidance of situations that could trigger the memory, negative alterations in cognition/mood, and hyperarousal. Particularly the cluster of negative alterations accommodates feelings of guilt and thoughts of self-blame that many with PTSD report, as well as negative expectations about the world and the future.

The estimation of the lifetime prevalence of PTSD strongly varies between countries and regions. The lifetime prevalence for American adults is estimated between 7–12% (DiGangi, Guffanti, McLaughlin, & Koenen, 2013; Kessler, Sonnega, Bromet, Hughes, & Nelson, 1995). Living in a region with higher exposure to traumatic events (crisis regions, refugee camps, etc.) increases the occurrence of PTSD (e.g., 58% after combat exposure; Kessler et al., 1995, 2005). According to the National Comorbidity Survey (NCS; Kessler et al., 1995), most US-American adults are confronted with leastwise one traumatic event. Professions with an increased risk of experiencing traumatic events, such as rescue workers, also experience a higher prevalence of PTSD (Fullerton, Ursano, & Wang, 2004). After one year, a 13% higher prevalence to develop PTSD occurred in workers with disaster operation experience. Confirmed by several studies, such numbers indicate a cumulative influence of traumatic events, otherwise known as the *building block effect* (Schauer et al., 2003). This effect suggests that anybody can develop PTSD; it is merely a matter of how many traumatic events a person experiences. Neuner and colleagues (2004) found in one sample of over 3,300 refugees living in the West Nile region, a positive correlation between traumatic load and PTSD prevalence, as well as symptom severity.

THE PSYCHOLOGY OF PTSD

While several theoretical frameworks exist and are considered important in the development of PTSD, only some of those, which can be connected to AAI, will be discussed here.

Fear Conditioning Theories

Many theories about PTSD emphasize the way the trauma is processed according to the functioning of memory. Regarding the main symptoms, such as intrusive memories (e.g., flashbacks that seem so vivid that the person feels like the traumatic event is happening again) or impaired concentration, the idea of PTSD as a memory disorder seems plausible. One of the most considered theories when it comes to anxiety disorders is Mowrer's two-factor theory (1960). According to Mowrer, previous neutral stimuli present at the time of the traumatic event become a determining factor in the development of PTSD; this is what is also known as *classical conditioning.* For example, a soldier's camouflage uniform (conditioned stimulus) becomes fear-associated with a particular traumatic event, such as the explosion of an improvised explosive device (IED) on patrol (unconditioned stimulus). When the person is confronted with the conditioned stimulus (i.e., the camouflage uniform), it evokes the memories of the explosion and linked emotions, such as fear. By avoiding the conditioned stimuli, and everything that reminds the person of the traumatic event, PTSD symptoms decrease on a short-term basis (operant conditioning), but over the long-term it maintains the disorder (Keane, Zimering, & Caddell, 1985).

Foa, Steketee, and Rothbaum (1989) and Foa and Rothbaum (1998) emphasized that traumatic events violate the basic beliefs of safety. This emotional processing theory assumes that the activation of one memory (e.g., a sudden bang) would automatically generate the fear that was related to this event, including the physiological (sweating, heart beating), emotional (fear), and behavioral (fight, flight, freeze) response. The fear network can be easily activated by a large number of environmental cues and has a low threshold.

Therapeutic interventions based on this theory would focus on the extinction of the conditioned response, by unlinking the conditioned stimulus from the unconditioned response by exposure, while trying to maintain a calm state (e.g., by using relaxation techniques, safety imagination, and/or AAI).

Cognitive Theory of PTSD

Threat appraisal is an essential factor in developing PTSD (Ehlers & Clark, 2000). In some cases, traumatic events may leave a person feeling like a constant and continuous threat exists. Ehlers and Clark (2000) describe pathological ways of coping and responding to such traumatic events. Negative appraisals about 1) the probability with which the life-threatening events will occur (overestimation, meaning that the world is a bad and dangerous place); 2) the capability of acting (self-efficacy) vs. being helpless (being helplessly exposed to threats); and 3) the self (bad things only happen to bad people, thoughts about being guilty) are most common. Ehlers and Clark (2000) suggest that the memory of the trauma is incompletely elaborated in matters of the context of time and place.

They also distinguish between two different memory functions, data-driven processing and conceptual processing. Data-driven processing focuses on the memory of sensory information and leads to perceptual priming, whereas conceptual processing focuses on embedding the information in the appropriate context (autobiographical knowledge). Many PTSD patients report feelings of continuous threat because they overestimate the probability of the occurrence of negative events. This can lead to overly cautious and seemingly paranoid behavior; for example, only leaving the house with weapons or making their homes into highly secure fortifications. Because of impaired autobiographical memory processes (highly associative and perceptual priming), PTSD patients often remember the worst moments of the trauma, but fail to complement the traumatic influences and impressions with knowledge they currently possess (e.g., "I survived and will see my family again"). This leads to continually experiencing the threat of the traumatic event instead of labeling it as a feeling of a past event.

NEUROLOGICAL THEORIES OF PTSD

The fear network model (Elbert & Schauer, 2002) explains how a higher number of traumatic stressful events sum up and intensify fearful memories. Elbert and Schauer (2002) assume traumatic memories are arranged in networks. Sensory, perceptual, and affective information, as well as cognitions and the physiological response, are stored in a highly interconnected manner within these networks. When exposed to traumatic stress, the body reacts with an alarm response with body and mind becoming extremely aroused and/or energized, with the purpose of survival. This highly adaptive process includes fight or flight, and if neither is possible, a freeze reaction (tonic immobility). Metcalfe and Jacobs (1996) refer to the sensory, emotional, cognitive, and physiological responses in the network as "hot memories." "Cold memories," on the other hand, indicate context information (spatial and chronological) and are stored separately (as opposed to the interconnections between the hot memory elements).

Within this model, it is evident that both the perceptional processes, as well as parts of the hot memory system, occur in the same area of the brain (e.g., amygdala, insula), whereas processes related to cold memories require hippocampus activity and medial temporal lobe structures (Brewin, Dalgleish, & Joseph, 1996; Brewin, Gregory, Lipton, & Burgess, 2010). With normal or nontraumatic/nonstressful experiences, both hot and cold information are usually well combined and stored in the auto-biographical memory. With traumatic experiences, this memory process is disturbed. First, the rush of the stress hormone cortisol (released with traumatic experiences and the resultant emotional state of alarm) affects the hippocampus and therefore could explain the deficiency in declarative memory (Elzinga & Bremner, 2002). Second, according to the fear network model, this network can grow, and single elements can gradually intertwine. Every single hot memory node (e.g., emotions such as fear or guilt; physical reactions such as trepidation; perceptions such as seeing blood; smells in the environment; or cognitions) can be concurrently part of different traumatic events. Different traumatic events can lead to the same reactions and share the same hot memory elements, and the fear network can contain elements of more than one traumatic event. Thus, the more traumatic events the person experiences, the wider the fear network grows. The activation of one node within this growing network can activate the whole fear network itself and, with it, strengthen the interconnections of the network.

As mentioned above, the declarative memory processes are disturbed during traumatic events and needed autobiographical representations of the event cannot take place. The lack of an autobiographical representation of the traumatic event explains the occurrence of intrusive symptoms, such as flashbacks (i.e., the ignition of one element of the network can lead to the activation of the whole structure with a feeling of actual circumstances in the "here and now"). In contrast, having a well-integrated autobiographical memory causes the feeling—after the hot memory has been triggered—to be accepted as having occurred in the past (Kolassa & Elbert, 2007; Wilker & Kolassa, 2013).

GENETIC AND EPIGENETIC FACTORS OF PTSD

The main factor in developing PTSD involves the exposure to a traumatic event. However, current research focuses on genetic risk factors and the interaction with traumatic load (Cornelis, Nugent, Amstadter, & Koenen, 2010; Wilker & Kolassa, 2013). Since the focus of this chapter is on the advantages of AAI for trauma, only genetic and epigenetic factors having a potential influence on the development of PTSD (i.e., the genes responsible for the neurotransmitters serotonin and dopamine) will be briefly discussed.

Serotonin inhibits the amygdala, thereby affecting emotional learning and memory (Meneses & Liy-Salmeron, 2012; Ressler & Nemeroff, 2000) and, in particular, fear conditioning (Greenberg et al., 1999; Heils et al., 1996; Lonsdorf et al., 2009; Munafò, Brown, & Hariri, 2008). Additionally, dopamine has a large influence on the formation of fear memories (Guarraci, Frohardt, Falls, & Kapp, 2000) and certain special genetic types that affect enzyme activity, thus indirectly leading to higher extracellular dopamine levels (Lachman et al., 1996) and impaired learning regarding fear extinction (Lonsdorf et al., 2009). Further research has investigated genes associated with the glucocorticoid system and the cortisol-binding affinity and PTSD (see Bachmann et al., 2005; Binder, 2009; Hauer et al., 2011). While much of this research has been conducted in animal experiments, first studies in humans confirm genetic and epigenetic influences on the development of PTSD (Metha et al., 2013).

STRUCTURAL AND FUNCTIONAL BRAIN ALTERATIONS IN CONNECTION TO PTSD

For the sake of understanding, structural and functional brain alterations related to trauma and PTSD must briefly be discussed. Three brain structures—the medial prefrontal cortex, the amygdala, and hippocampus—may be particularly influenced and modified by PTSD. Because of its connection with the amygdala and the functioning of the hippocampus (which is responsible for explicit learning and memory [Rauch, Shin, & Phelps, 2006]), the medial prefrontal cortex plays an important role in influencing the stress response. Alterations in volume of the hippocampus have been found in persons with trauma (Smith, 2005; Woon, Sood, & Hedges, 2010) or PTSD (Karl et al., 2006; Kitayama, Vaccarino, Kutner, Weiss, & Bremner, 2005), which could explain impaired autobiographical memory processes. Also, an increased amygdala reaction in PTSD patients was found when exposed to aggravation stimuli (Brohawn, Offringa, Pfaff, Hughes, & Shin, 2010; Hayes, Hayes, & Mikedis, 2012). This is associated with decreased activity in the medial prefrontal cortex after exposure to aversive cues (Hayes et al., 2012).

STANDARD PSYCHOTHERAPEUTIC INTERVENTIONS FOR PTSD

Prevention of PTSD

As mentioned above, experiencing traumatic events is likely to happen during a person's lifetime and most survivors, being highly resilient, will adjust without needing psychotherapeutic intervention. However, in order to help prevent the development of PTSD, debriefings such as Critical Incident Stress Debriefing (CISD) were developed for people having experienced stressful events. CISD (Everly & Mitchell, 1999) involves a standardized, single debriefing session that can last up to 3–4 hours. Research, however, reveals no differences between debriefing receivers and non-receivers (Bisson, Brayne, Ochberg, & Everly, 2007). Recommendations (Foa, Keane, Friedman, & Cohen, 2009) against the use of debriefing interventions now exist since the self-healing processes within the natural adaption skills after trauma would be disturbed. Today, psychological first aid (PFA) (Brymer et al., 2006), which focuses on fundamental strategies to provide safety and emotional support or information, as well as access to social support systems, is the preferred preventative PTSD method.

The following evidenced interventions are regularly employed today.

Prolonged Exposure Therapy (PE)

The underlying model of PE is the emotional processing theory (EPT; Foa & Kozak, 1985, 1986). The basic idea of EPT is that emotions, especially fear, are organized in the memory as cognitive networks. These networks include different kinds of information about the feared stimuli, the fear response, and the meaning associated with that stimuli and that response. This is a natural and highly adaptive fear response, which should help people avoid danger in the future. To change the malfunctioning fear structure in PTSD patients, Foa and Kozak (1985) suggest first activating the fear network and then replacing the unrealistic (fearful) information with realistic information. Main therapeutic techniques include imaginal exposure (reprocessing the traumatic experience) and in vivo exposure using trigger stimuli that the patient usually avoids.

The activation of negative emotions happens in a safe, therapeutic surrounding, and corrective learning happens by gaining a new perspective about what happened. Also, the repeated confrontation with the feared memory leads to the realization that the trauma remains in the past.

Revisiting the traumatic event may be stressful, but the patient does not fall apart because of it.

Cognitive Processing Therapy (CPT)

CPT for PTSD is based on the assumption of an assimilation of the traumatic event into already existing core beliefs (about the self, the others, and the world) in a way that tries to make it consistent with existing personal beliefs. CPT is divided into 12 different therapy sessions across five phases. Phase one is about the differential diagnosis, phase two is about psychoeducation about PTSD, and phase three consists of the reprocessing of the traumatic event. In phase four, the previous filtered beliefs and emotions regarding the trauma are challenged and, if needed, changed. Phase five involves the patient transitioning back to a functional life.

Eye Movement Desensitization and Reprocessing (EMDR Therapy)

On the basis of the Adaptive Information Processing (AIP) model, EMDR is an integrative therapy approach. Extremely stressful experiences can overwhelm the information processing system. Usually the system tries to integrate new experiences by linking them to already existing memory networks. The system processes aversive experiences in a mitigating way by linking them with the networks containing adequate information, such as: "I have survived" or "I have successfully handled these things before." Traumatic experiences fail to be integrated into the existing memory networks and, therefore, the needed adaptive associations cannot develop. These unprocessed (stressful) memories are accompanied by emotions, physical sensations, and thoughts that occurred at the time of the stressful event. The source of dysfunctional beliefs and core values, such as: "I am helpless and worthless," are manifestations of unprocessed experiences from the past. EMDR is a standardized eight-phase treatment (Shapiro, 2001). The patient is asked to follow the therapist's hand movement from side to side with their eyes (bilateral stimulation, also possible with acoustic or sensational stimulation) while thinking about the traumatic event. During the process, associations, feelings, thoughts, and beliefs arise and are processed by the trauma survivor. Schnyder and Cloite (2015) note, "The goal is to stimulate the inherent information processing system of the brain and, with as little clinical intrusion as possible, allow it spontaneously to make the appropriate connections" (p. 210).

Narrative Exposure Therapy (NET)

Based on the fear network model (Elbert & Schauer, 2002; Metcalfe & Jacobs, 1996), it is assumed that traumatic memories are stored in a "trauma network." Emotional, sensory, physiological, and cognitive representations of the traumatic experience are identified as hot memory and are unconnected with the information about the context in the cold memory system. The confrontation with environmental or even internal cues (e.g., noises, startle responses, cognitions) gives the impulse to activate the whole fear/trauma network, which leads to intrusive symptoms. Subsequently, PTSD patients suffer from an easily ignitable hot memory system, with severe difficulties in combining the appropriate cold memory (chronological, autobiographical, contextual) information (Schauer, Neuner, & Elbert, 2011). The reconnection of hot and cold memory is the main purpose of NET, and should result from constructing a chronological narrative or lifeline (Catani et al., 2009; Crombach & Elbert, 2015; Elbert, Hermenau, Hecker, Weierstall, & Schauer, 2012; Hermenau et al., 2012; Ruf et al., 2010; Schaal, Elbert, & Neuner, 2009; Schauer et al., 2004).

Following PTSD diagnosis and psychoeducation about the symptoms and how to handle them, the patient is asked to describe his or her lifeline. A long rope on the floor symbolizes the patient's life span, and the patient places objects that symbolize major events (rocks for negative events, flowers for positive events, and sticks for events about aggression) along the rope. In the next session, the narration beginning at the very first moment of life starts. Step by step the patient constructs a chronological narration of his or her life with a clear focus on traumatic events. The therapist asks in detail about emotional responses, thoughts, and sensations, and then links the memories to episodic facts (time, place), always ensuring that the trauma survivor never disconnects from the "here and now" while talking. At the end of therapy, the patient receives the complete narration of his or her life.

HUMAN-ANIMAL INTERACTIONS (HAI)— EFFECTS RELEVANT FOR TRAUMA AND PTSD

Several effects of HAI, which could be relevant for interventions for trauma and PTSD, have been documented by controlled research—be it as effects of companion animal ownership, interaction with animals in experiments or other settings, or as a result of AAI (primarily with dogs) (Beetz, Julius,

Turner, & Kotrschal, 2012a). It should be kept in mind that since research attempts to mimic and control optimal conditions, only the largely positive effects of HAI are demonstrated. In contrast, real-life HAIs might not always be positive, and thus probably will not have the same desired effects as research HAIs.

Social Effects

The company of friendly looking animals elicits positive social attention from others (Eddy, Hart, & Boltz, 1988; Hart, Hart & Bergin, 1987), and thus, people walking dogs often know more people in their neighborhood (Wood et al., 2015). Several studies have documented that the presence of animals increases verbal and nonverbal social interaction, which has been termed the "social catalyst effect" of animals. Furthermore, people in the company of animals receive more trust from others (Gueguen & Ciccotti, 2008), which could be important for psychotherapy, particularly when establishing a good therapeutic relationship with the client (Schneider & Harley, 2006).

Psychological Effects

The presence of dogs seems to promote concentration and motivation (Gee, Church, & Altobelli, 2010; Gee, Crist, & Carr, 2010; Hediger & Turner, 2014; Wohlfarth, Mutschler, Beetz, Kreuser, & Korsten-Reck, 2013; Wohlfarth, Mutschler, Beetz, & Schleider, 2014); reduce depression (Souter & Miller, 2007) and anxiety; and help establish a sense of calmness, particularly before and during stress-eliciting situations (such as psychotherapeutic or medical treatments) (Barker, Pandurangi, & Best, 2003; Barker, Rasmussen, & Best, 2003; Lang, Jansen, Wertenauer, Gallinat, & Rapp, 2010). Less established, but nevertheless documented by some HAI research, is the reduction of pain perception, aggression, and the promotion of empathy.

Neurobiological/Physiological Effects

As documented in numerous studies, interactions with animals can buffer human stress systems. Endocrinology indices as indicators of the hypothalamic-pituitary-adrenal system (HPA-axis), as well as cardiovascular parameters of the autonomic nervous system (ANS), are positively affected during HAI. Particularly in stressful situations, physical contact with a friendly dog buffers human cortisol levels (Beetz et al., 2011; Odendaal, 2000; Viau et al., 2010) and dampens the cardiovascular system

(Friedmann, Katcher, Thomas, Lynch, & Messent, 1983; Motooka, Koike, Yokoyama, & Kennedy, 2006) by lowering blood pressure and heart rate. Furthermore, contact with dogs, in particular familiar dogs, increases the level of the hormone oxytocin and the neurotransmitter dopamine (Odendaal, 2000; Odendaal & Meintjes, 2003). Also, positive effects on the general health of companion animal owners have been observed. These owners have fewer heart and sleeping problems, better fitness, fewer doctor visits, and have a higher survival rate after myocardial infarction (Headey, 1999; Headey & Grabka, 2007; Headey, Na, & Zheng, 2008).

THEORIES EXPLAINING THE EFFECTS OF HAI

Why animals can have the effects described above, frequently measured against the contact or standard treatments involving humans only, cannot be explained by a single all-inclusive theory. However, the following mechanisms and theoretical approaches might help explain what makes HAI different, and also possibly effective, for the treatment of trauma and PTSD (for a more detailed report, see Beetz, in press; Julius, Beetz, Kotrschal, Turner, & Uvnäs-Moberg, 2013).

Biophilia

Biophilia (Wilson, 1984) describes human affinity to nature in general, including animals, which developed during evolutionary history and contributed to the survival of humans (e.g., animals indicating danger or predators representing a threat), thus improving their fitness (Serpell, 1986; Wilson, 1984). This supposed interest is supported by the fact that children, already a few months old, show more interest in animals than objects (DeLoache, Pickard, & LoBue, 2011). Furthermore, the *biophilia-effect* (Julius et al., 2013) describes the linked phenomenon that on a subconscious level, humans seem to perceive calm and resting animals (specifically those non-dangerous to humans—a resting lion or black widow spider should not have this effect) in their immediate surroundings as a signal of a safe environment, and experience feelings of security or safety themselves, which is accompanied by psychological and physiological relaxation.

This concept could be further applied in trauma-informed AAI, especially in regard to animal welfare considerations. For example, if a horse demonstrates calm and relaxed behavior during the intervention, one could reasonably assume that he or she is not experiencing stress, at least not significantly. This is encouraging and important information for the therapist or handler to have as they monitor and support the animal's well-being throughout the session. Moreover, evidence that the horse feels comfortable in the therapeutic setting (via the absence of extreme alarm, arousal, or agitation) may likely convey to the client that the environment and therapist are safe and trustworthy. Interacting and connecting with a relaxed horse during therapy may generate feelings of calm or stillness in the client as well, which could be particularly beneficial for those coping with the aftermath of traumatic events. In other words, ensuring animal welfare during AAI (which is often a complex and subjective process prone to human error) is not only essential for supporting the participating animal, but also the integrity of the intervention.

Experiential vs. Verbal Symbolic System

An advantage of animals is their nonverbal way of communication and interaction. In processing information and related forms of motivating arousal, the experiential system and verbal-symbolic system (Schultheiss, 2001) can be distinguished (implicit-experiential functioning and explicit-cognitive functioning, respectively [Epstein, 1994]). The experiential system directly processes sensory input from the real world, like sounds, pictures, and smells. This input is usually closely linked to emotions and employs implicit memory or representations. In contrast, the verbal-symbolic system uses words and symbols to process information (Schultheiss, 2001) and is associated with analytic-rational thinking and declarative memory (Epstein, 1994). Professional settings, such as psychotherapy, mainly employ verbal communication about consciously represented experiences. However, when dealing with emotions, such as in the treatment of traumatization and PTSD, HAI, which emotionalizes while providing a focus of attention and a feeling of security (see biophilia above), may set an ideal stage for successful intervention. HAI promotes an advantageous balance between the verbal communication with the therapist, while addressing implicit-experiential processes and motivating clients.

Motivation

Similar to the information processing theories, in motivation theory intrinsic and extrinsic motivation (McClelland, 1985), or implicit and explicit motive systems (Schultheiss, Strasser, Rösch, Kordik, & Graham, 2012), are usually distinguished. While explicit motivation energizes behaviors depending on rewards or avoidance of punishment, implicit motivation promotes enjoying executing a task for itself and acting for one's own satisfaction. Implicit motives are triggered by natural incentives [(i.e., mostly nonverbal stimuli [Stanton, Hall, & Schultheiss, 2010]) on an unconscious level, and are closely connected with affect and behavior (McClelland, Koestner, & Weinberger, 1989). Accordingly, goals are pursued in an affectively charged, "hot" mode (Schultheiss, Jones, Davis, & Kley, 2008), while goals linked to explicit motivation are followed in a "cold" or neutral mode. Animals seem to mainly activate implicit motives (Wohlfarth et al., 2013), and thus promote intrinsic motivation, which is mainly aroused via the experiential system. All the sensory input that animals provide makes it more likely to activate intrinsic motivation via the experiential system. With traumatized patients, especially those with chronic PTSD, low motivation to participate in therapy might pose a problem. Via AAI, however, intrinsic motivation to participate in the intervention might be more easily achieved, and thus could be utilized to work specifically on the trauma, in particular the integration of the more accessible emotions and cognitions.

Activation of the Oxytocin System

A neurobiological mechanism, which might be key in explaining many of the positive physiological, but also psychological, effects of animals on humans, is the activation of the oxytocin system, mainly via touch (Beetz, Uvnäs-Moberg, Julius, & Kotrschal, 2012b; Julius et al., 2013). Comprehensive research in animals and humans has documented that the activation of the oxytocin system, meaning the release of the hormone oxytocin, includes many of the same effects of HAI, such as the promotion of communication, social interaction, trust, calmness, and a good mood, as well as a reduction of anxiety, stress-related parameters, and pain perception. Oxytocin, a neurotransmitter and hormone, is released via stimulations like breastfeeding, massage, stroking, or in general, pleasant physical contact and touch (Beetz et al., 2012b; Carter & Porges, 2016; Insel, 2010; Uvnäs-Moberg, 2003). In several studies, oxytocin levels rose after a person petted a friendly dog, and the effect further increased when petting the person's own dog (Handlin et al., 2011; Odendaal, 2000; Odendaal & Meintjes, 2003).

This mechanism also explains why animal-assisted settings can promote the above-mentioned effects and set a good stage for successful trauma-therapy, perhaps better than in a human-only setting. Patients in AAI should develop more trust toward their therapist early in therapy, be in a better mood, be more motivated, be ready to communicate, and be more relaxed. This is particularly important for patients with PTSD who mistrust others and are anxious and stressed in many social situations. While touch has no place in usual psychotherapy (and therefore the oxytocin system cannot be activated this way in these situations), touch is an immanent part of interacting with animals (Jegatheesan et al., 2015). In addition to the traumatization, some patients may also have an insecure or disorganized attachment, which is associated with an impaired ability to profit from social support and oxytocin-activation via touch from other humans (Julius et al., 2013).

Social Support and Caregiving

Touch can also be a form of social support, most often found in combination with emotional support (Ditzen et al., 2007). This combined form of social support is the most effective in buffering stress responses (Demakis & McAdams, 1994; Ditzen et al., 2007). Even though therapists provide different forms of social support, the aspect of touch is omitted and with it a very effective way of reducing stress, which often prevails in trauma-therapy where patients are asked to confront their trauma.

A further advantage of animal-assisted therapy (AAT) is the chance to provide caregiving to another living being. Caregiving behavior (George & Solomon, 2008; Solomon & George, 1999), which stems from the behavioral system developed to care for offspring (including holding, touching, and feeding), is accompanied by oxytocin release (Uvnäs-Moberg, 2003) and the positive effects thereof. However, in a therapeutic context, it would be inappropriate for a patient to show caregiving behavior toward his or her therapist, in particular any involving physical contact. Animals, in contrast, are typically willing recipients of caregiving (feeding, brushing, stroking). Thus, in their role as a provider of social support via their presence and as recipients of care by the patient, animals can effectively activate the oxytocin system. Importantly, providing care and affection for an animal shares many of the same positive effects as receiving social support (Dunbar, 2010; Julius et al., 2013).

Distraction and Mindfulness

Probably based on biophilia, as well as the fact that animals in our surroundings catch our attention, distraction might also be a mechanism to explain some positive effects of HAI. Distraction effects might be most prominent in the reduction of pain, anxiety, and negative mood (Beetz & Bales, 2016). Distraction effects have been found with music (Kleiber & Adamek, 2012), cartoons (Lee et al., 2012), clowns (Vagnoli, Caprilli, & Messeri, 2010), and engaging in video games (Nilsson, Enskar, Hallqvist, & Kokinsky, 2012; Patel et al., 2006). Additionally, the level of engagement with such distracting objects or experiences likely correlates with the buffering of stress and negative emotions. Animals could be highly engaging, and thus provide an optimal distraction for patients from such symptoms as hopelessness or despair.

At the same time, interacting with animals provides effortless training in mindfulness. Recently, mindfulness-based therapeutic approaches have become quite popular. When interacting with animals, humans need to concentrate on what happens in the present and AAI, in comparison to other mindfulness trainings, provides a relatively easy way to achieve this. Patients with PTSD, who suffer from intrusions of traumatic content and flashbacks, can certainly profit from mindfulness-based approaches. Their problems with concentration (due to sleeping issues, anxiety, and being in a group setting), however, make more traditional mindfulness trainings difficult. In contrast, simply interacting with animals, even if just going for a walk, grooming, or playing with an animal, is a very different but effective form of mindfulness training.

ANIMALS PROMOTE OPTIMAL PRECONDITIONS FOR THERAPY

Optimal learning experiences, in education and likely in therapy, need settings that promote attention, concentration, positive mood, motivation, and a relaxed and calm state. Animals can help to establish such a positive setting. In addition, even though they cannot take the role of the therapist, suitable animals in AAI can provide some aspects needed for successful therapy, described as core conditions of client-centered psychotherapy by C. Rogers (1951).

For example, animals usually present certain traits such as congruence, or genuineness, which allow clients to experience the therapist as they really are. Additionally, animals typically provide unconditional (or perceived unconditional) positive regard—they do not care about human norms and simply react to how the client acts toward or around them. In AAI, friendly animals interested in contact with humans and tolerant to some unusual behaviors are employed. Animals can also provide empathy since they often accurately perceive human emotions and states of clients (Albuquerque et al., 2016; Reid, 2009). PTSD patients, like most humans, might not show their weaknesses, fears, or tension openly. Animals, in contrast, usually pick up on a patient's current state and act empathically, yet accordingly (e.g., by also showing consoling behavior or apprehension toward subtle aggression, or by getting anxious with anxious patients).

Furthermore, since a prominent symptom of trauma is a lack of trust toward others, the effects of promoting trust toward the therapist using a friendly animal is particularly important for patients having experienced a trauma. Animals, therefore, could support the formation of a trusting therapeutic alliance (Tedeschi, Sisa, Olmert, Parish-Plass, & Yount, 2015), yet another key variable for successful therapy (Barber, Connolly, Crits-Christoph, Gladis, & Siqueland, 2000; Shirk, Karver, & Brown, 2011).

Given that PTSD patients are generally hypervigilant with alerted stress systems, which causes impairment of the information integration from the fear network and autobiographical memory, therapy remains a highly supported option. As mentioned above among the effects of HAI, some, even if rather scarce, evidence exists that animal interaction can increase serotonin levels in humans. If higher serotonin levels could be promoted within an AAI, this would be very useful for patients with trauma/PTSD, since the regulation of serotonin may be changed in these individuals. However, increased serotonin also inhibits the activity of the amygdala, which promotes an optimal physiological activation allowing for better integration of emotions and facts (of "hot" and "cold" memories, see above).

As mentioned above, integrating animals can support very different forms of trauma therapy, since it mainly affects the therapeutic setting. In particular, when working with memories and emotions, AAI can be useful since animals emotionalize patients and help to regulate the activation of the patient, calming them down or motivating them as needed. This optimal activation, in turn, is the precondition for optimal executive functions (Diamond & Lee, 2011; Miyake et al., 2000) including working memory and self-reflection, which are only optimal in the absence of stress indicators (e.g., high cortisol levels, high sympathetic activity).

EXAMPLES OF AAI FOR TRAUMA

Prevention: Psychological First Aid (PFA) With Dogs

When humans, in particular large groups, experience a traumatic event or critical incident, PFA attempts to prevent the development of a post-traumatic adjustment or stress disorder (Kaul & Welzant, 2005; Watson, Brymer, & Bonanno, 2011). Animals can be integrated in this prevention. In one example, the introduction of a specially trained dog after the homicide of a university student lifted the mood of the students attending the crisis intervention and provided comfort to the students. Another example of trained dogs providing support and calm in the context of crisis intervention is described for children who have lost someone and are grieving (both examples cited in Eaton-Stull, 2015). Also, in Manhattan after 9/11, dogs worked at Ground Zero with disaster relief to provide the people who worked and volunteered there with social support, as well as a chance to find distraction and connection to life during their breaks.

Interventions for Trauma and PTSD

While there may be many practice projects working with AAI for persons with trauma and/or PTSD, only a few studies have investigated their effectiveness. One field in which AAI is popular is the therapeutic work with those who have experienced abuse. Mainly equine-assisted interventions (Kemp, Signal, Botros, Taylor, & Prentice, 2013) or interventions with dogs (Dietz, Davis, & Pennings, 2012; Hamama et al., 2011) can be found, with only a few involving other species. Group sessions, as well as individual treatment conducted by psychotherapists and/or social workers, have been investigated. Effects (see O'Haire, Guerin, & Kirkham, 2015) include a reduction of depressive symptoms and PTSD symptoms (to include anxiety and dissociation) and the promotion of attachment security.

Another important field of AAI for PTSD is the work with war veterans. Here, both AAI with dogs and horses can be found (e.g., Döhrer, Schöfmann, & Beetz, 2014; Ernst, Schöfmann, & Beetz, 2016), with research documenting a decrease in PTSD symptoms and depression, as well as an increase in happiness, resilience, sleep, satisfaction, and social support (Nevins, Finch, Hickling, & Barnett, 2013).

While the work with survivors of abuse or military veterans usually consists of therapy, another form of AAI for traumatized persons is the support of traumatized witnesses via dogs during interrogation in court, by the police, or during clinical interviews. The calming and fear-reducing effect of dogs not only helps the person psychologically, but given that memory retrieval is optimal in the absence of stress, these effects also promote a more detailed and accurate account of events, which is important for the precision of legal proceedings.

PTSD Service Dogs

An additional form of animal support involves service dogs that permanently live with the person with trauma-related problems or PTSD. Such a long-term relationship provides the possibility of establishing a secure attachment. Companion animals indeed can develop into attachment figures for humans of all ages who seek social support from them when under stress (McConnell, Brown, Shoda, Stayton & Martin, 2011; McNicholas & Collis, 2006; Rost & Hartmann, 1994). PTSD service dogs are mostly found among military veterans and seem to improve their mental health, likely via the above-described effects and underlying mechanisms of HAIs. Additionally, service dogs (or assistance dogs) also support veterans with physical impairments due to injuries (amputations, blindness, etc.). Anecdotal reports of one program, which also includes the veterans in the training of service dogs, include improvements in patience, impulse control, emotion regulation, sleep, depression, sense of purpose, and further symptoms and problems related to PTSD (Yount, Olmert, & Lee, 2012).

CONCLUSIONS

Overall, theoretical considerations based on existing knowledge about trauma, PTSD, and the effects of HAI, as well as first experiences with animals in the treatment and prevention of PTSD, support the justification of AAI for trauma. More controlled and peer-reviewed studies to test these assumed effects, however, are needed. O'Haire, Guerin, and Kirkham (2015) reviewed the existing research (published in English) and found that, indeed, AAI (with dogs and horses specifically) for trauma and PTSD due to abuse and war trauma do have significant effects on PTSD symptoms and related problems. Since, at the moment, there are only few studies, AAI should be recommended as a complementary therapy and not the primary treatment for trauma and PTSD (see Ernst et al., 2016). Patients with trauma and PTSD need to undergo specific trauma therapy in order to integrate the emotional and physiological responses with the explicit memories of the relevant event(s).

ACKNOWLEDGMENT

We would like to thank Christiana Crawford for her input on a first draft of this chapter.

REFERENCES

Albuquerque, N., Guo, K., Wilkinson, A., Savalli, C., Otta, E., & Mills, D. (2016). Dogs recognize dog and human emotions. *Biology Letters*, *12*(1), 1–5.

Bachmann, A. W., Sedgley, T. L., Jackson, R. V., Gibson, J. N., Young, R. M., & Torpy, D. J. (2005). Glucocorticoid receptor polymorphisms and post-traumatic stress disorder. *Psychoneuroendocrinology*, *30*(3), 297–306.

Barber, J. P., Conolly, M. B., Crits-Christoph, P., Gladis, L., & Siqueland, L. (2000). Alliance predicts patients' outcome beyond in-treatment change in symptoms. *Journal of Consulting and Clinical Psychology*, *68*(6), 1027–1032.

Barker, S. B., Pandurangi, A. K., & Best, A. M. (2003). Effects of animal-assisted therapy on patients' anxiety, fear, and depression before ECT. *The Journal of ECT*, *19*(1), 38–44.

Barker, S. B., Rasmussen, K. G., & Best, A. M. (2003). Effect of aquariums on electroconvulsive therapy patients. *Anthrozoös*, *16*(3), 229–240.

Beetz, A. (in press). Theories and possible mechanisms of action in animal assisted interventions. *Applied Developmental Science*.

Beetz, A., & Bales, K. (2016). Affiliation and attachment in human-animal relationships. In L. Freund, S. McCune, P. McCardle, L. Esposito, & N. Gee (Eds.), *The Social Neuroscience of Human-Animal Interaction* (pp. 107–126). Washington, DC: American Psychological Association.

Beetz, A., Julius, H., Turner, D., & Kotrschal, K. (2012a). Effects of social support by a dog on stress modulation in male children with insecure attachment. *Frontiers in Psychology (Educational Psychology)*, *3*(352). https://doi.org/10.3389/fpsyg.2012.00352

Beetz, A., Kotrschal, K., Hediger, K., Turner, D., Uvnäs-Moberg, K., & Julius, H. (2011). The effect of a real dog, toy dog and friendly person on insecurely attached children during a stressful task: An exploratory study. *Anthrozoös*, *24*(4), 349–368.

Beetz, A., Uvnäs-Moberg, K., Julius, H. & Kotrschal, K. (2012b). Psychosocial and psychophysiological effects of human-animal interactions: The possible role of oxytocin. *Frontiers in Psychology/Psychology for Clinical Settings, 3*(234). https://doi.org/10.3389/fpsyg.2012.00234

Binder, E. B. (2009). The role of FKBP5, a co-chaperone of the glucocorticoid receptor in the pathogenesis and therapy of affective and anxiety disorder. *Psychoneuroendocrinology, 34*(Supplement 1), S186–S195.

Bisson, J. I., Brayne, M., Ochberg, F. M., & Everly, G. S. (2007). Early psychosocial intervention following traumatic events. *American Journal of Psychiatry, 164*(7), 1016–1019.

Brewin, C. R., Dalgleish, T., & Joseph, S. (1996). A dual representation theory of posttraumatic stress disorder. *Psychological Review, 103*(4), 670–686.

Brewin, C. R., Gregory, J. D., Lipton, M., & Burgess, N. (2010). Intrusive images in psychological disorders: Characteristics, neural mechanisms, and treatment implications. *Psychological Review, 117*(1), 210–232.

Brohawn, K. H., Offringa, R., Pfaff, D. L., Hughes, K. C., & Shin, L. M. (2010). The neural correlates of emotional memory in posttraumatic stress disorder. *Biological Psychiatry, 68*(11), 1023–1030.

Brymer, M., Layne, C., Pynoos, R., Ruzek, J. I., Steinberg, A., Vernberg, E., & Watson, P. J. (2006). *Psychological first aid: Field operations guide.* Washington, DC: US Department of Health and Human Services.

Carter, C. S., & Porges, S. W. (2016). Neural mechanisms underlying human-animal interaction: An evolutionary perspective. In L. S. Freund, S. McCune, L. Esposito, N. R. Gee, & P. McCardle (Eds.), *Social Neuroscience and Human-Animal Interaction* (pp. 89–106). Washington, DC: American Psychological Association.

Catani, C., Kohiladevy, M., Ruf, M., Schauer, E., Elbert, T., & Neuner, F. (2009). Treating children traumatized by war and tsunami: A comparison between exposure therapy and meditation-relaxation in north-east Sri Lanka. *BMC Psychiatry, 9*, 22. https://doi.org/10.1186/1471-244X-9-22

Cornelis, M. C., Nugent, N. R., Amstadter, A. B., & Koenen, K. C. (2010). Genetics of post-traumatic stress disorder: Review and recommendations for genome-wide association studies. *Current Psychiatry Reports, 12*(4), 313–326.

Crombach, A., & Elbert, T. (2015). Controlling offensive behavior using Narrative Exposure Therapy: A randomized controlled trial of former street children. *Clinical Psychological Science, 3*(2), 270–282.

DeLoache, J. S., Pickard, M. B., & LoBue, V. (2011). How very young children think about animals. In P. McCardle, S. McCune, J.A. Griffin, & V. Maholmes, V. (Eds.), *How animals affect us: Examining the influence of human-animal interaction on child development and human health* (pp. 85–99). Washington, DC: American Psychological Association.

Demakis, G. J., & McAdams, D. P. (1994). Personality, social support and well-being among first year college students. *College Student Journal, 28*(2), 235–243.

Diamond, A., & Lee, K. (2011). Interventions shown to aid executive function development in children 4 to 12 years old. *Science, 333,* 959–964.

Dietz, T. J., Davis, D., & Pennings, J. (2012). Evaluating animal-assisted therapy in group treatment for child sexual abuse. *Journal of Child Sexual Abuse: Research, Treatment, and Program Intervention for Victims, Survivors, and Offenders, 21*(6), 665–683.

DiGangi, J., Guffanti, G., McLaughlin, K. A., & Koenen, K. C. (2013) Considering trauma exposure in the context of genetics studies of posttraumatic stress disorder: A systematic review. *Biology of Mood & Anxiety Disorders, 3*(1), 2.

Ditzen, B., Neumann, I. D., Bodenmann, G., von Dawans, B., Turner, R. A., Ehlert, U., & Heinrichs, M. (2007). Effects of different kinds of couple interaction on cortisol and heart rate responses to stress in women. *Psychoneuroendocrinology, 32,* 565–574.

Döhrer, S., Schöfmann, I., & Beetz, A. (2014). H.I.T.—Hundegestützte Intervention in der Therapie PTBS-erkrankter Soldaten—Neue Wege, neue Möglichkeiten? *Wehrmedizin & Wehrpharmazie, 3,* 46–48.

Dunbar, R. I. (2010). The social role of touch in humans and primates: Behavioural function and neurobiological mechanisms. *Neuroscience and Biobehavioural Reviews, 34,* 260–268.

Eaton-Stull, Y. (2015). Crisis intervention with individual and groups—frameworks to guide social workers. In K. Corcoran & A. R. Roberts (Eds.), *Social Worker's Desk Reference* (3rd ed., pp. 217–222). Oxford, UK: Oxford University Press.

Eddy, J., Hart, L., & Boltz, R. P. (1988). The effects of service dogs on social acknowledgements of people in wheelchairs. *Journal of Psychology: Interdisciplinary and Applied, 122*(1), 39–45.

Ehlers, A., & Clark, D. M. (2000). A cognitive model of posttraumatic stress disorder. *Behaviour Research and Therapy, 38,* 319–345.

Elbert, T., Hermenau, K., Hecker, T., Weierstall, R., & Schauer, M. (2012). FORNET: Behandlung von traumatisierten und nicht-traumaisierten Gewalttätern mittels Narrativer Expositionstherapie. In J. Endrass, A. Rossegger & B. Borchard (Eds.), *Interventionen bei Gewalt-und Sexualstraftätern. Risk-Management, Methoden und Konzepte der forensischen Therapie* (S. 255–276). Berlin, Germany: MWV Medizinisch-Wissenschaftliche Verlagsgesellschaft.

Elbert, T., & Schauer, M. (2002). Burnt into memory—Psychological trauma. *Nature, 419,* 883.

Elzinga, B. M., & Bremner, J. D. (2002). Are the neural substrates of memory the final common pathway in posttraumatic stress disorder (PTSD)? *Journal of Affective Disorders, 70*(1), 1–17.

Epstein, S. (1994). Integration of the cognitive and the psychodynamic unconscious. *American Psychologist, 49,* 709–724.

Ernst, C., Schöfmann, I., & Beetz, A. (2016). Hundegestützte Intervention in der Therapie PTBS-erkrankter Soldaten—eine Pilotstudie: Wirkt der Helfer auf vier Pfoten? *Wehrmedizin & Wehrpharmazie, 1,* 48–51. Retrieved from http:// www.wehrmed.de/article/2846-hundegestuetzte-intervention-in-der-therapie -ptbs-erkrankter-soldaten.html

Everly, G. S., & Mitchell, J. (1999). *Critical incident stress management. CISM. A new era and standard of care in crisis intervention* (2nd ed.). Ellicott City, MD: Chevron Publishing Company.

Foa, E. B., Keane, T. M., Friedman, M. J., & Cohen, J. A. (Eds.). (2009). *Effective treatments for PTSD: Practice guidelines from the International Society of Traumatic Stress Studies* (2nd ed.). New York, NY: Guilford.

Foa, E. B., & Kozak, M. J. (1985). Treatment of anxiety disorders: Implications for psychopathology. In A. H. Tuma & J. D. Maser (Eds.), *Anxiety and the anxiety disorders.* (pp. 421–452). Hillsdale: Erlbaum.

Foa, E. B., & Kozak, M. J. (1986). Emotional processing of fear—Exposure to corrective information. *Psychological Bulletin, 99,* 20–35.

Foa, E. B., & Rothbaum, B. O. (1998). *Treating the trauma of rape.* New York, NY: Guilford Press.

Foa, E. B., Steketee, G., & Rothbaum, B. O. (1989). Behavioral/cognitive conceptualization of post-traumatic stress disorder. *Behavior Therapy, 20,* 155–176.

Friedmann, E., Katcher, A. H., Thomas, S. A., Lynch, J. J., & Messent, P. R. (1983). Social interaction and blood pressure: Influence of animal companions. *Journal of Nervous and Mental Disease, 171*(8), 461–464.

Fullerton, C. S., Ursano, R. J., & Wang, L. (2004). Acute stress disorder, posttraumatic stress disorder, and depression in disaster or rescue workers. *American Journal of Psychiatry, 161*(8), 1370–1376.

Gee, N. R., Church, M. T., & Altobelli, C. L. (2010). Preschoolers make fewer errors on an object categorization task in the presence of a dog. *Anthrozoös, 23*(3), 223–230.

Gee, N. R., Crist, E. N., & Carr, D. N. (2010). Preschool children require fewer instructional prompts to perform a memory task in the presence of a dog. *Anthrozoös, 23*(2), 173–184.

George, C., & Solomon, J. (2008). The caregiving system: A behavioral systems approach to parenting. In J. Cassidy & P. Shaver (Eds.), *Handbook of attachment: Theory, research and clinical applications* (pp. 833–856). New York, NY: Guilford.

Greenberg, B. D., Tolliver, T. J., Huang, S. J., Li, Q., Bengel, D., & Murphy, D. L. (1999).Genetic variation in the serotonin transporter promoter region affects serotonin uptake in human blood platelets. *American Journal of Medical Genetics, 88*(1), 83–87.

Guarraci, F. A., Frohardt, R. J., Falls, W. A., & Kapp, B. S. (2000). The effects of intra-amygdaloid infusions of a D2 dopamine receptor antagonist on Pavlovian fear conditioning. *Behavioral Neuroscience, 114*(3), 647–651.

Gueguen, N., & Ciccotti, S. (2008). Domestic dogs as facilitators in social interaction: An evaluation of helping and courtship behaviors. *Anthrozoös, 21*(4), 339–349.

Hamama, L., Hamama-Raz, Y., Dagan, K., Greenfeld, H., Rubinstein, C., & Ben-Ezra, M. (2011). A preliminary study of group intervention along with basic canine training among traumatized teenagers: A 3-month longitudinal study. *Children and Youth Services Review, 33*, 1975–1980.

Handlin, L., Hydbring Sandberg, E., Nilsson, A., Ejdeback, M., Jansson, A., & Uvnäs-Moberg, K. (2011). Short-term interaction between dogs and their owners: Effects on oxytocin, cortisol, insulin and heart rate—an exploratory study. *Anthrozoös, 24*(3), 301–315.

Hart, L. A., Hart, B., & Bergin, B. (1987). Socializing effects of service dogs for people with disabilities. *Anthrozoös, 1*(1), 41–44.

Hauer, D., Weis, F., Papassotiropoulos, A., Schmoeckel, M., Beiras-Fernandez, A., Lieke, J., Kaufmann, I., Kirchhoff, F., Vogeser, M., Roozendaal, B., Briegel, J., de Quervain, D., & Schelling, G. (2011). Relationship of a common polymorphism of the glucocorticoid receptor gene to traumatic memories and posttraumatic stress disorder in patients after intensive care therapy. *Critical Care Medicine, 39*(4), 643–650.

Hayes, J. P., Hayes, S. M., & Mikedis, A. M. (2012). Quantitative meta-analysis of neural activity in posttraumatic stress disorder. *Biology of Mood & Anxiety Disorders, 2*(1), 9.

Headey, B. (1999). Health benefits and health cost savings due to pets: Preliminary estimates from an Australian national survey. *Social Indicators Research, 47*, 233–243.

Headey, B., & Grabka, M. M. (2007). Pets and human health in Germany and Australia: National Longitudinal Results. *Social Indicators Research, 80*(2), 297–311.

Headey, B., Na, F., & Zheng, R. (2008). Pet dogs benefit owners' health: A "natural experiment" in China. *Social Indicators Research, 84*, 481–493.

Hediger, K., & Turner, D. (2014). Can dogs increase children's attention and concentration performance? A randomized controlled trial. *Human-Animal Interaction Bulletin, 2*(2), 21–39.

Heils, A., Teufel, A., Petri, S., Stöber, G., Riederer, P., Bengel, D., & Lesch, K. P. (1996). Allelic variation of human serotonin transporter gene expression. *Journal of Neurochemistry, 66*(6), 2621–2624.

Hermenau, K., Hecker, T., Ruf, M., Schauer, E., Elbert, T., & Schauer, M. (2012). Childhood adversity, mental ill-health and aggressive behavior in an African orphanage: Changes in response to trauma-focused therapy and the implementation of a new instructional system. *Child and Adolescent Psychiatry and Mental Health, 5*, 29.

Insel, T. R. (2010). The challenge of translation in social neuroscience: A review of oxytocin, vasopressin, and affiliative behavior. *Neuron, 65*(6), 768–779.

Jegatheesan, B., Beetz, A., Ormerod, E., Johnson, R., Fine, A. H., Yamazaki, K., Dudzik, C., Garcia, R. M., Winkle, M., & Choi, G. (2015). The IAHAIO definitions for animal assisted intervention and guidelines for wellness of animals involved. In A. H. Fine (Ed.), *Handbook on animal-assisted therapy: Foundations and guidelines for practice* (4th ed., pp. 415–418). New York, NY: Academic Press.

Julius, H., Beetz, A., Kotrschal, K., Turner, D., & Uvnäs-Moberg, K. (2013). *Attachment to Pets—An integrative view of human-animal relationships with implications for therapeutic practice.* New York, NY: Hogrefe.

Karl, A., Schaefer, M., Malta, L. S., Dörfel, D., Rohleder, N., & Werner, A. (2006). A meta-analysis of structural brain abnormalities in PTSD. *Neuroscience and Biobehavioral Reviews, 30*(7), 1004–1031.

Kaul, R. E., & Welzant, V. (2005). Disaster mental health: A discussion of best practices as applied after the Pentagon attack. In A. R. Roberts (Ed.), *Crisis intervention handbook: Assessment, treatment, and research* (pp. 200–220). New York, NY: Oxford University Press.

Keane, T. M., Zimering, R. T., & Caddell, R. T. (1985). A behavioral formulation of PTSD In Vietnam veterans. *Behavior Therapist, 8*, 9–12.

Kemp, K., Signal, T., Botros, H., Taylor, N., & Prentice, K. (2013). Equine facilitated therapy with children and adolescents who have been sexually abused: A program evaluation study. *Journal of Child and Family Studies, 23*, 558–566.

Kessler, R. C., Berglund, P., Demler, O., Jin, R., Merikangas, K. R., & Walters, E. E. (2005). Lifetime prevalence and age-of-onset distributions of DSM-IV disorders in the National Comorbidity Survey Replication. *Archives of General Psychiatry, 62*(6), 593–602.

Kessler, R. C., Sonnega, A., Bromet, E., Hughes, M., & Nelson, C. B. (1995). Posttraumatic stress disorder in the National Comorbidity Survey. *Archives of General Psychiatry, 52*(12), 1048–1060.

Kitayama, N., Vaccarino, V., Kutner, M., Weiss, P., & Bremner, J. D. (2005). Magnetic resonance imaging (MRI) measurement of hippocampal volume in posttraumatic stress disorder: A meta-analysis. *Journal of Affective Disorders, 88*(1), 79–86.

Kleiber, C., & Adamek, M. S. (2012). Adolescents' perceptions of music therapy following spinal fusion surgery. *Journal of Clinical Nursing, 22*(3/4), 414–22.

Kolassa, I. T., & Elbert, T. (2007). Structural and functional neuroplasticity in relation to traumatic stress. *Current Directions in Psychological Science, 16*(6), 321–325.

Lachman, H. M., Papolos, D. F., Saito, T., Yu, Y. M., Szumlanski, C. L., & Weinshilboum, R. M. (1996). Human catechol-O-methyltransferase pharmacogenetics: Description of a functional poly-morphism and its potential application to neuropsychiatric disorders. *Pharmacogenetics, 6*(3), 243–250.

Lang, U. E., Jansen, J. B., Wertenauer, F., Gallinat, J. & Rapp, M. A. (2010). Reduced anxiety during dog assisted interviews in acute schizophrenic patients. *European Journal of Integrative Medicine, 2*(3), 123–127.

Lee, J., Lee, J., Lim, H., Son, J.-S., Lee, J.-R., Kim, D.-C., & Ko, S. (2012). Cartoon distraction alleviates anxiety in children during induction of anesthesia. *Anesthesia and Analgesia, 115*, 1168–1173.

Lonsdorf, T. B., Weike, A. I., Nikamo, P., Schalling, M., Hamm, A. O., & Ohman, A. (2009). Genetic gating of human fear learning and extinction: Possible implications for gene-environment interaction in anxiety disorder. *Psychological Science, 20*(2), 198–206.

McClelland, D. C. (1985). How motives, skills, and values determine what people do. *American Psychologist, 40*, 812–825. https://doi.org/10.1037/0003-066X.40.7.812

McClelland, D. C., Koestner, R., & Weinberger, J. (1989). How do self-attributed and implicit motives differ? *Psychological Review, 96*, 690–702.

McConnell, A. R., Brown, C. M., Shoda, T. M., Stayton, L. E., & Martin, C. E. (2011). Friends with benefits: On the positive consequences of pet ownership. *Journal of Personality and Social Psychology, 101*(6), 1239–1252.

McNicholas, J., & Collis, G. M. (2006). Animals as social supports: Insights for understanding animal-assisted therapy. In A. H. Fine (Ed.), *Handbook on animal-assisted therapy: Theoretical foundations and guidelines for practice* (2nd ed., pp. 49–71). San Diego, CA: Academic Press.

Meneses, A., & Lily-Salmeron, G. (2012). Serotonin and emotion, learning and memory. *Reviews in the Neurosciences, 23*(5–6), 543–553.

Metcalfe, J., & Jacobs, W. (1996). A "hot-system/cool-system" view of memory under stress. *PTSD Research Quarterly, 1996*(7), 1–3.

Metha, D., Klengel, T., Conneely, K. N., Smith, A. K., Altmann, A., Pace, T. W., . . . Binder, E. B. (2013). Childhood maltreatment is associated with distinct genomic and epigenetic profiles in posttraumatic stress disorder. *PNAS 110*(20), 8302–8307. https://doi.org/10.1073/pnas.121775110

Miyake, A., Friedman, N. P., Emerson, M. J., Witzki, A. H., Howerter, A., & Wager, T. D. (2000). The unity and diversity of executive functions and their contributions to complex frontal lobe tasks: A latent variable analysis. *Cognitive Psychololgy, 41*(1), 49–100.

Motooka, M., Koike, H., Yokoyama, T., & Kennedy N. L. (2006). Effect of dog-walking on autonomic nervous activity in senior citizens. *Medical Journal of Australia, 184*(2), 60–63.

Mowrer, O. H. (1960). *Learning theory and behavior.* New York, NY: Wiley.

Munafò, M. R., Brown, S. M., & Hariri, A. R. (2008). Serotonin transporter (5-HTTLPR) genotype and amygdala activation: A meta-analysis. *Biological Psychiatry, 63*(9), 852–857.

Neuner, F., Schauer, M., Karunakara, U., Klaschik, C., Robert, C., & Elbert T. (2004). Psychological trauma and evidence for enhanced vulnerability for posttraumatic stress disorder through previous trauma among West Nile refugees. *BMC Psychiatry, 4*(1), 34.

Nevins, R., Finch, S., Hickling, E. J., & Barnett, S. D. (2013). The Saratoga War-Horse project: A case study of the treatment of psychological distress in a veteran of Operation Iraqi Freedom. *Advances in Mind/Body Medicine, 27*(4), 22–25.

Nilsson, S., Enskar, K., Hallqvist, C., & Kokinsky, E. (2012). Active and passive distraction in children undergoing wound dressing. *Journal of Pediatric Nursing, 28*(2), 156–166.

Odendaal, J. S. (2000). Animal-assisted therapy—magic or medicine? *Journal of Psychosomatic Research, 49*(4), 275–280.

Odendaal, J. S., & Meintjes, R. A. (2003). Neurophysiological correlates of affiliative behavior between humans and dogs. *Veterinary Journal, 165*, 296–301.

O'Haire, M. E., Guerin, N. A., & Kirkham, A. C. (2015). Animal-assisted intervention for trauma: A systematic literature review. *Frontiers in Psychology (for Clinical Settings), 6.* https://doi.org/10.3389/fpsyg.2015.01121

Patel, A., Scheible, T., Davidson, M., Tran, M. C., Schoenberg, C., Delphin, E., & Bennett, H. (2006). Distraction with a hand-held video game reduces pediatric preoperative anxiety. *Paediatric Anaesthesia, 16*, 1019–1027.

Rauch, S. L., Shin, L. M., & Phelps, E. A. (2006). Neurocircuitry models of post-traumatic stress disorder and extinction: Human neuroimaging research—past, present, and future. *Biological Psychiatry, 60*(4), 376–382.

Reid, P. J. (2009). Adapting to the human world: Dogs' responsiveness to our social cues. *Behavioural Processes, 80*(3), 325–333.

Ressler, K. J., & Nemeroff, C. B. (2000). Role of serotonergic and noradrenergic systems in the pathophysiology of depression and anxiety disorders. *Depression and Anxiety, 12*(Supplement 1), 2–19.

Rogers, C. (1951). *Client-centered therapy: Its current practice, implications and theory.* London, UK: Constable.

Rost, D. H., & Hartmann, A. H. (1994). Children and their pets. *Anthrozoös, 7*(4), 242–254.

Ruf, M., Schauer, M., Neuner, F., Catani, C., Schauer, E., & Elbert, T. (2010). Narrative exposure therapy for 7 to 16-year-olds: A randomized controlled trial with traumatized refugee children. *Journal of Traumatic Stress, 23*(4), 437–445.

Schaal, S., Elbert, T., & Neuner, F. (2009). Narrative exposure therapy versus interpersonal psychotherapy: A pilot randomized controlled trial with Rwandan genocide orphans. *Psychotherapy and Psychosomatic, 78*(5), 298–306.

Schauer, E., Neuner, F., Elbert, T., Ertl, V., Onyut, P. L., Odenwald, M., & Schauer, M. (2004). Narrative exposure therapy in children—A case study in a Somali refugee. *Intervention, 2*(1), 18–32.

Schauer, M., Neuner, F., & Elbert, T. (2011). *Narrative exposure therapy: A short-term treatment for traumatic stress disorders.* Cambridge, MA: Hogrefe-Verlag.

Schauer, M., Neuner, F., Karunakara, U., Klaschik, C., Robert, C., & Elbert, T. (2003). PTSD and the "building block" effect of psychological trauma among West Nile Africans. *European Society for Traumatic Stress Studies Bulletin, 10*(2), 5–6.

Schneider, M. S., & Harley, L. P. (2006). How dogs influence the evaluation of psychotherapists. *Anthrozoös, 19*(2), 128–142.

Schnyder, U., & Cloitre, M. (Eds.). (2015). *Evidence based treatments for trauma-related psychological disorders.* Heidelberg, Germany: Springer.

Schultheiss, O. C. (2001). An information processing account of implicit motive arousal. In M. L. Maehr & P. Pintrich (Eds.), *Advances in Motivation and Achievement* (Vol. 12), (pp. 1–4). Greenwich, CT: JAI Press.

Schultheiss, O. C., Jones, N. M., Davis, A. Q., & Kley, C. (2008). The role of implicit motivation in hot and cold goal pursuit: Effects on goal progress, goal rumination, and depressive symptoms. *Journal of Research in Personality, 42,* 971–987. https://doi.org/10.1016/jrp.2007.12.2009

Schultheiss, O. C., Strasser, A., Rösch, A. G., Kordik, A. & Graham, S. C. C. (2012). Motivation. In V. S. Ramachandran (Ed.), *Encyclopedia of Human Behavior* (2nd ed., pp. 650–656). Oxford, UK: Elsevier.

Serpell, J. A. (1986). *In the company of animals.* Oxford, UK: Blackwell.

Shapiro, F. (2001). *Eye movement desensitization and reprocessing: Basic principles, protocols, and procedures* (2nd ed.). New York, NY: Guilford Press.

Shirk, S. R., Karver, M. S., & Brown, R. (2011). The alliance in child and adolescent psychotherapy. *Psychotherapy (Chic), 48*(1): 17–24.

Smith, M. E. (2005). Bilateral hippocampal volume reduction in adults with post-traumatic stress disorder: A meta-analysis of structural MRI studies. *Hippocampus, 15*(6), 798–807.

Solomon, J., & George, C. (1999). *Attachment disorganization.* New York, NY: Guilford.

Souter, M. A., & Miller, M. D. (2007). Do animal-assisted activities effectively treat depression? A meta-analysis. *Anthrozoös, 20*(2), 167–180.

Stanton, A. J., Hall, J. L., & Schultheiss, O. C. (2010). Properties of motive-specific incentives. In O. C. Schultheiss & J. C. Brunstein (Eds.), *Implicit Motives* (pp. 245–278). New York, NY: Oxford University Press. https://doi .org/10.1093/acprof.oso/9780195335156.003.0009

Tedeschi, P., Sisa, M. L., Olmert, M. D., Parish-Plass, N., & Yount, R. (2015). Treating human trauma with the help of animals: Trauma informed intervention for child maltreatment and adult post-traumatic stress. In A. H. Fine (Ed.), *Handbook on animal-assisted therapy: Foundations and guidelines for animal-assisted interventions* (4th ed., pp. 305–319). New York, NY: Academic Press.

Uvnäs-Moberg, K. (2003). *The oxytocin factor: Tapping the hormone of calm, love, and healing.* Cambridge, MA: Da Capo Press.

Vagnoli, L., Caprilli, S., & Messeri, A. (2010). Parental presence, clowns, or sedative premedication to treat preoperative anxiety in children: What could be the most promising option? *Paediatric Anaesthiology, 20,* 937–943.

Viau, R., Arsenault-Lapierre, G., Fecteau, S., Champagne, N., Walker, C.-D., & Lupien, S. (2010). Effect of service dogs on salivary cortisol secretion in autistic children. *Psychoneuroendocrinology, 35*(8), 1187.

Watson, P. J., Brymer, M. J., & Bonanno, G. A. (2011). Postdisaster psychological intervention since 9/11. *American Psychologist, 66*(6), 482–494.

Wilker, S., & Kolassa, I. T. (2013). The formation of a neural fear network in posttraumatic stress disorder: Insights from molecular genetics. *Clinical Psychological Science, 1*(4), 452–469.

Wilson, E. O. (1984). *Biophilia.* Cambridge, MA: Harvard University Press.

Wohlfarth, R., Mutschler, B., Beetz, A., Kreuser, F., & Korsten-Reck, U. (2013). Dogs motivate obese children for physical activity: Key elements of a motivational theory of animal-assisted interventions. *Frontiers in Psychology (Frontiers in Movement Science and Sport Psychology), 4*(796). https://doi.org/10.3389 /fpsyg.2013.00796

Wohlfarth, R., Mutschler, B., Beetz, A., & Schleider, K. (2014). An investigation into the efficacy of therapy dogs on reading performance in 6–7 year old children. *Human-Animal Interaction Bulletin, 2*(2), 60–73.

Wood, L., Martin, K., Christian, H., Nathan, A., Lauritsen, C., Houghton, S., Kawachi, I., & McCune, S. (2015). The pet factor—companion animals as a conduit for getting to know people, friendship formation and social support. *PLOS One, 10*(4): e0122085. https://doi.org/10.1371/journal,pone.0122085

Woon, F. L., Sood, S., & Hedges, D. W. (2010). Hippocampal volume deficits associated with exposure to psychological trauma and posttraumatic stress disorder in adults: A meta-analysis. *Progress in Neuro-Psychopharmacology & Biological Psychiatry, 34*(7), 1181–1188.

Yount, R. A., Olmert, M. D., & Lee, M. R. (2012). Service dog training program for treatment of posttraumatic stress in service members. *U.S. Army Medical Department Journal*, 63–69.

ABOUT THE AUTHORS

Andrea M. Beetz holds an MA in psychology and a PhD in psychology and special education, and works as lecturer and researcher at the IUBH University of Applied Sciences, Deptartment of Health Care (Distance Learning), Bad Honnef, Germany, and the Department for Special Education at the University of Rostock, Germany. The focus of her work is on attachment theory, the human-animal relationship, and animal-assisted interventions, especially in (special) education. She serves on the board of the International Association of Human-Animal Interaction Organizations (IAHAIO) and as president of the International Society for Animal Assisted Therapy (ISAAT).

Ira Schöfmann-Crawford received a master's in clinical and health psychology from the University of Konstanz, Germany, in 2010, and is a licensed cognitive-behavioral psychotherapist (Academy of Psychotherapy, Cologne, Germany, 2018). She holds the rank of captain in the German Air Force and works as a clinical psychologist at the Bundeswehr Central Hospital in Koblenz, Germany.

CHAPTER 4

Implications of Animal-Assisted Psychotherapy for the Treatment of Developmental Trauma Through the Lens of Interpersonal Neurobiology

Nancy Parish-Plass, MA; and Jessica Pfeiffer, LCSW, SSW

There has been a growing interest in the contributions of animal-assisted psychotherapy (AAP) to the psychological healing process for children who suffer from developmental trauma—that is, children who have experienced abuse (physical, emotional, sexual) or severe neglect (Bachi, Terkel, & Teichman, 2012; Balluerka, Muela, Amiano, & Caldentey, 2014; Dietz, Davis, & Pennings, 2012; Muela, Balluerka, Amiano, Caldentey, & Aliri, 2017; Parish-Plass, 2008; Trotter, Chandler, Goodwin-Bond, & Casey, 2008; Eliana Gil in Sori & Schnur, 2015; Tedeschi, Sisa, Olmert, Parish-Plass, & Yount, 2015; VanFleet & Faa-Thompson, 2014). This interest has been extended to an attempt to understand how the integration of animals into the process of psychotherapy may have positive impacts on neurological processes that will further facilitate healing from the neurological effects of trauma (Bona & Courtnage, 2014; Perry, 2013; Trotter & Baggerly, 2019; Yorke, 2010). This chapter explores the therapy process through the lens of the principles of psychodynamic theory and psychotherapy, especially play therapy, and then through the lens of interpersonal neurobiology of developmental trauma and therapy for those having experienced such trauma. It will be shown how these two lenses are interlinked and mutually reinforcing. This discussion will be developed in the context of AAP as a form of therapy that integrates the psychological with the neurological, uniquely advancing both processes for survivors of developmental trauma.

DEVELOPMENTAL TRAUMA—NOT JUST A TYPE OF PTSD

Trauma expert Judith Herman (1992) found in the literature concerning adults with a history of trauma that there are many clinical manifestations of prolonged exposure to repeated trauma that do not fit neatly into the *Diagnostic and Statistical Manual of Mental Disorders* (DSM-5) criteria of post-traumatic stress disorder (PTSD). These effects included symptomology 1) appearing to be more complex, diffused, and tenacious; 2) involving characteristic personality changes, including deformations of relatedness and identity; and 3) involving further harm, inflicted both by self and others. The symptomology was characterized by a multiplicity of symptoms, somatization, dissociation, and affective changes. She referred to this phenomenon as *complex PTSD (cPTSD)* or *complex disorder of extreme stress (DESNOS)*. Van der Kolk (2005) expanded the definition of *complex trauma* to refer to "the experience of multiple, chronic and prolonged, developmentally adverse traumatic events, most often of an interpersonal nature [e.g., sexual or physical abuse, war, community violence] and early-life onset" (p. 402), and coined the term *developmental trauma disorder*. He emphasized that exposure to such trauma usually commenced in early childhood within the child's caregiving system and included neglect (physical, emotional, and educational) and abuse.

UNDERSTANDING THE PSYCHOLOGICAL EFFECTS OF DEVELOPMENTAL TRAUMA IN THE CHILD

In her groundbreaking book, *Trauma and Recovery*, Herman (1997) stated that disconnection from others is a core experience of psychological trauma. This statement is in line with perhaps the most extensive theoretical, as well as empirical, study of children with developmental trauma, initiated by John Bowlby. Bowlby studied the behavior of institutionalized infants and toddlers, and later of mother-child dyads. In the institutions, he noticed that, despite having been provided with warm clothes and proper food, these children failed to thrive physically, developmentally, cognitively, and emotionally. He concluded that this phenomenon grew out of the loss of original caretakers (parents) and the lack of emotional availability for the children, as well as insensitivity toward the emotional needs of the children on the part of the caretakers in the institution.

These observations led Bowlby (1969, 1973, 1980) to develop his theory of attachment, which, in turn, led to decades of intensive psychological and neurobiological research on the effects of various types of caretaker-child relationships on a child's development in all realms (psychological, behavioral, cognitive, neurological, and physical). Bowlby's theory of attachment is now the basis for understanding not only child development (both in healthy upbringing and in the face of developmental trauma), but also for the healing of developmental trauma—both psychologically and neurologically.

Bowlby proposed that for healthy psychological development, a child needs a primary caretaker who serves as a *secure base* from which she may feel safe enough to explore the environment, and as a *safe haven* to which the child may return in the case that she feels threatened. Caretakers of children suffering from developmental trauma served as neither. Not surprisingly, Bowlby (1988) devoted two chapters in his book, *A Secure Base*, to a discussion on the subject of violence in the family as an example of insensitive and inconsistent parenting, from the point of view of attachment theory and insecure or disorganized behavior patterns. From this discussion, it is clear that these patterns are a result of relational trauma.

From the research on the subject of the relationship between relational trauma (whether coming from abuse, neglect, divorce or separation, other traumatic family events, insensitive and/or inconsistent parenting, unresolved loss, or parental depression) and insecure or disorganized attachment, a picture has arisen of the pervasive psychological, emotional, and behavioral effects of relational trauma. In a review of the consequences of maltreatment, exposure to family violence and loss, Cook and colleagues (2005) found impairment in seven domains:

- Attachment (e.g., problems with boundaries, distrust and suspiciousness, social isolation, interpersonal difficulties, difficulty attuning to other people's emotional states, difficulty with perspective taking)

- Biology (e.g., sensorimotor development, somatization, increased medical problems)
- Affect regulation (e.g., difficulty with emotional self-regulation, difficulty labeling and expressing feelings, problems knowing and describing internal states, difficulty communicating wishes and needs)
- Dissociation (e.g., distinct alterations in states of consciousness, amnesia, impaired memory for state-based events)
- Behavioral control (e.g., poor modulation of impulses, aggression toward self and others, pathological self-soothing behaviors, difficulty understanding and complying with rules, reenactment of trauma in behavior or play)
- Cognition (e.g., difficulties in attention regulation and executive functioning, problems with processing novel information, problems focusing on and completing tasks, difficulty planning and anticipating, problems with orientation in time and space)
- Self-concept (e.g., lack of continuous, predictable sense of self, low self-esteem, shame and guilt)

Many children who have suffered from abuse and/or neglect during the preverbal stage of development may exhibit difficulty in symbolization (Thompson, 1999). Cicchetti (1990) outlined a number of deficits found in maltreated children, two of which were (a) deficits in children's emotional language, and (b) deficits in children's ability to decode facial expression of emotions in others.

Crittenden (2006) proposed that maltreated children might be warier of failure, knowing that they may not receive support in the case of misjudgment, and therefore be in danger. These children will be less likely to dare to attempt new strategies, leading to rigidity and preventing reflective integration as well as the development of alternative and more elaborate *dispositional representations* (*DRs*), developmental pathways that are the outcomes of the interaction between neurological maturation and experience. Such a child will be likely to stay with immature and often inappropriate strategies and behavioral responses in any given situation.

Van der Kolk (2005) notes that the effects of chronic maltreatment and trauma are further complicated when the source of the distress is the caregiver. These children are not likely to experience the external environment as a possible source of relief in distressing situations, and therefore will have trouble relying on others for help. This observation is reminiscent of the insecure anxious avoidant pattern of attachment defined by Ainsworth (1985).

NEUROLOGICAL EFFECTS OF TRAUMA: UNDERSTANDING THEIR PSYCHOLOGICAL IMPLICATIONS

Neuroscience research has a long and impressive history reaching back to ancient Egypt. From these ancient times and through the Middle Ages, it was clear that the brain was the source of mental illness. Already in the 19th century, neuron research was being conducted (Finger, 1994). In the 20th century, universities instituted the study of what they called psychobiology, which was later changed to neurobiology.

In recent times, the study of trauma has gained much ground in terms of psychological theory and research (as covered earlier in this chapter through the work of John Bowlby, Judith Herman, and Bessel van der Kolk), as well as in theory and research in what has come to be known as interpersonal neurobiology (as covered later in this chapter through the work of Louis Cozolino, Daniel Siegel, Stephen Porges, and Bruce Perry).

It is fascinating and even exciting to see how the study of interpersonal neurobiology reinforces these psychological theories, some of which were constructed through observation long before the current neurological study of trauma and others concurrently. In this section, we present the neurological underpinnings of the emotional, psychological, cognitive, and behavioral implications of trauma mentioned in the previous section.

Among theorists and researchers in the area of interpersonal neurobiology and trauma, it is now well-accepted that prolonged stress in general, and especially developmental trauma, causes major damage to the neurological system and leads to a lack of integration between parts of the system. In an extensive review of the neurological effects of maltreatment (Teicher et al., 2003), it can be seen that maltreatment ceases the development of, or injures, three integrative areas of the brain: 1) the corpus callosum (that links the left and right hemispheres); 2) the hippocampus (that links implicit memories to each other to form explicit memory); and

3) the prefrontal cortex (that links the cortex, the limbic area, and the brain stem, controlling the body and the social world). As a result, information flow will be disrupted.

Furthermore, maltreated children are more likely to suffer from problems with cortisol regulation, causing difficulties in social functioning (characterized by withdrawn or disruptive behavior) (Alink, Ciccetti, Kim & Rogosch, 2012). According to Prendiville (2016):

> The resulting lack of smooth integration contributes to difficulties in regulation and a compromised stress response system. When an individual is in a state of alarm, the frontal cortex (the thinking brain) and the limbic system (the emotional brain) shut down. Only the lower brain areas are activated, and the individual will struggle with establishing a feeling of safety, processing incoming information, successfully engaging with others, recognizing emotional states, self-regulating [and] organizing their thinking. (p. 52)

Cozolino (2017) discusses the importance of the default mode network (DMN), a coherent neural network of various regions of the brain, which continues to function even when we are in a resting state, until a novel situation or possible threat arises. The DMN allows us to "synthesize a sensory experience of the body and internal world that allows us to have a conscious experience of ourselves in imaginal space within the flow of time" (p. 158), as well as to focus on our relationships. In disorders characterized by anxiety, such as PTSD and developmental trauma, "The sustained hyperarousal and vigilance . . . is a core factor . . . [that] disrupts the ability to activate the DMN, exiling victims from their internal worlds, a coherent sense of self, and the ability to connect with others" (p. 163).

Providing further evidence of the damaging effects of trauma on neurological development and the DMN, Daniels and colleagues (2011) found that DMN connectivity observed in women with severe chronic PTSD due to prolonged maltreatment during childhood closely paralleled that observed in a study of children aged seven to nine years (Fair et al., 2008). Bluhm and colleagues (2009) found less precuneus connectivity (PCC) with the right amygdala (the emotional center of the brain) in subjects suffering from PTSD, negatively affecting the activity of the DMN.

De Bellis and Zisk (2014) suggest that childhood trauma causes dysregulation of executive or control circuits, negatively affecting networks responsible for one's ability to think and regulate sense of self, motivation, and behavior. De Bellis and Zisk (2014) conclude that, "the data to date strongly suggest that childhood trauma is associated with adverse brain development in multiple brain regions that negatively impact emotional and behavioral regulation, motivation, and cognitive function" (p. 205).

Suo and colleagues (2016) found in their study of pediatric PTSD that damage due to trauma of one area of the brain will dramatically affect connections with linked areas, and that trauma has adverse effects on brain maturation, as well as causing abnormalities in the intrinsic connectivity network. These phenomena, they pose, lead to decreased efficiency in the local and global network due to damage of linked regions of the brain. According to Siegel (2012), this breakdown of connectivity, or linkage, between areas of the brain prevents communication between these parts, causing impaired integration, leading to dysregulation and anxiety. The neural system is, thus, at risk to fall into a state of either chaos or rigidity.

Perry (2009) examines the consequences of child maltreatment on the neural connectivity from a neurodevelopmental lens. Crucial sets of neural networks originating in the lower, more primitive brain areas having developed in utero, project into every other part of the developing brain. That is, *the organization of the higher areas depends upon the input from the lower areas of the brain.* Perry (2009) writes, "If the patterns or incoming neural activity [from the lower areas] in these monoamine systems is regulated, synchronous, patterned, and of 'normal' intensity, the higher areas will organize in healthier ways; if the patterns are extreme, dysregulated, and asynchronous, the higher areas will organize to reflect these abnormal patterns" (p. 242). Each of these areas, or functional domains, mediates a distinct function: brainstem—sensory integration; diencephalon—regulation; limbic—relational; and cortex—cognitive.

The Neurobiological Effects of Developmental Trauma on Social Engagement

According to the *polyvagal theory* (Porges, 2011), during times of threat, our very neurons perceive and evaluate this threat (neuroception) *without any cognitive awareness*, directing the individual toward defensive strategies. Our higher-level neural systems (present in mammals) lead us to seek *social engagement* (the myelinated vagus parasympathetic circuit) for safety and lowering of anxiety. Should this strategy fail or not be available, neuroception leads us to devolve into a more primitive, sympathetic circuit leading to either fight (aggressive behavior) or flight (avoidant behavior). If this fails, the most primitive unmyelinated vagus circuit takes over, leading to freeze (immobilization, shutdown), when there is less blood flow to the brain, and dissociation may occur.

In connection with this dissociation, the breakdown in the functioning of the higher-level neural systems due to fear leads to cognitive impairment, thus compromising one's reactions, emotional responses, and thought (Prendiville, 2016). Rauch and colleagues (1996) found that a decrease in the transformation of subjective experience into speech occurs during the provocation of traumatic memories. That is, the traumatized person may be at a loss of words to describe, even to himself, his traumatic experiences. This research may explain what van der Kolk (1998) describes as a loss of explicit memories of certain events related to traumatic experiences. However, the implicit memories still may remain, in the form of emotional and behavioral reactions to a stimulus with associated perceptions without an accompanying explanation for these reactions and perceptions (van der Kolk, 1998). The presence of these reactions and perceptions are likely to be anxiety-producing and stressful without an understanding of their source or context.

According to Perry (2008), a prolonged stress response disrupts the neural system mediating this above response, possibly leading to a persistently activated state characterized by dysregulation and lack of ability to self-soothe. One example of such prolonged stress is that of inconsistent, abusive, or neglectful caregiving in early childhood, when the brain is most rapidly developing and organizing. Such experiences alter normal development of neural systems involving relationships, together with the stress response and disorganization of neural systems mediating social-emotional functioning (Ludy-Dobson & Perry, 2010).

There has been a great amount of research focusing on the neuropeptide oxytocin and its role in much of our social behavior and emotional well-being in the presence of others. Porges (2011) suggests that oxytocin supports emotional and autonomic processes, allowing for what he describes as *immobility without fear* (to be differentiated from immobilization or freeze due to helplessness). According to Carter (2017), immobility without fear is an important biobehavioral enabler providing opportunities to express attachment, a sort of "neural choice" to stay in one place. In the face of challenge, oxytocin and activation of its receptors signal psychological safety, permitting positive social behaviors and passive coping.

Among other findings, oxytocin has been found to be responsible for social affiliation and support (Carter, 1998; Heinrichs, von Dawans, & Domes, 2009; Theodoridou, Rowe, Penton-Voak, & Rogers, 2009), attachment security (Buchheim et al., 2009), trust (Kosfeld, Heinrichs, Zak, Fischbacher, & Fehr, 2005), sharing emotions (Lane et al., 2012), reduction of fear response (Huber, Veinante, & Stoop, 2005; Meyer-Lindenberg, 2008), and management of stress and anxiety (Heinrichs, Baumgartner, Kirschbaum, & Ehlert, 2003; Neumann, 2002).

However, maltreated subjects have been shown to be characterized by lower levels of oxytocin (Heim, Newport, Mletzko, Miller, Young, & Nemeroff, 2006) and oxytocin reactivity (Wismer Fries, Zigler, Kurian, Jacoris, & Pollak, 2005) than in controls. In a review article covering the literature concerning the connection between oxytocin, experience of maltreatment, and their effects on trust, sense of safety, fear response, anxiety, and social interaction, Olff, Langeland, Witteveen, and Denys (2010) suggest that, "Early stress and abuse experiences (particularly childhood emotional abuse and neglect and early parental separation) seem to disrupt the normal development of the oxytocin system in children, a mechanism critical to the regulation of emotional behaviors increasing the risk of developing PTSD. This may lead to long-term disruptions in the ability to be calmed and comforted by social bonding interactions" (p. 526).

Social connectedness and healthy relationships may serve as a buffer, or protective factor, from the neurobiological effects of child maltreatment, as well as a source of healing from maltreatment (Ludy-Dobson & Perry, 2010; Perry, 2009). Perry (2009) states that resilience and the ability to cope with trauma are related to healthy relationships. Indeed, Zimrin (1986) found that one factor predicting higher functioning among adults who were maltreated as children was either the presence of an empathetic adult at the time of the maltreatment, or alternately, long-term psychotherapy (that is, the long-term presence of an empathetic figure after the maltreatment).

These implications of social connectedness reinforce the importance of the role of social engagement as a protective strategy proposed in the polyvagal theory. Porges and Carter (2011) state that "systems that support sociality, because they are intertwined with restorative physiological states, also may be protective against the costly or destructive effects of *chronic* fear or stress" (p. 58). That is, social support and connectedness protect from the neurological damage usually occurring due to maltreatment, thus preventing developmental trauma.

GOALS AND PROCESS OF PSYCHOTHERAPY FOR TRAUMA

Taking into account the psychological and neurological origins and implications of developmental trauma, the literature recommends three major emphases for the therapy process for survivors of developmental trauma. The first emphasis involves psychotherapy based on a healing relationship built on support, understanding, acceptance, and trust, and which provides a sense of safety and presents a healthier model of relationships.

Herman (1997) states that, "recovery [from trauma] can take place only within the context of relationships" (p. 133). Similarly, Banks (2006) sees the destruction of relationships as the largest obstacle to healing from the effects of trauma. She feels that models of therapy striving for objectivity and neutrality, and attempting to help the client to overcome dependency, may in fact retraumatize the client with a history of childhood abuse. Banks recommends relational therapy with the goal of the development of a mutual, growth-fostering relationship.

Pearlman and Courtois (2005) expand on the relevance of relational therapy for complex trauma, noting the need to treat attachment disturbances and dissociative processes in the context of the therapeutic relationship. Pearlman and Courtois explain that an attachment-relational approach also emphasizes the formation of the therapeutic alliance[1], the establishment and maintenance of the framework of treatment and its boundaries, and the addressing of relational and behavioral reenactments of past attachments and trauma. Cloitre, Stovall-Mclough, Miranda, and Chemtob (2004) concluded from the results of their research that "the therapeutic relationship may be an especially 'active' ingredient in the remediation of childhood abuse-related PTSD" (p. 414).

Likewise, Ludy-Dobson and Perry (2010) refer to the "biological gift of the healing power of relationships" (p. 39). Siegel (2010) states that attunement with another allows for resonance with the inner world of the other, leading to a feeling of "feeling felt," resulting in the feeling of security found in close relationships. This relational attunement and resonance can be explained by a process called *brain-to-brain coupling* (Hasson, Ghazanfar, Galantucci, Garrod, & Keysers, 2012) in which signals are transmitted to the environment by one neural system and perceived by another neural system and synergy may be achieved.

The second emphasis involves recognition of the trauma itself, processing it, and forming a meaningful narrative. Both Herman (1997) and van der Kolk (2005) stress that, in order to heal, victims of trauma must remember, proclaim, mourn, and process their traumatic experiences. According to van der Kolk (2005), therapy must emphasize the recovery and integration of traumatic memories with their associated effects, as well as the necessity for validation of the patient's traumatic experiences. The validation of the trauma is a precondition for restoration of an integrated self-identity and the capacity for appropriate relationships with others.

Here, it is important to activate implicit memory (expressed in physical sensations, emotions, perceptions, and behaviors), which should be processed into explicit form in order to enable the trauma to be recognized and consequently be worked through, leading to a narrative that adds meaning and sense to the trauma.

The third emphasis, on the neurological level, is on the regrowth of neural connective tissue, or linkage, between regions of the brain, resulting in integration within the neural system (Siegel, 2012). According to Siegel (2012), the individual will then be able to achieve 1) emotional and behavioral self-regulation; 2) understanding of self, with the ability to express oneself and one's needs to others; and 3) participation in healthy relationships. These achievements will lead to lower anxiety and to higher and more satisfying functioning.

An interaction exists between these three emphases, each mutually reinforcing and facilitating each other, leading to the psychological and neurological healing of the effects of relational trauma. According to Geller and Porges (2014), "The capacity of the brain to develop new neural connections leading to calmer and healthier emotional states is facilitated when a safe therapeutic environment is promoted through the cultivation and expression of therapists' presence" (p. 188). One can see that the emphasis on interpersonal neurobiological principles will facilitate the healing relationship as well as the work dealing more directly with the trauma itself. Furthermore, participation in a healthy relationship in therapy, together with recognizing the trauma and the related narrative, as well as finding the words to express the sensations (that is, turning implicit knowledge into explicit knowledge), will in turn further the regrowth of neural connective tissue and neural integration.

Originating from his neurodevelopmental approach to interpersonal neurobiology and trauma, Perry (2009) created a therapy approach called Neurosequential Model of Therapeutics (NMT). In the first stage of NMT, deficits and the related systems and areas of the brain are first identified. The second stage involves targeting patterned, repetitive activation in the neural systems that mediate the dysfunction in the sequence that is identical to the normal sequential process of development. In other words, therapy should commence with deficits associated with the lowest area of the brain, sequentially moving up the brain to the next deficit as improvements are seen. For instance, self-regulation, anxiety, and impulsivity should be targeted before emotional problems, and then only afterward should cognitive problems be addressed. Perry emphasizes that a key component of the NMT model is the relational environment of the child in that it serves as the major mediator of therapeutic experiences.

PLAYING THE TRAUMA: PSYCHODYNAMIC RELATIONAL THERAPY WITH CHILDREN SUFFERING FROM DEVELOPMENTAL TRAUMA

Child psychotherapists have long known that the best way to peek into the inner world of the child is to be present for, or join in on, the child's play (Axline, 1969; Freud, 1946; Klein, 1932; Landreth, 2012; Winnicott, 1971). Play is a form of self-exploration and expression of experiences, emotions, and thoughts that children may have difficulty, or have a fear of, verbalizing to others (Landreth, 2012) or even to themselves.

Potential Space and Its Importance in Play Therapy

An element critical to play is the concept of *potential space*. According to Winnicott (1971), the *potential space* is the intermediate area of experiencing, or transitional space between one's outer reality and inner world, allowing for play that brings together elements of both worlds in such a way that helps the client work through conflictual and anxiety-producing issues. Potential space exists only in a setting that feels safe to the client, allowing for the reenactment and reexperiencing of feelings, thoughts, and experiences without fear of actual danger, as well as offering a safe environment for emotional expression, observation, and contemplation of thoughts, emotions, and dynamics, and for the freedom to consider options and possible solutions.

Thirty years after Winnicott coined the term *potential space*, Raichle and colleagues (2001) coined the term *default mode of brain function*, occurring when a person is not involved with goal-directed activities. As described earlier, only when the neurological network involved in the default mode (or DMN) is at rest, and there is no sense of threat, can one experience an imaginal space in the flow of time. This process may serve as the neurological explanation of Winnicott's concept of potential space.

Play occurring within the context of a facilitating and generative relationship with a psychotherapist permits the development of a sense of security within the therapy setting (Levy, 2011).

The Interpersonal Neurobiological Implications of Play Therapy for the Healing of Developmental Trauma

In the last century, Vygotsky (1976) posited that make-believe or sociodramatic play leads to self-regulation. Authors of literature review chapters (Gioia & Tobin, 2010; Whitebread, Coltman, Jameson, & Lander, 2009) discuss research that reinforces this observation, in terms of both behavioral and emotional self-regulation and especially when a supportive adult (such as a therapist) participates in this type of play together with the child.

The literature concerning trauma psychotherapy for children often refers to the play therapy approach (Gaskill & Perry, 2014; Gil, 2017; Gil & Terr, 2013; Goodyear-Brown, 2010). This is not surprising since a great amount of significance is attributed to the role of play in interpersonal neurobiology (Gaskill & Perry, 2014; Porges, 2015b; Siegel & Bryson, 2012), especially in the context of self-regulation.

Porges (2015b) states that play serves as a neural exercise of using the social engagement system to efficiently downregulate our fight/flight behaviors, requiring practice to become effective. The improvement of neural regulation of our social engagement system leads to resilience in dealing with disruptions in our lives. According to Porges (2001), "It may be possible that creating states of calmness and exercising the neural regulation of brainstem structures may potentiate positive social behavior by stimulating and exercising the neural regulation of the social engagement system" (p. 142). In this way, play enables the neural systems of maltreated children to become familiar with, and capable of, the regulation of their defensive systems, going back and forth between fight/flight and social engagement, and experiencing types of social engagement and recognizing its presence.

Siegel and Bryson (2012) note that reactivity, originating in the lower, more primitive brain, makes one feel shut down, upset, and defensive. The receptive state activates the social engagement system, related to the upper areas of the brain, and gives one a feeling of being safe and seen. Siegel and Bryson then posit that playfulness, in the presence of a supportive and involved adult, turns reactivity to receptivity.

Explaining play therapy in a way that combines psychological and neurobiological principles, Levy (2011) states that, "Affect regulation, self-awareness, and self-complexity is developed by the process of containing, regulating, and repairing the treatment relationship, the engendering of experimentation, and promoting the experience of self-states through play" (p. 53). Levy further explains that experiencing various self-states in the play therapy relationship is related to the promotion of greater complexity in the child's self-organization. These self-states become more elaborated, more flexibly experienced, and better integrated within the child's personality.

Siegel (2015) states that play cultivates integration, both relationally and neurologically. That is, integration actually links fibers between brain areas, allowing for neural communication and therefore creating balance. Play helps clients to start imagining, to search for meaning and narrative. Integration and finding meaning together increase neural regulation, lower anxiety, and provide a feeling of safety. Yet there are factors resulting from the experience of chronic maltreatment by an adult that are likely to prevent these processes from occurring. These are discussed in the following section.

BARRIERS TO PSYCHOTHERAPY IN CHILDREN WITH DEVELOPMENTAL TRAUMA

Poor Therapeutic Alliance

Many researchers and theorists point to the nature of the connection between attachment style and the therapeutic alliance, specifically that avoidant style of attachment (both dismissing and fearful) was related to poor therapeutic alliance (Eames & Roth, 2000; Kivlighan, Patton, & Foote, 1998; Mallinckrodt, Gantt, & Coble, 1995; Mallinckrodt,

McCreary, & Robertson, 1995; Mikulincer & Shaver, 2010; Parish & Eagle, 2003; Robbins, 1995; Satterfield & Lyndon, 1998). Research suggests that the client may project onto the therapist feelings, perceptions, expectations, and sensitivities from previously established working models formed by past relationships and experiences with abusive attachment figures, negatively affecting the establishment and development of the therapeutic alliance (Gelso & Carter, 1994; Green, 2006; Satterfield & Lyndon, 1998; Mallinckrodt, 1991).

In his research on the impact on neurobiological systems of child maltreatment as a social experience, Cicchetti (2002) found an interaction between cognitive, social, emotional, and biological systems to be a likely contributor to maltreated children's construction of their world as marked by fear and hypersensitivity to future maltreatment. Lack of trust in the intentions of others (Briere, 1988; Herman, Russell, & Trocki, 1986; Putnam, 2003; Somer & Szwarcberg, 2001; van der Kolk, 2005), as well as a lack of understanding of social cues and intentions of others (Cicchetti, 1990), is a common consequence of interpersonal trauma. Therapy, the very situation that is meant to heal, is often perceived as emotionally threatening. This phenomenon is likely to have a negative effect on the establishment of the therapeutic alliance.

Therefore, social engagement, which is meant to reduce anxiety and heal the brain from the effects of interpersonal trauma, instead is inhibited, activating the client's more primitive, sympathetic circuit of fight or flight. That is, the client is likely to be avoidant of a relationship with the therapist. Indeed, Lopez, Melendez, Sauer, Berger, and Wyssmann (1998) found a relationship between insecure attachment and dropout rate from therapy. Many other studies have found a high rate of attrition among maltreated children suffering from PTSD (Murphy et al., 2014). Chemtob, Novaco, Hamada, and Gross (1997) found that PTSD-related anger symptoms caused ruptures in the therapeutic relationship.

In order to uncover the root of trauma responses in children and successfully guide healing, the therapist must overcome resistance and defenses presented by the children toward the therapy process. The therapy setting must be perceived as safe, which will not occur if the therapist present is felt to be dangerous.

To remedy this situation, Zoicas, Slattery, and Neumann (2014) suggest that since the oxytocin system is associated with social fear, restoring balance to the oxytocin system may alleviate some of the symptoms. Olff and colleagues (2010) suggest that oxytocin may enhance a sense of safety and perception of the therapeutic relationship as a place providing support. They suggest administering oxytocin prior to therapy sessions with sufferers of PTSD in order to increase the building of the therapy alliance and enhance therapy outcome. A review by Striepens, Kendrick, Maier, and Hurlemann (2011) of studies employing the use of internasal oxytocin for its therapeutic potential notes the plethora of prosocial effects, including the domains of trust, generosity, socially reinforced learning, and emotional empathy.

This research seems to point to the benefit of the use of exogenous oxytocin, which would lead to immobilization without fear, allowing the client to stay in the therapy setting with the therapist, and letting the therapeutic alliance occur. However, Carter (2017) points out that conditions such as chronic use of exogenous oxytocin, or its use in exceptionally high doses, may downregulate the oxytocin's own receptors.

Collapse of Potential Space

Whether the medium for therapy is that of play (in the case of children) or direct discussion (in the case of adults), the existence of potential space is a critical element in the process of psychotherapy. However, contact with one's inner world of emotions and content related to the trauma is likely to raise the trauma survivor's anxiety, leading to reexperiencing the danger associated with the trauma, the collapse of the potential space, and escape from this emotionally dangerous content into the real world. When this occurs, the client often becomes emotionally unavailable for therapy.

In neurobiological terms, contact with a threatening inner world may cause the polyvagal system to inhibit the limbic (emotional and relational) and cortex (cognitive) areas of the neural system, leading to flight (from contact with the threatening content) or even dissociation.

Anxiety found in children suffering from developmental trauma may also originate from the lack of integration in the neurological system, as explained earlier in this chapter. Lack of words, deficits in ability to decode facial emotional expression, and lack of explicit memories make it difficult to ascribe meaning to experiences and prevent the formation of a coherent narrative. Fearing the emotional chaos in their inner world, these children will prefer the certainty of reality, resulting in the collapse of the potential space that is essential for self-expression through play.

Cozolino (2017) explains that the DMN is chronically inhibited after severe trauma in early childhood, significantly impairing one's ability to develop a coherent sense of self, affect regulation, introspection, and empathy for others. As a result, a child with developmental trauma may never achieve the ability to withdraw into an inner world for comfort. With no access to their inner world, play therapy is not an option. As a first step, the therapist must employ a treatment context involving the amygdala.

Deficit in Ability to Symbolize

Many children who suffered from maltreatment during the preverbal stage of development may exhibit difficulty in symbolization (Thompson, 1999). According to Siegel (2012), relationship histories may impair the development of the mentalizing reflective function as a result of impairment of the integrative function of essential associative neural pathways, specifically a blockage of the corpus callosal fibers interconnecting the two hemispheres, and of interconnections within the right hemisphere itself. Siegel (2012) writes, "This impairment can be pervasive and can lead to a child's generalized inability to mentalize, as revealed in impaired symbolic play" (p. 261), making the use of potential space difficult if not impossible.

Shame and the Presentation of False Self to Others

In research that focuses on trauma in general and abuse in particular, shame is a prevalent and significant factor resulting in the delay of disclosure of the abuse by the victim (Hershkowitz, Horowitz, & Lamb, 2005; Lev-Wiesel, Eisikovits, First, Gottfried, & Mehlhausen, 2016). Studies have shown that maltreated children suffer from low self-esteem (Pearce & Pezzot-Pearce, 1997) and see themselves as devalued and incompetent (Bretherton & Munholland, 1999). Furthermore, according to Feiring and Taska (2005), "Persistent shame may explain failure to process the abuse and the maintenance of posttraumatic stress disorder symptoms" (p. 337). The explanation behind this finding may lay in the unbearable shame the abuse survivor feels as a result of the abuse, and the need to hide that shame from others and also from oneself. This process leads the client to present a false self [2] in an attempt to hide the source of the shame, and to hide from the resulting emotional pain, resulting in the lack of authentic emotional expression and self-disclosure of thoughts and events. Instead, the client tries to appease the therapist and to present a more positive self to the therapist. As in the discussion above concerning the collapse of the potential space, the client will be less able to make use of the therapeutic relationship for healing, and she may even withdraw from it (Safran & Muran, 1996).

Loss of Touch With Self

A well-known consequence of trauma, especially in the case of sexual abuse, is the experience of emotional and sensory numbness. Dissociation may occur when either fight or flight fails to protect or is not an option. Yet another reaction to the trauma may involve the trauma survivor becoming emotionally overwhelmed and trying to hide the emotions or even the fact of the abuse from themselves or from others. In many cases, there will be a memory deficit concerning the trauma. Memory deficits may be explained by a disruption of neurological functioning caused by chemical responses to the trauma (U.S. Department of Health and Human Services, 2014).

Whether the reaction is numbness, dissociation, feeling of being emotionally overwhelmed, or lack of memory, the client will have a very difficult time in therapy recognizing and processing the trauma, and creating a coherent narrative surrounding it.

If the sensory issues related to the trauma (originating from the brainstem) are not recognized and processed, then the higher parts of the neural system will become poorly regulated and dysfunctional—emotionally, behaviorally, relationally, and cognitively. The client will be unable to cognitively make sense of the trauma she suffered and to work through it. This will likely lead to the client formulating an alternative and false explanation for the implicit memories (expressed in emotional and behavioral reactions), thereby preventing their translation to explicit memories and the process of healing.

Lack of Regulation

Though extreme dysregulation can be a symptom for a child who has experienced trauma and for a child who has experienced neglect, at the neurobiological level the roots of this symptom differ in the impact they have on the developing brain. Trauma, in simplistic terms, is the overactivation of the stress response system for extended periods of time, which in turn causes that system to change. Neglect is the opposite. Neglect is the absence of activation for the neurons in critical and sensitive periods during development. For both, the fact that the brain is a use-dependent organ and develops in a sequential fashion is at the center for each form of maltreatment (Perry, 2008).

According to Perry Pollard, Blakely, Baker, and Vigilante (1995), the acute adaptive states, during and following traumatic events, can become maladaptive traits if they persist long enough. Perry (2009) writes:

> When a child is threatened and the stress response is activated in an extremely prolonged or repetitive fashion, the neural networks involved in this adaptive response will undergo a 'use dependent' alteration. The very molecular characteristics of individual neurons, synaptic distributions, dendritic trees, and a host of other microstructural and microchemical aspects of these important neural networks will change. And the end effect is an alteration in the baseline activity and reactivity of the stress response systems in the traumatized individual. (p. 244)

Likewise, Perry (2002) states, "The earlier and more pervasive the neglect is, the more devastating the development problems for the child. Indeed, a chaotic, inattentive and ignorant caregiver can produce pervasive developmental delay" (p. 89). Due to the sequential development of key areas of the brain, neurotransmitters that run from the lowest part of the brain (the brainstem) to the highest part of the brain (the cortex) are affected in their ability to have healthy communication with one another. Child Welfare Information Gateway (2001) notes:

> If a child does not receive kindness as an infant, he may not know how to show kindness as an adult. If a child's cries for attention are ignored as a toddler, he may not know how to interact positively with others later. These capacities may not fully develop because the required neuronal pathways were not activated enough to form the 'memories' needed for future learning. (p. 10)

Children with developmental trauma have had little if any practice in using the social engagement system to downregulate, for the environment was more often than not dangerous or uncertain, and neuroception kept them in neurophysiological states supporting mobilization and shutdown (Porges, 2015b). In other words, their baseline state is that of hyperarousal or dissociation.

Engaging children in play therapy who are either hyperaroused or dissociative can be very challenging, and it may even be outside the child's capability to participate in play therapy. Motor hyperactivity, behavioral impulsivity, hypervigilance, avoidance, emotional volatility, and inability to maintain attention are just a few of the symptoms children who have experienced developmental trauma display. They may misinterpret prosocial behavior of other children as threatening, preventing reciprocal inhibition of fight/flight behaviors and/or reacting with either aggression or avoidance. These behaviors make sustainability in play with children suffering from developmental trauma extremely difficult.

Van der Kolk (2014) describes the effects of what happens when a child's (or adult's) baseline state becomes a heightened state of alarm or fear: "When that system breaks down, we become like conditioned animals: the moment we detect danger we automatically go into fight or flight mode" (p. 62). Play with a highly dysregulated child is very hard, due to their difficulty controlling their emotions and impulses. Van der Kolk (2014) continues, "They may startle in response to any loud sound, become enraged by small frustrations, or freeze when somebody touches them" (p. 63).

ANIMAL-ASSISTED PSYCHOTHERAPY

Although Freud was accompanied in therapy sessions by his dog Jofi (Grinker, 2013), animal-assisted psychotherapy (AAP) was only brought to the attention of the clinical community 40 years later by psychologist Boris Levinson, at a conference of the American Psychological Association (Levinson, 1962) and later through articles and books (e.g., Levinson, 1965, 1984; Levinson & Mallon, 1997). Levinson's insights into the mechanisms of AAP, through his work with maltreated children and accompanied by his dog Jingles, are still relevant today (Fine, 2017) and serve as a useful and credible base for current and ongoing clinical work, theoretical development, and research.

AAP is a clinical field based on accepted principles and goals of psychotherapy, and may be applied in the context of various theoretical frameworks and clinical approaches. AAP may be carried out in relation to attachment theory (Bachi, 2013; Balluerka et al., 2014; Zilcha-Mano, Mikulincer, & Shaver, 2011), intersubjectivity (Parish-Plass & Oren,

2013), Jung (Maayan, 2013), psychodynamic therapy (Parish-Plass, 2008, 2013a), gestalt (Kirby, 2010; Lac, 2016), cognitive therapy (Gonzalez-Ramirez, Ortiz, & Landero-Hernandez, 2013), play therapy (Parish-Plass, 2008, 2013b; VanFleet & Faa-Thompson, 2017), group therapy (Harel, 2013), parent-child (dyadic) therapy (Shani, 2017), and eye movement desensitization and reprocessing (EMDR) (Jenkins, 2013). Chandler (2017) systematically covers a number of psychotherapy approaches integrating animals into their setting.

The integration of animals into the therapy setting, by a therapist who understands the opportunities provided by the human–animal bond, may expand these principles to further advance the therapy process. The presence of animals in the psychotherapy setting may serve as a rich and multifaceted medium for the expression of the client's inner world (Oren & Parish-Plass, 2013). The fact that an animal is alive, breathes, walks, plays, is spontaneous, makes sounds, has smell, eats, has babies, gets sick, and even dies catalyzes the therapy process in many ways. For instance, the animal's genuineness and aliveness brings up many issues and emotions from the client's life, which makes the animal a more likely object for projection and transference than a doll or other inanimate object.

Fairbairn (1944) claimed that the basis for all psychopathological conditions could be found in disturbances in early childhood relationships. Similarly, Bowlby (1969) posited that all humans base their social interactions on internal working models formed in interactions with their parents. The client's ensuing relational style is carried into other relationships, as well as into the therapy situation. These models may be worked on within therapy. For this reason, psychotherapy is based on the exploration of the client's emotional issues through the utilization of the relationship in the therapy setting. In AAP, the presence of a number of potential relationships existing simultaneously allows for reenactment, within the therapy setting, of many other relational experiences. Thus, the inclusion of animals in the therapeutic setting expands this principle by providing opportunities in the here-and-now for processing past relational issues, identifying and working on underlying relational patterns and internal models, and offering adaptive alternatives (Parish-Plass & Oren, 2013).

Because the AAP setting may serve as a microcosm of one's social world due to the number of potential relationships that may occur (client-therapist, therapist-animal(s), client-animals(s), and even animal-animal), individual AAP has certain elements and advantages of group therapy (Ish-Lev

& Amit, 2013). As in group therapy, there are a number of participants (client, therapist, animals) in the setting, allowing for various dynamics to occur between them, and each participant may at any given time be an active participant or an observer. Yet in the case of AAP, the client is the only focus of the therapy process.

Chandler (2017) refers to various categories of significant human-animal relational moments (SHARMs) that occur during human-animal interaction: *greeting* (the therapist's facilitating the greeting between client and animal, commenting on the animal's body language and possible meaning or value of this body language), *acknowledgment* (the therapist acknowledging the animal's communication of something of value to the client, the therapist, or about the animal himself), *speculation* (the therapist wondering aloud about the animal's thoughts or feelings, which might provide insight or awareness to the client; asking the client to speculate, providing a medium through which the client may project the client's internal experience), *interpretation* (offering an interpretation of the animal's behavior or asking a client to interpret an animal's behavior to imply what the animal is experiencing or may be communicating), *assurance* (a client experiencing assurance or self-assurance due to the animal's behavior around the client or due to a client's observation of the animal's behavior), and *checking in* (a therapist's pointing out that the animal is checking in to make sure the client or therapist is okay; the therapist or client checking in with the animal to see if the animal is okay). These SHARMs provide opportunities for effective processing of those moments by a client and a therapist. The human-animal relational processing of a SHARM gives personal meaning and relevance to the relational moment.

These opportunities are especially salient for work with maltreated children, whose source of trauma was an injurious relationship.

AAP: ADVANCING THE PRINCIPLES OF PSYCHOTHERAPY AND INTERPERSONAL NEUROBIOLOGY IN THE HEALING OF TRAUMA

Similar to Herman's stance on trauma and recovery, Perry (2009) stresses the healing power of relationships in children suffering from trauma, stemming from research in the area of the interpersonal neurobiology of trauma and healing of trauma. Yet, as shown earlier in this chapter, many maltreated children are suspicious of relationships with adults and are avoidant of them, either dropping out of therapy, being unable to participate in the psychotherapy process, or refusing to attend therapy at all. Psychotherapy with such children is often characterized by a poor therapeutic alliance, the collapsing of potential space, a deficit in ability to symbolize, and/or shame and presentation of false self. Porges (2015b) writes, "The vulnerability of the Social Engagement System to environmental cues of danger and life threat is profound. Even with the removal of danger cues, the Social Engagement System may remain dormant unless it is appropriately stimulated with safety cues" (p. 120).

We will now suggest ways in which the integration of animals into the process of psychotherapy might provide solutions for these issues and therefore advance the process. The case examples provided are drawn from Pfeiffer's experience as a therapist at a facility school for children, ages 5–13 years old, who have experienced severe maltreatment.

Animals as Facilitators of the Therapeutic Alliance

Taking into account the research mentioned earlier, many maltreated children will find the therapy situation to be very threatening, and they will be unlikely to trust the therapist or her positive intentions toward them. These feelings make the establishment of the therapeutic alliance very difficult if not impossible. Yet recent research presents evidence that the therapeutic alliance with maltreated children can be established earlier and stronger in AAP in a play therapy setting than in non-AAP play therapy (Parish-Plass, 2018). This finding may explain the results found by Dietz and colleagues (2012) and Signal and colleagues (2017) that the addition of dogs to the therapy plan for maltreated children leads to higher rates of treatment completion. This research reinforces past studies that have shown that that the presence of an animal may serve as a facilitator of social interaction (Corson, Corson, Gwynne, & Arnold, 1977; McNicholas & Collis, 2000; Messent, 1983).

As mentioned above, the client may sometimes be an observer of the relationship between the therapist and the animals. It is our experience that through the therapist's genuine interactions with the animals, the client judges the therapist as to what type of person she is, if she can be trusted, and if she is respectful, protective, and caring. In addition, the client may notice the animals' behavior toward the therapist, such as looking for her attention and protection, trusting her, expecting to be fed by her, and appearing happy to see her. Due to children's tendency to identify with animals (as smaller and more helpless than adults),[3] their perception that the animals can trust the therapist may lead the child to feel that he can also trust the therapist and feel safe with her.[4]

Lockwood (1983) found that a situation portrayed in a picture that included an animal was perceived in a more positive light than that in an identical picture but without an animal. Similarly, a person shown in a picture accompanied by an animal was perceived with more positive regard than a person shown in an identical picture but not accompanied by an animal. One may infer from this research that the presence of an animal in therapy is likely to make the therapy setting less threatening, and the therapist will be perceived more positively.

There may be a number of possible explanations for these findings. Studies have found that an animal may serve both as a secure base (from which to explore) and as a safe haven (to which one may return in case of perceiving threat), both in general (Zilcha-Mano, Mikulincer, & Shaver, 2012) and specifically in the therapy setting (Zilcha-Mano, 2019). Thus, an animal's presence is likely to lead the client to perceive the therapy setting as safe and secure. Once the therapy environment is considered safe, that is that there is a neuroception of safety, the client may have access to neural circuits that enable one to socially engage and benefit from the physiological states associated with social support (Porges, 2003, 2006). The way is now paved for the establishment of the therapeutic alliance.

Geller and Porges (2014) emphasize the importance of a *mutual relational presence* that promotes relational depth, safety, and therapeutic change. For the relational presence to develop, there must be a felt, communicated, and received presence within and between therapist and client. As has been shown, many maltreated children resist therapy and refuse or seem to be incapable of creating a therapeutic alliance. They are unlikely to experience the therapist's presence.

Claire Winnicott (1968) discussed the importance of the "third thing," a common interest that draws the focus from the threatening therapist-client relationship and places it instead on something outside of the therapy dyad. The animals in the therapy setting may provide that common ground, both therapist and client taking care of the animals together, observing and discussing their behavior, and playing with them. Through the common caring and playfulness that occurs, and the multiple relationships developing in a nonthreatening way, the client may feel an atmosphere of relationships in the room to be less threatening and even natural and authentic. *Presence* by all in the setting may be communicated and felt by each other and for each other more strongly, contributing to the development of a *relational presence* between the therapist and client.

Both theory and research in the area of interpersonal neurobiology contributes much to the understanding of how animals may contribute to the establishment of the therapeutic alliance with clients suffering from developmental trauma. The *biophilia hypothesis* (Kellert & Wilson, 1993; Wilson, 1984) posits that humans have an innate need for deep and intimate association with animals, as well as an inclination to affiliate with life in order to achieve meaning and fulfillment. Support was found for this hypothesis in a study by Mormann and colleagues (2011). Using an fMRI brain scan, they found a preferential response for pictures of animals (as opposed to people or landmarks) in the neurons of the right amygdala, the area of the brain performing a primary role in the processing of emotional reactions. In turn, findings from recent research support the hypothesis that the amygdala is associated with social interactions (Bickart, Wright, Dautoff, Dickerson, & Barrett, 2011), and that oxytocin may regulate social behavior and prosocial tendencies partly through amygdala neuromodulation (Chang et al., 2015).

In light of this research, and research suggesting that interactions with animals cause the release of oxytocin in humans (Nagasawa, Kikusui, Onaka, & Ohta, 2009; Odendaal, 2000), there could be a relationship between the amygdala's preferential response for animals and the oxytocin released due to seeing the animals. Research would be needed to understand whether the relationship is causative (and in which direction) or correlational. Considering the connections within the neural system illustrated in Figure 2 in Porges (2001), it would seem that seeing the animal, recorded in the amygdala, is what reaches the hypothalamus and causes the release of oxytocin (if indeed, seeing animals results in the release of oxytocin). This would explain the "anti-stress" effect caused by being with animals, as seen both in research on state anxiety, lowering of blood pressure, and lowering of cortisol. Perhaps the presence of the animal, in a supportive and safe atmosphere, subdues the limbic activation (Porges, 2003), dampening the stress response system of the hypothalamic pituitary adrenal (HPA) axis (cortisol) and fight/flight mechanism (Porges, 2015a), thus allowing for immobilization without fear and social engagement behaviors. Carter and Porges (2016) further explain that humans may feel a sense of emotional safety with animals in that affection with an animal may be less complex to experience and return than with humans.

We suggest that the response to animals (due to the amygdala's reaction to them, and/or due to the release of oxytocin during interaction with them or even by just seeing them) increases the likelihood of social interaction, social behavior, and prosocial tendency, thus facilitating the establishment or strengthening of the therapeutic alliance.[5] In effect, the presence of animals in the AAP setting would provide a natural alternative to the administering of possibly dangerous exogenous oxytocin in order to return balance to the oxytocin system of the maltreated client, with all the positive emotional effects and implications for the therapy process that would ensue.

Carter (2017) asserts that, "Developmental exposure to social experiences and to peptides, including oxytocin and vasopressin, also can 'retune' the nervous system, altering thresholds for sociality, emotion regulation and aggression" (p. 499). Here, Carter points to the positive effect of the combination of social experiences and neuropeptides on the nervous system. Interaction with animals provides both in a way unique to AAP.[6]

According to Geller and Porges (2014), the detection of safety promotes receptivity toward others. We physiologically calm down and our defenses are inhibited and downregulated. Geller and Porges (2014) go on to say, "Defensive strategies are then replaced with gestures associated with feeling safe and with this state of safety there is a perceptional bias toward the positive. Appropriately executed prosocial spontaneous interactions reduce psychological and physical distance" (p. 183).

The feeling of safety brought about through the presence of and interaction with the animals, is therefore likely to facilitate the therapeutic alliance with the therapist, as well as promote receptivity to the therapy process. That is, in light of the above research, one may conclude that the presence of animals allows for social engagement for the purpose of preventing or healing the deleterious psychological and neurobiological effects of trauma. This helps us to understand why the avoidantly attached client will often cooperate with AAP therapists when they have not done so with other psychotherapists.

Not only will the therapeutic alliance be difficult to establish with maltreated children, but also ruptures in the alliance are more likely to occur (Chemtob et al., 1997). AAP provides unique opportunities for the resolution of alliance ruptures (Zilcha-Mano, 2017). For instance, as discussed by Zilcha-Mano (2017), an animal serving as a safe haven may allow the client to stay in therapy during the resolution process. The secure base provided by the animal may help clients explore their internal working models reflected in alliance ruptures with their therapists, leading to the repairing of the alliance with the therapist, as well as to the ability to form healthier relationships. A rupture in the client's relationship with the animal in therapy may be a psychologically safer way for the client to work through maladaptive relational patterns, with the help of the therapist.

CASE EXAMPLE

Surrounded by adults she had never met on her first day of school with us, Haley, age eight years old, was highly overwhelmed. Her anxieties were extremely high, and she did what she tended to do when she felt that out of control. She undressed and curled up in a ball, screaming and crying for her mom. New environments and new adults were so threatening to Haley that she moved immediately into a terror state. The adults were trying everything to let her know she was safe, but their actions and words were not enough. After a bit of time with no success, a staff member asked if perhaps my therapy dog, Charlie, could come out and walk by to see how she would respond. Charlie initially walked at a far distance from her, but close enough for her to see. Though there was not a major shift in behavior, the staff did notice that she began paying attention to the dog near her. Charlie slowly came closer and eventually, with permission from Haley, was able to sit by her. I asked if Charlie could walk her to my office with the staff member so she could get dressed and perhaps spend some time getting to know Charlie, to which Haley agreed. This became our first therapy session. Through her frequent reference to me as Charlie's mom, I felt Haley could trust me because she witnessed Charlie trusting me as her mother. Through her time with us, Charlie played a significant role in Haley's trauma treatment. Charlie was present in all our play sessions, and supported transitions in Haley's day when needed. Charlie was able to be a safe haven and secure base, which allowed Haley to stay in therapy. Prior to Haley joining us, she had been in four different schools and had at least five different therapists. I truly believe the presence of Charlie is why Haley was able to engage with me in therapy.

Expansion of Potential Space[7]

There are a number of ways in which the integration of animals in a play therapy setting might expand the potential space of children with developmental trauma. A necessary condition for the expansion of the client's potential space is the lowering of anxiety. Studies have found that the presence of animals reduces anxiety, as evidenced by lower cortisol levels (Barker, Knisely, McCain, & Best, 2005; Beetz et al., 2011; Odendaal, 2000;), lower state anxiety (Shiloh, Sorek, & Terkel, 2003), and lower blood pressure (Friedmann, Katcher, Thomas, & Lynch, 1983; Zilcha, Mikulincer, & Shaver, 2012). Based on the literature covered earlier in this chapter, this lowering of anxiety may be achieved through the presence of animals, observing them, or interacting with them in the following ways:

1. The animal may serve as a safe haven should anxiety-producing content become too difficult.
2. Social engagement with the animal has a calming effect on the child.
3. The animal may mediate the interactions between the child and the therapist, or serve as a bridge between the child and the therapist, leading to social engagement between them and eventually to the therapeutic alliance, which in turn lowers anxiety and contributes to the perception of the therapy setting as a safe place.
4. Interacting with the animals, as well as with the therapist, causes the growth of neurological fibers between areas of the brain, creating smoother communication between those areas and balance in the system. The client is better able to find meaning in his actions and emotions, which also leads to the lowering of anxiety and feeling safe (Siegel, 2010).

Once the client feels calmer and safer, she is better able to be open to the ways in which the animals more directly influence the potential space.

1. Serving as a secure base, the animal facilitates the client's exploration of her inner world.
2. Maltreated children are frightened and anxious by the chaos and dangerous content residing in their inner world. Imagination may lead to frightening places and images. They often prefer to stay as close as possible to a world that is predictable and concrete. Animals provide the opportunity for some for unbeknownst forays into the world of play, through interactions with animals who they perceive as concrete and real. Animals have much in common with humans, sharing many of the same characteristics, emotions, behavior, and health aspects. Yet they are not humans, thus, play with them occurs at a safe psychological distance from threatening content, making them safe objects for projection of the client's inner conflicts and confusion, feelings, thoughts, and experiences. The projection onto animals, that is observing their states, actions, and reactions and reflecting and judging them from her (the client's) own context but from the *outside*, can indeed be considered *play* for the sake of working through her issues. This AAP play situation can be considered to be *mindsight*,[8] leading to neural integration (D. Siegel, personal communication, October 4, 2016).
3. A virtual laboratory for relationships, AAP provides opportunities and stimulation for reenacting and working through many types of past and present relationships, within the context of multiple relationships in the here-and-now. Through the therapeutic alliance, the client will be able to receive support in the face of difficult content that arises. The therapist mediates between the child and animal, and between the child and her inner fears, allowing for the working through of the content. Together with the therapist, the client observes them and wonders about them, arrives at insights through this mediation, and tries new options and new strategies within these relationships.
4. Reenactment may sometimes come too close to reexperiencing, thus retraumatizing the client. The interaction with the animals

brings integration, allowing the memories to "move on" so they are sensed as in the past as opposed to in the present. The client may now reenact without refeeling.

5. Integrating animals into the psychotherapy setting allows implicit representations, whether emotions, bodily sensations, perceptions or behaviors, to become activated. When the representations are implicit only, the child does not have a sense of remembering. These emotions, bodily sensations, perceptions, and behaviors may be projected onto the animal. In the words of Daniel Siegel, in AAP,

> The implicit representations are being activated into consciousness, and the social child has enough trust that [the therapist has] created with [the] animal in the therapeutic setting to allow the dance of the implicit representations to enter into the interaction with the pet, with the animal. . . . This is the way mental models and priming also participate in implicit activations and then within consciousness. . . . In this way, clients] can work through their unresolved issues. . . . What is happening then is the hippocampus [underdeveloped due to trauma] of that child is watching the play with the animal and the resolution of . . . why a loving figure would be abusive and working it through in some play where the child goes from helplessness to being empowered, for example. [This] is a push towards integration completely, and a working through [of] these negative states of anger and sadness and fear. . . . Those are decreased states of integration, and the liberation of this working through within the play is actually a movement towards higher states of integration and that's where you get positive emotional states of joy, literally, and empowerment, of 'broaden and build' is what Barbara Frederickson would call it. [AAP offers an] opportunity to let the developmental trauma, with its blocked memory and narrative integration, be opened up. So, in the setting of therapy, integration can be created, neuroplasticity can allow changes to occur. Literally, memory retrieval becomes a memory modifier, as deeper and longer states of integration are created.[9]

Furthermore, this process allows for the translation of implicit knowledge into explicit knowledge, leading to newfound understanding of the origin of sensations and emotions.[10]

6. Mitchell and Aron (Ogden, 1999) state that therapists must "mine their [patient's] potentially rich yield of access points into the patient's inner world" (p. 461). The implications of developmental trauma (anxiety, loss of memory, the threatening nature of contact with traumatic memory of experiences and emotions) often prevent that access to the client's inner world. Due to posits of the biophilia hypothesis, backed up by research that shows that animals may serve as direct access in the inner emotional area of the brain, the right amygdala (Mormann et al., 2011), it can be supposed that clients may be more naturally disposed to be in contact with their inner world in the presence of an animal.

Cozolino (2017) explains that the right amygdala (in conjunction with the right cortex) is involved with the internal emotional experiences of self and other. Furthermore, the right amygdala is likely to be involved with emotional pain, such as shame and loneliness. The right amygdala is also a component of neural circuits related to attachment. Thus, when the right amygdala is activated by the sight of an animal (Mormonn et al., 2011), we can connect with and work on our emotional pain that is associated with attachment issues. This activation of the right amygdala assists us in accessing both positive and negative implicit memories associated with attachment issues that need to be addressed in therapy (L. Cozolino, personal communication, June 15, 2017).

CASE EXAMPLE

Developing safe and healthy relationships with children who have experienced complex trauma can be extremely difficult. Anna challenged me on this point as a therapist from the beginning. Though I worked hard to create a safe therapeutic space for her to engage in play, she was resistant and would not do anything more than engage in the same board game over and over. She even refused to have sessions in the play therapy room, and would only want to meet in my office. Due to her trauma history and explosive anger, I integrated Charlie slowly into our sessions. Initially, Charlie just being present was the focus. I didn't draw attention to it, and I let Charlie and Anna ebb and flow in their interactions. Anna might reach out and pet Charlie while playing the board game. Charlie might walk over to Anna at different times during our session, or she might just lay close by, watching. Or Charlie might come over to me and gently lay her head on my lap while I was focusing on the board game. After several sessions of these interactions, I slowly began to move our sessions to the play room. We would bring the board game with us and keep that consistent, but there was a shift in Anna's reaction to being in the room with Charlie. Anna would spontaneously get up and walk around the room with Charlie to explore the different toys together. Eventually, though the board game was still present, Anna would move right into play. Her play was extremely violent, and she would attack me with toy swords and guns the entire time. With Charlie being present, she was able to receive support and slowly begin to share her trauma history through play. She could attack me, but afterward Charlie was there, a nonthreatening, nonjudging, living being who would sit next to her and just be present. With the support of Charlie, her play was also able to change. In the beginning, her play was raw anger without much of a story. But that story slowly changed, and she began taking the role of protector and protecting Charlie from the "bad people." Though it took a long time, she was able to articulate that she wished she had someone to protect her like she was protecting Charlie. Anna kept a psychological distance from play because she was afraid of what my reactions might be if she truly shared her anger. Charlie was able to increase the safety of our therapeutic space and provide a relationship in which Anna was able to reenact and work through past relationships without fear of repercussion.

Deficit in Ability to Symbolize

Due to the inability of some maltreated children to symbolize, a doll is just a doll—a piece of plastic and cloth. It cannot represent a crying or frightened or happy child. A toy gun is only a piece of plastic with no symbolic meaning. Mentalization and symbolic play will not and cannot take place. Research in the area of mirror neurons helps us understand how clients may unknowingly project themselves onto an animal, allowing for symbolization and the mentalizing to take place for those who otherwise are not able to do so.

The mirror neuron system involves numerous parts of the brain, coding biological motion and integrating sensory information, allowing for actions by one person to become messages understood by another without any cognitive mediation (Acharya & Shukla, 2012). Findings by Iacoboni, Molnar-Szakacs, Gallese, Buccino, & Mazziotta (2005) suggest that mirror neurons hold an active part in understanding the intentions behind observed actions in others. Keysers and Gazzola (2014) suggest this process occurs when the neural substrates of our own actions are vicariously activated while witnessing the actions of others, causing one's mirror neuron system to project oneself onto others with an egocentric bias. Based on the research concerning mirror neurons, Pally (2017) asserts that we understand others based on what we believe we would do in the same situation, and that this process is related to the process of mentalization, or the reflective function.

For those unable to symbolize, it is impossible for them to see a doll as if alive, moving, or having intentions. The mirror neuron system will not be activated, and the client will not project onto the doll. Yet, like a human, an animal moves, breathes, eats, has facial expressions and other body language, approaches clients or hides from them. Animals certainly do have intentions. The movement and behavior of the animal may stimulate the mirror neurons to activity, likely causing the client to unconsciously calculate what she would do in a similar situation, and then ascribe intentions to the animal based on her own personal experience, emotions, needs, thoughts, and sensations.

It is the egocentric bias of the mirror neuron system that may be the basis of conclusions drawn by Pally (2010) that, "Since people use their own intentions to understand the intentions of others, there is often room for misunderstanding" (p. 399). In AAP, as well as other forms of psychodynamic psychotherapy, it is exactly the misunderstanding mentioned by Pally that we as therapists take advantage of. This misunderstanding is the client's projection that will advance the therapy process. We must remember that the AAP setting is not a lesson in animal behavior, nor a lesson in body language or social skills. Rather, we allow and even encourage clients to project their own needs, emotions, feelings, and thoughts onto the animal, and to interpret the animal's behavior according to those needs.[11]

The opportunity provided by the animals for the client to symbolize has both psychotherapeutic and neurobiological advantages. The opportunity to symbolize (albeit unknowingly) allows for the client to create his potential space to work through his issues of trauma. The use of animals to symbolize leads to neurological processes creating neural linkage, leading to integration and contributing to balance, reduction of anxiety, and increased positive functioning.

Justification for assuming parallel processes of mirror neuron activation, and projection of intentions onto humans as well as onto animals, can be found in research by Spunt, Ellsworth, and Adolphs (2017). Employing fMRI scans, they found that attributions of emotion to both humans and to nonhuman animals draw on the same neural mechanism. The researchers conclude that this mechanism is spontaneously activated by participants while observing nonhuman animal facial expressions, even in the absence of explicit verbal cues, which might have caused them to attribute emotion. Furthermore, in a study in which participants watched short video clips of geometric figures interacting with each other, Scheele and colleagues (2015) found that oxytocin concentrations were associated with anthropomorphic tendencies. Higher levels of oxytocin were related to the tendency to attribute social meaning to nonsocial agents and actions. As mentioned earlier, evidence points to a rise in oxytocin in humans when in the presence of animals.

CASE EXAMPLE

I had been trying to engage Brandon in EMDR for a few weeks with no luck. We were stuck in trying to develop a safe or special place as an internal resource. The concept of a safe or special place was to foreign for him; he had never experienced such a place and showed limited ability to use his imagination to create one for himself. In the play therapy setting, Brandon was not even able to relate to the idea of creating a safe place for one of the dolls. One day in session, I decided to ask Brandon if he thought that Charlie ever felt the need for a safe place. That session Brandon built an intricate fort around Charlie in which nothing bad could happen to her. There was no talking that session, and I decided to not use bilateral stimulation that week. The following week, we did the same thing. Brandon worked for an hour straight to build a safe place surrounding Charlie. Slowly over the next several weeks, without noticing, Brandon began to build the fort around himself as well. I was eventually able to introduce alternating bilateral stimulation, and Brandon was able to articulate why the space was so safe for Charlie and him. What was initially too dangerous to think about could now be addressed through the integration of Charlie in play. Brandon was able to initially keep his own defenses up, yet still work though his trauma by assuming what might be needed to keep a dog safe.

From Shame and Presentation of False Self to Self-Acceptance and Expression of True Self

"I'm a cute kid. I can be really nice. But sometimes I can be just like your cockatiel and attack other kids. I can't stop myself. I don't know what is happening to me, and it's so embarrassing!" Children with developmental trauma have often been shamed and humiliated—by others or by themselves—for their behavior, for being a victim, for their family's behavior, or even just for being who they are. In order to take advantage of the therapy process, these children must shed their false selves and be willing to accept and share their feelings about their true selves. This may be a near impossible task for children who feel shame.

According to Porges (2017c), when in a "mammal to mammal" social engagement state, the traumatized client carries within her internal voices that are kind and compassionate, rather than self-condemning. She will feel more self-respect and will be less judgmental toward herself. We feel that AAP facilitates the process in which social engagement leads the child to be less judgmental and more compassionate toward herself, in turn leading to the expression of true self in the therapy process.

In AAP, the client witnesses the relationship between the therapist and the animals, as well as the therapist's attitude toward the animals. While the child might try to hide parts of her true self from the therapist out of shame, the animals unapologetically express their true selves. The hamster might bite, the cockatiel might try to steal treats from a closed box, and the dog might be ugly. The therapist shows love and acceptance for them all, caring for them according to their needs, while openly talking about the full range of the animal's characteristics. Through the client's identification with the animals, and the atmosphere of open discussion in the session in which all subjects are acceptable, she is likely to feel accepted for all her parts. She may then be more willing to discuss them and exhibit them, and will feel less of a need to appease the therapist. Her true self is more likely to show itself, the therapeutic alliance will be strengthened, and then emotional content arising from the true self may be worked through in a more meaningful way.

CASE EXAMPLE

Homelessness, domestic violence, and methamphetamine abuse where just a few of the major experiences James had even before taking a breath in this world. It impacted not only his cognitive functioning, but his sense of self and how he presented to others. Within our therapy sessions, James worked hard for perfection and would not take a lot of chances in case a mistake might be made. His engagement was superficial and initially it was hard to make any therapeutic progress. My relationship with Charlie was the basis for how James began to open up to me. Throughout our sessions, he would see Charlie make "mistakes": spill water out of her bowl, run after a squirrel, bark at geese, and jump up on James to give him kisses, all things some might say a "good" therapy dog would not do.[12] However, those actions played a powerful role in building trust with James because he witnessed firsthand how I continued to accept and love Charlie, while recognizing her for all her different parts. James also noticed how I managed those actions with kind and gentle redirections. Charlie could just be herself without fear. James' internal messages began to shift, and he began to take chances in his play. He would show more affect and his body language was not as closed off.

Back in Touch With Oneself With the Help of AAP

As has been alluded to in many different ways in this chapter, the way back to oneself, from dissociation, from being more concerned with survival, is through social connection. However, when the child interprets danger even

is Charlie provided a stronger reward connection for Matt at a biological level. As a canine, Charlie was more eager to play, and her genuineness was very apparent. Her tail was wagging, and she would pull gently (yes she pulls the leash sometimes) because she was excited about walking with him. In turn, the reward neurons being released in Matt due to playing with Charlie began to help regulate him. Charlie also provided an opportunity for a bottom to top form of regulation (versus a top-down approach), which was very helpful in regulating Matt. She kept the environment safe, which focused on Matt's brainstem. Matt was engaged in a large motor activity that focused on his diencephalon, and the play was relational which, focused on his limbic system. All of these were crucial to help Matt become more regulated.

NEUROLOGICAL EFFECTS OF ALTRUISTIC, CARING, AND COMPASSIONATE BEHAVIOR BY THE THERAPIST AND THE CLIENT ON THE AAP PROCESS AND HEALING FOR THE CLIENT

In his book, *The Neuroscience of Psychotherapy*, Cozolino (2017) contributes greatly to the understanding of psychotherapy in the context of interpersonal neurobiology of trauma. His discussions hold many implications for the field of AAP with those suffering from developmental trauma. A discussion of these implications[13] provides an opportunity to present an integration of many points covered thus far into one coherent model.

There is one phenomenon of AAP that has thus far not been discussed in the context of interpersonal neurobiology, yet is present in every session and has important implications for psychotherapy with those having experienced developmental trauma. In the discussion of the therapeutic alliance, the effects on the client of watching the therapist's empathetic approach to the animals, and caring behavior of the therapist toward the animals, were noted. Cozolino adds more components to our understanding of this mechanism of AAP.

Inherent in AAP therapists is their love of animals in general, and especially for their own animals and those animals with whom they work closely. We often include our clients in the care of the animals, whether it be giving them food and water, cleaning cages, administering medical care, or even taking the client with us on a trip to the vet with a sick or injured animal. Many maltreated clients who live in residential care or in foster homes often work through their experiences of having lived in neglectful conditions at home, or having felt that their needs in their current living situations are not being met, by trying to make better homes for the animals in the therapy setting (i.e., building new cages, making them more fun, safe, comfortable, etc.).

It is this love and caring not only by the therapist, but also by the client that may have healing effects on the traumatized brain. Cozolino (2017) emphasizes the importance of guided altruism in the psychotherapy setting, leading to a cascade of positive effects enhancing success in therapy by activating certain neurobiological and psychological processes, including decreased stress, deeper therapy relationship, increased neural plasticity, increase in self-awareness, self-reflective capacity, perspective-taking, openness to feedback, deeper internalization of the therapeutic experience, increased self-esteem, self-agency, personal responsibility, and empathy.

Here, it is possible that mirror neurons are involved, becoming activated when the client sees the therapist relating empathetically and caring for the animal. Thus, the client feels altruistic through observing the therapist, and through activation of the orbital and medial prefrontal cortex (ompfc) circuitry. The ompfc is considered to be the apex of the attachment circuitry.

Cozolino (2017) writes, "The activation of ompfc circuitry through altruistic behavior will likely stimulate bonding and attachment in situations when the altruist feels safe. *This may explain why taking care of animals often serves as a valuable bridge with people for those with social anxiety or post-traumatic stress disorder. This could be a step toward connection that might allow clients to experiment with more risky relationships with people.* The circuits connecting the ompfc and the amygdala are a central neural target for change in psychotherapy" (p. 268, italics added by this chapter's authors). Here, Cozolino not only provides an explanation of the underlying neurological process involved in the animal serving as a facilitator of the therapeutic alliance in AAP with clients fearing the therapeutic relationship due to developmental trauma, but also points to this relationship as an activator of neural circuits that are essential for change in psychotherapy.

Another consequence of the stimulation by altruistic behavior of the ompfc is that "the ompfc is able to regulate the amygdala and other subcortical structures allowing proximity to caretakers and loved ones to modulate our anxiety and fears" (Cozolino, 2017, p. 268).

From this discussion, one may come to the conclusion that the presence of animals affects the amygdala from two directions: 1) the animals activate the amygdala in the first place (bringing up internal emotions concerning traumatic interactions with others, content that needs to be worked through); and 2) watching the therapist interacting compassionately with the animals permits the client to allow himself to become close to the therapist, modulating the anxiety and fears associated with that emotional content that otherwise would be too threatening and anxiety-producing to recognize and work through. It is the interaction of these two directions that advances the therapy process.[14]

Cozolino (2017) further suggests that since altruistic behaviors activate neural regions associated with bonding and secure attachment, client-therapist collaboration is enhanced, creating brain and mind states allowing for neural growth and learning. Psychological mindfulness inherent in the therapeutic relationship expands self and other awareness through the growth of the use of language[15] and self-reflection. Finally, the client's experience of self may be changed from helpless (a strong factor in trauma) to helpful, from victim to actor. These assertions reinforce and provide neurological bases for some of the roles mentioned in Oren and Parish-Plass (2013) and Parish-Plass and Oren (2013) of animals in AAP, as well as in this chapter, such as animals' roles in decreasing anxiety, facilitating the therapeutic alliance, facilitating play and flexibility through neural plasticity, and increasing the ability of mentalization.

Porges (2017a) suggests an additional therapeutic mechanism involved with showing compassion to others. Allowing and respecting another's right to "own" their experiences of pain and loss enables us to allow and respect our own pain and loss, without experiencing shame. If a child suffering from developmental trauma feels compassionate and acts on that compassion in her caring behavior toward the animal, she may also become compassionate toward herself, accepting and respecting her own loss and emotional pain. This process will enable her to own these feelings and experiences, talk about them with the therapist with whom she participates in the compassionate behavior toward the animals, and work them through within the safe environment provided by AAP. For compassion to develop, Porges emphasizes the need for a "neural platform" enabling one to feel safe when confronted with the pain and suffering of others. In AAP, this sense of safety is provided by the unique qualities of the therapeutic alliance found in AAP, as well as the psychological and physiological consequences of the presence of the animals in the therapy setting that lead to lowering anxiety and a sense of safety, as mentioned earlier in this chapter. This neural platform in AAP may also allow one to feel safe when confronted with one's own pain and suffering (allowing for self-compassion), and may have been found in research by Klimecki, Leiberg, Ricard, & Singer (2014), which showed that compassion training leads to neural plasticity and activation in a nonoverlapping brain network, which they conclude leads to resilience.

Another positive implication of compassionate behavior may be extrapolated from 2010 research by Feldman and her colleagues on the effects of fathers' active participation in childrearing. Whereas a mother's caretaking behavior toward her newborn infant is initiated by the release of oxytocin as a result of the birth process, the father has no such physiological impetus leading to caretaking behavior toward the infant. Feldman, Gordon, Schneiderman, Weisman, & Zagoory-Sharon (2010) found a bio-behavioral feedback loop in which a father's touch and contact with his infant increases his levels of oxytocin, which in turn results in more touch and contact within the attachment relationship. In light of this research, it may be assumed that the same bio-behavioral feedback loop exists in AAP when the client participates in compassionate care of an animal. The rise in oxytocin resulting from this compassionate care of animals is then likely to lead to the positive implications of oxytocin mentioned earlier for the therapy process, such as trust in the therapist, the ability to stay in the otherwise anxiety-producing therapy situation, sharing of emotions, regulation, and more.

Reinforcing the implications of compassionate behavior toward animals for the healing from trauma, Zimrin (1986) found in her study of childhood maltreatment survivors that two predictors of successful functioning later in life were: 1) the presence of an empathetic adult, either at the time of the trauma or later in long-term psychotherapy, and 2) if, as a child, the subject was responsible for taking care of a sibling or a pet.

CONCLUSIONS

Although the two areas, psychotherapy and interpersonal neurobiology, grew from different theoretical backgrounds and different research bases, they have reached many of the same conclusions, perhaps most notably in their emphasis on the need for social connection for both prevention of and healing from trauma. Many times, professionals in fields that may parallel each other are competitive, invested in proving how their field is unique and contributes more than others to the understanding of the issues. Certainly this is true today, for instance, in the ongoing struggle between cognitive behavioral therapy (CBT) and psychodynamic clinical psychology. Through mutual respect, openness, curiosity, a desire to learn from each other, and a genuine interest in helping survivors of trauma, today's neurobiology researchers and mental health clinicians have come together. They are finding commonality in such a way that encourages growth, integrating the two fields in such a way that raises both to higher levels of functioning. Similar to the concept posited by Dan Siegel (2012), the fields of neuroscience and psychotherapy are creating linkages while respecting differences, leading to growth and health.

One way we see the similarity between the two fields is through their emphases on similar concepts. While Bowlby discussed terms such as attachment, security vs. insecurity, anxious and avoidant, Porges and Siegel both discuss social engagement, safety, dysregulation, and flight. A child can use social engagement to diffuse the tendency toward fight/flight in a threatening situation. Bowlby refers to attachment figures as a safe haven in the time of threat. Herman posits that trauma heals only in the context of relationships. Porges and Siegel discuss the importance of relationships as they buffer the child with developmental trauma from the effects of trauma, and lead to neural integration and regulation in healing from trauma. Winnicott discusses the potential space as a way for the child to be in touch with her inner world and play it out within a safe relationship. Cozolino refers to the default mode network, which, when the client feels no threat, allows him to be in touch with his inner world and imaginal space in a flow of time.

A history of developmental trauma raises many barriers to therapy with these clients. The integration of animals into the psychotherapy setting circumvents some of these barriers and lowers others. In an attempt to help the clinician understand the mechanisms of AAP in working with clients with developmental trauma, we have described six barriers and delineated possible solutions provided by AAP to each one of them. However, the separation between them is artificial, made for the sake of clearer explanation, and they are all interconnected and even mutually influencing each other. In addition, any given solution often relies on a number of other solutions.

For instance, the creation of a narrative is dependent on the existence of potential space, for which the client must feel safe in the setting, and which is partially dependent upon the establishment of the therapeutic alliance. Once the client feels safe, she will be more likely to set aside the false presentation of her true self and allow for the expansion of potential space, as well as feel in touch with her inner self, where she can discover her own story through play. At this point, through integration, she will self-regulate.

However, the client with developmental trauma may have the inclination to refuse therapy, not take advantage of the therapy, or drop out of therapy, due to a sense of danger she feels when in a room alone with a therapist. How might animals facilitate the therapy process?

- An animal in the therapy may be a target for social engagement, helping to diffuse the flight impulse.
- The client will feel more secure to explore herself through this social engagement with the animal as a secure base, and will retreat to the animal as a safe haven when she feels too overwhelmed.
- The therapy setting itself will feel more authentic with the animal acting naturally in the room, and both the therapist and client interacting with the animal in a genuine and spontaneous way.
- The client notices the care given to the animals by the therapist, and that the animals look to the therapist for fun but also for compassion, help, and safety. The animal will thus facilitate the establishment of the therapeutic alliance with the therapist, making the therapy setting feel even safer.
- The client may find it very difficult to play due to the anxiety-producing content of her inner world. Interaction with the animals will have physiological, neurological, and psychological effects on the client, lowering the child's anxiety level.
- The activation of the right amygdala through being with the animals serves as an access point to the client's inner emotional experiences, especially as related to relationships with others.
- Altruistic behavior of the therapist, together with the client, stimulates a feeling of safety and bonding between the two, allowing the therapeutic relationship to modulate the client's

anxieties and fears, facilitating the ability of the client to face and work through difficult emotional content.

- The client may have difficulty symbolizing due to the early age of her trauma. The animals may serve as targets for her projections, through the activation of mirror neurons and her identification with the animals, allowing for play with the animals from a safe psychological distance.

- The potential space is expanded by the calming effect of the animal on the client, as well as by the default mode network activated in an environment perceived by the client as safe due to the relationships of the therapist with the animals. Due to the acceptance of the client by the animal and the therapist, the client will feel that she can present her real self that she had previously kept hidden due to shame.

- The client will now feel safe enough to be more in touch with herself, hidden inside even from herself. The animal's characteristics will stimulate the client's sensory system through smell, sound, touch, and movement. She will begin to find words for her experiences and her emotions, and will start to develop a narrative. The therapist will be present for the client, empathetically reflecting the content and helping the client make sense of the story that is developing.

- Through 1) social engagement with the therapist and also with the animal, 2) the expansion of the potential space and ability to play and find words for self-expression, 3) implicit representations that can be transformed into explicit memories and be worked through, and 4) the discovery of a coherent narrative, the client will achieve integration and self-regulation.

- The sight of, and a relationship with, an animal activate neural circuits (with the right amygdala as a component) related to attachment. The activation and development of this circuitry can possibly be used in subsequent relationships with others (L. Cozolino, personal communication, June 15, 2017). This process will allow social behavior learned in the therapy setting to be exported to the client's relationships outside of therapy.

Although the field of AAP is now becoming recognized by interpersonal neurobiologists and acknowledged as beneficial for those having experienced developmental trauma, only one neurobiologist, Bruce Perry of the ChildTrauma Academy, is known to actually employ AAP in his work. Perry's Neurosequential Model of Therapeutics (NMT) takes into account the key systems and areas in the brain affected by adverse developmental experiences. In his centers for maltreated children, Perry (2013) identifies therapeutic goals in four functional domains that are meant to reach these areas of the brain and have a reparative effect on them.

Perry suggests that AAP may help reach three of these domains (sensory integration, self-regulation, and relational), leading to the integration of the related areas of the brain, which is essential in the healing of the child suffering from trauma (Siegel, 2003). 1) Animals aid the sensory integration domain by helping the client get in touch with her true self through sensory stimulation (movement, smell, sight, sound, and touch). 2) Animals aid the self-regulation domain by helping the client present her true self through acting it out in play due to an expanded potential space, and learning to interact with the animals in an attuned and appropriate way. 3) Animals aid the relational domain by creating an atmosphere of participation in different relationships (between child and animals, between the therapist and animals, between the child and the therapist, and even between animals). The child learns to trust the therapist through observing the positive, caring, and respectful relationship between the therapist and the animals.

Porges (2017b) emphasizes the biological imperative for humans to achieve safety through coregulation of physiological state, enabled by relationships and interaction with other appropriate mammals. He queries as to how we can get the nervous system to spontaneously engage in a healthy way. In this context, Porges predicts that, "Trauma treatment may move to working with dogs, horses, and other mammals" (Porges, 2017b, p. 196). We claim that the future is already here.

Animal-assisted psychotherapy is a growing field worldwide; however, there are many misunderstandings surrounding the profession (Parish-Plass, 2017). It is important to expand the understanding of the mechanisms involved in this type of psychotherapy through theory-building, research, and clinical reporting. This chapter lends support to the view that AAP adds a unique contribution as a relational therapy for children who have experienced developmental trauma, especially for those children who are avoidantly attached and resist the establishment of the therapeutic alliance.

ACKNOWLEDGMENTS

We would like to warmly thank Daniel Siegel, Stephen Porges, Louis Cozolino, and Sue Carter for their generous and supportive comments on the ideas presented in this chapter.

NOTES

1. Considered to be the key to successful therapy, the therapeutic alliance is made up by the mutual agreement by the therapist and client concerning the goals of the therapy, the methods used to reach these goals, and therapist-client bond (Bordin, 1979). In children, this bond is the main, if not only, element of the therapeutic alliance (Fjermestad et al., 2012). For the therapeutic alliance to be established, the client must feel that the therapist is empathetic, supportive, trustworthy, authentic, and genuinely interested in the good of the client, and everything that the therapist does is toward that end. It could also be said that the therapist will serve as a safe haven and a secure base for the client.

2. Winnicott (1965) referred to the authentic and spontaneous real self vs. the false self, developed as a defense mechanism against impingement, as a painful and intrusive experience of the real self, leading to disconnectedness and a feeling of inner emptiness.

3. Bellak (Bellak & Abrams, 1996) developed the widely used projective Children's Apperception Test (similar to the adult Thematic Apperception Test—TAT) based on the tendency of children to identify with animals.

4. Examples of identification with animals in therapy facilitating the therapeutic alliance may be seen in Parish-Plass, 2008.

5. This assertion is dependent upon the degree to which the animals are perceived to be "safe" by the client.

6. This explanation throughout this chapter of the effects of oxytocin would be incomplete without a description of the interaction between oxytocin and vasopressin, and their receptors, both components of an integrated neural system regulating social behavior. The interactions of the two neuropeptides supply a more complete explanation of the importance of social behavior in the regulation of anxiety and responses to threats. At optimal levels, both oxytocin and vasopressin may contribute to the dampening of social

anxiety, which would permit the approach to unfamiliar others. Furthermore, both oxytocin and vasopressin systems are also affected by early life experiences, in turn affecting their regulation of social behavior across the life span. According to Sue Carter (personal communication, August 31, 2017), "These complex interactions are only now becoming apparent, but may in time help to predict when animal-assisted therapies will be most helpful." For further discussion, see Carter (2017).

7. For further discussion on the effects of animals on the potential space, see Parish-Plass, 2013b.

8. Mindsight is a term used by Daniel Siegel referring to insight into one's own mind and into the mind of others. It is a way of focusing on and being aware of the nature of one's inner world (Siegel, 2009, 2010).

9. This quote is taken from an online Q&A session (October 4, 2016), as part of an online course with Dr. Dan Siegel on the subject of the interpersonal neurobiology of trauma and healing of trauma. The quote is part of Siegel's answer to Parish-Plass's question: "I am an AAP therapist working in an emergency shelter for at-risk children. Many of these children are characterized by a high level of anxiety and are unable to play, for contact with their inner world is far too threatening. I often see the children projecting their emotions, their stories, onto the animals and working through their issues in this way. Can this be considered to be play (in the therapeutic sense), leading to integration? Any insights of yours will be helpful."

10. For further discussion on the subject of the mentalization and translation of implicit knowledge into explicit knowledge through AAP, see Shani, 2017.

11. While we are interested in the client fulfilling his own needs for the therapy process through the animals present in the setting, it is essential and ethically critical that the animal's needs are always kept in mind, and that they will always be protected. The AAP therapist must be constantly aware of the difference between projective play with the animal that is harmless and that which has the potential to cause any harm or unnecessary stress to the animal, and prevent that from occurring.

12. We prefer an untrained dog with a temperament appropriate for taking part in therapy, rather than a well-trained dog. We are more interested in dogs with authentic behavior, rather than obedient behavior.

13. This discussion is based on a series of personal communications with Cozolino, whose enthusiasm and willingness to help us arrive to a greater understanding of the material and its implications for AAP is highly appreciated.

14. It is important to realize that all of these processes involve not only the amygdala and the ompfc, but also the autonomic and polyvagal nervous systems as well (L. Cozolino, personal communication, June 15, 2017).

15. It was mentioned earlier that developmental trauma leads to a deficit in emotional language and a fear of verbalizing.

REFERENCES

Acharya, S., & Shukla, S. (2012). Mirror neurons: Enigma of the metaphysical modular brain. *Journal of Natural Science, Biology, and Medicine, 3,* 118–124.

Ainsworth, M. D. (1985). Patterns of infant-mother attachments: Antecedents and effects on development. *Bulletin of the New York Academy of Medicine, 61,* 771.

Alink, L., Cicchetti, D., Kim, J., & Rogosch, F. (2012). Longitudinal associations among child maltreatment, social functioning, and cortisol regulation. *Developmental Psychology, 48,* 224–236.

Aoki, J., Kazuhiko, I., Ishigooka, J., Fukamauchi, F., Numajiri, M., & Ohtani, N. (2012). Evaluation of cerebral activity in the prefrontal cortex in mood [affective] disorders during animal-assisted therapy (AAT) by near-infrared spectroscopy (NIRS): A pilot study. *International Journal of Psychiatry in Clinical Practice, 16*(3), 205–13.

Axline, V. (1969). *Play therapy.* New York, NY: Ballantine.

Bachi, K. (2013). Equine-facilitated psychotherapy: Practice, theory and empirical knowledge. In N. Parish-Plass (Ed.), *Animal-Assisted Psychotherapy: Theory, Issues, and Practice* (pp. 221–241). West Lafayette, IN: Purdue University Press.

Bachi, K., Terkel, J., & Teichman, M. (2012). Equine-facilitated psychotherapy for at-risk adolescents: The influence on self-image, self-control and trust. *Clinical Child Psychology and Psychiatry, 17*(2), 298–312.

Balluerka, N., Muela, A., Amiano, N., & Caldentey, M. A. (2014). Influence of animal-assisted therapy (AAT) on the attachment representations of youth in residential care. *Children and Youth Services Review, 42,* 103–109.

Banks, A. (2006). Relational therapy for trauma. *Journal of Trauma Practice, 5*(1).

Barker, S. B., Knisely, J. S., McCain, N. L., & Best, A. M. (2005). Measuring stress and immune responses in health care professionals following interaction with a therapy dog: A pilot study. *Psychological Report, 96,* 713–729.

Beetz, A., Kotrschal, K., Turner, D. C., Hediger, K., Uvnäs-Moberg, K., & Julius,

H. (2011). The effect of a real dog, toy dog and friendly person on insecurely attached children during a stressful task: An exploratory study. *Anthrozoös, 24*(4), 349–368.

Bellak, L., & Abrams, D. M. (1996). *The T.A.T., the C.A.T., and the S.A.T. in clinical use* (6th ed.). Needham Heights, MA: Allyn & Bacon.

Bickart, K. C., Wright, C. I., Dautoff, R. J., Dickerson, B. C., & Barrett, L. F. (2011). Amygdala volume and social network size in humans. *Nature Neuroscience, 14*(2), 163–164. https://doi.org/10.1038/nn.2724

Bluhm, R. L., Williamson, P. C., Osuch, E. A., Frewen, P. A., Stevens, T. K., Boksman, K., . . . Lanius, R. A. (2009). Alterations in default network connectivity in posttraumatic stress disorder related to early-life trauma. *Journal of Psychiatry & Neuroscience: JPN, 34*(3), 187–94.

Bona, E., & Courtnage, G. (2014). The impact of animals and nature for children and youth with trauma histories: Towards a neurodevelopmental theory. In T. Ryan (Ed.), *Animals in social work* (pp. 105–119). UK: Palgrave Macmillan.

Bordin, E. S. (1979). The generalizability of the psychoanalytic concept of the working alliance. *Psychotherapy: Theory, Research & Practice, 16*(3), 252–260. https://doi.org/10.1037/h0085885

Bowlby, J. (1969). *Attachment and loss: Attachment (Vol. 1).* New York, NY: Basic Books.

Bowlby, J. (1973). *Attachment and loss. Separation: Anxiety and anger (Vol. 2).* New York, NY: Basic Books.

Bowlby, J. (1980). *Attachment and loss: Sadness and depression (Vol. 3).* New York, NY: Basic Books.

Bowlby, J. (1988). *A secure base: Clinical applications of attachment theory.* London, UK: Routledge.

Bretherton, I., & Munholland, K. A. (1999). Internal working models in attachment relationships: A construct revisited. In J. Cassidy, & P. R. Shaver (Eds.), *Handbook of attachment: Theory, research and clinical applications* (pp. 226–248). New York, NY: Guilford Press.

Briere, J. (1988). The long-term clinical correlates of childhood sexual victimization. *Annals of the New York Academy of Sciences, 528,* 327–334.

Buchheim A., Heinrichs, M., George, C., Pokorny, D., Koops, E., Henningsen, P., O'Connor, M., & Gundel, H. (2009). Oxytocin enhances the experience of attachment security. *Psychoneuroendocrinology, 34,* 1417–1422.

Carter, C. (1998). Neuroendocrine perspectives on social attachment and love. *Psychoneuroendocrinology, 23,* 779–818.

Carter, C. S. (2017). The role of oxytocin and vasopressin in attachment. *Psychodynamic Psychiatry, 45,* 499–518.

Carter, C. S., & Porges, S. W. (2016). Neural mechanisms underlying human-animal interaction: An evolutionary perspective. In L. Freund, S. McCune, L. Esposito, N. Gee, & P. McCardle (Eds.), *The social neuroscience of human-animal interaction* (pp. 89–105). Washington, DC: American Psychological Association.

Chandler, C. (2017). *Animal-assisted therapy in counseling* (3rd ed.). New York, NY: Routledge.

Chang, S. W. C., Fagan, N. A., Toda, K., Utevsky, A. V., Pearson, J. M., & Platt, M. L. (2015). Neural mechanisms of social decision-making in the primate amygdala. *Proceedings of the National Academy of Sciences, 112*(52), 16012–16017. https://doi.org/10.1073/pnas.1514761112

Chemtob, C. M., Novaco, R. N., Hamada, R. N., & Gross, D. (1997). Cognitive-behavioral treatment of severe anger in posttraumatic stress disorder. *Journal of Consulting and Clinical Psychology, 65*, 184–189.

Child Welfare Information Gateway. (2001). *Understanding the effects of maltreatment on early brain development.* Retrieved from https://www.childwelfare.gov/pubPDFs/earlybrain.pdf

Cicchetti, D. (1990). The organization and coherence of socioemotional, cognitive, and representational development: Illustrations through a developmental psychopathology perspective on Down syndrome and maltreatment. In R.A. Thompson (Ed.), *Socioemotional Development* (pp. 256–366). Lincoln, NE: University of Nebraska Press.

Cicchetti, D. (2002). The impact of social experience on neurobiological systems: Illustration from a constructivist view of child maltreatment. *Cognitive Development, 17*, 1407–1428.

Cloitre, M., Stovall-McClough, C. K., Miranda, R., & Chemtob, C. M. (2004). Therapeutic alliance, negative mood regulation, and treatment outcome in child abuse-related posttraumatic stress disorder. *Journal of Consulting and Clinical Psychology, 72*(3), 411–6. https://doi.org/10.1037/0022-006X.72.3.411

Cook, A., Spinazzola, J., Ford, J., Lanktree, C., Blaustein, M., Cloitre, M., DeRosa, R., Hubbard, R., Kagan, R., Liautaud, J., Mallah, K., Olafson, E., & van der Kolk, B. (2005). Complex trauma in children and adolescents. *Psychiatric Annals, 35*(5), 390–398. https://doi.org/10.3928/00485713-20050501-05

Corson, S., Corson, E., Gwynne, P., & Arnold, E. (1977). Pet dogs as non-verbal communication links in hospital psychiatry. *Comprehensive Psychiatry, 18*, 61–72.

Cozolino, L. (2017). *The neuroscience of psychotherapy: Healing the social brain* (3rd ed.). New York, NY: W. W. Norton.

Crittenden, P. M. (2006). Why do inadequate parents do what they do? In O.

Mayseless (Ed.), *Parenting representations: Theory, research and clinical implications* (pp. 388–433). Cambridge, UK: Cambridge University Press.

Daniels, J., Frewen, P., McKinnon, M., & Lanius, R. (2011). Default mode alterations in posttraumatic stress disorder related to early-life trauma: A developmental perspective. *Journal of Psychiatry & Neuroscience, 36*, 56–59.

De Bellis, M. D., & Zisk, A. (2014). The biological effects of childhood trauma. *Child and Adolescent Psychiatric Clinics of North America, 23*(2), 185–222. https://doi.org/10.1016/j.chc.2014.01.002

Dietz, T. J., Davis, D., & Pennings, J. (2012). Evaluating animal-assisted therapy in group treatment for child sexual abuse. *Journal of Child Sexual Abuse, 21*(6), 665–683.

Eames, V., & Roth, A. (2000). Patient attachment orientation and the early working alliance—A study of patient and therapist reports of alliance quality and ruptures. *Psychotherapy Research, 10*(4), 421–434.

Fair, D., Cohen A., Dosenbach N., Church, J., Miezin, F., Barch, D., Raichle, M., Peterson, S., & Schlaggar, B. (2008). The maturing architecture of the brain's default network. *Proceedings of the National Academy of Sciences of the United States of America, 105*, 4028–32.

Fairbairn, W. R. D. (1944). Endopsychic structure considered in terms of object-relationships. *The International Journal of Psycho-Analysis, 25*, 70.

Feiring, C., & Taska, L. S. (2005). The persistence of shame following sexual abuse: A longitudinal look at risk and recovery. *Child Maltreatment, 10*(4), 337–349. https://doi.org/10.1177/1077559505276686

Feldman, R., Gordon, I., Schneiderman, I., Weisman, O., & Zagoory-Sharon, O. (2010). Natural variations in maternal and paternal care are associated with systematic changes in oxytocin following parent-infant contact. *Psychoneuroendocrinology, 35*, 1133–1141.

Fine, A. H. (2017). Standing the test of time: Reflecting on the relevance today of Levinson's pet-oriented child psychotherapy. *Clinical Child Psychology and Psychiatry, 22*(1), 9–15.

Finger, S. (1994). *Origins of neuroscience: A history of explorations into brain function.* Oxford, UK: Oxford University Press.

Fjermestad, K. W., McLeod, B. D., Heiervang, E. R., Havik, O. E., Öst, L. G., & Haugland, B. S. M. (2012). Factor structure and validity of the therapy process observational coding system for child psychotherapy-alliance scale. *Journal of Clinical Child and Adolescent Psychology, 41*(2), 246–254.

Freud, A. (1965). *The psych-analytical treatment of children.* New York, NY: International Universities Press.

Friedmann, E., Katcher, A. H., Thomas, S. A., Lynch, J. J., & Messent, P. R. (1983). Social interaction and blood pressure: Influence of animal companions. *Journal of Nervous and Mental Disease, 171*, 461–465.

Gaskill, R. L., & Perry, B. (2014). The neurobiological power of play. In C. Malchiodi, & D. Crenshaw (Eds.), *Creative Arts and Play Therapy for Attachment Problems* (pp. 178–194). New York, NY: Guilford Press.

Geller, S. M., & Porges, S. W. (2014). Therapeutic presence: Neurophysiological mechanisms mediating feeling safe in therapeutic relationships. *Journal of Psychotherapy Integration, 24*(3), 178–192. https://doi.org/10.1037/a0037511

Gelso, C., & Carter, J. (1985). The relationship in counseling and psychotherapy: Components, consequences, and theoretical antecedents. *The Counseling Psychologist, 13*, 155–243.

Gil, E. (2017). *Posttraumatic play in children.* New York, NY: Guilford Press.

Gil, E., & Terr, L. (2013). *Working with children to heal interpersonal trauma: The power of play.* New York, NY: Guilford Press.

Gioia, K., & Tobin, R. (2010). The role of sociodramatic play in promoting self-regulation. In C. Schaefer (Ed.), *Play therapy for preschool children* (pp. 181–198). Washington, DC: American Psychological Association.

González-Ramírez, T., Ortiz, X., & Landero-Hernández, R. (2013). Cognitive-behavioral therapy and animal-assisted therapy: Stress management for adults. *Alternative and Complementary Therapies, 19*, 270–275.

Goodyear-Brown, P. (2010). *Play therapy with traumatized children.* Hoboken, NJ: John Wiley & Sons.

Green, J. (2006). Annotation: The therapeutic alliance—A significant but neglected variable in child mental health treatment studies. *Journal of Child Psychology and Psychiatry and Allied Disciplines, 47*(5), 425–435.

Grinker, R. (2013). My father's analysis with Sigmund Freud. In J. A. Winer, & J. W. Anderson (Eds.), *The Annual of Psychoanalysis: Sigmund Freud and His Impact on the Modern World* (Vol. 29, pp. 35–50). Hillsdale, NJ: The Analytic Press.

Harel, O. (2013). Animal-assisted group therapy for children. In N. Parish-Plass (Ed.), *Animal-assisted psychotherapy: Theory, issues, and practice* (pp. 413–430). Lafayette, IN: Purdue University Press.

Hasson, U., Ghazanfar, A. A., Galantucci, B., Garrod, S., & Keysers, C. (2012). Brain to brain coupling: A mechanism for creating and sharing a social world. *Trends in Cognitive Sciences, 16*, 114–121.

Heim, C., Newport, D. J., Mletzko, T., Miller, A. H., Young, L. J., & Nemeroff, C. B. (2006). Decreased cerebrospinal fluid oxytocin concentrations associated with childhood maltreatment in adult women. *Developmental Psychobiology Abstract, 48*, 603–630.

Heinrichs, M., Baumgartner, T., Kirschbaum, C., & Ehlert, U. (2003). Social support and oxytocin interact to suppress cortisol and subjective responses to psychosocial stress. *Biological Psychiatry, 54*(12), 1389–1398. https://doi.org/10.1016/S0006-3223(03)00465-7

Heinrichs, M., von Dawans, B., & Domes, G. (2009). Oxytocin, vasopressin, and human social behavior. *Frontiers in Neuroendocrinology, 30*(4), 548–557.

Herman, J. (1997). *Trauma and recovery*. New York, NY: Basic Books.

Herman, J., Russell, R., & Trocki, K. (1986). Long-term effects of incestuous abuse in childhood. *American Journal of Psychiatry, 143*, 1293–1296.

Herman, J. L. (1992). Complex PTSD: A syndrome in survivors of prolonged and repeated trauma. *Journal of Traumatic Stress, 5*(3), 377–391.

Hershkowitz, I., Horowitz, D., & Lamb, M. E. (2005). Trends in children's disclosure of abuse in Israel: A national study. *Child Abuse and Neglect, 29*(11), 1203–1214. https://doi.org/10.1016/j.chiabu.2005.04.008

Huber, D., Veinante, P., & Stoop, R. (2005). Vasopressin and oxytocin excite distinct neuronal populations in the central amygdala. *Science, 308*(5719), 245–248.

Iacoboni, M., Molnar-Szakacs, I., Gallese, V., Buccino, G., & Mazziotta, J. C. (2005). Grasping the intentions of others with one's own mirror neuron system. In *PLOS Biology, 3*(3), e79. https://doi.org/10.1371/journal.pbio.0030079

Ish-Lev, H., & Amit, R. (2013). Elements of group psychotherapy found in individual animal-assisted psychotherapy. In N. Parish-Plass (Ed.), *Animal-assisted psychotherapy: Theory, issues, and practice* (pp. 145–169). Lafayette, IN: Purdue University Press.

Jenkins, S. (2013). The equiLateral protocol: The first EMDR protocol to integrate animal assisted therapy. Presentation at the 18th EMDR International Association Conference, Austin, TX.

Kellert, S. R., & Wilson, E. O. (Eds.). (1993). *The biophilia hypothesis*. Washington, DC: Island Press.

Keysers, C., & Gazzola, V. (2014). Hebbian learning and predictive mirror neurons for actions, sensations and emotions. *Philosophical Transactions of the Royal Society B: Biological Sciences, 369*, 20130175. https://doi.org/10.1098/rstb.2013.0175

Kirby, M. (2010). Gestalt equine psychotherapy. *Gestalt Journal of Australia and New Zealand, 6*, 60–68.

Kivlighan, D. M., Patton, M. J., & Foote, D. (1998). Moderating effects of client attachment on the counselor experience—working alliance relationship. *Journal of Counseling Psychology, 45*, 274–278.

Klein, M. (1932). *The psychoanalysis of children.* New York, NY: Delacorte Press.

Klimecki, O. M., Leiberg, S., Ricard, M., & Singer, T. (2014). Differential pattern of Functional brain plasticity after compassion and empathy training. *Social Cognitive and Affective Neuroscience, 9*, 873–879.

Kosfeld, M., Heinrichs, M., Zak, P. J., Fischbacher, U., & Fehr, E. (2005). Oxytocin increases trust in humans. *Nature, 435*(7042), 673–676.

Lac, V. (2016). Horsing around: Gestalt equine psychotherapy as humanistic play therapy. *Journal of Humanistic Psychology, 56*, 194–209.

Landreth, G. (2012). *Play therapy: The art of the relationship* (3rd ed.). New York, NY: Routledge.

Lane, A., Luminet, O., Rime, B., Gross, J., de Timary, P., & Mikolajczak, M. (2012). Oxytocin increases willingness to socially share one's emotions. *International Journal of Psychology, 48*, 676–681.

Levinson, B. (1962). The dog as a "co-therapist." *Mental Hygiene, 46*, 59–65.

Levinson, B. (1965). Pet psychotherapy: Use of household pets in the treatment of behavior disorder in childhood. *Psychological Reports, 17*, 695–698.

Levinson, B. (1984). Human/companion animal therapy. *Journal of Contemporary Psychotherapy, 14*, 131–144.

Levinson, B., & Mallon, G. (1997). *Pet-oriented psychotherapy* (2nd ed.). Springfield, IL: Charles C. Thomas Publisher.

Lev-Wiesel, R., Eisikovits, Z., First, M., Gottfried, R., & Mehlhausen, D. (2016). Prevalence of child maltreatment in Israel: A national epidemiological study. *Journal of Child & Adolescent Trauma, 11*(2), 141–150.

Levy, A. (2011). Psychoanalytic approaches to play therapy. In C. Schaefer (Ed.), *Foundations of play therapy* (2nd ed., pp. 43–59), Hoboken, NJ: John Wiley & Sons.

Lockwood, R. (1983). The influence of animals on social perception. In A. Katcher & A. Beck (Eds.), *New perspectives on our lives with companion animals.* Philadelphia, PA: University of Pennsylvania Press.

Lopez, F. G., Melendez, M. C., Sauer, E. M., Berger, E., & Wyssmann, J. (1998). Internal working models, self-reported problems, and help-seeking attitudes among college students. *Journal of Counseling Psychology, 45*, 79–83.

Ludy-Dobson, C. R., & Perry, B. D. (2010). The role of healthy relational interactions in buffering the impact of childhood trauma. In E. Gil, & L. Terr (Eds.), *Working with Children to Heal Interpersonal Trauma: The Power of Play* (pp. 26–43). New York, NY: Guilford Press.

Maayan, E. (2013). The therapy zoo as a mirror to the psyche. In N. Parish-Plass (Ed.), *Animal-assisted psychotherapy: Theory, issues, and practice* (pp. 171–220). West Lafayette, IN: Purdue University Press.

Mallinckrodt, B. (1991). Client's representations of childhood emotional bonds with parents, social support, and formation of the working alliance. *Journal of Counseling Psychology, 38,* 401–409.

Mallinckrodt, B., Gantt, D., & Coble, H. (1995). Attachment patterns in the psychotherapy relationship: Development of the client attachment to therapist scale. *Journal of Counseling Psychology, 42,* 307–317.

Mallinckrodt, B., McCreary, B., & Robertson, A. (1995). Co-occurrence of eating disorders and incest: The role of attachment, family environment, and social competencies. *Journal of Counseling Psychology, 42,* 178–186.

McNicholas, J., & Collis, G. (2000). Dogs as catalysts for social interactions: Robustness of the effect. *British Journal of Psychology, 9,* 61–70.

Messent, P. (1983). Social facilitation of contact with other people by pet dogs. In A. Katcher, & A. Beck (Eds.), *New perspectives on our lives with companion animals.* Philadelphia, PA: University of Pennsylvania Press.

Meyer-Lindenberg, A. (2008). Impact of prosocial neuropeptides on human brain function. *Progress in Brain Research, 170,* 463–470.

Mikulincer, M., & Shaver, P. (2010). Implications of attachment theory and research for counseling and psychotherapy. In M. Mikulincer, & P. Shaver (Eds.), *Attachment in adulthood: Structure, dynamics, and change* (pp. 405–432). New York, NY: Guilford Press.

Mormann, F., Dubois, J., Kornblith, S., Milosavljevic, M., Cerf, M., Ison, M., . . . Koch, C. (2011). A category-specific response to animals in the right human amygdala. *Nature Neuroscience, 14*(10), 1247–1249. https://doi.org/10.1038/nn.2899

Muela, A., Balluerka, N., Amiano, N., Caldentey, M. A., & Aliri, J. (2017). Animal-assisted psychotherapy for young people with behavioural problems in residential care. *Clinical Psychology & Psychotherapy, 24,* O1485-O1494.

Murphy, R. A., Sink, H. E., Ake, G. S., Carmody, K. A., Amaya-Jackson, L. M., & Briggs, E. C. (2014). Predictors of treatment completion in a sample of youth who have experienced physical or sexual trauma. *Journal of Interpersonal Violence, 29,* 3–19. https://doi.org/10.1177/0886260513504495

Nagasawa, M., Kikusui, T., Onaka, T., & Ohta, M. (2009). Dog's gaze at its owner increases owner's urinary oxytocin during social interaction. *Hormones and Behavior, 55*(3), 434–441. https://doi.org/10.1016/j.yhbeh.2008.12.002

Neumann, I. (2002). Involvement of the brain oxytocin system in stress coping: Interactions with the hypothalamo-pituitary-adrenal axis. *Progress in Brain Research, 139*, 147–162.

Odendaal, J. S. J. (2000). Animal-assisted therapy: Magic or medicine? *Journal of Psychosomatic Research, 49*, 275–280.

Ogden, T. H. (1999). The analytic third: Working with intersubjective clinical facts. In S. A. Mitchell, & A. Aron (Eds.), *Relational psychoanalysis: The emergence of a tradition* (pp. 459–92). Hillsdale, NJ: Analytic Press.

Olff, M., Langeland, W., Witteveen, A., & Denys, D. (2010). A psychobiological rationale for oxytocin in the treatment of posttraumatic stress disorder. *CNS Spectrums, 15*(8), 522–530.

Oren, D., & Parish-Plass, N. (2013). The integration of animals into the therapy process and its implications as a unique medium in psychotherapy. In N. Parish-Plass (Ed.) *Animal-assisted psychotherapy: Theory, issues, and practice* (pp. 3–45). West Lafayette, IN: Purdue University Press.

Pally, R. (2010). The brain's shared circuits of interpersonal understanding: Implications for psychoanalysis and psychodynamic psychotherapy. *Journal of the American Academy of Psychoanalysis and Dynamic Psychiatry, 38*, 381–412.

Pally, R. (2017). *The reflective parent: How to do less and relate more with your kids.* New York, NY: W. W. Norton.

Parish, M., & Eagle, M. (2003). Attachment to the therapist. *Psychoanalytic Psychology, 20*(2), 271–286.

Parish-Plass, N. (2008). Animal-assisted therapy with children suffering from insecure attachment due to abuse and neglect: A method to lower the risk of intergenerational transmission of abuse? *Clinical Child Psychology and Psychiatry, 13*(1), 7–30. https://doi.org/10.1177/1359104507086338

Parish-Plass, N. (Ed.) (2013a). *Animal-assisted psychotherapy: Theory, issues, and practice.* West Lafayette, IN: Purdue University Press.

Parish-Plass, N. (2013b). The contribution of animal-assisted psychotherapy to the potential space in play therapy. In N. Parish-Plass (Ed.), *Animal-assisted psychotherapy: Theory, issues, and practice* (pp. 79–109). West Lafayette, IN: Purdue University Press.

Parish-Plass, N. (2017). *Order out of chaos revised: A call for clear and agreed-upon definitions differentiating between animal-assisted interventions.* Retrieved from https://www.researchgate.net/profile/Nancy_ParishPlass/publication/307908063_Order_Out_of_Chaos_Revised_A_Call_for_Clear_and_AgreedUpon_Definitions_Differentiating_Between_Animal-Assisted_Interventions/links/57d172b508ae601b39a1c8e4/Order-Out-of-Chaos

-Revised-A-Call-for-Clear-and-Agreed-Upon-Definitions-Differentiating
-Between-Animal-Assisted-Interventions.pdf

Parish-Plass, N. (2018). *The influence of animal-assisted psychotherapy on the establishment of the therapeutic alliance with maltreated children in residential care* (Unpublished master's thesis). University of Haifa, Haifa, Israel. https://www.researchgate.net/publication/323944061_The_Influence_of_Animal-Assisted_Psychotherapy_on_the_Establishment_of_the_Therapeutic_Alliance_with_Maltreated_Children_in_Residential_Care

Parish-Plass, N., & Oren, D. (2013). The animal as a relational medium: An object relations approach to the therapy triangle in animal-assisted psychotherapy. In N. Parish-Plass (Ed.), *Animal-assisted psychotherapy: Theory, issues, and practice* (pp. 47–64). West Lafayette, IN: Purdue University Press.

Pearce, J. W., & Pezzot-Pearce. T. D. (1997). *Psychotherapy of abused and neglected children.* New York, NY: Guilford Press.

Pearlman, L. A., & Courtois, C. A. (2005). Clinical applications of the attachment framework: Relational treatment of complex trauma. *Journal of Traumatic Stress, 18*(5), 449–459. https://doi.org/10.1002/jts.20052

Perry, B. (2002). Childhood experience and the expression of genetic potential: What childhood neglect tells us about nature and nurture. *Brain and mind, 3*, 79–100.

Perry, B. (2008). Child maltreatment: A neurodevelopmental perspective on the role of trauma and neglect in psychopathology. In T. Beauchaine & S. Hinshaw (Eds.), *Child and Adolescent Psychopathology* (pp. 93–129). Hoboken, NJ: John Wiley & Sons.

Perry, B. (2009). Examining child maltreatment through a neurodevelopmental lens: Clinical applications of the Neurosequential Model of Therapeutics. *Journal of Loss and Trauma, 14*, 240–255.

Perry, B. (2013). The Neurosequential Model of Therapeutics: Application of a developmentally sensitive and neurobiology-informed approach to clinical problem solving in young maltreated children. In K. Brandt, B. D. Perry, S. Seligman, & E. Tronick (Eds.), *Infant & Early Childhood Mental Health: Core Concepts and Clinical Practice* (pp. 21–54). Washington, DC: American Psychiatric Publishing.

Perry, B., Pollard, R., Blakely, T., Baker, W., & Vigilante, D. (1995). Childhood trauma, the neurobiology of adaption, and "use-dependent" development of the brain: How "states" become "traits." *Infant Mental Health Journal, 16*, 271–291.

Porges, S. (2001). *The polyvagal theory: Phylogenetic substrates of a social nervous system. International Journal of Psychophysiology, 42*, 123–146.

Porges, S. (2003). Social engagement and attachment: A phylogenetic perspective. *Annals New York Academy of Sciences, 1008*, 31–47.

Porges, S. (2006). The role of social engagement in attachment and bonding. In S. Carter, L. Ahnert, K. Grossmann, S. Hardy, M. Lamb, S. Porges, & N. Sachser (Eds.), *Attachment and bonding: A new synthesis* (pp. 33–54). Cambridge, MA: MIT Press.

Porges, S. (2011). *The polyvagal theory: Neurophysiological foundations of emotions, attachment, communication and self-regulation.* New York, NY: W. W. Norton.

Porges, S. (2013, July). Human-animal interactions: A neural exercise supporting health. Plenary speech at the annual conference of IAHAIO—The International Association of Human-Animal Interaction Organizations.

Porges, S. (2015a). Making the world safe for our children: Down-regulating defence and up-regulating social engagement to 'optimise' the human experience. *Children Australia, 40*, 114–123.

Porges, S. (2015b). Play as a neural exercise: Insights from the polyvagal theory. Retrieved from https://cxservices.com/htx12/rrn16.php?module=FILEM ANAGER&command=DOWNLOAD&p1=porges-play-as-neural-exercise .pdf&p2=download

Porges, S. (2017a). Vagal pathways: Portals to compassion. In E. M. Seppala, E. Simon-Thomas, S. L. Brown, M. C. Worline, C. D. Cameron, & J. R. Doty (Eds.), *Oxford Handbook of Compassion Science* (pp. 289–204). New York, NY: Oxford University Press.

Porges, S. (2017b). The pocket guide to the polyvagal theory: The transformative power of feeling safe. New York, NY: W. W. Norton.

Porges, S. (2017c). Stephen Porges: Social engagement heals. Blog post. Retrieved from http://attachmentdisorderhealing.com/porges-polyvagal3/

Porges S., & Carter C. S. (2011). Mechanisms, mediators, and adaptive consequences of caregiving. In S. L. Brown, R. M. Brown, & L. A. Penner (Eds.), *Self-interest and beyond: Toward a new understanding of human caregiving* (pp. 53–71). New York, NY: Oxford University Press.

Prendiville, E. (2016, March). When words are not enough: Listening to the lessons of neuroscience and bringing creativity into the psychotherapy space. Paper presented at the Irish Association of Humanistic and Integrative Psychotherapy.

Putnam, F. (2003). Ten-year research update review: Child sexual abuse. *Journal of the American Academy of Child & Adolescent Psychiatry, 42*, 269–278.

Raichle, M. E., MacLeod, A. M., Snyder, A. Z., Powers, W. J., Gusnard, D. A., & Shulman, G. L. (2001). Inaugural article: A default mode of brain function. *Proceedings of the National Academy of Sciences, 98*(2), 676–82.

Rauch, S., van der Kolk, B. A., Fisler, R., Alpert, N. M., Orr, S. P., Savage, C. R., Fischman, A. J., Jenike, M. A., & Pitman, R. K. (1996). A symptom provocation study using position emission tomography and script driven imagery. *Archives of General Psychiatry, 53*(5), 380–387.

Robbins, S. B. (1995). Attachment perspectives on the counseling relationship: Comment on Mallinckrodt, Gantt, and Coble (1995). *Journal of Counseling Psychology, 42*, 318–319.

Safran, J. D., & Muran, J. C. (1996). The resolution of ruptures in the therapeutic alliance. *Journal of Consulting and Clinical Psychology, 64*, 447–458.

Satterfield, W. A., & Lyddon, W. J. (1998). Client attachment and the working alliance. *Counseling Psychology Quarterly, 11*(4), 407–415.

Scheele, D., Schwering, C., Elison, J. T., Spunt, R., Maier, W., & Hurlemann, R. (2015). A human tendency to anthropomorphize is enhanced by oxytocin. *European Neuropsychopharmacology, 25*(10), 1817–1825. https://doi.org/10.1016/j.euroneuro.2015.05.009

Shani, L. (2017). Animal-assisted dyadic therapy: A therapy model promoting development of the reflective function in the parent–child bond. *Clinical Child Psychology and Psychiatry, 22*(1), 46–58. https://doi.org/10.1177/1359104516672506

Shiloh, S., Sorek, G., & Terkel, J. (2003). Reduction of state-anxiety by petting animals in a controlled laboratory experiment. *Anxiety, Stress and Coping, 16*(4), 387–395. https://doi.org/10.1080/1061580031000091582

Siegel, D. (2003). An interpersonal neurobiology of psychotherapy: The developing mind and the resolution of trauma. In M. Solomon, & D. Seigel (Eds.), *Healing trauma: Attachment, mind, body, and brain.* New York, NY: W. W. Norton.

Siegel, D. (2009). Mindful awareness, mindsight, and neural integration. *The Humanistic Psychologist, 37*, 137–158.

Siegel, D. (2010). *Mindsight: The science of personal transformation.* New York, NY: Random House.

Siegel, D. (2012). *The developing mind: How relationships and the brain interact to shape who we are* (2nd ed.). New York, NY: Guilford Press.

Siegel, D. (2015). The role of play and creativity in psychotherapy. Seminar on DVD. PESI, Inc.

Siegel, D., & Bryson, T. (2012). *The whole-brain approach.* New York, NY: Bantam Books.

Signal, T., Taylor, N., Prentice, K., McDade, M., & Burke, K. (2017). Going to the dogs: A quasi-experimental assessment of animal assisted therapy for children who have experienced abuse. *Applied Developmental Science, 21*, 81–93.

Somer, E., & Szwarcberg, S. W. (2001). Variables in delayed disclosure of childhood sexual abuse. *American Journal of Orthopsychiatry, 71*(3), 332–341. https://doi.org/10.1037/0002-9432.71.3.332

Sori, C., & Schnur, S. (2014). Integrating a neurosequential approach in the treatment of traumatized children: An interview with Eliana Gil, Part II. *The Family Journal: Counseling and Therapy for Couples and Families, 22*, 251–257.

Spunt, R. P., Ellsworth, E., & Adolphs, R. (2016). The neural basis of understanding the expression of the emotions in man and animals. *Social, Cognitive and Affective Neuroscience, 12*(1), 95–105. https://doi.org/10.1093/scan/nsw161

Striepens, N., Kendrick, K. M., Maier, W., & Hurlemann, R. (2011). Prosocial effects of oxytocin and clinical evidence for its therapeutic potential. *Frontiers in Neuroendocrinology, 32*(4), 426–450. https://doi.org/10.1016/j.yfrne.2011.07.001

Suo, X., Lei, D., Chen, F., Wu, M., Li, L., Sun, L., . . . Gong, Q. (2016). Anatomic insights into disrupted small-world networks in pediatric posttraumatic stress disorder. *Radiology, 282*(3), 826–834. https://doi.org/10.1148/radiol.2016160907

Tedeschi, P., Sisa, M. L., Olmert, M. D., Parish-Plass, N., & Yount, R. (2015). Treating human trauma with the help of animals: Trauma informed intervention for child maltreatment and adult post-traumatic stress. In A. H. Fine (Ed.), *Handbook on animal-assisted therapy: Foundations and guidelines for animal-assisted interventions* (4th ed., pp. 305–320). San Diego, CA: Academic Press.

Teicher, M. H., Andersen, S. L., Polcari, A., Anderson, C. M., Navalta, C. P., & Kim, D. M. (2003). The neurobiological consequences of early stress and childhood maltreatment. *Neuroscience and Biobehavioral Reviews, 27*(1–2), 33–44. https://doi.org/10.1016/S0149-7634(03)00007-1

Theodoridou, A., Rowe, A. C., Penton-Voak, I. S., & Rogers, P. J. (2009). Oxytocin and social perception: Oxytocin increases perceived facial trustworthiness and attractiveness. *Hormones and Behavior, 56*(1), 128–132. https://doi.org/10.1016/j.yhbeh.2009.03.019

Thompson, R. A. (1999). Early attachment and later development. In J. Cassidy, & P. R. Shaver (Eds.), *Handbook of attachment: Theory, research and clinical applications* (pp. 265–287). New York, NY: Guilford Press.

Trotter, K. S., & Baggerly, J. N. (Eds.). (2019). *Equine-assisted mental health for healing trauma.* New York, NY: Routledge.

Trotter, K. S., Chandler, C. K., Goodwin-Bond, D., & Casey, J. (2008). A comparative study of the efficacy of group equine assisted counseling with at-risk children and adolescents. *Journal of Creativity in Mental Health, 3*(3), 254–284. https://doi.org/10.1080/15401380802356880

U.S. Department of Health and Human Services. (2014). *A treatment improvement protocol—trauma-informed care in behavioral health services—tip 57*. Rockville, MD: U.S. Department of Health and Human Services.

van der Kolk, B. (1998). Trauma and memory. *Psychiatry and Clinical Neurosciences, 52*, S52–S64.

van der Kolk, B. (2005). Developmental trauma disorder. *Psychiatric Annals, 35*(5), 401–409. https://doi.org/10.1038/472298a

van der Kolk, B. A. (2014). *The body keeps the score: Brain, mind, and body in the healing of trauma*. New York, NY: Penguin Group.

VanFleet, R., & Faa-Thompson, T. (2014). Animal Assisted Play Therapy to empower vulnerable children. In E. Green, & A. Myrick (Eds.), *Play therapy with vulnerable populations: No child forgotten* (pp. 85–103). Lanham, MD: Rowman & Littlefield.

VanFleet, R., & Faa-Thompson, T. (2017). *Animal Assisted Play Therapy^TM*. Sarasota, FL: Professional Resource Press.

Vygotsky, L. S. (1976). Play and its role in the mental development of the child. In J. S. Bruner, A. Jolly, & K. Sylva (Eds.), *Play—its role in development and evolution*. New York, NY: Basic Books, Inc., Publishers.

Whitebread, D., Coltman, P., Jameson, H., & Lander, R. (2009) Cognition and self-regulation: What exactly are children learning when they learn through play? *Educational & Child Psychology, 26*, 40–52.

Wilson, E. O. (1984). *Biophilia*. Cambridge, MA: Harvard University Press.

Winnicott, C. (1968). Communicating with children. In R. J. Tod (Ed.), *Disturbed children*. London, U.K.: Longmans, Green and Co.

Winnicott, D. (1971). *Play and reality*. London, UK: Hogarth Press.

Winnicott, D. W. (1965). Ego distortion in terms of true and false self. In D. W. Winnicott (Ed.), *The maturational process and the facilitating environment: Studies in the theory of emotional development* (pp. 140–157). New York, NY: International Universities Press.

Wismer Fries, A. B., Zigler, T., Kurian, J., Jacoris, S., & Pollak, S. D. (2005). Early experience in humans is associated with changes in neuro-peptides critical for regulating social behaviour. *Proceedings of the National Academy of Sciences of the United States of America, 102*, 17237–17240.

Yorke, J. (2010). The significance of human-animal relationships as modulators of trauma effects in children: A developmental neurobiological perspective. *Early Child Development and Care, 180*(5), 559–570. https://doi.org/10.1080/03004430802181189

Zilcha-Mano, S. (2017). Resolution of alliance ruptures: The special case of animal-assisted psychotherapy. *Clinical Child Psychology and Psychiatry, 22*(1), 34–45. https://doi.org/10.1177/1359104516677138.

Zilcha-Mano, S. (2019). A pet as a safe haven and secure base in the psychotherapy setting. Manuscript in preparation.

Zilcha-Mano, S., Mikulincer, M., & Shaver, P. R. (2011). Pet in the therapy room: An attachment perspective on animal-assisted therapy. *Attachment and Human Development, 13*(6), 541–561. https://doi.org/10.1080/14616734.2011.608987

Zilcha-Mano, S., Mikulincer, M., & Shaver, P. R. (2012). Pets as safe havens and secure bases: The moderating role of pet attachment orientations. *Journal of Research in Personality, 46*(5), 571–580. https://doi.org/10.1016/j.jrp.2012.06.005

Zimrin, H. (1986). A profile of survival. *Child Abuse and Neglect, 10*, 339–349.

Zoicas, I., Slattery, D., & Neumann, I. (2014). Brain oxytocin in social fear conditioning and its extinction: Involvement of the lateral septum. *Neuropsychopharmacology, 39*, 3027–3035.

ABOUT THE AUTHORS

Nancy Parish-Plass, MA social work, has completed studies in animal-assisted psychotherapy and advanced psychotherapy. Her positions include: senior staff member at the AHAVA Emergency Shelter for At-Risk Children, AAP clinical supervisor, editorial board member of HABRI Central, member of the IAHAIO International Task Force for the Development of Guidelines for Animal-Assisted Interventions and Animal Welfare, and chairperson of the IAAAP—Israeli Association of Animal-Assisted Psychotherapy. Her research focuses on the therapeutic alliance and self-disclosure in AAP with maltreated children.

Jessica Pfeiffer is a licensed clinical social worker, licensed school social worker, and a ChildTrauma Academy Education Fellow. She is the owner of Intricate Roots Educational Consulting Services supporting educational systems in implementing a trauma-informed lens and providing therapeutic services to children, adolescents, and families. Pfeiffer is also a faculty member at the Institute for Human-Animal Connection in the Graduate School of Social Work at the University of Denver. Currently, she is working toward her doctorate in clinical psychology in the School of Psychology at the University of Colorado Denver.

CHAPTER 5

The Power of Play and Animals: Animal Assisted Play Therapy as an Integrative Practice Model for Mental Health Treatment

Risë VanFleet, PhD, RPT-S, CDBC

BACKGROUND

Literary great Mark Twain once said, "Against the assault of laughter, nothing can stand." Child development theorist Erik Erikson said, "The playing adult steps sideward into another reality; the playing child advances forward to new stages of mastery." Physicist Albert Einstein said, "Play is the highest form of research." What did they all know that we might be missing?

Play is a much-overlooked resource in therapeutic work with people of all ages. It creates bonds, reduces stress, fosters an atmosphere of emotional safety, provides fresh perspective, allows one to practice new behaviors, encourages flexibility and creativity, and offers the opportunity to gain mastery. Gradually over the past 70 years, the use of play, laughter, and humor to help people overcome social, emotional, and behavioral difficulties has become more broadly accepted. Research has also shown its value in the formal therapeutic process (Bratton, Ray, Rhine, & Jones, 2005). Arguably, the benefits of animal-assisted interventions (AAIs) can be magnified when conducted more playfully (VanFleet & Faa-Thompson, 2012,

2015a, 2017). This chapter discusses the integration of animal-assisted therapy (AAT) with play therapy. Brief descriptions of play (including animal play), play therapy, and Animal Assisted Play Therapy™ (AAPT) are followed by details of the principles and procedures involved in AAPT, as well as considerations and case examples that highlight its application with children who have experienced complex trauma and attachment disruptions.

HISTORY AND TERMINOLOGY

Play offers certain benefits to the players. It usually is fun and filled with joy, providing a release from stress. It facilitates the development of physical, cognitive, social, and adaptive capacities and skills, and permits the nonverbal (and sometimes verbal or vocalized) expression of emotions, motivations, interests, and desires. Play also helps creates bonds in social animals, both human and nonhuman. Conversely, scholars note that the absence of play in a child's life may be linked with antisocial behavior (Brown, 2009). The American Academy of Pediatrics (Ginsburg, 2007) states, "Play allows children to use their creativity while developing their imagination, dexterity, and physical, cognitive, and emotional strength," while adding, "play is important in healthy brain development" (p. 183). These benefits apply to children and adults.

Play also serves many purposes for nonhuman animals (henceforth referred to as animals), both in the wild and in captivity. To date, the most complete definition of animal play is one proffered by Gordon Burghardt (2005). He has detailed a five-point definition to distinguish play from other similar patterns of animal behavior. In brief, his definition is as follows: "Play is repeated, incompletely functional behavior differing from more serious versions structurally, contextually, or ontogenetically, and initiated voluntarily when the animal is in a relaxed or low-stress setting" (Burghardt, 2005, p. 82). Play does not serve any immediate function, and it arises from within the animal in a spontaneous, voluntary, and enjoyable manner. It differs qualitatively from survival behaviors; play fighting is different from actual fighting in identifiable ways, even though they might look the same initially. There is much repetition in animal play, but there are at least some differences in the repetitions. Play takes precedence over other activities when it occurs, but it occurs only when animals feel safe.

Although the benefits of play are clear, its value in both human and animal life has long been overlooked. Perhaps it was seen as frivolous, or as something humans and animals engaged in only when more "serious" or "worthwhile" pursuits were completed. It was only when cognitive ethologists (e.g., Bekoff, 2018; Bekoff & Byers, 1998), as well as psychologists and neuroscientists (e.g., Burghardt, 2005; Panksepp, 2005, 2012), documented the pervasiveness of play in the animal world and the pathways for play in the brain, that the topic gained considerable traction. In the meantime, social scientists noted the value of play for children, adults, and whole societies, but continued to struggle with a clear definition (Brown, 2009; Chudakoff, 2007; Sutton-Smith, 1997).

Sutton-Smith (1997) has identified seven different forms of rhetoric to describe play, including: 1) as an adaptation that assists learning and development; 2) as a form of strategy or skill that establishes hierarchy; 3) as an optimistic mechanism that offsets pessimistic views; 4) as a means to transform the ordinary through pretense and exaggeration; 5) as an expression of one's identity; 6) as a way to establish social and community bonds; and 7) as fun, which contrasts with work. Over the last 20 years, the recognition of play as a subject of serious study has grown, with published books, articles, and research becoming increasingly prevalent (Brown, 2009; Burghardt, 2005; Käufer, 2013; Maestripieri, 2012; Panksepp, 2012; Pellegrini & Smith, 2005; Pellis & Pellis, 2009). Periodicals such as the *American Journal of Play*, the *British Journal of Play Therapy*, and the *International Journal of Play Therapy* have provided additional outlets for research about play and its application in therapeutic work.

Play therapy has been defined as a "broad field that uses children's natural inclination to play as a means of creating an emotionally safe therapeutic environment that encourages communication, relationship-building, expression, and problem resolution for the child" (VanFleet, 2004b, p. 5; VanFleet, Sywulak, & Sniscak, 2010, p. 11). There are many forms of play therapy that represent the major personality theories, such as psychodynamic play therapy, cognitive-behavioral play therapy, and child-centered play therapy (humanistic). Play therapy has increasingly been extended successfully to adults, adding the elements of playfulness and humor with other forms of intervention. Play and humor are important coping mechanisms that can be incorporated into therapy for a wide range of challenges. In addition, because play tends to increase motivation, it is a useful tool in other forms of intervention that may be onerous in nature, such as physical, occupational, and speech/language therapy, as well as diverse forms of education for people of every age (VanFleet, 2008; VanFleet & Faa-Thompson, 2017).

Moreover, play interventions have even been applied with animals suffering from fear or stress disorders, such as with puppy mill, unsocialized, and feral dogs. For example, VanFleet (2014b) created the conditions of safety for extremely fearful dogs to engage in natural play with other dogs specially selected to serve as social facilitators. These canine play interactions occur at the pace and full choice of the fearful dog, and are followed by invitations and opportunities for human-dog play as the fearful dog shows interest. Notably, this approach has resulted in the observation of increased social behaviors and reduced fear among unsocialized, anxious, or feral dogs.

AAPT harnesses the power of play, as well as the many benefits of including animals in human mental health, allied health, and educational therapies and interventions (i.e., AAI) (Chandler, 2017; Fine, 2015; Parish-Plass, 2013). Animals working in professional settings, including hospitals, nursing facilities for older adults, and schools (among others), can facilitate the achievement of client goals in many areas of therapeutic need, and are valuable for social support and connection. AAPT is defined as:

The integrated involvement of animals in the context of play therapy, in which appropriately trained therapists and animals engage with clients primarily through systematic playful interventions, with the goal of improving clients' psychosocial health, while simultaneously ensuring the animal's well-being and voluntary engagement. Play and playfulness are essential ingredients of the interactions and the relationships (VanFleet, 2004a; VanFleet & Faa-Thompson, 2015c, 2017, p. 17).

While the author of this contribution first engaged in AAPT-type activities over 35 years ago, and others are likely to have incorporated playfulness into their AAI work, the systematic and formal development of the AAPT field began in 2004 (VanFleet, 2008). Two years later, a professional collaboration between Risë VanFleet and Tracie Faa-Thompson, both mental health professionals and credentialed play therapists with similar approaches to working with animals (including equine-assisted interventions, in Faa-Thompson's case), began. This collaboration has since resulted in further articulation of the use of play in AAI, including in-depth training programs and a comprehensive, competence-based certification for mental health, allied health, and education professionals (International Institute for Animal Assisted Play Therapy® or IIAAPT, 2017).

ANIMAL ASSISTED PLAY THERAPY (AAPT)—AN OVERVIEW

AAPT differs from other forms of animal-assisted therapy (AAT) in its systematic incorporation of, and focus on, play and playfulness. The appropriate use of a lighter tone in therapy creates greater emotional safety for human clients by lifting intensity and offering acceptance, while also increasing the likelihood that the animals involved will genuinely enjoy the process. AAPT is beneficial for psychotherapy and family therapy clients across the life span. The playful environment reduces stress and builds connections, not only with the animals involved, but also between client and therapist (VanFleet & Faa-Thompson, 2017). AAPT heavily emphasizes relationships between therapists and animals, clients and animals, and therapists and clients. Clients then learn to extend what they learn about relationships in therapy to other relationships in their lives.

Importantly, AAPT also emphasizes the welfare of animals involved in this work. It is essential that animals be treated with respect throughout the process. At no time is an animal expected to "tolerate" the behaviors of humans. A substantial knowledge of the animal species being incorporated, including body language and behavior, as well as of the individual animal, is required of the practitioner. While animals are evaluated for their suitability for AAPT work, including being well-behaved and under control during play sessions, the burden of risk management is placed upon the therapists. For example, therapists must be able to accurately interpret their animal's body language and intervene at the first signs of stress or fatigue. This provides the animals with greater freedom to move and participate voluntarily without the use of leashes and other equipment that can dampen their behavior and choices. The therapist and animal are trained to such a degree that dogs work off-leash and horses work at liberty, in which they are free to go where they choose.

A training process created and tested specifically for AAPT is used to further prepare therapists and their animals for this more intensive and enduring work. Through online courses and hands-on training workshops, therapists learn to read their animals' behavioral cues fluently, improve their abilities to anticipate situations that might be stressful for their animals, and ensure that the animals can always move away from situations that they find uncomfortable. There is a strong emphasis on building positive and strong therapist-animal partnerships that are then shared with clients in a variety of playful ways while simultaneously ensuring animal well-being. Therapists also learn to split their attention skillfully between clients and their animals to ensure a valuable experience for all.

Principles

VanFleet and Faa-Thompson (2010, 2017) have outlined the following principles underlying AAPT:

- Mutual respect for clients and animals;
- Physical and emotional safety for both the human and animal;
- Enjoyment by all;
- Acceptance of clients and animals for who they are;
- Use of positive, nonaversive training and equipment for the animals;
- Healthy, mutually beneficial relationships;
- Process-orientation with measurable results, grounded in theory; *and*
- The importance of developing an empirical base.

In AAPT, the animals' needs and preferences are considered on par with those of the humans, and practitioners learn how to balance and respect both, including leveraging natural animal behaviors to help achieve therapeutic outcomes. For example, when animals in AAPT are selected for sociability and curiosity, and the therapist-animal relationship helps the animal see most humans as desirable companions, animals are able to make their own choices to approach or move away from clients. When they move away, clients might feel rejected or disappointed. Usually, clients' reactions reflect feelings they might experience in family or peer relationships, such as abandonment fears or feeling isolated. The therapist then helps clients work through their reactions in real time, using the therapeutic skills at their disposal. It is often during these spontaneous moments, where the animals are free to behave authentically and unexpectedly, that the most valuable therapy occurs.

Likewise, the natural behaviors of animals create rich opportunities for human learning and behavioral change. For instance, the AAPT therapist might call the child's attention to the animal's body language and behavior during play (i.e., the display of behavioral indicators of stress). Gradually, the child then learns to adjust his or her own behavior to accommodate and respect the needs of the animal. In other words, the therapy is not so much about getting the animals to do what the clients want all the time, but helping clients with their reactions to what naturally happens in sessions, even when the animals don't "play along" exactly as the clients would wish or expect. AAPT practitioners continuously help children develop two-way, mutually respectful relationships with the animal, whether they are engaging in obstacle course exercises or sitting quietly together while the child gives advice about a "problem" the dog is having (for example). Such lessons are anticipated to transfer to the client's social relationships outside of therapy, and the therapist facilitates this when it does not occur naturally. Additional examples of how AAPT principles play out in the actual work are described in greater detail later in this chapter and elsewhere (see VanFleet, 2014c, VanFleet & Faa-Thompson, 2017).

Primary Goals

The primary goal areas of AAPT include the development of self-efficacy, healthy attachment and relationship, empathy, self-regulation, and problem-resolution for a wide range of specific difficulties (VanFleet & Faa-Thompson, 2010, 2017). The approach is flexible and can be adapted to many different ways of working with clients. Often, multiple goal areas can be addressed with the same interventions. When applied by allied health and/or mental health professionals or educators, AAPT goals can differ according to the specific objectives of their profession, as well as their therapy and teaching methodology. In the mental health field, AAPT has been used to address such clinical targets as anxiety, attention deficits, autism spectrum disorder, chronic medical illness, delinquency and truancy, attachment problems, family tensions, depression, selective mutism, oppositional and conduct problems, obsessive compulsive disorder, grief, and trauma (VanFleet, 2008; VanFleet & Colţea, 2012; VanFleet & Faa-Thompson, 2014, 2015b, 2017). Furthermore, AAPT has often been applied to help clients who experience fears of dogs or horses. These fears might come from prior traumatic experiences with animals, or from overly cautious caretakers who demonstrate or "model" their own fears of animals with their children.

Trauma-Specific Applications

AAPT is particularly well-suited for working with children who have experienced trauma, but is also effective with adolescents, adults, and families. This chapter focuses on AAPT's application with maltreated and traumatized children with concomitant attachment difficulties. When children have experienced abuse, neglect, domestic violence, exposure to substance abuse, and attachment disruptions, they often develop mistrust of people, along with serious emotional, social, and behavioral problems (Gil, 2006; James, 1994; Terr, 1990; VanFleet, 2015; VanFleet & Sniscak, 2003b). Effective treatment must include the facilitation of healthy attachment experiences, while providing avenues for overcoming the sequelae of trauma. This can be particularly challenging because children are typically hurt most by adults and, therefore, have difficulty trusting them, including therapists.

AAPT offers an alternative to traditional forms of therapy by addressing these trust-related issues in two primary ways. First, using the language of play creates emotional safety. Children are not required to "talk" directly about their problems, which is often frightening and can run the risk of retraumatization. Instead, play therapy gives them opportunities to express themselves and to be understood, as well as symbolically work through and master their intense and often confused feelings. Second, the involvement of animals allows for trust and early experiences of healthy attachment relationships within the therapeutic process itself (VanFleet & Faa-Thompson, 2017). In the author's experience, directly with clients and in supervision of other AAPT practitioners, the connection between client and animal occurs quickly and, not long after, rapport with the therapist is facilitated by the presence of the animal. A consistent clinical finding is that traumatized children's ability to work on their problems in a non-defensive and open manner is considerably enhanced when animals are present in AAPT (as compared to play therapy without animals). Animals' social lubricant or catalyst effects (McNicholas & Collis, 2000, 2006) are significant when working with children with trauma and attachment problems, thereby helping them connect with human support systems more readily (VanFleet & Faa-Thompson, 2017).

THEORY AND POTENTIAL MECHANISMS

Psychology

Developmental research clearly shows the importance of animals for children (Jalongo, 2018; Melson, 2001; Melson & Fine, 2015). For many years, play therapists have noted the importance of animal figures, puppets, and toys in the therapeutic playroom. Children frequently select animal objects and roles in child-centered play therapy (VanFleet et al., 2010), and therapists typically include animal representations as part of their playrooms and sessions.

Adults also express interest in animals. In the author's shared family practice, a significant number of adult clients explain that the involvement of animals in therapy was the main reason this practice was chosen over others. Some theorists have suggested that people have a strong need to seek connection to nature (e.g., biophilia hypothesis; Wilson, 1984). Others (Louv, 2012; Olmert, 2009) believe that the connection to animals offers a route to connect with the environment at a time when people are disconnected from it and each other by busy schedules, disappearing opportunities to experience nature, and increasing involvement with electronic devices and online social experiences.

Clients of all ages who participate in AAPT can have attachment or relationship challenges. Change occurs in the context of relationships, and sometimes it is easier to develop a relationship with a nonhuman animal than a human one. It is important for therapists to remember that their relationships with their own animals serve as models and metaphors for their clients (VanFleet & Faa-Thompson, 2017), and that a key skill is to recognize the various relationship dynamics that occur during sessions so they can make the most of relational moments (Chandler, 2017).

The actual practice of AAPT spans a variety of psychological theories. Likewise, there are forms of play therapy that are derived from nearly all psychotherapeutic theories, including psychodynamic, humanistic, cognitive-behavioral, and family systems. The manner in which play is incorporated differs according to the theory being used. The same is true of AAPT. For example, AAPT can be conducted from a humanistic perspective in a nondirective manner in which the therapist creates safety and acceptance while the client decides the activities, expressions, and interactions. It can also be conducted from a cognitive-behavioral perspective in which the therapist suggests activities or interactions that are likely to meet a specific goal for that session. In nondirective AAPT, a child might dress up as a police officer and announce that the dog is a police dog. The child may want the dog to accompany her around the room to look for "bad guys." If the dog does not do this, the therapist can help, at the same time reflecting the play through the dog, as exemplified by: "Wow! Those bad guys are hiding around here somewhere. Rover, Mary wants you to help! Come here and look behind this chair! Now Mary wants you to sniff around those blocks. Good work, Rover!"

Such play themes of threat (i.e., the presence of "bad guys") and mastery (i.e., finding the "bad guys") are commonly used by children in nondirective AAPT, while the therapist conveys safety and support through the use of empathic responding and the animal participates.

Directive AAPT can take many forms. One intervention—with the goals of improving family communication and cohesion—asks a family to set up an obstacle course and then work together to get the dog to go through it, all without touching the dog and using no more than 10 treats. Another might be tasking a client to teach the dog a new trick, with the help of the therapist, for the purposes of enhancing the client's self-efficacy. There is great latitude in AAPT for therapists who operate from different theoretical bases. Perhaps the most relevant theories that guide AAPT interventions are life-span development (where humans are viewed as continuously developing from birth to death) and attachment/relationship/systems approaches, which emphasize the importance of caring and mutual relationships (VanFleet & Faa-Thompson, 2017).

As noted earlier, AAPT offers a very useful component in multimodal therapy that is typically needed for children who have experienced complex trauma and attachment disruptions. Through play, it provides the emotional and interpersonal safety that is needed for therapy to work well. The involvement of animals opens the door to communication, as well as to therapeutic processing (VanFleet & Faa-Thompson, 2017). As clients interact with the animals, they relax and begin to lower their defenses. One teen client told the author, "When I first came here, I was very suspicious. I didn't want to talk with a stranger about my problems. But I quickly began to trust you more because you were sharing Kirrie with me, plus you made it fun. You didn't put a lot of demands on me and you seemed to accept me for me."

In many ways, when animal involvement is skillfully facilitated by the therapist, it offers a secure base from which the child can explore. That exploration can go in many directions: exploration of the traumatic experiences and attached emotions of identity, of relationships, of hopes and wishes, and of the road ahead. The playful, active nature of AAPT stretches beyond traditional talk therapies, allowing children to form actual and genuine relationships with the animals and with the therapist, as they use the range of interventions to heal and make progress.

Physiology

Traumatized children often display emotional and behavioral dysregulation. Without the grounding of consistent relationships, they can end up in a downward spiral in which their misunderstood and externalized behaviors lead to even greater misunderstanding and possibly isolation (James, 1994). Play therapy offers them a means of expressing the feelings associated with trauma, as well as a way to master those feelings in developmentally appropriate ways. This, in turn, allows children to try out new, more adaptive behaviors in a safe and secure environment.

Neuroscience has provided considerable knowledge about trauma's effects in recent years, and it is well-established that expressive therapies, including play, are appropriate for treatment based upon the imprint of trauma in the brain (Perry & Szalavitz, 2010; van der Kolk, 2014). When the attachment system for the child has been compromised or damaged, there is a need for healthier "templates" of relationship. The importance of consistent, caring relationships for helping children overcome trauma and attachment problems has also been established (Garbarino, Kostelny, & Dubrow, 1991; Garbarino, Dubrow, Kostelny, & Pardo, 1992; Siegel, 2012; VanFleet & Sniscak, 2003a). The child needs a framework to realize that, in securely attached relationships, adults are focused on meeting their needs rather than ignoring, subjugating, or hurting them. In the case of AAPT, the animal may also serve as a reliable source of support and connection for children, which could further aid their ability to trust, and seek relationships with, others.

In addition, playful interactions with animals may result in the release of opioids in the body, as well as oxytocin (Olmert, 2009; Panksepp, 2012). Both can help provide a greater sense of safety and well-being as children begin to work through very difficult experiences and feelings.

Seeking and play, two of the emotional systems mapped through the brain by Panksepp (2012), are likely important in AAPT applications as well. Both of these neurological systems are thought to help counteract negative emotional experiences, and help people explore inwardly and outwardly in their relationships.

Interacting playfully with animals while the therapist facilitates also allows children to have genuine experiences with another living being. It allows them to touch, explore, teach, and respond to the animal. Touch, in particular, is important to social animals—both human and nonhuman. While touching between therapist and child is limited in therapy, there are many more opportunities to explore appropriate touch with an animal. Children can learn through direct experience how and where an animal likes to be touched. For example, in AAPT, the "three-second rule" is often used. With this, the child pets or scratches the animal for three seconds and then stops. The therapist and child watch for the animal's reaction. If the animal remains in place or looks at the child or nudges the child's hand, it is usually an indication that the animal would like more of that touch. If the animal shows stress signals (e.g., chewing or licking, turning his or her head or body away), it suggests that the animal is not interested in being touched further in that way. In AAPT, therapists help children use this rule to learn about the interests of the animal, and to show concern for the animal's feelings, reactions, and boundaries. Clinical and anecdotal evidence suggests that touching, and being touched by, animals may provide children with sensory stimulation; comfort, relaxation, and the relief of physiological stress; unique opportunities to engage in gentle and/or consensual physical contact, which may likely be uncommon for children who have been maltreated; and help in forming and maintaining respectful social relationships.

CURRENT AAPT RESEARCH

It is difficult to conduct good research until there are practitioners who fully understand the method and how to apply it in competent and consistent ways. With emerging fields, this takes time. Today, there is preliminary research on AAPT, as well as consistent clinical findings, but only recently have therapists been certified in the practice.

Play therapy and Filial Therapy (where parents learn to conduct special nondirective play sessions with their own children; see Guerney & Ryan, 2013 and VanFleet, 2014a) provide the foundations of AAPT, and are empirically supported and/or evidence-based approaches in both the United States and the United Kingdom (Bratton et al., 2005; VanFleet, Ryan, & Smith, 2005). Research on the impact of these two approaches has grown considerably over the past 20 years, although more research on play-based interventions is needed, especially in regard to the various forms and clinical outcomes of AAPT that integrate both of these models.

A first step in an emerging field is to see if the professional training is useful. Hansing (2014) studied 67 mental health professionals who had attended at least the Level 1, 48-hour workshop in AAPT (24 hours of which are hands-on), and found that the development of counselor self-efficacy was significantly higher for professionals who had participated in both the online and hands-on training when compared to those who had taken only the online courses. Additionally, Thompson (2009) conducted a preliminary study of AAPT using subjects as their own controls with animals present or absent from child-centered play therapy sessions; she found fewer play disruptions and overt signs of anxiety when the dogs were present.

VanFleet (2008) also completed a preliminary study of AAPT from the point of view of 21 child clients. In this assessment, children were asked to select an unlimited number of miniature toy figurines for their sandtray from a wall display of over 1,000 options (including animal and people items, as well as non-animal objects such as vehicles, houses, trees, and dishes). Researchers directed the children to base their choice of miniature on what they perceived to be the best parts of therapy. In all cases (i.e., 100% of the time), those children who had been previously involved with AAPT with dogs included at least one miniature of a dog in their sandtray. In contrast, children who had not received AAPT, but could play with all playroom items (animal and non-animal) in their therapy, included a dog figurine only 20% of the time. These findings suggest that the experience of connecting with dogs during AAPT is a meaningful aspect of therapy for children, and likely more so than playing with toy dogs alone. At present, this study is expanding with more therapists, a larger child sample, an analysis of horse miniatures for those in equine AAPT, and an external assessment of sandtray photos.

In related research, Faa-Thompson (2014) recently asked children in her AAPT trauma groups (designed to help children with their feelings, problematic behaviors, social relationships, and emotional regulation) to develop their own assessment of their AAPT experience, and to complete it at the end of their program. Each child provided five questions that they considered important to include in an AAPT program evaluation and answered them. Question examples included: "What were the best things you did?", "Which animals liked you the best?", and "What was it like doing [AAPT] with other kids you didn't always like before the program?" The current assessment survey, which has been informed by the children who participated in this process, has since been used effectively with other clients. Additionally, the feedback from children on these evaluations has been overwhelmingly positive, particularly in regard to their perceptions of AAPT participation as valuable.

Additionally, Wenocur (2018) studied the impact of AAPT when used with children in a homeless shelter. She used grounded constructivist theory to perform an integrated analysis of projective drawings, accompanying narratives, parent interviews, and the treatment records of 11 children, aged 6 to 11 years, who participated in AAPT sessions at the shelter. The study illustrated children's lived and wished-for experiences of attachment relationships. It also showed that tasks associated with taking care of the dogs were important to the children, and that parents identified the dogs' involvement as a component of the program's success for their children.

CASE STUDY: JAKE AND KIRRIE

Identifying information about clients has been changed to protect confidentiality.

Kirrie (a play therapy dog) eagerly greeted 12-year-old Jake when he arrived for his fifth AAPT session. Her tail wagged so strongly that her hips swung back and forth. Jake smiled broadly and said, "She's got her wiggle on again. That's how I know she's happy to see me!" He proceeded to pet her under the chin and said he wanted to play hide-and-seek with her. I reflected, "You're looking forward to more hide-and-seek with her!" and then assisted him as he set up the "game" they had played together for the first time in the prior session.

Jake proceeded to hide in various locations in the large play-room while I kept Kirrie's attention. When he was well-hidden, I gave Kirrie the cue, "Go find Jake!" She then moved around the room, sniffing and looking until she found him. I did not tell her where to go, but merely described aloud what was happening so Jake would know what she was doing: "She's over by the window, sniffing all around the stuffed animals. Now she's checking out under the table. Here she comes your way." Kirrie approached the chair in which Jake was hiding. It was an egg-shaped chair with a movable shade that pulled down in front to conceal him. Kirrie approached, pushed the shade up with her nose, and licked his arm as Jake got out laughing. I reflected his delight, "You really like it when she looks for you and finds you!" Jake (who rarely spoke unless he was in a session with Kirrie) replied, "Yep! She is *really* looking for me—not just pretending!" I empathically responded with, "It feels so good that she really, truly wants to find you. You can tell she cares for you and wants to find you when you're missing!" Jake hid several times during that session, and we repeated the process.

At the time, Jake was in foster care with a long history of extreme physical abuse from his mother's boyfriends. He had also been molested while in a prior foster placement. An adoption had fallen through because of the adoptive parents' inability to control his behavior. Another adoptive family was being considered, and this time the agency was willing to pay for therapy to address Jake's social, emotional, and behavioral difficulties associated with his trauma and attachment disruptions. He had already shown improvement with play therapy and family therapy with his foster mother. The work with Kirrie had been added to assist with his mistrust of people, attachment problems, self-esteem, and occasional attempts to be unkind to animals.

Jake's AAPT sessions involved a number of interventions that were designed to support him and his treatment goals. He helped teach Kirrie several new tricks using positive reward-based methods (clicker training), with the aim of improving his sense of competence and confidence. When I prompted him to check how Kirrie was reacting to his various behaviors, he learned about basic body language in dogs. He also learned how to create a kind and caring relationship with the dog, and to respect her boundaries and preferences. Emphasis on how the dog was feeling and responding helped him see her as the emotional, cognitive being that she was. As Jake developed skills and confidence, we held family sessions where he could show his foster mother what he had accomplished and learned with Kirrie. Before I tried specific interventions to help him transfer his ability to be kind to the dogs in his foster family, he generalized what he had learned on his own and began treating the family dog with the same regard as he did Kirrie.

Jake's sessions typically involved a period of nondirective AAPT, where he was able to select what and how to play, followed by more structured, or directive, AAPT held in a different room or in a private outdoor area. During the directive AAPT segments, I suggested more specific playful interactions (e.g., teaching her new tricks, scratching her favorite spots, giving her "advice" for problems that resembled his, playing games that involved taking turns or watching her reactions to new toys) that helped Jake build relationship, consider Kirrie's feelings, teach and help her with tasks, and provide nurturance to her. I also included some impulse-control activities where Jake and Kirrie did an energetic and exciting activity, followed by a calmer period where Jake's "job" was to help Kirrie settle down. Jake was always motivated to work in AAPT with Kirrie, and his foster mother, adoption worker, and teacher all noted differences in his behavior after just three sessions. The secure relationships Jake had with both the dog and therapist provided the context in which he could work on overcoming his trauma, developing coping strategies, and feeling more at ease in the world and with himself.

According to his foster mother, after 10 sessions with Kirrie, Jake showed improved self-regulation in daily life. His inappropriate and/or intrusive behavior with the family dog had disappeared entirely. She also reported that he seemed more at ease with himself. While the play therapy and family therapy had helped significantly, it seemed that his work with Kirrie opened new doors for him. He became better able to express himself and cope with life's challenges in more constructive ways. The process continued as he met and was eventually adopted by a second family.

In general, the different applications and therapeutic activities of AAPT allowed Jake to express his feelings in an accepting environment and to master them through something he genuinely enjoyed—play. AAPT also provided him with coping skills and increased confidence to handle the often considerable stresses in his life. Finally, it helped him learn about emotions in himself and others, and how to build mutually respectful relationships. AAPT allowed Jake to experience *being cared for* as well as *caring for* the dog, facilitated by the therapist. These are core features of healthy attachment and development (Bifulco & Thomas, 2013; Bowlby, 1988), and AAPT provided Jake a playful and safe environment in which to explore, perhaps for the first time, these very significant aspects of his life.

BEST PRACTICES

Protocols

AAPT is a form of play and family therapy. Its practice depends on the goals developed in tandem with families, so the specific methods selected in any given case are driven by that individual assessment. The methods used are also determined by the animal's personality, abilities, and preferences (which can vary from day to day). The Animal Appropriateness Scale (VanFleet & Faa-Thompson, 2017) is used to select animals, and positive reinforcement- and relationship-based methods of training are utilized. A "goodness of fit" model is also applied, whereby therapists consider their animals' characteristics, including energy level, curiosity, engagement, playfulness, sociability, and preferred activities. These are then matched with the type of AAPT being employed. For example, Grazie, the horse, had a relatively short attention span, so she was included in sessions that were shorter in duration. Magnum, however, was an extremely sociable and curious horse, always trotting to greet people when they approached the gate to his field. As such, he was included in more active interventions that integrated those features.

AAPT therapists watch carefully for any signs of stress in the animals, and they proactively ensure the comfort and safety of their therapy partners. Children are not permitted to intrude in the animals' space; if and when this happens, the situation is used to help the child think about the animal's needs and behave accordingly. If that is not possible, then the therapist can set limits. For more detailed information about AAPT standards of practice, please see VanFleet and Faa-Thompson (2017).

As mentioned previously, even carefully selected and well-trained animals do not always do as they are asked in therapy sessions, and unplanned animal behaviors are often expected. Horses might choose to graze rather than interact. Dogs might refuse to jump over an obstacle, or may back away when confronted with a new prop or toy. These situations are often of great therapeutic value and can provide important healing potential for clients. For example, the animal does not behave as the child wishes, and the child reacts with disappointment or anger. The AAPT therapist then processes that reaction with the child. There are various methods of processing, ranging from empathic listening to brief, guided questioning to explore the reasons behind the animal's reaction or to suggest that the client try again, using a different approach. In most cases, verbal discussions about the child's feelings or behaviors are not used or are kept short. The unique value in AAPT is in the doing, the experiencing.

Different forms of AAPT have their own methods, as is true of traditional play therapy. Nondirective AAPT follows the same standards and practices as child-centered play therapy, where activities are mostly led by the child. Cognitive-behavioral AAPT is conducted similarly to cognitive-behavioral play therapy, in that it incorporates more directive approaches designed to adjust perceptions and behaviors. There are different levels of structure in different interventions, and it is part of the therapy to consider what approaches are likely to work best to meet individual client goals while still suiting the animals and considering their well-being (VanFleet, Fine, O'Callaghan, Mackintosh, & Gimeno, 2015).

ANIMAL WELFARE

There are numerous considerations in AAPT, just as there are in all AAI, in the area of animal welfare. These include the fundamental care and health of the animals, but also reach far beyond their physical well-being. For example, AAPT practitioners must carefully evaluate whether a particular animal is well-suited or wants to be involved, and if he or she truly enjoys working with client populations. A keen understanding of the client and therapist behaviors, as well as environmental factors, that create either stress or comfort in the individual animal is essential. Likewise, practitioners must be able to recognize signs of animal stress, fatigue, and injury/illness, and respond in a manner that benefits or safeguards their animal before, during, and after the interaction takes place.

Likewise, AAPT practitioners must consider what benefit the animals are likely to get from their participation. Therapists must carefully consider what a reasonable workload is for each animal, and how that is influenced by their age, health, and development. Furthermore, AAPT practitioners must ensure that all activities and interactions respect the dignity and choices of the animals. It is important for animal welfare, but also for the integrity of therapeutic interventions and the well-being of clients, that animals are never depersonalized or devalued in the pursuit of helping people.

Finally, AAPT practitioners need to develop self-awareness to ensure that they are always modeling respectful interactions with the animals for their clients, both in therapy and in their home lives. This is accomplished by developing fluency in the body language and communications of the species with whom practitioners work, as well as actively attending to the specific behaviors and reactions of the therapy animal on an ongoing basis. In essence, the therapist learns to respond in an empathic manner to subtle changes in body language that suggest that human behaviors are too intrusive or threatening to the animal, and to adjust until the animal signals that the stress has been eliminated. This starts with practitioners' awareness of the impact of their own behavior with the animal, and extends into therapy sessions with clients.

This skill is taught and reinforced during AAPT training programs. For example, it is quite common for people, often without thinking, to use leash pops (i.e., quick yanks) or to steer dogs around on a tight leash. In AAPT training, therapists learn that these are ineffective ways to work with dogs, and instructors provide feedback in the moment to help improve the trainee's handling techniques and self-awareness. In such cases, incorporating off-leash alternatives with the dog to build relationship and connection helps offset these often natural human tendencies to push and pull dogs, and/or pop their leashes. If a dog wanders off, the therapist finds playful and dog-friendly ways of regaining the dog's attention, and provides clearer communication about his/her expectations.

These are just some of the animal welfare considerations that arise in this work. While most professionals readily agree that it is important to treat animals humanely in a general way, there is less agreement when it comes to details of practice. What are the implications of collars vs. harnesses for the well-being of dogs? Is control-oriented equipment, such as prong collars for dogs or knotted rope halters for horses, acceptable or should they be prohibited? Exactly how does one create a securely attached relationship with animals of different species? Are natural behaviors of animals permitted (such as grazing or sniffing), or is it better to prevent these from occurring? As the reader can see, once this discussion gains greater specificity, there is more room for disagreement, yet these are discussions that are critical to have. Details on this topic are explored fully in VanFleet and Faa-Thompson (2017).

All of the AAPT training programs and materials emphasize that animal welfare is equally as important as client considerations. The principles of AAPT are clear that animals should not merely be tolerating their involvement, but that they should enjoy it and show that in their behavior. Throughout the process, animals are given choices; they are never forced to participate. It is important from a welfare point of view, but also for the authenticity of the therapy, that the animals' participation in the interactions is voluntary. For example, handler training emphasizes that animals are always provided with an "escape route" or opportunity to rest. When ropes or leashes are used, therapists ensure that they are kept loose and that animals are never pulled. Overall, handlers must frequently advocate for their animals' needs and preferences whenever necessary (VanFleet & Faa-Thompson, 2017).

PROFESSIONAL CERTIFICATIONS

Professionals wishing to use AAPT must receive practice-specific training. They need working knowledge of, and hands-on skill development in, psychotherapy and play therapy, as well as animal behavior, welfare, and ethics. This requires not only training, but also supervision of actual work in the field. The International Institute for Animal Assisted Play Therapy® (IIAAPT, 2013) offers a stringent certification process based on demonstrated competencies (see "IIAAPT Requirements and Competencies"). There are different levels of certification, but all must demonstrate the core competencies. In addition to postgraduate degrees and credentials, professionals must complete several online courses and over 100 hours of in-person, hands-on training with dogs and horses that help develop these competencies. The supervision requirement involves discussion of cases and videos of the professional's work in AAPT with a supervisor who is certified by their primary profession and in AAPT specifically.

IIAAPT Requirements and Competencies

- Education, credentialing, and competence in psychotherapy and play therapy relevant to the client groups served
- Adherence to ethical standards of mental health practice (or the profession in which licensed)
- Work within one's scope of practice
- Adherence to AAPT guiding principles and humane guidelines
- Ability to select, conduct, and process therapeutic interventions in the service of client goals
- Ability to use humor and playfulness appropriately to facilitate therapeutic processes
- Knowledge of appropriate selection and socialization of animals
- Ability to develop and maintain securely attached, collaborative, humane relationships with therapy animals at all times
- Ability to carry out positive, nonaversive training and preparation of animals
- Adherence to the goodness-of-fit model for including animals in different forms of AAPT
- Ability to proactively ensure the well-being and comfort of clients and therapy animals
- Dedication to preserving the dignity of all humans and animals involved, and to avoiding any form of depersonalization of the animals
- Knowledge of two species' body language, and competence in reading and responding to these communications in real time
- Ability to focus on the well-being of clients and the animal partners simultaneously
- Ability to formulate treatment plans that conform to the highest standards of professional practice, while ensuring the welfare and humane treatment of animals

The certification program is conducted in a collaborative manner, which provides individualized feedback and assistance throughout.

Certification is also available for supervisors, instructors, and canine and equine support professionals.

GAPS AND NEXT STEPS

Research

There is a need for more qualitative and quantitative research on AAPT's effectiveness for people who have experienced trauma. To date, research findings have been anecdotal and/or largely quantified clinical outcomes, along with a small number of qualitative or mixed methods studies, with time being invested to ensure consistent training and competencies of therapists using the method. Encouragingly, a pool of highly trained and research-oriented AAPT therapists and animals is growing, and more studies in the field are now possible. As discussed earlier, preliminary research has been promising, and clinical results have been exciting. The IIAAPT has provided data-collection assistance to researchers engaged in several studies on AAI and AAPT, with initial results expected in 2019–2020. The IIAAPT welcomes inquiries about these and future studies, as the program values collaboration with universities, students, and other programs.

Practice

Perhaps the biggest gap resides with the many therapists who do not realize that they should obtain training before involving animals in their professional work. This is not only problematic in AAPT, but in AAI in general. When therapists understand that training is needed, they often underestimate to what degree, and they are satisfied taking only an online course or instruction geared toward volunteer visitation programs. AAI programs that offer social support and enrichment are extremely useful, but it is important to acknowledge that the work in professional practice is much more involved and complex. Specialized preparation is needed for the animals and the therapists, especially in terms of building their own relationships and in planning and facilitating effective AAPT with clients. When a therapist says, "The more I learn, the more I realize I have to learn," it indicates that he or she is aware of the true enormity of knowledge and hands-on skills needed to do this work.

For therapists who have met the required competencies in certification, there are needs for ongoing continuing education, as well as support for those involving other species beyond the most common (i.e., dogs, horses, cats, rats, and rabbits). The general principles of AAPT are the same across all species, but whenever a new species is involved, the practitioner must learn a substantial amount of information about that species and the particular animal they are now partnering with. New online courses are currently being developed to support many aspects of AAPT work, and 2019–2020 will see the addition of special educational opportunities beyond the core courses to help therapists develop the mutual, playful, and securely attached relationships with their animals that are needed for practice. AAPT therapists have been extremely creative to date, and future publications and conferences will feature their ideas and input.

CONCLUSIONS

Involving appropriately prepared animals in play therapy sessions with traumatized children combines the strengths of both approaches—AAI and play—and has the potential to greatly facilitate therapeutic outcomes. Clinical results using this emerging field demonstrate enhanced trust-building in therapy, as well as the ability to meet therapeutic goals in unique and creative ways. These therapeutic goals include the development of: competence and confidence; feeling cared for while learning about mutually respectful relationships; genuine empathy and concern for others; self-regulation; and solutions to a wide range of other trauma-specific challenges. The use of play-based approaches benefits traumatized clients as they safely "play out" and master the intense feelings related to their traumatic experiences (e.g., child maltreatment) and consequent attachment disruptions. At the same time, the playfulness of AAPT creates a welcoming, enjoyable environment for the animals, whose needs are considered equal to those of any human in the equation. Overall, the relationship and welfare emphases of AAPT make it a useful way to work with clients of all ages who struggle with trauma reactions and other difficulties.

AAPT has been evolving with considerable consumer input, as well as a strong sense of clinical quality and animal welfare. An in-depth training program and rigorous certification based on demonstrated competencies have been implemented for mental health and allied health professionals and educators. The AAPT field is now ready for evidence-based research to measure its effectiveness, with the hope that collaborative relationships can be formed to enable this next step forward.

REFERENCES

Bekoff, M. (2018). *Canine confidential: Why dogs do what they do.* Chicago, IL: University of Chicago Press.

Bekoff, M., & Byers, J. A. (Eds.). (1998). *Animal play: Evolutionary, comparative, and ecological perspectives.* Cambridge, UK: Cambridge University Press.

Bifulco, A., & Thomas, G. (2013). *Understanding adult attachment in family relationships: Research, assessment & intervention.* New York, NY: Routledge.

Bowlby, J. (1988). *A secure base: Parent-child attachment and healthy human development.* London, UK: Routledge.

Bratton, S. C., Ray, D., Rhine, T., & Jones, L. (2005). The efficacy of play therapy with children: A meta-analytic review of treatment outcomes. *Professional Psychology: Research and Practice, 36*(4), 376–390.

Brown, S. (2009). *Play: How it shapes the brain, opens the imagination, and invigorates the soul.* New York, NY: Avery.

Burghardt, G. M. (2005). *The genesis of animal play: Testing the limits.* Cambridge, MA: MIT Press.

Chandler, C. K. (2017). *Animal assisted therapy in counseling* (3rd ed.). New York, NY: Routledge.

Chudakoff, H. P. (2007). *Children at play.* New York, NY: New York University Press.

Faa-Thompson, T. (2014). Report on children's and adolescents' self-designed assessments of the Turn About Pegasus Program. In R. VanFleet, & T. Faa-Thompson (Eds.), *Animal Assisted Play Therapy training manual* (8th ed., pp. T17–T18). Boiling Springs, PA: International Institute for Animal Assisted Play Therapy®.

Fine, A. (Ed.). (2015). *Handbook on animal-assisted therapy: Foundations and guidelines for animal-assisted interventions* (4th ed.). London, UK: Elsevier.

Garbarino, J., Dubrow, N., Kostelny, K., & Pardo, C. (1992). *Children in danger: Coping with the consequences of community violence.* San Francisco, CA: Jossey-Bass.

Garbarino, J., Kostelny, K., & Dubrow, N. (1991). What children can tell us about living in danger. *American Psychologist, 46*(4), 376–383.

Gil, E. (2006). *Helping abused and traumatized children.* New York, NY: Guilford.

Ginsburg, K. R. (2007). The importance of play in promoting healthy child development and maintaining strong parent-child bonds. *Pediatrics, 119*(1), 182–191.

Guerney, L., & Ryan, V. (2013). *Group Filial Therapy: A complete guide to teaching parents to play therapeutically with their children*. London, UK: Jessica Kingsley.

Hansing, K. K. (2014). *Self-efficacy among counselors trained in Animal Assisted Play Therapy* (Unpublished doctoral dissertation). Auburn University, Auburn, AL.

International Institute for Animal Assisted Play Therapy®. (2013). *Certification manual forAnimal Assisted Play Therapy*™. Boiling Springs, PA: Author.

Jalongo, M. R. (Ed.). (2018). *Children, dogs and education: Caring for, learning alongside, and gaining support from canine companions*. New York, NY: Springer.

James, B. (1994). *Handbook for treatment of attachment problems in children*. New York, NY: The Free Press.

Käufer, M. (2013). *Canine play behavior: The science of dogs at play*. Wenatchee, WA: Dogwise Publishing.

Louv, R. (2012). *The nature principle: Reconnecting with life in a virtual age*. Chapel Hill, NC: Algonquin Books.

Maestripieri, D. (2012). *Games primates play*. New York, NY: Basic Books.

McNicholas, J., & Collis, G. M. (2000). Dogs as catalysts for social interaction: Robustness of the effect. *British Journal of Psychology, 91*(1), 61–70.

McNicholas, J., & Collis, G. M. (2006). Animals as social supports: Insights for understanding animal-assisted therapy. In A. H. Fine (Ed.), *Handbook on animal-assisted therapy:Theoretical foundations and guidelines for practice* (2nd ed., pp. 49–71). San Diego, CA: Academic Press.

Melson. G. F. (2001). *Why the wild things are: Animals in the lives of children*. Cambridge, MA: Harvard University Press.

Melson, G. F., & Fine, A. H. (2015). Animals in the lives of children. In A. H. Fine (Ed.), *Handbook on animal-assisted therapy: Foundations and guidelines for animal-assisted interventions* (4th ed., pp. 179–194). London, UK: Elsevier.

Olmert, M. (2009). *Made for each other: The biology of the human-animal bond*. Cambridge, MA: Da Capo Press.

Panksepp, J. (2005). *Affective neuroscience: The foundations of human and animal emotions*. New York, NY: Oxford University Press.

Panksepp, J. (2012). *The archaeology of mind: Neuroevolutionary origins of human emotions*. New York, NY: W. W. Norton.

Parish-Plass, N. (Ed.). (2013). *Animal-assisted psychotherapy: Theory, issues, and practice*. West Lafayette, IN: Purdue University Press.

Pellegrini, A. D., & Smith, P. K. (Eds.). (2005). *The nature of play: Great apes and humans*. New York, NY: Guilford Press.

Pellis, S., & Pellis, V. (2009). *The playful brain: Venturing to the limits of neuroscience*. Great Britain: Oneworld Publications.

Perry, B. D., & Szalavitz, M. (2010). *Born for love: Why empathy is essential—and endangered*. New York, NY: Harper.

Siegel, D. (2012). *The developing mind: How relationships and the brain interact to shape who we are*. New York, NY: The Guilford Press.

Sutton-Smith, B. (1997). *The ambiguity of play*. Cambridge, MA: Harvard University Press.

Terr, L. (1990). *Too scared to cry: How trauma affects children . . . and ultimately us all*. New York, NY: Basic Books.

Thompson, M. J. (2009). Animal-assisted play therapy: Canines as co-therapists. In G. R. Walz, J. C. Bleuer, & R. K. Yep (Eds.), *Compelling counseling interventions: VISTAS 2009* (pp.199–209). Alexandria, VA: American Counseling Association.

van der Kolk, B. (2014). *The body keeps the score: Brain, mind, and body in the healing of trauma*. New York, NY: Viking.

VanFleet, R. (2004a). *Animal Assisted Play Therapy™ training manual*. Boiling Springs, PA: Play Therapy Press.

VanFleet, R. (2004b). *It's only natural: Exploring the play in play therapy workshop manual*. Boiling Springs, PA: Play Therapy Press.

VanFleet, R. (2008). *Play therapy with kids & canines: Benefits for children's developmental and psychosocial health*. Sarasota, FL: Professional Resource Press.

VanFleet, R. (2014a). *Filial Therapy: Strengthening parent-child relationships through play*. Sarasota, FL: Professional Resource Press.

VanFleet, R. (2014b). Overcoming extreme fear in unsocialized dogs: A participant-observation study of the impact of safety and play in a home setting. *International Society for Anthrozoology Conference Proceedings*, Vienna, Austria, July 20.

VanFleet, R. (2014c). What it means to be humane in animal-assisted interventions. *The APDT Chronicle of the Dog, Fall*, 18–20.

VanFleet, R. (2015). Short-term play therapy for adoptive families. In H. G. Kaduson & C. E. Schaefer (Eds.), *Short-term play therapy for children* (3rd ed., pp. 290–322). New York, NY: The Guilford Press.

VanFleet, R., & Colţea, C. (2012). Helping children with ASD through canine-assisted play therapy. In L. Gallo-Lopez & L. Rubin (Eds.), *Play-based interventions for children and adolescents on the autism spectrum* (pp. 193–208). New York, NY: Routledge.

VanFleet, R., & Faa-Thompson, T. (2010). The case for using Animal Assisted Play Therapy. *British Journal of Play Therapy, 6*, 4–18.

VanFleet, R., & Faa-Thompson, T. (2012). The power of play, multiplied. *Play Therapy, 70*, 7–10.

VanFleet, R., & Faa-Thompson, T. (2014). Including animals in play therapy with young children and families. In M. R. Jalongo (Ed.), *Teaching compassion: Humane education in early childhood* (pp. 89–107). New York, NY: Springer.

VanFleet, R., & Faa-Thompson, T. (2015a). Animal Assisted Play Therapy. In D. A. Crenshaw & A. L. Stewart (Eds.), *Play therapy: A comprehensive guide to theory and practice* (pp. 201–214). New York, NY: Guilford.

VanFleet, R., & Faa-Thompson, T. (2015b). Animal Assisted Play Therapy to empower vulnerable children. In E. J. Green & A.C. Myrick (Eds.), *Play therapy with vulnerable populations: No child forgotten* (pp. 85–103). Lanham, MD: Rowman & Littlefield.

VanFleet, R., & Faa-Thompson, T. (2015c). Short-term Animal Assisted Play Therapy for children. In H. G. Kaduson & C. E. Schaefer (Eds.), *Short-term play therapy for children* (3rd ed., pp. 175–197). New York, NY: The Guilford Press.

VanFleet, R., & Faa-Thompson, T. (2017). *Animal Assisted Play Therapy™*. Sarasota, FL: Professional Resource Press.

VanFleet, R., Fine, A. H., O'Callaghan, D., Mackintosh, T., & Gimeno, J. (2015). Application of animal-assisted interventions in professional settings: An overview of alternatives. In A. H. Fine (Ed.), *Handbook on animal-assisted therapy: Foundations and guidelines for animal-assisted interventions* (4th ed., pp.157–177). London, UK: Elsevier.

VanFleet, R., Ryan, S. D., & Smith, S. K. (2005). A critical review of Filial Therapy interventions. In L. Reddy & C. E. Schaefer (Eds.), *Empirically-based play interventions for children* (pp. 241–264). Washington, DC: American Psychological Association.

VanFleet, R., & Sniscak, C. C. (2003a). Filial Therapy for attachment-disrupted and disordered children. In R. VanFleet & L. Guerney (Eds.), *Casebook of Filial Therapy* (pp. 279–308). Boiling Springs, PA: Play Therapy Press.

VanFleet, R., & Sniscak, C. C. (2003b). Filial Therapy for children exposed to traumatic events. In R. VanFleet & L. Guerney (Eds.), *Casebook of filial therapy* (pp. 113–137). Boiling Springs, PA: Play Therapy Press.

VanFleet, R., Sywulak, A. E., & Sniscak, C. C. (2010). *Child-centered play therapy*. New York, NY: The Guilford Press.

Wenocur, K. P. (2018). *It's the journey: The developmental and attachment implications of Animal Assisted Play Therapy for children in emergency housing* (Doctorate in Social Work (DSW) dissertation). Retrieved from https://repository.upenn.edu/edissertations_sp2/117

Wilson, E. O. (1984). *Biophilia*. Cambridge, MA: Harvard University Press.

ABOUT THE AUTHOR

Risë VanFleet, PhD, RPT-S, CDBC, is a licensed psychologist specializing in children and families, a registered play therapist-supervisor, and a certified dog behavior consultant with 46 years of experience from Boiling Springs, Pennsylvania. Well-known internationally for her extensive writing and teaching in play therapy, Filial Therapy, and AAPT, she is the cofounder, with Tracie Faa-Thompson, of the International Institute for Animal Assisted Play Therapy® (www.iiaapt.org). Their coauthored book, *Animal Assisted Play Therapy*, was awarded the Maxwell Award from the Dog Writers Association of America for the best book on the human-animal bond in 2018.

CHAPTER 6

Children and Animals: The Importance of Human-Other Animal Relationships in Fostering Resilience in Children

Sarah M. Bexell, PhD; Susan Clayton, PhD; and Gene Myers, PhD

BACKGROUND

History

This chapter offers a slightly different lens than that of most other chapters in this volume. Instead of a clinical lens, we present foundational insights into human child-other animal relationships, ways bonds between children and other animals develop naturally, ways they can be fostered by practitioners, and, importantly, why human child-other animal bonds are important both for typically developing children, as well as for children who have experienced traumatic events. We extend the analysis of human child-other animal bonds to include the importance of the natural environment for the full appreciation of biotic and abiotic factors in the world of all children, which support human health and well-being. Additionally, we touch upon the modern appreciation of the One Health nexus, which reminds humanity that human, other animal, and natural environment health must be simultaneously protected and maintained in order for sustained health to be obtained. Practical and tested protocols to allow for these bonds are shared.

Bonds between humans and individuals of other species have been important throughout human evolution. Humans, as relatively weak in physical form compared to other species, have always studied other species to protect ourselves, learn about the environment around us, and master how to kill for sustenance through the development of cunning and tools, for example. Over millennia, humans have also sought companionship with other species, and these friendships, or bonds, have enriched human lives so significantly as to warrant worry about human psychological well-being if suddenly we find ourselves alone through the destruction of others. Here, we would like to get away from asking questions such as why other animals are important in the lives and development of children. This line of inquiry often perpetuates the status quo of humanocentrism. We do not exist in an exclusively human world, and children seem to see this more clearly than most adults. As developing children study the world around them, each facet is important to attend to and understand, to find out what is safe, what is dangerous, and what provides the most comfort, stimulation or sustenance, for example. While all objects of a child's attention will find their way into the repertoire and understanding of the world of the child, perhaps the most concentrated subjects of interest are living and animate beings (including other humans) who can be perceived as possessing self-determination.

In observations of and interactions with other beings, there is a developing sense of "we are in this together" and a camaraderie that often is forgotten, in terms of relations with other animals, throughout the process of aging and within modern individual human development. If there is universal acceptance that relationships with other humans are essential to healthy development, why have we for so long thought of human-other animal relationships as different, and in many cases, nonessential? Practitioners of animal-assisted interventions (or interactions) (AAIs) capitalize on these innate understandings, without necessarily fully recognizing them or having the scientifically accepted terminology to describe what many of us feel. It is common to hear about the "magic" of encounters with other animals in therapeutic settings, and there is a sense of urgency to research and define these magical powers, down to the invisible chemicals that are produced in the human body that confer the comfort many humans feel in the company of other animals, especially domesticated companion animals. In our anthropocentric drive to make the lives of humans better, at all costs, perhaps we are blinded by our quest, and beautifully orchestrated evolutionarily beneficial relationships are blurred or, worse yet, distorted and destroyed.

We all inhabit the same planet, and it would be beneficial for adult humans to also accept that we truly are all in this together. Biodiversity on Earth is in steady and drastic decline. One solid indicator shows losses of vertebrate (animals with backbones, not including humans within this example) populations averaging 58% over the 40 years up to 2012 (World Wildlife Fund, 2016), making the worry of finding ourselves alone all too real. How will this impact normal child development? If we can create mutually beneficial relationships with all of life on Earth, likely more healing than just from traumatic events would ensue, and just maybe many of those traumatic events could be avoided in the first place. From an evolutionary perspective, all life has value, none above another. As humans have placed themselves above all others, the consequences have included mass extinction, epidemic social ills, dangerous transformations of Earth (our life source), and a growing sense that in the grand scheme, we as individuals no longer matter. There are too many of us, our societies are rapidly becoming less democratic, and our individual voices are obscured or even completely unheard. There perhaps can be nothing so damaging to a person as to realize they might not matter, from which psychological and social pathologies emerge that create trauma for both victims and perpetrators.

In step with the modern tendency to overlook the importance of other life forms (other than those abused for human sustenance) in the health of the developing child, recognition of the importance of other animals in the lives of children in scholarly works has been scarce, while their inclusion in folklore, children's stories, and in their actual lives has been rich. Provocative exceptions to the lack of inclusion of children's relationships with other animals in scholarly works include Myers' (1998/2007) *The Significance of Children and Animals: Social Development and Our Connections to Other Species*; Melson's (2001) *Why the Wild Things Are;* and Ascione's (2005) *Children and Animals: Exploring the Roots of Kindness and Cruelty*, among others, that will provide support here. An explanation for the sparse attention to the issue could be that it may seem too obvious: everyone knows or naturally assumes that children's knowledge of, and relationships with, other animals are paramount in their development and understanding of the world around them, for example through keeping or viewing animals (Myers, 2007). However, could the reasons also be more problematic, as alluded to above?

Today's children are raised in environments where the presence of wildlife is increasingly rare; being raised on a farm is uncommon; and life in housing often includes restrictions on companion animals, resulting in the lack of positive interactions to understand and connect with other species. However, the presence of companion animals in the lives of some children is growing exponentially, as covered in several chapters of this volume. But mixed messages about animals are often conveyed to children with little to no explanation or reconciliation (e.g., animal as companion, food, family member, marketing tool, object of entertainment, victim of domestic violence, victim of neglect, someone to be purchased, someone who was bred to be beneficial to humans), resulting in contradictory framings and confusion. The lack of attention to the importance of animals in the lives of children could also be a psychological protective measure. Many adults may not want to acknowledge the sixth mass extinction (Ceballos et al., 2015), or the modern-day abuses (e.g., factory farms, laboratories, circuses, rodeos, zoos, pollution, and mass habitat destruction such as land and water conversions) that we are all complicit in because our modern economies make it difficult to avoid our own participation.

Yet another reason could be that, both physically and emotionally, our modern urbanized communities have allowed us to forget animals' importance. While the technology that surrounds us is touted as simplifying or making our lives more convenient, it in fact consumes or backgrounds our every waking moment, distancing us ever further from other animals, including other humans. Additionally, adults who choose to have children (or did not have a choice) are under great pressure to make enough money to support the children they brought into the world, creating distancing from animals as well as their own children as they work long hours to make ends meet. Acknowledging the need for other animals in healthy child and human development could bring about another imperative to protect and preserve those with whom we share Earth. In order for interactions with other animals to be therapeutic, and especially to help a child recover from a traumatic event, the child must first be in a trusting relationship with the other animal. This chapter will focus on why and how these important relationships are formed in the context of wider social forces as outlined above.

THEORY AND POTENTIAL MECHANISMS

Psychology

Why are other animals psychologically important in the lives of children? There are many reasons, including development of self in relation to others (Shepard, 1996); having someone safe to care about and to take care of which increases responsibility, empathy, compassion, self-efficacy, and skill mastery (Wiens, Kyngas & Polkki, 2016); as social support (Brown, 2004); in learning how to be an ally for someone else; in developing an understanding of the world around them; in making sense of Earth and in finding their place in the world (Wilson, 1984); and the sheer human need for reliable relationships even when all is right in our personal lives (Blazina, Boyraz & Shen-Miller, 2011). Here we explore the psychological mechanisms of biophilia, empathy, prosocial moral development, continuity of care, and the need for nature, each of which provide support for the understanding of human child-other animal bonds.

Biophilia. An overarching psychological phenomenon underpinning the importance of other animals in child development is biophilia (Wilson, 1984). *Biophilia* is the term coined by sociobiologist Edward O. Wilson (1984) to describe what he believes is the innate human affinity for the natural world. Evolutionarily and biologically, humans are connected to nature and are hardwired to be attracted to nature (for safety as well as serenity). Wilson describes how a human tendency to focus on life and lifelike processes is a biologically based need, and integral to development as individuals and as a species (Kellert, 1993; Wilson, 1984). Today, most children globally have very few positive experiences in nature and with animals (Louv, 2005; Melson, 2001; Myers, 2012). In the absence of such experiences, children may feel personally ill-equipped to function in natural settings, perceiving nature as hostile and dangerous (Bixler & Floyd, 1997). Children need this exposure to sustain their interest, trust, and ultimately, concern for the well-being of other animals, as well as the natural world (Louv, 2005; Myers, 2007). Later, we will present examples of how practitioners can provide these experiences for children, as well as why they should.

Empathy. Young children naturally and willingly empathize with other humans (Eisenberg, Fabes & Spinrad, 2006; Quann & Wien, 2006) as well as other animals, and feel compelled to help animals in distress (Melson, 2001; Myers, 2007; Thompson & Gullone, 2003). This provides children with a strong sense of purpose. Experiences with animals for whom they can help provide care will deepen their ability to empathize with others, both of their own species and individuals of other species (Bexell, 2006). Child development specialists previously thought that children outgrew their affinity for, and connections to, animals. However, we worry that something else is happening, specifically, that by children's development of distancing mechanisms after exposure to socially normalized abuses or statements that diminish the lives of other animals, their empathy with animals weakens and allows them to treat animals and the environment with lack of true understanding, compassion, and respect. Normative experiences and programmatic planning should aim to reclaim and nurture those innate empathic feelings with animals in the hopes that children will understand their world, be kind to humans and other animals, maintain self-respect and self-love, and in the future understand and act to preserve the natural environment for the animals they have grown to love and admire.

Empathy and prosocial moral development. Theories of empathy and moral development have focused on either the behavioral, cognitive, or emotional dimensions of prosocial moral development (Hoffman, 2000). Hoffman (2000) combines the three dimensions and provides a framework of prosocial moral development in children. He states that the starting point for the development of morals is empathy—one feels what is appropriate for another's situation, rather than one's own. Hoffman (2000) believes that moral development is rooted in empathy, and that our highest morals are founded on empathic feelings we experience, often vicariously, with others who make us want to act with kindness toward them. While most of his research (see Hoffman, 2000, for a review) has focused on the development of moral behavior toward humans, we hypothesize that the same theories can be applied to children's relationships with other animals.

Specifically, Hoffman (1979) states that what he calls *empathic distress*, or awareness of another's distress, is a prosocial motivator. This is evidenced in his findings (Hoffman, 1979) that empathic distress not only correlates positively with people's helping behavior, but in many cases precedes and contributes to helping behavior. For example, when a child sees another child who is distressed because he cannot find his mother, she instinctually feels what the distressed child is experiencing and asks her own mother to help him. Once the other mother is found, the previously distressed child feels better and so does the helpful child, which reinforces the helpful behavior via the opportunity to have good feelings. Therefore, like other motives, empathic distress diminishes in intensity when one helps, but continues at a high level when one does not help (Hoffman, 2000). The same process occurs in healthy humans when one sees a distressed or injured member of another species and provides appropriate and needed help.

Some people think of animals as not sentient and therefore impossible to empathize with, and this has enabled extreme cases of animal abuse and insensitivity (Ratloff, 2005; Song, 2004). In contrast, within AAIs, practitioners often explain to children the type of care that the individual therapeutic animal needs. This explanation allows children to recognize the power differential between humans and the other animal, and to see that they are also in the position of holding the power to help provide for the other animal's needs for both physical and mental health. With this knowledge and understanding, children often participate in the care of the animal such as walking, feeding, brushing, and even consoling. A relationship built on trust and care forms, and both child and animal can begin to predict the needs of the other.

For example, on the side of a child who has experienced a traumatic event and is with a therapist to work through their concerns, a therapy animal will sense that the child may need their love and the comfort they provide. On the side of the animal, the child will learn the other animal's patterns of expressing their needs, such as going for a walk, seeking water or respite, or needing the child to be calm to help them both feel safe. This process of attunement between child and animal is reassuring to both, and for the child, the relationship may be one in which he or she feels the safest, as well as a valued contributor to someone who needs his or her love and understanding. For many children who have experienced maltreatment, these features of safety, reliability/trust, genuine communication, and feeling like a valued member of the relationship may be extremely rare, if not completely unique. They may have never felt this way in their other significant relationships (i.e., with their parents), making their new relationship with an individual of another species paramount in their healing and founding of their own self-worth and self-efficacy.

Human-other animal bond. Young children are able to identify other animals as social others (Myers, 2007). In identifying with animals on a social level, relationships form due to consistency of behavior and expectations that confer comfort and a caring bond. To connect with another animal, like with our own species, it is believed that children need to first understand and appreciate them (Sobel, 1996). Intervention programs can be designed to foster the human-animal bond in participants, as well as provide concrete ways to care for animals. Knowledge about other species (including their biology, habitats, emotions, cognition, abilities, traumas, and plights) both in the wild and under human care can be presented in appropriate contexts to develop realistic concern and connection. However, the focus should be on love and compassion for animals, and how to demonstrate care for them (Bexell, 2006). Later, we provide specific examples of protocols and programming that provide these experiences for children.

Another way to foster the human-other animal bond involves giving particular biographic information about animals and using names and personal pronouns even with those who are typically less "personalized" or considered to be unsafe (e.g., reptiles, insects), so children can see them as individuals and not just as a member of a species (Myers, 2007). Just as we know the dangers of stereotypes humans utilize to marginalize other humans, we tend toward the same generalizations in our thoughts of other animals (e.g., rats are dirty, bats are scary, the only use for a cow is as food, chickens are stupid). However, anyone who has had the chance to really get to know a cow, a rat, a bat, or a chicken finds it difficult to treat any member of those species according to today's socially normalized notions.

Interventions can highlight traits that are similar between children and other animals, while emphasizing special and exceptional traits of animals and the abilities of providing care that children possess. This strategy is commonly used in humane education (Bexell, 2006; Raphael, 1999; Weil, 2004). People often are more interested in, and in turn protective of, animals whom they can perceive as intelligent, strong, fast, cute, industrious, creative, kind, and/or protective of their children (for example) (Hoage, 1989). All living beings have special qualities that help them survive and create balance in their native ecosystem, so interventions can make those qualities apparent and inspiring to children. In this process, children can take a reprieve from their own history and pain and focus love and support toward others who need them. This is empowering for young children and gives them a sense of purpose to heal and to continue to be able to help others. When a child cares about another human or animal, that child also tends to care about that other's environment. It is hoped that by providing opportunities to form bonds with animals, children may begin a lifetime of care toward animals as well as the environment.

Multiple points of contact. Another supporting intervention modality is what we call *multiple points of contact between children and other animals* (Bexell, 2006; Bexell, Jarrett & Xu, 2013). The provision of multiple points of contact with the same animal builds trust through multiple planned or chance interactions between a person and another animal. According to Myers (2007) and Shepard (1996), children must develop trust of new animals they meet, and the animals must be allowed time to trust them. Children acquire this trust after observing how an animal reacts in different situations, just as the animal is doing with them. With multiple interactions building upon the other, both the child and the other animal can see consistency of behavior (involving intentions and personality of each other) and may be better able to predict each other's behavior in future interactions (Bexell, 2006; Myers, 2007). Providing multiple repeated experiences that allow a child and another animal to become familiar others, to become acquaintances or even friends, corresponds with how humans develop relationships with new people. Established human-other animal connections provide the experience of attunement: two beings responding to the core self of each other (Irvine, 2004; Lasher, 1998). Because relationships in the lives of maltreated children or those exposed to family violence are often not reliable, consistent, predictable, or stable, which can further reinforce hyperarousal for these children, the experience of consistently supportive relationships with animals can be of great benefit. In sum, relationships, including with animal companions, can provide a safe, responsive setting for inner growth (Lasher, 1998), and for healing in both children and other animals who have experienced trauma.

Cross-cultural continuity of concern. A hypothesis we feel has strong merit and promise for fostering bonds between children and other animals is that a cross-cultural continuity of concern for animals, and empathy with animals, may exist in children (Hoffman, 2000; Myers, 2007; Turiel, 1983). The literature documents young children across cultural lines expressing empathic feelings toward the suffering or discomfort of other people (Turiel, 1983). A study among Chinese and American preschool children strongly suggests that such empathy for other animals also exists (Bexell, Jarrett, Yang, & Tan, 2005). However, as children develop cognitively, they realize there are inconsistencies in what adults say and do to animals and the environment, causing discontinuity or lessening in children's concern (Myers, 2007). While some practitioners of AAIs may worry that children of some cultures may have trouble understanding and bonding with animals, we posit that every culture includes their own familial environments that vary greatly in their ability to hinder or enhance bonds with other animals.

In one study, six-year-old children of farm owners and farmworkers did not express concern for animals when the interests of the animals conflicted with interests of farming (Severson & Kahn, 2010). However, Severson and Kahn (2010) showed that when conflicts with humans were removed in a hypothetical dilemma, six-year-olds articulated empathy toward, and biocentric moral inclusion of, animals. Thus, family practices and beliefs may encourage attitudes ranging from distrust and disgust to respect and adoration of all species. This is likely confusing for children—that adults treat other animals (and other humans) differently depending upon situations these others find themselves in. However, Kahn (1997) found that children from multiple cultures express concern for and willingness to protect nature and other animals, with no contingencies on benefits to them, but for full consideration of the intrinsic value of nature and other animals. With a strong practitioner who has foremost in her/his mind and heart the well-being of the child and other animal, it is predicted that a therapeutic milieu can be fostered between almost any young child and animals.

Children's need for nature. It has been well-documented that for children, time in nature is important both physically and psychologically (e.g., Burriss & Boyd, 2005; Hart, 1997; Louv, 2005; Moore, 1997; Nabhan & Trimble, 1994). Adult recollections of special places and preferred play areas testify to the importance of nature in childhood (Chawla, 1994, 1999); many adults identify the most significant place in their childhood with the outdoors (Sebba, 1991). Natural areas have been found to satisfy some critical developmental needs of young children, and many scientists fear that without exposure to nature and outdoor play, development could be hindered (Burriss & Boyd, 2005; Louv, 2005). Increasingly, children have fewer opportunities to play outdoors, especially in natural or even semi-natural areas (Louv, 2005; Nabhan & Trimble, 1994). Many children never develop a personal bond with the natural world, and may grow up believing they are separate from, rather than a part of, nature (Louv, 2005). Children today also may never develop an awareness of the interrelationships that exist among all living things, and may never give thought to the fact that all their food, air, and water comes from nature (Miles, 1986/87; Partridge, 1984; Wilson, 1993, 1994). Realities such as these are dangerous because human health depends on the health of the natural environment, and in children's purposeful and conscientious awareness of this relationship.

Early years are significant in a child's development of his/her value system (Bredekamp & Copple, 1997; Kals, Schumacher, & Montada, 1999). Children are surrounded by materialistic cultural values that lead to overconsumption. Automobiles and technology keep them isolated and indoors. A plethora of disposable convenience items and public media convey that new is always better (De Graaf, Waan, & Naylor, 2001; Louv, 2005; Prévot-Julliard, Julliard, & Clayton, 2014; Schor, 1998). To help counter these influences, the ability of living beings to hold children's interest should be used to: help them understand the living environment, including themselves and other animals; respect the appearance and well-being of the world; and take responsibility for its care (Katcher & Wilkins, 1993). Children are likely to be receptive to such attempts; after all, many prefer natural areas to play in (Chawla, 1999; Korpela, 2002).

A number of studies have demonstrated the positive impact of green spaces on children's social and emotional well-being (Kuo & Faber Taylor, 2004; Wells & Evans, 2003; Wells & Rollings, 2012). The opportunity for children to develop an environmental identity—an underlying sense of self as interdependent with and connected to the natural world—is also likely to promote their attention to environmental issues (Clayton, 2012). A strong environmental identity is linked to early experiences with the natural world (Prévot, Clayton, & Mathevet, 2016). Among adults, it is associated not only with pro-environmental concern and behavior and support for animal rights (Clayton, 2008), but also with personal well-being (Olivos & Clayton, 2016).

BEST PRACTICES

Service Providers

Perhaps some of the best organizations providing the types of programming referred to throughout this chapter are local nature centers and sanctuaries in the case of rescued wild or farm animals, and humane societies in the case of domesticated companion animals. For example, the Zoology Foundation at Crooked Willow Farm in Larkspur, Colorado (zoology foundation.org/our-animal-sanctuary), in partnership with the Institute for Human-Animal Connection at the University of Denver (www.du.edu /humananimalconnection), provides a camp experience to typically developing children ages 8–12 years with the primary goal of fostering the human-animal bond (see procedures below) to improve animal and nature protection.

An important facet of the experience is that the individual animals have been rescued from human actions (e.g., hoarding, neglect, abandonment) and are now thriving under human love, proper care, and respect. The camp curriculum is based on one that was designed to work cross-culturally and originally implemented for children in China (Bexell, 2006; Bexell, Jarrett, Xu & Feng, 2009; Bexell et al., 2013) (see below for further description). The camp experience actively constructs the human-animal bond via multiple points of contact. It builds a *continuum of care* throughout the week of camp by first introducing the children and other animals in a way to foster relationships, then teaching how to provide care for each individual animal, then introducing experts (e.g., animal behaviorists, veterinarians, wildlife rehabilitators, conservation biologists) who become role models to the children, and finally learning what the animals need from humans in order to live well, and with as much self-determination as is safe for each individual.

Protocols

The protocol that was used at the Zoology Foundation at Crooked Willow Farm was originally created as a human-other animal bond intervention with children in China, and capitalizes on the above-mentioned multiple-points-of-contact and *continuum of care* (Bexell, 2006; Bexell &

Feng, 2013; Bexell et al., 2013). The original program in China consisted of a five-day, overnight camp experience developed for typically developing children, ages 8–12 years, and took them along the *continuum of care* (Bexell, 2006; Bexell et al., 2013). Students first intimately met small animals (e.g., rabbits, guinea pigs, hamsters, parakeets, and tortoises), whom the students were encouraged to recognize as individuals with distinctive personalities and feelings similar to their own. This was followed by less intimate exposure to more fully wild species (including giant pandas, red pandas, zebras, golden monkeys, giraffes, and lemurs).

Children were then given responsibilities for the care of the small animals and were allowed to bond with individual animals and think about their emotional states. Our hope was that these intimate experiences would not only instill caring feelings about individual animals, but also extend to a deepening feeling about the environment on which all animals depend, thus encouraging awareness that destroying an animal's environment is akin to directly harming individuals within a child's realm of care. Our hypothesis was that children would be able to make these intimate connections and thereby choose to change their own personal behaviors that harm the environment and wild animals. Near the end of camp, we asked children how activities that harm the environment might impact the animals they came to know, and we encouraged them to talk with their friends and family about their newly found respect for animals and worries about how their homes are treated.

The camp was designed to encourage the human–other animal bond in participants, as well as provide concrete ways to care for animals and nature. Knowledge about animals, both in the wild and in captivity, was presented in appropriate contexts to elicit emotional feelings from children in a safe environment wherein expressions of love and compassion for animals were not only acceptable, but preferred, behavior. Our curriculum highlighted those traits that are similar between humans and other animals, but also revealed specialized characteristics of animals to help pique students' interest in, and acceptance of, the unique natural history of our diverse world (Hoage, 1989).

This protocol could be adapted and added to AAIs with any individual or population that either has not had much positive interaction with other animals or in nature, or to enrich the lives of clients who currently do have relationships with other animals. For example, in AAI applications, practitioners typically work to first establish rapport between their clients and therapy animals; this protocol could provide direction in encouraging greater intimacy, trust, and mutual respect in these child-animal relationships.

It is important to note that the program in China used all the described mechanisms with children who had not experienced a known traumatic event. In other words, the program was not designed to address specific needs in regard to trauma or symptoms. But very similar practices, when done with rescued animals for children with trauma, could also work powerfully for therapeutic ends, as well as conservation and humane ones. Ensuring that individual animals utilized in therapeutic interventions are rescued and not purchased is critically important. The act of purchasing another being is a violation of their rights and sets the tone that other animals are not our equals and can be bought and sold, acquired and abandoned, nurtured or neglected, bred only to serve human interests. Children who have suffered from traumatic events could be retraumatized if they learn of the unethical treatment of animals they have come to love. Additionally, the life history of each individual rescued animal is important, just as the traumatic events that happened to traumatized children are, but also the journey to regaining trust in others, allowing yourself to be loved, and finding the sense of security that opens doors to happiness and well-being, can be shared between children and these individual animals.

Professional Certifications

There are at least three important certification options to date. Two are with the Institute for Human-Animal Connection at the University of Denver, which provides professional development certification in "Raising Compassionate Kids: Humane Education and Interventions for Early Learners," as well as in "Animals in Human Health." Additionally, the Institute for Humane Education offers workshops, certifications, and full graduate degree programs in humane education.

Relevant professional competencies in these areas include: 1) possession of a firm understanding of the interlinking of human, other animal, and environmental health (the One Health nexus); 2) deep empathy with, and passion for, working for the well-being of humans, other animals, and the natural world simultaneously; 3) learning how to foster the best qualities in young children, for their health and well-being and for that of the natural world; and 4) learning to create and implement high-quality animal-assisted and humane education programs and interventions guided by experienced and trained professionals who can offer ethical and skills-based certifications.

ANIMAL WELFARE

Challenges

The greatest challenge to animal welfare is in preparing adults to teach the correct information, and most importantly, to model the appropriate behavior toward any species, wild or domesticated, in interventions designed to facilitate the child-animal bond. Without training and correct knowledge of animals' species-specific and individual needs, in combination (usually) with empathy and compassion for other animals, adults can inadvertently teach fear, disgust, anxiety, or improper care or treatment, instead of respect, proper care, and love (Bexell & Feng, 2013).

Recommendations

How to Foster Relationships Between Children and Other Animals

Rachel Carson (1956) believed that for children to keep alive an inborn sense of wonder, they each need the companionship of at least one adult who can share it and rediscover with them the joy, excitement, and mystery of the natural world. A goal in intervention design to foster the human-animal bond is to prepare role models for children, models who exemplify new patterns of caring about and for animals, as well as protecting the environment in a way that encourages children to take responsibility for animal well-being. The ability to nurture other animals appears to be a universal of human nature; however, appropriate nurturing does not necessarily appear without role models acceptable to the local community, as well as adequate opportunities to engage in such behavior (Irwin, 2003). People who are passionate and knowledgeable about animals and who model care, concern, and admiration for them are needed to implement these interventions. The first step in providing proper care and respect of animals is an understanding of both who and what they are, knowledge best gained through the study of the natural history of the species a practitioner plans to work with, and a study of their individual behavior and personality.

Children should also study animal behavior, both through direct experience and anecdotally through experts. The awareness of an animal's behavior can give children insight into the animal's mind and feelings. Moreover, children can realize for themselves that animals have thoughts, intelligence, feelings, and behaviors similar to their own. As they recognize these similarities, their interest in, and appreciation of, the individual animal usually increases (Bexell, 2006). With the growth of solid scientific evidence showing qualities of animal minds and behavior akin to human animal minds and behavior (e.g., Bekoff, 2006; Darwin, 1998; de Waal, 2016; Fossey, 2000; Goodall, 2000; Griffin, 2001; Masson & McCarthy, 1996; McConnell, 2003; Mitchell, Thompson, & Miles, 1996; Moss, 2000; Poole, 1998, Shanor & Kanwal, 2011), practitioners can now confidently use the scientific literature to describe human similarities with other animals. Likewise, practitioners can use the findings from animal behavior research to engender human respect, care, and nurturance of our animal kin. The study of cognitive ethology, how animals use their minds to adapt and survive, is a young and positive area of science (Bekoff, 2006; de Waal, 2016). Understanding the minds of other animals opens children's eyes and hearts to create meaningful relationships with them.

In past training of program implementers in China, the first author and colleagues found that instructors were highly influenced by exposure to compassionate and knowledgeable trainers. New instructors readily changed their own attitudes and behavior toward animals (Bexell, Yu, Feng, Yang, & Xu, 2004), and were inspired to model for their participants care and interest in animals as sentient beings. This modeling of respect and admiration for animals is critical to success in fostering healthy human-other animal bonds.

The importance of modeling is based on social learning theory (Bandura, 1977). Bandura states that most learning occurs on a vicarious basis by observing other people's behavior and the consequences that behavior has for them. The capacity to learn by observation enables humans (and other animals) to acquire large, integrated patterns of behavior without having to form them by trial and error (Bandura, 1977). According to Bandura (1977), behavior change usually begins when someone receives extrinsic incentives for a particular behavior, but to become incorporated into a person's repertoire, intrinsic incentives are usually necessary. Reinforcement, perhaps in the form of approval by a respected model, acts as an extrinsic prerequisite for the development of intrinsic reinforcement, formed by the development of relationships between children and other animals in a program or intervention. A good deal of intrinsic reinforcement comes in the form of emotional feedback (Bandura, 1977). If that feedback is pleasant, in the case of emotionally satisfying relationships with animals, it should serve to reinforce and maintain the performance of caring behavior toward animals, thus fostering relationships that enhance resilience in both partners.

Role models can show that behaviors have consequences, and we want to exemplify the positive consequences that derive from compassionate care of other animals. This point applies not only on the level of immediate face-to-face intervention, but also (and simultaneously) on a societal level. Today, human societies globally have normalized extreme levels of abuse of other animals and of other humans. Models whose behaviors differ from these expected, predicted behaviors may be more influential than models that exhibit stereotyped conventional behaviors (Harris & Evans, 1973). In essence, everyone can widen their impact by modeling compassionate relationships.

CONCLUSION

The best way forward for AAI research and practice would be to move from questioning the importance of children's bonds with other animals to finding or developing and testing best evidence-based practices for allowing these bonds to occur naturally. We are still at the early stages of understanding questions like, what types of relationships with animals are therapeutic as well as humane? Are companion animals in the home the best model? Can relationships fostered through classroom-based curricula be as effective, or even more so? Are there certain species that are more appropriate, and is this different for healthy children as compared to those who have experienced trauma? Is there a critical period for these experiences? What are the best ways for adults and institutions to encourage mutually beneficial bonds between children and other animals?

Greater facilitation of healthy relationships between children, other animals, and the natural world would bring about systemic change in human health, animal protection, and preservation of Earth and her processes. The

One Health nexus asks us to examine our responsibilities toward human life, other life, and environmental health, and is changing our conceptions of resilience and what it will take to get us to a more pragmatic, as well as humane, human presence on Earth. Children rarely find difficulty in recognizing the worth of other animals, but rely on capable humane models to demonstrate how the animals should be treated to maintain respect and compassion. The growing body of AAI practitioners is one of the strongest groups demonstrating our need for sharing our lives with other species.

REFERENCES

Ascione, F. (2005). *Children and animals: Exploring the roots of kindness and cruelty.* West Lafayette, IN: Purdue University Press.

Bandura, A. (1977). *Social learning theory.* Upper Saddle River, NJ: Prentice-Hall.

Bekoff, M. (2006). *Animal passions and beastly virtues: Reflections on redecorating nature.* Philadelphia, PA: Temple University Press.

Bexell, S. M. (2006). *Effect of a wildlife conservation camp experience in China on student knowledge of animals, care, propensity for environmental stewardship, and compassionate behavior toward animals* (Dissertation). Georgia State University, Atlanta, Georgia.

Bexell, S. M., & Feng, R. X. (2013). Considering human development, socialization and enculturation in educational intervention design for wildlife conservation: A case for bats. In R. A. Adams & S. C. Pedersen (Eds.), *Bat evolution, ecology, & conservation* (pp. 343–361). New York, NY: Springer Science Press.

Bexell, S. M., Jarrett, O. S., & Xu, P. (2013). The effects of a summer camp program in China on children's knowledge, attitudes and behaviors toward animals: A model for conservation education. *Visitor Studies, 16*(1), 59–81.

Bexell, S. M., Jarrett, O. S., Xu, P., & Feng, R. X. (2009). Fostering humane attitudes toward animals: An educational camp experience in China. *Encounter, 22*(4), 25–27.

Bexell, S. M., Jarrett, O. S., Yang, J., & Tan, N. N. (2005). Children and animals: Exploring empathic feelings with animals in four year olds in China and the United States. Poster presented at the meeting of the Society for Research in Child Development, Atlanta, GA: 7–10 April 2005.

Bexell, S. M., Yu, J., Feng, R. X., Yang, X. Y., & Xu, P. (2004). Instructor camp evaluation journals. Unpublished raw data.

Bixler, R., & Floyd, M. (1997). Nature is scary, disgusting, and uncomfortable. *Environment and Behavior, 5*(2), 202–247.

Blazina, C., Boyraz, G., & Shen-Miller, D. (2011). Introduction: Using context to inform clinical practice and research. In C. Blazina, G. Boyraz, & D. Shen-Miller (Eds.), *The psychology of the human-animal bond* (pp. 3–24). New York, NY: Springer.

Bredekamp, S., & Copple, C. (Eds.). (1997). *Developmentally appropriate practice in early childhood programs servicing children from birth through age eight.* (Rev. ed.). Washington, DC: National Association for the Education of Young Children.

Brown, S. E. (2004). The human-animal bond and self psychology: Toward a new understanding. *Society & Animals 12*(1), 67–86.

Burriss, K. G., & Boyd, B. F. (Eds.). (2005). *Outdoor learning and play ages 8–12.* Olney, MD: Association for Childhood Education International.

Carson, R. (1956). *The sense of wonder.* New York, NY: HarperCollins.

Ceballos, G., Ehrlich, P. R., Barnosky, A. D., Garcia, A., Pringle, R. M., & Palmers, T. M. (2015). Accelerated modern human-induced species losses: Entering the sixth mass extinction. *Science Advances, 1,* e1400253.

Chawla, L. (1994). *In the first country of places: Nature, poetry, and childhood memory.* Albany, NY: State University of New York Press.

Chawla, L. (1999). Life paths into effective environmental action. *Journal of Environmental Education, 31*(1), 15–26.

Clayton, S. (2008). Attending to identity: Ideology, group membership, and perceptions of justice. In K. Hegtvedt & J. Clay-Warner (Eds.), *Advances in group processes: Justice* (pp. 241–266). Bingley, UK: Emerald.

Clayton, S. (2012). Environment and identity. In S. Clayton (Ed.), *Oxford handbook of environmental and conservation psychology* (pp. 164–180). New York, NY: Oxford University Press.

Darwin, C. (1998). *The expression of the emotions in man and animals* (3rd ed.). Oxford, UK: Oxford University Press.

De Graaf, J., Waan, D., & Naylor, T. H. (2001). *Affluenza: The all-consuming epidemic.* San Francisco, CA: Berrett-Koehler Publishers.

de Waal, F. (2016). *Are we smart enough to know how smart animals are?* New York, NY: W. W. Norton.

Eisenberg, N., Fabes, R. A., & Spinrad, T. L. (2006). Prosocial development. In W. Damon & R. Lerner (Eds.), *Handbook of child psychology* (6th ed., pp. 647–702). Hoboken, NJ: John Wiley & Sons.

Fossey, D. (2000). *Gorillas in the mist.* Boston, MA: Mariner Books.

Goodall, J. (2000). *In the shadow of man.* Boston, MA: Mariner Books.

Griffin, D. R. (2001). *Animal minds: Beyond cognition to consciousness.* Chicago, IL: University of Chicago Press.

Harris, M. B., & Evans, R. C. (1973). Models and creativity. *Psychological Reports*, *33*, 763–769.

Hart, R. (1997). *Children's participation: The theory and practice of involving young citizens in community development and environmental care.* London, UK: Earthscan Publications.

Hoage, R. J. (1989). Introduction. In: R. J. Hoage (Ed.), *Perceptions of animals in American culture.* Washington, DC: Smithsonian Institution Press.

Hoffman, M. L. (1979). Development of empathy and altruism. *Developmental Psychology*, *15*, 607–623.

Hoffman, M. L. (2000). *Empathy and moral development: Implications for caring and justice.* Cambridge, UK: Cambridge University Press.

Irvine, L. (2004). *If you tame me: Understanding our connection with animals.* Philadelphia, PA: Temple University Press.

Irwin, P. (2003). A strategic review of international animal protection. In *The state of the animals II: 2003* (pp. 1–8). Retrieved from http://files.hsus.org/web-files /PDF/soa_ii_chap01.pdf

Kahn, P. H. (1997). Developmental psychology and the biophilia hypothesis: Children's affiliation with nature. *Developmental Review*, *17*, 1–61.

Kals, E., Schumacher, D., & Montada, L. (1999). Emotional affinity towards nature as a motivational basis to protect nature. *Environment and Behavior*, *31*(2), 178–202.

Katcher, A., & Wilkins, G. (1993). Dialog with animals: It's nature and culture. In S. R. Kellert, & E. O. Wilson (Eds.), *The biophilia hypothesis* (pp. 173–197). Washington, DC: Island Press.

Kellert, S. R. (1993). Introduction. In S. R. Kellert, & E. O. Wilson (Eds.), *The biophilia hypothesis* (pp. 20–27). Washington, DC: Island Press.

Korpela, K. (2002). Children's environment. In R. B. Bechtel & A. Churchman (Eds.), *Handbook of environmental psychology* (pp. 363–373). New York, NY: John Wiley & Sons.

Kuo, F., & Faber Taylor, A. (2004). A potential natural treatment for attention-deficit/hyperactivity disorder: Evidence from a national study. *American Journal of Public Health*, *94*(9), 1580–1586.

Lasher, M. (1998). A relational approach to the human-animal bond. *Anthrozoös*, *11*(3), 130–133.

Louv, R. (2005). *Last child in the woods: Saving our children from nature-deficit disorder.* Chapel Hill, NC: Algonquin Books of Chapel Hill.

Masson, J. M., & McCarthy, S. (1996). *When elephants weep: The emotional lives of animals.* New York, NY: Delta Press.

McConnell, P. B. (2003). *The other end of the leash: Why we do what we do around dogs*. New York, NY: Ballantine Books.

Melson, G. F. (2001). *Why the wild things are*. Cambridge, MA: Harvard University Press.

Miles, J. C. (1986/1987). Wilderness as a learning place. *Journal of Environmental Education, 18*(2), 33–40.

Mitchell, R. M., Thompson, N. S., & Miles, H. L. (1996). *Anthropomorphism, anecdotes, and animals*. Albany, NY: State University of New York Press.

Moore, R. (1997). *Natural learning*. Berkeley, CA: MIG Communications.

Moss, C. (2000). *Elephant memories: Thirteen years in the life of an elephant family*. Chicago, IL: University of Chicago Press.

Myers, Jr. O. E. (2007). *The significance of children and animals: Social development and our connections to other species* (2nd ed.). West Lafayette, IN: Purdue University Press. Original work published in 1998.

Myers, Jr. O. E. (2012). Children and nature. In S. Clayton (Ed.), *The Oxford handbook of environmental and conservation psychology* (pp. 113–127). Oxford, UK: Oxford University Press.

Nabhan, G. P., & Trimble, S. (1994). *The geography of childhood: Why children need wild places*. Boston, MA: Beacon Press.

Olivos, P., & Clayton, S. (2016). Self, nature and well-being: Sense of connectedness and environmental identity for quality of life. In G. Fleury-Bahi, E. Pol, & O. Navarro (Eds.), *Handbook of environmental psychology and quality of life research* (pp. 107–126). New York, NY: Springer.

Partridge, E. (1984). Nature as a moral resource. *Environmental Ethics, 6*, 101–130.

Poole, J. (1998). An exploration of a commonality between ourselves and elephants. *Etica & Animalia, 9*, 85.

Prévot, A. C., Clayton, S., & Mathevet, R. (2016). The relationship of childhood upbringing and university degree program to environmental identity: Experience in nature matters. *Environmental Education Research*, 1–17.

Prévot-Julliard, A. C., Julliard, R., & Clayton, S. (2014). Historical evidence for nature disconnection in a 70-year time series of Disney animated films. *Public Understanding of Science, 6*, 672–680.

Quann, V., & Wien, C. (2006). The visible empathy of infants and toddlers. *Young Children 61*(4), 22–29.

Raphael, P. (1999). *Teaching compassion: A guide for humane educators, teachers, and parents*. Alameda, CA: Latham Foundation for the Promotion of Humane Education.

Ratloff, J. (2005). A galling business: The inhumane exploitation of bears for traditional Asian medicine. *Science News, 168*, 250–252.

Schor, J. B. (1998). *The overspent American: Why we want what we don't need*. New York, NY: HarperPerennial.

Sebba, R. (1991). The landscapes of childhood: The reflection of childhood's environment in adult memories and in children's attitudes. *Environment and Behavior, 23*(4), 395–422.

Severson, R. L., & Kahn, P. H., Jr. (2010). In the orchard: Farm worker children's moral and environmental reasoning. *Journal of Applied Developmental Psychology, 31*, 249–256.

Shanor, K., & Kanwal, J. (2011). *Bats sing, mice giggle: The surprising science of animals' inner lives*. London, UK: Icon Books.

Shepard, P. (1996). *The others: How animals made us human*. Washington, DC: Island Press.

Sobel, D. (1996). *Beyond ecophobia: Reclaiming the heart in nature education*. The Great Barrington, MA: Orion Society.

Song, W. (2004). Traditional Chinese culture and animals. In *Animal Legal and Historical Center*. Retrieved from www.animallaw.info/nonus/articles/arcnweiculturalatt2005.htm

Thompson, K. L., & Gullone, E. (2003). Promotion of empathy and prosocial behaviour in children through humane education. *Australian Psychologist, 38*(3), 175–182.

Turiel, E. (1983). *The development of social knowledge: Morality and convention*. Cambridge, UK: Cambridge University Press.

Weil, Z. (2004). *The power and promise of humane education*. Gabriola Island, BC: New Society Publishers.

Wells, N., & Evans, G. (2003). Nearby nature: A buffer of life stress among rural children. *Environment and Behavior 35*(3), 311–330.

Wells, N., & Rollings, K. A. (2012). The natural environment in residential settings: Influences on human health and function. In S. Clayton (Ed.), *The Oxford handbook of environmental and conservation psychology* (pp. 509–523). Oxford, UK: Oxford University Press.

Wiens, V., Kyngas, H., & Polkki, T. (2016). The meaning of seasonal changes, nature, and animals for adolescent girls' well-being in northern Finland: A qualitative descriptive study. *International Journal of Qualitative Studies on Health and Well-Being, 11*, 30160. https://doi.org/10.3402/qhw.v11.30160

Wilson, E. O. (1984). *Biophilia: The human bond with other species*. Cambridge, MA: Harvard University Press.

Wilson, R. A. (1993). *Fostering a sense of wonder during the early childhood years*. Columbus, OH: Greyden Press.

Wilson, R. A. (1994). (Ed.). *Environmental education at the early childhood level.*
Troy, OH: North American Association for Environmental Education.

World Wildlife Fund. (2016). *Living planet report 2016: Risk and resilience in a
new era.* Gland, Switzerland: WWF International.

ABOUT THE AUTHORS

Sarah Bexell, PhD, is a clinical associate professor at the Graduate School
of Social Work and director of Humane Education for the Institute for
Human-Animal Connection, both at the University of Denver. She teaches
sustainable development, humane education, and animal studies. She is
faculty with the Institute for Humane Education-Valparaiso University and
senior advisor at China's Chengdu Research Base of Giant Panda Breeding.

Susan Clayton, PhD, is the Whitmore-Williams Professor of Psychology at
the College of Wooster in Ohio. A social psychologist by training, her
research focuses on the importance of the human relationship with nature
and how it can be utilized to promote environmental concern. She has
written extensively about the implications of climate change for human
well-being.

Olin Eugene (Gene) Myers, Jr., PhD, is a professor of environmental studies at
Huxley College of the Environment, Western Washington University. His
work deals with four interrelated areas: the psychological foundations of
children's relation to animals; the ontogenetic development of environmental care and responsibility; the integration of psychology into conservation
and sustainability practice; and teaching environmental ethics for preparation of future eco-social justice educators.

CHAPTER 7

The Healing Power of Nature: The Impact of Interventions in Farm Settings

Michael Kaufmann; Miyako Kinoshita, M.S.Ed.; and Susan Puckett Teumer, MA

INTRODUCTION

A group of adults with Down syndrome participate in vocational animal care at a dairy farm with cattle; a child on the autism spectrum, accompanied by a therapist, observes a pair of Bactrian camels in a pasture; and war veterans with post-traumatic stress disorder (PTSD) participate in a guided self-reflection surrounded by a herd of horses. In each example, it is the farm setting and contact with animals and nature that is intended to serve as a catalyst for positive change in humans. At present, the potential of activities like these—those that enlist diverse farm environments for the purposes of learning and teaching, as well as facilitating health and well-being in a wide range of populations—is gradually being confirmed (Haubenhofer & Strunz, 2013).

The intent of this chapter is to provide an overview of how two specific farm settings contribute to the treatment and education of children with trauma histories, via reviewing the experiences of the former Our Farm Program and highlighting the example of present-day Green Chimneys School. Of note, we as authors do not intend this chapter to clinically guide the therapist treating trauma patients; rather, we will present program

potential through the lens of administrative structure, program implementation, and outcome observation, with a dual focus on intervention
activities and the evident impacts of animals and farm environments in a
practical human services context.

BACKGROUND AND SIGNIFICANCE

Children with trauma histories frequently display academic failure, emotional dysregulation, behavioral maladjustment, and social skill deficits.
Many of the elements inherent in farm- and nature-based therapeutic
programming have been demonstrated to address such needs. In his 2005
book, *Last Child in the Woods*, Richard Louv expressed concerns about
the lack of access that present-day children in most industrialized countries have to the natural world, coining the term *nature-deficit disorder*.
According to Louv (2005), studies suggest that exposure to nature may
reduce the symptoms of attention deficit hyperactivity disorder (ADHD),
and can improve cognitive abilities and resistance to negative stresses and
depression in children. Farms offer a variety of interaction opportunities
in nature that frequently present domesticated animals, maintain horticulture, and contain natural habitat for native wildlife.

In 2013, the American Academy of Pediatrics issued a policy statement
to support structured and unstructured recess/play as an essential, planned
respite from rigorous cognitive tasks to enhance subsequent academic
attentiveness and cognitive school performance (American Academy of
Pediatrics, 2013). Animals and nature in farm settings provide an enriched
environment for such recess and play activities for children who struggle
with traditional classroom environments. For example, Gee, Fine, and
Schuck (2015) discuss a number of research studies that suggest that the
presence of nature and animals reduces disruptive behaviors and increases
prosocial skills among students in both typical and special needs class-
rooms, from preschool through eighth grade.

In *The Walking Larder: Patterns of Domestication, Pastoralism, and
Predation*, Clutton-Brock made a case that nature and our symbiotic,
life-sustaining relationship with the natural world, particularly as related
to domesticated animals, have filled our myths and theology, and have
helped shape societies and culture (Clutton-Brock & World Archaeological
Congress, 1989). Likewise, Rollin refers to the loss in modern times of a

mystical connection to animals and nature (a relationship captured in ancient cave paintings), and how industrialization and urbanization threaten the intimate connection to animals in our consciousness (Fine, 2006).

In the latter part of the last century, an understanding evolved of a more purposeful therapeutic interaction with farm animal species in human services. According to Hildegard George (1988), "all farm animals are social by nature; this means that man can enter into a social relationship with these animals by taming them at certain critical stages within the animal's development" (p. 408). Describing her work as a therapist with adolescents, George (1988) concluded, "The practicalities of using animals—pets as well as farm animals—are as limitless as the creativity of the therapist" (p. 408).

More recently, Haubenhofer and Strunz (2013) offered comprehensive, evidence-based writings on the value of farm settings for children. Diverse authors explain how traditional animal-assisted therapy (AAT) and activity (AAA) concepts with companion animals (e.g., dogs) can be replicated with farm animal species, but also touch on the broader and more unique impacts of nature-based settings that farms provide (Haubenhofer & Strunz, 2013). While there are a great many practice models that might be used to incorporate these strategies in farm- and nature-based programming for children who have experienced trauma, we offer two select models for the reader's consideration.

THE OUR FARM MODEL

The competency-based model of animal-assisted interventions (AAIs) provided at Our Farm in central Texas from 2001–2006 offered an example of a farm program that was demonstrated to be highly successful in addressing the needs of children who had experienced early trauma. Public school students and staff from their schools participated in half-day programming each week at the farm, providing direct care for a variety of large and small animals. It is believed the improved self-efficacy of the students, as described below, provided the basis for a number of affective, cognitive, and academic improvements that were observed.

The brainchild of Dr. Aaron H. Katcher and a project of the nonprofit Animal Therapy Association, Our Farm served as a demonstration site for schools looking to effectively implement experiential learning with animals and nature into their curricula. The program's conceptual foundation was based on work done previously in the Devereux Foundation's Companionable Zoo, and documented in *The Centaur's Lessons: Therapeutic Education Through Care of Animals and Nature Study* (Katcher & Wilkins, 2000). The model used at Our Farm was unique, however, in that it established certain competencies—knowledge and skills to complete tasks successfully—and utilized these as the framework of the programming.

Staff at partnering schools selected students receiving special education services or deemed "at risk" of school failure to participate in this competency-based farm program. Students ranged from kindergarten through high school, with approximately 75% of them male. Over 90% of the participants were from special education classes, most carrying multiple diagnoses. Disabilities commonly seen included autism spectrum disorders, learning disabilities, ADHD, and severe emotional disability. Other students not otherwise served in special education were selected due to a lack of academic motivation, behavioral concerns, poor social skill development, and/or low self-esteem. While there was no attempt to look statistically at the number of participating students who had experienced trauma—and indeed such data would have been very difficult to collect—patterns of behavior and anecdotal data collected over time indicated trauma was likely quite prevalent among participants. In fact, one could argue that the very nature of having such a disability, especially in a neurotypical school environment where bullying might be a factor, could in and of itself be traumatic.

While program participants attended sessions at the farm in groups, generally 6 to 12 students at a time, each individual student selected a particular animal with whom to work. With support from the farm teacher and school staff (special educator, paraprofessional, counselor, or even principal—it varied from school to school), the student learned to appropriately handle, feed, and care for that animal, working week after week until he or she had achieved mastery of the skills and information deemed necessary to provide for the animal's needs.

Sessions always began and ended with group time, allowing for reminders of expectations, notices of changes at the farm, recognition of individual student accomplishments, and special activities related to the farm's seasonal work. However, work time was individual, and within one session students might engage in a variety of animal care activities, such as washing a rabbit cage, as well as feeding, holding, and brushing the rabbit; scooping the donkey's pen, providing fresh water and hay, and leading him around the yard; tidying a rat's enclosure, teaching the rat a new trick, and sitting to read a book with her; making a salad for the large desert tortoise, giving him exercise time beyond his typical pen, reviewing facts about that reptile's natural habitat, and discussing how we may accommodate for his needs within the current environment; setting up an obstacle course and leading an alpaca through it, while rewarding the animal's accomplishments with healthy treats the student had prepared; and collecting eggs, cleaning the coop, and providing fresh food and water to the chickens.

Animal care was guided by skill cards, giving basic information about each animal, including food, water, exercise, grooming, and natural environment. For very young or nonverbal students, picture skill cards were developed, giving the student a sequence of pictures to show the care of the animal. Once a student had mastered the competencies set for that particular animal, he or she was issued a license (modeled after the state's driver's license and including a picture of the student and animal together). The student was then free to "independently" handle and care for the animal, and even teach other students about the animal and its care. Equally important, once licensed, the student picked another animal of a different species and began to learn to care for it as well.

Although the students were focused on mastery of the established competencies—or at least the tangible rewards that accompanied that mastery—school and farm staff were simultaneously addressing specific goals established for each student. The range of these goals was as broad as each group was diverse, and included language development, motor skills, concept development, self-regulation, and social skills. So, while a student might be intent on earning a license with the pot-bellied pig, the school counselor working with that student might help guide interactions with the pig in a way that helped the student establish healthy boundaries, a skill that might later be discussed in terms of fostering and maintaining interpersonal and social relationships.

Growth toward mastery of competencies truly progressed at individual rates. Some students needed significant repetitions, and might license with only one or two animals during the course of a school year. Others needing more challenge could license with a different animal almost once a month. Students often engaged in added research about the animals, reading from the library provided at the farm or from other resources available at school.

Two students (from different schools), who were basically "nonwriters," each self-initiated research projects. One student wrote a successful proposal to add a snake to the program, while the other created two different, leveled versions of skill cards for the farm's bourbon red turkeys. This task was particularly useful, as skill cards had not yet been developed for the care of these animals. Among other skills, this particular student's work provided new and helpful directives to follow when handling the bourbon red turkeys (i.e., "Turkeys generally don't like to be handled, but if you move slowly and quietly, the toms may let you touch their feathers") (Our Farm, 2005). Often, the work required students to collaborate, allowing real-life opportunities for communication, turn-taking, sharing, perspective-taking/empathy, and problem solving. Progress toward individual goals was noted each session by both school and farm staff, and goals were adjusted as needed.

One integral component of the program was the celebration of success. Students were recognized within the group for reaching milestones, both "licensing" with a given animal as well as simply reaching personal bests, such as being able to halter an animal for the first time or even push the wheelbarrow independently. School staff began to identify each student's individual interests and competencies, often for the first time. In turn, the students also viewed themselves differently. This became evident in group sessions as conversations became more animated with students sharing stories of their successes, in individual work time when "I can't" was replaced by "Watch me," and in notes from school staff indicating students had proudly relayed their new knowledge and accomplishments to others. Our data showed that positive changes were noted very quickly at school, and anecdotal reports indicated these improvements were noted both at school and at home.

Utilizing the Achenbach Teacher Report Form (Achenbach, 1991) and the Behavior Assessment System for Children Teacher Rating Scales (BASC TRS; Reynolds & Kamphaus, 1998), there was an immediate and statistically significant decrease in all problematic behaviors at the farm as opposed to the school. These improved behaviors included those associated with externalizing problems, internalizing problems, hyperactivity, aggression, conduct, anxiety, depression, attention and learning problems, atypical behaviors, and withdrawal. Notably, quantitative measures did not substantiate additional improvement over time at the farm or a definite transfer of skills from the farm to school, although qualitative measures (including teacher reports) did indicate both occurred.

One possible explanation for the changes documented in the Our Farm program (and one that is quite relevant in working with individuals who have experienced trauma) can be found in the construct of self-efficacy. Albert Bandura, a leading researcher in this field, defines perceived self-efficacy as "people's beliefs about their capabilities to produce designated levels of performance that exercise influence over events that affect their lives" (Bandura, 1994, p. 71). In their review article, Benight and Bandura (2004) integrated findings from the existing literature regarding the role of self-efficacy in coping with trauma. In their concluding remarks, they state:

> The results yield consistent support for perceived coping self-efficacy as a focal mediator of posttraumatic recovery. People who believe they can surmount their traumatization take a hand in mending their lives rather than have their lives dictated by the adverse circumstances. The consistency of findings across diverse types of traumatizations speaks to the generality of the enabling and protective function of beliefs of personal efficacy to manage the impact of calamitous events. (p. 1144)

Bandura asserts there are four main factors influencing the development of self-efficacy, and each of these can be found in the competency-based model. The first of these factors is *mastery experiences*, which were present in the "license" system at Our Farm. High standards were set for licensing with each animal, and school and farm staff provided scaffolding to support students in achieving these goals. The next factor—*vicarious experiences of peers successfully completing difficult tasks*—was also an integral part of this model as groups celebrated participants' accomplishments. Through peer and adult coaching, participating students experienced the third factor, *social persuasion*, by coming to believe they could indeed persevere and reach their lofty goals. Bandura's fourth and final factor—*perceptions of strengths and vulnerabilities inferred from somatic and emotional states*—is addressed in the positive mood of students and school staff at the farm. As Relf and Lohr (2003) discuss in their review, people's positive responses to nature have been documented for decades, and they were certainly apparent at Our Farm.

Additionally, according to Bandura (1994), cognition, motivation, and affect are all influenced by one's perceived self-efficacy. One participant of Our Farm, George, had a severe learning disability that greatly impacted his sense of self-worth. Presumably due to frustration over his inability to achieve the high level of academic success he expected of himself (and as experienced by many of his peers), he had become quite aggressive toward other students, and therefore was placed in a self-contained classroom for students with severe emotional and behavioral disabilities. Ten years old when he first came to Our Farm, George thrived in the program and actively participated for each of the farm's five years of operation. In an interview two months after he had started at the farm, George's adoptive mother remarked, "He told me the other day that he's learned to like himself because he's found something he's good at."

Overall, the hundreds of students who received services at Our Farm over the course of five years showed a significant decrease in problematic symptoms often seen in individuals with a history of trauma. It is believed that the competency-based model of AAI employed at Our Farm, which included high levels of both adult support and farm-school communication, allowed the participating students to increase their self-efficacy, thus reducing symptomatic behavior typically associated with trauma—both at the farm and in other settings.

THE GREEN CHIMNEYS PROGRAM MODEL

Founded in 1947, Green Chimneys is accredited by New York State as a special education school, offering treatment services incorporating environmental and recreational programs, as well as AAIs and nature-based programming for students in its residential and therapeutic day treatment programs. Located on a rural campus, a farm and wildlife center and garden of considerable size are part of this residential treatment center for children. Currently, there are over 200 farm animals, permanently injured wildlife, horses, and a small number of shelter therapy dogs-in-training at the farm. Through strong academics, as well as recreational and clinical interventions (i.e., an enriched academic curriculum meeting New York State standards, an experiential learning environment, onsite clinical services and therapeutic support, and a focus on individual needs), children explore and discover strengths in a structured, nature-based setting. The primary goals of the program are to improve student self-esteem, compassion, coping, and social skills.

Green Chimneys has a long history as a leader and innovator in education and therapeutic treatment for children with special needs and, as such, the organizational philosophy supports a safe and healing environment. We at Green Chimneys integrate psychoeducational approaches in response to best practice models that identify trauma as a central aspect of human experience. Trauma-informed care has become an accepted standard in human services: "Every outpatient and inpatient mental health setting, child protection service, parenting program, domestic violence shelter, school, and homeless shelter today must contend with the issue of a past history of exposure to trauma in their clients" (Bloom, n.d., para. 1). Green Chimneys therapeutic treatment and management practices align with a trauma-informed approach of creating and maintaining an optimal environment for safety and recovery. Established universal values and a shared language help create an environment in which everyone feels safe, respected, and included. It is how we teach skills, set program activity priorities, and make decisions that ultimately impact those we serve.

The population at Green Chimneys currently consists of emotionally fragile boys and girls (ages 6–18 years, with a male to female student ratio of 9:1), who are coping with a variety of challenges related to anxiety disorders, ADHD, autism spectrum disorders and pervasive developmental disorder, bipolar disorder, impulse control disorder, mood disorder, post-traumatic stress disorder, and reactive attachment disorder. Utilizing the treatment team model, each child has a group of professionals who work together to provide consistent and diverse treatments during his or her stay at Green Chimneys. The average length of stay is 20–24 months.

Each child in the residential treatment center is assigned an individual psychiatrist who becomes a vital member of that child's treatment team. The primary function of the psychiatrist is to monitor and regulate the child's psychotropic medications, and to educate staff and families regarding his or her types of medications, target symptoms, and any possible side effects. The goal of youth mental health treatment at Green Chimneys is to stabilize a child's mood and behavior, thus enabling him or her to benefit from academic instruction, as well as develop self-regulation and effective coping skills.

Upon admission, each child is also assigned a therapist, who may be a licensed clinical social worker, mental health counselor, psychologist, or graduate- or PhD-level intern specializing in mental health. Therapists meet with each child for weekly individual psychotherapy sessions and also work with direct care staff in weekly living unit group sessions. Specialized small groups in areas such as trauma support, international adoptees, and children who are freed for adoption may also be offered.

Sessions are individualized to each child using a number of different therapeutic modalities including, but not limited to, dialectical behavior therapy, cognitive behavior therapy, AAT, and play therapy. All therapists practice within a family systems and trauma-informed framework. Psychoeducation groups on social skills and other topics are frequently held.

An enriched treatment milieu that brings people together with animals and plants in a mutually beneficial relationship forms the foundation of the Green Chimneys approach. Nature-based programs at Green Chimneys support the school and residences, as well as clinical approaches and the overall therapeutic process. The entire team of farm and clinical staff is part of the treatment process, and the nature-based activities provided each day are a cornerstone of each child's experience.

Animal interactions are divided into the following categories and all rely on structure and supervision:

- *Farm-Based Education Classes:* Credentialed special education teachers with a background in animal-assisted and/or horticulture education host scheduled classes in the various farm areas. Classroom teachers have the opportunity to integrate experiential learning on the farm and outside in their curriculum.

- *Learn and Earn Farm Jobs:* Non-therapist staff members—including animal caretakers, residential staff, and interns—work with individual children through a therapeutic AAA program. Understanding the difference between these animal activities and goal-directed therapy conducted by a licensed practitioner, these staff are trained to implement and facilitate for the children such meaningful activities as cleaning stalls, taking a calf for a walk, preparing animal food, or harvesting ripe tomatoes from the garden. All the activities are designed to support the overall social, emotional, behavioral, and academic treatment plan goals for individual students.

- *Therapy Sessions:* Formal AAT sessions are conducted by licensed mental health professionals at the farm for specific, goal-directed treatment involving animals. Occupational therapists and speech and language pathologists also utilize the farm setting, and incorporate interaction with animals in their treatment approaches.

Conceptual Philosophy of Nature-Based Programs

The Green Chimneys program brings people and animals together with a variety of philosophies, theories, and potential mechanisms at work. While these provide theoretical frameworks to the whole, it is critical to understand that the Green Chimneys approach relies on a complex amalgamation of organically blended approaches, as described below:

- *Milieu Therapy:* Milieu therapy refers to the organization of the entire social system (such as in a hospital or therapeutic community) as a therapeutic instrument, a planned environment exerting an independent force, and a total environment that can be structured to meet treatment goals (Soth, 1997). Milieu therapy can be conceptualized as a treatment procedure that attempts to make the total environment, including all personnel and patients of the therapeutic community, conducive to psychological improvement. In milieu therapy, the staff conveys to the patients/clients/students the expectation that they can and will behave more normally and responsibly.
- *Green Care:* Green care is an inclusive term for many complex interventions, such as care farming, AAT, therapeutic horticulture, and others. What links this diverse set of interventions is their use of nature and the natural environment as a framework in which to create these approaches (Sempkin, Hines, & Wilcox, 2010).
- *Eco-Psychology:* Eco-psychology is a concept situated at the intersection of a number of fields of inquiry, including environmental philosophy, psychology, and ecology, but is not limited by any disciplinary boundaries. At its core, eco-psychology suggests that there is a synergistic relation between planetary and personal well-being—that the needs of the one are relevant to needs of the other (Schroll, 2017).
- *Biophilia:* Coined by E.O. Wilson, biophilia describes the deep need people have to experience natural habitats and species. The term suggests that there is an instinctive bond between human beings and other living things. Wilson (1984) proposes that the strong and meaningful affiliations humans have with nature are rooted in biology.

- *Animal-Assisted Interventions (AAI):* AAIs are goal-oriented and structured interventions that intentionally incorporate animals in health, education, and human service for the purpose of therapeutic gains and improved human health and wellness. AAT, animal-assisted education (AAE), and AAA are all forms of AAIs. Across these interventions, the animal may be part of a volunteer therapy animal team working under the direction of a professional, an animal who belongs to and works with the professional himself or herself, or a service animal who lives with his or her handler full-time (Pet Partners, 2017).
- *Humane Education:* Humane education is the process of teaching and promoting humane attitudes toward people, animals, and the environment. Key elements of humane education include providing accurate information; fostering the three Cs: curiosity, creativity, and critical thinking; instilling the three Rs: reverence, respect, and responsibility; and offering positive choices and tools for problem solving (Institute for Humane Education, 2017).

Interactions With Animals and Plants in a Farm Setting

Children are encouraged by their treatment team to apply the lessons learned in the Green Chimneys Farm environment to everyday life. At family case conferences, it is often evident that life skills practiced in the barns, gardens, and on the farm are applied to interactions in other environments by students. They appear to learn patience while training a calf. Watching a bee pollinate a sunflower inspires academic curiosity. The process of living with animals becomes the basis of conversations with adults and peers, as well as self-reflection. The progression of growing vegetables from seed to harvest requires patience and persistence, as the rewards for garden care do not come instantly and may take months to actualize. Following the harvest, the children prepare the vegetables and herbs they have grown in culinary classes, and share the meals with others. Sharing the rewards of their patient and dedicated work with others who enjoy the food heightens the impact. The garden experience also offers opportunities for social cooperation and delayed gratification, and enhances the children's self-esteem.

These and other farm experiences can also awaken enthusiasm and support educational and therapeutic goals, as well as foster skill development.

Interest has been found to play an energizing role in cognitive functioning, with research indicating that interest has a strong effect on learner motivation and in predicting future intention (Alexander, Jetton, & Kulikowich, 1995). The fact that children identify the farm as "enjoyable" implies that they are interested and may be motivated to learn in that environment.

In order to understand the specific benefits offered at the farm for children with trauma histories (i.e., psychiatric hospitalizations, loss, academic failure, and in select cases, abuse and neglect), it may be helpful to break down intention and outcomes into separate goal areas, and outline how these may be met through interactions at the farm.

Academic Goals

Nature-based programs integrate skills such as reading, writing, mathematics, social studies, and history into "real-life," seemingly nonacademic situations. By connecting these academic subjects to something concrete and practical in daily life, the concepts students are learning become tangible and meaningful. For example, division on a math sheet in a classroom environment is a stress inducer and a child may shut down without trying. Dividing baby carrots into equal amounts to feed to the bunnies, on the other hand, is a much more motivating task, and children are willing to try it without necessarily realizing that they are engaging in an academic goal.

Process Goals

Nature- and animal-based activities help teach children who struggle with multistep instructions or who lack problem-solving skills. Measuring animal feed, distinguishing names of plants, or grading the size of eggs requires effort and results in incremental task mastery over time without being consciously focused on an outcome. As in all learning, the tasks can be broken down into small steps, but the child's motivation and the experiential aspect of the farm activities are a powerful support.

Character Goals

In Positive Youth Development Theory, Richard Lerner defines character as respect for societal and cultural norms, possession of standards for correct behaviors, a sense of right and wrong (morality), and integrity (Lerner, 2011). Upon entering Green Chimneys, children have an opportunity to build respectful relationships with animals. Adults and peers model caring treatment of animals, enforce high standards of animal welfare, and define rules of what is right or wrong to do with various species. Children learn to respect these cultural rules. For example, no one is ever to chase a peacock walking around campus, and animals are not to be fed treats by hand (in order to reduce begging and biting). These rules of relating to animals become the norm, are reinforced by the campus community, and integrate into broader milieu expectations required to effectively and successfully function in the academic and residential community. Moreover, when children have a chance to nurture an orphaned animal, care for an animal who requires geriatric care, or nurse an animal recovering from illness, they relate to those animals and become particularly and emotionally involved in the experience by accepting the responsible role of caregiver.

Conceptual Thinking

Students apply academic concepts learned in the classroom to work in the garden and with animals through measuring garden beds, experimenting with the effect of light on plant growth, calculating feed amounts, and weighing the animals. Complex conceptual relationships that eventually are taken for granted must first be comprehended. Various scientific and biological concepts must be understood for a child to grasp the correlation between how a daily increase in feed or calories, over time, results in the weight gain of a thin animal. Additional opportunities for concept application and self-reflection include recognizing how animals who have been injured or rescued from abuse situations require similar care and nurturing as people who have experienced their own trauma or injury (e.g., themselves or others they know).

Motor Coordination

Students hone fine motor coordination as they carefully spread seeds across a flat of soil, work with pressed flowers, and handle and groom animals. Proper tool usage in a stall while cleaning the barn strengthens fine and gross motor skills, and provides a productive release for energetic students who have trouble sitting still. Occupational therapists at Green Chimneys have counted more than 25 different padlocks, dead bolts, latches, and handles that children must master in the process of working with the animals and in the garden, offering fine and gross motor skill development, opportunity for sequencing, and mastery in navigating the complex barn environment.

Sensory Integration

Children with special needs often have different sensory integration challenges, but a common experience is to be overwhelmed. Some may not be able to tolerate the smell of a dog, while others have auditory oversensitivity to dog barking (Fine, Grandin, O'Haire, Carlisle, & Bowers, 2015). These same reactions can be observed in the barn with pigs, chickens, and other farm animals. The experience can also vary depending on the time of day. When the child enters the livestock barn in the morning, the noise, movement of hungry animals, and smells of the dirty stalls from the night before are much greater than at midday when all the stalls have been cleaned and the animals are resting and digesting their food. Depending on the moment, situation, and/or student, the barn can be either a soothing and enjoyable environment or an overwhelming sensory experience. That said, it has been observed that children at the farm increasingly tolerate sensory input as they get used to the animals, farm machinery, and various stimuli in the setting.

In addition, showing a child how a new horse gets acclimated to the farm—and how the animal, too, goes through a process of learning to cope with new noises, new smells, and new sights—often allows the student to observe the desensitizing process in action. It is possible that seeing how the horse acclimates, and how this may not always be easy for that animal, could help normalize the difficulties and anxious responses that children have when confronted with new environments and overwhelming sensory experiences. This could help children feel less abnormal or alone in their feelings and more connected to the horse, while also providing them with capacity skills and hope to better cope during future transitions.

Emotional Regulation

Work with farm animals in natural settings stimulates the senses (similar to work with companion animals), provides a quiet refuge for contemplation and internal renewal, and may enhance feelings of self-worth. In a review of mechanisms of effectiveness, Morrison (2007) suggests that, while frequently based on self-reports, children as a patient population appear to benefit from AAIs in the areas of self-esteem, decreased stress, and improved morale.

Emotional dysregulation is one of the most common causes of crisis for children at Green Chimneys. A goal of treatment at Green Chimneys is to deepen awareness among the children and families regarding the impact of trauma and its triggers, and to build a greater understanding of how different kinds of trauma impact emotions and behavior. The organizational structure and treatment framework of the program, at the farm and in all areas, encourages recognition of trauma and aims to educate and support clients in an open-ended and sincere process. Therapists often utilize the farm environment to explore self-regulation with children, to practice coping skills, to explore emotions, and to examine responses to various life situations.

While Green Chimneys utilizes the Cornell Based Therapeutic Crisis Intervention (TCI) model (Cornell University, 2017), which includes physical restraints as part of the intervention strategy in cases where a child endangers himself or others, we are increasingly aware of how any restraint may be dangerous to all participants and could reenact trauma. According to Sandra Bloom (2010), "One of the most important challenges to the therapeutic environment is the successful management of traumatic reenactment" (p. 4). Because of this understanding, one of our measurements of success is in the reduction and elimination of restraints during any period of time in the program, and we track these incidents throughout the day and week. This informal measurement tool validated positive behaviors, mood, and the absence of restraints at the farm while we reviewed critical incidents. Of note, the percentage of restraints in the farm setting is extremely low compared to the school, residential units, and other areas of the campus. Although it is impossible to know the specific cause of these data, they hint at a higher degree of emotional regulation in the nature-based environments due to farm staff, the animals, nature itself, or a combination of all three factors.

Turning Compassion Into Action

The interaction with individual animals who have special needs can encourage compassionate responses from children. By caring for an orphaned, ill, injured, weakened, or aging animal, children can express sympathy and are often compelled to assist with that animal's care voluntarily. In some cases, children who have experienced past trauma (e.g., psychiatric hospitalization, the loss of a family member, being given up for adoption) relate to a specific animal who reflects similar experience. Therapists often utilize these points of connection to help children cope and work through their own trauma. For example, a group of children with adoption histories bottle fed and helped raise orphaned lambs as part of their weekly adoptee support group. Guided by social workers, they processed their own experience as orphans, while also providing nurturance to young animals who had lost their families through separation.

CASE STUDY: THERAPY SESSIONS WITH A STUDENT AND TWO BACTRIAN CAMELS

Student: Jack, male, 11th grade day student
Admission to Green Chimneys program: During 6th grade
Presenting problems: Lack of self-confidence; anxiety; task avoidance; poor peer interactions; failure in multiple school placements due to explosive behaviors
Therapeutic services: Had his own psychiatrist and psychotherapist outside of school; during school, he received counseling twice a week with a school social worker

Jack, his therapist, and the farm staff and animals were all looking for a challenge that would motivate him and build his confidence. Typically, Jack would shut down and disengage whenever he faced a challenge. As he was easily overwhelmed—he often put his head down on a desk, refused to participate in schoolwork, or walked out of the classroom to avoid tasks. Originally, the plan to help Jack included a variety of species; however, when introduced to the camels, Phoenix and Sage, in the second session, the therapist noticed that Jack was fascinated by these large animals who were not very familiar to him. With Phoenix and Sage, he was more talkative and visibly more engaged, maintaining conversation and eye contact with both his therapist and the animal specialist (both of whom supervised each session). During sessions, the therapist and animal specialist would reflect back to Jack key experiences with the camels, such as how he helped Phoenix and Sage to learn new things and how he effectively demonstrated self-soothing skills during periods when the camels were tied. It was anticipated that the camels would motivate Jack and help him gain self-confidence, relationship and leadership skills, patience, and flexibility.

In a 12-month period, Jack built a deeper relationship with the camels, particularly Sage. Much time was spent on animal care activities, including grooming and bathing, feeding, walking on a lead, and clicker/target training for various behaviors. At the conclusion of each session, successes, setbacks, and impressions were discussed and processed.

Gradually, Jack became more engaged and came up with ideas for things to do with the camels during each session. He was encouraged, and his opinions and confidence grew along with his competence in understanding the camels' behaviors and emotions, as well as how to properly handle them. After a few sessions, Jack was transitioned into a leadership role by inviting preschool students to meet the camels, with Jack as the guide and the safe-keeper for the younger kids. Jack rose to this leadership challenge and was successful. The therapist reflected these experiences back to Jack, tying them to his treatment goals including self-regulation and awareness.

Over time, sessions with the camels offered Jack opportunities to conquer his fears, and gain a sense of empowerment in a safe and enjoyable environment. Repeated exposure resulted in increases in emotional regulation, distress tolerance skills, and mastery over anxiety. At the beginning of the school year, Jack refused to take his psychological or academic testing as he felt intense pressure and struggled with performance anxiety. After working closely with Sage, who also frequently exhibits emotional and anxious behavior in new situations, Jack explored various coping and self-regulation skills for both the camel and himself. In early spring of that year, Jack expressed that he was ready to take the psychological testing and complete it. As an extra support, we offered Jack a picture of Sage and a small toy camel to keep with him. When the time came for him to take the New York State regions exams, he asked for the toy camel as a tool to refocus and regulate his emotions when he became overwhelmed, thereby actively advocating for his own needs for the first time. We are happy to report that Jack successfully passed his exam.

CASE STUDY: FARM ACTIVITY SESSIONS AS AN ADJUNCT SUPPORT TO COPING WITH TRANSITIONS AND SELF-REGULATION

Student: Peter, male, 7th grade, resident at Green Chimneys
Admission to Green Chimneys program: During 6th grade
Presenting problems: Academic level of grade 2 with an IQ of 65; difficulty keeping up socially and academically in the classroom and residential unit; multiple behavioral crises a day; struggles with transitions, changes in routine, and peer interactions
Therapeutic services: Participated in individual, group, medication, and family therapy; targeted AAAs supplemented his therapy

Multiple farm activity sessions were scheduled as a support for Peter to coincide with his most challenging and anxiety-producing times of the day. One session was set for late morning when it was close to transitioning from the classroom to lunch. The other was scheduled just before or after the time when he transitioned from the dormitory to school. These transition times were particularly hard for Peter, as he tended to be triggered by noise and movements, and felt out of control as a result. His farm activities were 1:1 with specially trained farm staff focusing on general animal care in the wildlife center with birds of prey.

Peter required significant amounts of staff attention in order to be successful and to maintain his composure. Sharing the attention of adults with peers was very difficult for him. Peter enjoyed physical activities, was an experiential learner, and found the farm offered him opportunities to get outside away from the overwhelming classroom environment. Since the animal care activities were individualized for him, he was generally helpful, productive, and motivated to cooperate with his assigned staff. It also was suggested that Peter benefited from grounding activities in which he did some heavy lifting to calm his body. Caring for the hawks, eagles, and owls allowed incorporation of activities such as pushing heavy wheelbarrows with food. Staff carefully chose the activity that would both physically and emotionally benefit Peter.

By strategically offering him time at the wildlife center with the birds as an adjunct activity, we were able to support his overall therapy goals, resulting in a reduction of frequent behavioral crises caused by anxiety over transitions. The treatment team also created a calmer and quieter environment for his transitions, allowing him to do so after other students were settled, and when staff had more time to tend to his needs. With these interventions, Peter gradually became more stabilized within the overall program.

This kind of individualized and adjunct support at the farm is often applied for students with additional, various behavioral challenges, including attention and focus, completing a task/sequencing, distractibility, emotional stabilization, frustration tolerance, hyperactivity, impulsivity, and organizational skills and/or prioritization.

CONCLUSION

We have provided an overview of how farm settings—specifically the former Our Farm program in Texas and the existing Green Chimneys School in New York State—can aid in the treatment and education of children with trauma histories. Anecdotal and empirical evidence was presented to construct a defensible framework for farm-based program settings, suggesting positive impacts on cognition, motivation, and affect, as well as social, academic, and psychological progress for children with trauma histories when integrated into a more broad-based treatment approach. It would be premature to conclude that there is a sufficient evidence base in this area, as best practices are only slowly emerging regarding when and how to utilize farm settings in education and therapy for special populations.

However, the potential of this work to support children in special education and treatment settings is promising. To further the evidence base in this area, Green Chimneys partnered with the University of Denver's Institute for Human-Animal Connection in 2016 to thoroughly explore the influence of Green Care models on measures of Positive Youth Development (Lerner, 2011) for students ranging in age from 6 to 18 years. The research team will focus this multiyear study through the use of a Positive Youth Development lens to see if this unique Green Care-incorporative framework allows youth with behavioral, developmental, and/or environmental challenges to meet treatment goals and develop their individual strengths. As Bustad (1990) notes, "We must immerse students in living things. The growing interest in nourishing and caring for plants and animals must be encouraged, especially in our children, for we need to preserve and care for the life of the entire planet" (p. 124).

REFERENCES

Achenbach, T. M. (1991). *Manual for the child behavior checklist 14–16 and 1991 scoring profile.* Burlington, VT: University of Vermont.

Alexander, P. A., Jetton, T. L., & Kulikowich, J. M. (1995). Interrelationship of knowledge, interest, and recall: Assessing a model of domain learning. *Journal of Educational Psychology, 87*(4), 559–575. https://doi.org/10.1037// 0022-0663.87.4.559

American Academy of Pediatrics. (2013). The crucial role of recess in school. *Pediatrics, 131*(1), 183–188. Retrieved from http://pediatrics.aappublications .org/content/131/1/183

Bandura, A. (1994). Self-efficacy. In V. S. Ramachaudran (Ed.), *Encyclopedia of human behavior* (Vol. 4, pp. 71–81). New York, NY: Academic Press.

Benight, C., & Bandura, A. (2004). Social cognitive theory of posttraumatic recovery: The role of perceived self-efficacy. *Behaviour Research and Therapy, 42*(10), 1129–1148.

Bloom, S. L. (2010). *Reenactment.* Unpublished editorial. Community Works. Retrieved from http://sanctuaryweb.com/Portals/0/2010%20PDFs%20 NEW/2010%20Bloom%20Reenactment.pdf

Bloom, S. L. (n.d.). *S. E. L. F. group curriculum.* Retrieved from http://sanctuaryweb .com/Products/SELFGroupCurriculum.aspx

Bustad, L. K. (1990). *Compassion: Our last great hope.* Renton, WA: Delta Society.

Clutton-Brock, J., & World Archaeological Congress. (1989). *The walking larder: Patterns of domestication, pastoralism, and predation.* London, UK: Unwin Hyman.

Cornell University. (2017). *TCI system overview.* Retrieved from http://rccp .cornell.edu/tci/tci-1_system.html

Fine, A. H. (2006). *Handbook on animal-assisted therapy: Theoretical foundations and guidelines for practice.* San Diego, CA: Elsevier Academic Press.

Fine, A. H., Grandin, T., O'Haire, M., Carlisle, G., & Bowers, C. M. (2015). The roles of animals for individuals with autism spectrum disorder. In A. H. Fine (Ed.), *Handbook on animal-assisted therapy: Foundations and guidelines for animal-assisted interventions* (4th ed., pp. 225–236). San Diego, CA: Elsevier Academic Press.

Gee, N. R., Fine, A. H., & Schuck, S. (2015). Animals in educational settings: Research and practice. In A. H. Fine (Ed.), *Handbook on animal-assisted therapy: Foundations and guidelines for animal-assisted interventions* (4th ed., pp. 195–210). San Diego, CA: Elsevier Academic Press.

George, M. H. (1988). Child therapy and animals: A new way for an old relationship. In C. E. Schaefer (Ed.), *Innovative interventions in child and adolescent therapy* (pp. 400–419). New York, NY: John Wiley & Sons.

Haubenhofer, D., & Strunz, I. A. (2013). *Raus auf's Land!: Landwirtschaftliche Betriebe als zeitgemäße Erfahrungs-und Lernorte für Kinder und Jugendliche.* Baltmannsweiler: Schneider Hohengehren.

Institute for Humane Education. (2017). *What is humane education?* Retrieved from http://humaneeducation.org/become-a-humane-educator/what-is-humane -education/

Katcher, A. H., & Wilkins, G. G. (2000). The centaur's lessons: Therapeutic education through care of animals and nature study. In A. H. Fine (Ed.), *Handbook for animal-assisted therapy: Theoretical foundations and guidelines for practice* (1st ed., pp. 153–177). Pomona, CA: Academic Press.

Lerner, R. M. (2011). The positive development of the youth. Retrieved from http://ase.tufts.edu/iaryd/documents/4HPYDStudyWave7.pdf

Louv, R. (2005). *Last child in the woods: Saving our children from nature-deficit disorder.* Chapel Hill, NC: Algonquin Books of Chapel Hill.

Morrison, M. L. (2007). Health benefits of animal-assisted interventions. *Complementary Health Practice Review, 12*(1), 51–62. https://doi.org/10.1177 /1533210107302397

Our Farm. (2005). *Turkey skill card.* Taylor, TX: Author.

Pet Partners. (2017). Terminology. Retrieved from https://petpartners.org/learn /terminology/

Relf, P., & Lohr, V. (2003). Human issues in horticulture. *HortScience, 38*(5), 984–993.

Reynolds, C. R., & Kamphaus, R. W. (1998). *BASC behavior assessment system for children: Manual including preschool norms for ages 2–6 through 3–11.* Circle Pines, NM: American Guidance Service.

Schroll, M. A. (2017). *Remembering ecopsychology's origins: A chronicle of meetings, conversations, and significant publications.* Retrieved from http://www .ecopsychology.org/journal/ezine/ep_origins.html#top

Sempkin, J., Hines, R., & Wilcox, D. (2010). *Green care: A conceptual framework.* Leicestershire, England: Loughnorough University.

Soth, N. B. (1997). Milieu therapy and management. In N. B. Soth (Ed.), *Informed treatment: Milieu management in psychiatric hospitals and residential treatment centers* (pp. 1–9). Lanham, MD: Scarecrow Press.

Wilson, E. O. (1984). *Biophilia.* Cambridge, MA: Harvard University Press.

ABOUT THE AUTHORS

Michael Kaufmann is the farm and wildlife director at Green Chimneys and the director of the Sam and Myra Ross Institute, dedicated to research on human connection to animals and the natural world. He served the American Society for the Prevention of Cruelty to Animals (ASPCA) and the American Humane Association (AHA) as a key program director in animal-assisted activities/therapy, humane education, and animal welfare. Kaufmann has contributed to defining publications in the field of human-animal interaction, and serves on numerous national boards and committees. He lectures internationally, with a special focus on animal welfare and the practical/administrative animal management issues with diverse species involved in human-animal interaction programs.

Miyako Kinoshita is a farm education program manager at Green Chimneys. She holds a master's degree in education, and is a certified advanced-level therapeutic riding instructor with the Professional Association of Therapeutic Horsemanship International (PATH Intl.). Kinoshita specializes in prevention, early detection, and intervention of emotional and behavioral crisis in AAA settings, and has presented many workshops and lectures throughout the United States and Japan. She was a past committee member for the Equine Facilitated Mental Health Association (EFMHA), and served on the board for PATH. Having led Green Chimneys' equine programs for many years, she now focuses her work on the extensive intern training programs (including supervision of the international intern program), as well as the integration of farm programming with the educational, clinical, and residential programs.

Susan Puckett Teumer has been a public school educator for 30 years, and serves as adjunct faculty at the Institute for Human-Animal Connection at the University of Denver. She was the lead teacher for Animal Therapy Association's Our Farm program in Taylor, Texas, where she developed and instituted competency-based programming in animal-assisted education. With a Master of Arts in education, Teumer has taught students of all levels and of varying learning needs. She served as a volunteer, trainer, evaluator, and national board member for the Delta Society's Pet Partner program, and has worked as program coordinator, volunteer, instructor, and executive committee member for Human-Animal Bond in Colorado. Teumer has also spoken at numerous education forums, including lecturing internationally on AAI, and has contributed to a textbook on the subject.

CHAPTER 8

Horses in the Treatment of Trauma

Nina Ekholm Fry, MSSc., CCTP

INTRODUCTION

Advances in the field of neuroscience over the past 30 years have led to a more comprehensive view of the effects of trauma on the brain, mind, and body (van der Kolk, 2014; Siegel, 2012). Traumatic events and associated debilitating symptoms such as intrusive memories and thoughts, heightened arousal, dissociative states, and somatic issues all impact the ability to enjoy life and connect with others, leading to a life of distress if not addressed. Fortunately, awareness of trauma as an etiological factor in mental illness and addiction has led to more effective treatments that directly address trauma, and also the emergence of so-called trauma-informed care. This is a framework that encourages the recognition of symptoms of trauma, regardless of setting; realizes their prevalence in client populations, staff, and others; and seeks to integrate awareness of trauma in policy and practices (SAMHSA, 2015).

In addition to better understanding the nature of trauma, finding ways to help individuals seek treatment, to remain in treatment, and for practitioners to optimize treatment is crucial (Najavits, 2015; Sayer et al., 2009). The inclusion of horses in the treatment of trauma has the potential to address each of these three areas. However, more research is needed to support the emergence of equine interactions as an enhancement of trauma approaches, whether as part of treatment that directly addresses trauma or in strengthening functioning and coping skills more generally.

In this chapter, I discuss the inclusion of horses in the treatment of trauma through their benefit to central tasks in trauma recovery, organized in a tri-phasic framework (Herman, 1992).

DEFINITIONS

Equine-assisted therapy (EAT), also referred to as equine-assisted mental health (EAMH) when focusing on psychological treatment, is how mental health professionals appropriately credentialed to legally practice psychotherapy or counseling in their state or country include equine interactions and the equine environment to enhance their clinical treatment and assessment, within their scope of practice. It is not a standalone therapy. The mental health professional has received education, training, and supervision in equine-assisted mental health in order to practice ethically and effectively. Equine-assisted therapy will be used interchangeably with equine-assisted mental health, and, when used in this context, refers to psychotherapy, as opposed to other therapies (such as physical or occupational therapy). Terms such as therapeutic riding—which in the United States commonly refers to a recreational activity that is not provided by mental health professionals and cannot, as such, be referred to as therapy—will be defined at the time of mention (the American Hippotherapy Association recommends use of the term *adaptive riding* to avoid misunderstanding [2018]). Finally, equine refers to horse, mule, or donkey, and will be used interchangeably with horse.

BACKGROUND

History of Horses in Human Health

Since the domestication of horses approximately 6,000 years ago (Outram et al., 2009; Vilà et al., 2001), the versatility of *equus caballus* is thought to have contributed to the development of human civilization in many meaningful ways, most notably in transportation, trade, warfare, and agriculture (Johns, 2006). The ability to travel more efficiently with the help of horses made new communications and trade possible, which some scholars believe contributed to the development of modern languages (Anthony, 2007). Horses are still being used in farming, ranch work, and logging around the world, although to a much lesser extent (Brandt & Eklund, 2007; Pickeral, 2005). Horsemeat and other horse-related products, such as the urine of pregnant mares used in pharmaceutical compounds for human hormone replacement therapy, are produced around the world, although horses are not regarded as production animals. Increasing numbers of horses are part of sport and leisure, and most recently in physical and psychological therapy for humans (Edenburg, 1999). In the United States, miniature horses are permitted for use as service animals under the law (Americans with Disabilities Act, 2010).

In addition to their prominent role in art and mythology, the impact of the horse on human health has been discussed in medical literature as early as by the ancient Greeks (Bain, 1965). Accounts from the second century CE up to the late 1900s focused primarily on the effects of horseback riding on the human physique (see Ekholm Fry, 2013, for an overview). When discussing the history of horses as part of trauma treatment, or even psychiatric treatment as such, it is important to consider the history and development of mental health treatment itself (Porter, 2002). The faint beginnings of today's mental health treatment with horses can, perhaps, be traced to the 1800s, when institutions such as York Retreat in England emphasized "moral" and mental treatment over, but also alongside, the abusive confinement practices and crude medical procedures of the time, and when model asylums were designed to function like working farms in country settings with horses and other animals. Similar advances were made in France and other European countries, with early study of trauma taking place through doctors Charcot and Janet at the Hôpital du Salpêtrière in the late 1800s (van der Kolk, 2003). In Finland, Lappvikens Sjukhus in Helsinki, built in 1841, was modeled on the idea that the environment is important for treating mental illness, and patients at the hospital did have access to horses in stables and pastures, as they were used in farming and for transportation (K. Wahlbeck, personal communication).

The notion of psychological trauma came into focus through accounts of "shell shock" during World War I (see van der Kolk, 2014, for an overview). Some propose that horses were used in the rehabilitation of wounded soldiers during World War I; however, a reliable source for this is difficult to find. Since the study of trauma, and the understanding of it as an etiological factor in mental disorders, was not a focus until the late

1970s (van der Kolk, 2003), there are no accounts of including horses in the treatment of trauma until much later. By the 1990s, there was some indication of the emergence of horses as part of psychological treatment in the United States and Europe, but it is truly in the past 20 years that equine-assisted therapy has developed more formally.

Inclusion of Horses in Mental Health Treatment

Interacting with horses, both on the ground and on their backs, often inspires sayings such as "the horse is my therapist" (Davis, Maurstad, & Dean, 2014, p. 299). However, addressing trauma, either directly through the traumatic memory or through strengthening other aspects of functioning, relies on the presence of a skilled and appropriately credentialed therapy professional, just like in other treatment areas. Providing mental health services together with a horse without education, training, and supervision in doing so and, importantly, without specific training in the population or diagnosis (or client challenge), is not ethical practice and may cause scope of practice violations.

Equine-assisted mental health can be understood as having simultaneously experiential, somatic (mind-body focused), and relational elements. While there are benefits to including animals in treatment that are present regardless of species, discussed in Fine (2015) and in this book, there are some aspects unique to horses that are highlighted as follows.

Setting. Equine-assisted therapy takes place in a nontraditional environment that can seem a better alternative to some clients than meeting the therapist in a small, enclosed office space. The option of being outdoors in nature or indoors (in spaces such as the indoor arena or barn office), or both, during the session allows for some flexibility depending on client preference and the weather. The setting in which equine-assisted therapy takes place is often a natural one, bringing with it additional benefits discussed elsewhere (cf. Louv, 2008; Thompson-Coon et al., 2011). Human interactions with horses for leisure and work tend to have positive meanings in different cultural and religious settings (Frewin & Gardiner, 2005; Pickeral, 2008), and so participating in equine-assisted therapy can foster a connection to a larger equestrian culture for the client.

Touch and movement. As proposed by Schulz (1999), rhythm, touch, and skin contact, naturally present in equine-assisted therapy, are essential elements of human development. The horse not only presents an opportunity for touch that might not be feasible in typical therapy, but they also provide large surfaces for body interaction, and even the ability to physically carry the client. Brooks (2006) notes how the horse can provide a client with the experience of being held in an environment that is perceived as safe. Brooks also comments on how the client's use of touch with an animal can be part of diagnostic assessment. The perception of a safe relationship, together with non-noxious sensory stimulation, can stimulate the release of oxytocin, a hormone involved in stress-reduction, calm states, and a feeling of connectedness (Uvnäs-Moberg, Handlin, Petersson, 2014). In addition to general physical benefits, movement can help with attention, relaxation, and a sense of connection in the therapy session. Brushing, leading, and riding are common ways to move together with horses.

Relational influence. The biophilia hypothesis, proposed by Wilson (1984), theorizes that humans have an innate tendency to focus on life and lifelike processes. It does not suggest that humans have a natural affection for animals but that attention to, and knowledge of, environmental cues has been an important part of human evolution (Kruger & Serpell, 2010). In other words, events in nature may be associated with a sense of safety or a sense of danger for humans. The biophilia hypothesis is used to support the notion that low-intensity interaction with a relaxed horse can have a calming, de-arousing effect, and it is likely that other factors, such as rhythmic touch, are also part of reducing arousal and facilitating a state change (a shift from one state of mind to another) in the client. A major feature of equine-assisted mental health is the opportunity for the client to form a relationship with an other-than-human being (Esbjorn, 2006; Hayden, 2005). Direct behavioral feedback, as well as the invitation to engage in body-based communication, give the client new insights into their own relational behavior. The horse can also function as an ally to the client and be perceived as a source of nonjudgmental support. Wanting to see the horse and to practice new behaviors that facilitate a relationship with the horse (such as self-regulation) can be a source of motivation for many clients.

Practice. Equine-assisted mental health is experiential in nature and often involves the opportunity to practice behaviors. The use of metaphor is often employed to help create an isomorphic bridge between what is happening with the client and the horse to other contexts in the client's life. Helping to make the intangible, such as the client's feelings and thoughts, tangible through physical and visual representation in the session, can create new avenues for self-insight. This includes the valuable opportunity to experience and practice new behaviors in a less-threatening social setting. At the same time, equine interactions do come with a level of risk, and the client can practice taking emotional risks together with the therapist.

Joint venture. The therapeutic alliance has been determined as a consistent factor related to therapeutic outcome (Ardito & Rabellino, 2011; Lambert & Barley, 2001), so it makes sense to focus on ways to evaluate and strengthen this relationship. Clients consciously or unconsciously assess the therapist and the therapy situation for clues related to safety and need for self-protection; hearing how the therapist talks about the horse and seeing how he or she interacts with the horse can create a basis of trust for the client: "*This is also how I will be treated in this relationship.*" The opportunity for the therapist and client to actively do things together in equine-assisted therapy, rather than simply talk about the client's issues, may be a strengthening factor for the therapeutic alliance. As a result, the client may feel more buy-in from the therapist for the client's therapeutic journey, a sense of "joint venture."

The aspects described above are made possible by the nature of the horse as a social prey mammal, which has implications for their brain structure, relational behavior, and learning, specifically associative learning. Compared with horses, humans have an enlarged prefrontal cortex, and while other areas of the brain are similar in mammals, humans possess reasoning skills and self-insight as a result of this difference, which horses do not (McGreevy, 2012; Siegel, 2012). As a prey animal, horses pay close attention to self- and energy-preservation, and as a social animal, to interactions with others. Their sociosensual awareness, a concept first introduced by anthropologist E. Richard Sorenson (1978) and which is shared with humans, means that they benefit from orienting and responding to the states of others.

These and other aspects of how horses and their environment specifically help enhance trauma treatment are discussed in the next section.

THEORY AND POTENTIAL MECHANISMS

Tri-Phasic Model as a Framework for Trauma Recovery Tasks

The presentation of how horses can enhance the treatment of trauma in this section is based on current understanding of trauma from advances in neuroscience, promoted by practitioners and researchers such as van der Kolk (2014), Siegel (2012), Ogden (Ogden, Minton, & Pain, 2006), Lanius (Frewen & Lanius, 2015), Porges (2011), Gilbert (2010), Perry (2009), and Levine (2010). I utilize the tri-phasic approach to trauma treatment, first proposed by Herman (1992), as a framework within which integrative tasks related to trauma recovery such as memory processing, reducing hyper- or hypoarousal, working with the body, developing core mind skills, creating meaning making and new narratives, achieving response flexibility, and (re) experiencing connection through relationships can be organized. The three phases can be characterized as: *Phase I—Stabilization and Moving Toward a Sense of Safety*; *Phase II—Integration of Traumatic Memories and Events*; and *Phase III—Reconnection*. There is no set or "right" way to address trauma in each complex client situation as the impact of trauma on an individual, as well as the length of treatment, depends on a number of lived experiences. These include attachment history; existence of previous, untreated traumatic experiences; the developmental timing of the trauma; characteristics of the trauma; and other supportive or destabilizing factors.

There are a number of approaches employed in the treatment of trauma (Foa, Keane, & Friedman, 2010), and a distinction should be made between treatment models that directly address the traumatic memory, such as eye-movement desensitization and reprocessing (EMDR), prolonged exposure (PE), and cognitive processing therapy (CPT), and those that address coping skills and supportive factors (see Imel, Laska, Jakcupcak, & Simpson, 2013, for a discussion on issues in conducting meta-analyses of trauma treatment for this reason). In the tri-phasic model presented here, the third phase (with the central task of reconnection) and the first phase (where central tasks relate to stabilizing and managing the mind) could be thought of as supportive on their own, but it is important to note that mastery of tasks in phase I is a prerequisite for the second phase (where integration of traumatic memories and creation of coherent narratives are central tasks). Treatment tasks for each of the four diagnostic clusters related to behavioral symptoms for post-traumatic stress disorder (PTSD) in the DSM-5—intrusion (reexperiencing); avoidance; negative alterations in cognitions and mood; and arousal (disturbances in arousal and reactivity such as hyper- or hypoarousal) (American Psychiatric Association, 2013)—can also easily be found within the three phases of the trauma treatment framework.

I agree with van der Kolk (2014) that eventually addressing the traumatic memory is central to reducing trauma symptomology. The neurobiology and neuroanatomy related to the process of integrating traumatic memories is discussed at length by Siegel (2012), but can, in short, be described as follows: traumatic memories have certain features that separate them from non-traumatic, or typical, memories. Traumatic memories lack a "time stamp," causing a person to have the experience again in the present, as opposed to simply thinking back to the past when it happened. Ogden and colleagues (2006) call this "the here-and-now experience of the traumatic past" (p. 167). Traumatic memories are fragmented and disorganized, with images, smells, and sounds experienced without sequence. The reason why this occurs is the lack of involvement of parts of the brain responsible for time and perspective, as well as creation of a coherent story line, at the time of the overwhelming experience(s). Helping the mind process the event with all necessary parts active is facilitated by reducing arousal, the excess of which created the lack of integration in the first place, and means that flashbacks and the reliving of the trauma will cease to happen. The ability to maintain calm while accessing the sensations and emotions that have caused such pain in order for the memory integration to happen is practiced as part of tasks in phases I and III and specifically applied in phase II.

Risk of Re-Traumatization in EAMH

Therapists who are working with a population with identified trauma but not directly with trauma treatment, and who include horses in treatment and whose session content may fall within phases I and III, need to make sure that their approach is, at a minimum, trauma-informed. The risk of re-traumatization has to be taken into consideration in session planning. Rothschild (2000) addresses three situations where the traumatic event can be accidentally triggered in therapy: 1) in state-dependent recall, 2) in postural-dependent recall, and 3) during exercises that involve accelerated heart rate. State-dependent recall occurs when the current state replicates the internal state produced in conjunction with the traumatic event. Each client's trauma is different, but caution should be taken if facilitating equine-assisted interactions with a high level of mental discomfort (involving a lot of unknowns or little instruction) or where there is need to perform under time pressure (such as in group games). Postural-dependent recall is similar, but specifically relates to the body being in a position associated with the traumatic event. Sitting astride a moving horse might trigger traumatic memories of sexual activities due to movement in the hips, for instance. Therapists placing clients in sensory positions on the back of the horse, such as in a prone position facing the tail, need to keep in mind that immobilization without fear (Porges, 2003) can be difficult to achieve in that position for some clients with trauma. Finally, Rothschild (2000) notes that an accelerated heart rate is part of hyperarousal in PTSD. Activities that might involve running or moving quickly and that are not entirely within an individual's control (such as part of a game or group exercise), might, through state-dependent recall, act as a trigger (Kozlowska, Walker, McLean, & Carrive, 2015). For the same reason, dramatic evocation of emotion common in certain psycho-spiritual approaches to EAMH should also be done with caution with a trauma population. In addition, activities that intentionally evoke a flight response in horses have welfare implications and are discussed in the section on equine welfare.

Finally, the nontraditional setting and inclusion of a horse may lead to clients disclosing about their traumas more quickly, either by choice or through gaining access to previously unknown experiences. It is the therapist's responsibility to help the client pace their processing so that treatment does not become re-traumatizing (Rothschild, 2000).

How Horses Can Enhance Trauma Treatment

Each phase in the framework is explained with general intention and tasks, adapted from Herman (1992), along with the horse's role in optimizing the achievement of these tasks.

Phase I: Stabilization and Moving Toward a Sense of Safety

The feeling that the world, other people, relationships, and own thoughts and body are dangerous hinders a trusting connection with self and others. Re-experiencing traumatic events through fragmented flashbacks and experiencing disturbances in arousal leads to attempts to disconnect from these extreme emotions through withdrawal from relationships, from oneself, and from one's body. Use of drugs and substances, and excessive engagement in behaviors, also function as self-management strategies (van der Kolk, 2004). Lanius, Bluhm, and Frewen (2011) found that clients diagnosed with complex PTSD have deficits in brain functioning related to emotion regulation, social emotional processing, and self-awareness, among others.

Tasks in Phase I

Tasks in phase I relate to helping clients find safety in their bodies and relationships through exploring ways to manage their mind and emotions. Identifying sources of strength and understanding the function of traumatic symptoms are also in focus.

Establishing a therapeutic relationship and a roadmap for treatment. Since trauma affects the ability to build and maintain relationships, especially where traumatic events are related to other people, experiencing safety in the therapeutic relationship can be difficult for clients. Through the presence of the horse, clients can assess how others in relationship with the therapist are talked about and treated (see also studies of how animals affect the social perceptions of others, such as Lockwood, 1983, and Rossbach & Wilson, 1992). This likely contributes to the client feeling more comfortable in the early therapeutic relationship (Tedeschi, Sisa, Olmert, Parish-Plass, & Yount, 2015). When client and therapist jointly focus on the horse, through brushing or observing, initial conversations can feel less threatening. This nonconfrontational spatial relationship (unlike sitting and facing one another in a traditional therapy office) can facilitate the sense of safety for the client.

Psychoeducation. Helping clients understand what is happening in their minds and bodies as a result of what are initially adaptive responses to trauma can reduce shame and confusion (Ogden et al., 2006), and starts the process of meaning making (Siegel, 2012). Further normalization and understanding of behaviors come through observation of similar behaviors and biological functions in the horse. Relaying curiosity from the client about the horse's behavior to their own can be very effective in encouraging self-awareness and reflection. In addition, it might be easier for clients to initially talk about themselves through the safer focus on the horse(s).

Body access and awareness. Regardless of approach, the central role of the body in the treatment of trauma has been much recognized (*cf.* Levine,

2010; Rothschild, 2000, 1999; van der Kolk, 2014). The intense physical reactions coming from the body as a response to heightened emotional states can lead to numbing or disconnecting responses for self-protection. This creates temporary relief but has a side effect: it is hard to "feel alive" without accessing a major part of oneself. Some clients put themselves into dangerous situations in order to "feel," while others narrow their lives to an extreme due to the painful impact of constantly scanning for danger (van der Kolk, 2014). *Vertical integration*, a term proposed by Siegel (2012) for the integration of the mind and body, and the way the mind, body, and brain work in concert, is central to consider in the treatment of trauma. Interacting with one's body applies directly to interacting with horses. The horse creates a setting where the need for body access and awareness makes sense, and this can motivate clients to engage in something that might cause initial discomfort. Increased understanding of the role of the body in communication, as well as access to it through practicing with the horse, helps supply the client with tools that help regulate body sensations. The ability to calm the body, through affecting the functioning of the autonomic nervous system, is a necessary component of emotion regulation and traumatic memory integration (Baranowsky & Gentry, 2015; Siegel, 2012).

Developing mind skills. In order to start achieving a sense of safety within, it is important that clients start recognizing signs of internal escalation and de-escalation, where models such as the Window of Tolerance (Ogden et al., 2006) come into good use. Related to this is finding ways to reduce extreme emotional states without maladaptive avoidance strategies. Mind skills, such as focusing skills, self-observation, and self-support, help clients to "apply the brakes" (Rothschild, 1999), and create a way to both feel and observe, as opposed to being completely taken over by a feeling. The ability to self-observe and other metacognitive strategies are cut off when internal arousal reaches a certain point. Decreasing arousal is directly related to the ability to engage in self-observation (Siegel, 2012). Horses can enhance the practice of mind skills and emotion management in a number of ways. For instance, horses provide a compelling reason to focus on the present, and clients can use this both as an anchor in thought pendulation activities and as a way to practice tolerating a calm state (see Ekholm Fry, 2016, for a more detailed discussion). Engaging with horses in activities that require focus, such as leading the horse through an obstacle course, not only creates an opportunity for the client to consciously notice what focus feels like, but can also motivate them to practice when the setting makes it functional. Activities done together with the horse might create more buy-in from the client than a guided visualization or other less tangible strategies would on their own. State shifts happen naturally in interaction with another living being, and the therapist can help identify those happening between the client and the horse without needing to address them within the therapeutic relationship. The latter is likely less tolerated by the client until later in treatment. An additional benefit of practicing mind skills together with the horse is the opportunity for bonding. If the client perceives that the relationship between themselves and the horse is trusting and safe, the elements of touch and rhythmic movement that are not possible between the therapist and client can help facilitate a release of oxytocin (Uvnäs-Moberg et al., 2014).

Putting words to feelings and distress. Clients with PTSD often have difficulties identifying and labeling their emotions (Lanius et al., 2011). An early neuroimaging study by Rauch and colleagues (1996) showed decreased activity in Broca's area (a part of the brain with functions linked to speech and language) in participants with PTSD during exposure to a traumatic narrative. This suggests that it might be difficult for traumatized individuals to verbalize what they are feeling when becoming emotionally distressed. Putting words to experiences can help bring organization to sensations, facilitating the creation of a coherent narrative (Siegel, 2012). In addition to previously mentioned approaches to facilitating sharing by the client, such as allowing the client to project their own feelings onto the horse or describing their own emotional state through the identity of the horse, the dynamic nature of equine interaction brings up different emotions that can be identified and explored by the client in the moment. In addition, it is important for clients to start noticing that there is, in fact, some variation in the intensity of their distress, especially since distress without exploration can seem constant. The subjective units of distress (SUDs) scale, first developed by Wolpe and Lazarus (1966), is a helpful tool in achieving this. Through practice of identifying level of comfort or level of distress associated with lower-arousal tasks in the therapeutic setting (such as picking up a horse's feet or walking around the back of a horse), clients can practice without overwhelming emotional content hindering skill building. Positive experiences with the horse can facilitate the recognition of other sources of strength in the client's life.

Understanding orienting and appraisal—reducing disturbances in arousal. After a traumatic event, orienting and appraisal systems often become altered, leading to a narrowing of perception and an appraisal process sensitized to perception of threat. The constant scanning for an inner sense of threat, also referred to as neuroception (Porges, 2011), and outer cues of threat and danger cause abnormal levels of arousal. Disturbances in arousal, which is part of the DSM-5 diagnostic criteria for PTSD (American Psychiatric Association, 2013), has negative effects on mood and cognition (see Ogden et al., 2006, for an excellent overview to orienting responses). Observing how the client evaluates threat, what factors go into the appraisal, and how able the client is to rework the appraisal process are helpful assessment tools for trauma therapists (Ogden et al., 2006). Interaction with horses can help the client to start making voluntary choices about what to orient toward, to allow for new information to enter into the appraisal process. Being able to reflect on the orienting/appraisal process as it happens enables the client to start making strategic choices about how to respond. As mentioned in the previous task, there are interactions around horses that clients might have apprehension about, such as picking up the feet, which is necessary for their care, and walking around the back of the horse. Simply approaching a large animal can also feel daunting, especially if the client has no previous experience or poor past experiences with horses. This flexible environment provides an excellent experiential opportunity for the therapist and client to explore and make sense of the client's orienting responses.

An example of this that happens frequently in my practice is walking around the back of the horse, which naturally happens when interacting with horses. Walking around a horse that is fully comfortable with human interaction and trained for a number of tasks on the ground is best done by walking closely to the rump. Horses have a wide field of vision and a narrow blind spot near the rear, which can be accessed by the horse slightly moving their head (McGreevy, 2012). The trainability of horses and their energy-preserving nature means that they have no reason to kick back or step on the client. The exceptions to this would be if the horse startled, or displayed a response to pain or conflict.

Each of my clients receives brief instruction and demonstration with another human, if available, on how to pass behind a horse at the beginning of a session. Even when equipped with information they know is coming from a professional, and with horses that are trained, most clients might feel some apprehension when walking around the horse but are willing to try. But for some, the amount of hyperarousal and disruption to a typical orienting process as a result of their past traumatic experiences might not allow them to distinguish this situation from those in their past. Unless the client's arousal is much too high, the client now has a tangible opportunity in the therapy session to practice what to orient toward, to allow for new information to enter into the appraisal process, and to reflect on the orienting/appraisal process as it happens.

If the client asks that I go with them around the horse when they are not yet able to attempt this action with only verbal support from me, I position myself at the horse's side, facing their tail, and ask the client to stand behind me. Being positioned behind me, as opposed to in front, is a less threatening position for the client. I slowly walk to the tail of the horse, with the client following, and when I am standing by their back legs (this position seems the most risky to the client) I pause, and together with the client we appraise the situation so that we can make strategic decisions based on what is happening in that moment. I ask the client to notice their own internal state. I describe mine to the client. Then we assess what the horse's state might be, based on level of tension or relaxation in its body, how the horse holds its neck, where the ears are pointed, and whether there are any elements in the environment that might contribute to the horse moving, such as other horses approaching. Throughout this dual attention exercise together with the horse, I demonstrate a calm body state and might also encourage the client to slow down their breath. By paying attention to cues in the environment that are happening right now, and allowing *some* past experience to enter the decision-making process, clients can now start the process of reworking these acquired schemas. The knowledge that overwhelming experiences of the past have created some unhelpful biases in their thinking and feeling can be liberating for the client. The more cautious nature of horses, compared to dogs, for instance, can also help clients relate to their own experience of hyperarousal and hypervigilance.

As noted by Briere and Scott (2006), hope is not typically described as a therapeutic goal, but should be seen as a crucial therapeutic action. Hopelessness arises from the perception that negative things will remain constant, which, for those affected by traumatic experiences might be unbearable. New internal and external experiences made possible from the tasks in phase I facilitate the idea that change is possible (van der Kolk, 2004), and help prepare clients for the tasks in phase II. The task of phase

I should not be seen as "complete" when moving to the next phase, but as part of the ongoing therapy process.

Phase II: Integration of Traumatic Memories and Events

The integration of traumatic memories involves lessening their emotional intensity so that they can function as typical memories and not be relived or fragmented. This integrative process also includes making sense of what has happened through a narrative that can become part of the client's larger life story. The process can also involve mourning losses, such as not having a typical childhood, or living with injuries sustained in the course of the traumatic events (Herman, 1992). This is the phase of treatment least tolerated by clients (Najavits, 2015), so preparation and timing must be appropriate. Interactions with a preferred horse can help motivate the client to remain in treatment during the height of therapeutic intensity.

Tasks in Phase II

Integrating traumatic memories. The ability to maintain a calm body in response to experiencing fragments of traumatic memory will help the mind organize and store these experiences so that they can later be retrieved, as opposed to painfully and intrusively relived. In an early text, Wolpe (1958) proposed that by having people relax while they were in situations that provoked fear, subsequent exposures to the situations would become less distressing. The ability of the client to engage in dual awareness, keeping part of their focus on the present and part on the traumatic images and sensations is also necessary (Ogden et al., 2006). The horse can support this process in a number of ways: as a reminder and facilitator of a calm state, as a support for a distressing process, and as an appealing anchor to the present.

Constructing and integrating a narrative. Creating coherent narratives with descriptions of sensations associated with the trauma and sequence of events assists in memory integration and meaning making for the client (Rothschild, 2000). The narrative can then be integrated into the client's life story and is available for examination and reexamination. The therapist is responsible for helping the client pace the narrative process. Rothschild (2000) suggests stages to constructing the trauma narrative, and Briere and Scott (2006) recommend starting and ending each session with low therapeutic intensity. Interaction with the horse can function as a physical break for the client who is becoming too activated. In order to reinforce a connection to the present, the client can also create a visual representation of the trauma narrative in the arena together with the horse and therapist. By creating a physical representation of intangible experiences of the mind, dual attention and self-observation can be made easier. Incorporating movement and the connection to the horse can help clients tolerate the narration of fragmented details related to the trauma. Starting and ending with low therapeutic intensity can be easily achieved through interactions with the horse such as grooming, feeding, or leading the horse back to their pasture.

Phase III: Reconnection

When the acute effects of traumatic experiences are gradually fading, there is space and opportunity for the client to reconnect with themselves and others in their lives. Within this phase lies endless opportunity to pursue self-exploration, further integration and meaning making of the increasingly coherent trauma-related narrative, and creating connection through healthy relationships and meaningful activities that make life enjoyable. Including the horse facilitates experiential engagement in this process with a relational partner to the client.

Tasks in Phase III

Connecting with self. Tasks in Phase I initially helped the client to establish a basic sense of safety and management of their emotions. In Phase III, these tasks can be revisited through a new sense of agency. Exploring patterns of thinking and behaving in relation to overall goals in the client's life may also involve treatment for addictions and substance abuse that might arise as ways to cope with the trauma. The client is now faced with the task of establishing trust in themselves and compassion toward who they were before, during, and after the trauma. Herman (1992) calls this "reconciling with oneself." Equine-assisted therapy used as an enhancer in the treatment session provides an experiential, somatic, and relational space for the client to explore these and other tasks, and can easily be incorporated with other approaches such as art therapy. One of my clients said after a session in this phase: "I remember that there are all these different parts to me."

Connecting with others. Our neurobiology is designed to promote and reward social behavior, and our brain is reliant on others for development and survival (Siegel, 2012). So, without others, we cannot fully function. The symptoms of traumatic experiences not only hinder the ability to feel present and fully alive, but also largely prevent a feeling of connection with others (van der Kolk, 2014). The experience of an attuned relationship and the experience of repair after rupture, both part of secure attachment (Siegel, 2012), can be carefully fostered between therapist, client, and horse. Relational skills such as setting and maintaining boundaries, perspective taking, empathy, and communicating one's own needs can be practiced experientially through including equine interactions in treatment.

Connecting with community. Shapiro and Maxfield (2003) note, "Let me make it fruitful, let me be useful, let me help others" (p. 214). Taking part in community activities and being of service to others can be part of post-traumatic growth (Calhoun & Tedeschi, 2014). The connection to horses and the culture surrounding horses established through equine-assisted therapy as a treatment enhancer can provide a place for the client to engage in their larger community. Volunteering in programs that provide opportunity for individuals with physical disabilities to be around horses and learn to ride, or spending more time with horses by helping at barns or horse rescues can be satisfying avenues to be of service.

CONSIDERATIONS FOR EQUINE WELFARE IN TRAUMA TREATMENT

When including an animal in human therapy services, therapists have a responsibility to attend to the welfare of the animal. The nature of this responsibility can be seen from a number of perspectives, from that of One Health (Gibbs, 2014), meaning the understanding that the health of humans, the health of other animals, and the health of the environment are interconnected and interdependent; to ethical and moral reasons; to reasons related to therapeutic outcomes; and to risk management, all of which are interlinked.

How horses are managed and handled affects their levels of stress and pain, which in turn affect their behaviors. Horses that are fearful or aggressive pose a larger risk to humans (Popescu & Diugan, 2013). Since the treatment of horses and their overall demeanor in the therapy session affects the client's perception of safety, a connection between the welfare and treatment of the horse and therapeutic outcomes in equine-assisted therapy can be proposed (Ekholm Fry, 2014).

Challenges

Therapist knowledge, skills, and attitudes have the biggest impacts on the welfare of horses that are included in human trauma treatment. For instance, attitudes such as: "horses are called to heal trauma" or "my horse loves doing trauma work" fail to take into consideration actual mental abilities of horses, such as the lack of reasoning and self-reflection (McGreevy, 2012), and may cause the therapist to overlook signs of stress or discomfort in the horse. The belief that "the horse can take care of themselves" and allowing for so-called natural consequences in the session if a client acts inappropriately with the horse, also may cause stress due to inconsistent handling and lack of predictability and controllability for the horse (Weiss, 1971). Interactions between the client and the horse must be very closely monitored so as to not elicit high levels of stress in the horse, and the therapist should ensure that interactions do not run counter to a healthy relationship between the client and the horse. Activities that might elicit flight in the horse should be avoided altogether (McGreevy & McLean, 2010) as it does not make sense to work in a trauma treatment setting without a trauma-informed relationship with the horse.

Inadequate, inappropriate, or nonexistent work role preparation accounts for confusion and unwanted behaviors in horses, together with inappropriate management practices such as confinement, restricted access to hay or grass, and lack of access to other horses (McGreevy, 2012). Mental health practitioners who are not trained in equine behavior may not be able to recognize subtle cues that horses communicate when distressed, or might not know how to create a therapeutic environment that includes consideration for the horse. They might, in turn, not intervene soon enough or in a therapeutic way when interactions with the client are creating high levels of stress in the horse.

The effect on the horse from a human who exhibits symptoms of trauma are thought to be stressful, but based on inconsistent results from studies measuring the effects of a tense or anxious human on a horse, there is no clear evidence for this (Hama, Yogo, & Matsuyama, 1996; Keeling, Jonare, & Lanneborn, 2009; Merkies et al., 2014). For instance, Merkies and colleagues (2014) found that the horses in their study reacted more calmly to a human whose heart rate was elevated due to anxiety than to one whose heart rate was elevated due to physical exercise. Hama and colleagues (1996) found an elevation in equine heart rate initially when being stroked by study participants who had negative attitudes toward companion animals, but that heart rate then decreased. Keeling et al. (2009) found corresponding elevations in equine heart rate during a leading and riding task as a result of anticipatory stress in the human created for the purpose of the study. In addition, Gehrke, Baldwin, and Schiltz (2011) found no difference in heart rate variability (HRV) during a 24-hour period between horses engaging in unspecified equine-assisted therapy and thoroughbreds used for racing.

A study by Yorke and colleagues (2013) hypothesized that cortisol levels would correlate between children diagnosed with PTSD and their assigned therapeutic riding horse during a 12-day program period. Results were inconclusive and it is unclear whether the design of the study appropriately accounted for the variables involved. Only two studies to date have specifically measured responses of horses to individuals diagnosed with PTSD (Malinowski et al., 2018; Merkies, McKechnie, & Zakrajsek 2018). Malinowski and colleagues (2018) found that stress levels, demonstrated by equine plasma cortisol concentrations and heart rate variability in the study, did not change in horses involved in sessions with veterans who had been diagnosed with PTSD. The horses did not demonstrate increased levels of wellbeing after these interactions per analysis of plasma oxytocin via oxytocin immunoassays, either. It may be of relevance that the horses in the study were conditioned and experienced as adaptive riding horses, working in 8–10 lessons per week in addition to being ridden by volunteers 2–4 times per week. Merkies and colleagues (2018) found that behavioral and physiological responses of horses to humans, measured by equine heart rate and salivary cortisol, were more pronounced based on human experience with horses than whether the human was diagnosed with PTSD. It is likely that horses, similar to humans, have different thresholds of tolerance for tension and other states in others due to a variety of factors.

Recommendations

In the competencies for therapists using animal-assisted therapy in counseling, promoted by the American Counseling Association (Stewart, Chang, Parker, & Grubbs, 2016), the section on animal knowledge includes understanding species-specific behaviors and needs, animal training techniques, and paying attention to signals of stress. In addition, therapists working with horses in trauma treatment should know:

- How to establish an equine work role and prepare a horse for work in your therapy setting, using training based on learning theory (Doner & Ekholm Fry, 2015).
- How to select horses for the specific therapy work you do (that is, the work role you expect the horse to fill). This includes both assessing overall temperament and understanding the learned behaviors that help the horse avoid experiencing confusion or constant conflict in the therapy setting.
- How to assess, or simply understand, how and what horses communicate about their emotional and physical health (and continuously respond to this communication in a trauma-informed manner, as you would with humans).
- How to employ strategies that enhance welfare in horses and maintain a realistic appreciation of their cognitive capacities to avoid misinterpretation of behavior.
- How to recognize signs of mental and behavioral wellness in horses, not just welfare issues (see Waran & Randle, 2017, for a discussion).
- How to manage the horse's living environment so that species-specific needs in feeding and housing arrangements are met.
- How to recognize signs of pain and discomfort (especially related to the horse's limbs and back, and to the muscling needed to carry humans) that might warrant discontinuation of work.
- How to train and handle horses using practices that are based on learning theory, and which do not involve inescapable pressure, flight, or flooding. Therapists who include riding in their treatment should know how to develop and strengthen core muscles in horses.
- How to employ post-session strategies based on cognitive, emotional, and physical needs of horses.

Simply loving or owning horses is not enough to competently include them in therapy. Similarly, a focus on the term "relationship" does not prevent abusive training practices or misinformation about horses from occurring. The desire to maintain a relationship with the horse can, however, function as a motivator to take in information about handling, training, and management practices that will be in the best interest of the horse, but might not immediately fit human convenience or thinking.

There is a need to move beyond basic frameworks such as the Five Freedoms (Farm Animal Welfare Council, n.d.), developed for settings where animals are farmed, and to rethink our relationships with animals. In trauma treatment, it is important to be sensitive to features of equine interactions that perpetuate the power differences between humans and horses in a way that might introduce a sense of exploitation into the therapeutic environment. Just as therapists are aware of the power dynamic between themselves and their clients, this awareness must also be extended to relationships with horses in the session and beyond. Is it acceptable to refer to horses part of equine-assisted therapy as "partners," but simultaneously deny them basic needs in their living situation (for example, keeping horses separate in small spaces, sometimes isolated from each other; denying them constant access to fiber; and making them endure periods of fasting)? Is it acceptable for well-intended trainers to subject horses to training and handling that causes them pain and confusion, such as flooding, which has been abandoned in human trauma and phobia treatment practice? More discussion is needed around these issues; otherwise animal-assisted interventions, and specifically horses as part of therapy, simply represent additional avenues for humans to exploit animals.

GAPS AND NEXT STEPS

Research

Through examining results from a systematic literature review on animal-assisted interventions for trauma (O'Haire, Guérin, & Kirkham, 2015), and conducting extensive database searches, 25 journal articles with a primary focus on trauma and equine-assisted therapy published in English were identified. The articles varied greatly in content and methodological rigor; despite this, most of them are commonly cited. In addition, six doctoral dissertations on equine-assisted therapy and trauma were identified (Abrams, 2013; Beck, 2014; Gomez, 2016; Held, 2006; Mattson, 2015; McCullough, 2011).

Of the 25 articles, some included qualitative studies (Meinersmann, Bradberry, & Roberts, 2008; Schroeder, Stroud, Sherwood, & Udell, 2017; Thelle, 2010; Yorke, Adams, & Coady, 2008), and some described equine-assisted trauma-focused programs (Ferruolo, 2016; Froeschle, 2009; Mykhaylov, Serdiuk, Vodka, Aliieva, & Vashkite, 2016; Newton-Cromwell,

McSpadden, & Johnson, 2015; Porter-Wenzlaff, 2007). One study, where cortisol levels were measured, used the term equine-assisted therapy in its title (Yorke et al., 2013), but it appears a therapist was not involved in delivering the intervention. Based on this, the program might be better categorized as adaptive riding (therapeutic riding), see "Definitions," instead of therapy. Results from this study were inconclusive.

Fifteen articles presented quantitative research. One study (Schultz, Remick-Barlow, & Robbins, 2007), which has often been cited, consisted of a convenience sample of all children referred to a therapist over the course of 18 months, with diagnoses that included PTSD. Children's Global Assessment of Functioning (GAF) scores were assigned by the treatment team pre- and posttreatment. Children who had a history of physical abuse and neglect had a statistically significant greater percentage improvement in GAF scores after treatment than those who did not have a history of abuse and neglect. All children showed an improvement after receiving equine-assisted treatment based on assigned GAF scores. The remaining studies used evidence of trauma symptomology or identified childhood sexual abuse (CSA) as inclusion criteria for participants.

Two studies (Johnson et al., 2018; Lanning, Wilson, Woelk, & Beaujean, 2018) specifically discussed the use of adaptive riding (therapeutic riding) to reduce PTSD symptoms. Both studies emphasized that this non-therapy riding approach should be seen as a complement to trauma treatment.

Sample sizes ranged from 1 to 68, from a single case study (Nevins, Finch, Hickling, & Barnett, 2013) and collection of cases (Naste et al., 2017), to couples (Romaniuk, Evans, & Kidd, 2018) and group treatment (Earles, Vernon, & Yetz, 2015; Johnson et al., 2018; Kemp, Signal, Botros, Taylor, & Prentice, 2014; Lanning et al., 2018; McCullough, Risley-Curtiss, & Rorke, 2015; Mueller & McCullough, 2017; Shambo, Seely, & Vonderfecht, 2010; Signal, Taylor, Botros, Prentice, & Lazarus, 2013; Whittlesey-Jermone, 2014). Four studies involved children and adolescents (Naste et al., 2017; Kemp et al., 2014; McCullough et al., 2015; Mueller & McCullough, 2017), the rest had adult participants (Burton, Qeadan, & Burge, 2019; Earles et al., 2015; Johnson et al., 2018; Lanning et al., 2018; Malinowski et al., 2018; Nevins et al., 2013; Romaniuk et al., 2018; Shambo et al., 2010), and in one study the same program was delivered to all three age groups (Signal et al., 2013). Four studies had a control group (Burton et al., 2019; Johnson et al., 2018; Lanning et al., 2018; Mueller

& McCullough, 2017). In two of the studies with controls (Johnson et al., 2018; Lanning et al., 2018), clinically meaningful improvements in PTSD symptoms were found using the same measure (PCL-Military) in both studies, but no significant effect for other measures in either study was found. In a study by Burton and colleagues (2019), the PCL-Military was also used and garnered statistically significant improvements in PTSD symptoms, but no statistically significant difference was found when compared with the control group (wherein participants received treatment-as-usual for PTSD). The equine-assisted therapy provided in this study was not specifically designed to enhance existing trauma treatment approaches. In the study by Mueller and McCullough (2017), increased effectiveness of equine-assisted therapy treatment over office-based therapy (used as a control) was not found.

A study without a control group found significant reduction in PTSD symptoms (Malinowski et al., 2018). It is, however, unclear, how the intervention should be characterized, since it was described as a 5-day program called "Equine-Assisted Activities and Therapies," where incompatible language and terms were used (an intervention cannot simultaneously be both therapy and not).

Most studies had little to no description of session content or indication of a protocol, and in some cases only typical horsemanship activities were mentioned. Studies by Kemp et al. (2014) and Signal et al. (2013) had overlapping participants and design and appeared to use a set protocol for all, which was described by Kemp and colleagues as based on experiential learning with the help of horses and delivered by mental health professionals. Four articles included more detailed information on enhancing clinical theory through equine interactions to meet the needs of the population studied (Naste et al., 2017; Schroeder & Stroud, 2015; Schroeder et al., 2017; Shambo et al., 2010). Naste and colleagues (2017) also emphasized that existing EAMH treatments for trauma are limited with respect to their integration of existing evidence-based frameworks (which I address in this chapter). The distinction between treatment models that directly address traumatic memories and those focusing on supportive skills, as discussed in the earlier section on the "Tri-Phasic Model as a Framework for Trauma Recovery Tasks," is also evident when reviewing the current equine-assisted therapy studies. None of the approaches in these studies seem to engage the traumatic memory directly.

Along with more typical issues in methodology, such as lack of randomization and control, small sample size and quasi-experimental design (see O'Haire et al., 2015, for a discussion), additional challenges related to investigating the effectiveness of trauma treatment that includes horses are: 1) lack of replicable treatment protocols, 2) lack of integration with evidence-based treatment approaches, and 3) large differences in the background and training of therapists providing equine-assisted mental health services. It is likely that the latter significantly contributes to the lack of comparable research in this area.

As mentioned above, the American Counseling Association recently published competencies for practitioners who include animal-assisted therapy in their counseling practice (Stewart et al., 2016). This document constitutes an important step toward establishing a specific scope of practice for therapists providing animal-assisted interventions in the United States. The development of species-specific competencies seems a natural next step, and each country must work to establish similar documents and expectations for their practitioners through their own governing bodies. Increasing competence among practitioners will certainly help inform research protocols.

An example of comprehensive, academic training in equine-assisted therapy is the Equine-Assisted Mental Health Practitioner Certificate program at the University of Denver's Institute for Human-Animal Connection, which the author coordinates. This is a professional program for master's- and doctoral-level therapists who want to include equine interactions as a way to enhance treatment in their practice. The program meets the American Counseling Association's competency requirements for animal-assisted therapy and can function as a model for other programs. More agreement is needed, specifically in equine-assisted therapy, around length of training and basic competencies to further both research and practice. The equine-assisted EMDR approach EquiLateral, developed by Sarah Jenkins in the United States, shows promise in terms of producing a replicable protocol for examining the effects of horses in the treatment of trauma, as it follows an existing evidence-based and manualized treatment.

Scientific investigation of whether there are specific parts of trauma treatment that are, in fact, enhanced by equine-assisted therapy is necessary, since the inclusion of horses in therapy is more expensive than services taking place in a typical office. Services involving horses can also be more difficult to access with regards to transportation, and they do include an element of inherent risk. Research findings can help guide the development of more training opportunities for therapists who want to include horses in trauma treatment, after meeting basic competencies for animal-assisted therapy.

Practice

Therapists who include horses in their practice need education, training, and supervision in working with trauma before intentionally working with and addressing traumatic experiences in their clients. It is important to note that the horse themself is not the provider of the treatment; rather, it is the skill of the therapist that allows for the horse to be intentionally included in order to assist the client in meeting their goals.

It is necessary to disclose whether the treatment provided is meant to directly address the processing of the traumatic memory or strengthen other supportive skills, or both, when describing equine-assisted mental health to clients and other practitioners. When clients want horse interactions outside of formal treatment, adaptive riding (also known as therapeutic riding), which in the United States is an activity focused on riding and horsemanship skills taught by specifically trained riding instructors, is an option. Some adaptive riding centers offer groups specifically for veterans, for instance. There are also other recreational activities, such as trail riding and horse training clinics that therapists could recommend to their clients. However, quality does vary, especially in terms of the welfare of the horses involved, which can lead to counterproductive experiences.

Continued efforts to organize and professionalize related to practice with horses in treatment, including promoting collaboration and agreement on competencies, will strengthen current use and understanding of equine-assisted therapy and the inclusion of horses in the treatment of trauma. Honest recognition of, and willingness to discuss, issues related to the practice area, such as those detailed in the equine welfare section, is also necessary.

CONCLUSIONS

The inclusion of horses in the treatment of trauma as a way to enhance current clinical approaches, discussed in this chapter, could motivate clients to seek treatment and remain in treatment, both of which are central issues in trauma treatment overall (Najavits, 2015; Sayer et al., 2009).

The experiential, somatic, and relational nature of equine-assisted mental health meets the need for clients to have experiences in trauma treatment that are not solely based on talking, but that experientially address the despair and psychophysical burden of living with trauma (van der Kolk, 2004). Concerns among practitioners using PE and CPT regarding dropout rates and client tolerance for treatment (Najavits, 2015) could be mitigated by motivating and supportive aspects that equine interactions and the equine environment bring to treatment.

Variation in therapist competencies, skill, and training in equine-assisted mental health in general, and in trauma practice in particular, reflects a non-unified area with disagreements regarding competency. This is one of the potential barriers to investigating treatment of trauma that includes equine interactions, and likely accounts for gaps in the study of its effectiveness. Equally important to consider is the impact of the horse's health and needs on the therapeutic environment and on the quality of the therapy session. To gain more recognition for equine interactions as a way to enhance current treatment options for trauma, practitioners, organizations, and grant makers need to work together in establishing competencies, practice guidelines, and opportunities for research.

REFERENCES

Abrams, B. N. (2013). *Exploring therapists' conceptions of equine facilitated/assisted psychotherapy for combat veterans experiencing posttraumatic stress disorder* (Doctoral dissertation). Northcentral University, Scottsdale, AZ.

American Hippotherapy Association. (2018). *AHA Inc., Terminology guidelines.*

American Psychiatric Association. (2013). *Diagnostic and statistical manual of mental disorders* (5th ed.). Washington, DC: Author.

Americans With Disabilities Act. (2010). *U.S. Department of Justice: ADA requirements for service animals.* Retrieved from https://www.ada.gov/service_animals_2010.htm

Anthony, D. W. (2007). *The Horse, the wheel, and language.* Princeton, NJ: Princeton University Press.

Ardito, R. B., & Rabellino, D. (2011). Therapeutic alliance and outcome of psychotherapy: Historical excursus, measurements, and prospects for research. *Frontiers in Psychology, 2,* 270. https://doi.org/10.3389/fpsyg.2011.00270

Bain, A. M. (1965). Pony riding for the disabled. *Physiotherapy, 51*(8), 263–265.

Baranowsky, A. B., & Gentry, J. E. (2015). *Trauma practice: Tools for stabilization and recovery.* Boston, MA: Hogrefe.

Beck, D. H. (2014). *Trauma focused equine assisted psychotherapy: A phenomenological study of therapists' beliefs about components of effective treatment for children who have experienced abuse and neglect* (Unpublished doctoral dissertation). Capella University, Minneapolis, MN.

Brandt, N., & Eklund, E. (2007). *Häst-människa-samhälle: Om den nya hästhushållningens utveckling i Finland.* Notat 1/2007, Forskningsinstitutet SSKH. University of Helsinki. Retrieved from http://sockom.helsinki.fi/info/notat/notat107.pdf

Briere, J., & Scott, C. (2006). *Principles of trauma therapy: A guide to symptoms, evaluation, and treatment.* Thousand Oaks, CA: SAGE.

Brooks, S. M. (2006). Animal-assisted psychotherapy and equine-facilitated psychotherapy. In N. Webb (Ed.), *Working with traumatized youth in child welfare* (pp. 196–219). New York, NY: Guilford Press.

Burton, L. E., Qeadan, F., & Burge, M. R. (2019). Efficacy of equine-assisted psychotherapy in veterans with posttraumatic stress disorder. *Journal of Integrative Medicine, 17*(1), 14–19. https://doi.org/10.1016/j.joim.2018.11.001

Calhoun, L. G., & Tedeschi, R. G. (Eds.). (2014). *Handbook of posttraumatic growth: Research and practice.* New York, NY: Psychology Press.

Davis, D. L., Maurstad, A., & Dean, S. (2014). My horse is my therapist: The medicalization of pleasure among women equestrians. *Medical Anthropology Quarterly, 29*(3), 298–315.

Doner, E., & Ekholm Fry, N. (2015). Role of learning theory in training and handling the therapy horse. *Scientific and Educational Journal of Therapeutic Riding, 20*, 61–76.

Earles, J., Vernon, L., & Yetz, J. (2015). Equine-assisted therapy for anxiety and posttraumatic stress symptoms. *Journal of Traumatic Stress, 28*(2), 149–152.

Edenburg, N. (1999). Perceptions and attitudes towards horses in European societies. *Equine Veterinary Journal, 28*, 38–41.

Ekholm Fry, N. (2013). Equine-assisted therapy: An overview. In M. Grassberger, R. A. Sherman, O. S. Gileva, C. Kim, & K. Y. Mumcuoglu (Eds.), *Biotherapy: History, principles and practice* (pp. 255–285). New York, NY: Springer.

Ekholm Fry, N. (2014, October). *How horse culture affects sustainability and risk management.* Presented at the annual meeting of PATH International, San Diego, CA.

Ekholm Fry, N. (2016). *Building capacity for wellness through core mind skills.* Presentation at the 4th Healing with Horse Tele-Summit, Healing with Horse Collective.

Esbjorn, R. J. (2006). *When horses heal: A qualitative inquiry into equine facilitated psychotherapy* (Doctoral dissertation). Institute of Transpersonal Psychology, Palo Alto, CA.

Farm Animal Welfare Council. (n.d.). Five freedoms. Retrieved from http://webarchive.nationalarchives.gov.uk/20121010012427/http://www.fawc.org.uk/freedoms.htm

Ferruolo, D. M. (2016). Psychosocial equine program for veterans. *Social Work, 61*(1), 53–60.

Fine, A. H. (Ed.). (2015). *Handbook on animal-assisted therapy: Foundations and guidelines for animal-assisted interventions* (4th ed.). San Diego, CA: Academic Press.

Foa, E. B., Keane, T. M., & Friedman, M. J. (2010). *Effective treatments for PTSD: Practice guidelines from the International Society for Traumatic Stress Studies.* New York, NY: Guilford.

Frewen, P., & Lanius, R. (2015). *Healing the traumatized self: Consciousness, neuroscience, treatment.* New York, NY: W. W. Norton.

Frewin, K., & Gardiner, B. (2005). New age or old sage? A review of equine assisted psychotherapy. *Australian Journal of Counselling Psychology, 6,* 13–17.

Froeschle, J. (2009). Empowering abused women through equine assisted career therapy. *Journal of Creativity in Mental Health, 4*(2), 180–190.

Gehrke, E. K., Baldwin, A., & Schiltz, P. M. (2011). Heart rate variability in horses engaged in equine-assisted activities. *Journal of Equine Veterinary Science, 31*(2), 78–84.

Gibbs, E. P. (2014). The evolution of One Health: A decade of progress and challenges for the future. *Veterinary Record, 174,* 85–91. https://doi.org/10.1136/vr.g143

Gilbert, P. (2010). *Compassion focused therapy.* New York NY: Routledge.

Gomez, I. B. (2016). *Evaluating a program of equine therapy for veterans with PTSD symptoms* (Unpublished doctoral dissertation). Alliant International University, Los Angeles, CA.

Hama, H., Yogo, M., & Matsuyama, Y. (1996). Effects of stroking horses on both humans and horses heart rate responses. *Japanese Psychological Research, 38*(2), 66–73.

Hayden, A. (2005*). An exploration of the experiences of adolescents who participated in equine facilitated psychotherapy: A resiliency perspective* (Doctoral dissertation). Alliant International University, Los Angeles, CA.

Held, C. (2006). *Horse girl: An archetypal study of women, horses, and trauma healing* (Doctoral dissertation). Pacifica Graduate Institute, Carpinteria, CA.

Herman, J. (1992). *Trauma and recovery.* New York, NY: Basic Books.

Imel, Z. E., Laska, K., Jakcupcak, M., & Simpson, T. L. (2013). Meta-analysis of dropout in treatments for post-traumatic stress disorder. *Journal of Consulting and Clinical Psychology, 81*(3), 394–404.

Johns, C. (2006). *Horses: History, myth, art.* Cambridge, MA: Harvard University Press.

Johnson, R., Albright, D., Marzolf, J., Bibbo, J., Yaglom, H., Crowder, A., Carlisle, G., Willard, A., Russel, C., Grindler, K., Osterlind, S., Wassman, M., & Harms, N. (2018). Effects of therapeutic horseback riding on post-traumatic stress disorder in military veterans. *Military Medical Research, 5*(3), 1–13.

Keeling, L., Jonare, L., & Lanneborn, L. (2009). Investigating horse-human interactions: The effect of a nervous human. *Veterinary Journal, 181*(1), 70–1.

Kemp, K., Signal, T. Botros, H., Taylor, N., & Prentice, K. (2014). Equine facilitated therapy with children and adolescents who have been sexually abused: A program evaluation study. *Journal of Child and Family Studies, 23*(3), 558–566.

Kozlowska, K., Walker, P., McLean, L., & Carrive, P. (2015). Fear and the defense cascade: Clinical implications and management. *Harvard Review of Psychiatry, 23*(4), 263–287.

Kruger, K. A., & Serpell, J. A. (2010). Animal-assisted interventions in mental health: Definitions and theoretical foundations. In A. H. Fine (Ed.), *Handbook of animal-assisted therapy: Theoretical foundations and guidelines for practice* (3rd ed., pp. 33–48). San Diego, CA: Academic Press.

Lambert, M. J., & Barley, D. E. (2001). Research summary on the therapeutic relationship and psychotherapy outcome. *Psychotherapy: Theory, Research, Practice, Training, 38*(4), 357–361. https://doi.org/10.1037/0033-3204.38.4.357

Lanius, R. A., Bluhm, R. L., & Frewen, P. A. (2011). How understanding the neurobiology of complex post-traumatic stress disorder can inform clinical practice: A social cognitive and affective neuroscience approach. *Acta Psychiatrica Scandinavia, 124*, 331–348.

Lanning, B. A., Wilson, A., Woelk, R., & Beaujean, A. (2018). Therapeutic horseback riding as a complementary intervention for military service members with PTSD. *Human-Animal Interaction Bulletin, 6*(2), 58–82.

Levine, P. A. (2010). *In an unspoken voice: How the body releases trauma and restores goodness.* Berkeley, CA: North Atlantic Books.

Lockwood, R. (1983). The influence of social contact with other people by pet dogs. In A. H. Katcher & A. M. Beck (Eds.), *New perspectives on our lives with companion animals* (pp. 64–71). Philadelphia, PA: University of Pennsylvania Press.

Louv, R. (2008). *Last child in the woods: Saving our children from nature-deficit disorder.* Chapel Hill, NC: Algonquin Books.

Malinowski, K., Yee, C., Tevlin, J. M., Birks, E. K., Durando, M. M., Pourna-jafi-Nazarloo, H., Cavaiola, A. A., & McKeever, K. H. (2018). The effects of equine assisted therapy on plasma cortisol and oxytocin concentrations and heart rate variability in horses and measures of symptoms of post-traumatic stress disorder in veterans. *Journal of Equine Veterinary Science, 64,* 17–26.

Mattson, L. (2015). *The impact of equine assisted activities and therapies on trauma recovery: Stories of United States military veterans who have participated in equine assisted activities and therapies programs* (Unpublished doctoral dissertation). Plymouth State University, Plymouth, NH.

McCullough, L. M. (2011). *Effect of equine-facilitated psychotherapy on posttrau-matic stress symptoms in youth with history of maltreatment and abuse* (Unpub-lished doctoral dissertation). Northcentral University, Scottsdale, AZ.

McCullough, L., Risley-Curtiss, C., & Rorke, J. (2015). Equine facilitated psycho-therapy: A pilot study of effect on posttraumatic stress symptoms in maltreated youth. *Journal of Infant, Child, and Adolescent Psychotherapy, 14*(2), 158–173.

McGreevy, P. (2012). *Equine behavior: A guide for veterinarians and equine scientists* (2nd ed.). London, UK: Saunders.

McGreevy, P. D., & McLean, A. N. (2010). *Equitation science.* UK: Wiley-Blackwell.

Meinersmann, K. M., Bradberry, J., & Roberts, F. B. (2008). Equine-facilitated psychotherapy with adult female survivors of abuse. *Journal of Psychosocial Nursing & Mental Health Services, 46*(12), 36–42.

Merkies, K., McKechnie, M., & Zakrajsek, E. (2018). Behavioural and physio-logical responses of therapy horses to mentally traumatized humans *Applied Animal Behaviour Science, 205,* 61–67.

Merkies, K., Sievers, A., Zakrajsek, E., MacGregor, H., Bergeron, R., & Köning von Borstel, U. (2014). Preliminary results suggest an influence of psychologi-cal and physiological stress in humans on horse heart rate and behavior. *Journal of Veterinary Behavior, 9,* 242–247.

Mueller, M., & McCullough, L. (2017). Effects of equine-facilitated psychother-apy on post-traumatic stress symptoms in youth. *Journal of Child and Family Studies, 26*(4), 1164–1172.

Mykhaylov, B. V., Serdiuk, A. I., Vodka, M. E., Aliieva, T. A., & Vashkite, I. D. (2016). The use of equine assisted psychotherapy among the demobilized mem-bers of the antiterrorist operation with PTSD, located on rehabilitation in san-atorium conditions. *Psychiatry, Neurology, and Medical Psychology (Психіатрія, Неврологія Та Медична Психологія), 1*(5), 112–117.

Najavits, L. M. (2015). The problem of dropout from "gold standard" PTSD therapies. *F1000Prime Report, 7*, 43. https://doi.org/10.12703/P7-43

Naste, T., Price, M., Karol, J., Martin, L., Murphy, K., Miguel, J., & Spinazzola, J. (2017). Equine facilitated therapy for complex trauma (EFT-CT). *Journal of Child and Adolescent Trauma, 11*(3), 289–303. https://doi.org/10.1007/s40653-017-0187-3

Nevins, R., Finch, S., Hickling, E. J., & Barnett S. D. (2013). The Saratoga WarHorse Project: A case study of the treatment of psychological distress in a veteran of Operation Iraqi Freedom. *Advances in Mind/Body Medicine, 27*(4), 22–25.

Newton-Cromwell, S. A., McSpadden, B. D., & Johnson, R. (2015). Incorporating experiential learning for equine-assisted activities and therapies with an in-house equine therapy program for veterans. *Journal of Equine Veterinary Science, 35*(5), 458.

Ogden, P., Minton, K., & Pain, C. (2006). *Trauma and the body: A sensorimotor approach to psychotherapy*. New York, NY: W. W. Norton.

O'Haire, M. E., Guérin, N. A., & Kirkham, A. C. (2015). Animal-assisted intervention for trauma: A systematic literature review. *Frontiers in Psychology, 6*, 1121. https://doi.org/10.3389/fpsyg.2015.01121

Outram, A. K., Stear, N. A., Bendrey, R., Olsen, S., Kasparov, A., Zaibert, V., Thorpe, N., & Evershed, R. P. (2009). The earliest horse harnessing and milking. *Science, 323*(5919), 1332–1335. https://doi.org/10.1126/science.1168594

Perry, B. D. (2009). Examining child maltreatment through a neurodevelopmental lens: Clinical application of the Neurosequential Model of Therapeutics. *Journal of Loss and Trauma, 14*, 240–255.

Pickeral, T. (2005). *The encyclopedia of horses and ponies*. London, UK: Parragon.

Pickeral, T. (2008). *The horse: 30,000 years of the horse in art*. London, UK: Merrell.

Popescu, S., & Diugan, E. A. (2013). The relationship between behavioral and other welfare indicators of working horses. *Journal of Equine Veterinary Science, 33*(1), 1–12.

Porges, S. (2011). *The polyvagal theory: Neurophysiologial foundations of emotions, attachment, communication, and self-regulation*. New York, NY: W. W. Norton.

Porges, S. W. (2003). Social engagement and attachment: A phylogenetic perspective. *Annals of the New York Academy of Science, 1008*, 31–47.

Porter, R. (2002). *Madness: A brief history*. New York, NY: Oxford University Press.

Porter-Wenzlaff, L. (2007). Finding their voice: Developing emotional, cognitive, and behavioral congruence in female abuse survivors through equine facilitated therapy. *Explore, 3*(5), 529–534.

Rauch, S., van der Kolk, B. A., Fisler, R., Alpert, N., Orr, S., Savage, C., Jenike, M., & Pitman, R. (1996). A symptom provocation study of posttraumatic stress disorder using positron emission tomography and script-driven imagery. *Archives of General Psychiatry, 53,* 380–387.

Romaniuk, M., Evans, J., & Kidd, C. (2018). Evaluation of an equine-assisted therapy program for veterans who identify as "wounded, injured or ill" and their partners. *PLOS One, 13*(9), 1–16. https://doi.org/10.1371/journal.pone.0203943

Rossbach, K. A., & Wilson, J. P. (1992). Does a dog's presence make a person more likable? Two studies. *Anthrozoös, 5*(1), 40–51.

Rothschild, B. (1999). Making trauma therapy safe. *Self and Society, 27*(2), 17–23.

Rothschild, B. (2000). *The body remembers: The psychophysiology of trauma and trauma treatment.* New York, NY: W. W. Norton.

SAMHSA. (2015). *Substance abuse and mental health service administration: Trauma-informed approach and trauma-specific interventions.* Retrieved from http://www.samhsa.gov/nctic/trauma-interventions

Sayer, N. A., Friedemann-Sanchez, G., Spoont, M., Murdoch, M., Parker, L. E., Chiros, C., & Rosenheck R. (2009). A qualitative study of determinants of PTSD treatment initiation in veterans. *Psychiatry: Interpersonal and Biological Processes, 72*(3), 238–255.

Schroeder, K., & Stroud, D. (2015). Equine-facilitated group work for women survivors of interpersonal violence. *Journal for Specialists in Group Work, 40*(4), 365–386.

Schroeder, K., Stroud, D., Sherwood, D., & Udell, M. (2017). Therapeutic factors in equine facilitated group psychotherapy for women survivors of interpersonal violence. *The Journal for Specialists in Group Work, 43*(4), 326–348.

Schultz, P. N., Remick-Barlow, G., & Robbins, L. (2007). Equine-assisted psychotherapy: A mental health promotion/intervention modality for children who have experienced intra-family violence. *Health & Social Care in the Community, 15*(3), 265–271.

Schulz, M. (1999). Remedial and psychomotor aspects of the human movement and its development: A theoretical approach to developmental riding. *Scientific and Educational Journal of Therapeutic Riding, 17,* 44–57.

Shambo, L., Seely, S., & Vonderfecht, H. R. (2010). A pilot study on equine-facilitated psychotherapy for trauma-related disorders. *Scientific and Educational Journal of Therapeutic Riding, 17,* 11–25.

Shapiro, F., & Maxfield, L. (2003). EMDR and information processing in psychotherapy treatment: Personal development and global perspectives. In M.

Solomon & D. J. Siegel (Eds.), *Healing trauma: Attachment, mind, body, and brain* (pp. 196–220). New York, NY: W. W. Norton.

Siegel, D. (2012). *The developing mind: How relationships and the brain interact to shape who we are* (2nd ed.). New York, NY: W. W. Norton.

Signal, T., Taylor, N., Botros, H., Prentice, K., & Lazarus, K. (2013). Whispering to horses: Childhood sexual abuse, depression and the efficacy of equine facilitated therapy. *Sexual Abuse in Australia and New Zealand, 5*(1), 24–32.

Sorenson, E. R. (1978). Cooperation and freedom among the Fore of New Guinea. In A. Montagu (Ed.), *Learning non-aggression: The experience of non-literate societies* (pp. 12–30). New York, NY: Oxford University Press.

Stewart, L. A., Chang, C. Y., Parker, L. K., & Grubbs, N. (2016). *Animal-assisted therapy in counseling competencies*. Developed in collaboration with the Animal-Assisted Therapy in Mental Health Interest Network of the American Counseling Association. Retrieved from https://www.counseling.org/docs/default-source/competencies/animal-assisted-therapy-competencies-june-2016.pdf?sfvrsn=6

Tedeschi, P., Sisa, M. L., Olmert, M. D., Parish-Plass, N., & Yount, R. (2015). Treating human trauma with the help of animals: Trauma informed intervention for child maltreatment and adult post-traumatic stress. In A. H. Fine (Ed.), *Handbook on animal-assisted therapy: Foundations and guidelines for animal-assisted interventions* (4th ed., pp. 305–320). San Diego, CA: Academic Press.

Thelle, M. (2010). Horse power helps: Evaluation of horse assisted psychotherapeutic treatment with severely traumatized inpatients, a pilot study. *Scientific and Educational Journal of Therapeutic Riding, 17*, 25–35.

Thompson-Coon, J., Boddy, K., Stein, K., Whear, R., Barton, J., & Depledge, M. H. (2011). Does participating in physical activity in outdoor natural environments have a greater effect on physical and mental wellbeing than physical activity indoors? A systematic review. *Environmental Science and Technology, 45*(5), 1761–72.

Uvnäs-Moberg, K., Handlin, L., & Petersson, M. (2014). Self-soothing behaviors with particular reference to oxytocin release induced by non-noxious sensory stimulation. *Frontiers in Psychology, 5*, 1529.

van der Kolk, B. (2003). Posttraumatic stress disorder and the nature of trauma. In M. Solomon & D. J. Siegel (Eds.), Healing trauma: Attachment, mind, body, and brain (pp. 168–195). New York, NY: W. W. Norton.

van der Kolk, B. (2014). *The body keeps the score: Brain, mind, and body in the healing of trauma*. New York, NY: Viking.

van der Kolk, B. A. (2004). Psychobiology of posttraumatic stress disorder. In

J. Panksepp (Ed.), *Textbook of biological psychiatry* (pp. 319–345). New York, NY: Wiley.

Vilà, C., Leonard, J. A., Götherström, A., Marklund, S., Sandberg, K., Liden, K., Wayne, R. K., & Ellegren. H. (2001). Widespread origins of domestic horse lineages. *Science, 291*(5503), 474–477.

Waran, N., & Randle, H. (2017). What we can measure, we can manage: The importance of using robust welfare indicators in Equitation Science. *Applied Animal Behavior Science: Special Issue on Equitation Science in Practice, 190*, 74–81.

Weiss, J. M. (1971). Effects of coping behavior in different warning signal conditions on stress pathology in rats. *Journal of Comparative and Physiological Psychology, 77*, 1–13.

Whittlesey-Jermone, W. K. (2014). Adding equine-assisted psychotherapy to conventional treatments: A pilot study exploring ways to increase adult female self-efficacy among victims of interpersonal violence. *The Practitioner Scholar: Journal of Counseling and Professional Psychology, 3*(1), 82–101.

Wilson, E. O. (1984). *Biophilia*. Cambridge, MA: Harvard University Press.

Wolpe, J. (1958). *Psychotherapy by reciprocal inhibition*. Stanford, CA: Stanford University Press.

Wolpe, J., & Lazarus, A. A. (1966). *Behavior therapy techniques: A guide to the treatment of neuroses*. Oxford, UK: Pergamon Press.

Yorke, J., Adams, C., & Coady, N. (2008). Therapeutic value of equine–human bonding in recovery from trauma. *Anthrozoös, 21*(1), 17–30.

Yorke, J., Nugent, W., Strand, E., Bolen, R., New, J., & Davis, C. (2013). Equine assisted therapy and its impact on cortisol levels of children and horses: A pilot study and meta-analysis. *Early Child Development and Care, 183*(7), 874–894.

ABOUT THE AUTHOR

Nina Ekholm Fry, MSSc., CCTP, is the director of Equine Programs at University of Denver's Institute for Human-Animal Connection, and adjunct professor in the Graduate School of Professional Psychology and the Graduate School of Social Work. She has a background as a mental health practitioner providing clinical services; as a competitive rider and equine behavior consultant; and as an academic professional engaged in national and international organizations for therapeutic equine interactions. She has a particular interest in ethics and social justice perspectives within the human-animal connection.

CHAPTER 9

Why the Dog?

Ann R. Howie, MSW; Aubrey H. Fine, EdD; and Lindsay A. Rojas, LSW, MSW, AASW

Companion and working canines have become integral to many people's 21st-century lives. Arguably, the process of domestication has helped dogs become wonderful companion, therapy, and service animals (Ensminger, 2010). Dogs have been found to be a viable support for individuals suffering from trauma by serving as a buffer from physical and emotional challenges, and helping them indirectly manage stress (Carter & Porges, 2016). This chapter intends to focus on the importance of our relationships with dogs and to explain some of the benefits that dogs provide to people in general, as well as to those who face trauma. Important canine welfare considerations and strategies in animal-assisted intervention (AAI) are also discussed.

FIRST THINGS FIRST

It is important to first clarify terminology, as several terms related to working dogs are currently used and easily confused by the public and professionals alike:

Service Animals: The Americans with Disabilities Act (ADA) (1990) defines *service animals* as animals "individually trained to do work or perform tasks for the benefit of a person with a disability" (para. 3). These disabilities may be physical or psychiatric (i.e., post-traumatic stress disorder or

PTSD, anxiety, depression, and others). Through the ADA, service dogs are legally entitled to be in public places with their partner (the person with a disability) as long as they are well-controlled (including housetrained) and do not cause a fundamental alteration in the business. After an amendment to the ADA effective in 2011, only dogs and miniature horses are now legally recognized as service animals. The ADA uses the term *service animal*, rather than *assistance animal*, even though many organizations use those terms interchangeably. Some people incorrectly refer to police "K9s" (and other working dogs) as "service dogs." While it is true that these working dogs provide an important service, they are not considered service dogs under the ADA.

Therapy Animals: The United States has no legal definition of a therapy animal. As a result, therapy animals (including dogs) are legally considered pets. Therapy animals are generally domesticated species who have been trained and screened for appropriateness to a) visit facilities with their handler to brighten people's days, or b) work with therapists to help clients meet specific therapy goals. Handlers must obtain permission to go into public places with their therapy animals.

Emotional Support Animals: Emotional support animals (ESAs) provide comfort or emotional support to their person. The person is considered to have a disability, but the animal is not held to ADA standards for service animals. Rather, ESAs are considered pets or companions and are not covered by the ADA. Many people, including human health care professionals, incorrectly call ESAs "therapy animals."

Notably, ESAs may be recognized by landlords under the Fair Housing Act. The U.S. Department of Housing and Urban Development (2013) considers ESAs to be "assistance animals," which can cause confusion among people who consider "service animal" and "assistance animal" to mean the same thing. ESAs may be many species and do not require specific training other than general good behavior and housetraining. ESAs are allowed in housing where pets are not permitted unless the animal poses a threat to the health or safety of others through its conduct. The landlord may require documentation of need for the ESA.

ESAs of only domesticated species may be recognized by airlines under the Air Carrier Access Act. Airlines may require people who wish to fly with an ESA to notify the airline in advance of the flight and provide documentation of their need for an ESA by a mental health professional. The Air Carrier Access Act allows airlines to require highly specific documentation related to both the person and the animal.

This chapter specifically focuses on *dogs* working as therapy animals as part of a client's treatment plan, and also includes select references to canine pet companions. Given the potential for confusion regarding terminology, the authors have made every effort to clarify the roles of dogs discussed in this chapter.

A JOURNEY TOGETHER

As Anatole France noted, "Until one has loved an animal, a part of one's soul remains unawakened." Human affinity for canine interaction has remained significant over time. Excavation of ancient burial grounds reveals that dogs were sometimes buried next to people, occasionally with collars or other mementos, indicating that those dogs were held in high esteem (Archaeology Magazine, 2016). Egyptian Pharaoh Ramses the Great built a tomb for his dog, Pahates, with the inscription, "Bed Companion to the Pharaoh." Likewise, Queen Victoria of England died in bed next to Turi, her Pomeranian (Coren, 2014). This inclination for humans to share their beds or private spaces with dogs still holds true today. In fact, a 2015 Harris Interactive Poll reported that 71% of dog owners allow their dogs to sleep on their beds, suggesting a high degree of affection and regard between people and their pet dogs.

This same Harris Interactive Poll also reported that 95% of pet owners consider their companion animals to be members of their family, with 96% of dog owners identifying their dogs as family members (Harris Interactive Poll, 2015). The strength of these close kinships was brought to light in 2005, following Hurricane Katrina, when many faced with leaving their animals behind or staying in unsafe conditions chose to endanger themselves by remaining with their animal companions. Such accounts led to the passage of the Pets Evacuation and Transportation Standards (PETS) Act in 2006, which directed the Federal Emergency Management Administration (FEMA) to develop emergency preparedness plans that took into account the needs of people with pets and service animals (Hodges, 2011). Indeed, positive differences in how people with animals were treated in shelters were evident during the 2017 Hurricanes Harvey and Irma, as compared to Katrina.

Yet still there remains room for improvement. Arguably, recognizing animals as members of the family (for instance) could be a promising step for employers to better support their workforce. People often need leave from work to care for a sick family member or bereavement leave after a death in the family, yet few employers designate companion animals as family members. Consequently, when a dog is in need of medical care or passes away, pet owners may not be allotted the time to address the concern or to grieve their loss in ways that correspond with the depth of that connection. This may be particularly pertinent for those who are socially isolated and consider their relationship with their pet(s) as primary.

There currently is a plethora of research supporting the impact of interacting with canines on human-health-related variables, such as lowering rates of cardiovascular disease (Levine et al., 2013) and cholesterol (Serpell, 1991). These particular health outcomes may have much to do with increased activity through walking and play among people who live with dogs (Cutt, Giles-Corti, Knuiman, & Burke, 2007). Indeed, many people—including this chapter's authors—freely admit that they will get up when feeling ill to exercise their companion dogs when they would rather stay in bed. Select research has also demonstrated the positive well-being effects of touching an animal (Olmert, 2013), as well as laughing and feeling joy by way of their behavior and personality. Importantly, study findings continually acknowledge the impacts of laughter on people's emotion-related behavior, in that it both decreases stress and improves immune functioning (Bennett, Zeller, Rosenberg, & McCann, 2003).

As much as we like being around dogs, it is doubtful that our strong relationships with them would persist if dogs did not respond positively to our attention (Call, Bräuer, Kaminski, & Tomasello, 2003). Canines obtain information, often accurately, from human facial cues and can use audiological and visual information to identify emotions in both canines and humans (Albuquerque et al., 2016). Furthermore, Nagasawa and colleagues (2015) recently found that mutual gaze, a behavior most commonly signifying attachment between mother and child, is also observed in human-pet dog relationships.

Furthermore, research is now demonstrating more precisely that dogs are capable of understanding human words. An imaging study demonstrated that dogs' brains respond to actual words, not just the tone in which they are said or communicated (Andics et al., 2016). In this study, brain scans on dogs utilizing functional magnetic resonance imaging (fMRI) found that dogs processed purposeful words (i.e., the phrase "well done" in Hungarian) in the left hemisphere of the brain, similar to the way humans process language (Andics et al., 2016). Miklósi and Kubinyi (2016) recently reported that selective forces during domestication may have supported the emergence of the canine brain structure underlying this capability. Remarkably, it is now believed that some dogs are able to recognize more than 1,000 human words.

UMWELT

Von Uexkull (1934/1957) conceptualized the term *umwelt* as the "phenomenal world or the self-world of the animal" (p. 319). The ways in which dogs perceive and relate to the world that surrounds them has been described as their umwelt (von Uexkull, 1934/1957). Humans who are aware of and respect a dog's umwelt appreciate that he or she responds to, and learns from, environmental elements that humans do not perceive as well, such as auditory and olfactory stimuli. Moreover, understanding how a dog perceives the world, through considering his or her umwelt, is critical for humans to strengthen their interactions and relationships with dogs. For example, although canine vision is in lower resolution than human vision, dogs' abilities to smell and to hear are profoundly better than our own.

In regard to human-animal interaction (HAI) and AAI, canine umwelt can be consulted to further substantiate empirical evidence in the field. For example, from a research perspective, Horowitz and Hecht (2014) argue that canine umwelt be considered in a study's design and methodology. Ways in which this may be realized are discussed later in this chapter.

THEORETICAL BACKGROUND AND POTENTIAL MECHANISMS

There are three primary, respected theories that help explain the strong and transformative qualities of the human-canine bond: biophilia, social support, and attachment. Here, we discuss them individually, first highlighting the theory of biophilia. Of note, the order in which these theories are presented does not reflect our opinion of which theory more strongly explains the bond, but rather that each of the orientations helps provide a different way of viewing the relationship between humans and dogs. The figure shown illustrates the relationship between these three theories as a metaphoric three-legged stool.

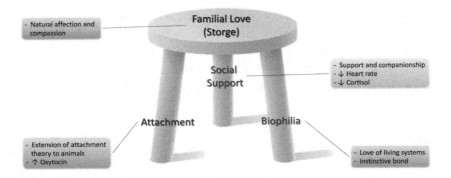

The analogy of the three-legged stool can be used to describe the relationship between the three human-animal bond theories and the Storge concept of familial love. (Fine & Mackintosh, 2016; reprinted with permission.)

Biophilia Hypothesis

The biophilia hypothesis argues that humans possess an inherent desire to connect with nature and other life-forms (Kellert & Wilson, 1995). Fine (2014) and Fine and Weaver (2018) suggest that biophilia connects humans to the external world. Additionally, interacting with animals in the home (or in a clinical setting) may replicate the feeling of being in nature, which, in turn, enriches well-being (Fine, 2014).

Seemingly, humans will subconsciously feel safer and less threatened in social settings when in the presence of a safe animal, supposedly because of that animal's connection to nature. For those who have experienced trauma, especially in the case of individuals with PTSD, social disengagement and avoidance of certain stimuli are common (Hopper, Frewen, Van der Kolk, & Lanius, 2007; Williamson, Porges, Lamb, & Porges. 2014). According to the biophilia effect, the physical presence or existence of a close bond with a canine can provide a sense of safety that may allow these individuals to engage in situations (social, outside of the home) that they typically would avoid otherwise (Kellert & Wilson, 1995).

Attachment Theory

Attachment theory argues that humans are genetically predisposed to form attachments with others, especially parent to child (Ainsworth & Bowlby, 1991; Goldberg, Grusec, & Jenkins, 1999). In the context of HAI, Payne,

Bennett and McGreevy (2015) argue that the human-canine relationship is mutually beneficial, with humans providing access to basic needs (such as food, water, and shelter) and both species providing a source of emotional fulfillment for each other. Payne and colleagues (2015) and Payne, DeAraugo, Bennett, and McGreevy (2016) highlight that bonding behaviors, such as petting a dog, can enhance the attachment between the human and his/her dog. Additionally, dogs often exhibit behaviors characteristic of attachment relationships, such as proximity seeking where a dog "seeks out" the attachment figure as a way to manage stress (Payne et al., 2015). In regard to individuals experiencing trauma from failed attachments, dogs can present a new or unique opportunity to form a successful and reliable attachment bond (Zilcha-Mano, Mikulincer, & Shaver, 2011).

As noted earlier, mutual gazing can often be found in relationships between humans and their pet dogs. This "looking into one another's eyes" causes oxytocin release in both humans and canines (an "interspecies oxytocin-mediated positive loop"), which produces social rewarding effects and may be indicative of strong attachment with underlying coevolutionary components (Nagasawa et al., 2015, p. 333). Likewise, Fine (2014) identifies research proposing that oxytocin released by mutual gaze may also affect dopamine (a neurotransmitter with functions related to pleasure and reward), which results in both the dog and the person wanting to be with each other on a frequent and regular basis.

In their study of potential stress relief effects of connecting with dogs, Miller and colleagues (2009) measured levels of serum oxytocin in men and women after interacting with pet dogs with whom they had reported emotional attachments, as well as after a period of reading nonfiction material without the dog present. Data were collected after the participants returned home from work in order to evaluate potential stress effects of both conditions. Findings showed that oxytocin levels increased significantly more when women interacted with their dog as compared to when they were in the reading condition. Interestingly, these effects were not noted in male participants. These findings suggest that the release of oxytocin during human-canine interaction may decrease stress and anxiety, and that these effects could be dependent on human sex/gender. One may also infer from this study's findings that individuals with close canine attachments may experience greater physiological benefits and stress reduction than those without canine attachments or where the connection with their dog is not as deep. However, this presumption, as well as the role of gender in human-canine bonding and interactions, should be fully investigated and validated by future research.

Social Support Theory

In the context of the human-animal bond, this theory proposes that social support can be found in interactions between humans and nonhuman animals. Social supports buffer against loneliness, anxiety, depression, and related illnesses (Ozbay et al., 2007). In humans, social support enriches quality of life by improving physical and mental well-being (McNicholas & Collis, 2006). Some pet owners have reported believing that their companion animals offer social support that is greater than, or equal to, that found in human-to-human relationships (Beck & Madresh, 2008).

Animals who provide social support can help people manage stress and handle difficult life transitions that accompany traumatic experiences (Maharaj, Kazanjian, & Haney, 2016). In regard to PTSD, several studies have found that symptoms such as anger and social withdrawal may result in the erosion of social support from people (Clapp & Beck, 2009). When considering these effects, it is important not to underestimate or trivialize research indicating the role of canines as reliably nonjudgmental, comforting, or affectionate; one could argue that the social support provided by pet dogs is indispensable to people who may be isolating themselves from others (Fine, 2015). Likewise, canine social support may be especially valuable for people with PTSD, as their symptoms of anger, flashbacks, or social withdrawal, for example, may alienate the humans who might have previously served as support networks.

A 2013 study conducted with veterans by Stern and colleagues reported that service and emotional support canines, referred to as *canine companions* in this study, acted as supportive confidants for individuals with PTSD, thus providing an opportunity to discuss difficult issues without fear of interruption, criticism, or judgment. Moreover, the veterans in this study reported that their dogs acted as social supports by reducing their fear and improving their level of comfort in social situations (Stern et al., 2013).

In a related case example, Kyle, a man in his mid-twenties returning from serving a combat tour in Afghanistan, was discharged after a gunshot wound with a Purple Heart military decoration. When he attempted to reenter nonmilitary life, he found it difficult to stay grounded and to reintegrate himself into his previous, preservice lifestyle. His friends did not know how to help him. Often startled by loud noises and uncomfortable in novel situations, he would retreat emotionally and psychologically, finding solace in his newly adopted mixed-breed Labrador, Scarlet. Kyle had heard of ESAs and had dogs and pets throughout his life. Consequently, he felt that having an ESA dog as part of his new life as a veteran would not only provide needed companionship, but could also be beneficial in terms of his health and well-being.

Kyle's initial beliefs about the value of getting a dog came to fruition, both anecdotally and practically. As examples, he definitely viewed Scarlet as an important and positive dimension in his life, and was able to recognize how she supported him. The two became inseparable; wherever Kyle went, Scarlet would be right next to him. Kyle relished having her company, and it was apparent that he was more at ease when Scarlet was near. When he slept, Scarlet rested next to him. When he became restless and anxious, Scarlet immediately came closer to him, often by lying on his legs and applying necessary pressure with her weight. With the support of Scarlet by his side, Kyle felt calmer and better able to cope through relaxation and reassurance.

Similarly, children living in abusive or neglectful households may also find the presence of a pet animal to be socially supportive. According to McDonald and colleagues (2015), children experience close bonds with companion animals and rely on pets as a way of managing stress. McDonald et al. (2015) note that pets may serve as security—providing attachment figures, offering comfort, consistency, and support to children who are coping with adverse environments. Furthermore, the animal's presence in such situations could also act as a buffer against the negative impacts that domestic and intimate-partner violence have on the child. Given this supportive relationship, it is particularly traumatic for such children to observe incidences of their pet being abused or mistreated (McDonald et al., 2015).

In addition, therapy dogs serve not only as a source of social support for children with trauma histories, but also as a motivator to share their experiences. According to the American Society for the Prevention of Cruelty to Animals (ASPCA), simply the nearby presence of a therapy animal seems to provide comfort and enhances healing and recovery for children who have experienced maltreatment (Phillips, 2014). In many states, the legal system has taken note of the social support a dog provides by allowing children to testify while accompanied by a court facility dog (Holder, 2013). These dogs commonly provide a calming presence during this painful and distressing experience (Dellinger, 2008).

As the following case account exemplifies, the supportive roles of dogs in the lives and treatment of children who have experienced maltreatment are both ample and multifaceted. Susan had visited many therapists over the years, but seemed resistant to accept support. She had built up numerous defense mechanisms, such as avoidance, repression, and anger. Susan's father had sexually assaulted her when she was quite young, and he had minimal contact with her following his release from prison.

Over time, Susan's relationship with her mother worsened; she felt betrayed by her mother for not protecting her and resented her greatly. Home life was dysfunctional, and Susan had a hard time getting along with her younger siblings. At home, her main source of comfort was her young pet dog, with whom she spent time walking and playing. Although she had seen several therapists, Susan did not open up to them. However, when introduced to AAI, the therapy dog's presence in her sessions provided Susan with social support that helped ease her tension. Both immediately and over time, Susan's facial expressions reflected her comfort with being supported by the therapy dog. The dog seemed to ameliorate her anxiety, promoted safety and security, and boosted her confidence to open up emotionally.

It is worth noting here that clinicians must be mindful of not only how a therapy dog is incorporated into a treatment plan, but also of the client's response to the animal. Clinicians can structure interventions that provide an opportunity for the client to respond to the therapy dog in ways that reflect how the client responds to the world in general. Such interactions then become grist for the therapeutic process. The clinician must also ensure that the client does not "hide" behind the animal to avoid focusing on difficult subject areas that need attention. When integrated effectively in therapy sessions, a therapy dog can be supportive, which may promote engagement and rapport. For example, Susan was able to open up and reveal some of her significant emotional conflicts and traumas when in the presence of the therapy dog. In particular, the dog helped her feel more comfortable, and made coming to therapy more appealing for her.

This simple snapshot of Susan is highly reflective of children who have been abused. Therapy dogs change the therapeutic milieu, enhance rapport between therapists and clients, and provide support when needed. Additionally, they may act not only as emotional confidants, but also as friends and playmates. Over the past 20 years, an increasing number of mental health clinicians have incorporated therapy dogs in individual and group therapy. For example, there are numerous programs throughout the country that use AAI (including dog-training programs) to treat youth with troubled pasts, including maltreatment or involvement in the juvenile justice system (e.g., the Pairing Achievement With Service [PAWS] Program in Brownwood, Texas [Ward, 2013]). In some cases, youth are asked to help train shelter dogs to improve the dogs' adoptability. Clinicians who have used this approach now realize that, although children believe the primary purpose of the intervention is teaching the dogs, they ultimately learn more about themselves and how they can become loving and responsible caregivers through these mutually beneficial and supportive relationships (Ward, 2013).

EVIDENCE-BASED RESEARCH ON HUMAN-CANINE INTERACTIONS AND TRAUMA

Research on HAI with dogs in the context of trauma is emerging. Owen, Finton, Gibbons, and DeLeon (2016) conducted interviews with veterans with PTSD who had participated in therapeutic treatment plans involving canines, and found the veterans experienced greater reductions in psychological distress and improved overall functioning as compared to those who did not receive AAI. Likewise, Hamama and colleagues (2011) assessed the impact of a canine-assisted intervention with adolescent girls with a history of abuse. The AAI group demonstrated a reduction in several PTSD symptoms in comparison to the non-AAI group. Dietz, Davis, and Pennings (2012) also found that children with a history of sexual abuse who interacted with therapy dogs in group therapy had greater decreases in trauma symptoms (i.e., anger, anxiety, and depression) than did similarly situated children who did not interact with dogs during therapy.

In animal-assisted prolonged exposure (Lefkowitz, Prout, Bleiberg, Pahiria, & Debiak, 2005), AAI is paired with prolonged exposure (PE) treatment, which involves a client reliving or revisiting his or her individual trauma incident(s). By including therapy dogs in the client's exposure to his or her trauma-related stimuli, clinicians seek to "reduce [the client's] anxiety, lower physiological arousal, enhance the therapeutic alliance, and promote social lubrication" (Lefkowitz et al., 2005, p. 275). Further, in their study with sexual assault survivors, Lefkowitz and colleagues (2005) sought to reduce attrition from traditional PE treatment by incorporating therapy dogs into sessions. Therapy dog involvement in treatment appeared to reduce trauma symptoms, making sessions more tolerable.

An additional noteworthy application of canines in trauma recovery is the field of animal-assisted crisis response (AACR). Following emergencies such as natural and community disasters (i.e., fires, floods, hurricanes, shootings, and accidents), therapy dogs are deployed with their handlers as a team to provide comfort for individuals and communities (Hall et al., 2004). These AAI approaches, which are still in their infancy and, to date, lack a substantial evidence base, are discussed in greater depth later in this book.

The health benefits that humans receive from our relationships with dogs are now more scientifically accepted than ever before. However, whether or not dogs likewise benefit from these interactions remains, at this stage, relatively uncertain. Not surprisingly, current research comes predominantly from a human-centered (anthropocentric) perspective rather than a canine-centered one. For example, whereas anthropocentric research focuses on (human-preferred) vision or verbal language, canine-centered research might measure a dog's use of scent or behavior (Horowitz & Hecht, 2014).

Allowing for dogs' umwelt in AAI is an area of focus for future investigation. However, research that examines canine umwelt can be challenging due to the individual nature of each dog and his or her behaviors and subjective perceptions. As such, it is essential for both clinicians and handlers to not only know general canine displacement behaviors (i.e., those in response to a stressor), but also to be familiar with how their individual dog typically expresses himself or herself. Counting displacement behaviors in a research study is invaluable, yet if a particular canine expresses himself in a way that is not included on a predetermined checklist, then the results may be skewed away from umwelt. This example demonstrates how critically important it is to consider each therapy dog as an individual rather than as a member of any category (like "therapy dog"), just as we do for our human clients.

NEUROBIOLOGICAL MECHANISMS ATTRIBUTED TO HUMAN-ANIMAL INTERACTION

The exact mechanisms underlying HAI are only beginning to be the focus of serious study. Notably, one mechanism of increasing interest is that of social neuroscience, with several human brain structures being implicated. Mormann and colleagues (2011) found that, in humans, the right side of the amygdala (involved in emotions and memory) reacted differently to pictures of animals than it did to pictures of people, suggesting that this specific side of this brain region evolved to allow humans to process information relating exclusively to animals. Furthermore, Sugawara and colleagues (2012) reported decreased activity in the putamen, thalamus, the fusiform gyrus, and the left middle frontal gyrus, regions of the brain typically associated with stress, when people interacted with their pet dogs.

Beetz and Bales (2016) suggest that similar neurobiological mechanisms that drive interactions between humans are implicated in interactions between pet dogs and owners. Key players in the biological functions of interactions between humans and canines are the hormones oxytocin and vasopressin; the steroid hormone cortisol, which serves as a biomarker for stress in most mammals; and the neurotransmitter dopamine (Odendaal & Meintjes, 2003; Olmert, 2013).

Odendaal and Meintjes (2003) were among the first to recognize the influence of the human-animal bond on physiological stress. Following positive interactions between humans and canines, oxytocin nearly doubled in both species and cortisol concentrations decreased significantly in humans (Odendaal & Meintjes, 2003). As discussed previously, oxytocin is involved with positive social and nurturing behaviors and produces a calming effect (Beetz & Bales, 2016). Specifically, the nerves in the hypothalamus that generate oxytocin join with the vagal nerve. Activation of the parasympathetic nervous system is what ultimately stops the production of stress hormones, such as cortisol, and lowers both blood pressure and heart rate (Beetz & Bales, 2016). Furthermore, oxytocin may increase an individual's tolerance for pain and help wounds heal more quickly (Fine,

2014; Olmert, 2013). Given that the majority of research in this area has focused on oxytocin effects of human-pet dog relationships (Handlin et al., 2011; Nagasawa et al., 2015; Odendaal & Meintjes, 2003), further exploration into how oxytocin is released in the context of AAI with less familiar dogs would be useful. For example, such studies may provide potential explanation for why our connections with canines often serve as a resource for helping individuals tolerate emotional and physical pain, and heal faster than they would on their own.

SUGGESTED BEST PRACTICES

Suggested best practices in the field of AAI include therapist and volunteer handler training, as well as experience with the client population (i.e., diagnosis and treatment) and the specific animal species with whom they are partnering. In order to practice ethically with a therapy animal, the therapist and handler require additional education and supervision specific to working with animals. Necessary training includes observation and interpretation of animal behavior, humane training methods and husbandry, respectful relationship building, animal selection, and animal health considerations (Delta Society, 1999; Fine, 2015; Howie, 2015).

Thoughtful therapists' and handlers' experiences show that therapy dogs can absorb client projections and imbalances. Recent research supports these observations, calling them emotional contagion (Huber, Barber, Faragó, Muller, & Huber, 2017). One of the benefits of working with a therapy animal is to help clients, including those struggling with trauma, learn how to regulate their emotions and act toward a therapy animal and toward people responsibly and respectfully when emotional. It is crucial that therapists and handlers remember that the therapeutic environment exposes therapy dogs to clients' emotions, which may be unpredictable. Moreover, unlike humans, therapy dogs often do not have the ability to leave the interaction at will when feeling overwhelmed or uncomfortable.

Accordingly, ethical practitioners must ensure that therapy animals are not used as shock absorbers for clients' emotions. It is unfortunately easy for a well-meaning therapist or handler to expose a therapy dog to excessive emotion simply by seeing client after client day after day. This risk is exacerbated by the benevolent desire to help people, which can lead to prioritizing the client's needs over the animal's, even unintentionally.

Clients experiencing trauma require a safe place to discharge emotion, and the therapist's office is one of those safe places. Importantly, the therapeutic setting also needs to be safe for the therapy dog. Making the office a safe place begins by considering the individual dog's umwelt. Such strategies may include choosing which client(s) the dog will work with, designing interventions to accommodate the dog's strengths, having a client-free zone to which the dog can freely retreat, having a less-than-daily work schedule, and working shifts of limited length so as not to fatigue or overwork the dog (King, Watters, & Mungre, 2011).

The therapist is also responsible for helping the therapy dog discharge the emotional energy that accumulates during therapy sessions. This discharge must be done in a way that the dog as an individual finds useful (again, respecting his/her umwelt), and not solely according to the therapist or handler. The dog will have an important opinion on how to effectively help with this release. Therapists and handlers who have developed a relationship of emotional intimacy with their dog know how to read their canine partner's subtle behavioral communications much like they do with a human friend or partner. For example, depending on context, a slight head turn, a quick lick of the lips, a delicate ear flick, a seemingly happy grin, a lowered tail or head, relaxed eyes, forward ears, and particular foot positions all can indicate how the dog may be feeling at that very moment. Just as every human may not enjoy a five-mile run after his or her workday, neither does every dog after AAI. Rather, s/he may prefer quiet rest, aerobic or intellectual exercise, play, eating a favorite food, or any number of activities specific to that particular dog. Using a medical metaphor, AAI practitioners in Japan refer to this process as "recovery" (Yamazaki, personal communication, April 10, 2016); similar to the importance of recovery after a medical procedure, recovery after AAI is indispensable for the therapy dog (and for any working dog after a period of service or exertion).

Obtaining a therapy dog's consent to participate in AAI is also essential, and must be considered a continual and ongoing process, not something that merely happens with a formal evaluation every two years. Clothier (2014) teaches that there are six Elemental Questions when asking for a therapy dog's consent before and during each AAI session. To ask these questions, the therapist or handler must become centered and prepared to listen by watching. To understand the dog's answers, the practitioner must be fluent in general canine behavior, as well as the particular behaviors of his or her therapy dog. Those who do not know how to ask these questions or how to interpret a dog's answers to them lack crucial training and/or experience.

- *Hello?* When asked as a question, this means "Do you want to interact with me?" "Do you want to interact with other people today?" A dog who turns his head away (or acts in any way that creates distance) is answering, "No."
- *Who are you?* When we start a conversation with people, we often first ask who they are. We need to know who our therapy dogs are, too—not just when we first meet, but throughout our relationship with them. When we have an emotionally intimate relationship with our dogs, we know from their behavior what they like, dislike, and/or merely tolerate. In other words, we know who they are. This knowledge affects what we ask them to do. People who have a respectful relationship with their dogs ask them to do only work that is congruent with their essential nature.
- *How is this for you?* This question is completely about the therapy dog (not about the handler or the client). It is a question to be asked continuously throughout the session. Once again, a happy or contented dog expresses his emotional state through behavior. The therapist or handler must observe the dog's behavior and adjust his or her therapeutic technique according to the dog's comfort with the interaction.
- *May I?* Here the therapist or handler is asking permission to do things with the therapy dog, such as pet him, be near him, and/or put equipment on him. A dog who creates distance between himself and the therapist, handler, or client is doing so to communicate his preference to be away from, rather than immersed in, an interaction.
- *Can you?* This question is about the dog's ability: physical, intellectual, and emotional. Fido may be physically able to move nearer to a client, and he may be willing, but he may not understand the handler's cue. Or perhaps he understands the cue, but emotionally he does not want to get close to that particular person. It is incumbent upon therapists and handlers to respect all aspects of a dog's ability. Respecting a dog's ability

(and opinion) is the opposite of pushing a dog into a desired position next to a client, even with gentle effort.

- *Can we?* This question invites a mutual decision about what to do rather than the therapist or handler making a unilateral decision. Just like the "how is this for you?" question, it is essential to continuously ask this throughout the interaction. A dog who was enthusiastic at the beginning of a session may not remain so through the end. Again, ethical practitioners demonstrate their respect for the dog's opinion by changing therapeutic technique, or making arrangements for the dog to go to a client-free zone, or both.

CANINE WELFARE

In addition to the practices and competencies discussed in the previous section, therapists and handlers must advocate for and protect their therapy dogs by helping to manage the client's expectations of and interactions with them. Again, individuals struggling with PTSD may have difficulties sustaining close relationships with humans and nonhumans, and may exhibit erratic or highly emotional behaviors that impact their sense of trust and social problem solving. It is easy to see how these behaviors may be a source of stress for therapy dogs, ESAs, and service dogs who work or are otherwise connected with people who have experienced trauma. As such, it is incumbent upon the therapist and handler to foster an environment of mutual respect for the needs of both parties. Just as the client is allowed to express his or her personality and behaviors in individual ways, the therapy dog must be given ample opportunities to communicate his or her needs, and to have those needs respected during therapy sessions. Fine, Albright, Nu, and Peralta (2013), as well as Serpell, McCune, Gee, and Griffin (2017), report that as the field of AAI becomes more established and accepted, attention must be given to safeguard not only the well-being of the humans who are being served, but also the therapy animals involved. Fine and Mackintosh (2016) argue that those involved with AAI must take a moral and ethical stand to deliver a treatment that ensures the welfare of all parties involved.

Notably, Haubenhofer and Kirchengast (2006, 2007) have reported that more than 50% of handlers volunteering with their therapy dog thought that AAI sessions were possibly or could be stressing or straining for their dog. Furthermore, their research revealed that those therapy dogs had increased levels of salivary cortisol concentrations on working days as compared to nonworking days, and that the level of cortisol increased with more sessions per week without respite and relaxation. Further, Glenk and colleagues (2013) indicate that a potential way to decrease therapy dog stress (i.e., cortisol) is to give the dog more choice about approach and avoidance movements during sessions (which coincides with Clothier's Elemental Questions [2014], as described above). These are essential factors to take into account when working with therapy dogs. Clinicians must be considerate of a dog's work schedule, as well as experience during sessions, so that he or she will not be placed into unduly stressful situations. Overall, therapists and handlers must act as their animals' advocate, as highlighted in the Pet Partners acronym YAYABA: You Are Your Animal's Best Advocate (Pet Partners, 2017).

Fine and colleagues (2013) point out that, even though selected for their behavioral traits and consistency, therapy dogs will likely show some of the following behaviors recognized by canine behavior experts as signs of stress: panting, pacing, startle responses, pupillary dilation, trembling, whining, excessive licking, yawning, and/or hiding. If these or other behaviors are noted, practitioners must ask themselves what factors may be contributing to the dog's stress, including client behavior, environmental stimuli, therapist/handler behavior (including unrealistic expectations or inattention to canine needs), insufficient training for the dog, or possibly a dog who is unsuited for the work. No matter how earnest or well-intentioned, a poor fit between job and dog, whether from the structure of the job or the temperament of the dog, is nonetheless stressful and may even go so far as to create illness (Heimlich, 2001).

King and colleagues (2011) found that therapy dogs under two years of age showed more behavioral signs of stress than therapy dogs who were older and had more experience. Their research also reported significant elevations in canine salivary cortisol levels in 21 dogs from baseline to after one hour of AAI in a hospital environment (King et al., 2011). These findings suggest that dogs in working roles need outlets for good behavioral health, and that canine age or AAI experience may play a large role in their levels of stress. In essence, handlers must regularly consider their particular dog's sensitivity and responses to environmental stimuli (i.e., their umwelt), as well as their needs, and provide longer quiet time-out periods for calm and respite.

Peralta, Fine, Goldman, and Melco (2017) recently initiated a study evaluating the impact on therapy dogs participating in a program with children with attention deficit hyperactivity disorder (ADHD). The dogs involved in the study demonstrated only a mild behavioral response and no significant findings in cortisol or heart rate changes while in the program. Likewise, findings from a recent study by McCullough et al. (2018) indicated no significant differences in salivary cortisol levels between baseline and AAI sessions among 26 therapy dogs visiting pediatric oncology patients and their families. These results seem to indicate that, with proper supervision and well-trained therapy staff and handlers, canine stress can be minimal and/or reduced in a therapy setting.

It should be noted that the settings for therapy dog work vary widely. A private office is quite different from a busy hospital, with a spectrum of options in between. As has been described in this chapter, many factors are involved when considering the stress placed on the therapy dog, and setting, supervision, and training are just three of them.

The authors believe that it is impossible to completely avoid stress for a therapy dog, yet it is entirely possible to avoid therapy dog distress. Avoiding distress requires that the therapist take several steps. "Therapist Strategies for Canine Welfare" (below) is a summary of the steps presented in this section. Additionally, "The Therapy Animal's Bill of Rights" (following) highlights important considerations and responsibilities for AAI handlers.

THERAPIST STRATEGIES FOR CANINE WELFARE

1. Become educated about, and have experience observing and interpreting, canine behavior.
2. Choose with intention which client(s) the therapy dog will work with based on the dog's strengths, abilities, and temperament.
3. Develop skill in dividing attention between the client and the therapy dog during sessions.
4. Develop handling skills that support the individual dog rather than increase stress.
5. Allow the dog to have client-free zones and as much freedom of movement as possible within the setting.
6. Formulate a plan to assure the therapy dog's welfare within a session and after a session, including building recovery time into the therapy dog's schedule.

7. Be willing to implement that plan should the dog's welfare or well-being become threatened or compromised.

8. Ask the dog to work a less-than-daily work schedule, with time-limited working shifts, and give the dog vacations from work.

THE THERAPY ANIMAL'S BILL OF RIGHTS

As a therapy animal, I have the right to a handler who:

- Obtains my consent to participate in the work
- Provides gentle training to help me understand what I'm supposed to do
- Is considerate of my perception of the world
- Helps me adapt to the work environment
- Guides the client, staff, and visitors to interact with me appropriately
- Focuses on me as much as the client, staff, and visitors
- Pays attention to my nonverbal cues
- Takes action to reduce my stress
- Supports me during interactions with the client
- Protects me from overwork
- Gives me ways to relax after sessions
- Provides a well-rounded life with nutritious food, physical and intellectual exercise, social time, and activities beyond work
- Respects my desire to retire from work when I think it is time

(Howie, 2015; reprinted with permission from Purdue University Press.)

CONCLUSION

Our understanding of the human-canine bond and how it relates to healing following traumatic experiences continues to expand. Research demonstrates that people have strong and exceptional connections with dogs, although the reasons why these relationships provide certain therapeutic advantages are not altogether certain. In this chapter, we have discussed how the socially supportive attachments we have long shared with dogs are often beneficial for our emotional and physical health. Studies have begun to demonstrate the various therapeutic effects of this bond in the context of trauma, such as in the case of individuals experiencing PTSD and abuse (O'Haire, Guerin, & Kirkham, 2015). The exact psychological and neurological mechanisms responsible for these changes represent areas for continued research attention. Equally important is further research to identify the well-being effects of AAI work for therapy dogs. Going forward, it may be of interest and benefit to specifically examine canine personalities and temperaments, and how they may best fit with meeting the needs of specific traumas through AAI.

Best practices emphasize the need for AAI practitioners to have a foundation of knowledge and continuing education about the species with whom they work, and the populations they are serving. Several colleges and universities now offer single courses or certificate programs, which begin to address this need, including the University of Denver's Graduate School of Social Work and the University of Tennessee at Knoxville's Veterinary Social Work program. Canine-specific education is also easily available through webinars and seminars provided by canine professional organizations, such as Animal Behavior Associates, iSpeakDog, E-Training for Dogs, Raising Canine, Pet Professional Guild, and more. Many of these are available for the general public, as well as for canine professionals.

At the time of this writing, the American Psychological Association's Section on Human-Animal Interaction (Section 13 of Division 17) is developing competencies for psychologists providing AAI. Likewise, the American Counseling Association has accepted Stewart, Chang, Parker, and Grubbs' (2016) list of competencies for AAI practitioners providing mental health services. And, in 2014, the International Association for Human-Animal Interactions Organizations (IAHAIO) published a white paper addressing definitions and procedures to assure animal welfare in AAI (individual countries have also published similar documents) (Jegatheesan et al., 2014). Such informational resources are currently available for public use.

AAI practitioners need to continue to seek increased awareness of effective, evidence-based applications for trauma recovery as they become available and more established, as well as properly assure the well-being of therapy dogs who take part in human mental health treatment. Such knowledge is not only important ethically, but is key to ensuring that both client and therapy dog well-being are integral to AAI practice and research without waver or hesitation.

REFERENCES

Ainsworth, M. S., & Bowlby, J. (1991). An ethological approach to personality development. *American Psychologist, 46*(4), 333.

Albuquerque, N., Guo, K., Wilkinson, A., Savalli, C., Otta, E., & Mills, D. (2016). Dogs recognize dog and human emotions. *Biology Letters, 12*(1), 20150883.

Americans with Disabilities Act (ADA). (1990). U.S. Department of Justice—Civil Rights Division. Retrieved from https://www.ada.gov/ada_intro.htm

Andics, A., Gábor, A., Gácsi, M., Faragó, T., Szabó, D., & Miklósi, Á. (2016). Neural mechanisms for lexical processing in dogs. *Science, 353*(6303), 1030–1032.

Archaeology Magazine. (2016, March 3). *Siberia's Ancient Dog Burials.* Retrieved from https://www.archaeology.org/news/4230-160303-siberia-domesticated-dogs

Beck, L., & Madresh, E. A. (2008). Romantic partners and four-legged friends: An extension of attachment theory to relationships with pets. *Anthrozoös, 21*(1), 43–56.

Beetz, A., & Bales, K. L. (2016). Affiliation in human-animal interaction. In L. S. Freund, S. McCune, L. Esposito, N. R. Gee, & P. McCardle (Eds.), *Social Neuroscience and Human-Animal Interaction* (pp. 107–126). Washington, DC: American Psychological Association.

Bennett, M., Zeller, J., Rosenberg, L., & McCann, J. (2003). The effect of mirthful laughter on stress and natural killer cell activity. *Alternative Therapies in Health and Medicine, 9*(2) 38–45.

Call, J., Bräuer, J., Kaminski, J., & Tomasello, M. (2003). Domestic dogs (Canis familiaris) are sensitive to the attentional state of humans. *Journal of Comparative Psychology, 117*(3), 257.

Carter, C. S., & Porges S. W. (2016). Neural mechanisms underlying human-animal interaction: An evolutionary perspective. In L. S. Freund, S. McCune, L. Esposito, N. R. Gee, & P. McCardle (Eds.), *Social Neuroscience and Human–Animal Interaction* (pp. 89–106). Washington, DC: American Psychological Association.

Clapp, J. D., & Beck, J. G. (2009). Understanding the relationship between PTSD and social support: The role of negative network orientation. *Behaviour Research and Therapy, 47*(3), 237–244.

Clothier, S. (2014, August). Presentation for the reflected relationship seminar. St. Johnsville, NY.

Coren, S. (2014, September 23). *Is that a dog in your bed?* Retrieved from https://www.psychologytoday.com/blog/canine-corner/201409/is-dog-in-your-bed

Cutt, H., Giles-Corti, B., Knuiman, M., & Burke, V. (2007). Dog ownership, health and physical activity: A critical review of the literature. *Health & Place, 13*(1), 261–272.

Dellinger, M. (2008). Using dogs for emotional support of testifying victims of crime. *Animal Law Review, 15,* 171.

Delta Society (currently Pet Partners) (Ed.). (1999). *Standards of practice for animal-assisted activities and therapy.* Renton, WA: Delta Society.

Dietz, T. J., Davis, D., & Pennings, J. (2012). Evaluating animal-assisted therapy in group treatment for child sexual abuse. *Journal of Child Sexual Abuse, 21*(6), 665–683.

Ensminger, J. J. (2010). *Service and therapy dogs in American society: Science, law and the evolution of canine caregivers.* Springfield, IL: Charles C Thomas Publisher LTD.

Fine, A. H. (Ed.). (2015). *Handbook on animal-assisted therapy: Foundations and guidelines for animal-assisted interventions* (4th ed.). San Diego, CA: Academic Press.

Fine, A. H. (2014). *Our faithful companions: Exploring the essence of our kinship with animals.* Loveland, CO: Alpine Publications.

Fine, A. H., Albright, J., Nu, J., & Peralta, T. (2013). *Our ethical and moral responsibility: Ensuring the welfare of therapy animals.* Paper presented at the 2013 American Veterinary Medical Association Conference, Chicago, IL.

Fine, A. H., & Mackintosh, T. (2016). Animal-assisted interventions: Entering a crossroads of explaining an instinctive bond under the scrutiny of scientific inquiry. In H. Friedman (Ed.), *The encyclopedia of mental health* (2nd ed., pp. 68–73). San Diego, CA: Elsevier.

Fine, A. H., & Weaver, S. (2018). The human-animal bond and animal assisted intervention. In M. van den Bosch & W. Bird (Eds.), *Oxford textbook of nature and public health* (pp. 132–138). Oxford, UK: Oxford University Press.

Glenk, L. M., Kothgassner, O. D., Stetina, B. U., Palme, R., Kepplinger, B., & Baran, H. (2013). Therapy dogs' salivary cortisol levels vary during animal-assisted interventions. *Animal Welfare, 22,* 369–378.

Goldberg, S., Grusec, J. E., & Jenkins, J. M. (1999). Confidence in protection: Arguments for a narrow definition of attachment. *Journal of Family Psychology, 13*(4), 475.

Hall, M. J., Ng, A., Ursano, R. J., Holloway, H., Fullerton, C., & Casper, J. (2004). Psychological impact of the animal-human bond in disaster preparedness and response. *Journal of Psychiatric Practice, 10*(6), 368–374.

Hamama, L., Hamama-Raz, Y., Dagan, K., Greenfeld, H., Rubinstein, C., & Ben-Ezra, M. (2011). A preliminary study of group intervention along with basic canine training among traumatized teenagers: A 3-month longitudinal study. *Children and Youth Services Review, 33*(10), 1975–1980.

Handlin, L., Hydbring-Sandberg, E., Nilsson, A., Ejdebäck, M., Jansson, A., & Uvnäs-Moberg, K. (2011). Short-term interaction between dogs and their owners: Effects on oxytocin, cortisol, insulin and heart rate—an exploratory study. *Anthrozoös, 24*(3), 301–315.

Harris Interactive Poll. (2015, July 16). More than ever, pets are members of the family. Retrieved from https://www.prnewswire.com/news-releases/more-than -ever-pets-are-members-of-the-family-300114501.html

Haubenhofer, D. K., & Kirchengast, S. (2006). Physiological arousal for companion dogs working with their owners in animal-assisted activities and animal-assisted therapy. *Journal of Applied Animal Welfare Science, 9*(2), 165–172.

Haubenhofer, D. K., & Kirchengast, S. (2007). "Dog handlers" and dogs' emotional and cortisol secretion responses associated with animal-assisted therapy sessions. *Society & Animals, 15*(2), 127–150.

Heimlich, K. (2001). Animal-assisted therapy and the severely disabled child: A quantitative study. *Journal of Rehabilitation, 67*(4), 48–54.

Hodges, C. (2011). *Brief summary of state emergency planning laws for animals.* Animal Legal & Historical Center. Retrieved from https://www.animallaw .info/intro/state-and-federal-disaster-planning-laws-and-pets

Holder, C. (2013). All dogs go to court: The impact of court facility dogs as comfort for child witnesses on a defendant's right to a fair trial. *Houston Law Review, 50*, 1155.

Hopper, J. W., Frewen, P. A., van der Kolk, B. A., & Lanius, R. A. (2007). Neural correlates of reexperiencing, avoidance, and dissociation in PTSD: Symptom dimensions and emotion dysregulation in responses to script-driven trauma imagery. *Journal of Traumatic Stress, 20* (5), 713–725.

Horowitz, A., & Hecht, J. (2014). Looking at dogs: Moving from anthropocentrism to canid umwelt. In A. Horowitz (Ed.), *Domestic dog cognition and behavior* (pp. 201–219). Berlin, Germany: Springer-Verlag Berlin Heidelberg.

Howie, A. (2015) *Teaming with your therapy dog.* West Lafayette, IN: Purdue University Press.

Huber, A., Barber, A. L. A., Faragó, T., Muller, C. A., & Huber, L. (2017). Investigating emotional contagion in dogs (Canis familiaris) to emotional sounds of humans and conspecifics. *Animal Cognition, 20*(4), 703–715.

Jegatheesan, B., Beetz, A., Ormerod, E., Johnson, R., Fine, A., Yamazaki, K., Dudzik, C., Garcia, R. M., Winkle, M., & Choi, G. (2014). *The IAHAIO definitions for animal assisted intervention and guidelines for wellness of animals involved*

[White paper]. International Association for Human-Animal Interactions Organizations. Retrieved from http://iahaio.org/new/fileuploads/9313IAHAIO%20WHITE%20PAPER%20TASK%20FORCE%20-%20FINAL%20REPORT.pdf

Kellert, S. R., & Wilson, E. O. (1995). *The biophilia hypothesis*. Washington, DC: Island Press.

King, C., Watters, J., & Mungre, S. (2011). Effect of a time-out session with working animal-assisted therapy dogs. *Journal of Veterinary Behavior: Clinical Applications and Research, 6*, 232–238.

Lefkowitz, C., Prout, M., Bleiberg, J., Pahiria, I., & Debiak, D. (2005). Animal-assisted prolonged exposure: A treatment for survivors of sexual assault suffering posttraumatic stress disorder. *Animals & Society, 13*(4), 275–295.

Levine, G. N., Allen, K., Braun, L. T., Christian, H. E., Friedmann, E., Taubert, K. A., Thomas, S. A., Wells, D. L., & Lange, R. A. (2013). Pet ownership and cardiovascular risk: A scientific statement from the American Heart Association. *Circulation, 127*(23), 2353–2363.

Maharaj, N., Kazanjian, A., & Haney, C. J. (2016). The human-canine bond: A sacred relationship. *Journal of Spirituality in Mental Health, 18*(1), 76–89.

McCullough, A., Jenkins, M. A., Ruehrdanz, A., Gilmer, M. J., Olson, J., Pawar, A., . . . O'Haire, M. E. (2018). Physiological and behavioral effects of animal-assisted interventions for therapy dogs in pediatric oncology settings. *Applied Animal Behaviour Science, 200*, 86–95.

McDonald, S. E., Collins, E. A., Nicotera, N., Hageman, T. O., Ascione, F. R., Williams, J. H., & Graham-Bermann, S. A. (2015). Children's experiences of companion animal maltreatment in households characterized by intimate partner violence. *Child Abuse & Neglect, 50*, 116–127.

McNicholas, J., & Collis, G. M. (2006). Animals as social supports: Insights for understanding animal-assisted therapy. In A. H. Fine (Ed.), *Handbook on animal-assisted therapy: Theoretical foundations and guidelines for practice* (2nd ed., pp. 49–71). San Diego, CA: Academic Press.

Miklósi, Á., & Kubinyi, E. (2016). Current trends in canine problem-solving and cognition. *Current Directions in Psychological Science, 25*(5), 300–306.

Miller, S. C., Kennedy, C. C., DeVoe, D. C., Hickey, M., Nelson, T., & Kogan, L. (2009). An examination of changes in oxytocin levels in men and women before and after interaction with a bonded dog. *Anthrozoös, 22*(1), 31–42.

Mormann, F., Dubois, J., Kornblith, S., Milosavljevic, M., Cerf, M., Ison, M., Tsuchiya, N., Kraskov, A., Quiroga, R. Q., Adolphs, R., Fried, I., & Koch, C. (2011). A category-specific response to animals in the right human amygdala. *Nature Neuroscience, 14*(10), 1247–1249.

Nagasawa, M., Mitsui, S., En, S., Ohtani, N., Ohta, M., Sakuma, Y., Onaka, T., Mogi, K., & Kikusui, T. (2015). Oxytocin-gaze positive loop and the coevolution of human-dog bonds. *Social Evolution, 348*(6232), 333–336.

Odendaal, J. S., & Meintjes, R. A. (2003). Neurophysiological correlates of affiliative behaviour between humans and dogs. *The Veterinary Journal, 165*(3), 296–301.

O'Haire, M. E., Guerin, N. A., & Kirkham, A. C. (2015). Animal-assisted intervention for trauma: A systematic literature review. *Frontiers in Psychology (for Clinical Settings), 6.*

Olmert, M. D. (2013). *Made for each other: The biology of the human-animal bond.* Boston, MA: Da Capo Press.

Owen, R. P., Finton, B. J., Gibbons, S. W., & DeLeon, P. H. (2016). Canine-assisted adjunct therapy in the military: An intriguing alternative modality. *Journal for Nurse Practitioners, 12*(2), 95–101.

Ozbay, F., Johnson, D. C., Dimoulas, E., Morgan III, C. A., Charney, D., & Southwick, S. (2007). Social support and resilience to stress: From neurobiology to clinical practice. *Psychiatry (Edgmont), 4*(5), 35.

Payne, E., Bennett, P. C., & McGreevy, P. D. (2015). Current perspectives on attachment and bonding in the dog–human dyad. *Psychology Research and Behavior Management, 8,* 71–79.

Payne, E., DeAraugo, J., Bennett, P., & McGreevy, P. (2016). Exploring the existence and potential underpinnings of dog-human and horse-human attachment bonds. *Behavioural Processes, 125,* 114–121.

Peralta, J., Fine, A., Goldman, L., & Melco, A. (2017). (Submitted for publication). Investigation of stress-induced physiological and behavioral responses in registered therapy dogs participating in animal-assisted therapy with children diagnosed with ADHD.

Pet Partners. (2017). Home page. Retrieved from https://petpartners.org/volunteer/our-therapy-animal-program/

Phillips, A. (2014). *Understanding the Link between violence to animals and people: A guidebook for criminal justice professionals.* Alexandria, VA: National District Attorneys Office Association. Retrieved from http://www.ndaa.org/pdf/The%20Link%20Monograph-2014.pdf

Serpell, J. (1991) Beneficial effects of pet ownership on some aspects of human health and behaviour. *Journal of the Royal Society of Medicine, 84*(12), 717–720.

Serpell, J., McCune, S., Gee, N., & Griffin, J. A. (2017). Current challenges to research on animal-assisted interventions. *Applied Developmental Science, 21*(3), 223–233.

Stern, S. L., Donahue, D. A., Allison, S., Hatch, J. P., Lancaster, C. L., Benson, T. A., Johnson, A. L., Jeffreys, M. D., Pride, D., Moreno, C., & Peterson, A. L. (2013). Potential benefits of canine companionship for military veterans with posttraumatic stress disorder (PTSD). *Society & Animals, 21*(6), 568–581.

Stewart, L. A., Chang, C. Y., Parker, L. K., & Grubbs, N. (2016). *Animal assisted therapy in counseling competencies.* Developed in collaboration with the Animal Assisted Therapy in Mental Health Interest Network of the American Counseling Association. Retrieved from https://www.counseling.org/docs/default-source/competencies/animal-assisted-therapy-competencies-june-2016.pdf?sfvrsn=6

Sugawara A., Masud, M. M., Yokoyama, A., Mizutani, W., Watanuki, S., Yanai, K., Itoh, M., & Tashiro, M. (2012). Effects of presence of a familiar pet dog on regional cerebral activity in healthy volunteers: a positron emission tomography study. *Anthrozoös, 25*(1), 25–34.

U.S. Department of Housing and Urban Development (2013). Fair Housing and Equal Opportunity Notice 2013–01. Retrieved from https://www.hud.gov/sites/documents/SERVANIMALS_NTCFHEO2013-01.PDF

von Uexkull, J. (1934/1957). A stroll through the worlds of animals and men. In C. H. Schiller (Ed.), *Instinctive behavior: The development of a modern concept* (pp. 5–80). New York, NY: International Universities Press.

Ward, M. (2013). Juvenile-justice corrections program trains dogs, youths. Retrieved from https://www.statesman.com/news/20130207/juvenile-justice-corrections-program-trains-dogs-youths

Williamson, J. B., Porges, E. C., Lamb, D. G., & Porges, S. W. (2014). Maladaptive autonomic regulation in PTSD accelerates physiological aging. *Frontiers in Psychology, 5*, 1571.

Zilcha-Mano, S., Mikulincer, M., & Shaver, P. R. (2011). Pet in the therapy room: An attachment perspective on animal-assisted therapy. *Attachment & Human Development, 13*(6), 541–561.

ABOUT THE AUTHORS

Ann R. Howie, MSW, is an adjunct professor with the University of Denver and is director of their Canine-Assisted Intervention Specialist Program. She has worked professionally with both animals and humans since 1987, and has pioneered competency-based team evaluations for AAI. Howie has a private counseling practice, and her focus on animal welfare now includes providing physical fitness training for canines.

Aubrey H. Fine, EdD, is a professor of education at California State Polytechnic University and a licensed psychologist. Fine is the author of several books, including Our Faithful Companions, Give a Dog Your Heart, The Handbook on Animal-Assisted Therapy, and Afternoons with Puppy. His research pertains to the human-animal bond (HAB), animal-assisted interventions (AAIs) and children, and social skills training with children with ADHD.

Lindsay A. Rojas, LSW, MSW, AASW, is a licensed social worker in the state of Colorado. She currently works in community mental health and private practice with her therapy dog, Dante, specializing in animal-assisted therapy. She earned her undergraduate degree in psychology and Latino studies from the University of Notre Dame in 2014. In 2017, she graduated with her master of social work degree and animal-assisted social work certification from the University of Denver.

CHAPTER 10

Animals in Action: Therapeutic Roles in Healing Military Trauma

Cheryl A. Krause-Parello, PhD, RN, FAAN; Allison E. Boyrer, MS, MA, BSN, RN; and Eleni Padden, BA

Throughout history, dogs have consistently and fondly been regarded as "man's best friend." This relationship takes on an increasingly meaningful role in the context of wartime, when humans and dogs often depend upon one another for survival. Vitally, bonding with dogs has been shown to be invaluable to many military members and veterans as they work to cope with the trauma of combat and other hardships, both from anecdotal accounts and through recent scientific investigations evaluating the effects of the human-animal interaction (HAI).

In exploring the myriad ways that animals, and specifically dogs, impact military and veteran health, we first provide an overview of the history of military working dogs, thus establishing the reliable alliance that often exists between these animals and active duty service members. The continuous loyalty and sense of safety that a military working dog provides often resembles a service dog's consistent, integrative support of veterans with service-connected conditions as they return home and transition back to civilian life.

The reciprocal relationship of trust and mutual respect between dogs and service members has been well established over decades of high-stakes interaction in military settings and during wars and conflicts, which we will consider in-depth in the following first sections. Concurrently, we lay the groundwork for further discussion later in this chapter regarding the utility and healing impact of dogs and other animals in ameliorating the physical, physiological, and psychological symptoms of trauma within the military and veteran population.

HISTORY OF MILITARY WORKING DOGS IN THE UNITED STATES

Military working dogs have saved countless lives in war and conflicts since they first began serving with their military comrades (Mott, 2003). These dogs not only serve side by side with their human military partner, but many also provide a sense of comfort and safety on the battlefield's front-lines (Reporter's Notebook & Russo, 2011). Military working dogs have held and continue to play both official (e.g., alerting) and unofficial (e.g., providing solace) roles in the military, and have been used by the United States military since World War I. Along with their volunteer handlers, these dogs are trained in teams as scouts, trackers, sentry dogs, mine/booby-trap/tunnel dogs, and in the water for the detection of hostile forces (US War Dogs, n.d.).

Scouts serve as the "eyes and ears" for the military unit. Scouts typically monitor environments for threats, such as booby trap trip wires, ambushes, hidden stashes of weapons or food, and enemy snipers. Trackers are used when military units want to reestablish contact visually or olfactorily in order to locate missing personnel who may be wounded or dead, or to locate the enemy. Sentry dogs are trained to walk the perimeter of base camps for enemy combatants, predominantly during nighttime hours. The sentry dog's mission is to detect, detain, and destroy. The mine/booby-trap/tunnel dog's role is to detect land mines, booby-traps, trip wires, and underground hideaways and tunnels. These dogs also search villages for enemy supplies, such as weapons and ammunition. Over several decades, military working dogs have gained notoriety for their service in World War I, World War II, Korea, Vietnam, the Persian Gulf, Bosnia, Kosovo, and Afghanistan and Iraq. The history and achievements of several of these honorable dogs are highlighted in the sections that follow.

World War I and Stubby

The most decorated military working dog who served in WWI was named Stubby. In 1917, while training for combat at Yale University, Private Robert Conroy came across a wandering Boston bull terrier puppy with a brindle coat (Bausum, 2014). Due to the dog's short tail, he dubbed him Stubby. Stubby became the official mascot of the 102nd Infantry Regiment, assigned to the 26th Yankee Division. Stubby learned how to salute, and, importantly, it was noted by many that he boosted the troop's morale (Russell, 2017). When the infantry received orders to set sail for France, Private Conroy snuck Stubby on the ship (since dogs were forbidden on base camp and missions), and brought him up onto the deck once they were far off land so that Stubby would not have to disembark.

The American army dog Sergeant Stubby (ca. 1916–1926). (Photo from the U.S. National Archives.)

Due to his acute sense of smell—a dog's sense of smell is roughly 40 times greater than that of a human (Tyson, 2012)—Stubby would promptly alert the troops when gas was launched in the trenches. Additionally, his precision hearing allowed him to notify the troops of danger and impending raids by barking and running around the base camp to signal his fellow brothers in arms. Stubby was the first military dog to ever be given rank, and then promoted to sergeant, in the US Army based on his contributions to an operation that successfully captured an enemy spy. Stubby served for 18 months overall. By the end of the war, he had served in 17 battles on the Western Front, receiving many metals of heroism and bravery throughout his service.

World War II and Chips

The most decorated (unofficially) military working dog who served in WWII was named Chips. During WWII, there was a call for private citizens to donate their family dogs for military duty (Zimmerman, 2014). Chips' family answered the call and donated him for military service. In 1942, Chips, a German shepherd-collie-Siberian husky mix, was shipped out to the War Dog Training Center in Front Royal, Virginia, for training as a sentry dog. Chips served with the 3rd Infantry Division overseas in

Chips, the most decorated dog of World War II, November 19, 1943. (Photo from the U.S. National Archives.)

Europe. During his time in the military, he specifically served as a tank guard dog. Chips would alert his military counterparts of impending ambushes. Based on Chips' valor, he received many distinguished military awards and honors including the Silver Star for valor and a Purple Heart (Estrada, n.d.). However, these awards were ultimately taken away based on the perception that a dog receiving military awards and honors was demeaning to the soldiers who received the same recognitions. In 1945, Chips was discharged from the military and sent home to his family, who later gave the dog to his military handler upon discharge. Subsequently, in 1980, Disney made a movie entitled *Chips, the War Dog* based on his colorful life.

Operation Neptune Spear and Cairo

In 2011, Cairo, a Belgian Malinois, became instrumental in Operation Neptune Spear, which was responsible for the raid on Osama bin Laden's compound in Abbottabad, Pakistan (Schmidle, 2011). Cairo was trained to sniff out bombs, attack enemy combatants, slide down ropes, and repel and jump from 5,000 feet, amongst other tasks. Cairo was consistently equipped with a Kevlar vest, a harness for repelling, a drainage system for waterborne assaults, and a night vision camera. During this mission, Cairo assisted the US Navy Seals by scaling the compound and looking for hidden rooms and doors. He also alerted the Seals if anyone tried to escape, and warned them of approaching Pakistani security forces (Dozier, 2011).

There are many more military working dogs who have served and currently serve our country with great pride and loyalty who, out of necessity, are not highlighted here. Moreover, dogs have also played a significant role in the military not only in their combat roles, but also in their ability to improve troop morale during times of uncertainty (Foliente, 2009). In fact, military working dogs and other classifications of dogs often continue to serve our military even after they are discharged, including via work as service dogs, emotional support dogs, and companion animals. Considered cumulatively, the noble history of military working dogs, their integral place in military culture, and their critical importance to the very livelihood of so many members of our nation's armed forces underscore the fundamental capacity of dogs to aid in the healing of trauma for military service members and veterans.

Dogs, War, and Wellness

During WWI, foreign Red Cross societies employed dogs who greatly aided the Allied Forces (Browe, 2014). Dogs were present to help find wounded soldiers and bring them first aid supplies within their saddle bags. This was important in that the dogs could reach soldiers, while navigating through dangerous territory, without alerting the enemy. The dogs were trained to bring something back of the injured soldier to alert the Red Cross staff of a soldier down, and to provide messenger and delivery services, carry ammunition, and scout out weapon factories.

Following WWII, the American Red Cross began the use of therapy dogs in the Army Air Forces Convalescent Center in Pawling, New York. Seven hundred acres of farmland were acquired by the US government in the 1940s, and were turned into a working farm (including dairy operations) with many farm animals. This marked one of the first times animal-assisted therapies were employed to assist returning soldiers in their recovery from the visible and invisible wounds of war.

Military Wounds of War

Mental health disorders are the leading cause of disability in the United States and Canada, accounting for 25% of all years of life lost to disability and premature mortality (World Health Organization, 2004). Harrowingly, suicide is a leading cause of death in the United States. A recent 2018 Centers for Disease Control (CDC) report posited that suicide is responsible for the deaths of a staggering 45,000 Americans each year (Stone et al., 2018). In many states, these data represent an average 30% increase in suicide rates over the past two decades, with the rates among veterans being some of the highest in a subpopulation (Department of Veterans Affairs, 2016b). Military members have significant reintegration needs, including physical, physiological, and psychological. Musculoskeletal injuries and pain, infectious diseases, noise and vibration exposure, and mental health issues are just some of the ailments our veterans must cope with when returning from service.

Injuries from recent operations, such as Operation Enduring Freedom in Afghanistan and Operation Iraqi Freedom in Iraq, are profound, with an estimated 19% to 42% of veterans being diagnosed with a mental health condition (Hoge, Auchterlonie, Milliken, 2006). The long conflicts, which have required many troops to deploy multiple times and operate under an almost constant threat of attack, have exacted a far more widespread emotional toll than previously recognized by most government studies and independent assessments (Chandrasekaren, 2014). As such, it is of significant importance to research a range of viable non-pharmacological mental health interventions, such as animal-assisted interventions (AAI) and animal-assisted therapy (AAT). Specifically, it is critical that the scientific community work toward establishing evidence-based treatment mechanisms with the potential to be implemented in a highly personalized manner to our nation's veterans.

Invisible Wounds of War: Post-Traumatic Stress Disorder and Traumatic Brain Injury

Veterans have often experienced inhumane events that one would not necessarily see in the everyday world. Post-traumatic stress disorder (PTSD) is a trauma and stress-related condition that can occur after a traumatic event such as war, assault, or disaster (American Psychiatric Association, 2013). Events such as mass suicides, mortar attacks, combat exposure, physical abuse, terrorist attacks, sexual or physical assault, and other heinous acts against humanity are just a handful of the atrocities that may be witnessed or experienced by military members at war. Notably, many noncombat veterans may similarly experience extreme and traumatizing events, sexual or physical trauma, and moral injury. Whether the injury sustained is from shrapnel, a roadside bomb or witnessing carnage, the pain and suffering of servicewomen and men is real and, for many, chronic (Weinmeyer, 2015).

Such actions seen in combat are difficult to "erase" from memory, and may result in hypervigilance and agitated states during a service member's return to civilian life. Military members and veterans may also experience detachment and estrangement from others, difficulty with concentration, and sleep/wake cycle disturbances. During a PTSD event, the veteran may believe that his or her life is in danger, and may feel he/she has minimal to no control over the situation, thus causing heightened anxiety. If this belief does not subside, psychological and/or physiological changes may disrupt the person's life, making it exceedingly difficult or even impossible to continue activities of daily living. The nature of PTSD (e.g., avoiding situations and stimuli that may trigger symptoms) means many individuals in need of help will eschew discussing their struggles (Furst, 2016).

Alongside PTSD, traumatic brain injury (TBI) has been coined an "invisible wound of war," frequently giving rise to emotional and cognitive problems. TBI is an acute brain event where symptoms may occur immediately, or present days or weeks following an injury or traumatic experience. Classified as either mild or severe, TBI has also been found to coexist with chronic pain conditions, depression, PTSD, and sleep problems (Lee et al., 2017). At times, the person is not even aware they have had a brain injury, such as one sustained from shock wave blasts or falls. Regardless of the type of TBI diagnosed, the consequences to a person's life, family, social circle, community, and occupation can be devastating.

Often, service members suffering from TBI concurrently suffer from PTSD, thus complicating treatment regimens and compounding such TBI-related symptoms as cognitive impairments and memory dysfunction. Although psychotherapy and pharmacotherapy are known as the current best practices for the treatment of PTSD, a significant proportion of individuals with PTSD do not seem to respond to these treatments (Vincent et al., 2017). This underscores the pressing necessity for identifying and developing non-pharmacological interventions—such as AAI involving therapy and service animals—to aid in lessening PTSD symptoms. Potential effects of canine assistance may be both social and physiological (Krause-Parello, Sarni, & Padden, 2016). Several military- and veteran-specific interventions in hospital and deployed settings report benefits from therapeutic human-canine interactions, including increased assertiveness, improved stress management, improved communications and parenting interactions, expanded affect and emotional regulation, and improved morale for participants and health care workers/staff (Owen, Finton, Gibbons, DeLeon, 2016).

Military Sexual Trauma

Severe or threatening forms of sexual harassment and sexual assault sustained during military service are referred to within the Veterans Health Administration as military sexual trauma (MST) (Kimerling, Gima, Smith, Street, & Frayne, 2007). Since 2002, the VA has implemented universal screening for MST using a standard clinical reminder within the electronic medical record. Veterans who screen positive for MST are more likely to have a history of suicide attempts documented in their VA medical record (Kimerling et al., 2007).

Despite the expanding roles for women within the military (Street, Vogt, & Dutra, 2009), MST affects far more women than men; approximately 41% of women and 4% of men reported experiencing MST during a recent study surveying 60,000 veterans (Barth et al., 2016). Veterans with sexual trauma are likely to experience detachment and estrangement from others, sleep disturbances, and problems with concentration (Graham et al., 2016). For women who enter the military with significant previous trauma histories and are exposed to additional traumatic events (such as MST) during the course of military service, risk for cumulative trauma exposure, significant occupational stress, and related mental and physical health problems is high (Zinzow, Grubaugh, Monnier, Suffoletta-Mairle & Frueh, 2007). Worse yet, if the ability to cope is lost, one may also lose his/her independence and be unable to maintain personal and professional relationships or forge new ones. The feelings of safety induced by a canine companion may help a survivor of MST challenge those fears, leading to a reevaluation of the world as relatively safe and of himself or herself as strong and competent (Lefkowitz, Paharia, Prout, Debiak & Bleiberg, 2005).

IMPACTS OF HUMAN-CANINE INTERACTIONS

As Bern Williams notes, "There's no psychiatrist in the world like a puppy licking your face." The physiological and psychological effects that animals have on humans have been documented consistently throughout history, and the utilization of canines to comfort service members in military hospital settings, such as the Army Air Forces Convalescent Center in Pawling, is a compelling early demonstration of how animals have a profound and historically noted impact on the health of active duty military and veterans. Findings in recent years have developed robustly. Here, we intend to add to this discussion by taking a specific look at the biology of PTSD, as well as the impact that animals, and, in particular, canines, have on the physical and psychological health of traumatized military service members and veterans.

Current treatment methods for PTSD are lacking. While treatments such as cognitive behavioral therapy (CBT) (Harvey, Bryant, & Tarrier, 2003), prolonged exposure (PE) therapy (Rauch et al., 2009; Tuerk et al., 2011), and pharmacotherapy (Ipser & Stein, 2012) have been evidenced as efficacious for some patients, it remains a hard reality of the contemporary clinical field that these methods do not work for all individuals with PTSD. Moreover, there exist a variety of shortfalls with prevailing treatment methodologies, and nonresponse to treatment is common (Haagen, Smid, Knipscheer, & Kleber, 2015; Richardson et al., 2014; Schottenbauer, Glass, Arnkoff, Tendick, & Gray, 2008; Shalev, Bonne, & Eth, 1996; Watts et al., 2013). Further investigation and investment in alternative ways to ameliorate this condition and improve quality of life for patients is of extreme and pressing importance to researchers, health care professionals, patients, and caregivers alike.

Canine Welfare and Well-Being

Before fully delving into an examination of canine impacts on human health, there is a need to recognize and reflect upon the ways in which the reverse interaction may function. That is to say, are there benefits or consequences (recognized in the literature) that canines receive or suffer from by interacting with humans? In particular, does a robust body of data currently exist to suggest that there may be negative health impacts on canines as a result of their roles as key players in AAT/AAI, and, in particular, as psychiatric service dogs? If so, how does this alter the ways in which health professionals should responsibly manage AAT/AAI, specifically the care for the canines involved?

It seems that the jury, for the most part, is still out. Interestingly, a 2006 study on the physiological stress levels in shelter dogs found that human contact—defined as "taking the dog into an outdoor enclosure, playing with the dog, grooming, petting and reviewing basic obedience commands"—had a beneficial impact on stress and reduced salivary cortisol levels in these canines significantly (Coppola, Grandin, & Enns, 2006,

p. 537). Although this study was conducted with shelter dogs, the actual tasks (e.g., exercising, grooming, petting, and obedience) carried out are not dissimilar from many daily interactions that a service dog owner or a health care professional handling a therapy dog for AAI/AAT might perform; thus, these tasks may not be overly taxing to working dogs, at least from a stress perspective. In regard to the growing body of AAI-specific research in this area, the results are generally mixed; some investigators have found indicators of behavioral and/or physiological stress among therapy dogs after participating in AAI sessions with a variety of populations (Haubenhofer & Kirchengast, 2007; King, Watters, & Mungre, 2011), while the evidence of such in other studies is minimal or absent (Glenk et al., 2013; McCullough et al., 2018).

Likewise, a lack of specific evidence exists with regard to stress-related impacts for service dogs paired with people diagnosed with PTSD. It is suggested that this be an area for future research. Interestingly, some evidence does exist with regard to the well-being of service dogs who work with children with autism. In fact, two 2008 studies examined this question, and the challenges that families faced when integrating service dogs into their lives. Potential canine stressors were identified, and included such factors as minimal access to rest and recovery time after working, lack of predictability in daily routines, insufficient time for recreational activities, and bonding with the parent instead of the child originally (Burrows, Adams, & Millman, 2008). It could reasonably be assumed that some of the above stressors could also exist within the context of PTSD. Of note, the same research group also determined in a congruent qualitative study that although there were challenges with service dog integration into a home and working environment—such as public access issues, added work/training for the family, and financing of dog care—ultimately families "overwhelmingly" felt that these challenges were worth it given the benefits provided to their children (Burrows & Adams, 2008, p. 559).

Anecdotal evidence and common sense tell us that dogs need time to relax and partake in "vest-off" activities—or, as patients with service dogs sometimes put it, to have time to "just be a dog." For example, military working dogs, in particular, have been shown to benefit from enrichment, including exercise coupled with human contact (Lefebvre, Giffroy, & Diederich, 2009). The proper amount of "vest-off" time has yet to be quantified empirically, and is likely highly variable depending on individual factors such as the particular tasks the dog is required to do, the dog's daily working environment, the age of the dog, the stage of training that the dog is in, and so forth. However, the takeaway here is that psychiatric service dogs and therapy dogs involved in AAI/AAT should not be expected to be working 100% of the time. Rather, they require care and compassion in order to do their jobs correctly and accurately. Specifically, dogs need designated time for rest and play; opportunities to engage in natural and relaxed species-specific behaviors and activities; affectionate attention; physical exercise; a consistent and nutrient-rich diet; proper medical care; and routine check-ups. Additionally, psychiatric service dogs may likely need reinforcement and upkeep in training for their specific tasks. If mobility-related equipment or any other equipment worn by the dog is utilized, it should ideally be properly fitted by professionals who specialize in the ergonomics of service dog equipment, and be kept in good working condition as well as updated as per the growth of the dog. Improper fitting of equipment is not only a potential health concern for the dog, but it can also impede the proper execution of service-related tasks.

Physiological and Psychological Effects of AAIs on Human Health

Bearing in mind these considerations of canine well-being, let us proceed in examining the potential impacts that dogs may have on human health, and, particularly, the amelioration of trauma in vulnerable populations. A growing body of research suggests that interactions with dogs have a significant effect on the human body's stress response mechanisms, and may contribute markedly to various domains of psychological well-being. Considering the nature of PTSD and its classification in the DSM-5 as a trauma and stress-related disorder, the capacity for dogs to influence physical and psychological stress in humans may have a particularly profound impact on this condition.

Encouragingly, various contemporary reviews of efficacy have cited AAT/AAI as a putative mechanism to improve mental and physical health in numerous populations, including children with histories of sexual abuse, college-aged students experiencing stress, older adults, patients living with chronic or terminal illnesses, and individuals who have experienced additional challenges and/or other forms of trauma (Kamioka et al., 2014; Krause-Parello & Friedmann, 2014; Nimer & Lundahl, 2007; O'Haire, Guérin, & Kirkham, 2015; Krause-Parello, Sarni, & Padden, 2016). Such research has documented significant improvements in areas including, but not limited to, reducing loneliness (Banks & Banks, 2002; Krause-Parello & Gulick, 2013); decreasing anxiety in hospitalized psychiatric patients (Barker & Dawson, 1998); improving cardiovascular wellness in older adults (Krause-Parello & Kolassa, 2016); and reducing depression (Friedmann, Thomas, & Son, 2011; Krause-Parello, 2012; Souter & Miller, 2007) and stress (Allen, Shykoff, & Izzo, 2001; Barker, Knisely, McCain, Schubert, & Pandurangi, 2010). In a recent study, service dogs were found to improve veteran physical and psychological health and aid in positive reintegration into civilian life (Krause-Parello & Morales, 2018).

Based on the growing body of evidence suggesting that AAT/AAI is a dynamic, empirically sound method by which to improve human health and well-being, an upwelling of recent interest has developed with regard to the investigation of how these interventions may be applied toward facilitating patient recovery from trauma and PTSD, particularly within the military and veteran population. A hallmark of PTSD biology is the documented alteration of cortisol (Lehrner, Daskalakis, & Yehuda, 2016; Yehuda, 2002), a hormone tied to stress perception and reactivity. Notably, cortisol levels impact the functionality of the hippocampus and the amygdala, two brain regions that play a central role in how we experience emotions and process memory (Lehrner et al., 2016; Myers, McKlveen, & Herman, 2012; Rauch, Shin, & Phelps, 2006; Shin et al., 2004; Shin, Rauch, & Pitman, 2006; Starcevic et al., 2014).

Difficulty with cortisol regulation is thought to be a significant factor in both the neuropathology of PTSD, as well as the stress-related symptoms that are characteristic of this condition. Recent investigations and reviews have suggested that dysregulated levels of cortisol found in patients with PTSD may play an important role in the neurodegeneration of the hippocampus (Bremner & Bremner, 2016; Daskalakis, McGill, Lehrner, & Yehuda, 2016; Lehrner et al., 2016), which has historically been found to be significantly smaller in individuals with PTSD (Woon, Sood, & Hedges, 2010). This is not altogether surprising, given that people with PTSD often display difficulty controlling emotional responses (e.g., extreme irritability or sadness) and with memory functioning (e.g., reexperiencing the traumatic event through flashbacks).

An additional key hormone to consider in the context of trauma is oxytocin. Oxytocin is a neuropeptide historically implicated in social interaction and bonding. In recent years, the capacity of administering oxytocin to diminish the fear response has been evaluated as a way to potentially aid in lessening trauma symptoms (Frijling et al., 2016; Olff, Langeland, Witteveen, & Denys, 2010). In a groundbreaking 2016 study, Koch and colleagues (2016a) found that intranasal administration of oxytocin dampened amygdala reactivity (i.e., fear response) toward all emotional faces in male and female patients with PTSD, suggesting a therapeutic potential of oxytocin for this population. Strikingly, a study by the same researchers found that the administration of intranasal oxytocin normalized functional connectivity in the amygdalae of patients with PTSD, and resulted in decreased subjective anxiety and nervousness in these individuals (Koch et al., 2016b). These research findings strengthen the case that oxytocin may potentially have clinical applications for patients coping with fear response dysregulation in conditions such as PTSD.

Importantly, contemporary research indicates that interactions with canines may naturally impact levels of both cortisol and oxytocin in humans. A recent study found short-term interactions with dogs to have a quick, significant effect on decreasing levels of cortisol in humans 15 and 30 minutes after they began an interaction with a dog (Handlin et al., 2011). Furthermore, the presence of a dog attenuated cortisol levels among undergraduate students in the Trier Social Stress Test (Polheber & Matchock, 2014), while participation in a dog-visitation program consistently lowered the salivary cortisol levels of inmates in a Japanese prison (Koda et al., 2016). Reductions in cortisol levels after interactions with a therapy dog have also been recently cited in populations of college students (Krause-Parello, Tychowski, Gonzalez, & Boyd, 2012).

In a recent study, the effects of a facility dog on hospitalized veterans seen by a palliative care psychologist were examined. Participants received a visit from a VA facility dog, a clinical psychologist, and the dog's handler (experimental condition), or an unstructured visit with the clinical psychologist alone (control condition). The veteran's heart rate (HR) and salivary cortisol were measured before, just after, and 30 minutes after both the experimental and control conditions. A significant decrease in cortisol was found when comparing the before time period to the 30 minutes after time period for both the experimental ($p = 0.007$) and control condition ($p = 0.036$). A significant decrease in HR was also found when comparing the before time period to the 30 minutes after time period for both the experimental ($p = 0.0046$) and control ($p = 0.0119$) condition. While both conditions saw physiological indicators of stress reduction, results do support that a VA facility dog, matched with a palliative care psychologist, had a significant, positive impact on salivary cortisol levels and HR in hospitalized veterans on the palliative care service (Krause-Parello, Levy, Holman, & Kolassa, 2016).

In addition, close bonds between people and their pet dogs may be further facilitated by an increase in oxytocin. In fact, research shows that human-canine interactions, including those involving mutual gaze, have been linked to increased oxytocin in both species (Handlin, Nilsson, Ejdebäck, Hydbring-Sandberg, & Uvnäs-Moberg, 2012; Nagasawa et al., 2015). Taken together, existing evidence delineating the oxytocin-eliciting and cortisol-altering effects of human-canine interactions provides a solid foundation upon which to develop viable mechanistic explanations regarding the effects that these relationships may have within the context of PTSD neuropathology and symptomology. Biologically, stress-reducing aspects of interacting with dogs may have the therapeutic effect of disallowing environmental triggers to have catastrophic impacts on the stress response, thereby exerting protection over the neuroendocrine system, and consistently serving to facilitate reregulation to typical levels of stress response. The less the system is retriggered and forced to react to negative inputs, perhaps the more likely it is that the system will be able to minimize dysregulation. Accordingly, human-canine interaction—and, in particular, interaction with highly trained psychiatric service dogs (discussed next)—may decrease the likelihood that triggered episodes or intrusive memories of traumatic stress will recur, and may function to curtail the emotional impact that these triggers have on individuals. In turn, these effects may serve to protect from extreme episodes of stress compensation and, in theory, promote reregulation and "healing" of the chronically dysregulated system.

Psychiatric service dogs, in particular, have the ability to quite literally be constantly present in the lives of individuals coping with PTSD. From a therapeutic standpoint, this differentiates AAIs with service dogs from approaches such as animal-assisted group therapy, CBT, PE, and other clinician-led therapies that require an assigned timeline in which to accomplish goals. Service dogs represent a sustained mechanism of support for individuals with PTSD, with the capacity to extend far beyond a clinician's office and, indeed, into every realm of an individual's life. By default, this sustained contact allows for an individual to consistently experience not only the psychological benefits of bonding and interacting with the dog, but also the nuanced physiological effects that this interaction facilitates (e.g., alterations of endogenous cortisol and oxytocin levels) and the stress-regulating benefits that result from the interplay of such physiological processes.

This "all-the-time" therapeutic effect may only truly be achieved otherwise by pharmacological interventions. Current pharmacological approaches are limited, and various systematic reviews of pharmacological usefulness in PTSD treatment have concluded a stark lack of efficacy (Haagen et al., 2015; Watts et al., 2013). Thus, interaction with psychiatric service dogs represents a highly consistent and ecologically valid modality by which to deliver therapeutic effects to individuals with PTSD in a functional, real-world setting, and should be considered seriously as a powerful adjunctive treatment mechanism by service providers.

CASE STUDY
LYNDON AND ICE: FOUR-LEGGED LOVE

The following is an excerpt from a piece written by marine veteran, Lyndon Villone, who has worked for the past several years to establish Heel the Heroes, a charitable 501(c)(3) organization with the mission of providing innovative programs and services uniting specially trained dogs and horses with holistic therapies to aid in the recovering, reclaiming, and refining of veterans' lifestyles, and ultimately facilitating the empowerment and enrichment of veteran lives. From January 2011–November 2012, Villone was stricken with grief over the loss of six people he considered to be family/brothers in arms, including the loss of his Marine mentor to overdose medications. None of these deaths were from combat activities per se; all of them happened stateside. From January of 2013 until present day, Villone has been working to improve his lifestyle, along with the mental and physical health needed to once again obtain a satisfactory quality of life. When five-week-old Siberian husky "Ice" came into his life from a bad breeding situation six days after the loss of Villone's best friend, there was no way to predict the lifeline Ice would ultimately become for Villone.

> "Ice, come!" As the paws of a 60-pound Siberian husky glide through the air springing from the ground with excitement in your direction, it's easy to admire the physical nature of a striking "wolf like" canine. Further beneath the skin, though, is a living, breathing, intelligent canine that is visibly happy in his efforts

to obey your one simple cue to return. These are personal experiences I've enjoyed while being fortunate enough to get to know this animal. This canine has such an enhanced personality, and definitive things that he likes and dislikes. He gets happy, he gets sad, and he gets sick. He needs proper nutrition, health maintenance, and love. Most every parent I've spoken with said having kids changed their lives. Caring for this amazing creature has required me to get better as a person, and has changed my life forever.

Lyndon and Ice: "The love from a dog is unconditional; our love to them should be the same. With a bond that strong, there will always be a positive influence taking place." Corporal (CPL) Lyndon R. Villone; Fallujah, Iraq, from March–October 2006, again from October 2007–May 2008; United States Marine Corps; Parris Island, Camp LeJeune; Amphibious Assault Vehicle crewman (AAV) MOS = 1833.

A gigantic reason I've been able to understand my service dog Ice so well is because we bonded through socializing him appropriately with people, sights, sounds, things, and other well-behaved dogs. I studied proper introduction techniques for letting my dog meet other dogs for the first time as required of service dogs. It is only fair to our dogs that we know what we are asking from them. They operate differently than we do, but still have feelings. Ice does more than brace for my vertigo spells, and apply pressure points after nightmares and anxiety attacks. It's mentally healing getting to know another living animal's personality in such a wholesome and humbling presence. He's changed me as a person.

It's been my experience that I can take a peek into a person's character and personality by the way they care for their dog. We live in a world where lack of trust is evident. You will always be able to trust a dog; they share blind faith and trust in you.

IMPLICATIONS FOR PRACTICE AND POLICY:
A CALL TO ACTION

There is sufficient preliminary research regarding the psychological and physiological benefits of HAI, and its potential and specific usefulness in impacting PTSD symptomology, to warrant the funding of large-scale controlled and longitudinal studies in order to further evaluate these effects. It is the critical responsibility of private and governmental funding agencies to recognize the potential for clinical impact in this field of research, and to commit significant future funding to support researchers and projects with the intent of understanding how precisely the stress systems of our bodies react to animals, and how these interactions may be utilized therapeutically to aid both military and civilian populations struggling profoundly with trauma.

Veterans diagnosed with PTSD often utilize the assistance of dogs to cope with their fundamental human needs for safety, affiliation, and succorance (Taylor, Edwards, & Pooley, 2013). However, veterans with PTSD and TBI who acquire a service dog are not reimbursed, as service dogs are not considered a medical expense (Krause-Parello et al., 2016). The VA currently has a clinician review process to evaluate each veteran and determine if he or she qualifies for a service dog. Veterans who are approved for a service dog are currently referred to Assistance Dogs International-accredited agencies. There is no charge for the dog or the associated training. The VA provides veterinary care and equipment through VA Prosthetics and Sensory Aids, yet does not pay for boarding, grooming, food, or other routine expenses that come with owning a dog. According to the VA, protecting someone, giving emotional support, or being a companion does not qualify the dog as being "of service." Therefore, a service dog is not a reimbursable expense, which is a significant health care disparity (Department of Veterans Affairs, 2016a).

The Puppies Assisting Wounded Service members (P.A.W.S.) Act of 2017, H.R. 2327, is currently under review in the House of Representatives to direct the Secretary of Veterans Affairs to make grants available to eligible organizations to provide service dogs to veterans with severe PTSD and for other purposes. To be eligible for a service dog under the pilot program, a veteran needs to be enrolled in the patient enrollment system of the Department of Veterans Affairs under section 1705 of Title 38 of the United States Code. Additional eligibility criteria include: 1) the veteran has to have completed an established evidence-based treatment for

PTSD by a qualified health care provider (checklist PCL-5); 2) the health care provider or VA team needs to have determined that the veteran may potentially benefit from a service dog; and 3) the veteran must agree to complete training successfully with the service dog by an eligible organization. The veteran must also see the health care provider or VA clinical team at least once every six months to determine if he/she continues to benefit from a service dog.

Joining Forces is an initiative from the White House, former First Lady Michelle Obama, and Dr. Jill Biden to help raise awareness of the needs of veterans. Joining Forces has collaborated with various nursing organizations to raise awareness of health issues with returning veterans, specifically PTSD and TBI. Their goal is for *every nurse* to recognize signs and symptoms of these conditions, and to support veterans in obtaining quality referrals for treatment (Halderman, 2013).

Canines Providing Assistance to Wounded Warriors (C-P.A.W.W.) is a Health Research Initiative for Veterans in the Christine E. Lynn College of Nursing at Florida Atlantic University. The C-P.A.W.W. initiative was established in 2013 to advance the health and well-being of members of the armed forces. The mission of C-P.A.W.W. is to comprehensively advance interdisciplinary research, education, and practice protocols for wounded warriors and veterans through the development of evidence-based and restorative interventions; to support military-related health initiatives by building community partnerships; to investigate therapeutic interventions—particularly those involving canine assistance—that positively influence health outcomes; and to emphasize system planning, innovative public policy making, and thorough protocols of care development for the armed forces. One of C-P.A.W.W.'s goals is to continue to conduct research on the efficacy of service dogs by examining both biological and psychological correlates in order to provide the empirical evidence needed to support change in public policy regarding the reimbursement of service dogs for our military veterans (Krause-Parello, 2015). More information about this program can be found at www.nursing.fau.edu/c-paww.

Over time, dogs have played (and will continue to play) an important role in the lives of military service members and veterans. Initiatives like the P.A.W.S. Act (P.A.W.S. Act, 2017), Joining Forces, and C-P.A.W.W., as well as the growing number of dedicated grassroots service dog training organizations, are instrumental for promoting public education and awareness; providing supportive evidence regarding the benefits of service dogs for military members and veterans recovering from invisible wounds of war; and ultimately aiding veterans and other populations in obtaining service dogs at little or no cost. Creative, effective, and highly personalized interventions are urgently needed to help facilitate readjustment and post-deployment mental health and well-being in military and veteran populations. AAIs are an important step in the right direction to help change the lives of veterans—such as Corporal Lyndon R. Villone, with Ice by his side.

REFERENCES

Allen, K., Shykoff, B. E., & Izzo, J. L. (2001). Pet ownership, but not ACE inhibitor therapy, blunts home blood pressure responses to mental stress. *Hypertension, 38*(4), 815–820.

American Psychiatric Association. (2013). *Diagnostic and statistical manual of mental disorders: DSM-5*. Washington, DC: American Psychiatric Association.

Banks, M. R., & Banks, W. A. (2002). The effects of animal-assisted therapy on loneliness in an elderly population in long-term care facilities. *The Journals of Gerontology Series A: Biological Sciences and Medical Sciences, 57*(7), M428–M432.

Barker, S. B., & Dawson, K. S. (1998). The effects of animal-assisted therapy on anxiety ratings of hospitalized psychiatric patients. *Psychiatric Services, 49*(6), 797–801.

Barker, S. B., Knisely, J. S., McCain, N. L., Schubert, C. M., & Pandurangi, A. K. (2010). Exploratory study of stress-buffering response patterns from interaction with a therapy dog. *Anthrozoös, 23*(1), 79–91.

Barth, S., Kimerling, R., Pavao, J., McCutcheon, S., Batten, S., Dursa, E., Peterson, & M., Schneiderman, A. (2016). Military sexual trauma among recent veterans: Correlates of sexual assault and sexual harassment. *American Journal of Preventative Medicine, 50*(1), 77–86. https://doi.org/10.1016/j.amepre.2015.06.012

Bausum, A. (2014). *Sergeant Stubby: How a stray dog and his best friend helped win World War I and stole the heart of a nation*. Washington, DC: National Geographic.

Bremner, J. D., & Bremner, J. G. (2016). *Posttraumatic stress disorder: From neurobiology to treatment*. Hoboken, NJ: John Wiley & Sons.

Browe, A. (2014). From the archives: Red Cross dogs. American Red Cross. Retrieved from http://redcrosschat.org/2014/04/21/from-the-archives-red-cross-dogs/

Burrows, K. E., & Adams, C. L. (2008). Challenges of service-dog ownership for families with autistic children: Lessons for veterinary practitioners. *Journal of Veterinary Medical Education, 35*(4), 559–566.

Burrows, K. E., Adams, C. L., & Millman, S. T. (2008). Factors affecting behavior and welfare of service dogs for children with autism spectrum disorder. *Journal of Applied Animal Welfare Science, 11*(1), 42–62.

Chandrasekaran, R. (2014). A legacy of pain and pride. *Washington Post.* Retrieved from https://www.washingtonpost.com/sf/national/2014/03/29/a-legacy -of-pride-and-pain/?noredirect=on

Coppola, C. L., Grandin, T., & Enns, R. M. (2006). Human interaction and cortisol: Can human contact reduce stress for shelter dogs? *Physiology & Behavior, 87*(3), 537–541.

Daskalakis, N. P., McGill, M. A., Lehrner, A., & Yehuda, R. (2016). Endocrine aspects of PTSD: Hypothalamic-pituitary-adrenal (HPA) axis and beyond. *Comprehensive Guide to Post-Traumatic Stress Disorders,* 245–260.

Department of Veterans Affairs. (2016a). *Rehabilitation and prosthetic services.* Retrieved from http://www.prosthetics.va.gov/ServiceAndGuideDogs.asp

Department of Veterans Affairs. (2016b). *Suicide among veterans and other Americans: 2001–2014.* Data file. Retrieved from http://www.mentalhealth.va.gov /docs/2016suicidedatareport.pdf

Dozier, K. (2011, May 17). AP sources: Raiders, White House knew secret bin Laden raid was a one-shot deal. *Associated Press.* Retrieved from https://www.yahoo .com/news/ap-sources-raiders-knew-mission-one-shot-deal-070246711.html

Estrada, S. (n.d.). *Chips: Decorated war hero.* Retrieved from http://www.military .com/NewContent/0,13190,K9_051605,00.html

Foliente, R. (2009). Battle buddies' provide companionship, security in Iraq. *U.S. Department of Defense: DoD News.* http://archive.defense.gov/news/news article.aspx?id=52819

Friedmann, E., Thomas, S. A., & Son, H. (2011). Pets, depression and long-term survival in community living patients following myocardial infarction. *Anthrozoös, 24*(3), 273–285.

Frijling, J. L., van Zuiden, M., Koch, S. B., Nawijn, L., Veltman, D. J., & Olff, M. (2016). Intranasal oxytocin affects amygdala functional connectivity after trauma script-driven imagery in distressed recently trauma-exposed individuals. *Neuropsychopharmacology, 41*(5), 1286–1296.

Furst, G. (2016). Helping war veterans with posttraumatic stress disorder: Incarcerated individuals' role in therapeutic animal programs. *Journal of Psychosocial Nursing, 54*(5), 49–57.

Glenk, L. M., Kothgassner, O. D., Stetina, B. U., Palme, R., Kepplinger, B., & Baran, H. (2013). Therapy dogs' salivary cortisol levels vary during animal-assisted interventions. *Animal Welfare, 22*(3), 369–378. https://doi.org/10.7120/09627286.22.3.369

Graham, J., Legarreta, M., North, L., DiMuzio, J., McGlade, E., & Yurelun-Todd, D. (2016). A preliminary study of DSM-5 PTSD symptom patterns in veterans by trauma type. *Military Psychology, 28*(2), 115–122. https://doi.org/10.1037/mil0000092

Haagen, J. F., Smid, G. E., Knipscheer, J. W., & Kleber, R. J. (2015). The efficacy of recommended treatments for veterans with PTSD: A metaregression analysis. *Clinical Psychology Review, 40,* 184–194.

Halderman, F. (2013). Ben's story: A case study in holistic nursing and veteran trauma. *Holistic Nursing Practice, 27*(1), 34–36. https://doi.org/10.1097/HNP.0b013e318276fbb1

Handlin, L., Hydbring-Sandberg, E., Nilsson, A., Ejdebäck, M., Jansson, A., & Uvnäs-Moberg, K. (2011). Short-term interaction between dogs and their owners: Effects on oxytocin, cortisol, insulin, and heart rate—An exploratory study. *Anthrozoös, 24*(3), 301–315.

Handlin, L., Nilsson, A., Ejdebäck, M., Hydbring-Sandberg, E., & Uvnäs-Moberg, K. (2012). Associations between the psychological characteristics of the human–dog relationship and oxytocin and cortisol levels. *Anthrozoös, 25*(2), 215–228.

Harvey, A. G., Bryant, R. A., & Tarrier, N. (2003). Cognitive behaviour therapy for posttraumatic stress disorder. *Clinical Psychology Review, 23*(3), 501–552.

Haubenhofer, D. K., & Kirchengast, S. (2007). Dog handlers' and dogs' emotional and cortisol secretion responses associated with animal-assisted therapy sessions. *Society & Animals, 15,* 127–150. https://doi.org/10.1163/156853007x187090

Hoge, C., Auchterlonie J., & Milliken C. (2006). Mental health problems, use of mental health services, and attrition from military service after returning from deployment to Iraq or Afghanistan. *The Journal of the American Medical Association, 295*(9), 1023–1032.

Ipser, J. C., & Stein, D. J. (2012). Evidence-based pharmacotherapy of posttraumatic stress disorder (PTSD). *International Journal of Neuropsychopharmacology, 15*(6), 825–840.

Kamioka, H., Okada, S., Tsutani, K., Park, H., Okuizumi, H., Handa, S., Oshio, T., Park, S. J., Kitayuguchi, J., Abe, T., Honda, T., & Mutoh, Y. (2014). Effectiveness of animal-assisted therapy: A systematic review of randomized controlled trials. *Complementary Therapies in Medicine, 22*(2), 371–390.

Kimerling, R., Gima, K., Smith, M., Street, A., & Frayne, S. (2007). The Veterans Health Administration and military sexual trauma. *American Journal of Public Health, 97*(12), 2160–2166. https://doi.org/10.2105/AJPH.2006.092999

King, C., Watters, J., & Mungre, S. (2011). Effect of a time-out session with working animal-assisted therapy dogs. *Journal of Veterinary Behavior: Clinical Applications and Research, 6*(4), 232–238. https://doi.org/10.1016/j.jveb.2011.01.007

Koch, S. B., van Zuiden, M., Nawijn, L., Frijling, J. L., Veltman, D. J., & Olff, M. (2016a). Intranasal oxytocin administration dampens amygdala reactivity towards emotional faces in male and female PTSD patients. *Neuropsychopharmacology, 41*(6), 1495–504. https://doi.org/10.1038/npp.2015.299

Koch, S. B., van Zuiden, M., Nawijn, L., Frijling, J. L., Veltman, D. J., & Olff, M. (2016b). Intranasal oxytocin normalizes amygdala functional connectivity in posttraumatic stress disorder. *Neuropsychopharmacology, 41*(8), 2041–51. https://doi.org/10.1038/npp.2016.1

Koda, N., Watanabe, G., Miyaji, Y., Kuniyoshi, M., Miyaji, C., & Hirata, T. (2016). Effects of a dog-assisted intervention assessed by salivary cortisol concentrations in inmates of a Japanese prison. *Asian Journal of Criminology,* 1–11.

Krause-Parello, C. A. (2012). Pet ownership and older women: The relationships among loneliness, pet attachment support, human social support, and depressed mood. *Geriatric Nursing, 33*(3), 194–203.

Krause-Parello, C. A. (2015). Nurses answer the call to enhance veteran and military health. *American Nurse Today, 10*(5).

Krause-Parello, C. A., & Friedmann, E. (2014). The effects of an animal-assisted intervention on salivary alpha-amylase, salivary immunoglobulin A, and heart rate during forensic interviews in child sexual abuse cases. *Anthrozoös, 27*(4), 581–590.

Krause-Parello, C. A., & Gulick, E. (2013). Situational factors related to loneliness and loss over time among older pet-owners. *Western Journal of Nursing Research, 35*(7), 905–919.

Krause-Parello, C. A., & Kolassa, J. (2016). Pet therapy: Enhancing social and cardiovascular wellness in community dwelling older adults. *Journal of Community Health Nursing, 33*(1), 1–10.

Krause-Parello, C. A., Levy, C., Holman, E., & Kolassa, J. (2016). Effects of VA facility dog on hospitalized veterans seen by a palliative care psychologist: An innovative approach to impacting stress indicators. *American Journal of Hospice and Palliative Medicine,* 1–10.

Krause-Parello, C. A., & Morales, K. (2018). Military veterans and service dogs: A qualitative inquiry using interpretive phenomenological analysis. *Anthrozoös, 31*(1), 65–75.

Krause-Parello, C. A., Sarni, S., & Padden, E. (2016). Military veterans and canine assistance for post-traumatic stress disorder: A narrative review of the literature. *Nurse Education Today-Special Edition: Military.*

Krause-Parello, C. A., Tychowski, J., Gonzalez, A., & Boyd, Z. (2012). Human–canine interaction: Exploring stress indicator response patterns of salivary cortisol and immunoglobulin A. *Research and Theory for Nursing Practice, 26*(1), 25–40.

Lee, C., Felix, E., Levitt, R., Eddy, C., Vanner, E., Feuer, W., Sarantopoulos, C. & Galor, A. (2017). Traumatic brain injury, dry eye and comorbid pain diagnoses in US veterans. *British Journal of Ophthalmology, 0,* 1–7. https://doi.org/10.1136/bjophthalmol-2017-310509

Lefebvre, D., Giffroy, J. M., & Diederich, C. (2009). Cortisol and behavioral responses to enrichment in military working dogs. *Journal of Ethology, 27*(2), 255.

Lefkowitz, C., Paharia, I., Prout, M., Debiak, D., & Bleiberg, J. (2005). Animal-assisted prolonged exposure: A treatment for survivors of sexual assault suffering posttraumatic stress disorder. *Society & Animals, 13*(4), 275–295.

Lehrner, A., Daskalakis, N., & Yehuda, R. (2016). Cortisol and the hypothalamic-pituitary-adrenal axis in PTSD. *Posttraumatic Stress Disorder: From Neurobiology to Treatment,* 265.

McCullough, A., Jenkins, M. A., Ruehrdanz, A., Gilmer, M. J., Olson, J., Pawar, A., . . . O'Haire, M. E. (2018). Physiological and behavioral effects of animal-assisted interventions for therapy dogs in pediatric oncology settings. *Applied Animal Behaviour Science, 200,* 86–95.

Mott, M. (2003). Dogs of war: Inside the U.S. military's canine corps. *National Geographic News.* Retrieved from http://news.nationalgeographic.com/news/2003/04/0409_030409_militarydogs.html

Myers, B., McKlveen, J. M., & Herman, J. P. (2012). Neural regulation of the stress response: The many faces of feedback. *Cellular and Molecular Neurobiology, 32*(5), 683–694.

Nagasawa, M., Mitsui, S., En, S., Ohtani, N., Ohta, M., Sakuma, Y., Onaka, T., Mogi, K., & Kikusui, T. (2015). Oxytocin-gaze positive loop and the coevolution of human-dog bonds. *Science, 348*(6232), 333–336.

Nimer, J., & Lundahl, B. (2007). Animal-assisted therapy: A meta-analysis. *Anthrozoös, 20*(3), 225–238.

O'Haire, M. E., Guérin, N. A., & Kirkham, A. C. (2015). Animal-assisted intervention for trauma: A systematic literature review. *Frontiers in Psychology, 6.*

Olff, M., Langeland, W., Witteveen, A., & Denys, D. (2010). A psychobiological rationale for oxytocin in the treatment of posttraumatic stress disorder. *CNS Spectrums, 15*(08), 522–530.

Owen, R., Finton, B., Gibbons, S., & DeLeon, P. (2016). Canine-assisted adjunct therapy in the military: An intriguing alternative modality. *Journal for Nurse Practitioners*, *12*(2), 95–101.

P.A.W.S. Act. (2017). Puppies Assisting Wounded Service members (PAWS) Act of 2017—H.R. 2327. Retrieved from https://www.congress.gov/115/bills /hr2327/BILLS-115hr2327ih.pdf

Polheber, J. P., & Matchock, R. L. (2014). The presence of a dog attenuates cortisol and heart rate in the Trier Social Stress Test compared to human friends. *Journal of Behavioral Medicine*, *37*(5), 860–867.

Rauch, S. A., Defever, E., Favorite, T., Duroe, A., Garrity, C., Martis, B., & Liberzon, I. (2009). Prolonged exposure for PTSD in a Veterans Health Administration PTSD clinic. *Journal of Traumatic Stress*, *22*(1), 60–64.

Rauch, S. L., Shin, L. M., & Phelps, E. A. (2006). Neurocircuitry models of post-traumatic stress disorder and extinction: Human neuroimaging research—past, present, and future. *Biology Psychiatry*, *60*(4), 376–382.

Reporter's Notebook, & Russo, K. (2011) War dogs: U.S. Soldiers talk about the comfort of having dogs with their unit in Afghanistan. Retrieved from https://abcnews .go.com/International/war-dogs-us-soldiers-afghanistan-talk-comfort-dogs /story?id=13537829

Richardson, J. D., Contractor, A. A., Armour, C., Cyr, K. S., Elhai, J. D., & Sareen, J. (2014). Predictors of long-term treatment outcome in combat and peacekeeping veterans with military-related PTSD. *The Journal of Clinical Psychiatry*, *75*(11), 1299–1305.

Russell, S. (2017). Sergeant Stubby: An unlikely hero of WWI. *War History Online*. Retrieved from https://www.warhistoryonline.com/world-war-i/sergeant -stubby-unlikeliest-hero-wwi.html/2

Schmidle, N. (2011). Getting Bin Laden: What happened that night in Abbottabad. *New Yorker*. Retrieved from https://www.newyorker.com/magazine /2011/08/08/getting-bin-laden

Schottenbauer, M. A., Glass, C. R., Arnkoff, D. B., Tendick, V., & Gray, S. H. (2008). Nonresponse and dropout rates in outcome studies on PTSD: Review and methodological considerations. *Psychiatry*, *71*(2), 134–168.

Shalev, A. Y., Bonne, O., & Eth, S. (1996). Treatment of posttraumatic stress disorder: A review. *Psychosomatic Medicine*, *58*, 165–182.

Shin, L. M., Rauch, S. L., & Pitman, R. K. (2006). Amygdala, medial prefrontal cortex, and hippocampal function in PTSD. *Annals of the New York Academy of Sciences*, *1071*(1), 67–79.

Shin, L. M., Shin, P. S., Heckers, S., Krangel, T. S., Macklin, M. L., Orr, S. P., . . .

Rauch, S. L. (2004). Hippocampal function in posttraumatic stress disorder. *Hippocampus, 14*(3), 292–300.

Souter, M. A., & Miller, M. D. (2007). Do animal-assisted activities effectively treat depression? A meta-analysis. *Anthrozoös, 20*(2), 167–180.

Starcevic, A., Postic, S., Radojicic, Z., Starcevic, B., Milovanovic, S., Ilankovic, A., Dimitrijevic, I., Damjanovic, A., Aksic, M., & Radonjic, V. (2014). Volumetric analysis of amygdala, hippocampus, and prefrontal cortex in therapy-naive PTSD participants. *BioMed Research International*, Article ID 968495.

Stone, D. M., Simon T. R., Fowler K. A,. Kegler, S. R., Yuan, K., Holland, K. M., Ivey-Stephenson, A. Z., & Crosby, A. E. (2018). Vital signs: Trends in state suicide rates—United States, 1999–2016 and circumstances contributing to suicide—27 states, 2015. *Morbidity Mortality Weekly Report, 67*, 617–624. https://doi.org/10.15585/mmwr.mm6722a1

Street, A., Vogt, D., & Dutra, L. (2009). A new generation of women veterans: Stressors faced by women deployed to Iraq and Afghanistan. *Clinical Psychology Review, 29*, 685–394. https://doi.org/10.1016/j.cpr.2009.08.007

Taylor, M., Edwards, M., & Pooley, J. (2013). "Nudging them back to reality:" Toward a growing public acceptance of the role dogs fulfill in ameliorating contemporary veterans' PTSD symptoms. *Anthrozoös, 26*(4), 593–611.

Tuerk, P. W., Yoder, M., Grubaugh, A., Myrick, H., Hamner, M., & Acierno, R. (2011). Prolonged exposure therapy for combat-related posttraumatic stress disorder: An examination of treatment effectiveness for veterans of the wars in Afghanistan and Iraq. *Journal of Anxiety Disorders, 25*(3), 397–403.

Tyson, P. (2012). *Dogs' dazzling sense of smell*. NOVA scienceNOW. Retrieved from http://www.pbs.org/wgbh/nova/nature/dogs-sense-of-smell.html

US War Dogs (n.d.). Types of war dogs. Retrieved from http://www.uswardogs .org/war-dog-history/types-war-dogs/

Vincent, C., Belleville, G., Gagnon, D., Dumont, F., Auger, E., Lavoie, V., Besemann, M., Champagne, N. & Lessart, G. (2017). Effectiveness of service dogs for veterans with PTSD: Preliminary outcomes. In P. Cudd and L. de Witte (Eds.), *Harnessing the power of technology to improve lives* (pp. 130–136). Amsterdam: IOS Press. https://doi.org/10.3233/978-1-61499-798-6-130

Watts, B. V., Schnurr, P. P., Mayo, L., Young-Xu, Y., Weeks, W. B., & Friedman, M. J. (2013). Meta-analysis of the efficacy of treatments for posttraumatic stress disorder. *The Journal of Clinical Psychiatry, 74*(6), 541–550.

Weinmeyer, R. (2015). Service dogs for veterans with posttraumatic stress disorder. *American Journal Association Journal of Ethics, 17*(6), 547–552.

Woon, F. L., Sood, S., & Hedges, D. W. (2010). Hippocampal volume deficits associated with exposure to psychological trauma and posttraumatic stress disorder in adults: A meta-analysis. *Progress in Neuro-Psychopharmacology and Biological Psychiatry*, *34*(7), 1181–1188.

World Health Organization. (2004). *The World Health Report 2004: Changing history. Annex Table 3: Burden of disease in DALYs by cause, sex, and mortality stratum in WHO regions, estimates for 2002; A126–A127*. Geneva: WHO Publishing.

Yehuda, R. (2002). Post-traumatic stress disorder. *New England Journal of Medicine*, *346*(2), 108–114.

Zimmerman, D. J. (2014). *Chips: War dog hero of the 3rd infantry*. Defense Media Network. Retrieved from https://www.defensemedianetwork.com/stories /chips-war-dog-hero-of-the-3rd-infantry-division/

Zinzow, H., Grubaugh, A., Monnier, J., Suffoletta-Maierle, S., & Frueh, B. (2007). Trauma among female veterans: A critical review. *Trauma, Violence, & Abuse*, *8*(4), 384–400. https://doi.org/10.1177/1524838007307295

ABOUT THE AUTHORS

Cheryl A. Krause-Parello, PhD, RN, FAAN is a professor at Florida Atlantic University in the Christine E. Lynn College of Nursing (CELCON), and a faculty fellow in the Institute for Healthy Aging and Lifespan Studies (I-HeAL). Krause-Parello completed her PhD in nursing research at Rutgers University, where she developed a program of human-animal interaction research. She has also developed, and is the director of, a university-based health research initiative for veterans (C-P.A.W.W.; www.nursing.fau .edu/c-paww). The long-term goal of her program of research is to implement effective interventions to modulate the long-term effects of PTSD on returning active duty military and veterans, and to identify additional populations where this intervention will be effective. One of Krause-Parello's prospective goals is to provide the evidence to support changes in public policy so that service dogs will be covered as a reimbursable medical expense for those recovering from invisible service connected conditions.

Allison E. Boyrer, MS, MA, BSN, RN is a faculty member at the University of Colorado, College of Nursing at the Anschutz Medical Campus. She is a graduate of Syracuse University (BSN); the University of South

Florida (MA in physical education); and the University of Colorado (MS in nursing: veteran and military health care). She is currently pursuing her doctoral degree in education (EdD) for executive leadership at the University of Colorado School of Education and Human Development. Boyrer serves as the coordinator of Strategic Partnerships for the College of Nursing, connecting community to practice.

Eleni Padden, BA, is a graduate of Johns Hopkins University in Baltimore, Maryland. After obtaining her bachelor's degree in 2015, Padden served as a research assistant for the Canines Providing Assistance for Wounded Warriors (C.P.A.W.W.) nonprofit research initiative, under the supervision of Dr. Cheryl Krause-Parello at the Anschutz Medical Campus. She is currently working toward becoming a clinical social worker and public health scientist, and hopes to serve the veteran population over the course of her career via therapy and innovative policy making.

CHAPTER 11

The Battle for Hearts and Minds: Warrior Canine Connection's Mission-Based Trauma Recovery Program

Rick A. Yount, LSW; Robert Koffman, MD; and Meg D. Olmert

Fourteen years of war in Afghanistan and Iraq have taken a devastating toll on a large percentage of the 2.7 million service members who carried out these military missions. Post-traumatic stress disorder (PTSD) and traumatic brain injury (TBI) are the signature wounds of these wars, and among the most difficult to treat. Despite the billions of dollars being spent on medical care for veterans, hundreds of thousands continue to suffer the debilitating effects of these "invisible wounds." Warrior Canine Connection's (WCC's) *Mission Based Trauma Recovery*^{SM} (MBTR) program is an innovative animal-assisted therapy initiative now offered within major military and VA medical centers. This chapter will present MBTR's clinically based methodology, scientific rationale, and one case study that will demonstrate the program's therapeutic impact and success.

BACKGROUND AND SIGNIFICANCE

The United States deployed 2.7 million service members in military operations in Afghanistan and Iraq between 2001 and 2011. A 2015 Congressional Research Service Report estimates that since the start of combat operations, 177,461 service members were diagnosed with PTSD, and an additional 327,299 suffered TBI (Fischer, 2015). A 2012 report to Congress found that 26% of returning veterans who sought medical treatment through the Veteran's Health Administration (VHA) were diagnosed with PTSD. This report cautioned that these numbers do not reflect the true physical and mental toll of combat trauma, since almost 50% of veterans do not seek medical care through the VHA (Congressional Budget Office, 2012). Nor do these statistics factor in the disruption to military families when spouses/partners and relatives need to alter their lives and employment schedules to care for loved ones (Bilmes, 2013).

Despite the $23.6 billion dollars spent on veteran health care between 2001 and 2013 (Fischer, 2013), many veterans continue to suffer from PTSD and TBI. Recent US Army studies reveal that less than 50% of soldiers with a PTSD diagnosis receive treatment and, of those who do, 20–40% drop out before completion (Levin, 2012). According to Major Gary Wynn, a PTSD research psychiatrist at the Uniformed Services University of Health Sciences in Bethesda, Maryland, veterans' treatment resistance and dropout rates result mainly from a lack of trust in health care providers and the stigma of a PTSD diagnosis. Major Wynn sees these disturbing statistics as a mandate to better match therapies with patient preference, and to "disguise" mental health care as primary care or thorough alternative interventions (Levin, 2012).

THE TROJAN DOG EFFECT

In 2008, licensed social worker and professional service dog trainer Rick Yount set out to do exactly that. Yount recognized that mobility service dog training could provide unique experiential opportunities to learn, or relearn, emotional and behavioral skills impaired by combat trauma. He also knew that thousands of veterans were waiting years to be partnered with skilled service dogs that are trained to provide the mobility and/ or emotional support that can change their lives. Under the legitimate guise of a mission to train a service dog for another wounded warrior, Yount created a service dog training program that inspired even the most treatment-resistant patients to pick up a leash and discover the therapeutic benefits embedded in training great dogs for the purpose of helping a fellow wounded veteran.

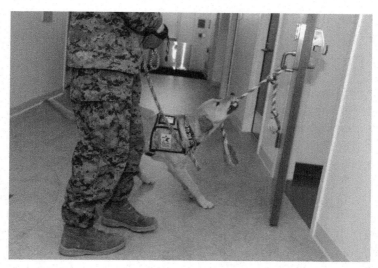

A Warrior Trainer (MS) works with service dog-in-training, Ron. (Photo by Bonnie Grower/WCC. Used with permission from WCC.)

Yount was invited to launch this innovative mission-based trauma program at the Men's and Women's Trauma Recovery Program at the Veterans Hospital in Menlo Park, California. Over the next two years, this volunteer program—operating as part of Recreation Therapy Services—proved to be highly popular, as indicated by participant and caregiver feedback and its very low dropout rate. Approximately 200 service members participated in the initial pilot program, five service dogs were placed with veterans, and two program volunteers went on to become accredited, professional service dog trainers.

In 2009, Yount and the Menlo Park VA team were asked to present anecdotal observations of the pilot program's success at the Veterans Administration National Mental Health Conference, and at the annual meeting of the International Society for Traumatic Stress Studies. The following are the clinical observations they presented that support the program's ability to reduce a wide range of combat PTSD symptoms (Yount, Olmert, & Lee, 2012):

- Increased patience, impulse control, and emotional regulation
- Improved ability to display affect and decreased emotional numbness

- Improved sleep
- Decreased depression and increased positive sense of purpose
- Decreased startle responses
- Decreased pain perception
- Increased sense of belonging/acceptance
- Increased assertive communication skills
- Improved parenting skills and family dynamics
- Fewer war stories and more in-the-moment thinking
- Lower stress levels, and an increased sense of calm

In 2009, Yount was invited to establish this program model at the Warrior Transition Brigade at Walter Reed Hospital, in Washington, DC. In 2011, he established the nonprofit Warrior Canine Connection, Inc., to support, expand, and constantly improve the quality of WCC's unique MBTR model. WCC's MBTR program is staffed by professional service dog trainers and purpose-bred dogs. Currently, MBTR is a highly valued complementary intervention supporting goal achievement in traditional PTSD and TBI treatment modalities, such as cognitive and behavioral health; substance abuse treatment; and occupational, recreational, and family therapies at the National Intrepid Center of Excellence (NICoE) in Bethesda, Maryland; the Menlo Park, Virginia Hospital; and the Marcus Institute for Brain Health in Denver, Colorado.

WCC is also reaching out to help the many thousands of veterans whose struggles have resulted in serious legal trouble, and has become a highly effective component of Veterans Treatment Court (VTC) programs across the country. VTC programs provide treatment and rehabilitative restitution programs as alternatives to incarceration for veterans with combat trauma. WCC's model was first piloted in the Albuquerque, New Mexico, VTC program in 2015 by WCC's partners, Assistance Dogs of the West. Additionally, WCC launched MBTR programming in three California VTC programs (San Francisco, Santa Clara, and San Mateo) in 2016, and was invited to bring MBTR to the Baltimore City, Maryland and Asheville, North Carolinal, VTC programs in 2018. VTC judges, parole officers, and court officials have embraced the WCC MBTR model as a powerful and popular mission that enhances the veterans' sense of well-being and purpose on their road to recovery, restitution, and a meaningful, productive life.

MBTR: IT'S A FAMILY AFFAIR

According to the VA's National Center for PTSD, the emotional toll on military families struggling with PTSD has been shown to be severe and pervasive (Price & Stephens, 2017). The negative effects of PTSD on family relations create a debilitating feedback effect that exacerbates the veteran's PTSD symptoms, and further erodes family stability. The results can include compromised parenting, family violence, divorce and sexual problems, aggression, and caregiver burden (Price & Stephens, 2017). This knock-on effect reverberating through military families suffering from PTSD extends the tragic cost of war into generations to come. As such, MBTR considers supporting military families as a "no-fail mission."

Service members go through intense experiential training to become warfighters, including tasks to become acutely reactive to threat, as well as able to suppress emotions that would inhibit their performance in battle. This military training often creates challenges when highly vigilant, emotionally numb warfighters return home to their families.

WCC's warrior trainers are taught service dog training skills that are based on the values and best practices of family-focused social work. Bonding with and shaping the behavior of young dogs offer unlimited

MS walking with Birdie, his daughter, and RY's daughter. (Photo by Bonnie Grower/WCC. Used with permission from WCC.)

experiential training opportunities for wounded warriors to practice patience, empathy, and consistency. Service members are also coached to use positive expressions of emotion and praise to enhance their dog's training performance. Expressing—even feeling—positive emotions can be very challenging for our volunteer trainers. However, through the training process, they see how their emotional efforts immediately capture their dog's attention and improve their ability to perform a command. Both partners are rewarded with a sense of accomplishment and joy. Many program participants have reported that regaining their ability to express positive emotions with the dogs has improved their sense of well-being and has had a significant impact on their family dynamics (Tedeschi, Sisa, Olmert, Parish-Plass, & Yount, 2015).

ENSURING HEALTHY AND HAPPY SERVICE DOG/VETERAN BONDS

Given the large number of service members who will potentially work with a WCC dog over the two-year training cycle, it is critically important to choose the right dogs for this work, and to prepare them for the various tasks they will perform. WCC has a very well developed breeding program that breeds Golden and Labrador retrievers, with a focus on canine health and temperament. WCC puppies receive a tremendous amount of early socialization from a multitude of devoted volunteers, thereby instilling in the pups a sense of trust and love for humans. Careful breeding selection and early socialization set the dogs up for success, as well as ensure that they will thrive from the attention that they receive from their multiple warrior trainers.

In addition to the nature/nurture considerations described above, WCC dogs benefit from our close partnership with the staff of Olney-Sandy Spring Veterinary Hospital (an accredited member of the American Animal Hospital Association), who provide expert medical care and consultation throughout the life cycle of the dogs. Furthermore, WCC dogs are also examined annually by board certified ophthalmologists and cardiologists. Preplacement veterinary exams that include the veteran partner who will receive the dog (whenever possible) help establish the important relationship between the veterinarian and veteran recipient. Likewise, WCC's Dog Program specialists provide ongoing support to the veteran/dog team, and maintain communication with them throughout the life of the dog.

Ensuring a successful match between the dog and veteran recipient is another critical consideration. WCC carefully assesses both task needs and individual personalities prior to placement. Instead of "E-Harmony," WCC uses "D-Harmony" to ensure that veteran and dog profiles are a match. Expert screening of veteran recipients by qualified mental health professionals is also essential in determining how the partnership dynamic can enhance the well-being of both the veteran and the dog.

Over the last decade, WCC has been able to reach out across the country to an increasing number of warriors in-need. Over 5,000 service members, veterans, and their families have volunteered to be part of this vital healing mission, with the overwhelming majority reporting an increased sense of well-being and purpose from participation in the program. This growing "canine corp" of warrior-trainers has also helped WCC partner (at no cost) 62 Assistance Dogs with veterans in need of mobility, psychosocial, and/or family support.

CASE STUDY OF MBTR

The following is a case study of a former WCC Warrior Trainer (henceforth referred to as "MS") whose experience illustrates the ways in which this innovative service dog training program can reduce a wide range of psychosocial and behavioral effects of combat-related PTSD. The case study includes (in italics) the volunteer testimony of MS and excerpts from "Training a Dog to Train Me," a paper MS wrote for a college psychology class he completed while in treatment at Walter Reed. In addition, we present case notes from the two authors who participated in his treatment for PTSD. Rick Yount ("RY") was MS's clinical service dog trainer, and Captain Robert Koffman, MD ("RK") was senior consultant for integrative medicine and behavioral health at NICoE during the patient's course of treatment (Koffman, now retired, serves as WCC's chief medical advisor).

RK: MS, a 25-year-old marine sergeant, served eight years of active military duty, including three combat deployments to Iraq and Afghanistan, during which he engaged in numerous firefights and endured the loss of several fellow marines. He was also exposed to multiple blast events, the most significant in 2010 when an IED detonated, destroying his vehicle and causing loss of consciousness for approximately three to five minutes. Following his third and most traumatic deployment, he experienced persistent hypervigilance, marked arousal, reexperiencing phenomena (i.e., nightly nightmares), and profound emotional blunting. While at the military treatment facility at his home base, he was diagnosed with PTSD, mild TBI with chronic headache, and insomnia. The service member began standard PTSD treatment, including pharmacotherapy with selective serotonergic uptake inhibitors (SSRIs) and cognitive behavioral therapy.

In July 2011, MS was referred to NICoE's intensive four-week treatment plan due to worsening symptoms of PTSD and TBI, including persistent and intractable headaches, near syncope (or the temporary loss of consciousness due to low blood pressure that worsens with exertion) and, perhaps most troubling, irritability, anger, marked hyperarousal, and startle. Insomnia was also chronic and unmanageable. Chronic pain exacerbated all neuropsychiatric conditions. During treatment at NICoE, MS lived in Fischer House apartments on the Walter Reed base.

MS's psychological testing at NICoE revealed short-term memory and processing speed deficits, most likely associated with his TBI. While at NICoE, MS was offered group, individual, and supportive psychotherapy. He was also given the opportunity to engage in various integrative modalities including expressive arts therapy (i.e., mask-making and journaling), yoga, meditation, acupuncture, biofeedback (i.e., autogenic training and breathing exercises), and WCC's Mission-Based Trauma Recovery Program.

MS: When I first arrived at NICoE in 2011, I hadn't slept decent in months. I would go days on end with no sleep, before finally crashing and getting a couple hours of broken sleep. Pills didn't help, and none of the other sleep hygiene stuff was working. It affected everything I did. I didn't have any energy, was always in a bad mood. I was always in pain and irritated and had very little patience, which was likely exacerbated by the sleep deficiencies, and I was generally just frustrated with life.

About a week into my treatment, I told a nurse I liked dogs better than people, and she suggested I check out the Warrior Canine Connection program. I agreed and met with Rick Yount and several of the dogs in the program. We discussed his program, and how the dogs needed training so they could be placed with veterans coming back with physical impairments. I have always loved dogs—so just getting to spend time with them, it seemed like a no-brainer for me.

RY: On MS's first visit to our WCC office, I gave him an overview of what he would need to do to help train a service dog for a fellow veteran, including practicing patience and learning to praise the dog with positive affect. When I referred to the praise voice as similar to "Richard Simmons," MS hesitated a bit, but agreed to participate, knowing that he would be able to have a positive impact on another veteran's life by training a service dog for him/her.

MS: One of my favorite memories of the program was the day I was introduced to [WCC dogs] Olive and Birdie. Both were about a year old, but with vastly different personalities. Olive was a sweetheart and had lots of energy, while Birdie was a little different than the dogs I knew when I was growing up. He was a bit more mellow and laid back, but had a mind of his own sometimes, which I figured would require a lot more patience and motivation—things I didn't think I still had at the time. Rick let me work with both dogs in the beginning on basic tasks like sit and down. After a few days, Rick had asked which dog I preferred working with, and I instantly responded Olive. Rick seemed to think otherwise, and proceeded to tell me I would be working with Birdie primarily. He was a wise man.

RY: MS seemed to take pride in the service dog training skills he was acquiring. He was learning how to include effective communication, patience, and to express positive affect to reinforce the dogs' behaviors. The WCC dogs that MS helped to train gave honest and immediate feedback that let him know what worked and didn't work. We coached MS to build his relationships with the dogs, and to try to sound as genuinely happy as possible (even when he wasn't), because the dogs would respond better to this level of encouragement. Not only did this positive effort improve

MS's attitude, but he clearly saw how quickly it improved his dog training skills as well.

MS: After a week or so working with the dogs, and mostly Birdie, I looked forward to coming in each day, and made it a point to get to the office in between my appointments to see the dogs and work with Birdie. We had developed a bond and he was as eager to work with me as I was with him. It is a tedious process some-times, breaking larger tasks into smaller ones, and it didn't always click for him right away, which challenged a lot of the issues I was struggling with. But, while frustrating at times, watching him succeed in performing tasks was exciting.

RK: Heart rate variability (HRV)—the heart's ability to effectively respond to, and recover from, stress—is essential to healthy heart function. Dysregulation of HRV is a common condition in those with PTSD and TBI (Edmondson & Cohen, 2013). MS's HRV patterns were consistently irregular. Two measures were taken to compare MS's HRV profile after breathing relaxation techniques and while accompanied by a WCC dog. Only the presence of the WCC dog produced significant improvement of MS's HRV functioning.

MS: Recently a nurse monitored my HRV measures while I had one of the WCC dogs on my lap. My heart rate was in the green zone—the healthy zone—for the first time.

RK: MS's case was one of the most challenging we had seen at NICoE. While at NICoE, MS experienced an acute worsening of his depression, accompanied by periods of suicidal ideation. MS's aggravated headaches and lack of sleep likely contributed to his increased sense of hopelessness and subsequent despair. He was transferred to a general medical ward for a full dihydoergotamine (DHE) protocol for intractable headaches, and to try different medications to control his PTSD symptoms. Even the DHE pro-tocol was not very successful. Due to his symptom severity and need for additional treatment, his four-week stay at NICoE was doubled. Up until MS's arrival, no patient had remained in our care for that long.

MS: After a few more weeks, Birdie started coming with me to my appointments. Just having him in the room with me made me a lot less anxious.

RY: MS would come to our office and sleep with the dogs on their beds. At Menlo Park, I had seen how patients with severe insomnia were able to get a good night's sleep with a program dog at their side. In anticipation of MS's ultimate discharge, realizing that usual care for PTSD and TBI was not entirely effective in MS's case, I discussed the idea of documenting the benefit of sleeping with a WCC dog that MS initially reported at NICoE. MS's sleep doctor agreed. Through actigraphy, the sleep doctor confirmed MS's severe insomnia markedly improved with Birdie by his side. Subsequently, we were able to get permission from the Fischer House manager for Birdie to sleep with MS on an ongoing basis.

RK: Actigraphy measures taken on two nights with sleep medication showed that, despite medication, MS had frequent movement during the sleep periods. The next night, MS took sleep medication but also slept with Birdie. Actigraph readings showed that, with Birdie, MS had a more consolidated sleep period, less activity, and improved sleep efficiency.

MS: With Birdie at my side—sleep! Almost every night! It was magnificent! And it progressed my treatment tenfold. I was slowly becoming more like Birdie—the mellow, more laid back dog. Birdie had taught me patience, and gave me motivation to get up each morning. He had almost single-handedly corrected many of my sleep problems.

RK: MS was legally separated from his wife following his stay at NICoE. He maintained shared custody of his four-year-old daughter throughout his treatment while residing both on base and at an off-base apartment.

RY: MS was often accompanied by his four-year-old daughter. MS was in an impossible position of caring for a four-year-old while in treatment and only getting two hours of sleep on a good night. His daughter would sit solemnly in a chair in our office and appeared to be shut down as a result of her father's parenting style, which at this point was authoritative and lacking patience. I decided to try having MS take Birdie overnight while his daughter was visiting. The sleepovers with Birdie turned out to have a profound impact, not just on MS's sleep, but also on his relationship with his daughter and other family members.

MS: I was also given the opportunity to take the dog I bonded with overnight while my four-year-old daughter was visiting. She could see a different side of me. Instead of being a strict father, she and the dog were getting praised for doing something right, rather than being punished for something they did wrong. It brought to light a different parenting technique that she responded to better. The dog allowed us to connect in a very positive way. Working with the dog has taught me patience, which also carries over to being a parent. I credit the judge's favorable decisions in the custody case of my daughter to the parenting skills I mastered while working with Birdie.

RK: MS's symptom reduction improvement followed his involvement with WCC's Birdie. As reported and demonstrated by actigraphy, the service member enjoyed restorative sleep for the first time since his redeployment years earlier. Moreover, improvements in his mood, sleep, and concentration, as well as increased energy, indicated that he was experiencing a decrease in his depression. MS also reported a decrease in pain. MS was discharged after completing the extended NICoE treatment course in significantly better condition. After, MS began the process of applying for a medical retirement from the military. He remained on medical hold for the next 12 months and continued to be treated at Walter Reed.

RY: MS's involvement in the WCC program increased over the months as he prepared to transition out of the military. This led to his decision to request permission from his commanding officer to work full-time as an intern with WCC. MS's internship was supported by the Marine Corps' Wounded Warrior Regiment.

MS: The dogs have a drive to work and take care of people. They do so because they care, not because they have to. It's great knowing that I am helping to train a service dog for a service member who has physical disabilities.

RY: MS's personal and medical progress was paralleled by his success as a service dog trainer. Not only did he become an advanced service dog trainer, but he helped teach other WCC participants on how to train the dogs. MS volunteered to participate in dozens of MBTR public presentations and speaking engagements to senior military and civilian community leaders to share the benefits he felt he gained from the program. MS was also able to attend and complete a college psychology class. The class paper he wrote, "Training a Dog to Train Me," was an account of how the WCC program was helping him regain control of his life, and teaching him how to be the father his daughter needed. As MS's training skills improved and the relationship with Birdie deepened, he was given permission to become Birdie's foster parent and keep the dog with him in his room during the 14 months MS was on medical hold at Walter Reed.

MS: Birdie reduced a lot of the abrasive personality I had accrued over the past year, and allowed me to be able to be out in public without being overwhelmed.

RY: After nearly two years of MS's increasing involvement with WCC, the time came to decide which veteran would receive Birdie as a service dog partner. This can be an emotional time for the trainers who have developed strong, healing bonds with the dogs. It is our experience that the pride of being part of the mission to train a dog for another warrior in need proves greater than any sense of personal loss of that particular relationship. In the few cases where patients felt significant sadness, clinicians found those emotions provided therapeutic insight into deeper loss the patient had experienced in combat, but had not yet processed. This is especially significant in treating veterans who are struggling with survivor's guilt. MS, on the other hand, had made his peace with passing Birdie's leash on to another deserving veteran. But MS's pending retirement and therapeutic recovery presented another option. The undeniable synchrony of social style, assertiveness, and responsiveness that had developed between him and Birdie made the choice clear: MS and Birdie were a perfect match.

MS: About the time Birdie was finishing his training, I was leaving Walter Reed. He was going to be heading on to bigger and better things, and I was moving forward as well. The bulk of my treatment was done, and I was moving back home to be with my daughter and start the next chapter in my life. To my surprise, I got a phone call from WCC shortly before I left, informing me that Birdie was going to be placed with me as my service dog. I couldn't believe it!

RY: With Birdie at his side, MS returned home and to civilian life. Since then, he has introduced this program to his local Veteran's Administration Medical Center. MS continues to work with WCC, doing public outreach and sharing his experiences with Birdie and the WCC program to offer hope for other veterans who are struggling with the invisible wounds of war. MS maintains primary custody of his daughter and has established a very healthy relationship with her, along with a stable relationship with his current girlfriend and her younger son.

MS: My family has also noticed a difference in the way I interact with them as a result of what I learned and experienced while training my service dog. I am patient with my children when they are around, I haven't yelled at them in several months, and they aren't afraid of me when I'm around. I think that is a direct result of working with my dog. I remain so grateful to everyone at WCC for such a great gift! And I will forever be grateful to the big black behemoth lying next to me as I write this. Birdie has changed me back to the person I once was, and maybe even better. While I will likely always struggle with some of my deficiencies, he hasn't skipped a beat in being there right beside me helping me through them and to overcome them.

GIVING THE DOG ITS SCIENTIFIC DUE

Given the dire need for compelling, safe, and effective treatment for PTSD, as well as the long wait and high cost for skilled service dogs, the WCC model offers a clinically sound, cost-effective, and non-pharmaceutical way to help meet these critical military goals. The therapeutic success of WCC's MBTR program has garnered unprecedented military, veteran, and Congressional support.

In 2014, WCC's research partners at the Uniformed Services University of Health Science (USU) Consortium for Health and Military Performance were awarded funding by the U.S. Army Medical Research and Materiel Command to conduct a randomized (wait-list) controlled trial to investigate the psychological, physiological, and neurobiological effects of six hours of MBTR participation on 20 Walter Reed patients with PTSD. The effects of MBTR on the HRV performance of this pilot's subjects were recently presented at the 2018 Walter Reed Research Forum Analysis, and the data suggested that HRV was significantly improved within 10 minutes and at the end of the 60-minute MBTR session (Bonner et al., 2018). HRV (as described in the case study above) is a well-established measure of autonomic nervous system function and reflects one's ability to respond to and recover from stressful experiences.

This significant finding offers objective evidence that participation in MBTR can produce acute improvement in the autonomic nervous system of patients with PTSD. This change in physiologic status may contribute to our other preliminary findings that MBTR participants also experienced a significant reduction in pain and perceived stress and reported improvement in cognitive, emotional, and social functioning. The findings from this study are expected to be published later in 2019.

WCC is also the focus of a larger, biopsychosocial prospective study, conducted by researchers at the Walter Reed National Military Medical Center (WRNMMC), the NICoE, USU, and the University of Maryland. This research examines the biopsychosocial effects of 6–12 hours of MBTR on 220 PTSD patients from Department of Defense (DoD) treatment centers in the Greater Capital Region. Follow-up measures will be taken three months after completion of the MBTR research sessions. This study will also investigate MBTR's effect on sleep behavior, social interactions, and family dynamics. Results are scheduled for 2020.

It is our hope that these rigorous research protocols will further establish the scientific and therapeutic integrity of our Mission-Based Trauma Recovery model, as well as provide clinical and scientific guidelines for the appropriate training of the new class of service dogs for psychological support of veterans with PTSD.

REFERENCES

Beetz, A., Uvnäs-Moberg, K., Julius, H. & Kotrschal, K. (2012). Psychosocial and psychophysiological effects of human-animal interactions: The possible role of oxytocin. *Frontiers in Psychology/Psychology for Clinical Settings*, *3*(234). https://doi.org/10.3389/fpsyg.2012.00234

Bilmes, L. J. (2013, March). The financial legacy of Iraq and Afghanistan: How wartime spending decisions will constrain future national security budgets. *Harvard Kennedy School of Government: Faculty Research Working Paper Series*. Retrieved from http://web.hks.harvard.edu/publications

Bonner, J., Abraham, P., Kazman, J., Silverman, M., Hagin, J., & Deuster, P. (2018). Service dog training program effects on heart rate variability. Poster presentation at the Walter Reed National Military Medical Center Research Forum, Bethesda, MD.

Congressional Budget Office. (2012, February). *The Veterans Health Administration's treatment of PTSD and traumatic brain injury among recent combat veterans* (CBO publication No. 4097, pp. 10). Washington, DC: U.S. Government Printing Office. Retrieved from https://www.cbo.gov/sites/default/files/cbofiles/attachments/02-09-PTSD.pdf

Edmondson, D., & Cohen, B. E. (2013). Posttraumatic stress disorder and cardiovascular disease. *Progress in Cardiovascular Diseases*, *55*(6), 548–56. https://doi.org/10.1016/j.pcad.2013.03.004

Fischer, H. (2013, February 5). *U.S. Military casualty statistics: Operation New Dawn, Operation Iraqi Freedom, and Operation Enduring Freedom* (Congressional Research Service Report for Congress). Retrieved from https://journalistsresource.org/wp-content/uploads/2013/02/RS22452.pdf

Fischer, H. (2015, August 7). *A guide to U.S. military casualty statistics: Operation Freedom's Sentinel, Operation Inherent Resolve, Operation New Dawn, Operation Iraqi Freedom, and Operation Enduring Freedom* (Congressional Research Service Report for Congress). Retrieved from https://fas.org/sgp/crs/natsec/RS22452.pdf

Levin, A., (2012, July 20). Army psychiatrist makes case for collaborative care. *Psychaitric News, 47*(14). Retrieved from http://psychnews.psychiatryonline.org/doi/10.1176/pn.47.14.psychnews_47_14_10-a

Price, J. L., & Stevens, S. P. (2017). Partners of veterans with PTSD: Research findings. National Center for PTSD, U.S. Department of Veterans Affairs. Retrieved from https://www.ptsd.va.gov/professional/treat/specific/vet_partners_research.asp

Quintana, D. S., Kemp, A. H., Alvares, G. A., & Guastella, A. J. (2013). A role for autonomic cardiac control in the effects of oxytocin on social behavior and psychiatric illness. *Frontiers in Neuroscience, 7*, 48. https://doi.org/10.3389/fnins.2013.00048

Tedeschi, P., Sisa, M. L., Olmert, M. D., Parish-Plass, N., & Yount, R. (2015). Treating human trauma with the help of animals: Trauma informed intervention for child maltreatment and adult post-traumatic stress. In A. H. Fine (Ed.), *The handbook on animal-assisted therapy: Foundations and guidelines for animal-assisted interventions* (4th ed., pp. 305–319). New York, NY: Academic Press.

Yount, R. A., Olmert, M. D., & Lee, M. R. (2012). Service dog training program for treatment of posttraumatic stress in service members. *Army Medical Department Journal*, 63–69.

ABOUT THE AUTHORS

Rick A. Yount, LSW, is the founder and CEO of Warrior Canine Connection, Inc. He synthesized decades of social work experience and service dog training expertise to create a unique animal-assisted intervention to help service members with post-traumatic stress disorder. He has lectured and published on the therapeutic observations and potential of WCC's Mission-Based Trauma Recovery program.

Retired Navy Captain **Robert Koffman,** MD, was the director for psychological health to the Navy Surgeon General and Chief of Clinical Operations at NICoE, as well as the recipient of the US Special Operations Command Patriot Award for significant, enduring support to wounded warriors and their families. As chief medical advisor for WCC, he provides critical support for our service dog partnering process and research protocols.

Meg Daley Olmert is a world-renowned expert on the human-animal bond and its therapeutic effects. Author of *Made for Each Other: The Biology of the Human-Animal Bond*, Daley Olmert serves as director of Research for Warrior Canine Connection, Inc., and is scientific advisor to The Comfort Dog Project in Uganda.

CHAPTER 12

Animal-Assisted Crisis Response: Offering Opportunity for Human Resiliency During and After Traumatic Incidents

Raquel Lackey, CPA, CMA, CGMA; and Gehrig Haberstock, MSW, AASW

INTRODUCTION

On March 22, 2014, at 10:37 a.m., the normally peaceful community of Oso, Washington, was hit by a monumental mudslide that engulfed 49 homes and other buildings, killing 43 people and devastating the community. With urgency, over 600 personnel, including first responders and volunteers from across the country, arrived on the scene. Exhausted and missing their families, search and rescue (SAR) workers from Sacramento, California, took a short break during their complex mission. Sitting with elbows resting on his knees, eyes cast downward, and feeling weary, one of the workers did a double take when he saw Pickles, an animal-assisted crisis response (AACR) black Labrador retriever.

Accepting the worker's repeated glances as an invitation, the AACR team approached the resting SAR worker. Once near the worker, Pickles leaned on and nestled next to him. For a brief moment amidst the anguish, the SAR worker's tense shoulders relaxed as he delighted in the presence of his new friend. After talking for several minutes, the worker embraced Pickles and finished his final few hours on the job, remarking how Pickles had given him the needed energy to finish his deployment.

Pickles provided this SAR worker with comfort by establishing rapport, offering a calm and helpful distraction, and building a therapeutic bridge through being fully present (something that is difficult for even the most experienced human professionals and rescue workers to do), thereby acting as the catalyst to propel the worker through his final hours of searching for survivors in the mud.

The practice of incorporating dogs into crisis response first emerged in 1995, when the Federal Emergency Management Agency (FEMA) requested them on-scene to provide comfort following the Murrah Building bombings in Oklahoma City, Oklahoma (Shubert, 2012). A few years later, the National Organization for Victim Assistance summoned AACR teams to the 1998 Thurston High School shooting in Oregon. While on scene, counselors who were unsuccessful using traditional techniques watched in amazement as the human-canine teams broke down the walls of isolation among previously withdrawn students (HOPE AACR, 2017). Soon after returning from her Oregon call-out with her canine partner, Bear, Cindy Ehlers founded Hope Pets in 1999, which in 2001 became Hope Animal-Assisted Crisis Response (HOPE). Ehlers' newly formed nonprofit organization, the first of its kind in the United States, was a foundational step in formalizing what is commonly known today as animal-assisted crisis response or AACR, particularly in setting the precedent for specialized training and a concentrated focus on the welfare and well-being of participating canines (HOPE AACR, 2017).

AACR volunteers were also present following one of the most tragic days in US history, and one that none of us living at the time will soon forget—September 11, 2001. Teams consisting of human handlers and canine partners were present at Ground Zero following the terrorist attacks (Shubert, 2012), and were called in by the American Red Cross to support the efforts of counselors and chaplains as they provided care and comfort to individuals and families awaiting updates about their loved ones at Manhattan's Pier 94 Family Assistance Center. The response to September 11 prompted Ehlers to develop a comprehensive, multiday training program to better prepare human-canine teams for the various hardships often encountered during deployments, including precarious environments, human fragility, and emotional and physical exhaustion. Shortly thereafter, National Animal Assisted Crisis Response (presently known as NATIONAL Crisis Response Canines) was founded in 2003.

NATIONAL offers similar services as HOPE, and collaborated in the development of the 2010 AACR national standards.

WHAT IS ANIMAL-ASSISTED CRISIS RESPONSE (AACR)?

As defined by this chapter's authors, AACR is the utilization of certified canine-and-handler teams assisting in crisis interventions to support the psychological and physiological needs of individuals affected by, and responding to, crises and disasters in complex, unpredictable environments. These interventions, which provide needed respite during periods of unimaginable turmoil, are becoming all the more important due to the growing number of annual Stafford Act Disaster Declarations (since 1953) within the United States; when averaging 2000 to 2009 data, the original figure of 19 annual declarations has increased to 56 per year (Lindsay & McCarthy, 2015). Likewise, on a global scale, there has been a documented increase in weather-related events, particularly flooding and storm-related events. Between 2005 and 2014, an average of 335 weather-related events per year occurred, representing a 14% increase from the previous decade (UNISDR, 2015). Looking toward the future, we must recognize that climate-related disasters are on the rise, and be diligent in understanding the interconnectedness of growing population exposure and vulnerability, and the ongoing expansion of climate-related hazards (Thomas & Lopez, 2015).

Given that natural disasters are known to lead to an increase in the prevalence of mental illness, these growing trends have problematic implications (Canino, Bravo, Rubio-Stipec, & Woodbury, 1990; Madakasira & O'Brien, 1987). Specifically, weather-related disaster incidents, as well as those associated with community violence and acts of terrorism, are placing emergency responders and those personally impacted by these events at an elevated risk of experiencing trauma. Through human-animal interactions (HAIs), AACR provides comfort and encouragement for individuals affected by crisis and disasters, including those who have lost all of their personal possessions; first responders working through tiresome days and dangerous conditions; workers coordinating a response in an emergency operation center (EOC); and volunteers making a difference in the lives of affected individuals.

EVIDENCE SUPPORTING ANIMAL-ASSISTED CRISIS RESPONSE

Due to the somewhat indescribable nature of the human-animal bond, which archaeological evidence suggests has existed for thousands of years, it is understandable how AACR could look and even feel like magic to the untrained eye (Wenzl, 2017). One example of this perceived "magic" is indicated in a 2013 doctoral dissertation by Filomena Bua. In her interviews with AACR handlers and crisis counselors who had worked on the ground with AACR teams in Australia, Bua (2013) reported that her study participants "believed that AACR dogs have an innate ability to find the people in crisis who appear to need the most support" (p. 94). While such abilities and sensitivities to human emotion may indeed be present in dogs, especially those who work in close connection with people, there is a need to acknowledge the significant training, skills, and qualifications necessary to perform and implement AACR work safely and effectively. Currently, substantial evidence exists to warrant the continuation of these services, while simultaneously demanding further and more rigorous exploration to fully validate AACR protocols.

Whether or not someone develops a mental illness (i.e., post-traumatic stress disorder or PTSD; depression and anxiety; prolonged and traumatic grief; secondary grief reactions; suicide or suicidal ideation; substance abuse or dependency; and/or stress-related health problems) following a traumatic disaster or crisis is contingent on numerous personal and environmental factors (Bonanno, Brewin, Kaniasty, & La Greca, 2010). While many variations of these influences exist, Bonanno and colleagues (2010) provide a comprehensive overview of factors that may impact an individual's resiliency across the entire crisis event (i.e., pre-disaster, disaster, and the aftermath of disaster):

- The pre-disaster context considers the following factors: the individual's age, gender, and race/ethnicity; preparation and prior exposure; social support; economic resources; and personality.
- The disaster event factors primarily relate to proximal exposure, referring to the "events and consequences that occur during the approximate period of the disaster itself" (p. 20).
- Factors related to the aftermath of the disaster are mainly related to distal exposure, including economic resources lost; displacement and relocation; and media coverage.

Of all factors mentioned, AACR is best able to directly impact a person's level and quality of social support (specifically *received* support or actual support provided), which hopefully has a positive influence on *perceived* support (or the personal, subjective experience of feeling supported) and a subsequent reduction in distress (Bonanno et al., 2010). As Bua (2013) proffers, humans and canines are social complements, enabling the fulfillment of each other's needs for connection and social adaptability, leading to successful and supportive attachments. Given that the aforementioned concepts stem largely from attachment theory, it must be noted that there are also other commonly accepted AAI theoretical perspectives possibly at play, namely the biophilia hypothesis and the notion of animals as being *mediums*, or bridges, in the therapeutic relationship (Scott, 2015).

Coupled with enriching an individual's social support system and resources (even if only temporarily), AACR teams offer psychological and physiological benefits to promote short-term resiliency, while acting as a grounding mechanism to root the client back to reality. When individuals experience traumatic events, they are susceptible to both immediate and delayed emotional reactions. AACR aims to empower individuals to be mindful of their immediate reactions, such as numbness and detachment; disorientation; elevated heart rate, respiration, and blood pressure; racing thoughts; and distortion of time and space, in order to limit the development of delayed reactions (Center for Substance Abuse Treatment, 2014). When faced with crises, humans have a tendency to close down and isolate, a phenomenon that AACR dogs and handlers are able to help individuals overcome through the establishment of rapport and creating a sense of safety and support. The presence of a dog can also promote security, comfort, and stabilization, thus regrounding an individual who has experienced a crisis in the present (Chandler, 2012) and facilitating resiliency.

Arguably, dogs may have a grounding and supportive impact because their presence prompts neurochemical releases, such as oxytocin, in our circulatory system and brain (Bua, 2013; Olff, 2012). Often referred to as the love or social bonding hormone, oxytocin is commonly released due to sensory stimulation, such as "breastfeeding, labor, sex, but also touch, warmth, and stroking" (Beetz, Uvnäs-Moberg, Julius, & Kortrschal, 2012, p. 11). There is also recent evidence that mutual gazing between dogs and their owners increases oxytocin levels for both the human and canine (Nagasawa et al., 2015). As summarized by Beetz and colleagues in their 2012 literature review, oxytocin has been shown to influence how connected we are with others; increase trust and social skills; decrease depression, blood pressure, heart rate, and glucocorticoid levels; induce calmness; and potentially even increase pain thresholds (Handlin et al., 2011; Heinrichs, Baumgartner, Kirschbaum, & Ehlert, 2003; Kaminski, Pellino, & Wish, 2002; Petersson, Eklund, & Uvnäs-Moberg, 2005; Rimmele, Hediger, Heinrichs, & Klaver, 2009).

However, oxytocin is not the only neurochemical active in the body during interactions with animals. Whether in a crisis situation or not, stress reductions as measured by decreased salivary cortisol and blood pressure have been observed in those interacting with an animal (Friedmann & Son, 2009). Furthermore, increases in beta-endorphins, prolactin, and dopamine can occur in both humans and canines during positive human-animal interactions (Odendaal & Meintjes, 2003). Lastly, and potentially significant in grounding individuals, the presence of a canine engages all five of our senses, facilitating a powerful bond and contact (i.e., touch and/or physical affection) not customarily present or always appropriate amongst strangers, such as first responders or mental health providers.

Looking specifically at the potential long-term benefits of AACR as observed anecdotally, the comforting presence of a canine partner may facilitate trust that allows the client to begin to process his or her experience and/or loss, as well as identify coping strategies that will help the person move toward a "new normal." For example, AACR teams may play an important role in confidential briefings for individuals who have recently lost family members in an event, and/or who are awaiting news of their

Rex, an AACR canine, joins a family at a reunification site following a school shooting. Photograph by Elizabeth Lyon, NATIONAL Crisis Response Canines.

loved one's fate or safe return. Below is a case study that illustrates the application of AACR in such situations.

CASE STUDY

Less than 24 hours after a shooting, and prior to families receiving confirmation of the deceased, an AACR team entered an emotionally charged room where individuals anxiously awaited information about their loved ones. Engaging with individuals in the room was met with varying degrees of success. As each person responds differently to trauma and grief, some people embraced Areya, an AACR husky working with her human handler, while others nonverbally refused contact. While navigating the room, the handler recognized one woman's interest in engaging with Areya. The woman, who self-identified as a cat person, was given brief respite while digging her fingers into Areya's soft fur, petting her head, and gazing into her eyes, all while talking with the handler about matters unrelated to the present traumatic experience. After receiving confirmation that her loved one was killed in the shooting, Areya and her handler gradually and respectfully reengaged the grieving woman as she began processing her untimely loss. During such extreme grief reactions, our human instincts tell us to say comforting words or offer soothing touches. However, following the lessons of AACR trainings and the quiet example of Areya, the handler sat on the floor with the woman and provided appropriate support by being silent, yet fully present (J. Jackson, personal communication, September 30, 2016).

Unlike traditional therapy, the brief and urgent nature of crisis intervention requires rapport to be established nearly instantaneously for a meaningful dialogue to commence. This is where the presence of a canine can be immensely beneficial. According to Graham (2009), the "dog serves as an entrée to the establishment of a relationship and a venue for the affected individuals to talk" (p. 76). Cynthia Chandler echoes Graham when recalling her experiences of engaging with clients in Red Cross shelters during the aftermath of Hurricane Katrina. After her first two days of

deployment, Chandler and other Red Cross disaster mental health volunteers shared a mutual frustration of not being able to effectively connect
and converse with evacuees (Chandler, 2012). However, things changed
on the third day when Chandler's two dogs were allowed to accompany
her into the shelter. As she walked the aisles of the shelter, clients' faces
and affect turned from shocked and grief-stricken to smiles and laughs,
sparking conversations between volunteers and clients (Chandler, 2012).
Simply put, Chandler's dogs were able to remove "the barriers that had
been impeding the sharing process by evacuees" (Chandler, 2012, p. 274).

Similarly, Reverend Michael Rogers, a mental health professional with
over 35 years of field experience, has remarked that it takes a recipient approximately one quarter of the time to open up and share with him when
an AACR team is present. Rogers (2014) summarized his response work
when coupled with AACR teams by stating:

> These highly trained dogs are a treasure. Not only are more peo-
> ple reached through their presence, the potential quality of each
> human interaction is enhanced. Sharing a crisis response dog ex-
> perience together is like sharing a meal. Defenses are lowered. Care
> is enhanced through open hearts. (para. 4)

Establishing safety and trust through rapport is the basis upon which
one can empower healing and change within traumatized individuals. An
acceleration in this foundational step, a concept Rogers (2014) calls *rapid
rapport*, is made possible when working with a canine partner. As reported
by the experience of some AACR responders, the presence of a specially
trained and well-groomed dog allows the client to see the handler as a
trustworthy individual, as the canine provides a visual representation of
the handler's ability to care for another living being. Similarly, in Schneider
and Harley's (2006) study on client perceptions of psychotherapists, findings showed that, when accompanied by a dog, psychotherapists were
responded to more positively, with clients indicating a greater willingness
to disclose private information. Empirical and anecdotal findings such as
these may be related to the ability of animals, particularly dogs, to serve
as catalysts or facilitators in creating "affiliation[s] and relations in social
interactions" (Guéguen & Ciccotti, 2008, p. 339; McNicholas & Collis,
2000, 2006).

Furthermore, select research has demonstrated that interaction with
animals may have salient calming effects for people through the reduction

of stress and anxiety, two symptoms almost always present in traumatized individuals. When utilizing a visiting canine animal-assisted intervention (AAI) with psychiatric patients receiving electroconvulsive therapy, Barker, Pandurangi, and Best (2003) determined that interacting with a therapy dog significantly reduced treatment-related anxiety and fear. In fact, some of the major physiological effects a dog can bring to a therapeutic relationship are reductions in heart rate and blood pressure, both of which are typically elevated in stress-prone conditions, as well as in unfamiliar or uncomfortable social situations (Beetz et al., 2012; Bua, 2013). In their 2012 literature review, Beetz and colleagues discuss additional research findings regarding the stress-related benefits of AAIs, including those interventions that are brief in nature:

- Reductions in stress after a five-minute interaction with a therapy dog among health care professionals (Barker, Knisely, McCain, & Best, 2005).
- Reduced state-anxiety after petting both hard-shelled animals (e.g., a turtle) and soft animals (e.g., a rabbit); notably these state-anxiety effects were not observed in participants after they petted toy turtles and rabbits (Shiloh, Sorek, & Terkel, 2003).
- Improvements in cardiopulmonary pressures, neurohormone levels, and anxiety in adult patients hospitalized with heart failure after a 12-minute visit with a therapy dog (Cole, Gawlinski, Steers, & Kotlerman, 2007).

In many cases, AACR interventions occur with little to no verbal communication between the handler and human recipient. However, all AACR handlers are trained in psychological first aid (PFA) to further enhance the overall AACR experience and impact. The Minnesota Department of Health (2016) defines PFA as, "[A]n evidence-informed approach that is built on the concept of human resilience. PFA aims to reduce stress symptoms and assist in a healthy recovery following a traumatic event, natural disaster, public health emergency, or even a personal crisis" (para. 1).

PFA employs "five elements of psychological response"—1) sense of safety, 2) calming, 3) a sense of self and community efficacy, 4) connectedness, and 5) hope—that are crucial to address when responding to clients impacted by a disaster (McIntyre & Goff, 2012, p. 724). When an AACR team engages with an individual utilizing PFA (which emphasizes the importance of active listening and keen observation), they are

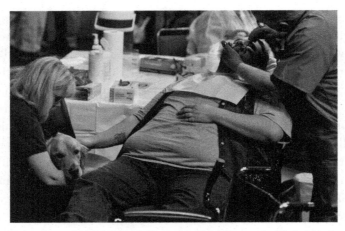

During a free medical clinic in Seattle, Washington, this gentleman arrived for dental work. After waiting for hours, his anxiety soared and he felt unable to receive treatment. Upon request from clinic organizers, Sierra and her handler (a HOPE AACR team) accompanied him while the dental procedure was performed. He was able to receive his needed treatment by keeping his hand on Sierra throughout the entire procedure. Photograph by Auston James, courtesy of Seattle King County Clinic (SKCC).

able to offer the benefits of a personalized intervention enriched by the presence of the dog to empower the development of individual resiliency. For example (and mirroring Chandler's [2012] experience), one of this chapter's authors was able to stabilize a distraught shelter resident into the present moment using PFA techniques with her AACR canine partner, thereby aiding in the reunification of this individual with her family after a period of separation.

NATIONAL STANDARDS AND BEST PRACTICES

In 2010, the founding AACR organizations of HOPE and NATIONAL collaborated to create the *Animal-Assisted Crisis Response National Standards* (National Standards Committee for Animal-Assisted Crisis Response, 2010). These standards provide guidance on handler and dog training, evaluation, experience, certification, standards of conduct, and AACR organizations. Of note, AACR teams need to integrate seamlessly with the broader response to minimize confusion. To do so, it is recommended that handlers take and successfully pass four foundational FEMA courses:

FEMA IS-100.c, IS-200.b, IS-700.b, and IS-800.c. These courses, each of which is currently available online, provide responders with an operational framework of the Incident Command System (ICS), a component of the National Incident Management System (NIMS) utilized in the United States that defines command, control, and coordination to facilitate effective response efforts (FEMA, 2008).

It must be noted here that AACR is not considered therapy or treatment, but rather a specialist intervention and support service for people in crisis (Bua, 2013; Robinson, 2004). Currently (and as taught in certification workshops), PFA is the preferred minimum crisis intervention skill used by AACR handlers, especially by those without a mental health background (Brymer et al., 2006). With continuing education required by the AACR National Standards, trainings that this chapter's authors have seen as beneficial in enhancing handler skills include Critical Incident Stress Management (CISM) and Applied Suicide Intervention Skills Training (ASIST). Building upon skills possessed by many already, PFA training equips AACR responders with the ability to foster resiliency in those impacted by trauma, as well as support their own self-care and psychological well-being during and after deployments (Minnesota Department of Health, 2016).

As with any helping professional working with traumatized and distressed individuals, AACR team members may be susceptible to experiencing trauma vicariously, which can lead to compassion fatigue and/or burnout (Boscarino, Figley, & Adams, 2004). To reduce or address this potential issue, confidential debriefings conducted by a trained CISM peer with the oversight of a mental health professional are becoming a regular occurrence for AACR teams following a deployment. While the symptoms of vicarious trauma are abundant and individualized, some affirmed by AACR responders include difficulty falling or staying asleep, fluctuations in eating or alcohol consumption, and intrusive dreams (American Counseling Association, 2011).

Accordingly, an AACR responder, or even a disaster response counselor, must be able to process and tolerate high levels of compounded stress, possess strong organizational and assertiveness skills, and excel at collaborating with countless other response stakeholders, all while being able to make decisions independently (Chandler, 2012). Although AACR handlers have a responsibility to serve those in trauma and themselves, their primary role is to ensure and advocate for the physical and psychological well-being of their canine partner (National Standards Committee for Animal-Assisted Crisis Response, 2010). Due to human reliance on verbal communication and/or their attention to event specifics and the needs of AACR recipients, handlers should be careful not to overlook their dogs' behavioral indicators of stress and fatigue during a deployment. Knowing this, handlers need to develop an advanced understanding of their canine partner's behavioral and personality traits prior to being deployed. Correspondingly, having a strong relationship with their dog further enables handlers to advocate for his or her needs both during and after highly stressful work.

While certain signs of canine stress—such as body shaking, panting, lip licking, increased locomotion, and restlessness, to name a few—are well-documented (Glenk, 2017), it is important to note that dogs participating in AACR might display additional manifestations. Through discussions with AACR responders, some specific signs of stress, fatigue, or being overworked among AACR dogs include refusing to wear their working vests when given the option, turning their heads to avoid engaging with visitors, or lying down and facing away from activity. Handlers must remember that advocating for their canine partner is a complex endeavor that encompasses more than simply watching for stress signals during interactions. Indeed, careful planning and preparedness on the part of the handler needs to occur. Factors to consider beforehand include the mode of transportation to, and during, deployments, as well as weather condition variations between home- and deployment-life.

Moreover, the handler's role as canine advocate becomes increasingly important during extended deployments, as stress is typically cumulative. Not only is the team entering into a chaotic environment, but the canines may be continuously exposed to potentially stressful stimuli, including unfamiliar surroundings, new sights and smells, and the high intensity of need presented by individuals seeking their comfort (National Standards Committee for Animal-Assisted Crisis Response, 2010). It cannot be overstated that dogs, even more so than humans, respond differently to stressors and manage their stress in unique ways.

Prior to becoming an AACR team, the handler and dog must be a certified therapy team with at least one year of experience (National Standards Committee for Animal-Assisted Crisis Response, 2010). After gaining this experience, the team can begin the process of determining whether or not they would make a favorable AACR team. Experience has shown

Oscar (left) and Pickles (right) pausing to take a break from their AACR work during the Highway 530 mudslide response in Oso, Washington. Photograph by Raquel Lackey, HOPE Animal-Assisted Crisis Response.

that proper canine selection not only strengthens the potential for positive human outcomes, but also is crucial for the dog to enjoy his or her job (Jegatheesan et al., 2014). In complementing earlier research conducted by Odendaal and Meintjes (2003), Marcus (2013) concludes that therapy dogs included in AAIs experience these visits as work. The study's inference that these activities require work and intentional effort on the part of AAI animals is logical when one considers that therapy dogs must calmly, willingly, and obediently accept petting and other forms of physical contact from strangers, rather than taking part in play or other enjoyable activities (Marcus, 2013). With this in mind, and understanding that work and stress can have both positive and negative aspects, some ethicists suggest that when balanced appropriately, the benefits received by dogs through human-animal connection support their continued participation in AAIs, such as AACR (Zamir, 2006). Given the unpredictability and high intensity of disaster deployments and settings, one could reasonably contend that the sense of work (and therefore stress) felt by AACR teams is comparatively greater than that experienced by handlers and therapy dogs who participate in more traditional AAIs (e.g., in a therapist's private office).

Likewise, the importance of a strong, reciprocal relationship between handler and dog is elevated within AACR work, and teams must be able to enter chaotic, unknown situations with a mutual trust to ensure each other's safety and well-being. As indicated by AACR responders, it is easy to sometimes overlook the fact that enjoying human contact and taking pleasure in being petted by a wide variety of people is also taxing, even for carefully selected and trained AACR canine partners.

Even though difficult to quantify, canine partners on deployment should also be prepared for, aware of, and be able to respond to environmental hazards that could place the team in danger (National Standards

Committee for Animal-Assisted Crisis Response, 2010). The following account about one author's experience depicts how a strong connection between handlers and their canine partners may have mutually beneficial implications in AACR work.

CASE STUDY

Within 24 hours of the Highway 530 mudslide, an AACR team was deployed to provide comfort, care, and temporary respite to those staffing the emergency operation center (EOC). Being conscious to not overwork her canine partners, the handler alternated workdays between her two AACR dogs. However, as she served as the sole handler for both dogs, the emotional work slowly began to take its toll on her. Ten days and countless hours into the deployment, her canine partner communicated behaviorally a request to not work for the remainder of the day, displayed by a slowing of the gait and taking a long pause before entering the main EOC room. This happened to be the same day that the handler began fighting a cough and cold. Within a few days, and while supporting teams remotely, the handler's condition worsened, initiating a trip to urgent care and antibiotic treatment. This account is indicative of how the close connections between AACR handlers and dogs can manifest, including through potential mirroring of experience/symptoms, as well as being in tune with each other's subtle changes in affect, mood, and behavior.

In regard to canine selection, Chandler (2012) explains how and why only certain dogs are suitable for AACR work. Chandler (201) writes, "A therapy dog should not be brought to a crisis and disaster scene unless they have a high tolerance for stress, chaos, and noise; a consistent and reliable response to commands; and a highly sociable attitude towards all people" (p. 287), all of which will be tested and verified during certification to ensure the prospective canine partners are qualified AACR dogs. AACR canines, partnering with their advocate handlers, must be able to manage the unpredictable environments surrounding traumatic events, as exemplified in the following selected scenarios:

- AACR canines need to be adaptable in a variety of environments. For example, when taking part in a school presentation on depression and suicide prevention following a school shooting, an AACR dog will likely be confronted with a gymnasium full of large crowds and loud noises. However, that dog may also participate in quieter, yet still potentially stressful and emotionally charged interactions, such as being present during student group sessions focused on suicide and self-harm prevention.
- AACR canines often accompany their handler when in the presence of media personnel after a disaster has occurred. These situations often involve urgent questioning about the traumatic event and the nature of AACR work from large and eager groups of people, as well as the stress of public speaking (for the handler, which could impact his/her dog), cameras, and hot lights.

CONCLUSIONS AND NEXT STEPS

Given the increased frequency of traumatic events, both natural and "manmade," the need and demand for AACR is growing. Concurrently, there is increasing interest and publicity surrounding AACR, as well as an increasing number of organizations attempting to provide these services. At present, AACR work is mostly carried out by volunteers. As experienced daily by one of the authors, volunteers are often equally as capable of performing this specialized work as their paid staff counterparts. Whether their volunteerism is driven by professional experience or personal passion, trained and qualified volunteers are indispensable in crisis response, including, but not limited to, firefighting, search and rescue, and AACR.

With increased attention to the field comes greater need to attend to the following: 1) to uphold (and revise as necessary) the existing national standards to keep professionals, volunteers, canines, and clients safe; and 2) to conduct more focused and rigorous research evaluating the human, canine, and community health outcomes associated with AACR interventions. As with other crisis response services, interventions like AACR and PFA are difficult to study. Some of these challenges include the inability to gather baseline data, the complexities of ethically or practically studying individuals in a state of crisis, and the relatively short nature of the AACR intervention (Lyon, & Sullivan, 2007; Pekevski, 2013). Further challenges of conducting ethical research in AACR include creating control groups, ensuring participant consent, and establishing adequate sample sizes and randomization of participants (Dieltjens, Moonens, Van Praet, De Buck, & Vandekerckhove, 2014; Pekevski, 2013; Stern & Chur-Hansen, 2013). However, these challenges of scientific inquiry must be met in order to accurately determine both the benefits and risks of working with animals under these most demanding and strenuous of conditions. For example, there is urgent need to understand, and then properly set, the expectations that can be reasonably and ethically asked of an AACR canine partner, particularly in regard to how long they can humanely work (i.e., length of workday, deployment, and overall AACR career).

Additional studies specifically measuring the impacts and outcomes of AACR would also help to solidify trauma-informed interventions, while simultaneously validating their utility. In order to make strides toward this end, we propose that researchers first focus on one particular area in need of investigation: the inclusion of AACR canines in CISM methodologies (i.e., those that center on immediate and concrete issues). For example, studies examining how AACR dogs may impact the stress-related outcomes and trauma symptoms of those who have experienced disaster or crisis (as compared to the use of CISM without the inclusion of an AAI) would be of great benefit to this emerging area of study and practice. Ultimately, there is an intrinsic responsibility to ensure that responders, both human and canine, are properly supported and equipped to meet the needs of the individuals with whom they interact, with research being an important component of establishing reliability and validity of AACR effectiveness.

As detailed above, responding to emergencies is not for all people or dogs, and those individuals who are interested should seek both knowledge and experience before first volunteering with their therapy dog for deployment. One of the best ways to gain exposure in this area is by volunteering with the American Red Cross or for another disaster relief organization. Volunteering in this area offers a valuable opportunity to gain experience in responding to emergencies, interacting with clients who have recently experienced a traumatic incident, and being ready to respond promptly after receiving an urgent call to action. These hands-on experiences will help determine whether or not someone has the skillset to appropriately manage both the short- and long-term effects of stress associated with AACR work.

In summary, while further research is certainly needed, there currently exists evidence and scientific validity to support the incorporation of therapy dogs into crisis response efforts to benefit individuals and communities who have experienced trauma. We propose that adherence to the following four key principles will be important in further improving these emerging practices and their comprehensive outcomes. First of all, handlers must never self-deploy when disaster strikes; rather, responders should always follow ICS structure to avoid additional chaos or causing harm to themselves or their canine partner. Secondly, much like finding the "right" canine to become a successful service dog is a challenging endeavor, so too is the case with working AACR dogs. Acknowledging that it takes a very special dog and human handler to excel in this service, the relationship between the canine and human must be built on unquestionable trust and respect. The third principle pertains to the importance of educating the general population on the *Animal-Assisted Crisis Response National Standards* so that the health and safety of all involved—including those responding to, and impacted by, the traumatic events; the AACR handlers; and especially the canines—are fully supported. Finally, and perhaps most importantly, the welfare of the canine partner before, during, and after each deployment is paramount. Our canine partners must have a particularly strong advocate to ensure that their well-being is safeguarded while working in the unpredictable midst of chaos and devastation, and that they emotionally, mentally, and physically enjoy their participation in serving traumatized populations during each and every AACR deployment.

REFERENCES

American Counseling Association. (2011). Fact sheet 9: Vicarious trauma. Retrieved from https://www.counseling.org/docs/trauma-disaster/fact-sheet-9 ---vicarious-trauma.pdf?sfvrsn=2

Barker, S. B., Knisely, J. S., McCain, N. L., & Best, A. M. (2005). Measuring stress and immune responses in health care professionals following interaction with a therapy dog: A pilot study. *Psychological Reports, 96*(3 Pt 1), 713–729.

Barker, S. B., Pandurangi, A. K., & Best, A. M. (2003). Effects of animal-assisted therapy on patients' anxiety, fear, and depression before ECT. *The Journal of ECT, 19*(1), 38–44.

Beetz, A., Uvnäs Moberg, K., Julius, H., & Kotrschal, K. (2012). Psychological and psychophysiological effects of human-animal interactions: The possible role of oxytocin. *Frontiers in Psychology: Psychology for Clinical Settings, 3*, 1–15. https://doi.org/10.3389/fpsyg.2012.00234

Bonanno, G. A., Brewin, C. R., Kaniasty, K., & La Greca, A. M. (2010). Weighing the cost of disaster: Consequences, risks, and resilience in individuals, families, and communities. *Psychological Science in the Public Interest, 11*(1), 1–49.

Boscarino, J. A., Figley, C. R., & Adams, R. E. (2004). Compassion fatigue following the September 11 terrorist attacks: A study of secondary trauma among New York City social workers. *International Journal of Emergency Mental Health, 6*(2), 57–66.

Brymer, M., Jacobs, A., Layne, C., Pynoos, R., Ruzek, J., Steinberg, A., Vernberg, E., & Watson, P. (2006). *Psychological first aid: Field operations guide* (2nd ed.). National Child Traumatic Stress Network & National Center for PTSD. Retrieved from https://www.nctsn.org/sites/default/files/resources/pfa_field_operations_guide.pdf

Bua, F. (2013). *A qualitative investigation into dogs serving on animal assisted crisis response (AACR) teams: Advances in crisis counseling* (Unpublished doctoral dissertation). Retrieved from http://arrow.latrobe.edu.au:8080/vital/access/manager/Repository/latrobe:35600

Canino, G., Bravo, M., Rubio-Stipec, M., & Woodbury, M. (1990). The impact of disaster on mental health: Prospective and retrospective analyses. *International Journal of Mental Health, 19*(1), 1951–1969.

Center for Substance Abuse Treatment. (2014). Understanding the impact of trauma. In Substance Abuse and Mental Health Services Administration (US), *Trauma-informed care in behavioral health* (pp. 59–90). Rockville, MD: Substance Abuse and Mental Health Services Administration.

Chandler, C. K. (2012). *Animal assisted therapy in counseling* (2nd ed.). New York, NY: Routledge Taylor & Francis Group.

Cole, K. M., Gawlinski, A., Steers, N., & Kotlerman, J. (2007). Animal-assisted therapy in patients hospitalized with heart failure. *American Journal of Critical Care, 16*(6), 575–585.

Dieltjens, T., Moonens, I., Van Praet, K., De Buck, E., & Vandekerckhove, P. (2014). A systematic literature search on psychological first aid: Lack of evidence to develop guidelines. *PLOS One, 9*(12). https://doi.org/10.1371/journal.pone.0114714

Federal Emergency Management Agency (FEMA). (2008, May). *Incident Command System training: Review material.* Retrieved from https://training.fema.gov/emiweb/is/icsresource/assets/reviewmaterials.pdf

Friedmann, E., & Son, H. (2009). The human-companion animal bond: How humans benefit. *Veterinary Clinics of North America: Small Animal Practice*, *39*(2), 293–326.

Glenk, L. M. (2017). Current perspectives on therapy dog welfare in animal-assisted interventions. *Animals*, *7*(2), 7.

Graham, L. (2009). Dogs bring comfort in the midst of a natural disaster. *Reflections: Narratives of Professional Helping, S.I., 15*(1), 76–84.

Guéguen, N., & Ciccotti, S. (2008). Domestic dogs as facilitators in social interaction: An evaluation of helping and courtship behaviors. *Anthrozoös, 21*(4), 339–349.

Handlin, L., Hydbring-Sandberg, E., Nilsson, A., Ejdebäck, M., Jansson, A., & Uvnäs-Moberg, K. (2011). Short-term interaction between dogs and their owners: Effects on oxytocin, cortisol, insulin and heart rate—an exploratory study. *Anthrozoös, 24*(3), 301–315.

Heinrichs, M., Baumgartner, T., Kirschbaum, C., & Ehlert, U. (2003). Social support and oxytocin interact to suppress cortisol and subjective responses to psychosocial stress. *Biological Psychiatry, 54*(12), 1389–1398.

HOPE Animal-Assisted Crisis Response (AACR). (2017). *About HOPE AACR.* Retrieved from http://hopeaacr.org/about-hope/

Jegatheesan, B., Beetz, A., Choi, G., Dudzig, C., Fine, A., Garcia, R. M., Johnson, R., Ormerod, E., Winkle, M., & Yamazaki, K. (2014). *The IAHAIO definitions for animal assisted intervention and animal assisted activity and guidelines for wellness of animals involved* [White paper]. International Association of Human-Animal Interaction Organizations. Retrieved from http://iahaio.org/new/fileuploads/9313IAHAIO%20WHITE%20PAPER%20TASK%20FORCE%20-%20FINAL%20REPORT.pdf

Kaminski, M., Pellino, T., & Wish, J. (2002). Play and pets: The physical and emotional impact of child-life and pet therapy on hospitalized children. *Children's Health Care, 31*(4), 321–335.

Lindsay, B. R., & McCarthy, F. X. (2015, July 14). *Stafford Act declarations 1953–2014: Trends, analyses, and implications for Congress* (Congressional Research Service Report for Congress). Retrieved from https://fas.org/sgp/crs/homesec/R42702.pdf

Lyon, E., & Sullivan, M. C. (2007, November). *Outcome evaluation strategies for domestic violence service programs receiving FVPSA funding: A practical guide.* National Resource Center on Domestic Violence. Retrieved from http://www.ocjs.ohio.gov/FVPSA_Outcomes.pdf

Madakasira, S., & O'Brien, K. F. (1987). Acute posttraumatic stress disorder in victims of natural disaster. *Journal of Nervous and Mental Disease, 175*(5), 286–290.

Marcus, D. A. (2013). The science behind animal-assisted therapy. *Current Pain and Headache Reports, 17*(4), 322.

McIntyre, J., & Goff, B. S. N. (2012). Federal disaster mental health response and compliance with best practices. *Community Mental Health, 48,* 723–728.

McNicholas, J., & Collis, G. M. (2000). Dogs as catalysts for social interaction: Robustness of the effect. *British Journal of Psychology, 91*(1), 61–70.

McNicholas, J., & Collis, G. M. (2006). Animals as social supports: Insights for understanding animal-assisted therapy. In A. H. Fine (Ed.), *Handbook on animal-assisted therapy: Theoretical foundations and guidelines for practice* (2nd ed., pp. 49–71). San Diego, CA: Academic Press.

Minnesota Department of Health. (2016, July 5). *Psychological first aid (PFA)*. Retrieved from https://www.health.state.mn.us/communities/ep/behavioral /pfa.html

Nagasawa, M., Mitsui, S., En, S., Ohtani, N., Ohta, M., Sakuma, Y., Onaka, T., Mogi, K., & Kikusui, T. (2015). Oxytocin-gaze positive loop and the coevolution of human-dog bonds. *Social Evolution, 348*(6232), 333–336.

National Standards Committee for Animal-Assisted Crisis Response. (2010). *Animal-assisted crisis response national standards*. Retrieved from http://www .hopeaacr.org/wp-content/uploads/2010/03/AACRNationalStandards 7Mar10.pdf

Odendaal, J. S., & Meintjes, R. A. (2003). Neurophysiological correlates of affiliative behavior between humans and dogs. *Veterinary Journal, 165*(3), 296–301.

Olff, M. (2012). Bonding after trauma: On the role of social support and the oxytocin system in traumatic stress. *European Journal of Psychotraumatology, 3.* https://doi.org/10.3402/ejpt.v3i0.18597

Pekevski, J. (2013). First responders and psychological first aid. *Journal of Emergency Management, 11*(1), 39–48.

Petersson, M., Eklund, M., & Uvnäs-Moberg, K. (2005). Oxytocin decreases corticosterone and nociception and increases motor activity in OVX rats. *Maturitas, 51,* 426–433.

Rimmele, U., Hediger, K., Heinrichs, M., & Klaver, P. (2009). Oxytocin makes a face in memory familiar. *The Journal of Neuroscience, 29*(1), 38–42.

Robinson, R. (2004). Counterbalancing misrepresentations of critical incident stress debriefing and critical incident stress management. *Australian Psychologist, 39*(1), 29–34.

Rogers, M. E. (2014, April 4). *Disaster mental health field work enhanced by animal-assisted crisis response.* Retrieved from www.hopeaacr.org/wp-content /uploads/ 2011/11/Rapid-Rapport-via-Therapy-Dogs.docx

Schneider, M. S., & Harley, L. P. (2006). How dogs influence the evaluation of psychotherapists. *Anthrozoös, 19*(2), 128–142.

Scott, S. K. (2015). *Walking the dog when talking is too much: Mental health workers' implementation of animal assisted interventions with adult survivors of potentially traumatic events* (Doctoral dissertation). Available from ProQuest Dissertations and Theses database (UMI No. 10153581).

Shiloh, S., Sorek, G., & Terkel, J. (2003). Reduction of state-anxiety by petting animals in a controlled laboratory experiment. *Anxiety Stress Coping, 16*(4), 387–395.

Shubert, J. (2012). Therapy dogs and stress management assistance during disasters. *The Army Medical Department Journal,* 74–78.

Stern, C., & Chur-Hansen, A. (2013). Methodological considerations for designing and evaluating animal-assisted interventions. *Animals, 3,* 127–141. Retrieved from https://www.ncbi.nlm.nih.gov/pmc/articles/PMC4495515/

Thomas, V., & Lopez, R. (2015). *Global increase in climate-related disasters* (No. 466, ADB Economics Working Paper Series). Manila, Philippines: Asian Development Bank. Retrieved from https://www.adb.org/sites/default/files /publication/176899/ewp-466.pdf

UNISDR. (2015). *The human cost of weather related disasters: 1995–2015.* Retrieved from http://www.unisdr.org/files/46796_cop21weatherdisastersreport2015.pdf

Wenzl, R. (2017, April 2). Our devotion to dogs goes way back in time. *Wichita Eagle.* Retrieved from http://www.kansas.com/news/local/article142279974.html

Zamir, T. (2006). The moral basis of animal-assisted therapy. *Society & Animals, 14*(2), 179–199.

ABOUT THE AUTHORS

Raquel Lackey is a certified public accountant with over 25 years of experience in both public and private accounting. She is currently the president of Washington State Volunteer Organizations Active in Disaster, and serves on the boards of HOPE Animal-Assisted Crisis Response and Reading with Rover. Along with her two dogs, Pickles and Bungee, Lackey has volunteered in the area of crisis response since 2010, often serving more than 400 hours annually. Lackey is a certified field traumatologist and compassion fatigue educator with Green Cross Academy of Traumatology, and has recently become a certified instructor with the International Critical Incident Stress Foundation.

Gehrig Haberstock, MSW, graduated from Harding University and the University of Denver with degrees in social work. Currently, he serves as disaster program manager in Wyoming for the American Red Cross, with a particular interest in chaos management. In this role, he also provides facilitative volunteer leadership in disaster relief and response. Haberstock is an avid cyclist, passionate outdoorsman, and loves investing in his community and the people in it.

CHAPTER 13

Loss, Grief, and Bereavement in the Context of Human-Animal Relationships

Susan Cohen, DSW; and Adam Clark, LCSW, AASW

INTRODUCTION

Our relationships with animals can be a cause of trauma or a buffer against it. As this chapter will show, most human-animal interaction (HAI) research has explored the benefits of interacting with animals, especially in our homes and in therapeutic settings. Less scholarly work has focused on the effects for people when pets, therapy and service animals, wildlife, livestock, or captive animals are lost or, more specifically, pass away.

This chapter discusses trauma in the context of grief, while exploring the role of other animals in supporting humans through periods of loss. In particular, we consider the special challenges of losing an animal companion, including the social devaluation and stigma of pet loss, as well as the meaningful place of animals in the lives of vulnerable people and what the loss of those relationships brings. Further, we discuss how animals can support those in bereavement, as well as how the loss of a beloved animal can be in and of itself traumatic, especially if disparaged or minimized. Additionally, we consider recently publicized traumatic losses of certain wild and captive animals, and how their deaths galvanized thousands of people who never knew them, becoming a vehicle for grieving, as well as political and often racial commentary. Finally, through clinical insight and case examples from our experiences as counselors in both veterinary and academic settings, we discuss potential ways to frame these experiences so as to not only protect those involved from enduring further trauma, but to also make loss an opportunity for growth.

TRAUMA IN THE CONTEXT OF LOSS

As discussed at length throughout this book, traumatic events are often so far outside previous or typical experience that one is often forced to revise his or her worldview in response. Some such events seem obvious (i.e., shootings, assault, watching your house burn to the ground). And yet, people react differently to similar misfortune. What is devastating to one can be inspiring and motivating to another.

Generally speaking, a traumatic event is one that overwhelms the person's perceived resources to cope with it. It is the kind of experience that can alter our memory functioning, and cause us to be hypervigilant of potential indicators of peril or misery. In small doses, attention to such warning signals can be protective. However, when they turn chronic or overwhelming, they become unmanageable and detrimental to a person's overall quality of life. For example, the traumatized individual may find that ordinary, everyday events or stimuli—such as a helicopter flying overhead, a comment heard on television, or a song playing on the radio—can trigger the traumatic memory in full force, disrupting normal activity, as well as mood (McCann & Pearlman, 2015).

The distinctly emotional, and often traumatic, pain that comes with losing someone we love (whether human or animal) is a universal experience, although grieving itself is highly subjective (Clements, DeRanieri, Vigil, & Benasutti, 2004; Saavedra Perez et al., 2015; Shear, 2015; Simon, 2013); an individual will process loss according to his or her own lens, including personal histories, supportive networks, characteristics of the lost relationship, and preferred or customary ways of coping (both positive and negative). The experience of grieving also typically varies depending on cultural upbringing, race/ethnicity, gender, economic resources, and religious or spiritual background.

Further, the manner in which we lose or say goodbye to someone (or not, in some cases) is also important. Some people will lose a loved one who gradually grows old and passes peacefully, while others will experience the shock of an unexpected or sudden loss, such as the suicide, homicide, or unexpected accident or illness of a friend or family member (Clements et al., 2004). Other significant losses, such as through divorce or separation, the end of friendship, the regretful relinquishment of companion animals to shelters, or pets running away from home, may also be profoundly traumatic for individuals, both human and animal alike. Taken together, these myriad factors often influence opinions regarding how long the grieving process should last. Generally, strong emotional response within the first year of loss is typical, although some research indicates that a two-year timeframe is still considered to be a very "normal" grieving process (Simon, 2013).

However long the process lasts may not be as important as the integration of experience, which is highly individualized and expressive of the grieving individual (Corr & Corr, 2012). Most grief counselors and clinicians, in an effort to respect differences in how people experience and manage grief, hesitate to assign specific timeframes to such duration, but they do consider the level of negative impact that a grief experience is having on the patient's or client's life. Indeed, the full weight of experiencing loss is often substantial, and impacts a person in all aspects of living: mentally, spiritually, physically, socially, and financially (Corr & Corr, 2012). Grief changes the way we have been living life, regardless of whether the loss is of relationship, of job, of plans and dreams for the future, or of loved ones through death or other permanent separation. After loss, we are now faced with the absence of someone or something we expected would be present in our lives for a long time, possibly forever. Consequently, our perspectives and the stories we tell ourselves will (need to) shift, often in rather abrupt, unpredictable, and complex ways.

Moreover, significant grief and loss will nearly always adjust (or shatter, even if temporarily) a person's sense of self and reality, as the loved one or activity is no longer present in day-to-day life. Assumptions and routines may be altered or halted, which, depending on the circumstance and type of loss, can cause the bereaved to question one's purpose in life and even one's very existence (Shear, 2015). People may also grapple with the reality and uncertainty of their own mortality, whether it happens today or years in the future, when working through their feelings of loss.

COMPLICATED GRIEF

When grief turns from a natural, although difficult, response to a more complex experience leading to long-term challenges or adverse health effects, a person may be suffering from what is known as *complicated grief.*

A traumatic loss can lead to expressions of complicated grief, which primarily include intrusive or uncontrollable thoughts about the deceased or individual who is no longer present (Saavedra Perez et al., 2015; Shear, 2015; Simon, 2013; Supiano & Luptak, 2013). In other words, a person with complicated grief tends to ruminate on the loss, and his or her pain associated with it. These thoughts and memories may take on a repetitive or cyclical pattern and can significantly lessen the bereaved person's quality of life, causing increased suffering or negative consequences to occur (Clements et al., 2004; Shear, 2015; Simon, 2013). For example, grieving may be so intense as to cause someone to stay home and miss multiple days of work due to feeling overwhelmed and unable to function. As a result, the person might experience the additional losses of their job, financial security, relationships with valued colleagues, and sense of professional purpose or identity.

One of the primary theoretical perspectives underlying complicated grief is that of Bowlby's Theory of Attachment (Bowlby, 1969/1982). Within his work, Bowlby summarizes that it is the level of perceived attachment between individuals that dictates the strength of that particular bond (Bowlby, 1969/1982). Hence, it may be suggested that with stronger bonds or attachments comes greater risk of complicated grieving when the bond is broken or lost (Bowlby, 1969/1982; Brown & Symons, 2016).

As suggested below, the levels of perceived attachment between humans and their pets may arguably be greater than that between humans in certain cases, thus highlighting the potential for complicated grief when a beloved animal is lost (Brown & Symons, 2016). Those who are socially isolated or who have come to depend on their pets for comfort and companionship may find themselves doubly bereaved when the loss of their animal companion compounds other emotional pains.

The following case study exemplifies how a complicated grief response to animal loss can manifest, especially in cases where the bereaved individual was isolated socially, and relied heavily on her pet for support and relationship.

CASE STUDY

Cindy is a 32-year-old working professional who finds community in regularly attending religious services, as well as bringing her dog, Sage, to the dog park every day after work. Cindy spends many hours at the office, and is fortunate enough to be able to bring Sage to work with her. In fact, Sage goes almost everywhere that Cindy does and serves as an important and constant companion in her life. Although she gets out for religious services, Cindy is busy, and her social circle is fairly small.

One day, Cindy has an important meeting at the office and is unable to bring Sage with her. When she returns home, she is shocked and dismayed to find Sage lying on the floor, not breathing. Cindy rushes to the veterinarian, but Sage's life unfortunately cannot be saved. Immediately, Cindy is distraught with all-encompassing grief, unable to grasp that her best friend and primary companion is suddenly gone. She blames herself for leaving Sage on that day, and feels desperately alone as she continuously contemplates what she could and "should" have done differently.

Eventually, months pass and Cindy hardly leaves her home, much less her bed. Social isolation, changed routines, and longed-for and painful memories of Sage have collectively decreased her quality of life and engagement in the world. She has used up her time off from work and is late on deadlines, while the caliber of her work and work ethic suffers immensely. Soon, Cindy's employer fires her due to her diminished work performance. This only makes her feel worse and more isolated, as she refuses visitors over the shame of her grief and losing her job. As a result, Cindy starts to fall behind on her bills (including rent), and her health suffers due to inconsistent and unhealthy eating patterns.

Depending on an individual's grief reaction, it can be very normal to stay in bed for days, if not weeks, during the acute phase of grief or period of time directly after a loss event (Diminich & Bonanno, 2014). However, in the case study above, Cindy's prolonged duration of grieving over Sage's passing led to increasing complications. Notably, a grief reaction can be frequently compounded with other previous experiences of loss, and whether or not the individual has adequately processed these. It is reasonable, then, to assume that Cindy may have been struggling from compounded loss, with potential factors such as a recent divorce, loss of a parent, or failure to be promoted at work, underlying her relatively intense response.

When working with clients who are experiencing complicated grief, it is important to first ensure that their basic needs of living are being met. As such, checking on eating and sleeping habits, safety, shelter, and hygiene can be important. In the beginning, small tasks can feel like major accomplishments.

THE SIGNIFICANCE OF ANIMALS, ANIMAL BONDING WHEN GRIEVING, AND ANIMAL LOSS

Increasingly, studies and polling have indicated that humans believe their pets serve integral and meaningful roles as members of the family, including as surrogate children (Cohen, 2002; Field, Orsini, Gavish, & Packman, 2009; Harris Poll, 2015; Parker, 2016). Likewise, research shows that pets often improve the functioning and quality of our lives, including overall emotional well-being, physical health and activity, and social connections with others (Fine, 2015; Suthers-McCabe, 2001). Indeed, many turn to their pets as sources of secure and reliable connection, often giving them human-like characteristics (see "surrogate children" above) in order to fulfill this need (Field et al., 2009).

Trends such as these suggest an increasing attachment (Bowlby, 1969/1982) expression among humans for our pets and other animals. Pet owners often expend significant time, money, and other resources to keep their animal companions happy and comfortable (Cain, 1985; Josephson, 2015). Likewise, many people form strong attachments to animals that do not live with them. In a study of how clients at a large, urban veterinary teaching hospital view their social network, both men and women often included their friends' pets as part of their support system (Cohen, 1998). As we discuss later in this chapter, these attachments may even extend to wildlife, as well as livestock and captive animals.

Importantly, such connections with companion, emotional support, therapy and service animals, as well as those we merely observe in nature or through media, can provide unique healing to those suffering with the effects of loss. For example, in cases of human loss, our pets can offer us a comforting presence and strong impetus to begin moving through the stages of grief. As pet owners, we typically structure our day by the needs and routines of our animal companions. We wake, feed, walk, touch, play with, talk to, and express affection for our pets, all of which can be incredibly comforting and uplifting. What is more, providing care for our animal companions grounds us in what is still good and important in life. In essence, animals may force us to take the first necessary steps toward healing and recovery.

However, when a beloved animal passes away or is lost, it is the absence of these very characteristics that often pains us the most. The trauma of losing a pet is profoundly life-changing for many, especially given the length and depth of most human-pet relationships. Increasing evidence has shown that the death of a companion animal can be just as severe and prolonged as the death of a human counterpart or loved one (Clements, Benasutti, & Carmone, 2003). Particular challenges can arise when an animal passes away due to his or her role as innocent and dependent in the relationship/family, as well as the person's role as primary guardian responsible for the animal's survival and well-being (Podrazik, Shackford, Becker, & Heckert, 2000). Feeling responsible for the loss or losing one's purpose of caregiving likely complicates the bereavement response of a grieving individual (Lagoni, Butler, & Hetts, 1994), especially if the animal was ill or injured and required the owner to administer at-home medical treatment prior to death.

Likewise, the loss of an animal companion can disrupt our daily schedules and routines, our social and family lives, our degree of loneliness, and even our sense of meaning regarding getting up in the morning or leaving the house (as observed in the case study with Cindy and Sage) (Lagoni et al., 1994). Importantly, a potential risk for retraumatization and complicated grieving exists when the pain that comes from losing an animal is discounted, ridiculed, or disregarded by others. Feeling uncertainty or guilt regarding the unique decision to euthanize a pet can also heighten any trauma associated with the overall loss (Adams, Bonnett, & Meek, 2000).

THE IMPACTS OF COMPANION ANIMAL LOSS FOR SELECT VULNERABLE POPULATIONS

Elders

Older adults in American society and throughout the world often suffer unique social disadvantages. They may live without human companions, physical touch, or structure in their daily lives. Children move away, partners and friends die, and chronic illness, pain, and disability make going out difficult. Financial constraints can also limit social activity. As a result, older people frequently become isolated from their broader community (Valtorta & Hanratty, 2012).

Pets and animal relationships can help fill many of these social needs. For example, pets curl up with you on the couch, and are excited to see you when you return home or rise in the morning. Moreover, elders who live alone can talk to, and be affectionate with, their companion animal. Research indicates that interacting with animals helps alleviate loneliness and supports mental health in older adults (Banks & Banks, 2002; Fick, 1993), with one study finding that adults over 60 years of age who had a pet were 36% less likely to report feeling lonely than non-pet owners (Stanley, Conwell, Bowen, & Van Orden, 2013).

To date, research has also indicated the positive health impacts of pets for elders, including reduced agitation and other symptoms associated with dementia (Bernabei et al., 2013; Johnson & Meadows, 2002). Dogs, in particular, may provide the impetus for mobility and routine, and their need for exercise and nourishment presents older adults with a purposeful, healthy outlet. In fact, studies show that people who walk their dogs get more exercise and even walk faster (Curl, Bibbo, & Johnson, 2017). Likewise, one long-term study found a relationship between current or previous pet ownership and improved cardiovascular disease survival among older adults (Chowdhury, Nelson, Jennings, Wing, & Reid, 2017), while another noted increased eating and better nutrition in those with Alzheimer's disease when in the presence of aquarium fish (Edwards & Beck, 2002).

After losing a pet (primarily via moves to assisted living environments or through the pet's death), older adults of a certain age, health status, or ability level may feel it is inappropriate to adopt another. Indeed, while walking is beneficial for both people and dogs, some research indicates that dog walking among older adults is not very common (Thorpe et al., 2006). Since elders cannot predict the future, and may not know of anyone who could care for the pet after they become ill or pass away, adopting again may be daunting. For many older adults, this can mean that when a pet dies, it is the end of their pet keeping life and the myriad benefits that come with animal companionship. While some older people may feel relieved to shed the responsibility of pet keeping, for others, the consequences of losing that affectionate focus may be severe.

Children

Pet loss may also have a significant effect on children, as relationships with animals are often monumental for their healthy development (Melson, 2001). In one of the author's clinical experience, the death of a pet is often a child's first exposure to losing someone close to them. While US society is generally more open about death than it used to be, many parents may still be reluctant to openly discuss the impending or actual loss of a family pet with their children due to discomfort or uncertainty of what to say. For example, parents may conceal the pet's death until the child returns home from camp, or downplay the circumstances of the pet's death to make it easier for the child to understand and cope with the loss.

Additionally, parents may remain stoic for the perceived benefit of their children, which could inadvertently leave the children feeling alone in their grief, and that the life and loss of their pet is not important. In such cases, children may also wonder how people would react if something tragic happened to them, and could be concerned because they seem to be more emotionally distraught about the loss than other members of the family (Fudin & Cohen, 1988). Overall, such research and clinical findings demonstrate the importance of having forthright, age-appropriate discussions with children about animal loss in order to assist them through the necessary grieving process.

Traumatized Individuals

People with existing trauma histories may also have a particularly difficult time coping with the loss of a pet. Trauma has long-lasting effects, which animals can help relieve. For example, veterans often rely on service dogs for guidance and protection, both at home and in public settings (Brulliard, 2018). Other individuals who have experienced trauma simply appreciate the comfort of safe touch, undemanding companionship, and the opportunity to socialize with ease that comes from being in the presence of trusted animals. The loss of such important social support not only causes grief, but may also trigger setback for people already coping with the present threat or aftermath of trauma.

Of note, animals can also be the cause of trauma. An individual may have been hurt by an animal or witnessed one being harmed or injured. In fact, accounts of people reporting symptoms of post-traumatic stress (PTS) after seeing and hearing their animals in pain have been documented (Watters, Ruff, & Jamora, 2013). In addition, forced separations from pets—whether through the trauma of natural disasters or family violence, for example—only intensify the devastation of losing that animal relationship. It is hard to accept that any one of us—young or old—may face unexpected changes in living arrangements (including homelessness) that require the relinquishment of a pet.

Attachment to pets can be so strong that people are often reluctant to leave their animals behind when natural disaster strikes, even if staying with them greatly endangers their own safety (Hunt, Al-Awadi, & Johnson, 2008). Likewise, adolescents living on the street are more likely to engage in treatment if provisions are made for their pets (Rew, 2000). And people faced with the threat or actual harm to pets by an abuser (i.e., in select cases of domestic violence and child maltreatment) often choose to stay in personally abusive situations rather than abandon their pet by fleeing to a nearby shelter that does not allow animals. Encouragingly, the Urban Resource Institute in New York City recently made national news for opening three shelters that include pet-friendly apartments for individuals and families escaping abuse at home (Newman, 2016). Special attention and accommodations must be paid to those with preexisting psychological injury who face further traumatization through the loss of a pet or other animal to whom they are attached.

CULTURAL STIGMA OF GRIEVING THE LOSS OF ANIMALS

The loss of pets continues to be devalued as compared to human death, despite ample evidence demonstrating the often important role that animals play in our lives. Further, there exists a relative lack of research concerning specific impacts of losing a pet, which is unexpected given the growing recognition of close human-animal relationships as central to many people's health and well-being. While mental health professionals and scholars have been working in the HAI field for over 50 years, research pertaining to the effects of animal loss among veterinarians, social workers, and other relevant practitioners also remains limited.

Some faced with the loss of a beloved animal have recently fared better through increasingly supportive resources and networks. Today, there are now sympathy cards specifically designed for pet loss, online supportive chat groups, and opportunities to connect with others who are grieving via social media. Recently one man made a post through Facebook, asking for fellow dog lovers/owners to join him at the beach for his dog's last visit before euthanasia. As a result, hundreds of people and their dogs—many of them strangers—showed up, offering their support through signs and warm embraces. A video recording shows the man expressing his gratitude for those who came to the beach, as well as for the many more who wrote to him from around the world (ABC News, 2016). Furthermore, select veterinary settings offer mental health care services to clients in an effort to help those coping with animal illness and injury, natural and unexpected death, and the unique decisions and emotions concerning pet euthanasia.

Yet, even with these promising developments, people who have lost their pets too often feel pressure, even subtly, to justify the depth of their pain and grief, or even of the connection once shared with the animal itself. This process of advocating for something dear that will never return, all while receiving support that lacks in comparison to reactions to human loss, can be incredibly heartbreaking. Additionally, depending on the animal's species, those who are grieving may experience a response that reflects a further hierarchy of loss, such as, "I could understand being so upset if it were a dog, but a bird?" Others may also find their wish to be buried alongside their pet's remains halted by legal restrictions, although New York State has just recently allowed pet ashes to be buried in human caskets (Maslin, 2016). According to the Green Burial Society (Green, 2017), a handful of states have introduced bills to allow for joint burial, but most of those few are either currently pending or have failed to pass.

In the United States today, many do not experience death or the normalization of the death process on a regular basis. Thus, clients may have an underlying uncertainty or dread when faced with an impending death, regardless of whether this death is of a human or companion animal. When a death occurs, many cultures and communities have a prescribed way of memorializing a grief experience and beginning the steps to process through a loss. When faced with the loss of a companion animal, some people face no cultural norm for pet memorialization. In some cases, they may feel guilt or shame for even considering it to be a devastation or trauma on par with the loss of human life (Turner, 2003).

The presence of guilt may also be strong when difficult euthanasia decisions need to be made; indeed, this may be the only or first situation where an individual is called upon to make such a permanent and heartbreaking choice about ending the life of someone he or she loves. There appears to be a lack of scientific evidence regarding the impact of euthanasia decisions on the bereavement process (Podrazik et al., 2000). It has been historically presented that having to process through a euthanasia decision and procedure may cause significant emotional distress, including depression, guilt, and anxiety (Adams et al., 2000; Podrazik et al., 2000).

Although research is limited in this area, it is the authors' experience that guilt plays a strong role in the grief experienced by pet owners. Anecdotally, there are often questions and personal turmoil regarding making the right choice or whether it is the appropriate time to move forward with euthanasia. Understandably, many want to hold on to their companion animal for as long as possible. After their animal has passed, some may believe that they killed their pet or, conversely, that they waited too long to act, both of which can cause people to internalize the pain and blame themselves. However, a common and helpful reframe may be to view euthanasia as a truly humane gift that we can provide to our beloved animal companions, one that reduces their pain and suffering without causing or prolonging distress.

Given these unique factors, it may be even more important for those grieving the chronic illness, death (both actual and anticipated), and loss of a companion animal to receive appropriate support through their communities or via professional intervention. With specific and proper training, mental health and other helping professionals—such as social workers, therapists, and counselors—can guide those experiencing pain and grief through critical decision making (i.e., regarding the medical treatment and euthanasia of a companion animal); memorialization, burial, and cremation; normalization of the loss experience; and reflective listening focusing on life review (or the thoughts and memories of the pet throughout their lifetime), including other ways to conceptualize the loss and its meaning for them. The bereavement or trauma experienced by the loss of a companion animal is profound and impactful, and should always be considered as such by any helping professional or practice.

THE LOSS OF A WORKING ANIMAL

The involvement and potential benefits of animals in healing applications for humans in distress is well documented. Pets, as well as service and therapy animals, increasingly assist people with disabilities, comfort those traumatized by personal and large-scale disaster, and provide cheer when times are too hard to bear (Brown & Katcher, 1997; Yorke, 2008). Recently, increasing evidence has shown that animals present a form of perceived unconditional love and authentic support to the homes and facilities in which they live and work (Bryan et al., 2014; Clements et al., 2003; Suthers-McCabe, 2001), including a nonjudgmental presence that can be crucial for helping professionals foster rapport and therapeutic benefit for clients through animal assisted intervention (AAI). Notably, the loss of an

AAI service or therapy animal can greatly affect not only his or her handler, but also all those whom the animal is trained to help.

Service Animals

Service animals (either dogs or miniature horses) are trained to assist someone with a disability (either physical or psychiatric) by performing specific tasks that the person would not otherwise be able to do alone, such as opening doors, retrieving medication, and alerting to the onset of a panic attack. One service animal can impact many lives and even help foster relationships between people. For example, people with service animals have reported that more people speak to them, and engage in more topics of conversation, when they are with their service animal (Eddy, Hart, & Boltz, 1988; Mader, Hart, & Bergin, 1989). According to handler Bob Vogel, when he is with his service dog, Schatzie, conversations with others are improved: "Trite comments like 'no speeding' and 'you are such an inspiration' are replaced by compliments about your beautiful dog and its stellar obedience" (Vogel, 2014, para. 1). Vogel adds that Schatzie wakes his (able-bodied) daughter from bad dreams, and often joins the two of them in mobility events. Overall, it is important to note that, while service animals help their handlers execute critical tasks, they are not mere "tools"; in addition to helping the person with a disability navigate through the world, service animals also provide comfort and, as described above, attract friendly company (Mader et al., 1989).

Losing a relationship with a loyal and affectionate companion who provides constant support—both vital and emotional—can devastate. Large breed service dogs who are able to pull a wheelchair or navigate through city sidewalks typically need to retire by age ten, after a working life of seven to eight years (Finke, 2010). Service dog retirement often leads to painful separation or a change in the previous human-animal relationship (Fischler, 2014).

Additionally, once a service dog retires and becomes a pet without legal recognition, it may become subject to housing rules that forbid pets, potentially leading to a need to rehome the dog. Even if dogs can stay in the family, they may be confused about the change in their role and relationship with their person (e.g., being left behind at walk time could be puzzling or potentially stressful) (Fischler, 2014). A group of experienced service dog handlers recently described what led them to retire service animals with whom they felt close, and how hard the process was to accept (Fischler, 2014). Becky Barnes Davidson, partnered with her Golden retriever, Rowan, explains, "People who don't work with a guide don't understand the depth of emotions we share with them. A pet dog isn't going to retire. When you say goodbye to a pet it's one thing, but a guide who has been with you 24 hours a day and has traveled everywhere with you is a lot different" (Fischler, 2014, para. 51).

Whether a retired service dog stays with the handler as a pet or moves to a new home, eventually there will be a permanent separation when the animal passes. Vogel described his painful discovery that Schatzie had incurable cancer with perhaps hours to live, by saying: "Surgery was out—I wouldn't put her through that kind of trauma. I was at the point that every dog person dreads" (Vogel, 2014, para. 6). Notably, Vogel chose euthanasia to prevent or limit any further discomfort or distress for Schatzie. However, judging from his self-described sobbing for hours after losing her, that choice was a heartbreaking one for him to have to make.

Therapy Animals

Working as an AAI practitioner to help enrich the lives of others can be an incredibly rewarding experience. Many individuals have an underlying passion for both humans and animals when they enter AAI practice. Few clinicians, however, have considered the powerful impact of losing their therapeutic animal partner, and continuing their practice alone, after bonding and working closely together as a team with clients. In the case study, we describe such an experience, told from the perspective of one of this chapter's authors.

CASE STUDY

It was just another day of work at my local equine organization, and the morning was sunny and crisp. Per usual, I was checking the herd before partnering with a selected horse, Wilma, to help guide a family therapy session with clients. Wilma was a beautiful choice for this family due to her rock solid nature, comforting presence, and patience. She was a "go-to" for many challenging families, as well as children with attachment concerns and complex diagnoses. In particular, Wilma did not typically present with discomfort when heavy human emotion or raised voices characterized a session. This family struggled with two children who expressed difficulty concentrating and were easily distracted. The parents had large levels of tension between them and often became frustrated when trying to engage with each other or their children.

To my dismay, when I went to find Wilma that morning, she was lying down in the field, not moving. She had passed at some point overnight. Unfortunately, the cause and circumstances of her death were unknown, but raised concern as she was not an extremely old horse. I was consumed with my own grief over the loss of Wilma, as I had been growing as a clinician with her for over four years, and we had come to trust each other. She was my friend. After the initial shock, I realized that in 20 minutes the family was about to arrive, expecting to work with her. How then, would this situation be handled?

In what follows we describe several clinical considerations for properly managing situations such as those described in the above case study. That is, how AAI practitioners may be gentle with themselves and their own feelings of grief, while properly supporting their clients in coping with the loss of a therapy animal through careful preparation and necessary precautions:

1. At the start of therapy with clients, begin therapeutic rapport building with a discussion of endings. Even if the clinician is not talking about death, per se, there may be times when an animal may not be available to participate in a session. For example, the animal may be sick, injured, or simply not in the mood to participate that day (i.e., showing signs of anxiety, fatigue, annoyance, withdrawal); whatever the reason may be, the animal's preferences should be respected. In preparation of such situations, AAI clinicians should create therapeutic interventions that do not include the animal, such as biofeedback or mood/feeling inventories that use animals as examples.

2. Have a plan implemented should a medical emergency happen with the therapy animal partner. Whether AAI involves a canine, horse, or smaller animal, being ready in an urgent or stressful situation is extremely important. One's rational mind can become overwhelmed during shock or crisis, making an

existing, documented plan to address the animal's well-being and client concern essential. For example, have veterinarian contact information available at all times, and write down the "steps" to take for assessment of the animal's condition.

3. Have conversations ahead of time with clients to let them know what the steps may be in case of an animal medical emergency during session or, less urgently, if the AAI animal partner cannot attend session that day. Having these conversations with clients in a manner that supports a healthy processing experience for them can help integrate their work into practice by modeling it yourself. Important components of these client discussions will be to promote creation or engagement of healthy coping skills. Reflecting on past losses may also be useful in helping clients prepare for future medical emergencies involving either their human or animal loved ones.

4. Take time to consider what memorialization and euthanasia options might look like when the time comes. Although it may be extremely difficult to think about the loss of a beloved companion and therapeutic partner, this process is very important. Being ready with one's own assessment of animal suffering and what memorialization to pursue can reduce the amount of anxiety (and plausibly panic) during a crisis or emergency.

5. Carefully consider the level of disclosure with clients in the event that a therapy animal becomes ill, is injured, or dies outside of their presence. This will, of course, vary depending upon the client's particular situation. Such questions as, "How will you hold your own heart throughout the grieving process, and hold the heart of your client in a clinically appropriate way?" may be particularly pertinent for practitioners. If the therapy animal is also the clinician's family pet, this may be even more important to consider, as personal grief and impact will be pervasive. Additionally, when clinicians integrate their own companion animal into their clinical identity and professional self, their clients will likely grieve the impact of this loss. Clients may mourn in unhealthy ways due to their coping mechanisms and diagnostic influence—the very reasons they came to therapy in the first place.

6. Have a "back-up" plan. Should something happen to the animal, know how clients might be contacted and informed. Additionally, be prepared to engage with the client on your own, without the assistance of a therapy animal.

7. Evaluate whether or not to cancel sessions due to personal distress or the need to support other companion animals and family members. A clinician who forces himself or herself to engage in work while facing his or her own intense grief may be doing a disservice to themselves and their clients. Thus, taking time for self-care is not only essential for the therapist, but may model the importance of doing so for the client(s). Furthermore, other animals who shared their lives with the deceased or ill therapy animal may likely be experiencing their own sense of loss and grief, so it would be inappropriate to ask them to "stand-in" or engage in therapeutic work with a client. Only if the clinician feels they are able do so safely and professionally should sessions continue.

MOURNING FOR WILDLIFE, LIVESTOCK, AND CAPTIVE ANIMALS

While the loss of pets or working animals touches the lives of those who knew and loved them well, the publicized mistreatment or killing of lesser known animals in the wild, in captivity, or on factory farms (e.g., through hunting, poaching, slaughter, etc.) often cut just as deep, and cause a number of reactions from hundreds, if not millions, of people. In this section, we discuss these various reactions in the cases of Cecil (a wild lion) and Harambe (a captive gorilla), and the complexity of grieving the loss of these particular animals.

On July 1, 2015, a "trophy" hunter shot (with an arrow) and killed a lion, who normally lived in a protected sanctuary, on private land. Cecil was a well-known lion to researchers and the public alike. Once the hunter's name was released, reporters, animal lovers, activists, and the courts pursued him with outrage, thereby forcing the closure of his dental practice. Cecil became a worldwide concern, with over 695,000 social media hits and approximately 94,000 hits in the editorial media between July 1 and September 30, 2015 (Macdonald, Jacobsen, Burnham, Johnson, &

Loverage, 2016). The loss of Cecil was felt on a profound level for people all across the globe.

Much like Cecil, another tragic shooting in 2016 demonstrated that the death of an animal, even one previously unfamiliar, can be traumatizing for those who witnessed it, those who read about it, and those who were affected by the conversation and symbols that came of it. Harambe, a 17-year-old endangered lowland gorilla, was the pride of the Cincinnati Zoo. On May 28, a 3-year-old boy climbed a fence and fell into the moat surrounding the gorilla exhibit. Much to the concern of onlookers, Harambe proceeded to drag the child around the enclosure. People had varying opinions regarding Harambe's behavior, and the motivation behind it. Despite their great affection for the gorilla and his potential valuable role in replenishing the species, the zookeepers felt the need to end Harambe's life in order to protect the child. Since Harambe's interaction with the child took place in front of dozens of zoo patrons, video surfaced early. Within hours, the public had turned on both the zoo and the child's parents as responsible for the tragedy. In an outpouring of rage and grief, social media commenters accused the parents of failing to adequately supervise their child (McPhate, 2016a).

Harambe's death deeply distressed both eyewitnesses and people who learned of it later. Onlookers worried about what might happen with the boy, but they also felt sorrow for the gorilla. Brittany Nicely, a mother who happened to be present with her family, posted online, "Witnessing this situation and hearing them shoot him has been one of the most horrific things I have ever been a part of" (Shammas, 2016, para. 6).

The staff of both the zoo where Harambe was raised as a young gorilla, and the one where he lived and died, needed support. One zookeeper remarked, "We're the ones who took the loss on this . . . it doesn't affect anyone as much as it does the people here at the zoo" (McPhate, 2016b, para. 32). The director of Harambe's original zoo, Jerry Stones, who had raised Harambe nearly all of his life, was perhaps the most grief-stricken (Bult, 2016): "An old man can cry, too . . . Harambe was my heart. It's like losing a member of the family" (para. 5).

In addition, the large-scale grieving response to the deaths of Harambe and Cecil also triggered other forms of heartache and anger, particularly in regard to race and racial tensions. For example, for some in the Black Lives Matter movement and other social justice communities, the outpouring of grief and media coverage for Cecil and Harambe felt disproportionately large (and thus disrespectful and hurtful) in comparison to the concern over the many recent and tragic killings of black men, women, and youth by police officers. A tweet from Roxane Gay, a renowned Haitian American writer, professor, and commentator, exemplified much of these sorts of feelings: "I'm personally going to start wearing a lion costume when I leave my house so if I get shot, people will care" (Adams, 2015).

At the same time, much of the news and social media backlash against those grieving Harambe and Cecil criticized or disparaged the legitimacy of these emotional reactions, thereby echoing common stigmas associated with animal loss (i.e., "People are dying. PEOPLE"; "It's a gorilla, get over it") (Blatchford, 2016; Young, 2015). Not surprisingly, political commentators on both sides of the aisle used these particular animal deaths for their own purposes, and much painful and, in some cases, racist debate ensued. Some in the media proposed that people may be more vocal about the death of an animal than that of a black person because doing so is relatively apolitical. According to Joshua Adams (2015), a writer with the *Huffington Post*, "There's a huge risk in saying #BlackLivesMatter, on social media or elsewhere. There's zero risk in mourning a lion. Even if we don't agree with one or the other or both, let's stop acting like we don't know exactly why we talk about certain issues and not others" (para. 10).

While Adams' point is well taken, many would argue that expressing pain about the loss of an animal, particularly our own as previously discussed here, is not always safe (at least emotionally) or met with respect and understanding either. This heated debate, while certainly useful in many respects, undoubtedly reinforced or triggered further grieving on both "sides" of the argument.

FOSTERING RESILIENCE AFTER ANIMAL LOSS

As the authors have discussed, preparing for the loss of a pet, service, or therapy animal—or even livestock, wild (like Cecil), or captive (like Harambe) animals—can help clients and practitioners recover and cope with the grieving process. Practitioners may receive questions and inquiries from anxious pet owners about quality of life decisions, euthanasia choices, and what to do should the "time" come. Clinicians, even those without a pet loss or AAI specialty, should be familiar with the impact of companion animal loss and its unique influence on the bereavement and quality of life for clients. As stated within this chapter, normalization of a commonly stigmatized experience of loss is extremely important, as is having resources available regarding grief, support, emergency preparedness, and memorialization.

Additionally, clinicians should be familiar with signs of complicated grief and complex bereavement, and be able to recognize when referrals to trauma specialists are warranted. In addition to reviewing the clinical considerations offered in this chapter, practitioners should tailor specific solutions according to the client population they are serving. Elders, for example, who can no longer have a personal pet may benefit from caring for the animal companions of neighbors. Likewise, they may participate in animal-assisted activities or receive visits from family pets. While some elders may be relieved to have less responsibility after the last pet dies, others may be reminded of their own mortality. Clinicians should be open to all possibilities, and be prepared to respond. Practitioners can also help older adults with their grief by reminiscing and finding meaning in their animal relationships.

Likewise, children need honest communication about animal loss delivered in age-appropriate language. Parents and clinicians need to explain what death is, why euthanasia may be the best and most humane choice, and what will happen to their beloved animal's remains. When appropriate, children should be offered a chance to say goodbye or perhaps be present for the pet's last moments. The animal should also be actively remembered, not forgotten or disregarded just because he or she has passed. Pictures of the pet or their treasured objects and toys should also not be disposed of if they are important to the child (Tousley, 2017). In addition, since death in some form will inevitably enter every child's life, adults should be prepared for discussions about death with books, videos, and other resources designed for children of different ages (Fudin & Cohen, 1988).

The loss of a service animal often means more than the loss of a meaningful relationship. In addition to officially trained service dogs, many people live with animals who provide help or feel therapeutic. Without them, the person may be unable to cope with anxiety, or easily navigate and engage with the social world. When such an animal dies, the bereaved person often cannot wait for his or her grief to subside. Helping professionals should give mourners an opportunity to describe their relationship and loss, while simultaneously helping them locate and bond with a new animal (either service or companion) when the time is opportune (Cohen, 2015). Likewise, losing a therapy animal can be devastating for the handler and client. Taking time to grieve is important for AAI handlers and therapists in order to best support and serve their clientele through this loss, as well as other life challenges.

The loss of an animal can also present opportunities for growth. Researchers have begun to examine resilience in the face of stress, including the death of a loved one. There is growing evidence that most people survive potentially traumatic events without developing significant, long-lasting mental health disorders. In one study of women who had been physically assaulted, two factors predicted resilience: 1) the feeling that one is in control of life's circumstances and 2) social support networks (Rusch, Shvil, Szanton, Neria, & Gill, 2015). As such, in the case of trauma related to animal loss, mental health professionals might direct the bereaved to services such as pet loss support groups. These could provide a safe place to explore how much influence the grieving person had over his or her animal companion's medical situation. These services can also help clients acknowledge control, while recognizing that all living things will die, no matter how much they are loved. In a group setting, whether formal or ad hoc, the grieving person can also receive the social support that research shows can help.

The authors have been asked about whether or not the presence of a therapy or comfort animal, or someone's personal pet, in pet loss group meetings is helpful. To some degree, this is a matter of clinical judgment, based on where the participants in the group are at in terms of grieving and recovery. Funeral homes have begun to include a friendly dog in the office or even during the ceremony (Lu, 2015), because mourners may find it soothing. However, in a pet loss situation, seeing someone else's pet companion may only intensify one's own lack or loss of relationship, so involving animals in these applications should be done so cautiously.

Resilience and growth after the loss of a significant human-animal relationship will be a fruitful area for further research. One of the most recent studies to explore this focus specifically is a paper by Packman, Field, Carmack, and Ronen (2011). After losing a beloved pet, some study participants reported an improved ability to relate to others and feel empathy for their problems; an enhanced sense of personal strength; and a greater appreciation of life (Packman et al., 2011).

DISCUSSION

Everyone's life includes a certain amount of pain and suffering. For many, animals not only improve everyday existence, but also serve as a comfort during the worst that life has to offer. In addition to the pleasures of touch, companionship, and humor that pets provide, some animals serve a formal therapeutic function. They allow people with disabilities to function more easily, while restoring physical and mental well-being to people recovering from illness, injury, and emotional pain.

In cases where life's events overwhelm a person's resources, trauma may occur. Animals can either be at the root of that trauma or part of the healing process. One treasured animal may die, retire from service or therapy work, or run away, causing immense pain. Another may come into one's life and transform it for good. The loss of such a buffer to hardship and difficulty uncovers old wounds and creates new ones. Therapists, counselors, and other helping professionals should be prepared to work with those whose interactions with animals form an important function in getting through the challenges of day-to-day life. Such institutions as the College of Social Work at the University of Tennessee in Knoxville, the Graduate School of Social Work at the University of Denver in Colorado, and the Argus Institute in Fort Collins, Colorado, all provide important academic professional training resources in this area for interested practitioners.

As this chapter demonstrates, our relationships with animals have also changed over time. Some animals have lived peacefully with us for thousands of years, while others have been subjected to maltreatment and violence. In recent times, some animals have moved from working partners to pets to members of the family. This affection for companion animals has perhaps changed how we view the natural world. The earth finds itself under stress from climate change. Current communication technology and social media allow us to learn about remote events and happenings from afar in ways we never could before. The death of a lion in Africa and the shooting of a gorilla in another city become worldwide knowledge, the cause of grief and pain, the focus of heated political rhetoric, and spurs to action. As a result, more people seem passionately interested both in individual animals and in the larger issues of animal keeping and species preservation.

The HAI field continues to be rich with opportunities for learning. In particular, scholars need to further explore the specifics of grief and mourning after various types of animal loss. Potential questions for future discussion include the following: What effects do different animal relationships have on the nature, duration, and recovery from grief? Under what circumstances does the death of a loved one (either human or animal) become a trauma? How can the pain of animal loss be more broadly accepted as legitimate and life changing for those in mourning? How can animals best help humans recover from the trauma associated with loss? Which animals (i.e., species) are best suited for this type of work, why, and how can we best protect their welfare needs in the process? Can our affection for individual animals inspire a wider concern for other living things? The authors hope that the many social workers, counselors, and other practitioners working in the field of HAI can continue to partner with researchers to explore these and other questions, thereby validating the impact of these powerful relationships, as well as the tremendous grief that comes from losing them.

REFERENCES

ABC News. (2016, November 14). *Walk to remember.* Retrieved from https://www.facebook.com/ABCNews/videos/10155017370813812/?hc_ref=NEWSFEED

Adams, C., Bonnett, B., & Meek, A. (2000). Client expectations of veterinarians. *Journal of the American Veterinary Medical Association, 217*(9), 1303–1309.

Adams, J. (2015, August 3). Context for Cecil the lion vs. #BlackLivesMatter debate. *Huffington Post.* Retrieved from http://www.huffingtonpost.com/joshua-adams/context-for-cecil-the-lion-vs-blacklivesmatter-debate_b_7906124.html

Banks, M. R., & Banks, W. A. (2002). The effects of animal-assisted therapy on loneliness in an elderly population in long-term care facilities. *The Journals of Gerontology, Series A, Biological Sciences and Medical Sciences, 57*(7), M428–M432.

Bernabei, V., De Ronchi, D., La Ferla, T., Moretti, F., Tonelli, L., Ferrari, B., Forlani, M., & Atti, A. R. (2013). Animal-assisted interventions for elderly patients affected by dementia or psychiatric disorders: A review. *Journal of Psychiatric Research, 47*(6), 762–773.

Blatchford, C. (2016, May 31). *It's a gorilla, get over it.* National Post. Retrieved from http://nationalpost.com/opinion/christie-blatchford-its-a-gorilla-get-over-it

Bowlby, J. (1969/1982). *Attachment: Attachment and loss volume one.* New York, NY: Basic Books.

Brown, O. K., & Symons, D. K. (2016). "My pet has passed": Relations of adult attachment styles and current feelings of grief and trauma after the event. *Death Studies, 40*(4), 247–255.

Brown, S., & Katcher, A. H. (1997). The contribution of attachment to pets and attachment to nature to dissociation and absorption. *Dissociation: Progress in the Dissociative Disorders, 10*(2), 125–129.

Brulliard, K. (2018, March 27). For military veterans suffering from PTSD, are service dogs good therapy? *Washington Post.* Retrieved from https://www .washingtonpost.com/national/health-science/for-military-veterans-suffering -from-ptsd-are-service-dogs-good-therapy/2018/03/27/23616190-2ec1-11e8 -b0b0-f706877db618_story.html?utm_term=.581d6ee0e257

Bryan, J. L., Quist, M. C., Young, C. M., Steers, M. N., Foster, D. W., & Lu, Q. (2014). Canine comfort: Pet affinity buffers the negative impact of ambivalence over emotional expression on perceived social support. *Personality and Individual Differences, 68*, 23–27.

Bult, L. (2016, May 29). Former caretaker mourns death of Harambe, gorilla killed after toddler fell into his cage; family thanks Cincinnati Zoo for "quick action." *New York Daily News.* Retrieved from http://www.nydailynews.com/news /national/caretaker-gorilla-killed-cincinnati-zoo-mourns-loss-article-1.2653971

Cain, A. O. (1985). Pets as family members. In M. B. Sussman (Ed.), *Pets and the family* (pp. 5–10). New York, NY: The Hayworth Press.

Chowdhury, E. K., Nelson, M. R., Jennings, G. L. R., Wing, L. M. H., & Reid, C. M. (2017). Pet ownership and survival in the elderly hypertensive population, *Journal of Hypertension, 35*, 769–775.

Clements, P. T., Benasutti, K. M., & Carmone, A. (2003). Support for bereaved owners of pets. *Perspectives in Psychiatric Care, 39*(2), 49–54.

Clements, P. T., DeRanieri, J. T., Vigil, G. J., & Benasutti, K. M. (2004). Life after death: Grief therapy after the sudden traumatic death of a family member. *Perspectives in Psychiatric Care, 40*(4), 149–154.

Cohen, S. P. (1998). *The role of pets in some urban American families* (Unpublished doctoral dissertation). Columbia University, New York, NY.

Cohen, S. P. (2002). Can pets function as family members? *Western Journal of Nursing Research, 24*, 621–638.

Cohen, S. P. (2015). Loss of a therapy animal. In A. H. Fine (Ed.), *Handbook on animal-assisted therapy: Foundations and guidelines for animal-assisted interventions* (4th ed., pp. 341–356). London, UK: Academic Press.

Corr, C., & Corr, D. (2012). *Death & dying, life & living* (7th ed.). Boston, MA: Cengage Learning.

Curl, A. L., Bibbo, J., & Johnson, R. A. (2017). Dog walking, the human-animal bond and older adults' physical health. *The Gerontologist*, 57(5), 930–939.

Diminich, E. D., & Bonanno, G. A. (2014). Faces, feelings, words: Divergence across channels of emotional responding in complicated grief. *Journal of Abnormal Psychology*, *123*(2), 350–361.

Eddy, J., Hart, L., & Boltz, R. (1988). The effects of service dogs on social acknowledgements of people in wheelchairs. *The Journal of Psychology*, *122*, 39–45.

Edwards, N. E., & Beck, A. M. (2002). Animal-assisted therapy and nutrition in Alzheimer's disease. *Western Journal of Nursing Research*, *24*, 697–712.

Fick, K. M. (1993). The influence of an animal on social interactions of nursing home residents in a group setting. *American Journal of Occupational Therapy*, *47*, 529–534.

Field, N. P., Orsini, L., Gavish, R., & Packman, W. (2009). Role of attachment in response to pet loss. *Death Studies*, *33*, 334–355.

Fine, A. H. (Ed.) (2015). *Handbook on animal-assisted therapy: Foundations and guidelines for animal-assisted interventions* (4th ed.). San Diego, CA: Academic Press.

Finke, B. (2010, March 25). How old are guide dogs when they retire? *Beth-Finke*. Retrieved from http://bethfinke.com/blog/2010/03/25/how-old-are-guide-dogs-when-they-retire/

Fischler, B. (2014, August 7). What happens to guide dogs when they retire? *Dogster*. Retrieved from http://www.dogster.com/lifestyle/guide-service-dogs-what-happens-retire

Fudin, C., & Cohen, S. (1988). Helping children and adolescents cope with the euthanasia of a pet. In W. Kay, S. Cohen, C. Fudin, A. Kutsche, H. Nieburg, R. Grey, & M. Osman (Eds.), *Euthanasia of the companion animal: The impact on pet owners, veterinarians, and society* (pp. 79–86). Philadelphia, PA: The Charles Press.

Green, E. (2017, June 7). *Whole-family cemeteries*. Green Pet Burial Society. Retrieved from https://greenpetburial.org/projects/whole-family_cemeteries/

Harris Poll. (2015, July 16). More than ever, pets are members of the family. Retrieved from http://www.theharrispoll.com/health-and-life/Pets-are-Members-of-the-Family.html

Hunt, M., Al-Awadi, H., & Johnson, M. (2008). Psychological sequelae of pet loss following Hurricane Katrina. *Anthrozoös*, *21*(2), 109–112.

Johnson, R. A., & Meadows R. L. (2002). Older Latinos, pets, and health. *Western Journal of Nursing Research*, *24*, 609–620.

Josephson, A. (2015, December 25). *The economics of the pet industry.* Smart Asset. Retrieved from https://smartasset.com/personal-finance/the-economics-of-the-pet-industry

Lagoni, L., Butler, C., & Hetts, S. (1994). *The human-animal bond and grief.* Philadelphia, PA: Saunders.

Lu, J. (2015, June 19). Comfort dogs at funeral homes. *The Bark.* Retrieved from http://thebark.com/content/comfort-dogs-funeral-homes

Macdonald, D. W., Jacobsen, K. M., Burnham, D., Johnson, P. J., & Loverage, A. J. (2016, April 25). Cecil: A moment or a movement? Analysis of media coverage of the death of a lion, anthera leo. *Animals, 6*(5), 26.

Mader, B., Hart L. A., & Bergin, B. (1989). Social acknowledgments for children with disabilities: Effects of service dogs. *Child Development, 60,* 1529–1534.

Maslin, S. (2016, October 6). New York burial plots will now allow four-legged companions. *New York Times.* Retrieved from https://www.nytimes.com/2016/10/07/nyregion/new-york-burial-plots-will-now-allow-four-legged-companions.html

McCann, I. L., & Pearlman, L. A. (2015). *Psychological trauma and the adult survivor: Theory, therapy, and transformation* (2nd ed.). New York, NY: Routledge.

McPhate, M. (2016a, May 29). Gorilla killed after child enters enclosure at Cincinnati Zoo. *New York Times.* Retrieved from https://www.nytimes.com/2016/05/30/us/gorilla-killed-after-child-enters-enclosure-at-cincinnati-zoo.html

McPhate, M. (2016b, May 30). Zoo's killing of gorilla holding a boy prompts outrage. *New York Times.* Retrieved from https://www.nytimes.com/2016/05/31/us/zoos-killing-of-gorilla-holding-a-boy-prompts-outrage.html

Melson, G. F. (2001). *Why the wild things are.* Cambridge, MA: Harvard University Press.

Newman, A. (2016, April 14). Where the abused, and their pets, can be safe. *New York Times.* Retrieved from https://www.nytimes.com/2016/04/17/nyregion/where-the-abused-and-their-pets-can-be-safe.html

Packman, W., Field, N. P., Carmack, B. J., & Ronen, R. (2011). Continuing bonds and psychosocial adjustment in pet loss. *Journal of Loss and Trauma, 16,* 341–357.

Parker, M. (2016, September 2). *In the U.S. pets are family, global survey reveals.* Pets Best—Pets Health Insurance. Retrieved from https://www.petsbest.com/blog/how-we-share-homes-with-pets-varies-worldwide/

Podrazik, D., Shackford, S., Becker, L., & Heckert, T. (2000). The death of a pet: Implications for loss and bereavement across the lifespan. *Journal of Personal and Interpersonal Loss, 5*(4), 361–395.

Rew, L. (2000). Friends and pets as companions: Strategies for coping with loneliness among homeless youth. *Journal of Child and Adolescent Psychiatric Nursing, 13,* 125–140.

Rusch, H. L., Shvil, E., Szanton, S. L., Neria, Y., & Gill, J. M. (2015). Determinants of psychological resistance and recovery among women exposed to assaultive trauma. *Brain and Behavior, 5*(4), e00322. https://doi.org/10.1002/brb3.322

Saavedra Perez, H. C., Ikram, M. A., Direk, N., Prigerson, H. G., Freak-Poli, R., Verhaaren, B. F., & Tiemeier, H. (2015). Cognition, structural brain changes and complicated grief: A population-based study. *Psychological Medicine, 45,* 1389–1399.

Shammas, J. (2016, May 30). Eyewitness says seeing gorilla shot dead at zoo "was the most horrific thing I've ever witnessed." *Mirror.* Retrieved from http://www.mirror.co.uk/news/world-news/eyewitness-says-seeing-gorilla-shot-8081827

Shear, K. (2015). Complicated grief. *New England Journal of Medicine, 372*(2), 153–160.

Simon, N. M. (2013). Treating complicated grief. *Clinical Review & Education, 310*(4), 416–423.

Stanley, I. H., Conwell, Y., Bowen, C., & Van Orden, K. A. (2013). Pet ownership may attenuate loneliness among older adult primary care patients who live alone. *Aging & Mental Health, 19*(3), 394–399.

Supiano, K. P., & Luptak, M. (2013). Complicated grief in older adults: A randomized controlled trial of complicated grief group therapy. *The Gerontologist, 54*(5), 840–856.

Suthers-McCabe, H. M. (2001). Take one pet and call me in the morning. *Generations, 25*(2), 93–95.

Thorpe, R., Simonsick, E. M., Brach, J. S., Ayonayon, H., Satterfield, S., Harris, T. B., Garcia, M., & Critchevsky, S. B. (2006). Dog ownership, walking behavior, and maintained mobility in late life. *Journal of the American Geriatrics Society, 54*(9), 1419–1424.

Tousley, M. (2017, August 14). Children and pet loss: Following their lead. *Grief Healing.* Retrieved from http://www.griefhealingblog.com/2017/08/children-and-pet-loss-following-their.html.

Turner, W. G. (2003). Bereavement counseling: Using a social work model for pet loss. *Journal of Family Social Work, 7*(1), 69–81.

Valtorta, N., & Hanratty, B. (2012). Loneliness, isolation and the health of older adults: Do we need a new research agenda? *Journal of the Royal Society of Medicine, 105*(12), 518– 522.

Vogel, B. (2014, November 1). Grieving the loss of a service dog. *New Mobility: Life Beyond Wheels.* Retrieved from http://www.newmobility.com/2014/11/grieving-service-dog/

Watters, N., Ruff, R., & Jamora, C. W. (2013). Can a posttraumatic stress disorder be caused by a traumatic injury to a companion pet? *International Journal of Psychological Studies, 5*(3), 182–186.

Yorke, J. (2008). The significance of human-animal relationships as modulators of trauma effects in children: A developmental neurobiological perspective. *Early Child Development and Care, 180,* 559–570.

Young, D. (2015, July 30). Why does Cecil the lion receive more humanity than slain black lives? *Hello Beautiful.* Retrieved from https://hellobeautiful.com/2805866/cecil-the-lion-vs-black-lives-matter/

ABOUT THE AUTHORS

Susan Cohen, DSW, has helped people make critical decisions about the health care of their pets for over 35 years. She currently serves as vice chairperson of SWAHAB (Social Workers Advancing the Human-Animal Bond), and facilitates support groups for veterinarians (VIN Foundation Vets4Vets) and animal welfare groups. Cohen also currently lectures widely to veterinary colleges and conferences, colleges of social work, veterinary technician programs, and human health groups on communication, pet loss and bereavement, human-animal interaction, client relations, and compassion fatigue.

Adam Clark, LCSW, AASW, is a published writer, educator, and adjunct professor at the University of Denver's Graduate School of Social Work. Clark focuses his work on the psychology underlying the human-animal bond, specializing in endings and transitions. He is passionate about reducing the cultural stigma associated with pet loss, supporting pet owners, and educating veterinary professionals.

CHAPTER 14

The Global and Cross-Cultural Reach of Trauma-Informed Animal-Assisted Interventions

Betty Jean Curran, LMSW, AASW; Molly A. Jenkins, MSW, AASW; and Philip Tedeschi, MSSW, LCSW

INTRODUCTION

In this book's preceding chapters, animal-assisted interventions (AAIs) are mainly presented from a Western-centered framework, focusing primarily on the psychotherapeutic processes that take place between a therapy or service animal and an individual diagnosed with symptoms of post-traumatic stress (PTS). However, without acknowledging cultural difference, understandings or even impacts of human-animal interactions (HAIs) in the context of international trauma recovery risk being undermined by the false universality of a Eurocentric framework. For instance, the etiology and defining symptoms of trauma, the construct of the individual psyche, and characteristics of the human-animal bond may be understood differently through the discursive formations—historically situated and contextualized systems of meaning—of non-Western cultures (Hall, 1997).

While it is important to note that the field of animal-assisted therapy (AAT) originated in, and assumes most of its philosophical tenets from, Western mental health traditions, HAI programs and practices are located across all continents. The International Association of Human-Animal

Interaction Organizations (IAHAIO) has over 90 organizations registered in their database, which represents just a small fraction of HAI programs taking place throughout the world (IAHAIO, 2017). Many of these programs and practitioners undoubtedly navigate complex cultural contexts in a variety of nuanced ways. To be sure, a number of underrepresented programs may veer away from what is traditionally considered the norm by mental health communities in Western countries, specifically with regard to trauma and the role of the human-animal bond in therapeutic processes. Often, these programs are obscured due to a lack of financial resources, knowledge, and/or local champions of AAIs. Yet, it is important for practitioners and researchers to recognize how these dynamic cultural contexts may inform a variety of international HAI programs (including those that are well-established), as they provide insight into effective, place-based social work practices and broaden normative conceptions of AAIs through promoting cultural inclusivity.

Today, the biomedical approach is the dominant model used by mental health practitioners and researchers of trauma (Breslau, 2004; Flouri, 2005; Suarez, 2016; Zur, 1996). Emphasizing biological and behavioral correlates in trauma response, this model characterizes post-traumatic stress disorder (PTSD) as a neurophysiological reaction that results from "exposure to actual or threatened death, serious injury, or sexual violence" (either directly or indirectly, such as via witnessing or learning that a traumatic event or threat has occurred) (American Psychiatric Association, 2013, p. 271). The assumed universality of trauma response from the lens of the biomedical model allows the mental health community to build an evidence base around a defined set of criteria, which are centered on neurophysiological processes that seem to transcend culture. Humanitarian and international aid workers, governments, and nongovernmental organizations utilize this model because it is seemingly generalizable across cultures, "legitimizes suffering" in the political arena, and often justifies the allocation of international aid (Breslau, 2004, p. 115). The biomedical model is thus a powerful discourse that is anchored by the "full authority of science" (Breslau, 2004, p. 114).

However, it is imperative to note that trauma response is also mediated by a number of historically rooted discursive practices, and that "[c]ore physiological responses to trauma are usually translated into a diverse array of expressions depending on the socio-cultural context of the experience" (Suarez, 2016, p. 144). Thus, while cross-culturally, a similar set of biological processes take place in response to actual or perceived threat (Zambrano-Erazo et al., 2017), phenomenological responses to trauma are shaped by a number of cultural variables, such as ontological conceptions of self (Zur, 1996), understandings of destiny or fate (Zur, 1996), and conceptions of memory (Breslau, 2004), to name a few. For instance, Kohrt and Hruschka (2010) note that, in the wake of the Maoist civil war, Nepali and ethnic Nepali-Bhutanese trauma survivors blamed traumatic events on the karma of past incarnations. The sins of past incarnations—both of self and family members—manifest in experiences of personal loss and suffering. Because karma is associated with the shame of personal and familial sins, some people choose not to seek help for their psychological symptoms (Kohrt & Hruschka, 2010). In this way, cultural narratives and cosmologies are woven into the ontologies of trauma (de Jong & Reis, 2010), shaping expressions of, and responses to, psychological suffering. As such, trauma response cannot be reduced to merely its neurophysiological processes; it must be understood within the relational context of culture and the production of meaning within specific sign systems.

Research in cultural anthropology provides useful insight into cross-cultural accounts of trauma. In particular, studies centered on "idioms of distress," or expressions of suffering that are culture-bound and contextually specific, highlight the way in which all trauma response manifests through "embodied symbolic language . . . that derives its legitimacy from its shared metaphors, meaning and understanding in a group" (de Jong & Reis, 2010, p. 302; Nichter, 2010). Researching culturally specific accounts of trauma response challenges the universality of the biomedical model insofar as it points to the formative nature of discourse. While studies of trauma in cross-cultural contexts reference the multifaceted nature of trauma response, many scholars note that certain idioms of distress highly overlap with symptoms of PTSD (Chhim, 2013; Hinton, Pich, Marques, Nickerson, & Pollack, 2010; Kohrt & Hruschka, 2010). In a sample of Cambodian refugees, Hinton and colleagues (2010) found that the cultural syndrome referred to as "*khyâl* attack," or the "dysregulation of wind flow," which causes psychosomatic problems for its victims, overlaps with reported symptoms of trauma, panic attacks, and panic disorders (p. 273). Hinton and colleagues (2010) note that it is important to understand the formative nature of *khyâl* attacks, because they are "a key part of the reticulum that unites trauma event[s], social experience, and somatic experience" (p. 273). Discursive practices and customs thus shape the framework through which external, traumatic events are assimilated into individual and community narratives.

Just as the experience of, and response to, trauma is mediated by cultural contexts, a person's perceptions of animals and, consequently, HAIs are often shaped by his or her distinct cultural histories, cosmologies, values, and customary practices. This means that any HAI program, no matter the location or clients served, will need to navigate these cultural factors, which are often embedded in a person's or community's religious beliefs and teachings (Jegatheesan, 2015). According to Serpell (2004), attitudes toward animals are generally based on two primary "motivational determinants": 1) *affect* for animals, manifested via love, sympathy, and identification; and 2) perceived *utility* of animals to benefit humans and their interests (p. 145). Moreover, these determinants may be further modified by specific attributes of the particular animal or animals (e.g., intelligence, appearance, usefulness), characteristics of the individual person (e.g., personality, gender, age), and a variety of cultural factors (e.g., history, folklore, and religion/expressions of faith) (Serpell, 2004). Singular or noteworthy incidents involving particular animals, such as pit bull bites or rat infestations that lead to human illness, may, for example, also translate to broad community fear or aversion to dogs and rodents in general.

Religion, in particular, appears to play a foremost role in molding cultural traditions and belief systems, including a culture's view of the importance of animals, their welfare, and people's relationships with them. The reasons underlying the cultural influence of religion in regard to animals are many, and far too extensive to be wholly covered here. That said, these influences are likely due, in part, to the deep-rooted role of religion in "[establishing] codes of morality that influence what is acceptable as thought, [behavior], and action" (Jegatheesan, 2015, p. 37). While most religions acknowledge the intrinsic value of animal life, certain religions—namely Judaism, Islam, and Christianity—attest to the concepts of human superiority or dominion over nonhuman animals (Szűcs, Geers, Jezierski, Sossidou, & Broom, 2012; World Animal Net, 2017). This is in stark contrast to Hinduism, for example, which believes that animals and humans have souls in equal measure (World Animal Net, 2017). Through the passage of time, such beliefs (both animal-positive and -negative) are powerful narratives that become ingrained in cultural traditions and everyday practices. As such, these cultural factors have strong implications for a person's estimation of, and affection for, animals, as well as his or her ability to conceptualize animals in roles that do not conform to these beliefs (i.e., as supportive therapy animals aiding in human recovery and treatment).

To date, AAIs have been traditionally centered on a particular conception of animals as companions or even family members. While over $40 billion are spent annually in pet-industry goods and services in the United States, pet keeping is characterized differently across the world (Gray & Young, 2011). It is important to note that divergent notions of animals and their corresponding "place" in homes and communities are not necessarily indicative of the strength or quality of bonds that people share with them. However, these dynamics do provide insight into the cultural factors that shape HAIs. For instance, Gray and Young (2011) examined human-pet dynamics across 60 cultures. Their results show that dogs were only considered pets in 22 of the societies, while cats were considered pets in 11 societies. With regard to their function, dogs were primarily used for hunting and defense, and most often lived and roamed outdoors (Gray & Young, 2011). This study contextualizes various pet keeping dynamics, and decenters the common Western notion that companion animals who live inside, and thus presumably in close connection with humans, are the norm. Of course, this form of pet keeping is commonplace in the United States, which informs how most AAI programs are designed. However, HAI programs in both national and international contexts must take into account varying cultural views and roles of animals, while at the same time working against certain perspectives, biases, and practices within that culture that place animals at risk of harm.

OVERVIEW AND PURPOSE OF THIS CHAPTER

In this chapter, we highlight international HAI programs that are engaged in important work with individuals and communities that, to a large extent, have experienced trauma. Over the course of one year (2016–2017), we interviewed four programs from Uganda, Romania, Hong Kong, and Costa Rica in order to both elevate and explore in-depth an array of interventions that are implemented in diverse cultural contexts. Programs were chosen to participate in this effort based upon the quality of their work, as well as their wide geographical representation on four continents; if time and space had allowed, we would have asked additional programs to take part. All interviews were conducted in English, and took place with organizational leaders over the telephone or via video conferencing for approximately one hour. Each interview was audio-recorded (with interviewee permission) for the purposes of accurate transcription; in select cases, the interviewees also provided the authors with written answers to the questions we posed (see the following section).

While these programs present unique and culturally relevant frameworks for HAIs, these interventions are not intended to be representative of all programs taking place in their respective countries. Indeed, there is great variety and creativity in international HAI programs, and these interviews give only a snapshot representation of four exceptional interventions. Likewise, it may be important to note that these programs, while having certain Western AAI influences, were all implemented within their own cultural contexts, with primary direction and/or partnership from local experts and community members.

In what follows, we describe each program and organize the interviews according to seven important themes that arose across the board: 1) driving factors for choosing HAIs as a point of intervention; 2) prominent cultural views toward mental health and trauma, specifically; 3) cultural stereotypes and views of animals; 4) challenges of running an HAI program; 5) welfare considerations for participating animals; 6) outcomes at the individual and community levels; and 7) advice for people who wish to start an AAI program in a non-Western culture where these practices may be rare or underappreciated. These themes reflect, in large part, the questions we asked each interviewee; however, they also represent important connector points that emerged more organically from the conversations themselves. For this reason, we attempt to remain as faithful to the original content of the interviews as possible.

INTERVIEW QUESTIONS

Below are questions that we posed to the program representatives during the interview process. Of note, not all questions were asked or discussed with each interviewee, as to allow for natural, engaged, and nondirective conversation.

1. Briefly describe your program.
2. What influenced your decision to work in this field?

3. How did your program get started?
4. How do you describe your program to others in your professional community, to stakeholders, and to potential clients?
5. How widely accepted is your work with animals?
6. How are animals viewed in your country?
7. How would you describe pet keeping practices in your country?
8. In your program, what standards or efforts are made to protect the animals or respond to their well-being needs (if any)?
9. How is trauma viewed in your country?
10. Are there ways in which you have seen program participants (or staff) infuse these practices with their own cultural practices, values, and belief systems?
11. What are your recommendations for people interested in starting their own AAI practice in locations where this work is either not common or not widely supported?

THE PROGRAMS AND INTERVIEWEES

The Comfort Dog Project, Uganda
Sarah Schmidt, Program Coordinator

Based in the Gulu District of northern Uganda, The Comfort Dog Project centers on psychosocial rehabilitation for survivors of war trauma through the facilitation of human-dog companionship. As part of the larger animal welfare organization, The Big Fix Uganda, this program pairs participants, including former Lord's Resistance Army (LRA) abductees, Uganda People's Defense Force (UPDF) veterans, and other war-affected community members, with dogs who have been donated by community members or rescued as strays (The Comfort Dog Project, 2017). Each participant vows to be a lifelong guardian of his or her designated dog, ultimately learning to provide nutritious food and ample shelter, training, and companionship to the dog. The human-canine bond becomes the therapeutic means through which participants heal from psychological and social symptoms of PTS that resulted from the devastating violence and displacement of the civil war between the LRA and the Ugandan government. In our interview, Sarah Schmidt, the program coordinator, described the most common type of trauma encountered by their clients:

All the people we work with intensively have either themselves been forced to kill another person or have witnessed the killing of family members. And there are so many other atrocities. There is one woman in our program who was abducted and given to a rebel leader as a wife. So, she was basically raped for ten years. There were not just murders, but torture followed by murder. And, several people of the program were, themselves, tortured in unspeakable ways.

Schmidt also described how traumas related to twenty years of displacement from the war impacted whole communities:

As part of the effort to control the rebel forces, the Ugandan military basically herded up all the people into IDPs, or internally displaced persons camps. The conditions in those camps were just horrible. There were widespread disease and death and insufficient infrastructure and people would stay in line all day long to get a jerrican of water. The atrocities that were faced by people for over twenty years were really unimaginable.

The traumas experienced during the civil war left a lasting impact on the communities in northern Uganda. Accordingly, "it has been estimated by mental health professionals that 7 in 10 people . . . have been traumatically affected by the war" (The Comfort Dog Project, 2017). Schmidt noted that the legacy of trauma is reflected in the rising suicide rate in northern communities (personal communication, September 14, 2016).

An integrative approach to psychosocial healing, The Comfort Dog Project is comprised of six phases: community sensitization and participant recruitment; client assessments; counseling and the development of dog-guardian bonds; dog-guardian bonding activities; final assessments and community integration; and service as mentors and program ambassadors (The Comfort Dog Project, 2017). These phases of the program target important facets of the healing process by facilitating the human-animal bond while promoting social integration and, ultimately, animal welfare advocacy and community education. Insofar as entire families are typically living with the guardian and their dog, many people are peripherally "included in the counseling and the project, but the guardian, him or herself, is the primary focus of [the] work" (Schmidt, personal communication,

CDP participants walking their comfort dogs in Uganda. (Used with permission from the CDP.)

September 14, 2016). In this way, the program not only targets the psychosocial health of its participants, but also impacts attitudes toward both mental health and dog welfare in local communities.

Dogs for People, Romania
Victor Chitic, Staff Psychologist and Research Coordinator

Located in Bucharest, Romania, Dogs for People is a project of the larger animal welfare organization, Four Paws (Vier Pfoten), and aims to train stray dogs for therapeutic interventions with youth with special needs and older populations. Started in 2004, this program seeks to foster healing relationships between individuals with special needs and stray-turned-therapy dogs through animal-assisted activities (AAAs) that promote mutually beneficial human-animal bonds. Twice a week, dogs visit with children under the guidance of a psychologist. During this time, "the children perform non-failure activities with the dog," which can lead to increases in self-esteem and improvements in communication skills and concentration abilities (Dogs for People, 2017). AAAs are also incorporated into communities that serve older adults, such as retirement homes, in order to engage individuals who are experiencing the physical and psychological challenges of aging. According to Victor Chitic, staff psychologist and research coordinator at Dogs for People, the goals of this program are twofold: to promote the value of stray dogs by training them to be therapy dogs. As stray dogs in Romania face many welfare challenges, this program provides

A child and psychologist work together in the presence of a stray-turned-therapy dog in Romania. (Used with permission from Dogs for People.)

a step toward reframing the attitudes regarding animals and, consequently, their living conditions.

Dogs for People collaborates with multiple institutions in order to reach their target and clinical populations. In our interview with Chitic, he noted the various types of traumas experienced by Dogs for People clients:

> In elders, traumatic experience can range from domestic abuse, abandonment by family or loss of family members. In children, we often work with children that are orphans, so abandonment is a recurrent issue, sometimes even peer abuse in state-operated facilities. Other times we work with children from families who are more protected. Children with disabilities perceive trauma in a different way. Things that are usually normal for children can be traumatic for them and things that are traumatic for normal children can pass unnoticed for children with mental disabilities.

Animals Asia, Hong Kong
Karina O'Carroll, Animal Welfare Education Manager

Based in Hong Kong, Animals Asia Foundation is a large animal welfare organization that focuses on three key issues: ending bear bile farming, cat and dog welfare, and captive animal welfare (Animals Asia, 2017).

Dr. Dog and Professor Paws are two important volunteer-based programs developed by Animals Asia to promote the human-animal bond and animal welfare, in general. Dr. Dog launched in 1991 as an AAA program that brings certified therapy dogs to clients in "hospitals, disabled [centers] and homes for the elderly" for regular visits (O'Carroll, personal communication, July 25, 2017). The Dr. Dog program is located across Hong Kong and China, and volunteer handlers and their therapy dogs engage with different populations, including older, underprivileged, youth, and special needs communities to foster understanding and improve wellbeing (Dr. Dog, 2017). The primary aim of Dr. Dog is to facilitate positive human-animal interactions that translate into forms of social support for vulnerable populations.

Professor Paws, a school-based animal welfare education program, was started in 2004. The program is comprised of educational sessions where a number of animal welfare topics are discussed with the intention of raising awareness; humane pet keeping is a major focus of this educational program. Accordingly, therapy dogs visit schools in Hong Kong and China where students have the opportunity to overcome their fear of dogs, learn safe and responsible handling practices, and engage in other lessons that promote compassion for all animals (Professor Paws, 2017). According to Karina O'Carroll, animal welfare education manager for Animals Asia, many people in Hong Kong and China "have never even seen a dog" because they live in remote areas where "pet ownership is low," or they live in certain Hong Kong housing where tenants "are forbidden to have pets" (O'Carroll, personal communication, July 25, 2017). In this way, Professor Paws focuses on introducing young people to dogs in positive and educational encounters and settings that ultimately promote compassionate interactions in the future.

Both Professor Paws and Dr. Dog seek to transform attitudes toward dogs and other animals through the facilitation of positive HAIs. Impacting attitudes through these interactions contributes to changing the culture of cruelty toward all animals in Hong Kong and China. While Animals Asia works to change policies that are inhumane, Dr. Dog and Professor Paws are important programs that engage the public on an experiential level, ultimately bringing these welfare issues to the fore in a number of direct (educating students about the issues) and indirect (facilitating positive HAIs in supportive settings) ways.

Dr. Dog handlers and their therapy dogs. (Used with permission from Animals Asia.)

Centro de Intervenciones Asistidas con Animales (Centro IAA), Costa Rica
María José Rodríguez, Psychologist

Located in Heredia, Costa Rica, Centro de Intervenciones Asistidas con Animales provides AAA, animal-assisted education (AAE), and AAT services to both individuals and groups. Therapy dogs are integrated mostly into traditional one-on-one and group psychotherapy sessions, thereby enhancing the therapeutic relationship between the therapist and client and contributing to a calming atmosphere (Centro IAA, 2017). Centro IAA also provides spaces for tutoring schoolchildren with a therapy dog present, which can contribute to lowered stress and better concentration in academics (Centro IAA, 2017). An additional AAE program of Centro IAA is a monthly preschool class on values and developing emotional intelligence, including interactions with a therapy dog. Furthermore, Centro IAA also partners with a number of private and public institutions, like schools, colleges, senior living centers, and special education schools, to engage large groups of people in AAAs.

María José Rodríguez, psychologist and AAI specialist at Centro IAA, leads a number of group activities and individual psychotherapy sessions where she works with individuals who have experienced trauma:

> In my private practice, I work mainly with children dealing with grief for their parent's divorce, [and] persons with emotional crises. I also work with hospitalized children with diverse physical

María José Rodríguez and her therapy dog, Afra. (Used with permission from M. J. Rodríguez.)

and emotional traumas. We do different projects in . . . facilities throughout the year. Some of those [projects include] a 10-session project in a mental health institution for women with autism, and a workshop for children in temporal shelters.

Overall, Centro IAA integrates therapy dogs as part of their team in order to capitalize on the benefits of this nontraditional and unique modality. With four psychologists and a number of volunteers and therapy dogs, Centro IAA is able to reach across the three domains of AAI: AAA, AAT, and AAE.

INTERVIEWS

Below we provide select content and context from our discussions with each of the four programs, according to the aforementioned interview themes.

Theme 1: Driving Factors for Choosing HAIs as a Point of Intervention

By asking each program interviewee why he or she chose to center interventions on HAIs (and/or animal welfare), we sought to understand what specific factors compelled them to enter this field. While a variety of animals have been used in HAIs, all four programs specifically integrate dogs into their interventions. For The Comfort Dog Project (CDP), Animals Asia (AA) and Dogs for People (DFP), animal welfare was described as a driving force for implementing dog-centered HAIs. This motivation makes sense, as these programs originally sprang from larger welfare organizations. Interestingly, however, these programs focused on different dimensions of welfare when describing their purpose for incorporating dogs.

Karina O'Carroll noted that, while some related organizations in China and Hong Kong utilize other animals in HAIs, Animals Asia specifically integrates dogs in their Dr. Dog and Professor Paws programs because it may be the most ethical choice.

> **K. O'Carroll, AA, Hong Kong:** We have 25 years of experience with dogs . . . and their behavior is something we know well and can appropriately assess pre- and during visits. . . . We have concerns that other species of animals may not be as adaptive as dogs can be, but also that the visit situations, such as transport and handling, could be traumatic to other species . . . the welfare of the animals is something we hold paramount; it is one of the main reasons why we work with dogs and their owners.

According to Victor Chitic, Dogs for People works primarily to redefine the role of stray dogs in Romanian culture.

> **V. Chitic, DFP, Romania:** We are using former stray dogs saved from various life-threatening or difficult conditions, thoroughly selected and trained to become therapy dogs, in order to change the Romanian public's mentality about stray dogs. So, although the beneficiaries are people, on the long-term animals also benefit from this project.

Sarah Schmidt described how The Comfort Dog Project saw a unique opportunity in northern Uganda where the human-dog bond was already a relatively strong cultural attribute, distinguishing these communities from others in Uganda.

> **S. Schmidt, CDP, Uganda:** Dogs were selected because—though in general in Uganda, dogs have terrible lives—we saw that in the north with the Acholi people, there were people who had really strong bonds with their animals. I talked with people in the villages who told me stories about living with their dogs in IDP camps, and the fact that it was very difficult to keep your dogs

in the camps. But, you know, they considered them part of the family, so they endured the hardship. . . . I have also repeatedly seen people who will carry their dogs on their backs for literally miles just to have their wound treated or will wait all day long for a rabies vaccination.

Additionally, the healing potential of the human-animal bond was experienced firsthand by the community psychologist, Francis Okello Oloya, an integral figure in the development and implementation of CDP in Uganda.

S. Schmidt, CDP, Uganda: The use of dogs in our program really came about because of Francis [who] is a war trauma survivor. He was blinded as a child by a bomb blast and lost his sight. [In high school], he really faced a lot of challenges, because the sleeping quarters were quite a distance from the latrine, and being a blind person . . . he had to find some way in the middle of the night to navigate himself from the sleeping quarters to the latrine. There were two dogs who lived next to the school who started to make a habit of watching out for Francis. When he would come out of his sleeping quarters at night, the dogs would come running over to him, letting him know they were there, and actually lead him to the latrine. And this happened every night for the years that he was in Gulu High School. Francis told me that having those dogs there to help him gave him such comfort and confidence that he could navigate the world.

The unwavering support, as well as the emotional and physical security, that Oloya received from these dogs contributed to his social and psychological well-being, ultimately inspiring him to formally incorporate dogs into the psychosocial rehabilitation of Northern Uganda's trauma survivors.

All programs expressed some level of rigor with regard to requirements for dog selection and implementation. Centro IAA, AA, and DFP all utilize a basic obedience and temperament test. For some, these tests are borrowed from established AAI organizations.

M. J. Rodríguez, Centro IAA, Costa Rica: My dog, Afra, was an offspring of an assistance dog from Spain. Since her birth, she was selected and trained to be a therapy dog; she is the one whom I work with daily. Currently, I own an eight-month-[old] Golden retriever that is training to become a therapy dog, too. For the other dogs that are volunteers, we apply a selection test based on the Pet Partners Program from the USA, and every six months we do a reevaluation . . . meeting . . . [that includes] role-plays and work[shops] for good handler-dog work.

V. Chitic, DFP, Romania: When we started the program in 2004, there was no other AAT program in Romania, so we had absolutely no idea what we were doing. We just knew that we wanted to do it for the children and for the animals. At the time, there were no books available (at least not in Romania), and not many Internet resources either. We searched for a long time for the perfect recipe—the perfect selection test. After a while, we realized we were chasing our own shadow. There was no perfect test. So, we made our own test by combining criteria from the American Kennel Club's "Good Citizenship" test and the Delta Society (at the time) tests. The result was a new generation of dogs that had never displayed any aggressiveness toward humans.

In Uganda, the selection of dogs for the CDP was described as a collaborative effort with community members who seek better homes for their dogs and know that this program can provide their animals with needed resources, such as food, hygiene, and veterinary health care.

S. Schmidt, CDP, Uganda: The [participating] dogs come from homes where there just isn't enough food or resources to take care of them. [Because] there was no veterinary care in northern Uganda for more than 20 years, the population of dogs grew very large. When people have a litter of puppies, some kill them. But, most people just let the dogs hang around. . . . As you can imagine, then, if a man can't feed his own children, the dog isn't going to see food very often. So, when you see dogs in the villages, they are usually very thin; they are full of worms and . . . parasites. It is not always a reflection that the people don't care about them. It is just that they don't have the resources. They don't have the money. They don't have food to be able to care for the dogs better.

So, whenever we indicate on the radio that we are looking for dogs for The Comfort Project, we usually have many, many people come forward who really care about their dogs [and] want to see a better life for their dogs. . . . We actually select the dogs who seem to have the calmest, friendliest personalities. And then we bring them back to the Big Fix and they undergo what we call "health rehabilitation." . . . We spay and neuter them, vaccinate them fully, deworm them, treat them for fleas and ticks, and try to get them in good condition, and start working with them to better socialize them and then the dogs will be ready for placement.

While the CDP does not utilize a specific test in dog selection, their process takes into account the needs of the community and the welfare of the animals, providing them with essential resources. In this way, the dogs, the community members, and the program participants all contribute to, and benefit from, the CDP's model, which enhances broader public health opportunities and outcomes.

Theme 2: Prominent Cultural Views Toward Mental Health and Trauma

All programs described cultural stigmas toward mental health, and expressed the need for expanding public education and awareness of trauma's psychosocial effects. Accordingly, interviewees noted that many people do not seek counseling for a number of reasons related to both cultural stigma and lack of opportunity.

K. O'Carroll, AA, Hong Kong: [In Hong Kong], people can still be quite "stoic" about traumatic events, brushing things under the carpet or just expecting individuals to "get over it."

V. Chitic, DFP, Romania: Unfortunately, [the stigma toward mental health in Romania] has a lot to do with gender roles. Traditionally, men are taught that they have to withstand anything in order to be "real men." Until roughly ten years ago, military service was mandatory. Going to the army was considered a lot like a rite of passage for boys to become men. In fairness, men were oftentimes subjected to abuse and then taught to inflict the same onto newcomers. Apparently, that made them "real men." Women, on the other hand, are sometimes taught the same thing, as long as it suits men. My view is that, for the most part, Romania is still a very patriarchal, traditional, religious, misogynistic society. It is true that things are starting to change, especially in the urban society with more access to education and information, but this change has come excruciatingly slow.

Chitic also noted that the stigmas regarding mental health prevent individuals from seeking help.

V. Chitic, DFP, Romania: In general, seeing a psychotherapist is still seen as a weakness. So, no, most men do not seek help. . . . The social pressure of mental vulnerability, as well as admitting even for one's self any kind of psychological vulnerability, is synonym to utter failure.

According to Rodríguez, both access to, and attitudes toward, mental health care in Costa Rica are split down the lines of socioeconomic status, thereby potentially creating marked disparities in recovery and treatment.

M. J. Rodríguez, Centro IAA, Costa Rica: Parents of a high or middle-high class usually seek professional help for their children when they suffered from some traumatic experience. What I have been able to observe in my professional experience is that there is no culture of commitment [to the therapeutic process]. People expect me, as . . . the therapist, to perform magic . . . in 3 or 4 sessions, everything [to be] addressed and all issues . . . healed. [For low-income families], usually the [stress] of poverty and violence impede them from visualizing the importance of . . . professional care to grow and overcome [mental health difficulties].

In countries like Uganda, however, mental health care is nearly impossible to attain:

S. Schmidt, CDP, Uganda: The mental health resources in Uganda are practically nonexistent. The entire country has one national mental health institution, which is the hospital, and that . . . is about 275 kilometers from Gulu. So, if you have a mental illness in northern Uganda, you have to get yourself into Gulu town, which for some people is more than two hours transport by vehicle. And people walk there. They don't get to ride in vehicles. And even if you get to Gulu . . . hospital, [it] is the [only] facility for over two million people. They have just a handful of mental health professionals. So, you can see that even getting to the hospital is a challenge, and even if you get there, seeing someone would be a challenge. And, if you get there, getting the kind of treatment that you need is nearly impossible.

Because mental health care is scarce in the communities of northern Uganda, many people have not been exposed to the "medicalized" discourse of PTSD and, therefore, have not connected their psychological suffering to past traumatic events from within this framework.

S. Schmidt, CDP, Uganda: What's very interesting to me is that while symptoms of post-traumatic stress disorder were widespread in the region, Francis told me that a lot of people didn't understand those things they were experiencing, like hypervigilance, nightmares . . . outbursts of anger, outbursts of sadness . . . they didn't know that those things were actually caused by what they had experienced in the war. No one had ever explained what post-traumatic stress disorder is, or that it has certain symptoms. So, people would just try to live with these symptoms and not even understand why they were having them.

Schmidt continued to explain how the organization provides initial and continuous community psycho-education to both inform the local people about trauma and its symptoms, as well as recruit those who may be interested in participating in the CDP.

S. Schmidt, CDP, Uganda: Francis held a number of meetings in the villages, and he encouraged people to come who had suffered during the war. He had large turnouts of people, and he basically sat down and explained to them that people who go through wartime experiences may now have these symptoms. He would talk about what these symptoms are: the nightmares, the flashbacks, the hypervigilance, the outbursts of anger, the withdrawal from society. And, people were recognizing, "Yes, I have that!" Now they were being provided with an explanation for why they were suffering with those things. Then, in the course of holding these village counseling sessions, Francis begins to introduce the concept of The Comfort Dog Project.

Still, Schmidt noted that there continues to be stigma associated with mental health and symptoms resulting from traumatic experiences.

> **S. Schmidt, CDP, Uganda:** I think that [trauma is] generally viewed as being a weakness, something that is shameful. The people I've known in Uganda have a real resilience, which has always impressed me. Life here is extremely difficult. It takes most of the day to cook a meal, because it is so involved—carrying the water, going to pick the things . . . life is very, very difficult. So, there is sort of this attitude that there is no time to have any personal problems. You've got to take care of your work; you get food to your family that day, and that's enough to worry about. . . . People are just expected to go on with their lives.

Notably, most of these programs counter the cultural stigmas associated with mental health and trauma through facilitating interventions that ultimately educate individuals and communities about the needs of animals, as well as the therapeutic power of animals and the human-animal bond. As such, attention to mental health concerns likely becomes more normalized in the process.

Theme 3: Cultural Stereotypes and Views of Animals

Those involved in all four programs spoke extensively about the various views and stereotypes of animals and animal roles in their respective countries and how these views impacted their AAI practices. A common theme that emerged was the perception of animals—particularly dogs or certain types of dogs (i.e., strays)—as unclean, diseased, and thus, menacing or undesirable.

> **S. Schmidt, CDP, Uganda:** Oftentimes, when people see dogs just running loose, they think that the dog is rabid. So, we'd [see] a desire [amongst some] to want to just kill that dog that is running loose.

V. Chitic, DFP, Romania: I guess the most common cultural variable is the prejudice regarding dogs. They bite, they are dirty, they spread disease . . . it is mainly about fear, and I believe this fear comes from lack of proper education regarding dogs.

In Uganda, fear was also based on the traditional role of dogs as the family protector, as well as their participation in wartime operations. As such, prior to the program's implementation, dogs in Uganda were often perceived as aggressive, which initially hindered the acceptability of their inclusion in services designed to help people.

S. Schmidt, CDP, Uganda: There are a lot of people who really fear dogs within northern Uganda, especially those who served in the rebel army, because dogs were fierce protectors of their homes and families. So, the rebel soldiers routinely came across very viscous dogs . . . and many of them were attacked by those dogs. Many [dogs] lost their lives during the war because of their protective instincts. Nowadays, still, many people keep dogs for protection. Those dogs are not socialized; they're just there to be aggressive and to scare off intruders. . . . So, the idea of having a dog as a best friend really seemed crazy to those people. And then the idea that a dog could actually help you with your problems . . . that really seemed [strange].

Views such as these were challenging when the concept of AAI was initially introduced. However, many of the interviewees believed these stereotypes had lessened over time, and were, in many cases, impacted by the projects' activities.

M. J. Rodríguez, Centro IAA, Costa Rica: One barrier has been the perception that dogs are dirty and can transmit diseases, even if this is not the case, since we comply with a protocol for cleaning and prevention of zoonosis . . . [however], something that supports this type of therapy is that dogs now are considered part of the families; this change has come about in the last few decades. This makes parents more comfortable with using dogs as a therapeutic tool in supporting their children's therapy program.

S. Schmidt, CDP, Uganda: So, when we started our project, a lot of our initial guardians were ridiculed for, you know, walking with a dog on a leash, going to a dog training class, you know, wearing a shirt saying you were part of a dog project—they were ridiculed for that. And, they really had to undergo some hardship just to be part of the project. But now, over time, people have started noticing that Comfort Dogs are very clean, healthy-looking dogs . . . that has created a desire for other people to have dogs like those Comfort Dogs—those dogs who look so nice, and are so well-behaved and obedient, and will sit down and come, and will do all these things when asked. . . . People are really starting to see that dogs do have a nice purpose; that they are protective, but that they are also friendly.

A CDP participant and his dog. (Used with permission from the CDP.)

K. O'Carroll, AA, Hong Kong: Culturally, I would say in both [Hong Kong and broader China], there is definitely—in the last ten years, I would say—a growing interest and increase in animal welfare issues and knowledge. And, people are paying more attention to what is happening with animals, and realizing, obviously, that animals are sentient, and they do deserve our respect and care, [including] how we treat them in all different industries as well.

These evolving attitudes have promising implications for animal welfare, animal involvement in mental health treatment, and enhanced relationships between community members and animals.

In addition, individual and community attitudes toward animals help shape pet keeping practices. Interviewees noted that these practices were directly tied to shifting cultural attitudes regarding animal sentience, and consequently, increased awareness of animal welfare issues.

K. O'Carroll, AA, Hong Kong: We've got a bit of an overpopulation of [companion] animals issue in Hong Kong at the moment. So, we're always promoting adopting over buying. . . . Obviously, China's a much bigger place than Hong Kong, so they have more rural communities. . . . They've got a rapid increase currently in pet ownership and companionship. So, awareness of animal welfare issues is rising. But, I think for China, unfortunately, the legislation in regard to animal welfare policy is still . . . lacking, but we hope that soon there will be change in that area. In Hong Kong, we actually have good . . . animal legislation for animal care and welfare and animal cruelty, but sometimes there are issues with enforcement of those laws.

While O'Carroll noted that the increase in pet keeping has raised awareness around animal sentience and welfare considerations, Chitic claimed that, in Romania, awareness of animal sentience does not always translate to humane practices.

V. Chitic, DFP, Romania: Pet owners certainly share [the] view [that dogs are sentient], but sometimes there are : . . logical inconsistencies like: "I love dogs, I have a pet dog, but I hate stray dogs, I think they should all be killed."

Indeed, pet keeping trends in Romania bring new welfare concerns to the fore, particularly around ethical care practices.

V. Chitic, DFP, Romania: I would say [pets are] very common, at least in an urban environment. Although, it is just my opinion, since there is no official statistic on pet ownership [in Romania] . . . most people have cats or dogs. Parrots or other caged birds, or sweet water tropical fish are also common and [were common] during the Communist regime. The new pets that came in the latest years with the proliferation of pet stores and especially [the] online pet trade—which is largely not regulated and raises major welfare concerns—are reptiles, amphibians, and rodents. It seems there is a rising demand for ferrets recently.

Noting his concerns about pet keeping and animal welfare issues, Chitic continued to speculate on the factors driving irresponsible practices in pet keeping, including often inappropriate attitudes regarding animals and their particular attributes.

V. Chitic, DFP, Romania: [I've] found that people rarely go through [the] process of informing themselves before getting a pet, or, if they do, they tend to disregard the information related to specific potential problematic behavior in favor of—most often—how the animal looks. Regarding pet keeping in Romania, there is also a history of successive 'fashion' trends, as I mentioned about the ferrets earlier. At some point during the Communist regime, for example, Airedale terriers were in high demand and were considered something of a social status. Only rich and [influential] people could afford to get and raise one. It might be worth mentioning here the fact that that period—[the] mid- to late 1980s—was marked by food shortages, especially meat. Airedales are big dogs that require a lot of food, hence their exclusive nature among Romanians at the time. Now, you can hardly see a few such dogs in the parks or streets of Bucharest.

Problematic trends in pet keeping, and animal welfare in general, are certainly not endemic to Romania, as all four programs point to notable shortcomings with regard to welfare practices in their respective countries. By seeking to challenge harmful cultural stereotypes of animals, these programs are forging spaces for creative alternatives in multiple domains of animal and public health.

Theme 4: Challenges of Running an HAI Program

Throughout these discussions, interviewees identified two key challenges of running an HAI program in their respective countries: cultural stereotypes of animals and the lack of information and resources pertaining to AAIs.

S. Schmidt, CDP, Uganda: The general stereotype about dogs [has] been our most challenging [issue]. One of our loveliest first-year Comfort Dogs was actually murdered because of those beliefs. It was just a tragedy. The young client who had this dog was so devoted . . . loved her so much. They were doing just so well together. And, because of either jealousy or bad feelings toward dogs in general, the dog was just brutally attacked by someone in the village.

V. Chitic, DFP, Romania: Most challenges stemmed from the way people regarded dogs in general and stray dogs in particular. In 2004, when we started, there were a lot more prejudices against dogs than there are now. The program was well received by the public and the press because it was a novelty and exploited the good image of anybody doing anything for free for children with disabilities. From this point of view, the program has always been beyond critiques.

While cultural attitudes and prejudices regarding animals are a major challenge to these programs, lack of resources and information also presents barriers. Chitic noted how limited AAI information and resources required him to prepare for the challenges posed by skeptics largely on his own.

V. Chitic, DFP, Romania: One of the challenges we faced in the be-ginning was the scarcity of information regarding this field. Fortunately, [that is] not the case anymore. That forced us to be creative, [to] develop selection procedures for dogs and targeted interventions with the dogs . . . another challenge was the reluc-tance of institutions to collaborate with us. The main concerns were dog biting, zoonosis, and lack of efficiency. I managed to convince them by always being prepared with an answer, up-to-date proof of health checks of the dogs, scientific papers of the benefits of interaction with dogs, and explaining in detail our selection process for dogs.

Likewise, Rodríguez explains how she navigated the lack of AAI re-sources, information, and professional partnerships in Costa Rica.

M. J. Rodríguez, Centro IAA, Costa Rica: The main difficulty in Costa Rica is the lack of formal education in AAI. There were no universities or educational centers to provide a formal training in this field. So, I had to search for a foreign university to get the proper certification [the Institute for Human-Animal Connection at the University of Denver]. When I came to Costa Rica with my certificate, I tried to join an organization who were working on AAI here, but they didn't want people with a different preparation, so I started from my own.

Theme 5: Welfare Considerations

Interviewees described specific steps taken to prevent welfare issues among participating animals from emerging. For example, the CDP has an extensive process through which they screen participants, and ensure the home environment will be safe and welcoming for a Comfort Dog.

S. Schmidt, CDP, Uganda: Francis spends time counseling each person before they are even considered for the program. So, he knows the person, whether they are stable, whether they are going to be able to provide a good home for the dog, whether the families can be supportive of the idea. . . . We have them interact with our dogs, so we can witness for ourselves: Are they afraid of dogs? . . . Then we go to the house and Francis talks to all the family members and makes sure everybody is on board with the idea.

We talk to the local leader [as well]. In Uganda, the local leaders . . . are very important. The LC1 [Local Council Leader] knows everybody in the village intimately. So, we talk to the LC1s. We make sure the house is a safe environment for the dog. And, then, if a person passes all that criteria, they attend an animal care class and they have to complete that successfully. If they complete that class successfully, then they're paired with a mentor who is a graduate of our program. . . . That mentor is actually paid a small compensation to follow up regularly with the new guardian and their dog, to visit the home, and make sure things are going well. Also, we have a humane officer who goes regularly to visit the new guardians after the dogs have been placed. And, then, the guardians attend a weekly training class where they come with the dogs. . . . So, we observe them with their dogs. We have one of our vet doctors who is always present at the weekly training, so . . . we are making sure that any illness or injuries are being addressed regularly as it comes about. The dogs will continue to receive free veterinary care for life from the Big Fix as well. . . . The only problem we have is that a lot of our dogs are overweight. People actually overfeed them, so we are having to monitor the food a little bit. It's 'funny' because some of our clients are so, so thin, but some of our dogs are so, so fat, because that's a way of showing your love. You feed the one that you love.

Schmidt also described an important cultural practice that anchors the guardian's life commitment to the Comfort Dog within the community.

S. Schmidt, CDP, Uganda: We also have a very, very serious guardian commitment that the guardian has to sign before the dog is placed. And the signing of that guardian commitment occurs in the presence of the LC1. So, that guardian commitment is signed not only with all the comforts of having people present, but also the LC1 is present. So, it adds a very serious thing, culturally. That guardian commitment provides that person with a lifelong commitment to their dogs, that they will always carry out for the dog with certain criteria, and [that] there are consequences if that's not carried out.

Indeed, for the CDP, working closely with the cultural traditions and structures of local communities ensures that welfare practices will be internalized and codified within local networks of meaning.

Theme 6: Outcomes at the Individual and Community Level

Interviewees described various outcomes and/or mechanisms of change—both for the people and for the animals—associated with their HAI program. The stories and anecdotes they shared point to impacts across individual and community scales. For instance, Schmidt explained how involvement with caretaking practices reframes the guardians' basic understanding of the human-dog bond, which ultimately filters out into the community through outreach projects. These observations are in line with research (Wood, Giles-Corti, Bulsara, & Borsche, 2007, p. 43) demonstrating that companion animals have a "ripple effect"; that is, pets have meaningful benefits not only for their owners, but also for the broader communities in which they live.

> **S. Schmidt, CDP, Uganda:** We actually teach dog grooming and washing. And, when we first started doing this people thought we were absolutely insane, because nobody ever washed a dog or thought of doing that. The problem is that most of the dogs living in the village or in the bush are very dirty, smelly, most have mange, and they are all covered with fleas and ticks. . . . [After grooming and bathing], we found that not only did [people] want to touch their dogs, but they didn't want to put their dogs on the ground again when they were clean. There were people who actually would carry their dogs home. They were so delighted that their dogs were clean, and they began touching and petting their dogs and interacting more with their dogs. So, we really felt like that was helping us to accomplish one of our main goals, which was to promote good human-animal bond. So, now we have our CDP people going out and teaching grooming and washing. And, now, we're running into, you know, teaching basic obedience as part of their [grooming] time and having people interacting in a good way with their dogs. Before . . . dogs were guard dogs; they were used for hunting, and that was it. They were not touched or handled or invited into the house or treated as friends. And now, we've seen it changing, . . . because of [this] education.

Dog grooming, according to Schmidt, becomes a means through which the human-animal bond is strengthened, contributing to the therapeutic process in the guardian's psychosocial rehabilitation. One author/ interviewer asked Schmidt about the significance of the human-animal bond for other areas of the guardians' lives.

> **Author/Interviewer:** Do you, as a program, believe that the emphasis—almost metaphorical emphasis—on animal well-being then translates to the client's human application of that to themselves or their families?

CDP participants train and work with their comfort dogs. (Used with permission from the CDP.)

S. Schmidt, CDP, Uganda: Yes, our observation is that . . . all of our guardians love their dogs so much. They think of them as children. They refer to them as my son or my daughter. There is really strong affection. We have had people who come to us and say, "My dog is sick. You have to come see him right away!" And we'll go visit the dog and find that actually . . . the dog is not really in that bad of condition. The dog might have a cough or a cut or something. . . . [But], we find that the person is actually very sick, but that is not their concern at all. The guardian's concern is the dog. So, even when they aren't able to acknowledge their own issue because they're recognizing something in the dog, they're able to make an improvement.

Let me tell you a great story to illustrate that: One of our clients suffered terrible atrocities—lost his wife and two children in the war, right in front of him. He was suffering from terrible depression and flashbacks. To try to cope . . . he [became addicted to] alcohol. We brought him to The Comfort Dog Project, and he immediately formed a strong bond with his dog. . . . [Soon] he became very, very ill, [and] he couldn't get out of his house or get any help. His dog went and got help for him. He ended up being in the hospital for a month. He believes the dog saved his life. So, he's very strongly bonded with this dog. Last time I saw him, I was told he was no longer drinking alcohol, which had been his major problem. One of his major things was avoidance of his symptoms through his use of alcohol. He stopped drinking alcohol. And I said, 'What? How did that come about?' . . . He said that his dog didn't like the smell of alcohol, so he had to stop drinking it.

This story reveals the power of a therapeutic human-animal bond, and the unique, yet indirect, way individuals can heal through the often uncomplicated relational dynamics shared with their animal companion. What is more, this particular connection was likely strengthened through this individual's enhanced perceptions of his dog (and thus the dog's worth and utility)—from serving as a helpful companion to a literal savior. In this way, the importance of the bond with his dog superseded his dependence on alcohol. It is unknown whether this healthy change in behavior and self-care stemmed from his desire to be a good guardian for his dog, from concern for his dog's welfare if he continued drinking, and/or via the replacement of alcohol with a far more effective source of solace and comfort—canine companionship. However, what is evident and remarkable is the level of trust and commitment that both he and his dog had for each other, and how these elements strengthened the potential for recovery through mutuality. As Schmidt noted, "If we magnify the value of the life of these dogs, if we reject the notion that their lives are disposable, and we value them, then . . . the guardians also feel valued in their own life" (personal communication, September 14, 2016).

Many stories shared by the interviewees referred to individual, therapeutic breakthroughs that resulted from HAIs.

M. J. Rodríguez, Centro IAA, Costa Rica: Recently, in a hospital there was a little girl [who] was about eight years old who was bitten by their house dog; her head had numerous stitches. When we [arrived] with the dogs, she was playing in the games room. When she saw us, she became alarmed and suspicious. We didn't approach her or seek to contact her; instead, we started by interacting with the other kids. About 15 minutes later, she came with her mother and asked for a brush to pet the dog and the magic began! Silently, she reached out for the dog's ears and the dog carefully allowed her to caress [its] ears. Over the course of 30 minutes, she was giving the dog a prize for being so good and obedient. She and her mother learned about dog body language, and began healing the fear from being [bitten].

Another anecdote is that of a boy who was in my office because of the divorce of his parents. He started to cry because he did not understand why his dad would not come back to the house. At that moment, Afra looked at him and licked the tear that ran down his cheek. He, with a slight smile, [embraced] her and [said], "Afra, you understand me. You know that I miss my dad very much."

V. Chitic, DFP, Romania: I would say that the most spectacular case was this 12-year-old girl that had been sexually abused by her stepfather. At the time, she was being brought daily by her mother to this daycare center owned by an NGO. She never talked about what happened to her to anybody and she was very withdrawn. After a few sessions of working with one of our dogs, she developed a fantastic relationship with the dog, and she started talking with the dog and sharing things about herself. She started sharing details about her abuse to the dog.

Throughout these accounts, the nonthreatening interactions with therapy dogs seemed to invite individuals to safely process important aspects of their trauma experiences—a breakthrough that could be attributed to the therapeutic nature of the human-animal bond.

Furthermore, O'Carroll noted that animal welfare outcomes empowered community members in Hong Kong and China through exposure and humane education.

K. O'Carroll, AA, Hong Kong: Our main aim was to originally promote animal welfare through people welfare. It was giving people a positive experience with animals to change their . . . beliefs and the way they think about animals. But, as more people were coming to understand that dogs have feelings . . . they were then changing their attitudes toward those animals and standing up to cruel trades, for example, in dog and cat meat eating . . . and the rise of adoptions, and not buying animals from pet shops. They're not commodities, they're not toys. . . . There was more animal

Children participate in a Professor Paws activity. (Used with permission from Animals Asia.)

welfare focus initially, but over the years, people can see the positive change in people as well.

Indeed, the promotion and implementation of humane practices is intimately connected to human public health and well-being. All of these programs demonstrate that positive HAIs can facilitate healing, reframe attitudes about animals and animal connections, and promote humane and conscientious behaviors—outcomes that are intrinsically interconnected.

Theme 7: Advice for Practitioners

When asked to reflect on the challenges their organizations faced when implementing their HAI programs, interviewees offered important advice on creating programs that are both well-informed and culturally competent.

> **S. Schmidt, CDP, Uganda:** You need the advice of an expert. . . . The other recommendation I would have is that actual on the ground-work must be [closely] involved with a local person who is intimately familiar with the local culture, because as an outsider, we can never fully create those cultural idiosyncrasies that are so

important to being effective. . . . Another really important thing is education. The Comfort Dog Project didn't start until early 2015, The Big Fix had already been working for three years doing education in the schools and in the villages about the Five Animal Freedoms . . . about the sentience of animals. If we hadn't had that work already done, it would have been very challenging to come in and just start the program. But, people in the Gulu district had already been exposed to these ideas for several years. So, that was important.

K. O'Carroll, AA, Hong Kong: I think, on the ground, the volunteers that we have for Dr. Dog and Professor Paws, most of them are local community members, so they have their networks of friends and their networks of people that we can go and visit, too. It definitely helps to have a sort of local knowledge and an understanding of culture as well. In Hong Kong, we don't really have a cat and dog eating issue here, because it is illegal. But it is . . . still happening in China and obviously other parts of Asia as well. So, trying to do education work on those topics, and having your volunteer staff [be] aware of the cultural sensitivity, and . . . to still be able to do the education work while understanding all that is definitely critical. . . . Having local staff and local knowledge . . . really does make a difference when you're trying to tailor your education or tailor your impact—or what you're trying to get across to the local community.

V. Chitic, DFP, Romania: Be aware of any cultural factors and prejudices against animals in general, and dogs in particular. Get to know other people involved in HAI locally—view them as colleagues and partners, not as competitors . . . there's room for everyone.

The advice provided by the interviewees highlights the necessary collaborations with local people, organizations, and institutions for effective HAI programs that are culturally inclusive and responsible. Cultural competence, as an ongoing process, allows for a program that is well integrated with local systems and values, and is therefore empowering for the community members who are involved.

DISCUSSION

In this chapter, we highlighted four international HAI programs that are integrated in different cultural contexts, and are seeking to improve the conditions and welfare of animals, as well as the mental health care and/or trauma recovery of people in their countries and local communities. The Comfort Dog Project in Uganda, Dogs for People Program in Romania, Animals Asia Foundation in Hong Kong, and Centro IAA in Costa Rica offer insights that underscore the unique ways that HAI programs are implemented in cultures traditionally unfamiliar with this modality. Cultural contexts, viewpoints, and traditions clearly shape conceptions of mental health, trauma, animals, and human-animal interactions, broadly. As these four programs—and others doing similar work—navigate these contexts in ethical and nuanced ways, they also contribute exponentially to the field by making it more culturally inclusive, relevant, and informed.

While these programs undoubtedly experience challenges in implementing therapeutic and welfare interventions in countries with certain stereotypes about animals, specifically dogs, they have found creative ways to develop their HAI interventions to ultimately benefit the individuals, the animals, and the communities as a whole. These HAI programs have thus forged important paths into complicated cultural situations and, through inviting collaboration with local knowledge sources, have developed new and effective organizational and practice models. These models thereby provide the field of AAI with important, and in some cases even novel, information on the therapeutic application of the human-animal bond, and should be widely recognized, invested in, and studied accordingly.

In addition, the interviews included in this chapter have raised a number of important questions that may inform the broader field of AAI research and practice. For instance, most interviewees described how they push against negative cultural stereotypes of animals, which ultimately mediates the implementation of AAIs. Once positive AAIs are facilitated, powerful therapeutic outcomes may take place, such as increased client/participant self-efficacy and support during therapy, reduction of trauma symptoms, and attitudinal shifts with regard to humane practices, animal welfare, and trauma recovery. In other words, the bond enables the outcomes. One must ask, then: Is there a transcultural understanding of the human-animal bond as a phenomenon? Do these programs tap into a natural affiliation by facilitating these positive encounters? By examining

HAIs in international contexts, we gain insight into these important questions via the human-animal bond from a variety of perspectives, not merely our own.

Another important question pertains to the mechanisms of change associated with the human-animal bond, particularly in different cultural contexts. The Western-centered approach to psychotherapy is focused on the individual—the psyche—and often AAT is directed with this framework in mind. However, some international programs—such as The Comfort Dog Project, discussed here—do not approach psychosocial rehabilitation from trauma in this way. Rather, they facilitate powerful bonds between the guardians and the comfort dogs, and allow the therapeutic outcomes (for individual people and animals, as well as the community) to unfold in the process. Thus, an important question about the mechanisms of change involved in these processes is raised: How do indirect aspects of AAIs contribute to therapeutic outcomes, both on the individual and community level? Are there parallel psychological processes that take place when an individual grooms, feeds, trains, nurtures, visits with, or simply observes a companion animal that help them process traumas? Do indirect AAIs, based on the relational (and often nonverbal) aspects of the human-animal bond, create a dynamic and flexible space for cultural difference that traditional, Western models of psychotherapy do not? And, does the indirect, nonthreatening nature of these AAIs normalize mental health and illness in communities where it has traditionally been stigmatized? Clearly, we are just beginning to scratch the surface in understanding the implications of HAI programs and applications—both international, as well as more well-known Westernized practices—for the field of AAI.

Insofar as the AAI field is influenced by Euro-American mental health traditions, implementing HAI programs cross-culturally or in locations where AAI is not yet broadly supported requires important ethical and practical considerations. Jegatheesan (2015) recommends three primary components for "a culturally responsive framework for AAI" when working with diverse clients, although these can certainly apply to program implementation as well: 1) cultural self-awareness, with an emphasis on one's own cultural biases, assumptions, prejudices, and privileges; 2) knowledge of clients gained through "dialogue-based" interactions; and 3) skill development, so that services are provided in a culturally respectful, inclusive, and effective manner.

Across the board, the four participating interviewees highlighted specific considerations, or competencies, for implementing a successful HAI program in a non-Western culture. Cultural competence and animal welfare were the most highly noted considerations. Cultural competence includes continuous collaborative dialogues with local cultures to learn about customs, attitudes toward animals, and histories. The Comfort Dog Project, for example, demonstrates the importance of infusing local traditions and knowledge into one's organization. Understanding the role of the local leaders (LC1s) in the communities allowed the program to develop an appropriate contract for the guardians that ensures a lifelong commitment to their comfort dog. This contract is weighted by the cultural significance of having the LC1 witness its signing; the guardian thus feels empowered by the weight of this commitment and the expectations of revered leaders, as he or she is supported by the community in maintaining his or her own integrity. This program ritual also helps to ensure that the tenets of the program are aligned with the local values and belief systems, which ultimately contributes to the program's success.

The other major consideration for a successful HAI program is the promotion of animal welfare. Ensuring humane practices is intrinsically tied to positive therapeutic outcomes for people; if animal well-being is compromised, so too are any potential benefits of the interaction. Indeed, a number of these programs noted beneficial outcomes across individual, animal, and community levels. These transformations are undoubtedly due to the integrative nature of these programs in that they pair animal welfare with human welfare in an expanded model that ultimately promotes public health.

The programs interviewed in this chapter also model the important interconnections between human and animal health and well-being that are highlighted by the One Health model (One Health Initiative, 2017). This model, originating with the interdisciplinary study of zoonosis, asserts that "human health (including mental health via the human-animal bond phenomenon), animal health, and ecosystem health are inextricably linked," and calls for collaborations across disciplines to ensure health and well-being for all species (One Health Initiative, 2017, para. 1). Programs that are informed by the One Health framework may thus avoid the asymmetrical power relations that often result from the imposition of missionary-like agendas in international contexts. Indeed, within the One Health framework, one species/one cultural framework/one ideology cannot be elevated above the rest, because health outcomes (including mental health) are contingent upon the well-being of the ecosystem as a whole. It is no surprise, then, that many of these featured programs, which were initially animal welfare-focused, have developed human welfare and mental health agendas. Integrating animal welfare with human health agendas via the framework of One Health allows HAI programs to facilitate trailblazing interventions that are ultimately humane and culturally inclusive. The four programs outlined in this chapter provide a glimpse of the unique ways that such interventions can be implemented across the globe with profound outcomes.

ACKNOWLEDGMENTS

We would like to thank our four interviewees (Victor Chitic, Karina O'Carroll, María José Rodríguez, and Sarah Schmidt and their respective organizations) for their time and interest in participating in this chapter, and for sharing with us the very good work they do each and every day. We also extend our sincere gratitude to their clients and animal participants.

REFERENCES

American Psychiatric Association. (2013). *Diagnostic and statistical manual of mental disorders* (5th ed.). Arlington, VA: Author.

Animals Asia. (2017). *Who we are.* Retrieved from https://www.animalsasia.org/us/about-us/who-we-are.html

Breslau, J. (2004). Cultures of trauma: Anthropological views of posttraumatic stress disorder in international health. *Culture, Medicine and Psychiatry, 28,* 113–126.

Centro de Intervenciones Asistidas con Animales. (2017). *Proyectos de TAA.* Retrieved from https://www.centroiaa.com

Chhim, S. (2013). Baksbat (broken courage): A trauma-based cultural syndrome in Cambodia. *Medical Anthropology, 32*(2), 160–173.

de Jong, J. T., & Reis, R. (2010). Kiyang-yang, a west-African postwar idiom of distress. *Culture, Medicine, and Psychiatry, 34,* 301–321.

Dogs for People. (2017). *Four paws: More humanity towards animals.* Retrieved from http://www.four-paws.org.uk/projects/stray-animals/dogs-for-people/

Dr. Dog. (2017). *Animals Asia*. Retrieved from https://www.animalsasia.org/us/our-work/cat-and-dog-welfare/what-we-do/dr-dog.html

Flouri, E. (2005). Post-traumatic stress disorder (PTSD): What we have learned and what we still have not found. *Journal of Interpersonal Violence*, *20*(4), 373–379.

Gray, P. B., & Young, S. M. (2011). Human-pet dynamics in cross-cultural perspective. *Anthrozoös*, *24*(1), 17–30.

Hall, S. (1997). Foucault: Power, knowledge, and discourse. In M. Wetherell, S. Taylor, & S. J. Yates (Eds.), *Discourse theory and practice: A reader* (pp. 72–81). London, UK: Sage.

Hinton, D. E., Pich, V., Marques, L., Nickerson, A., & Pollack, M. H. (2010). *Khyâl* attacks: A key idiom of distress among traumatized Cambodia refugees. *Culture, Medicine, and Psychiatry*, *34*, 244–278.

IAHAIO. (2017). *Overview of our member organizations*. Retrieved from http://iahaio.org/overview-of-members/

Jegatheesan, B. (2015). Influence of cultural and religious factors on attitudes toward animals. In A. H. Fine (Ed.), *Handbook on animal-assisted therapy: Foundations and guidelines for animal-assisted interventions* (4th ed., pp. 37–41). San Diego, CA: Academic Press.

Kohrt, B. A., & Hruschka, D. J. (2010). Nepali concepts of psychological trauma: The role of idioms of distress, ethnopsychology and ethnophysiology in alleviating suffering and preventing stigma. *Culture, Medicine, and Psychiatry*, *34*, 322–352.

Nichter, M. (2010). Idioms of distress revisited. *Culture, Medicine, and Psychiatry*, *34*, 401–416.

One Health Initiative. (2017). Mission statement. Retrieved from http://www.onehealthinitiative.com/mission.php

Professor Paws. (2017). Animals Asia. Retrieved from https://www.animalsasia.org/us/our-work/cat-and-dog-welfare/what-we-do/professor-paws.html

Serpell, J. A. (2004). Factors influencing human attitudes to animals and their welfare. *Animal Welfare*, *13*, 145–151.

Suarez, E. B. (2016). Trauma in global contexts: Integrating local practices and socio-cultural meanings into new explanatory frameworks of trauma. *International Social Work*, *59*(1), 141–153.

Szűcs, E., Geers, R., Jezierski, T., Sossidou, E. N., & Broom, D. M. (2012). Animal welfare in different human cultures, traditions and religious faiths. *Asian-Australasian Journal of Animal Sciences*, *25*(11), 1499–1506.

The Comfort Dog Project. (2017). *Promoting human-animal bonds.* Retrieved from http://www.thebigfixuganda.org/the-comfort-dog-project.html

Wood, L., Giles-Corti, B., Bulsara, M. K., & Bosch, D. A. (2007). More than a furry companion: The ripple effect of companion animals on neighborhood interactions and sense of community. *Society & Animals, 15,* 43–56.

World Animal Net. (2017). *Animal welfare in context: Religion.* Retrieved from http://worldanimal.net/documents/4_Religion.pdf

Zambrano-Erazo, S., Guzmán-Villa, D. C., Hurtado-González, C. A., Seminec, D., De la Cruz-Cifuentes, Triviño, O., & Olayo, J. (2017). Neuropsychological abnormalities in patients diagnosed with post-traumatic stress disorder. *Biomedical Research, 28*(6), 2609–2616.

Zur, J. (1996). From PTSD to voices in context: From an "experience-far" to an "experience-near" understanding of responses to war and atrocity across cultures. *International Journal of Social Psychiatry, 42*(4), 305–317.

ABOUT THE AUTHORS

Betty Jean Curran, LMSW, AASW, is the director of Student Services at EPEC's The Grooming Project in Kansas City, Missouri, a 501c3 nonprofit that trains parents living in poverty to become successful dog groomers. Earning her Master of Social Work from the University of Denver, Curran had the opportunity to work closely with the Institute for Human-Animal Connection on a number of research projects. It was here that she became passionate about understanding and utilizing the powerful and therapeutic potential of the human-animal bond in a variety of contexts.

Biographical sketches for **Molly A. Jenkins** and **Philip Tedeschi** can be found on p. 12 of this volume.

Conclusions

Molly A. Jenkins, MSW, AASW; and Philip Tedeschi, MSSW, LCSW

With this book, we and the contributing chapter authors sought to shed light on the ever-evolving fields of animal-assisted intervention (AAI) practice and research, particularly in regard to the inclusion of animals in various modes of human trauma treatment and recovery. This domain is currently experiencing swift attention and growth, expanding in ways that we are likely not even aware of. This is both exciting and a bit daunting, and as editors of the first book to highlight these specific applications, we have felt a great responsibility to facilitate the provision of material that is as practically useful as it is intriguing.

However, we feel it is important to acknowledge that this volume is not intended to be a comprehensive review of trauma-informed AAI practice but, rather, a presentation of some of the key theoretical models, methodologies, research findings, and scientific pursuits that exist today, as well as how each of these adds to the knowledge base and lays the foundation for further understanding. To be sure, an updated edition will likely be needed in the near future to account for the breadth of promising and complex work currently underway in this area. Just as the types and impacts of trauma are incredibly vast, so too are our relationships with animals and the potential avenues for healing through human-animal connection. It is, in fact, the depth of this very connection—in all of its resonant, genuine, and indescribable forms—that makes the AAI field so exciting, and so promising for those facing the hardships of trauma, in the first place.

Across the preceding chapters, a certain commonality regarding AAI applications and their effects became apparent. Whether through pairing service dogs with military veterans facing post-traumatic stress (PTS); help-ing children take responsibility for the care and/or training of camels and other animals in nature-based settings; offering therapy dog visitation for those in crisis in the wake of disaster; or incorporating play with animals in a therapeutic context with children who have been maltreated, it was clear that connecting with animals provided an overwhelming, and largely unique, sense of security for people with trauma. Relationships charac-terized by both physical and emotional safety, as well as trust nourished by reliable support, are often exactly what traumatized individuals and communities need the most.

Research and anecdotal accounts widely attest to the comfort and ac-ceptance people experience when in the presence of animals; with animals, we are free from the anxiety of self-doubt or second-guessing the unknown, and can feel assured in the tender stability of the bond we have collec-tively forged. In the trauma-informed practices covered in this volume, the benefits of *animal-assisted safety* and/or *bio-affiliative safety* manifested in a number of ways, including (but not limited to) directly or indirectly creating comfort and even joy with the therapist and throughout the ther-apeutic process; serving as a grounding force and secure base of which to focus or return to when discussing or (re-) experiencing traumatic events; providing opportunities and impetus for calm during periods of distress, emotional dysregulation, or hyperarousal; offering a sense of physical se-curity; and facilitating greater ease when (re-) engaging with others and the social and natural world.

Moreover, several authors discussed how animals can enhance people's feelings of self-efficacy, -worth, and -purpose, all of which may have been stifled by trauma and loss. Often, this took the form of mastery through learning about the behavior, preferences, and sensitivities of a particular species and its habitat; teaching or training an animal to perform certain tasks; practicing empathic and relational skills with animals for use in other social contexts; and actively attending to the needs of animals by ensuring they were healthy, clean, well-fed, and treated with kindness. As several chapter authors discussed, the importance of being cared for by someone we trust, while also providing care and compassion for that someone with neither shame nor trepidation, cannot be overstated.

Throughout each of these activities and achievements, the element of connection with the animal was always a steady fixture. In this sense, one could argue that, through healthy and humane attachment to animals, we may be more apt to question our assumptions about them, and empathize with them through recognition of their unique strengths and capabilities, as well as the common experiences we share. In turn, advocacy for animal welfare on a broad scale could likely advance by way of AAI participation and, as Bexell, Clayton and Myers highlight in their chapter, through observing "care, concern, and admiration for [animals]" as modeled by therapists, handlers, and other AAI interventionists.

Potential evidence of such developments was discernible across various chapters in this book, including in our interviews with four international AAI programs. For example, through dog bathing in Uganda, project participants (the majority of them war trauma survivors) were able to care for, and bond with, their individual comfort dogs, all while transforming common cultural and community perceptions of dogs as dirty and unsafe. Interestingly, most of the international programs featured in this book first stemmed from animal welfare initiatives, which then later led to the incorporation of a human mental health focus. Thus, these interventions, whether primarily human- or animal-centered, have ample potential for bidirectional and mutual benefits, granted that the welfare of animals be given equal footing. These features can assist in the healing and progress of individuals and communities alike, and could even help encourage the respectful treatment of a wide variety of animals who, they themselves, may be burdened with the aftermath of trauma or cruelty.

Despite these positive accounts, study findings, and a general common faith in the effectiveness of AAI, the field still struggles considerably with credibility. Indeed, there has not yet been a strong integration of AAI concepts into modern psychology, medicine, or academics, although this is most certainly changing. Many cite the limited number of rigorously designed HAI studies—with their methodological challenges, historically anecdotal slant, and somewhat ambiguous or tenuously supportive results—as primary underlying reasons for this. Others speak to the difficulty of accurately and logistically studying the impact of animals for people in need. We do not disagree with either assessment. The challenges of conducting sound and replicable research in this field are many, including restricted animal access to select clinical settings due to safety and health concerns, an overall lack of validated HAI instrumentation, researcher expectancy biases, potential human handler effects, and the complicated nature of stipulating specific intervention protocols that encompass the various needs and proclivities of multiple living beings at once, to name just a few.

Nevertheless, ensuring high-quality research studies that are both exact and adaptable enough to have meaning outside of the "laboratory" are essential for this field to gain serious recognition and broader, more relevant implementation. To date, this has been a difficult goal to achieve, partly because of the relatively sparse (in terms of both the number of opportunities and the amount of available awards) and stringent nature of research funding in this area. To be competitive, many grant applicants are called upon to incorporate a fairly consistent research design methodology into their proposals, including the use of a control cohort or third comparison group to account for any novelty effects of AAIs; randomization; a large sample size, including multiple study sites; validated instrumentation and/ or physiological measures; quantitative vs. qualitative data; treatment protocol fidelity; and longitudinal designs.

While we do not wish to undermine the importance or value of these research elements, and believe they do have a central role to play in this arena, we worry that an absolute expectation of their inclusion may be quite costly on the whole, as well as prohibitive for a number of prospective researchers. This may not only prevent the contribution of potentially valuable research findings, but could serve to exclude these individuals from gaining a seat at the table. As such, the good work of underrepresented and often underresourced programs is at risk of remaining in these positions, or worse, being further marginalized and disparaged as comparatively subpar because they lack the ability to evaluate their practices in ways deemed acceptable. We hope that, going forward, a commitment to high research standards and integrity can be augmented by an expanded view of what is considered worthy of our time, attention, and monetary support.

In truth, all approaches to research have their unique up- and downsides. For example, some have argued that the very specific conditions or factors present in rigorous studies that report positive HAI findings often lack practicality in "real-world" settings and scenarios. As Beetz and Schöfmann indicate in chapter 3, research in which optimal conditions are intentionally applied and controlled may not be representative of actual human-animal interactions and, thus, may not have the observed positive effect once practice implementation efforts are made. In other words, what is the advantage of studying the effectiveness of a certain intervention if that intervention is not actually able, or struggles significantly, to have the desired effect? "Practice-to-research-to-practice" models and implementation science approaches, in which feasible and diverse practices are assessed through an array of quality research methods with the aim of then optimizing further practice, may be particularly fruitful ways forward. As evident throughout this book, AAI practices to support those impacted by trauma has, to date, far outpaced research demonstrating their effects. We believe there may be reasons for this, as well as ways to expand and enrich opportunities in this area for the betterment of those in need, as well as the field's standing and reach.

In addition to the aforementioned research factors, we contend that the slowly emerging estimation of AAIs as credible may have much to do with how we collectively view the worth and capabilities of animals themselves. Nonhuman animals, as a whole, are still not universally held in high regard, even in societies and communities where some are adored as companions and kin. This complexity of what we believe about animals, and how those beliefs impact our connections with them, is explored in great depth by Hal Herzog in his 2010 book, *Some We Love, Some We Hate, Some We Eat: Why It's so Hard to Think Straight About Animals.* Arguably, inconsistent attitudes about various animal species—which are often heavily influenced by historical, cultural, religious, economic, and personal factors—also shape our behaviors toward them, and our stance on their general attributes and merit. According to Herzog (2010), "One reason behavioral scientists have shied away from studying human-animal interactions is that for many of them the topic seems trivial" (pp. 16–17). We agree with Herzog that perspectives such as these are mistaken, and even arrogant in their homocentrism and disregard of the often vital significance of animals in our lives. After all, not only is the utilization of therapy and service animals growing and diversifying, but pet ownership across the world is also on the rise. These relationships make up much of how people spend their time, and thus have significant implications for human physical, social, behavioral, and emotional health.

Encouragingly, there has recently been growing acknowledgment and even celebration of animals as sentient, emotive, and cognitively complex (Bekoff, 2007; Grandin & Johnson, 2009; Masson & McCarthy, 1994; others). While still controversial in some circles, the notions that animals can experience such feelings as grief, guilt, pride, shame, and jubilation, or that their memory and problem-solving skills serve as key components to their survival, are now well-documented. And yet, despite this progress, animals are still largely viewed through a hierarchal lens of "other"; other, or rather less than, in their needs and preferences, in their privileges, in their legal standing, and in their aptitudes. Until respect for animals and their capabilities are elevated, people will continue to take issue with human-animal connection as truly transformative, and the AAI field will lack serious appreciation. Nussbaum's Capabilities Approach (2006), originally conceived as an ethical framework for democracies to use when conceptualizing and securing individual human dignity, has strong applications for nonhuman animals as well (as discussed in chapter 1). For example, animals, like humans, are equally entitled to the following justice-based capabilities: 1) life; 2) bodily health; 3) bodily integrity; 4) senses, imagination, and thought; 5) emotions; 6) practical reason; 7) affiliation; 8) other species; 9) play; and 10) control over one's environment. In the context of AAI, these shared human and animal capabilities are notably pertinent for practitioners when considering how to support the welfare of all participants.

While the "otherness" of animals may hinder the level of credence that AAI practice and research have thus far received, we posit that this actually is what makes our relationships with animals so profound and healing, and that their unique qualities should be upheld as we seek both greater professional credibility for the field and justice for them. Indeed, animals are not exactly like us and, although anthropomorphism has played a valuable and undervalued role in helping people see an empathic commonality with other species, excessive anthropomorphism may ultimately do animals a disservice. According to renowned ethologist Marc Bekoff (2013), "we should replace the notion of human exceptionalism with species exceptionalism or individual exceptionalism, moves that will force us to appreciate other animals for who they are, not who or what we want them to be."

The perception of animal as "other" may also have fitting clinical applications when working with traumatized populations, individuals who—through isolation, shame, guilt, and social bias or misunderstanding—may spend much of their physical and emotional lives at the margin. These points of shared connection, of bonding through similar experience or adversity, have the potential of strengthening the therapeutic processes and outcomes of AAI. Throughout this volume, this concept of *comparable otherness* as clinically useful was demonstrated in a number of ways and settings. As just one example, Sarah Schmidt from The Comfort Dog Project shared the following anecdote with us during her interview:

[During the war], . . . the rebel soldiers were forced to carry out horrible atrocities, including killing their own family members. So, for these people to come back, even though the villages don't directly ostracize them, they feel ostracized based on their life experience. They feel like people hate them. They feel like they've been rejected, that they're not looked upon the same as other people. . . . I think that some of them have found special [connection] with the dogs, because historically, they know that dogs are looked upon in the same way. So, I have felt like there's a little extra kinship in those cases.

Moreover, certain strands of human-animal connections are simply not always present in similar bonds shared between humans, including perceived nonjudgmental support and acceptance; reliable companionship; quiet solace through nonverbal communication; sincere and unbridled affection; hormonal (e.g., oxytocin) synchronization; and emotional safety through mutual caregiving and trust. Alongside these benefits are also subtleties that are much more nebulous and subjective. Those who have ever had a friendship with an animal can surely attest to the "magic" of the human-animal bond. It is this way of being with animals that is at the heart of AAI work, and likely contributes to the efficacy of these interventions to foster resiliency and growth in people with trauma histories. As such, well-intentioned efforts to "professionalize" the AAI field—whether through regimented practice standards or research protocols—should not overlook or interfere with the natural nuances of these connections, for they are what truly underlie positive and therapeutic change.

For example, in chapter 4 of this volume, Parish-Plass and Pfeiffer provide a case study account of a therapy dog licking the face of a child receiving animal-assisted play therapy after a previous suicide attempt. The spontaneous behavior of licking, which current therapy dog practice standards generally discourage in an attempt to limit the spread of zoonoses, served an unforeseen clinical purpose by grounding the child in the present through sensory touch experience and preventing him from dissociating. It is worth noting that such an experience in therapy would not be possible or appropriate without the presence of an animal, as physical contact between therapists and clients is nearly always prohibited. Had the therapist stopped or discouraged the dog from licking the client, these benefits would not have been realized. Worse yet, this could have confused the child, damaged his authentic interaction with the dog, and, perhaps most importantly, even harmed his self-image and esteem by reinforcing core beliefs of being unlovable in any relationship. Accordingly, it may be time for the field to think critically about the ongoing use of current AAI guidelines by objectively weighing their potential advantages and risks (i.e., are the benefits of preventing the unlikely transmission of zoonosis through dog licking fundamentally worth the potential risk of a young client not feeling cared for in therapy?). Likewise, animal-assisted research protocols that specify the sequence or length of session activities be just so make good sense on paper, but could inadvertently impede or cut short something just as, or even more, meaningful from happening. In essence, while the caliber and precision of AAI programming and scientific inquiries are crucial and we advocate for them wholeheartedly, they should also not come at the expense of the individualized authenticity of the connection.

Currently, many HAI researchers are grappling with how to reconcile these two worthy objectives; that is, how best to establish a sound evidence base regarding the impacts of the indistinct, but consistent, phenomena that characterize our relationships with animals. But, how do you reliably measure something that most people have trouble describing, if not naming? And, if these subtleties cannot be measured, what does that mean in terms of demonstrating the effectiveness of AAI? Do the effects of our interactions with animals, however modest, need to be quantified in order to be "real"? Undoubtedly, there may be more than one "way of knowing" how and why these relationships impact us. As the AAI field continues to grow (particularly in the realm of trauma recovery), addressing questions like these will become all the more pressing. It is up to us, as HAI practitioners and researchers, to seek ways to further understand just how the intricacies of our bonds with animals can promote recovery and consolation when everything else in our lives feels fragile and threadbare. To quote Victor Chitic from Dogs for People in Romania:

> Ever since I saw that [AAI] works, I've been preoccupied in understanding how and why it does. To this day I feel like we're just scratching the surface, but this desire to understand more about these mechanisms is what's keeping me going. It's a puzzle, and I like solving puzzles.

One area where the impact of connection may be particularly apparent is not in interactions with unknown or relatively unfamiliar animals (i.e., therapy animals), but with the ones with whom we share our homes and private lives. Despite the prevalence of domesticated animals in the United States (for example), there are only 10,000 or so established AAI programs. Thus, one could reasonably argue that much of the way we relate to, and benefit from, animals is through pet ownership, companionship, and inter-action through nature. What would happen, then, if we no longer had the ability to see thriving animals in our environment, or be in close connec-tion with them? How would this type of "relational poverty" impact our well-being? As Cohen and Clark discuss at length in chapter 13, the loss of various animals (both familiar and unfamiliar, but especially pets) can devastate a person with grief and sorrow, thus exemplifying the profound importance of the human-animal bond. As such, the relationships people share with their companion animals could arguably offer the greatest po-tential in terms of healing, as well as bond-specific research opportunities. As humans exist within several, interconnected social environments, many factors—including pet ownership—play an important contributing role in our health and wellness.

Accordingly, it may be advantageous to evaluate the effects of pet ownership as a formal therapeutic intervention—an HAI deemed appro-priate and advised by a therapist or other mental health professional—for people who have experienced trauma. We are presently seeing a version of this with trained psychiatric service dogs who, after a typically long, costly, and demanding waiting period, live with those they serve (e.g., veterans diagnosed with PTSD) and provide trauma-specific purposes. However, would certain benefits remain if the relationship between hu-man and animal was more "casual," or if the only therapeutic goal was the connection itself? And, what possible impacts would such a process have on the countless number of animals currently in need of adoptive homes? Could enhanced partnerships between the mental health, shelter, and veterinary communities be established? Further, would such research drive a revisiting or reframing of current ADA requirements in ways that more fully support human-service dog attachments that are adaptive and productive in the long-term? We believe these may be valuable research avenues to pursue in the future.

We would also like to see greater interest in how AAI and HAI may impact people living with additional forms of trauma, such as those originating from sexual assault, domestic violence, divorce, chronic pain and disease, eating disorders, bullying or discrimination, extreme poverty and homelessness, incarceration, and displacement or migration due to conflict and environmental change. These additional research foci may not only expand notions of what qualifies as trauma, but could also clarify the varying roles and specific capacities of animals in human trauma response and recovery. In the case of displaced populations, for example, their migration may pose a unique cultural challenge in this area due to issues of potential unfamiliarity with typical AAI and companion animals in their new country. In future editions, we are also committed to including more in-depth discussions of the traumas experienced by, and inflicted upon, nonhuman animals by such inhumane practices as poaching, "trophy" and other forms of hunting, and factory farming. The relentless nature of these atrocities for animals, and animals' often complex and emotionally painful responses to them (Masson & McCarthy, 1994, and others), warrant our steadfast attention and advocacy.

Likewise, as noted extensively throughout this volume, the vast majority of current AAI practice and research concerns the use of just two primary species—canine and equine. As the two focused chapters on these animals (dogs: chapter 9, Howie, Fine, and Rojas; horses: chapter 8, Ekholm Fry) demonstrate, certain traits of these particular animals make them aptly suited for AAI participation. However, let us take this opportunity to call out the dog and horse in the room: studies with diverse animal species, whether they be dogs, cats, goats, horses, or swallows in nature, are salient to increasing our understanding of the subtle and unique hallmarks of human-animal connection, as well as the appreciation of the inherent worth of nonhuman animal life and our environmental surroundings.

Finally, throughout this book (and particularly in Ng's chapter), we made a point of calling attention to our abiding moral obligation to the animals whose participation in this work we seek and beseech. It bears repeating that animals who serve our interests and needs through AAI do not do so as a matter of choice; rather, their involvement is contingent on the actions and motivations of their human handlers. As such, we owe them our gratitude, our respect, and our commitment to their own personalized sense of well-being. Readers of certain portions of this book may walk away questioning whether or not placing animals in these circumstances, particularly ones in which trauma is at the center, is altogether appropriate. We welcome such quandaries as we believe they are critical in setting the stage for understanding both concrete welfare risks, as well as strategies to ensure the ethical inclusion of animals in AAI. In addition to the discussion and recommendations offered by Ng in chapter 2, we hope that, with proper attention to advocacy, greater appreciation of species-specific considerations, and concentrated knowledge of the therapy or service animal's individual needs and behaviors through close handler-animal partnership, the benefits of AAI will indeed outweigh the risks. As mentioned above, one of the chief benefits of AAI may, in fact, be a greater commitment to animal welfare and altruism. However, in order for this to become a confirmed reality, interventionists must not waver in their support of animal well-being as a focused priority. The AAI field would provide a great benefit if it were to develop more in-depth, species-specific resources regarding animal welfare, and make them intentionally and readily accessible to AAI practitioners and those in training.

In sum, we feel both fortunate and excited to have played a part in editing, and writing portions of, this volume on trauma-informed AAIs. The field is expanding in such ways and at such speeds that are indicative of just how promising our connections with animals can be for traumatized populations. Relationships with animals often have inherent qualities of caring, love, mutuality, trust and safety, all of which can serve as key components in an individual's trauma recovery. As discussed above, further and more diverse research that integrates innovative practices, methods, and inquiries are necessary to validate how, and under what circumstances, animals can assist in trauma treatment. Indeed, we believe that if further evidence can support the efficacy of AAI, the field could lend a powerful voice to the rich importance of other animal lives, thereby reframing our connections with them and socially shifting how we think, treat, and behave toward a variety of species and the world we share. At the same time, we are compelled to acknowledge the existence of unintended, adverse consequences that may likely accompany favorable AAI research findings. For example, if we succeed in demonstrating the fundamental effectiveness of AAI, we worry that the field could broadly serve as yet another way to exploit animals for the purpose of serving human priorities. It is therefore upon us—as practitioners, researchers, and members of communities—to be steadfast in our commitment to ensuring that AAIs and HAIs be conceived of ethically, and conducted in mutually beneficial ways that celebrate the transformative nature of human-animal connection.

REFERENCES

Bekoff, M. (2007). *The emotional lives of animals: A leading scientist explores animal joy, sorrow, and empathy—and why they matter.* Novato, CA: New World Library.

Bekoff, M. (2013, December 13). Human-animal relationships: Where we are and where we're going. *Huffington Post.* Retrieved from http://www.huffingtonpost.com/marc-bekoff/humananimal-relationships_b_4439038.html

Grandin, T., & Johnson, C. (2009). *Animals make us human: Creating the best life for animals.* New York, NY: Houghton Mifflin Harcourt.

Herzog, H. (2010). *Some we love, some we hate, some we eat: Why it's so hard to think straight about animals.* New York, NY: HarperCollins.

Masson, J., & McCarthy, S. (1994). *When elephants weep: The emotional lives of animals.* London, UK: Jonathan Cape.

Nussbaum, M. C. (2006). *Frontiers of justice: Disability, nationality, species membership.* Cambridge, MA: Belknap Press of Harvard University Press.

ABOUT THE AUTHORS

Biographical sketches for **Molly A. Jenkins** and **Philip Tedeschi** can be found on p. 12 of this volume.

Selective Index